CS
1-82

WW
3-35
415-425
95-127 T
162-181 art Tr
271-288 {

Essay
181-271

398-412 Tr

334-350
359-398
408-412

289

THE WORLD AS WILL AND REPRESENTATION

by

ARTHUR SCHOPENHAUER

Translated from the German
by
E. F. J. Payne

In two volumes:
VOLUME I

Dover Publications, Inc.
New York

This Dover edition, first published in 1966, is a
republication, with minor corrections, of the work
originally published by The Falcon's Wing Press,
Indian Hills, Colorado, in 1958. This edition is un-
abridged with the exception that the General
Editor's Preface to the original edition has been
omitted.
This edition is published by special arrangement
with The Falcon's Wing Press.

Library of Congress Catalog Card Number: 66-29058

International Standard Book Number

ISBN-13: 978-0-486-21761-1
ISBN-10: 0-486-21761-2

Manufactured in the United States by Courier Corporation
21761227
www.doverpublications.com

Translator's Introduction

Arthur Schopenhauer was born in the Hanseatic City of Danzig in 1788. His father was a well-to-do merchant of rugged independence and wide cultural interests, and his mother a woman of considerable intellectual gifts who in her day won fame as an authoress. At an early age, the son showed outstanding mental qualities, and soon embarked on an intensive study of the humanities, the empirical sciences, and philosophy at the Universities of Göttingen and Berlin. In 1813 he wrote his first work, *On the Fourfold Root of the Principle of Sufficient Reason,* a thesis which gained for him the degree of doctor of philosophy of Jena University, and in which he expounded his epistemology based on the Kantian doctrine of the ideality of space, time, and the categories.

From 1814 to 1818 Schopenhauer lived in Dresden, where his creative genius conceived and gave birth to a philosophical work which, for its depth and range of thought as well as for the clarity and brilliance of its style, was an outstanding achievement for so young a man. It was the more remarkable in that, during the forty-one years he was still to live after its publication, he did not consider it necessary to modify or recast in any way the basic idea underlying this work. Like Plato, he was deeply stirred by θαῦμα, by the wonder that impels men to philosophize, and he instinctively viewed the world with the objective eye of the genuine thinker. In his youth, he began to keep note-books in which from time to time throughout his life he recorded ideas as they occurred to him. Thus all such notes stemmed from the original fundamental conception round which the whole of his philosophical structure was built.

In 1844 a second edition of this main work was published in two volumes, the first of which was virtually a reprint of the first edition of 1819, whilst the second contained in fifty chapters supplementary discussions on the theme of the first. The encyclopaedic range of this supplementary volume is an indication of the depth and maturity of Schopenhauer's thought, and stamps it as one of the most eminent works in the whole province of philosophical literature. Like the first a quarter of a century earlier, this second edition evoked little or no response from the learned world of that time, which was still under the influence of Hegel and other post-Kantian philosophers. After 1851, when his last major work was published, Schopenhauer ultimately acquired fame, and the interest that was now awakened in his philosophy stimulated a demand for new editions of his works. In 1859, the year before his death, a third edition of *Die Welt als Wille und Vorstellung* was published.

Schopenhauer himself has stated that his philosophy is the natural continuation and completion of the Kantian, for he has taken as the foundation of his own system of thought the ideality of space and time and the Kantian thing-in-itself as expounded in the *Critique of Pure Reason.*

In his essay *On the Fourfold Root of the Principle of Sufficient Reason,* to which Schopenhauer frequently refers in this major work, he discusses in detail the *intellectual* nature of perception and shows that, from the meagre data supplied by our senses, our faculty of cognition creates immediately and automatically a mental picture of the external world in all its variegated wealth of detail. This mental picture is a "re-presentation" of the data of the senses, a *Vorstellung* of the intellect, and is something totally different from a mere figment of the imagination. Of the twelve Kantian categories, Schopenhauer rejects eleven as redundant, and retains only the category of causality. He then discusses the *a priori* nature of time, space, and causality, and shows that they are essentially the three innate functions of our intellect, inasmuch as they enter inevitably and inseparably into the framework of all possible experience, and are, in fact, the prerequisite of all knowledge of this. Our knowing consciousness, says Schopenhauer, is divisible solely into subject and object. To be object for the subject and to be our representation or mental picture are one and the same. All our representations are objects for the subject, and all objects of the subject are our representations. These stand to one another in a regulated connexion which in form is determinable *a priori,* and by virtue of this connexion nothing existing by itself and independent, nothing single and detached, can become an object for us. It is this connexion which is expressed by the principle of sufficient reason in general. All our representations are divisible into four classes which impart to the principle of sufficient reason its fourfold root. The first aspect of this principle is that of becoming, where it appears as the law of causality and is applicable only to *changes.* Thus if the cause is given, the effect must of necessity follow. The second aspect deals with concepts or abstract representations, which are themselves drawn from representations of intuitive perception, and here the principle of sufficient reason states that, if certain premisses are given, the conclusion must follow. The third aspect of the principle is concerned with being in space and time, and shows that the existence of one relation inevitably implies the other, thus that the equality of the angles of a triangle necessarily implies the equality of its sides and *vice versa*. Finally, the fourth aspect deals with actions, and the principle appears as the law of motivation, which states that a definite course of action inevitably ensues on a given character and motive. Thus the principle of sufficient reason deals only with our *representation* in the widest sense, that is to say, with the *form* in which things *appear* to us, not with that inscrutable metaphysical entity which appears through this form, and which Kant calls the "thing-in-itself." Because this "thing-in-itself" transcends the physical framework of time, space, and causality, and therefore of our cognitive functions, Kant regarded a knowledge of it as impossible. Schopenhauer admitted this up to a point, although, by identifying the Kantian thing-in-itself with the will in ourselves, he maintained that experience itself as a whole was capable of explanation; yet he did not imply by this that no problems remained unsolved.

The first volume of this work contains the basic idea of Schopenhauer's system divided into four books and followed by an appendix consisting of a masterly criticism of the Kantian philosophy which greatly facilitates the study of the three Critiques, and in which Schopenhauer readily acknowledges his indebtedness to his master, and just as readily subjects to a searching criticism those points in which he considers that Kant has gone astray. The picture emerging from a study of this first volume is that of an organically consistent structure of thought based on inner and outer *experience,* and culminating in three towers, in the metaphysics of nature, of art or aesthetics, and of morality.

The second volume supplements the discussions in each of the four books of the first, and represents the mature fruit of a lifetime's reflection on the many problems raised by the main theme of Schopenhauer's philosophy. The great all-embracing idea of the first volume with all its ramifications is further investigated, developed and corroborated in the second through the many references to art, life, and the empirical sciences. On the one hand, we discern the shrewdness of Schopenhauer's observation of the world and its many relations, a quality in which he is unique, and, on the other, we are struck by the psychological force and even fierceness with which he reveals the deepest recesses of the human heart. Many have complained that his philosophy is sombre and pessimistic, but an impartial examination will lead to the conclusion that it is neither more nor less pessimistic than the teachings of Brahmanism, Buddhism, and Christianity, all of which agree in preaching as the supreme goal deliverance from this earthly existence.* In the history of philosophy Schopenhauer's name will always be associated with a correct distinction between knowledge of perception and abstract knowledge, with a proper analysis of consciousness, of the so-called psyche, into will and intellect, with the correct interpretation and utilization of the Platonic Ideas, and finally with a true insight into the real nature of Christianity from both the religious and philosophical points of view.

It is universally acknowledged by all who have read Schopenhauer's works, even by those who do not share his views, that his prose is second to none in beauty of style and in power and lucidity of expression. Long periods are occasionally met with in his works, but there is never a doubt as to the precise meaning of what he wrote. He thought clearly and concisely, and expressed himself in clear and concise language. He was discriminating in the choice of words and expressions, and paid great attention even to punctuation. No translator can take liberties with his prose without adversely affecting the translation, which should aim at being as faithful as possible to the author's original work, and yet avoid being too literal and therefore unreadable. On the other hand, the translator must resist the temptation to "correct" and touch up his author under the mistaken impression that he is "improving" the work, a practice that was strongly condemned by Schopenhauer.

One of the difficulties in rendering a German philosophical work into English comes from the inability of the English language to reproduce adequately and accurately some of the philosophical terms and expressions of which there are so many in German. This language is an admirable medium for the precise expression of abstract philosophical ideas, and the translator must endeavour to keep as close as possible to the meaning of the original. It is pertinent to the matter to mention here one or two German words by way of showing that the translator's task is not always easy, despite the fact that Schopenhauer rarely resorted to the involved and long periods so characteristic of the style of many German philosophers.

Anschauung is used by Schopenhauer to describe what occurs when the eye perceives an external object as the cause of the sensation on the retina. "Perception" has been selected as the nearest English

---

* *Cf.* "East-West Fire . . . Schopenhauer's Optimism and the Lankavatara Sutra," C. A. Muses, 1955, *passim*.

equivalent, although it may also be translated "intuition" in the sense of an immediate apprehension.

Wahrnehmung is used to convey the idea of perception through any or all of the five senses.

Vernehmen has no exact equivalent in English, and is philologically related to *Vernunft*, the faculty of reason peculiar to man which enables him to form concepts and words from the countless objects perceived in the world of experience. *Vernehmen* means more than mere sensuous hearing, and implies hearing by means of the faculty of reason.

Grund and *Vernunft* are almost always translated by the word "reason," yet the two German words differ widely in meaning. The context usually enables one to see in which sense the word "reason" is used.

Willkür means free will, free choice, arbitrary power, or caprice. The expression "free will" is likely to give rise to a misconception, since Schopenhauer uses the word to indicate will with the power of choice, will determined by motives, conscious will as opposed to blind impulse. Such will, however, is not absolutely free in the metaphysical sense, in as much as a will determined by motives cannot be free. Schopenhauer uses the expression *liberum arbitrium indifferentiae* to convey the meaning of a will that is absolutely free in the metaphysical sense before it has assumed the phenomenal form. He emphatically denies the existence of such a freedom in the world of phenomena.

Vorstellung is important, for it occurs in the German title of this work. Its primary meaning is that of "placing before," and it is used by Schopenhauer to express what he himself describes as an "exceedingly complicated physiological process in the brain of an animal, the result of which is the consciousness of a *picture* there." In the present translation "representation" has been selected as the best English word to convey the German meaning, a selection that is confirmed by the French and Italian versions of *Die Welt als Wille und Vorstellung*. The word "idea" which is used by Haldane and Kemp in their English translation of this work clearly fails to bring out the meaning of *Vorstellung* in the sense used by Schopenhauer. Even Schopenhauer himself has translated *Vorstellung* as "idea" in his criticism of Kant's philosophy at the end of the first volume, although he states in his essay, *On the Fourfold Root of the Principle of Sufficient Reason*, that "idea" should be used only in its original Platonic sense. Moreover, confusion results in the translation of Haldane and Kemp from printer's errors in the use of "Idea" with a capital letter to render the German *Idee* in the Platonic sense and of "idea" for the translation of *Vorstellung* as used by Schopenhauer. In the present translation *Idee* has been rendered by the word "Idea" with a capital letter.

After the publication of each of his works, Schopenhauer was in the habit of recording in an interleaved copy additions and modifications for incorporation in future editions. In the last ten years of his life, he was engaged on these interleaved copies the blank pages of which were gradually filled with additions and amendments. In many instances these were completely edited and incorporated into the original text. In some cases, however, they were fragmentary and indefinite in form, whilst in others a brief reference was made to a passage in Schopenhauer's manuscript-books which formed the storehouse of his ideas and furnished essential material for all his works after 1819.

In his last years, Schopenhauer had considered the possibility of a complete edition of his works, but the rights of the six publishers ruled out the realization of such a plan during his lifetime. Not till 1873 was it possible for Julius Frauenstädt, the philosopher's literary executor, to publish an edition of the works which for many years remained the standard, a reprint of it appearing as recently as 1922.

Until Schopenhauer's works were out of copyright, scholars had to rely on Frauenstädt's edition as the standard, but with the suggestion that it contained a number of errors, attempts were made to replace it by a better and more reliable edition. By this time, however, editors no longer had at their disposal all the material that Frauenstädt had had as Schopenhauer's literary executor. After Frauenstädt's death in 1879, Schopenhauer's manuscript-books went to the Berlin Library, but by an oversight the interleaved copies of the works were sold and for many years were not accessible to scholars. Only gradually and by stages was it possible for them to complete their task of the textual criticism and emendation of Schopenhauer's works.

The first stage was the publication in 1891 of Eduard Grisebach's edition. At the time, scholars were surprised to learn from him that the edition of Frauenstädt contained many hundreds of errors, whereas his own gave not only the correct order of the works, in accordance with Schopenhauer's wishes, but also a text that had been compared with Schopenhauer's final editions and with the manuscript-books. However, it was not long before G. F. Wagner discovered that Grisebach himself had incorporated in his own edition many textual inaccuracies from the edition of Frauenstädt.

The second stage came when the interleaved copies of the works were again accessible to scholars. In 1911 Paul Deussen and his collaborators were able to begin their fine edition of Schopenhauer's works, and full advantage was taken of the possibility of obtaining an accurate text from the interleaved copies and the manuscript-books.

The third and final stage in the work of textual criticism and correction was taken up with an examination of the original manuscripts of most of the works. In 1937 Dr. Arthur Hübscher was able for the first time to use such manuscripts for the production of a new edition with a text representing the last word in accuracy. By carefully comparing these manuscripts with the traditional texts, he succeeded in eliminating many errors and inaccuracies from the earlier editions, and in producing a text that would have accorded with Schopenhauer's views. A reprint of this edition appeared between 1946 and 1950, and it is the text of this which has been used in making the present translation.

Reference has already been made to the only other English translation of *Die Welt als Wille und Vorstellung,* which was made by R. B. Haldane (later Lord Haldane) and J. Kemp between 1883 and 1886, and was freely consulted in the preparation of this new English version of Schopenhauer's main work. However, the interests of truth and the importance of this work in the history of philosophy require that attention be drawn to the many errors and omissions in their translation, over a thousand of which came to light when it was compared with the German text, and which seriously detract from its merit as a work of scholarship.

In conclusion, the translator would like to express his deep appreciation and gratitude to his many friends who, by their kindness and encouragement, have sustained him in the long task of translation, and in particular to his friend Dr. Arthur Hübscher of Munich, the President of the Schopenhauer-Gesellschaft and one of the most eminent living authorities on Schopenhauer and his philosophy, for his valuable advice always so generously given, and for the benefits of his wide scholarship in this field which have contributed so much to the work of translation.

LONDON, 1957.

Preface to the First Edition

I propose to state here how this book is to be read, in order that it may be thoroughly understood. What is to be imparted by it is a single thought. Yet in spite of all my efforts, I have not been able to find a shorter way of imparting that thought than the whole of this book. I consider this thought to be that which has been sought for a very long time under the name of philosophy, and that whose discovery is for this very reason regarded by those versed in history as just as impossible as the discovery of the philosophers' stone, although Pliny had already said to them: *Quam multa fieri non posse, priusquam sint facta, judicantur?* (*Historia naturalis,* 7, 1).[1]

According as we consider under different aspects this one thought that is to be imparted, it appears as what has been called metaphysics, what has been called ethics, and what has been called aesthetics; and naturally it was bound to be all these, if it is what I have already acknowledged it to be.

A *system of thought* must always have an architectonic connexion or coherence, that is to say, a connexion in which one part always supports the other, though not the latter the former; in which the foundation-stone carries all the parts without being carried by them; and in which the pinnacle is upheld without upholding. On the other hand, *a single thought*, however comprehensive, must preserve the most perfect unity. If, all the same, it can be split up into parts for the purpose of being communicated, then the connexion of these parts must once more be organic, i.e., of such a kind that every part supports the whole just as much as it is supported by the whole; a connexion in which no part is first and no part last, in which the whole gains in clearness from every part, and even the smallest part cannot be fully understood until the whole has been first understood. But a book must have a first and a last line, and to this extent will always remain very unlike an organism, however like one its con-

---

[1] "How many things are considered impossible until they are actually done!" [Tr.]

tents may be. Consequently, form and matter will here be in contradiction.

It is self-evident that in such circumstances, in order that the thought expounded may be fathomed, no advice can be given other than *to read the book twice,* and to do so the first time with much patience. This patience is to be derived only from the belief, voluntarily accorded, that the beginning presupposes the end almost as much as the end the beginning, and that every earlier part presupposes the later almost as much as the later the earlier. I say "almost," for it is by no means absolutely so; and whatever it was possible to do to give priority to that which is in any case explained by what follows, and generally whatever might contribute to the greatest possible comprehensibility and clearness, has been honestly and conscientiously done. Indeed, I might to a certain extent have succeeded, were it not that the reader, as is very natural, thinks when reading not merely of what is at the moment being said, but also of its possible consequences. Thus besides the many contradictions of the opinions of the day, and presumably of the reader also, that actually exist, as many others may be added that are anticipated and imaginary. That, then, which is mere misunderstanding, must show itself as lively disapproval, and it is the less recognized as misunderstanding because, while the laboriously attained clearness of explanation and distinctness of expression never leave one in doubt about the direct meaning of what is said, yet they cannot express its relations to all that remains. Therefore, as I have said, the first reading demands patience, derived from the confidence that with a second reading much, or all, will appear in quite a different light. Moreover, the earnest desire for fuller and even easier comprehension must, in the case of a very difficult subject, justify occasional repetition. The structure of the whole, which is organic and not like a chain, in itself makes it necessary sometimes to touch twice on the same point. This construction and the very close interconnexion of all the parts have not allowed of that division into chapters and paragraphs which I usually value so much, but have obliged me to be content with four principal divisions, four aspects, as it were, of the one thought. In each of these four books we have specially to guard against losing sight, among the details that must needs be discussed, of the principal thought to which they belong, and of the progress of the exposition as a whole. And thus is expressed the first, and like those that follow, absolutely necessary, demand on the reader, who is unfriendly towards the philosopher just because he is one himself.

The second demand is that the introduction be read before the book itself, although this is not a part of the book, but appeared five years previously under the title *On the Fourfold Root of the Principle of Sufficient Reason: a Philosophical Essay*. Without an acquaintance with this introduction and propaedeutic, it is quite impossible to understand the present work properly, and the subject-matter of that essay is always presupposed here as if it were included in the book. Moreover, if it had not preceded this work by several years, it would not be placed at the front of it as an introduction, but would be incorporated in the first book, since this book lacks what was said in the essay, and exhibits a certain incompleteness because of these omissions, which must always be made good by reference to that essay. However, my dislike of quoting myself, or of laboriously expressing once again in different words what had already been said adequately once, was so great that I preferred this course, despite the fact that I could now give the subject-matter of that essay a somewhat better presentation, particularly by clearing it of many conceptions which arose from my excessive preoccupation at that time with the Kantian philosophy, such as categories, outer and inner sense, and the like. But even there those conceptions occur only because I had as yet never really entered deeply into them, and therefore only as a secondary affair quite unconnected with the principal matter. For this reason, the correction of such passages in that essay will come about quite automatically in the reader's thoughts through his acquaintance with the present work. But only if through that essay we have fully recognized what the principle of sufficient reason is and signifies, where it is valid and where it is not, that it is not prior to all things, and that the whole world exists only in consequence of and in conformity to it, as its corollary so to speak; that rather it is nothing more than the form in which the object, of whatever kind it may be and always conditioned by the subject, is everywhere known in so far as the subject is a knowing individual; only then will it be possible to enter into the method of philosophizing which is here attempted for the first time, differing completely as it does from all previous methods.

But the same dislike to quote myself word for word, or to say exactly the same thing a second time in other and less suitable terms, after I had already made use of better ones, has been the cause of yet a second omission in book one of this work. For I have left out all that is to be found in the first chapter of my essay *On Vision and Colours,* which otherwise would have found its place here, word for word. Therefore an acquaintance with that short earlier work is also presupposed.

Finally, the third demand to be made on the reader might even be taken for granted, for it is none other than an acquaintance with the most important phenomenon which has appeared in philosophy for two thousand years, and which lies so close to us, I mean the principal works of Kant. Indeed, I find, as has already been said on other occasions, that the effect those works produce in the mind to which they really speak is very like that of an operation for cataract on a blind man. If we wish to continue the simile, my purpose can be described by saying that I wanted to put into the hands of those on whom that operation has been successful a pair of cataract spectacles, for the use of which that operation itself is the most necessary condition. Therefore, while I start in large measure from what was achieved by the great Kant, serious study of his works has nevertheless enabled me to discover grave errors in them. I had to separate these and show them to be objectionable, in order that I might presuppose and apply what is true and excellent in his doctrine, pure and clarified of them. But in order not to interrupt and confuse my own exposition by frequent polemics against Kant, I have put this into a special appendix. And just as, according as I have said, my work presupposes an acquaintance with the Kantian philosophy, so too does it presuppose an acquaintance with that appendix. Therefore, in this respect, it would be advisable to read the appendix first, the more so as its subject-matter has special reference to book one of the present work. On the other hand, it could not from the nature of the case be avoided that even the appendix should refer now and again to the main text. The result of this is simply that the appendix, as well as the main part of the work, must be read twice.

Kant's philosophy is therefore the only one with which a thorough acquaintance is positively assumed in what is to be here discussed. But if in addition to this the reader has dwelt for a while in the school of the divine Plato, he will be the better prepared to hear me, and the more susceptible to what I say. But if he has shared in the benefits of the *Vedas,* access to which, opened to us by the *Upanishads,* is in my view the greatest advantage which this still young century has to show over previous centuries, since I surmise that the influence of Sanskrit literature will penetrate no less deeply than did the revival of Greek literature in the fifteenth century; if, I say, the reader has also already received and assimilated the divine inspiration of ancient Indian wisdom, then he is best of all prepared to hear what I have to say to him. It will not speak to him, as to many others, in a strange and even hostile tongue; for, did it not sound too conceited, I might assert that each of the individual and disconnected utterances that make up the *Upanishads* could be derived as a consequence from the thought I am to impart, although conversely my thought is by no means to be found in the *Upanishads*.

*   *   *

But most readers have already grown angry with impatience, and have burst into a reproach kept back with difficulty for so long. Yet how can I dare to submit a book to the public under demands and conditions of which the first two are presumptuous and quite immodest, and this at a time when there is so general an abundance of characteristic ideas that in Germany alone such ideas are made common property through the press every year, in three thousand substantial, original, and absolutely indispensable works, as well as in innumerable periodicals, and even daily papers; at a time when in particular there is not the slightest deficiency of wholly original and profound philosophers, but in Germany alone there are more of them living simultaneously than several successive centuries have had to show? How are we to reach the end, asks the indignant reader, if we must set to work on a book with so much trouble and detail?

As I have not the least thing to say in reply to such reproaches, I hope only for some gratitude from such readers for having warned them in time, so that they may not waste an hour on a book which it would be useless for them to read unless they complied with the demands I make, and which is therefore to be left alone, especially as on other grounds one could wager a great deal that it can say nothing to them, but on the contrary will always be only *paucorum hominum,* and must therefore wait in calm and modesty for the few whose unusual mode of thought might find it readable. For apart from its intricacies, difficulties, and the efforts it demands of the reader, what cultured man of this age, whose knowledge has almost reached the magnificent point where the paradoxical and the false are all one and the same to him, could bear to meet on almost every page thoughts which directly contradict what he himself has nevertheless established once for all as true and settled? And then how unpleasantly disappointed will many a man find himself, when he comes across no mention of what he thinks he must look for just in this place, because his way of speculating coincides with that of a great philosopher still living.[2] This man has written truly pathetic books, and his single trifling weakness is that he regards as fundamental inborn ideas of the human mind everything that he learnt

---

[2] F. H. Jacobi.

and approved before his fifteenth year. Who could endure all this? Therefore, my advice is simply to put the book aside.

I am afraid, however, that even so I shall not be let off. The reader who has got as far as the preface and is put off by that, has paid money for the book, and wants to know how he is to be compensated. My last refuge now is to remind him that he knows of various ways of using a book without precisely reading it. It can, like many another, fill a gap in his library, where, neatly bound, it is sure to look well. Or he can lay it on the dressing-table or tea-table of his learned lady friend. Or finally he can review it; this is assuredly the best course of all, and the one I specially advise.

* * *

And so, after allowing myself the joke to which in this generally ambivalent life hardly any page can be too serious to grant a place, I put my book forth in profound seriousness, confident that, sooner or later, it will reach those to whom alone it can be addressed. For the rest, I am resigned in patience to the fact that the same fate will befall it in full measure which has always fallen to the lot of truth in every branch of knowledge, in the most important branch most of all. To truth only a brief celebration of victory is allowed between the two long periods during which it is condemned as paradoxical, or disparaged as trivial. The author of truth also usually meets with the former fate. But life is short, and truth works far and lives long: let us speak the truth.

Dresden, August 1818

Preface to the Second Edition

Not to my contemporaries or my compatriots, but to mankind I consign my now complete work, confident that it will not be without value to humanity, even if this value should be recognized only tardily, as is the inevitable fate of the good in whatever form. It can have been only for mankind, and not for the quickly passing generation engrossed with its delusion of the moment, that my mind, almost against my will, has pursued its work without interruption throughout a long life. As time has passed, not even lack of sympathy has been able to shake my belief in its value. I constantly saw the false and the bad, and finally the absurd and the senseless,[1] standing in universal admiration and honour, and I thought to myself that, if those who are capable of recognizing the genuine and right were not so rare that we can spend some twenty years looking about for them in vain, those who are capable of producing it might not be so few that their works afterwards form an exception to the transitoriness of earthly things. In this way, the comforting prospect of posterity, which everyone who sets himself a high aim needs to fortify him, would then be lost. Whoever takes up and seriously pursues a matter that does not lead to material advantage, ought not to count on the sympathy of his contemporaries. But for the most part he will see that in the meantime the superficial aspect of such matter becomes current in the world and enjoys its day; and this is as it should be. For the matter itself also must be pursued for its own sake, otherwise there can be no success, since every purpose or intention is always dangerous to insight. Accordingly, as the history of literature testifies throughout, everything of value needs a long time to gain authority, especially if it is of the instructive and not of the entertaining sort; and meanwhile the false flourishes. For to unite the matter with the superficial aspect of the matter is difficult, if not impossible. Indeed, this is just the curse of this world of want and need, that everything must serve and slave for these. Therefore it is not so constituted that any noble and

---

[1] The Hegelian philosophy.

sublime endeavour, like that after light and truth, can thrive in it unhindered, and exist for its own sake. But even when such an endeavour has once been able to assert itself, and the idea of it is thus introduced, material interests and personal aims will at once take possession of it to make it their tool or their mask. Accordingly, after Kant had brought philosophy once more into repute, it was bound to become very soon the tool of political aims from above, and of personal aims from below: though, to be accurate, not philosophy, but its double that passes for it. This should not even surprise us, for the incredibly great majority of men are by their nature absolutely incapable of any but material aims; they cannot even comprehend any others. Accordingly, the pursuit of truth alone is a pursuit far too lofty and eccentric for us to expect that all or many, or indeed even a mere few, will sincerely take part in it. But if we see, as we do for instance in Germany at the moment, a remarkable activity, a general bustling, writing, and talking on matters of philosophy, then it may be confidently assumed that, in spite of all the solemn looks and assurances, only real, not ideal, aims are the actual *primum mobile*,[2] the concealed motive, of such a movement; that is, that it is personal, official, ecclesiastical, political, in short material interests which are here kept in view, and that in consequence mere party ends set in such vigorous motion the many pens of pretended philosophers. Thus intentions, not intelligence, are the guiding star of these disturbers; and truth is certainly the last thing thought of in this connexion. It finds no partisans; on the contrary, it can pursue its way as silently and unheeded through such philosophical contention and tumult as through the winter night of the darkest century, involved in the most rigid faith of the Church, where it was communicated only as esoteric doctrine to a few adepts, or even entrusted only to parchment. In fact, I might say that no time can be more unfavourable to philosophy than that in which it is shamefully misused as a political means on the one hand, and a means of livelihood on the other. Or are we to believe that, with such effort and turmoil, the truth, by no means their aim, will also come to light? Truth is no harlot who throws her arms round the neck of him who does not desire her; on the contrary, she is so coy a beauty that even the man who sacrifices everything to her can still not be certain of her favours.

Now, if governments make philosophy the means to their political ends, then scholars see in professorships of philosophy a trade that nourishes the outer man just as does any other. They therefore crowd after them in the assurance of their good way of thinking,

---

[2] "First motive." [Tr.]

in other words, of the purpose or intention to serve those ends. And they keep their word; not truth, not clarity, not Plato or Aristotle, but the aims and ends they were appointed to serve are their guiding star; and these at once become the criterion both of what is true, valuable, and worthy of consideration, and of its opposite. Therefore whatever does not comply with these aims, be it even the most important and extraordinary thing in their department, is either condemned, or, where this seems precarious, suppressed by being unanimously ignored. Look only at their concerted indignation at pantheism; will any simpleton believe that this proceeds from conviction? How could philosophy, degraded to become a means of earning one's bread, generally fail to degenerate into sophistry? Just because this is bound to happen, and the rule "I sing the song of him whose bread I eat" has held good at all times, the making of money by philosophy was among the ancients the characteristic of the sophist. We have still to add that, since everywhere in this world nothing is to be expected, nothing can be demanded, and nothing is to be had for money except mediocrity, we have to put up with this here also. Accordingly, in all the German universities we see the cherished mediocrity straining to bring about from its own resources, and indeed in accordance with a prescribed standard and aim, the philosophy that still does not exist at all; a spectacle at which it would be almost cruel to mock.

While philosophy has long been obliged to serve to such an extent generally as a means to public ends on the one hand, and to private ends on the other, I have followed my course of thought, undisturbed by this fact, for more than thirty years. This I have done simply because I was obliged to, and could not do otherwise, from an instinctive impulse which, however, was supported by the confidence that anything true that a man conceives, and anything obscure that he elucidates, will at some time or other be grasped by another thinking mind, and impress, delight, and console it. To such a man we speak, just as those like us have spoken to us, and have thus become our consolation in this wilderness of life. Meanwhile, the matter is pursued on its own account and for its own sake. Now it is a strange thing as regards philosophical meditations that only that which a man has thought out and investigated for himself is afterwards of benefit to others, and not that which was originally destined for those others. The former is conspicuously nearest in character to perfect honesty, for we do not try to deceive ourselves, or offer ourselves empty husks. In this way, all sophistication and all idle display of words are then omitted, and as a result every sentence that is written at once repays the trouble of reading. Accordingly, my writings bear the stamp of honesty and openness so distinctly on their face, that they are thus in glaring contrast to those of the three notorious sophists of the post-Kantian period. I am always to be found at the standpoint of *reflection,* in other words, of rational deliberation and honest information, never at that of *inspiration,* called intellectual intuition or even absolute thought; its correct names would be humbug and charlatanism. Therefore, working in this spirit, and meanwhile constantly seeing the false and the bad held in general acceptance, indeed humbug[3] and charlatanism[4] in the highest admiration, I long ago renounced the approbation of my contemporaries. It is impossible that an age which for twenty years has extolled a Hegel, that intellectual Caliban, as the greatest of philosophers so loudly that the echo was heard throughout Europe, could make the man who looked at this eager for its approbation. No longer has it any crowns of honour to bestow; its applause is prostituted, its censure signifies nothing. I mean what I say here, as is obvious from the fact that, if I had in any way aspired to the approbation of my contemporaries, I should have had to strike out twenty passages that wholly contradict all their views, and indeed must in part be offensive to them. But I should reckon it a crime on my part to sacrifice even a single syllable to that approbation. My guiding star has in all seriousness been truth. Following it, I could first aspire only to my own approval, entirely averted from an age that has sunk low as regards all higher intellectual efforts, and from a national literature demoralized but for the exceptions, a literature in which the art of combining lofty words with low sentiments has reached its zenith. Of course, I can never escape from the errors and weaknesses necessarily inherent in my nature as in that of everyone else, but I shall not increase them by unworthy accommodations.

Now, as regards this second edition, in the first place I am glad that after twenty-five years I find nothing to retract; my fundamental convictions have been confirmed, at any rate as far as I myself am concerned. Accordingly, the alterations in the first volume, which contains only the text of the first edition, nowhere touch what is essential, but relate to matters of only secondary importance. For the most part, indeed, they consist of very short explanatory additions inserted here and there. The criticism of the Kantian philosophy alone has received important corrections and lengthy additions, for these could not be brought into a supplementary book, like those that have been received in the second volume by each of the four

---

[3] Fichte and Schelling.
[4] Hegel.

books representing my own teaching. In the case of these, I have chosen the latter form of enlargement and improvement, because the twenty-five years that have elapsed since they were written have produced so marked a change in my method of presentation, and in the tone of my exposition, that it would not do to amalgamate the contents of the second volume with those of the first into one whole, as both would inevitably have suffered from such a fusion. I therefore present the two works separately, and in the earlier exposition, even in many places where I should now express myself quite differently, I have altered nothing. This I have done because I wanted to guard against spoiling the work of my earlier years by the carping criticism of old age. What might need correction in this respect will set itself right in the reader's mind with the aid of the second volume. Both volumes have, in the full sense of the word, a supplementary relation to each other, in so far as this is due to one age in man's life being, in an intellectual regard, the supplement of another. We shall therefore find that not only does each volume contain what the other does not, but also that the merits of the one consist precisely in what is wanting in the other. If therefore the first half of my work excels the second half in what can be vouchsafed only by the fire of youth and the energy of first conception, then the second will surpass the first in the maturity and complete elaboration of the ideas, which belongs only to the fruit of a long life, and of its application and industry. For when I had the strength originally to grasp the fundamental idea of my system, to pursue it at once into its four branches, to return from these to the unity of their stem, and then to make a clear presentation of the whole, I could not yet be in a position to work through all the parts of the system with that completeness, thoroughness, and fulness which are attained only by many years of meditation on it. Such meditation is required to test and illustrate the system by innumerable facts, to support it by proofs of the most varied nature, to throw a clear light on it from all sides, and then to place in bold contrast the different points of view, to separate the manifold materials clearly and present them in a systematic order. Therefore, although it was certainly bound to be more pleasant for the reader to have the whole of my work in one piece, instead of its consisting as now of two halves to be brought together in use, let him reflect that this would have required my achieving at one period of my life what is possible only in two, since for this I should have had to possess at one period of life the qualities which nature has divided between two quite different periods. Accordingly, the necessity for presenting my work in two halves supplementing each other is to be compared to the necessity by which an achromatic object-glass, since it cannot be made out of one piece, is produced by making it up out of a convex lens of crown-glass and a concave lens of flint-glass, the combined effect of which above all achieves what was intended. On the other hand, the reader will find some compensation for the inconvenience of using two volumes at the same time in the variety and relief afforded from the treatment of the same subject by the same mind, in the same spirit, but in very different years. For the reader who is not yet acquainted with my philosophy, however, it is generally advisable to read first of all through the first volume without dragging in the supplements, and to use these only on a second reading. For otherwise it would be too difficult for him to grasp the system in its continuity, as only in the first volume is it presented as such, while in the second the principal doctrines are established individually in greater detail, and developed more completely. Even the reader who might not decide on a second reading of the first volume will find it better to read through the second volume by itself, and only after the first volume. This he can do in the ordinary sequence of its chapters, which certainly stand to one another in a looser connexion, and the gaps in this will be completely filled by recollection of the first volume, if the reader has really grasped that. Moreover, he will everywhere find reference to the corresponding passages of the first volume. For this purpose, in the second edition of the first volume I have furnished with numbers the paragraphs which in the first edition were divided only by lines.

I have already explained in the preface to the first edition that my philosophy starts from Kant's, and therefore presupposes a thorough knowledge of it; I repeat this here. For Kant's teaching produces a fundamental change in every mind that has grasped it. This change is so great that it may be regarded as an intellectual rebirth. It alone is capable of really removing the inborn realism which arises from the original disposition of the intellect. Neither Berkeley nor Malebranche is competent to do this, for these men remain too much in the universal, whereas Kant goes into the particular. And this he does in a way which is unexampled either before or after him, and one which has quite a peculiar, one might say immediate, effect on the mind. In consequence of this, the mind undergoes a fundamental undeceiving, and thereafter looks at all things in another light. But only in this way does a man become susceptible to the more positive explanations that I have to give. On the other hand, the man who has not mastered the Kantian philosophy, whatever else he may have studied, is, so to speak, in a state of innocence; in other words, he has remained in the grasp of that natural and childlike realism in which we are all born, and which qualifies one for every possible thing except philosophy. Consequently, such a man is related to the other as a person under age is to an adult. That nowadays this truth sounds paradoxical, as it certainly would not have done in the first thirty years after the appearance of the *Critique of Reason*, is due to the fact that there has since grown up a generation that does not really know Kant. It has never done more than peruse him hastily and impatiently, or listen to an account at second-hand; and this again is due to its having, in consequence of bad guidance, wasted its time on the philosophemes of ordinary, and hence officious and intrusive, heads, or even of bombastic sophists, which have been irresponsibly commended to it. Hence the confusion in the first conceptions, and generally the unspeakable crudity and clumsiness that appear from under the cloak of affectation and pretentiousness in the philosophical attempts of the generation thus brought up. But the man who imagines he can become acquainted with Kant's philosophy from the descriptions of others, labours under a terrible mistake. On the contrary, I must utter a serious warning against accounts of this kind, especially those of recent times. In fact in the most recent years in the writings of the Hegelians I have come across descriptions of the Kantian philosophy which really reach the incredible. How could minds strained and ruined in the freshness of youth by the nonsense of Hegelism still be capable of following Kant's profound investigations? They are early accustomed to regard the hollowest of verbiage as philosophical thoughts, the most miserable sophisms as sagacity, and silly craziness as dialectic; and by accepting frantic word-combinations in which the mind torments and exhausts itself in vain to conceive something, their heads are disorganized. They do not require any *Critique of Reason* or any philosophy; they need a *medicina mentis*, first as a sort of purgative, *un petit cours de senscommunologie*,[5] and after that one must see whether there can still be any talk of philosophy with them. Thus the Kantian doctrine will be sought in vain elsewhere than in Kant's own works; but these are instructive throughout, even where he errs, even where he fails. In consequence of his originality, it is true of him in the highest degree, as indeed of all genuine philosophers, that only from their own works does one come to know them, not from the accounts of others. For the thoughts of those extraordinary minds cannot stand filtration through an ordinary head. Born behind the broad, high, finely arched brows from under which beaming eyes shine forth, they lose all power and life, and no longer appear like themselves, when moved into the narrow

---

[5] "A short course in common sense." [Tr.]

lodging and low roofing of the confined, contracted, and thick-walled skulls from which peer out dull glances directed to personal ends. In fact, it can be said that heads of this sort act like uneven mirrors in which everything is twisted and distorted, loses the symmetry of its beauty, and represents a caricature. Only from their creators themselves can we receive philosophical thoughts. Therefore the man who feels himself drawn to philosophy must himself seek out its immortal teachers in the quiet sanctuary of their works. The principal chapters of any one of these genuine philosophers will furnish a hundred times more insight into their doctrines than the cumbersome and distorted accounts of them produced by commonplace minds that are still for the most part deeply entangled in the fashionable philosophy of the time, or in their own pet opinions. But it is astonishing how decidedly the public prefers to grasp at those descriptions at second-hand. In fact, an elective affinity seems to be at work here by virtue of which the common nature is drawn to its like, and accordingly will prefer to hear from one of its kind even what a great mind has said. Perhaps this depends on the same principle as the system of mutual instruction according to which children learn best from other children.

*   *   *

Now one more word for the professors of philosophy. I have always felt compelled to admire not only the sagacity, the correct and fine tact with which, immediately on its appearance, they recognized my philosophy as something quite different from, and indeed dangerous to, their own attempts, or in popular language as something that did not suit their purpose; but also the sure and astute policy by virtue of which they at once found out the only correct procedure towards it, the perfect unanimity with which they applied this, and finally the determination with which they have remained faithful to it. This procedure, which incidentally commended itself also by the ease with which it can be carried out, consists, as is well known, in wholly ignoring and thus in secreting—according to Goethe's malicious expression, which really means suppressing what is of importance and of significance. The effectiveness of this silent method is enhanced by the corybantic shouting with which the birth of the spiritual children of those of the same mind is reciprocally celebrated, shouting which forces the public to look and to notice the important airs with which they greet one another over it. Who could fail to recognize the purpose of this procedure? Is there then nothing to be said against the

maxim *primum vivere, deinde philosophari?* [6] The gentlemen want
to live, and indeed to live by *philosophy.* To philosophy they are
assigned with their wives and children, and in spite of Petrarch's
povera e nuda vai filosofia, [7] they have taken a chance on it. Now
my philosophy is certainly not so ordered that anyone could live by
it. It lacks the first indispensable requisite for a well-paid professorial
philosophy, namely a speculative theology, which should and must be
the principal theme of all philosophy—in spite of the troublesome
Kant with his *Critique of Reason;* although such a philosophy thus
has the task of for ever talking about that of which it can know
absolutely nothing. In fact, my philosophy does not allow of the
fiction which has been so cleverly devised by the professors of philosophy and has become indispensable to them, namely the fiction of
a reason that knows, perceives, or apprehends immediately and
absolutely. One need only impose this fiction on the reader at the
very beginning, in order to drive in the most comfortable manner
in the world, in a carriage and four so to speak, into that region
beyond all possibility of experience, wholly and for ever shut off
from our knowledge by Kant. In such a region, then, are to be found,
immediately revealed and most beautifully arranged, precisely those
fundamental dogmas of modern, Judaizing, optimistic Christianity.
My meditative philosophy, deficient in these essential requisites,
lacking in consideration and the means of subsistence, has for its
pole star truth alone, naked, unrewarded, unbefriended, often per-
secuted truth, and towards this it steers straight, looking neither to
the right nor to the left. Now what in the world has such a philosophy to do with that *alma mater,* the good, substantial university philosophy, which, burdened with a hundred intentions and a thousand
considerations, proceeds on its course cautiously tacking, since at all
times it has before its eyes the fear of the Lord, the will of the
ministry, the dogmas of the established Church, the wishes of the
publisher, the encouragement of students, the goodwill of colleagues,
the course of current politics, the momentary tendency of the public,
and Heaven knows what else? Or what has my silent and serious
search for truth in common with the yelling school disputations of
the chairs and benches, whose most secret motives are always personal aims? On the contrary, the two kinds of philosophy are fundamentally different. Therefore with me there is no compromise and
there is no fellowship, and no one derives any advantage from me,
except perhaps the man who is looking for nothing but the truth;
none, therefore, of the philosophical parties of the day, for they all

---

[6] "First live, then philosophize." [Tr.]

[7] "Philosophy, thou goest poor and nude!" [Tr.]

pursue their own aims. I, however, have only insight and discernment to offer, which suit none of those aims, because they are simply not modelled on any of them. But if my philosophy itself were to become susceptible to the professor's chair, there would have to be a complete change in the times. It would be a fine thing, then, if such a philosophy, by which no one can live at all, were to gain light and air, not to mention universal regard! Consequently, this had to be guarded against, and all had to oppose it as one man. But a man has not so easy a game with disputing and refuting; moreover, these are precarious and uncertain means, for the very reason that they direct public attention to the matter, and reading my works might ruin the public's taste for the lucubrations of the professors of philosophy. For the man who has tasted the serious will no longer relish the comic, especially when it is of a tedious nature. Therefore the system of silence, so unanimously resorted to, is the only right one, and I can only advise them to stick to it, and go on with it as long as it works—in other words, until ignoring is taken to imply ignorance; then there will still just be time to come round. Meanwhile, everyone is at liberty to pluck a little feather here and there for his own use, for the superfluity of ideas at home is not usually very oppressive. Thus the system of ignoring and of maintaining silence can last for a good while, at any rate for the span of time that I may yet have to live; in this way much is already gained. If in the meantime an indiscreet voice here and there has allowed itself to be heard, it is soon drowned by the loud talking of the professors who, with their airs of importance, know how to entertain the public with quite different things. But I advise a somewhat stricter observance of the unanimity of procedure, and, in particular, supervision of the young men, who at times are terribly indiscreet. For even so, I am unable to guarantee that the commended procedure will last for ever, and I cannot be answerable for the final result. It is a ticklish question, the steering of the public, good and docile as it is on the whole. Although we see the Gorgiases and Hippiases nearly always at the top; although as a rule the absurd culminates, and it seems impossible for the voice of the individual ever to penetrate through the chorus of foolers and the fooled, still there is left to the genuine works of all times a quite peculiar, silent, slow, and powerful influence; and as if by a miracle, we see them rise at last out of the turmoil like a balloon that floats up out of the thick atmosphere of this globe into purer regions. Having once arrived there, it remains at rest, and no one can any longer draw it down again.

Frankfurt a. M., February 1844.

Preface to the Third Edition

The true and the genuine would more easily obtain a footing in the world, were it not that those incapable of producing it were at the same time pledged not to let it gain ground. This circumstance has already hindered and retarded, if indeed it has not stifled, many a work that should be of benefit to the world. For me the consequence of this has been that, although I was only thirty years of age when the first edition of this book appeared, I live to see this third edition not until my seventy-second year. Nevertheless, I find consolation for this in the words of Petrarch: *Si quis tota die currens, pervenit ad vesperam, satis est* (*De Vera Sapientia*, p. 140).[1] If I also have at last arrived, and have the satisfaction at the end of my life of seeing the beginning of my influence, it is with the hope that, according to an old rule, it will last the longer in proportion to the lateness of its beginning.

In this third edition the reader will miss nothing that is contained in the second, but will receive considerably more, since, by reason of the additions made to it, it has, though in the same type, 136 pages more than its predecessor.

Seven years after the appearance of the second edition, I published the two volumes of the *Parerga and Paralipomena*. What is to be understood by the latter name consists of additions to the systematic presentation of my philosophy, which would have found their rightful place in these volumes. At that time, however, I had to fit them in where I could, as it was very doubtful whether I should live to see this third edition. They will be found in the second volume of the aforesaid *Parerga*, and will be easily recognized from the headings of the chapters.

Frankfurt a. M., September 1859.

---

[1] "If anyone who wanders all day arrives towards evening, it is enough." [Tr.]

Selected Bibliography

German Editions:

Schopenhauers sämtliche Werke. Ed. Paul Deussen. 13 vols. Munich: R. Piper, 1911–42.

Schopenhauers sämtliche Werke. Ed. Arthur Hübscher. 7 vols. Wiesbaden: F. A. Brockhaus, 1946–50.

Schopenhauers handschriftlicher Nachlass. Ed. Arthur Hübscher. 5 vols. Frankfurt am Main: Waldemar Kramer, 1966——(vols. 1, 2 and 5 already published).

Translations:

On the Fourfold Root of the Principle of Sufficient Reason. On the Will in Nature. Trans. E. F. J. Payne (to be published by Open Court Publishing Co. in one volume).

On the Freedom of the Will. Trans. Konstantin Kolenda. Library of Liberal Arts, Bobbs-Merrill, New York, 1960.

On the Basis of Morality. Trans. E. F. J. Payne. Library of Liberal Arts, Bobbs-Merrill, New York, 1965.

Selected Essays of Arthur Schopenhauer. Trans. and ed. E. Belfort Bax. G. Bell & Sons, London, 1926.

The Pessimist's Handbook: A Collection of Popular Essays. Trans. T. Bailey Saunders. Ed. Hazel Barnes. Bison Books, Lincoln: University of Nebraska Press, 1964.

Beer, Margrieta. *Schopenhauer.* London: T. C. & E. C. Jack, 1914.

Copleston, Frederick. *Arthur Schopenhauer: Philosopher of Pessimism.* London: Burns, Oates and Washbourne, 1947.

[xxix]

Deussen, Paul. *The Elements of Metaphysics.* London: Macmillan & Co., 1894.

Döring, W. O. *Schopenhauer.* Hamburg: Hansischer Gildenverlag, 1947.

Gardiner, Patrick. *Schopenhauer.* Baltimore: Penguin Books, 1963.

Hübscher, A. *Arthur Schopenhauer: Mensch und Philosoph in seinen Briefen.* Wiesbaden: F. A. Brockhaus, 1960.

——. *Schopenhauer: Biographie eines Weltbildes.* Stuttgart: Reclam, 1967.

——. *Schopenhauer-Bildnisse: Eine Ikonographie.* Frankfurt am Main: Waldemar Kramer, 1968.

Pfeiffer, K. *Arthur Schopenhauer: Persönlichkeit und Werk.* Leipzig: A. Kröner, 1925.

Saltus, Edgar E. *The Philosophy of Disenchantment.* New York: Belford Co., 1885 (New York: AMS Press, Inc.).

Schmidt, K. O. *Das Erwachen aus dem Lebens-Traum.* Pfullingen: Baum Verlag, 1957.

Taylor, Richard. *The Will to Live.* New York: Anchor Books, 1962.

Wagner, G. F. *Schopenhauer-Register.* Stuttgart: Fr. Frommann, 1960.

Whittaker, Thomas. *Schopenhauer.* London: Constable, 1920.

Zimmern, Helen. *Arthur Schopenhauer: His Life and His Philosophy.* London: Longmans, Green & Co., 1876.

Zint, Hans. *Schopenhauer als Erlebnis.* Munich: E. Reinhardt, 1954.

Contents, Volume I

First Book: The World as Representation. First Aspect   1

Second Book: The World as Will. First Aspect   93

Third Book: The World as Representation. Second Aspect   167

Fourth Book: The World as Will: Second Aspect   269

Appendix: Criticism of the Kantian Philosophy   413

FIRST BOOK

THE WORLD AS REPRESENTATION

FIRST ASPECT

The Representation subject to the Principle of Sufficient
Reason: The Object of Experience and of Science.

Sors de l'enfance, ami, réveille-toi!
Jean-Jacques Rousseau

("Quit thy childhood, my friend, and wake up." [Tr.])

§ 1.

The world is my representation": this is a truth valid with reference to every living and knowing being, although man alone can bring it into reflective, abstract consciousness. If he really does so, philosophical discernment has dawned on him. It then becomes clear and certain to him that he does not know a sun and an earth, but only an eye that sees a sun, a hand that feels an earth; that the world around him is there only as representation, in other words, only in reference to another thing, namely that which represents, and this is himself. If any truth can be expressed *a priori,* it is this; for it is the statement of that form of all possible and conceivable experience, a form that is more general than all others, than time, space, and causality, for all these presuppose it. While each of these forms, which we have recognized as so many particular modes of the principle of sufficient reason, is valid only for a particular class of representations, the division into object and subject, on the other hand, is the common form of all those classes; it is that form under which alone any representation, of whatever kind it be, abstract or intuitive, pure or empirical, is generally possible and conceivable. Therefore no truth is more certain, more independent of all others, and less in need of proof than this, namely that everything that exists for knowledge, and hence the whole of this world, is only object in relation to the subject, perception of the perceiver, in a word, representation. Naturally this holds good of the present as well as of the past and future, of what is remotest as well as of what is nearest; for it holds good of time and space themselves, in which alone all these distinctions arise. Everything that in any way belongs and can belong to the world is inevitably associated with this being-conditioned by the subject, and it exists only for the subject. The world is representation.

This truth is by no means new. It was to be found already in the sceptical reflections from which Descartes started. But Berkeley was the first to enunciate it positively, and he has thus rendered an immortal service to philosophy, although the remainder of his doctrines cannot endure. Kant's first mistake was the neglect of this principle, as is pointed out in the Appendix. On the other hand, how early this basic truth was recognized by the sages of India, since it appears as

[3]

the fundamental tenet of the Vedânta philosophy ascribed to Vyasa, is proved by Sir William Jones in the last of his essays: "On the Philosophy of the Asiatics" (*Asiatic Researches,* vol. IV, p. 164): "The fundamental tenet of the Vedânta school consisted not in denying the existence of matter, that is, of solidity, impenetrability, and extended figure (to deny which would be lunacy), but in correcting the popular notion of it, and in contending that it has no essence independent of mental perception; that existence and perceptibility are convertible terms." These words adequately express the compatibility of empirical reality with transcendental ideality.

Thus in this first book we consider the world only from the above-mentioned angle, only in so far as it is representation. The inner reluctance with which everyone accepts the world as his mere representation warns him that this consideration, quite apart from its truth, is nevertheless one-sided, and so is occasioned by some arbitrary abstraction. On the other hand, he can never withdraw from this acceptance. However, the one-sidedness of this consideration will be made good in the following book through a truth that is not so immediately certain as that from which we start here. Only deeper investigation, more difficult abstraction, the separation of what is different, and the combination of what is identical can lead us to this truth. This truth, which must be very serious and grave if not terrible to everyone, is that a man also can say and must say: "The world is my will."

But in this first book it is necessary to consider separately that side of the world from which we start, namely the side of the knowable, and accordingly to consider without reserve all existing objects, nay even our own bodies (as we shall discuss more fully later on), merely as representation, to call them mere representation. That from which we abstract here is invariably only the *will,* as we hope will later on be clear to everyone. This will alone constitutes the other aspect of the world, for this world is, on the one side, entirely *representation,* just as, on the other, it is entirely *will.* But a reality that is neither of these two, but an object in itself (into which also Kant's thing-in-itself has unfortunately degenerated in his hands), is the phantom of a dream, and its acceptance is an *ignis fatuus* in philosophy.

§ 2.

That which knows all things and is known by none is the *subject*. It is accordingly the supporter of the world, the universal condition of all that appears, of all objects, and it is always presupposed; for whatever exists, exists only for the subject. Everyone finds himself as this subject, yet only in so far as he knows, not in so far as he is object of knowledge. But his body is already object, and therefore from this point of view we call it representation. For the body is object among objects and is subordinated to the laws of objects, although it is immediate object.[1] Like all objects of perception, it lies within the forms of all knowledge, in time and space through which there is plurality. But the subject, the knower never the known, does not lie within these forms; on the contrary, it is always presupposed by those forms themselves, and hence neither plurality nor its opposite, namely unity, belongs to it. We never know it, but it is precisely that which knows wherever there is knowledge.

Therefore the world as representation, in which aspect alone we are here considering it, has two essential, necessary, and inseparable halves. The one half is the *object*, whose forms are space and time, and through these plurality. But the other half, the subject, does not lie in space and time, for it is whole and undivided in every representing being. Hence a single one of these beings with the object completes the world as representation just as fully as do the millions that exist. And if that single one were to disappear, then the world as representation would no longer exist. Therefore these halves are inseparable even in thought, for each of the two has meaning and existence only through and for the other; each exists with the other and vanishes with it. They limit each other immediately; where the object begins, the subject ceases. The common or reciprocal nature of this limitation is seen in the very fact that the essential, and hence universal, forms of every object, namely space, time, and causality, can be found and fully known, starting from the subject, even without the knowledge of the object itself, that is to say, in Kant's language, they reside *a priori* in our consciousness. To have discovered this is

---

[1] *On the Principle of Sufficient Reason*, 2nd ed., § 22.

one of Kant's chief merits, and it is a very great one. Now in addition to this, I maintain that the principle of sufficient reason is the common expression of all these forms of the object of which we are *a priori* conscious, and that therefore all that we know purely *a priori* is nothing but the content of that principle and what follows therefrom; hence in it is really expressed the whole of our *a priori* certain knowledge. In my essay *On the Principle of Sufficient Reason* I have shown in detail how every possible object is subordinate to it, that is to say, stands in a necessary relation to other objects, on the one hand as determined, on the other as determining. This extends so far that the entire existence of all objects, in so far as they are objects, representations, and nothing else, is traced back completely to this necessary relation of theirs to one another, consists only in that relation, and hence is entirely relative; but more of this later. I have further shown that this necessary relation, expressed in general by the principle of sufficient reason, appears in other forms corresponding to the classes into which objects are divided according to their possibility; and again that the correct division of those classes is verified by these forms. Here I constantly assume that what was said in that essay is known and present to the reader, for had it not already been said there, it would have its necessary place here.

§ 3.

The main difference among all our representations is that between the intuitive and the abstract. The latter constitutes only one class of representations, namely concepts; and on earth these are the property of man alone. The capacity for these which distinguishes him from all animals has at all times been called *reason* (*Vernunft*).[2] We shall consider further these abstract representations by themselves, but first of all we shall speak exclusively of the *intuitive representation*. This embraces the entire visible world, or the whole of experience, together with the conditions of its possibility. As we have said, it is one of Kant's very important discoveries that these very conditions, these forms of the visible world, in other words, the most

[2] Only Kant has confused this conception of reason, and in this connexion I refer to the Appendix as well as to my *Grundprobleme der Ethik,* "Grundlage der Moral," § 6, pp. 148-154 of the first edition (pp. 146-151 of the second).

universal element in its perception, the common property of all its
phenomena, time and space, even by themselves and separated from
their content, can be not only thought in the abstract, but also directly
perceived. This perception or intuition is not some kind of phantasm,
borrowed from experience through repetition, but is so entirely independent of experience that, on the contrary, experience must be
thought of as dependent on it, since the properties of space and time,
as they are known in *a priori* perception or intuition, are valid for all
possible experience as laws. Everywhere experience must turn out in
accordance with these laws. Accordingly, in my essay *On the Principle of Sufficient Reason*, I have regarded time and space, in so far as
they are perceived pure and empty of content, as a special class of
representations existing by itself. Now this quality of those universal
forms of intuition, discovered by Kant, is certainly very important, the
quality, that is, that they are perceivable in themselves and independently of experience, and are knowable by their entire conformity
to law, on which rests mathematics with its infallibility. Not less remarkable, however, is the quality of time and space that the principle
of sufficient reason, which determines experience as the law of causality and of motivation, and thought as the law of the basis of judgements, appears in them in quite a special form, to which I have given
the name *ground of being*. In time this is the succession of its moments, and in space the position of its parts, which reciprocally determine one another to infinity.

Anyone who has clearly seen from the introductory essay the complete identity of the content of the principle of sufficient reason, in
spite of all the variety of its forms, will also be convinced of the importance of the knowledge of the simplest of its forms as such for an
insight into his own inmost nature. We have recognized this simplest
form to be *time*. In time each moment is, only in so far as it has
effaced its father the preceding moment, to be again effaced just as
quickly itself. Past and future (apart from the consequences of their
content) are as empty and unreal as any dream; but present is only
the boundary between the two, having neither extension nor duration.
In just the same way, we shall also recognize the same emptiness in
all the other forms of the principle of sufficient reason, and shall see
that, like time, space also, and like this, everything that exists simultaneously in space and time, and hence everything that proceeds from
causes or motives, has only a relative existence, is only through and
for another like itself, i.e., only just as enduring. In essence this view
is old; in it Heraclitus lamented the eternal flux of things; Plato spoke
with contempt of its object as that which for ever becomes, but never
is; Spinoza called it mere accidents of the sole substance that alone

is and endures; Kant opposed to the thing-in-itself that which is known
as mere phenomenon; finally, the ancient wisdom of the Indians
declares that "it is Mâyâ, the veil of deception, which covers the eyes of
mortals, and causes them to see a world of which one cannot say
either that it is or that it is not; for it is like a dream, like the sunshine on the sand which the traveller from a distance takes to be
water, or like the piece of rope on the ground which he regards as a
snake." (These similes are repeatedly found in innumerable passages
of the *Vedas* and *Puranas*.) But what all these meant, and that of
which they speak, is nothing else but what we are now considering,
namely the world as representation subordinated to the principle of
sufficient reason.

§ 4.

H e who has recognized the form of the principle
of sufficient reason, which appears in pure time as such, and on which
all counting and calculating are based, has thereby also recognized
the whole essence of time. It is nothing more than that very form of
the principle of sufficient reason, and it has no other quality or attribute. Succession is the form of the principle of sufficient reason in
time, and succession is the whole essence and nature of time. Further,
he who has recognized the principle of sufficient reason as it rules in
mere, purely perceived space, has thereby exhausted the whole nature
of space. For this is absolutely nothing else but the possibility of the
reciprocal determinations of its parts by one another, which is called
position. The detailed consideration of this, and the formulation of
the results flowing from it into abstract conceptions for convenient
application, form the subject-matter of the whole of geometry. Now
in just the same way, he who has recognized that form of the principle of sufficient reason which governs the content of those forms (of
time and space), their perceptibility, i.e., matter, and hence the law
of causality, has thereby recognized the entire essence and nature of
matter as such; for matter is absolutely nothing but causality, as anyone sees immediately the moment he reflects on it. Thus its being is
its acting; it is not possible to conceive for it any other being. Only as
something acting does it fill space and time; its action on the immediate object (which is itself matter) conditions the perception in which

alone it exists. The consequence of the action of every material object on another is known only in so far as the latter now acts on the immediate object in a way different from that in which it acted previously; it consists in this alone. Thus cause and effect are the whole essence and nature of matter; its being is its acting. (Details of this are to be found in the essay *On the Principle of Sufficient Reason,* § 21, p. 77.) The substance of everything material is therefore very appropriately called in German *Wirklichkeit,*[3] a word much more expressive than *Realität.* That on which it acts, again, is always matter; thus its whole being and essence consist only in the orderly and regular change produced by one part of it in another; consequently, its being and essence are entirely relative, according to a relation that is valid only within its limits, and hence just like time and space.

Time and space, however, each by itself, can be represented in intuition even without matter; but matter cannot be so represented without time and space. The form inseparable from it presupposes *space,* and its action, in which its entire existence consists, always concerns a change, and hence a determination of *time.* But time and space are not only, each by itself, presupposed by matter, but a combination of the two constitutes its essential nature, just because this, as we have shown, consists in action, in causality. All the innumerable phenomena and conditions of things that can be conceived could thus lie side by side in endless space without limiting one another, or even follow one another in endless time without disturbing one another. Thus a necessary relation of these phenomena to one another, and a rule determining them according to this relation, would then not be at all needful, or even applicable. Thus, in the case of all juxtaposition in space and of all change in time, so long as each of these two forms by itself, and without any connexion with the other, had its course and duration, there would be no causality at all, and as this constitutes the real essence of matter, there would also be no matter. But the law of causality receives its meaning and necessity only from the fact that the essence of change does not consist in the mere variation of states or conditions in themselves. On the contrary, it consists in the fact that, at the *same place in space,* there is now *one* condition or state and then *another,* and at *one* and the same point of time there is *here* this state and *there* that state. Only this

---

[3] *Mira in quibusdam rebus verborum proprietas est, et consuetudo sermonis antiqui quaedam efficacissimis notis signat.* Seneca, *Epist.* 81.

"The appropriateness of expression for many things is astonishing, and the usage of language, handed down from the ancients, expresses many things in the most effective manner." [Tr.]

mutual limitation of time and space by each other gives meaning, and at the same time necessity, to a rule according to which change must take place. What is determined by the law of causality is therefore not the succession of states in mere time, but that succession in respect of a particular space, and not only the existence of states at a particular place, but at this place at a particular time. Thus change, i.e., variation occurring according to the causal law, always concerns a particular part of space and a particular part of time, *simultaneously* and in union. Consequently, causality unites space and time. But we found that the whole essence of matter consists in action, and hence in causality; consequently, space and time must also be united in this, in other words, matter must carry within itself simultaneously the properties and qualities of time and those of space, however much the two are opposed to each other. It must unite within itself what is impossible in each of those two independently, the unstable flight of time with the rigid unchangeable persistence of space; from both it has infinite divisibility. Accordingly, through it we find *coexistence* first brought about. This could not be either in mere time, that knows no juxtaposition, or in mere space, that knows no before, after, or now. But the *coexistence* of many states constitutes in fact the essence of reality, for through it *permanence or duration* first becomes possible. Permanence is knowable only in the change of that which exists simultaneously with what is permanent; but also only by means of what is permanent in variation does variation receive the character of *change,* i.e., of the alteration of quality and form in spite of the persistence of substance, i.e., of *matter.*[4] In mere space, the world would be rigid and immovable, with no succession, no change, no action; but with action arises also the representation of matter. Again, in mere time everything would be fleeting, with no persistence, no juxtaposition, and therefore no coexistence, consequently no permanence or duration, and thus also once more no matter. Only through the combination of time and space arises matter, that is to say, the possibility of coexistence, and so of duration; and again, through duration the possibility of persistence of substance with change of states and conditions.[5] As matter has its essential nature in the union of time and space, it bears in all respects the stamp of both. It shows its origin from space partly through the form that is inseparable from it, and particularly through its persistence (substance), (since variation belongs to time alone, but in it alone and for it nothing is per-

---

[4] It is explained in the Appendix that matter and substance are one.

[5] This shows the ground of the Kantian explanation of matter "that it is what is movable in space," for motion consists only in the union of space and time.

manent). The *a priori* certainty of persistence or substance is therefore to be wholly and entirely derived from that of space.[6] Matter reveals its origin from time in quality (accident), without which it never appears, and which is positively always causality, action on other matter, and hence change (a concept of time). The conformity to law of this action, however, always has reference to space and time simultaneously, and only thus has meaning. The legislative force of causality relates solely and entirely to the determination as to what kind of state or condition must appear *at this time and in this place.* On this derivation of the basic determinations of matter from the forms of our knowledge, of which we are *a priori* conscious, rests our knowledge *a priori* of the sure and certain properties of matter. These are space-occupation, i.e., impenetrability, i.e., effectiveness, then extension, infinite divisibility, persistence, i.e., indestructibility, and finally mobility. On the other hand, gravity, notwithstanding its universality, is to be attributed to knowledge *a posteriori,* although Kant in his *Metaphysical Rudiments of Natural Science* (p. 71: Rosenkranz's edition, p. 372) asserts that it is knowable *a priori.*

But as the object in general exists only for the subject as the representation thereof, so does every special class of representations exist only for an equally special disposition in the subject, which is called a faculty of knowledge. The subjective correlative of time and space in themselves, as empty forms, was called by Kant pure sensibility, and this expression may be retained, as Kant was the pioneer here, although it is not quite suitable; for sensibility presupposes matter. The subjective correlative of matter or of causality, for the two are one and the same, is the *understanding,* and it is nothing more than this. To know causality is the sole function of the understanding, its only power, and it is a great power embracing much, manifold in its application, and yet unmistakable in its identity throughout all its manifestations. Conversely, all causality, hence all matter, and consequently the whole of reality, is only for the understanding, through the understanding, in the understanding. The first, simplest, ever-present manifestation of understanding is perception of the actual world. This is in every way knowledge of the cause from the effect, and therefore all perception is intellectual. Yet one could never arrive at perception, if some effect were not immediately known, and thus served as the starting-point. But this is the action or effect on animal bodies. To this extent these bodies are the *immediate objects* of the subject; through them the perception of all other objects is brought about. The changes experienced by every animal body are immedi-

---

[6] Not, as Kant holds, from the knowledge of time, as is explained in the Appendix.

ately known, that is to say, felt; and as this effect is referred at once
to its cause, there arises the perception of the latter as an *object*. This
relation is no conclusion in abstract concepts, it does not happen
through reflection, it is not arbitrary, but is immediate, necessary,
and certain. It is the cognitive method of the *pure understanding*,
without which perception would never be attained; there would remain only a dull, plant-like consciousness of the changes of the
immediate object which followed one another in a wholly meaningless
way, except in so far as they might have a meaning for the will either
as pain or pleasure. But as with the appearance of the sun the visible
world makes its appearance, so at one stroke does the understanding
through its one simple function convert the dull meaningless sensation
into perception. What the eye, the ear, or the hand experiences is not
perception; it is mere data. Only by the passing of the understanding
from the effect to the cause does the world stand out as perception
extended in space, varying in respect of form, persisting through all
time as regards matter. For the understanding unites space and time
in the representation of *matter*, that is to say, of effectiveness. This
world as representation exists only through the understanding, and
also only for the understanding. In the first chapter of my essay *On
Vision and Colours,* I have explained how the understanding produces perception out of the data furnished by the senses; how by
comparing the impressions received by the different senses from the
same object the child learns perception; how this alone throws light
on so many phenomena of the senses, on single vision with two eyes,
on double vision in the case of squinting, or in the case where we
look simultaneously at objects that lie behind one another at unequal
distances, and on every illusion produced by a sudden alteration in
the organs of sense. But I have treated this important subject much
more fully and thoroughly in the second edition of my essay *On the
Principle of Sufficient Reason* (§ 21). All that is said there has its
necessary place here, and therefore ought really to be said again. But
as I am almost as reluctant to quote myself as to quote others, and as
I am unable to explain the subject better than it is explained there, I
refer the reader to that essay instead of repeating it, and here assume
that it is known.

The process by which children, and persons who are born blind
and have been operated on, learn to see; single vision of whatever is
perceived with two eyes; double vision and double touch, occurring
when the organs of sense are displaced from their usual position; the
upright appearance of objects, whereas their image in the eye is inverted; the attributing of colour to external objects, whereas it is
merely an inner function, a division, through polarization, of the

activity of the eye; and finally also the stereoscope; all these are solid and irrefutable proofs that all *perception* is not only of the senses, but of the intellect; in other words, *pure knowledge through the understanding of the cause from the effect.* Consequently, it presupposes the law of causality, and on the knowledge of this depends all perception, and therefore all experience, by virtue of its primary and entire possibility. The converse, namely that knowledge of the causal law results from experience, is not the case; this was the scepticism of Hume, and is first refuted by what is here said. For the independence of the knowledge of causality from all experience, in other words, its *a priori* character, can alone be demonstrated from the dependence of all experience on it. Again, this can be done only by proving, in the manner here indicated, and explained in the passages above referred to, that the knowledge of causality is already contained in perception generally, in the domain of which all experience is to be found, and hence that it exists wholly *a priori* in respect of experience, that it does not presuppose experience, but is presupposed thereby as a condition. But this cannot be demonstrated in the manner attempted by Kant, which I criticize in the essay *On the Principle of Sufficient Reason* (§ 23).

§ 5.

Now we must guard against the grave misunderstanding of supposing that, because perception is brought about through knowledge of causality, the relation of cause and effect exists between object and subject. On the contrary, this relation always occurs only between immediate and mediate object, and hence always only between objects. On this false assumption rests the foolish controversy about the reality of the external world, a controversy in which dogmatism and scepticism oppose each other, and the former appears now as realism, now as idealism. Realism posits the object as cause, and places its effect in the subject. The idealism of Fichte makes the object the effect of the subject. Since, however—and this cannot be sufficiently stressed—absolutely no relation according to the principle of sufficient reason subsists between subject and object, neither of these two assertions could ever be proved, and scepticism made triumphant attacks on both. Now just as the law of causality already precedes, as condition, perception and experience, and thus cannot be learnt from these (as Hume imagined), so object and subject precede all knowledge, and hence even the principle of sufficient reason in general, as the first condition. For this principle is only the form of every object, the whole nature and manner of its appearance; but the object always presupposes the subject, and hence between the two there can be no relation of reason and consequent. My essay *On the Principle of Sufficient Reason* purports to achieve just this: it explains the content of that principle as the essential form of every object, in other words, as the universal mode and manner of all objective existence, as something which pertains to the object as such. But the object as such everywhere presupposes the subject as its necessary correlative, and hence the subject always remains outside the province of the validity of the principle of sufficient reason. The controversy about the reality of the external world rests precisely on this false extension of the validity of the principle of sufficient reason to the subject also, and, starting from this misunderstanding, it could never understand itself. On the one hand, realistic dogmatism, regarding the representation as the effect of the object, tries to separate these two, representation and object, which are but one, and to assume a cause quite different from the representation, an object-in-itself independent of the subject, something that is wholly inconceivable; for as object it presupposes the subject, and thus always remains only the representation of the subject. Opposed to this is scepticism, with the same false assumption that in the representation we always have only the effect, never the cause, and so never real *being;* that we always know only the *action* of objects. But this, it supposes, might have no resemblance whatever to that being, and would indeed generally be quite falsely assumed, for the law of causality is first accepted from experience, and then the reality of experience is in turn supposed to rest on it. Both these views are open to the correction, firstly, that object and representation are the same thing; that the true *being* of objects of perception is their *action;* that the actuality of the thing consists exactly in this; and that the demand for the existence of the object outside the representation of the subject, and also for a real being of the actual thing distinct from its action, has no meaning at all, and is a contradiction. Therefore knowledge of the nature of the effect of a perceived object exhausts the object itself in so far as it is object, i.e., representation, as beyond this there is nothing left in it for knowledge. To this extent, therefore, the perceived world in space and time, proclaiming itself as nothing but causality, is perfectly real, and is absolutely what it appears to be; it appears wholly and without reserve as representation, hanging together according to the law of causality. This is its empirical reality. On the other hand, all causality is only in the understanding and for the understanding. The entire actual, i.e., active, world is therefore always conditioned as such by the understanding, and without this is nothing. Not for this reason only, but also because in general no object without subject can be conceived without involving a contradiction, we must absolutely deny to the dogmatist the reality of the external world, when he declares this to be its independence of the subject. The whole world of objects is and remains representation, and is for this reason wholly and for ever conditioned by the subject; in other words, it has transcendental ideality. But it is not on that account falsehood or illusion; it presents itself as what it is, as representation, and indeed as a series of representations, whose common bond is the principle of sufficient reason. As such it is intelligible to the healthy understanding, even according to its innermost meaning, and to the understanding it speaks a perfectly clear language. To dispute about its reality can occur only to a mind perverted by over-subtle sophistry; such disputing always occurs through an incorrect application of the principle of sufficient reason. This principle combines all representations, of whatever kind they be, one with another; but it in no way connects these with the subject, or with something that is neither subject nor object but only the ground of the object; an absurdity, since only objects can be the ground of objects, and that indeed always. If we examine the source of this question about the reality of the external world more closely, we find that, besides the false application of the principle of sufficient reason to what lies outside its province, there is in addition a special confusion of its forms. Thus that form, which the principle of sufficient reason has merely in reference to concepts or abstract representations, is extended to representations of perception, to real objects, and a ground of knowing is demanded of objects that can have no other ground than one of becoming. Over the abstract representations, the concepts connected to judgements, the principle of sufficient reason certainly rules in such a way that each of these has its worth, its validity, its whole existence, here called *truth,* simply and solely through the relation of the judgement to something outside it, to its ground of knowledge, to which therefore there must always be a return. On the other hand, over real objects, the representations of perception, the principle of sufficient reason rules as the principle not of the ground of *knowing,* but of *becoming,* as the law of causality. Each of them has paid its debt to it by having *become,* in other words, by having appeared as effect from a cause. Therefore a demand for a ground of knowledge has no validity and no meaning here, but belongs to quite another class of objects. Thus the world of perception raises no question or doubt in the observer, so long as he remains in contact with it. Here there is neither error nor truth, for these are confined to the province of the abstract, of reflection. But here the world lies open to the senses and to the understanding; it presents itself with naïve truth as that which it is, as representation of perception that is developed in the bonds of the law of causality.

So far as we have considered the question of the reality of the external world, it always arose from a confusion, amounting even to a misunderstanding, of the faculty of reason itself, and to this extent the question could be answered only by explaining its subject-matter. After an examination of the whole nature of the principle of sufficient reason, of the relation between object and subject, and of the real character of sense-perception, the question itself was bound to disappear, because there was no longer any meaning in it. But this question has yet another origin, quite different from the purely speculative one so far mentioned, a really empirical origin, although the question is always raised from a speculative point of view, and in this form has a much more comprehensible meaning than it had in the former. We have dreams; may not the whole of life be a dream? or more exactly: is there a sure criterion for distinguishing between dream and reality, between phantasms and real objects? The plea that what is dreamt has less vividness and distinctness than real perception has, is not worth considering at all, for no one has held the two up to comparison; only the *recollection* of the dream could be compared with the present reality. Kant answers the question as follows: "The connexion of the representations among themselves according to the law of causality distinguishes life from the dream." But even in the dream every single thing is connected according to the principle of sufficient reason in all its forms, and this connexion is broken only between life and the dream and between individual dreams. Kant's answer might therefore run as follows: the *long* dream (life) has complete connexion in itself according to the principle of sufficient reason; but it has no such connexion with the *short* dreams, although each of these has within itself the same connexion; thus the bridge between the former and the latter is broken, and on this account the two are distinguished. To institute an inquiry in accordance with this criterion as to whether something was dreamt or really took place would, however, be very difficult, and often impossible. For we are by no means in a position to follow link by link the causal connexion between any experienced event and the present moment; yet we do not on that account declare that it is dreamt. Therefore in real life we do not usually make use of that method of investigation to distinguish between dream and reality. The only certain criterion for distinguishing dream from reality is in fact none other than the wholly empirical one of waking, by which the causal connexion between the dreamed events and those of waking life is at any rate positively and palpably broken off. An excellent proof of this is given by the remark, made by Hobbes in the second chapter of *Leviathan*, that we easily mistake dreams for reality when we have unintentionally fallen asleep in our clothes, and particularly when it happens that some undertaking or scheme occupies all our thoughts, and engrosses our attention in our dreams as well as in our waking moments. In these cases, the waking is almost as little observed as is the falling asleep; dream and reality flow into one another and become confused. Then, of course, only the application of Kant's criterion is left. If subsequently, as is often the case, the causal connexion with the present, or the absence of such connexion, cannot possibly be ascertained, then it must remain for ever undecided whether an event was dreamt or whether it really occurred. Here indeed the close relationship between life and the dream is brought out for us very clearly. We will not be ashamed to confess it, after it has been recognized and expressed by many great men. The *Vedas* and *Puranas* know no better simile for the whole knowledge of the actual world, called by them the web of Mâyâ, than the dream, and they use none more frequently. Plato often says that men live only in the dream; only the philosopher strives to be awake. Pindar says (*Pyth.* viii, 135): σκιᾶς ὄναρ ἄνθρωπος (*umbrae somnium homo*),[7] and Sophocles:

'Ορῶ γὰρ ἡμᾶς οὐδὲν ὄντας ἄλλο, πλὴν
Εἴδωλ', ὅσοιπερ ζῶμεν, ἢ κούφην σκιάν.
Ajax, 125.

(*Nos enim, quicunque vivimus, nihil aliud esse comperio, quam simulacra et levem umbram.*)[8] Beside which Shakespeare stands most worthily:

> "We are such stuff
> As dreams are made on, and our little life
> Is rounded with a sleep."
> *The Tempest*, Act IV, Sc. 1.

Finally, Calderón was so deeply impressed with this view, that he sought to express it in a kind of metaphysical drama, *Life a Dream* ('La Vida es Sueño').

---

[7] "Man is the dream of a shadow." [Tr.]

[8] "I see that we who are alive are nothing but deceptive forms and a fleeting shadow-picture." [Tr.]

After these numerous passages from the poets, I may now be permitted to express myself by a metaphor. Life and dreams are leaves of one and the same book. The systematic reading is real life, but when the actual reading hour (the day) has come to an end, and we have the period of recreation, we often continue idly to thumb over the leaves, and turn to a page here and there without method or connexion. We sometimes turn up a page we have already read, at others one still unknown to us, but always from the same book. Such án isolated page is, of course, not connected with a consistent reading and study of the book, yet it is not so very inferior thereto, if we note that the whole of the consistent perusal begins and ends also on the spur of the moment, and can therefore be regarded merely as a larger single page.

Thus, although individual dreams are marked off from real life by the fact that they do not fit into the continuity of experience that runs constantly through life, and waking up indicates this difference, yet that very continuity of experience belongs to real life as its form, and the dream can likewise point to a continuity in itself. Now if we assume a standpoint of judgement external to both, we find no distinct difference in their nature, and are forced to concede to the poets that life is a long dream.

To return from this entirely independent empirical origin of the question of the reality of the external world to its speculative origin, we have found that this lay firstly in the false application of the principle of sufficient reason, namely between subject and object, and then again in the confusion of its forms, since the principle of sufficient reason of knowing was extended to the province where the principle of sufficient reason of becoming is valid. Yet this question could hardly have occupied philosophers so continuously, if it were entirely without any real content, and if some genuine thought and meaning did not lie at its very core as its real source. Accordingly, from this it would have to be assumed that, first by entering reflection and seeking its expression, it became involved in those confused and incomprehensible forms and questions. This is certainly my opinion, and I reckon that the pure expression of that innermost meaning of the question which it was unable to arrive at, is this: What is this world of perception besides being my representation? Is that of which I am conscious only as representation just the same as my own body, of which I am doubly conscious, on the one hand as *representation,* on the other as *will?* The clearer explanation of this question, and its answer in the affirmative, will be the content of the second book, and the conclusions from it will occupy the remaining part of this work.

§ 6.

Meanwhile for the present, in this first book we are considering everything merely as representation, as object for the subject. And our own body, which is the starting-point for each of us in the perception of the world, we consider, like all other real objects, merely from the side of knowableness, and accordingly it is for us only a representation. Now the consciousness of everyone, which is already opposed to the explanation of other objects as mere representations, is in even greater opposition when his own body is said to be mere representation. Thus it happens that to everyone the thing-in-itself is known immediately in so far as it appears as his own body, and only mediately in so far as it is objectified in the other objects of perception. But the course of our investigation renders necessary this abstraction, this one-sided method of consideration, this forcible separation of two things that essentially exist together. Therefore this reluctance must for the time being be suppressed, and set at rest by the expectation that the following considerations will make up for the one-sidedness of this one, towards a complete knowledge of the nature of the world.

Here, therefore, the body is for us immediate object, in other words, that representation which forms the starting-point of the subject's knowledge, since it itself with its immediately known changes precedes the application of the law of causality, and thus furnishes this with the first data. The whole essence of matter consists, as we have shown, in its action. But there are cause and effect only for the understanding, which is nothing but the subjective correlative of these. The understanding, however, could never attain to application, if there were not something else from which it starts. Such a something is the mere sensation, the immediate consciousness of the changes of the body, by virtue of which this body is immediate object. Accordingly the possibility of knowing the world of perception is to be found in two conditions; the first is, *if we express it objectively,* the ability of bodies to act on one another, to bring about changes in one another. Without that universal property of all bodies no perception would be possible, even by means of the sensibility of animal bodies. If, however, we wish to express this same first condition *sub-*

jectively, we say that the understanding first of all makes perception possible, for the law of causality, the possibility of effect and cause, springs only from the understanding, and is valid also for it alone; hence the world of perception exists only for it and through it. The second condition, however, is the sensibility of animal bodies, or the quality possessed by certain bodies of being directly objects of the subject. The mere changes sustained from without by the sense-organs through the impression specifically appropriate to them can themselves be called representations, in so far as such impressions stimulate neither pain nor pleasure, in other words; have no immediate significance for the will, and yet are perceived, i.e. exist only for *knowledge.* To this extent, therefore, I say that the body is immediately *known, is immediate object.* The conception of object, however, is not to be taken here in the fullest sense, for through this immediate knowledge of the body, which precedes the application of the understanding and is mere sensation, the body itself does not exist really as *object,* but first the bodies acting on it. For all knowledge of an object proper, in other words, of a representation of perception in space, exists only through and for the understanding, and thus not before, but only after, the application of the understanding. Therefore the body as object proper, in other words, as representation of perception in space, is first known indirectly, like all other objects, through the application of the law of causality to the action of one of its parts on another, as by the eye seeing the body, or the hand touching it. Consequently the form of our own body does not become known to us through mere ordinary feeling, but only through knowledge, only in the representation; in other words, only in the brain does our own body first present itself as an extended, articulate, organic thing. A person born blind receives this representation only gradually through data afforded him by touch. A blind man without hands would never get to know his form, or at most would infer and construct it gradually from the impression on him of other bodies. Therefore, if we call the body immediate object, we are to be understood as implying this restriction.

Moreover, it follows from what has been said that all animal bodies are immediate objects, in other words starting-points in the perception of the world for the subject that knows all, and, for this very reason, is never known. *Knowledge,* therefore, with movement consequent on motives conditioned by it, is the proper *characteristic of animal life,* just as movement consequent on stimuli is the characteristic of the plant. But that which is unorganized has no movement other than that produced by causes proper in the narrowest sense. I have discussed all this at length in the essay *On the Principle of*

Sufficient Reason (second ed., § 20), in the *Ethics* (first essay, iii), and in my *Vision and Colours* (§ i), to which therefore I refer the reader.

It follows from what has been said that all animals, even the most imperfect, have understanding, for they all know objects, and this knowledge as motive determines their movements. The understanding is the same in all animals and in all men; everywhere it has the same simple form, that is to say, knowledge of causality, transition from effect to cause and from cause to effect, and nothing else. But the degree of its acuteness and the extent of its sphere of knowledge vary enormously, with many different gradations, from the lowest degree, which knows only the causal relation between the immediate object and indirect ones, and hence is just sufficient to perceive a cause as object in space by passing from the impression experienced by the body to the cause of this impression, up to the higher degrees of knowledge of the causal connexion among merely indirect objects. Such knowledge extends to the understanding of the most complicated concatenations of causes and effects in nature; for even this last degree of knowledge still belongs always to the understanding, not to the faculty of reason. The abstract concepts of reason can only serve to handle what is immediately understood, to fix and arrange this, but never to bring about understanding itself. Every force and law of nature, every case in which such forces and laws are manifested, must first be known immediately by the understanding, must be intuitively apprehended, before it can pass into reflected consciousness *in abstracto* for the faculty of reason. Hooke's discovery of the law of gravitation, and the reference of so many important phenomena to this one law, were intuitive, immediate apprehension through the understanding, and this was also confirmed by Newton's calculations. The same may be said also of Lavoisier's discovery of acids and their important role in nature, and of Goethe's discovery of the origin of physical colours. All these discoveries are nothing but a correct immediate return from the effect to the cause, which is at once followed by recognition of the identity of the natural force which manifests itself in all causes of the same kind. This complete insight is an expression, differing merely in degree, of the same single function of the understanding, by which an animal perceives as object in space the cause affecting its body. Therefore all those great discoveries are, just like perception and every manifestation of understanding, an immediate insight, and as such the work of an instant, an *aperçu*, a sudden idea. They are not the product of long chains of abstract reasoning; these, on the contrary, serve to fix the immediate knowledge of the understanding for the faculty of reason by setting down such knowledge in the abstract concepts of such reason, in other words, to make it clear, to be in a position to point it out and explain it to others. That keenness of the understanding in apprehending the causal relations of objects indirectly known finds its application not only in natural science (all the discoveries of which are due to it), but also in practical life, where it is called *good sense* or *prudence*. But in its first application it is better called acuteness, penetration, sagacity. Strictly speaking, *good sense* or *prudence* signifies exclusively understanding in the service of the will. However, the boundaries of these concepts are never to be drawn sharply, for it is always one and the same function of the same understanding at work in every animal when perceiving objects in space. In its greatest keenness, it accurately investigates in natural phenomena the unknown cause from the given effect, and thus provides the faculty of reason with the material for conceiving general rules as laws of nature. Again, it invents complicated and ingenious machines by applying known causes to intended effects. Or, applied to motivation, it sees through and frustrates subtle intrigues and machinations, or suitably arranges even the motives and the men susceptible to each of them, sets them in motion at will as machines are set in motion by levers and wheels, and directs them to its ends. Want of understanding is called in the proper sense *stupidity,* and it is just *dulness in applying the law of causality,* incapacity for the immediate apprehension of the concatenations of cause and effect, of motive and action. A stupid person has no insight into the connexion of natural phenomena, either when they appear of their own accord or when they are intentionally controlled, in other words made to serve machines. For this reason, he readily believes in magic and miracles. A stupid man does not notice that different persons, apparently independent of one another, are in fact acting together by agreement; he is therefore easily mystified and puzzled. He does not observe the concealed motives of proffered advice, expressed opinions, and so on. But it is invariably only one thing that he lacks, namely keenness, rapidity, ease in applying the law of causality, in other words, power of the understanding. The greatest and, in this respect, the most instructive example of stupidity that I ever came across was that of a totally imbecile boy of about eleven years of age in an asylum. He certainly had the faculty of reason, for he spoke and comprehended, but in understanding he was inferior to many animals. When I came, he noticed an eye-glass which I was wearing round my neck, and in which the windows of the room and the tops of the trees beyond them were reflected. Every time he was greatly astonished and delighted with this, and was never tired of looking at it with surprise. This was because he did not understand this absolutely direct causation of reflection.

As the degree of acuteness of understanding varies a great deal as between men, so does it vary even more as between the different species of animals. In all species, even those nearest to the plant, there exists as much understanding as is sufficient for passing from the effect in the immediate object to the mediate object as cause, and hence for perception, for the apprehension of an object. For it is just this that makes them animals, since it gives them the possibility of movement consequent on motives, and thus of seeking, or at any rate of grasping, nourishment. Plants, on the other hand, have only movement consequent on stimuli, the direct influence of which they must await or else droop; they cannot go after them or grasp them. In the most accomplished animals we marvel at their great sagacity, such as the dog, the elephant, the monkey, or the fox, whose cleverness has been described by Buffon in so masterly a way. In these most sagacious animals we can determine pretty accurately what the understanding is capable of without the aid of reason, that is to say, without the aid of abstract knowledge in concepts. We cannot find this out in ourselves, because in us understanding and the faculty of reason are always mutually supported. Therefore we find that the manifestations of understanding in animals are sometimes above our expectation, sometimes below it. On the one hand, we are surprised at the sagacity of that elephant which, after crossing many bridges on his journey through Europe, once refused to go on one, over which he saw the rest of the party of men and horses crossing as usual, because it seemed to him too lightly built for his weight. On the other hand, we wonder that the intelligent orang-utans, warming themselves at a fire they have found, do not keep it going by replenishing it with wood; a proof that this requires a deliberation that does not come about without abstract concepts. It is quite certain that the knowledge of cause and effect, as the universal form of the understanding, is *a priori* inherent in animals, because for them as for us it is the preliminary condition of all knowledge of the external world through perception. If we still want a special proof of this, let us observe, for example, how even a quite young dog does not venture to jump from the table, however much he wants to, because he foresees the effect of the weight of his body, without, however, knowing this particular case from experience. Meanwhile, in judging the understanding of animals, we must guard against ascribing to it a manifestation of instinct, a quality that is entirely different from it as well as from the faculty of reason; yet it often acts very analogously to the combined activity of these two. The discussion of this, however, does not belong here, but will find its place in the second book, when we are considering the harmony or so-called teleology of nature. The twenty-seventh chapter of the supplementary volume is expressly devoted to it.

Lack of *understanding was called stupidity;* deficiency in the application of the faculty of *reason* to what is practical we shall later recognize as *foolishness;* deficiency in *power of judgement* as *silliness;* finally, partial or even complete *lack of memory* as *madness.* But we shall consider each of these in its proper place. That which is correctly known through the faculty of *reason* is *truth,* namely an abstract judgement with sufficient ground or reason (essay *On the Principle of Sufficient Reason,* § 29 *seqq.*); that which is correctly known by *understanding* is *reality,* namely correctly passing from the effect in the immediate object to its cause. *Error* is opposed to *truth* as deception of *reason; illusion* is opposed to *reality* as deception of *understanding.* The detailed discussion of all this is to be found in the first chapter of my essay *On Vision and Colours. Illusion* comes about when one and the same effect can be brought to pass by two entirely different causes, one of which operates very frequently, the other very rarely. The understanding, having no datum for determining which cause operates in a given case, since the effect is identical, always presupposes the ordinary cause, and because the activity of the understanding is not reflective and discursive, but direct and immediate, such false cause stands before us as perceived object, which is just the false illusion. I have shown, in the essay referred to, how in this way double sight and double touch occur, when the organs of sense are brought into an unusual position, and I have thus given an irrefutable proof that perception exists only through the understanding and for the understanding. Examples of such deception of understanding, or illusion, are the stick that seems broken when dipped in water, the images of spherical mirrors appearing with convex surface somewhat behind them, with concave surface well before them. To this class of examples also belongs the apparently greater extension of the moon at the horizon than at the zenith. This is not optical, for, as the micrometer proves, the eye apprehends the moon at the zenith at an even greater angle of vision than at the horizon. It is the understanding that assumes the cause of the feebler brightness of the moon and of all stars at the horizon to be their greater distance, treating them like earthly objects in accordance with atmospheric perspective. Therefore it regards the moon at the horizon as very much larger than at the zenith, and at the same time also considers the vault of heaven to be more extended, and hence flattened out, at the horizon. The same estimation, falsely applied according to atmospheric perspective, leads us to suppose that very high mountains, whose summits are visible to us only in pure transparent air, are nearer than they really are, to the detriment of their height; as for example, Mont Blanc seen from Salenche. All such deceptive illusions stand before us in immediate perception which cannot be removed by any arguments of reason. Such arguments can prevent merely error, that is to say, a judgement without sufficient ground or reason, by forming an opposite judgement that is true; for instance, knowing in the abstract that the cause of the weaker light of the moon and stars in the case cited is not the greater distance, but the cloudier atmosphere at the horizon. But the illusion remains unshakable in all the cases mentioned, in spite of all abstract knowledge; for the understanding is completely and totally different from the faculty of reason, a cognitive faculty that has been added to man alone; and indeed the understanding is in itself irrational, even in man. Reason can always only *know;* perception remains free from its influence, and belongs to the understanding alone.

§ 7.

With regard to the whole of our discussion so far, we must still note the following. We started neither from the object nor from the subject, but from the *representation,* which contains and presupposes them both; for the division into object and subject is the first, universal, and essential form of the representation. We therefore first considered this form as such; then (though here we refer mainly to the introductory essay) the other forms subordinate to it, namely time, space, and causality. These belong only to the *object,* yet because they are essential to the object *as such,* and as the object again is essential to the subject *as such,* they can be found also from the subject, in other words, they can be known *a priori,* and to this extent are to be regarded as the boundary common to both. But they can all be referred to one common expression, the principle of sufficient reason, as is shown in detail in the introductory essay.

This procedure distinguishes our method of consideration wholly and entirely from every philosophy ever attempted. All previous systems started either from the object or from the subject, and therefore sought to explain the one from the other, and this according to the principle of sufficient reason. We, on the other hand, deny the relation between object and subject to the dominion of this principle, and leave to it only the object. One might regard the philosophy of identity, which has arisen and become generally known in our day, as not coming within the contrast above mentioned, in so far as it makes its real first starting-point neither object nor subject, but a third thing, namely the Absolute, knowable through reason-intuition, which is neither object nor subject, but the identity of the two. As I am completely lacking in all reason-intuition, I shall not venture to speak of the aforesaid revered identity and of the Absolute. Yet, since I take my stand merely on the manifestoes of the reason-intuiters, which are open to all, even to profane persons like us, I must observe that the aforesaid philosophy cannot be excepted from the above-mentioned antithesis of two errors. For it does not avoid those two opposite errors, in spite of the identity of subject and object, which is not thinkable, but is merely intellectually intuitable, or is to be experienced through our being absorbed in it. On the contrary, it combines them both in itself, since it is itself divided into two branches; first, transcendental idealism, that is Fichte's doctrine of the ego; and consequently, according to the principle of sufficient reason, the object can be produced from the subject or spun out of it; and secondly, the philosophy of nature, which likewise represents the subject as coming gradually out of the object by the application of a method called construction, about which very little is clear to me, though enough to know that it is a process according to the principle of sufficient reason in various forms. I renounce the deep wisdom itself contained in that construction, for as I wholly lack reason-intuition, all those expositions which presuppose it must be to me like a book with seven seals. To such a degree is this the case that, strange to relate, with those doctrines of deep wisdom it always seems to me as if I were listening to nothing but atrocious and what is more extremely wearisome humbug.

The systems that start from the object have always had the whole world of perception and its order as their problem, yet the object which they take as their starting-point is not always this world or its fundamental element, namely matter. On the contrary, a division of these systems can be made in accordance with the four classes of possible objects set out in the introductory essay. Thus it can be said that Thales and the Ionians, Democritus, Epicurus, Giordano Bruno, and the French materialists started from the first of those classes, or from the real world. Spinoza (because of his conception of substance, as merely abstract and existing only in his definition), and before him the Eleatics, started from the second class, or from the abstract concept. The Pythagoreans and the Chinese philosophy of the *I Ching* started from the third class, namely from time, and consequently from numbers. Finally, the scholastics, teaching a creation out of nothing through the act of will of an extramundane personal being, started from the fourth class, namely from the act of will, motivated by knowledge.

The objective method can be developed most consistently and carried farthest when it appears as materialism proper. It regards matter, and with it time and space, as existing absolutely, and passes over the relation to the subject in which alone all this exists. Further, it lays hold of the law of causality as the guiding line on which it tries to progress, taking it to be a self-existing order or arrangement of things, *veritas aeterna*, and consequently passing over the understanding, in which and for which alone causality is. It tries to find the first and simplest state of matter, and then to develop all the others from it, ascending from mere mechanism to chemistry, to polarity, to the vegetable and the animal kingdoms. Supposing this were successful, the last link of the chain would be animal sensibility, that is to say knowledge; which, in consequence, would then appear as a mere modification of matter, a state of matter produced by causality. Now if we had followed materialism thus far with clear notions, then, having reached its highest point, we should experience a sudden fit of the inextinguishable laughter of the Olympians. As though waking from a dream, we should all at once become aware that its final result, produced so laboriously, namely knowledge, was already presupposed as the indispensable condition at the very first starting-point, at mere matter. With this we imagined that we thought of matter, but in fact we had thought of nothing but the subject that represents matter, the eye that sees it, the hand that feels it, the understanding that knows it. Thus the tremendous *petitio principii*[9] disclosed itself unexpectedly, for suddenly the last link showed itself as the fixed point, the chain as a circle, and the materialist was like Baron von Münchhausen who, when swimming in water on horseback, drew his horse up by its legs, and himself by his upturned pigtail. Accordingly, the fundamental absurdity of materialism consists in the fact that it starts from the *objective;* it takes an *objective* something as the ultimate ground of explanation, whether this be *matter* in the abstract simply as it is *thought,* or after it has entered into the form and is empirically given, and hence *substance,* perhaps the chemical elements together with their primary combinations. Some such thing it takes as existing absolutely and in itself, in order to let organic

---

[9] "Begging of the question." [Tr.]

nature and finally the knowing subject emerge from it, and thus completely to explain these; whereas in truth everything objective is already conditioned as such in manifold ways by the knowing subject with the forms of its knowing, and presupposes these forms; consequently it wholly disappears when the subject is thought away. Materialism is therefore the attempt to explain what is directly given to us from what is given indirectly. Everything objective, extended, active, and hence everything material, is regarded by materialism as so solid a basis for its explanations that a reduction to this (especially if it should ultimately result in thrust and counter-thrust) can leave nothing to be desired. All this is something that is given only very indirectly and conditionally, and is therefore only relatively present, for it has passed through the machinery and fabrication of the brain, and hence has entered the forms of time, space, and causality, by virtue of which it is first of all presented as extended in space and operating in time. From such an indirectly given thing, materialism tries to explain even the directly given, the representation (in which all this exists), and finally even the will, from which rather are actually to be explained all those fundamental forces which manifest themselves on the guiding line of causes, and hence according to law. To the assertion that knowledge is a modification of matter there is always opposed with equal justice the contrary assertion that all matter is only modification of the subject's knowing, as the subject's representation. Yet at bottom, the aim and ideal of all natural science is a materialism wholly carried into effect. That we here recognize this as obviously impossible confirms another truth that will result from our further consideration, namely the truth that all science in the real sense, by which I understand systematic knowledge under the guidance of the principle of sufficient reason, can never reach a final goal or give an entirely satisfactory explanation. It never aims at the inmost nature of the world; it can never get beyond the representation; on the contrary, it really tells us nothing more than the relation of one representation to another.

Every science invariably starts from two principal data, one of which is always the principle of sufficient reason in some form as organon; the other is its special object as problem. Thus, for example, geometry has space as problem, the ground of being in space as organon. Arithmetic has time as problem, and the ground of being in time as organon. Logic has as problem the combinations of concepts as such, the ground of knowledge as organon. History has the past deeds of men as a whole as its problem, and the law of motivation as organon. Now natural science has matter as problem, and the law of causality as organon. Accordingly, its end and aim on the guiding line of causality is to refer all possible states of matter to one another and ultimately to a single state, and again to derive these states from one another, and ultimately from a single state. Thus in natural science two states stand opposed as extremes, the state of matter where it is the least direct object of the subject, and the state where it is the most direct object, in other words, the most dead and crude matter, the primary element, as one extreme, and the human organism as the other. Natural science as chemistry looks for the first; as physiology for the second. But as yet the two extremes have not been reached, and only between the two has something been gained. Indeed, the prospect is fairly hopeless. The chemists, assuming that the qualitative division of matter is not, like the quantitative, an endless process, are always trying to reduce the number of their elements, of which there are still about sixty; and even if they eventually reached two, they would want to reduce these two to one. For the law of homogeneity leads to the assumption of a first chemical state of matter which belongs only to matter as such, and which preceded all others, these being not essential to matter as such, but only accidental forms and qualities. On the other hand, it cannot be seen how this state could ever experience a chemical change, if there did not exist a second state to affect it. Thus the same dilemma here appears in the chemical realm that Epicurus met with in the mechanical, when he had to state how the first atom departed from the original direction of its motion. In fact this contradiction, developing entirely of itself and not to be avoided or solved, might quite properly be set up as a chemical *antinomy*. Just as an antinomy is to be found in the first of the two extremes sought in natural science, so will there appear in the second a counterpart corresponding to it. There is also little hope of reaching this other extreme of natural science, for we see more and more clearly that what is chemical can never be referred to what is mechanical, and that what is organic can never be referred to what is chemical or electrical. But those who today once more take this old misleading path will soon slink back silent and ashamed, as all their predecessors have done. This will be discussed in more detail in the next book. The difficulties mentioned here only casually, confront natural science in its own province. Regarded as philosophy, it would be materialism; but, as we have seen, it carries death in its heart even at its birth, because it passes over the subject and the forms of knowledge that are presupposed just as much with the crudest matter from which it would like to start, as with the organism at which it wants to arrive. For "No object without subject" is the principle that renders all materialism for ever impossible. Suns and planets with no eye to see them and no understanding to know them can of course be spoken of in words, but for the representation these words are a *sideroxylon,* an iron-wood.[10] On the other hand the law of causality, and the consideration and investigation of nature which follow on it, lead us necessarily to the certain assumption that each more highly organized state of matter succeeded in · time a cruder state. Thus animals existed before men, fishes before land animals, plants before fishes, and the inorganic before that which is organic; consequently the original mass had to go through a long series of changes before the first eye could be opened. And yet the existence of this whole world remains for ever dependent on that first eye that opened, were it even that of an insect. For such an eye necessarily brings about knowledge, for which and in which alone the whole world is, and without which it is not even conceivable. The world is entirely representation, and as such requires the knowing subject as the supporter of its existence. That long course of time itself, filled with innumerable changes, through which matter rose from form to form, till finally there came into existence the first knowing animal, the whole of this time itself is alone thinkable in the identity of a consciousness. This world is the succession of the representations of this consciousness, the form of its knowing, and apart from this loses all meaning, and is nothing at all. Thus we see, on the one hand, the existence of the whole world necessarily dependent on the first knowing being, however imperfect it be; on the other hand, this first knowing animal just as necessarily wholly dependent on a long chain of causes and effects which has preceded it, and in which it itself appears as a small link. These two contradictory views, to each of which we are led with equal necessity, might certainly be called an *antinomy* in our faculty of knowledge, and be set up as the counterpart to that found in the first extreme of natural science. On the other hand, Kant's fourfold antinomy will be shown to be a groundless piece of jugglery in the criticism of his philosophy that is appended to the present work. But the contradiction that at last necessarily presents itself to us here finds its solution in the fact that, to use Kant's language, time, space, and causality do not belong to the thing-in-itself, but only to its appearance or phenomenon, of which they are the form. In my language, this means that the objective world, the world as representation, is not the only side of the world, but merely its external side, so to speak, and that the world has an entirely different side which

---

[10] A word coined by Schopenhauer from two Greek words to express a contradiction or absurdity. [Tr.]

is its innermost being, its kernel, the thing-in-itself. This we shall consider in the following book, calling it 'will' after the most immediate of its objectifications. But the world as representation, with which alone we are dealing here, certainly begins only with the opening of the first eye, and without this medium of knowledge it cannot be, and hence before this it did not exist. But without that eye, in other words, outside of knowledge, there was no before, no time. For this reason, time has no beginning, but all beginning is in time. Since, however, it is the most universal form of the knowable, to which all phenomena are adapted by means of the bond of causality, time with its whole infinity in both directions is also present in the first knowledge. The phenomenon which fills this first present must at the same time be known as causally connected with, and dependent on, a series of phenomena stretching infinitely into the past, and this past itself is just as much conditioned by this first present as, conversely, this present is by that past. Accordingly, the past, out of which the first present arises, is, like it, dependent on the knowing subject, and without this it is nothing. It happens of necessity, however, that this first present does not manifest itself as the first, in other words, as having no past for its mother, and as being the beginning of time; but rather as the consequence of the past according to the principle of being in time, just as the phenomenon filling this first present appears as the effect of previous states filling that past according to the law of causality. Anyone who likes mythological interpretations may regard the birth of Chronos (Χρόνος), the youngest of the Titans, as the description of the moment here expressed, when time appears, although it is beginningless. As he castrates his father, the crude productions of heaven and earth cease, and the races of gods and men now occupy the scene.

This explanation at which we have arrived by following materialism, the most consistent of the philosophical systems that start from the object, helps at the same time to make clear the inseparable and reciprocal dependence of subject and object, together with the antithesis between them which cannot be eliminated. This knowledge leads us to seek the inner nature of the world, the thing-in-itself, no longer in either of those two elements of the representation, but rather in something entirely different from the representation, in something that is not encumbered with such an original, essential, and therefore insoluble antithesis.

Opposed to the system we have discussed, which starts from the object to make the subject result from it, is the system that starts from the subject and tries to produce the object therefrom.

The first has been frequent and general in all philosophy hitherto; the second, on the other hand, affords us only a single example, and that a very recent one, namely the fictitious philosophy of J. G. Fichte. In this respect, therefore, he must be considered, however little genuine worth and substance his teaching had in itself. Taken on the whole, it was a mere piece of humbug, yet it was delivered with an air of the profoundest seriousness, with a reserved tone and keen ardour, and was defended with eloquent polemic against weak opponents, so that it was able to shine, and to seem to be something. But genuine earnestness, which, inaccessible to all external influences, keeps its goal, truth, steadily in view, was completely lacking in Fichte, as in all philosophers who like him adapt themselves to circumstances. For him, of course, it could not be otherwise. The philosopher always becomes such as the result of a perplexity from which he tries to disengage himself. This is Plato's θαυμάζειν,[11] which he calls a μάλα φιλοσοφικὸν πάθος.[11] But what distinguishes ungenuine from genuine philosophers is that this perplexity comes to the latter from looking at the world itself, to the former merely from a book, a philosophical system which lies in front of them. This was also the case with Fichte, for he became a philosopher merely over Kant's thing-in-itself, and had it not been for this would most probably have concerned himself with quite different things with much greater success, for he possessed considerable rhetorical talent. If he had penetrated only to some extent the meaning of the *Critique of Pure Reason,* the book that made him a philosopher, he would have understood that its principal teaching was in spirit as follows. The principle of sufficient reason is not, as all scholastic philosophy asserts, a *veritas aeterna;* in other words, it does not possess an unconditioned validity before, outside, and above the world, but only a relative and conditioned one, valid only in the phenomenon. It may appear as the necessary nexus of space or time, or as the law of causality, or as the law of the ground of knowledge. Therefore the inner nature of the world, the thing-in-itself, can never be found on the guiding line of this principle, but everything to which it leads is always itself also dependent and relative, always only phenomenon, not thing-in-itself. Further, this principle does not concern the subject, but is only the form of objects, which are for this very reason not things-in-themselves. With the object the subject exists forthwith, and with the subject the object; hence the object cannot be added to the subject or the subject to the object, merely as a consequent to its ground or reason. But Fichte did not take up

---

[11] "Astonishment—a very philosophical emotion." [*Theaetetus,* 155D. Tr.]

the least fragment of all this. The only thing that interested him in the matter was *setting out from the subject,* which Kant had chosen in order to show the falsity of the previous setting out from the object, which had thus become the thing-in-itself. Fichte, however, took this setting out from the subject to be the chief thing, and, like all imitators, imagined that if he were to outdo Kant in this, he would also surpass him. Now in this direction he repeated the mistakes which the previous dogmatism had made in the opposite direction, and which had thus been the cause of Kant's *Critique.* Thus in the main nothing was changed, and the old fundamental mistake, the assumption of a relation of reason or ground and consequent between object and subject, remained just the same as before. Hence the principle of sufficient reason retained as before an unconditioned validity, and the thing-in-itself was now shifted into the subject of knowing instead of into the object as previously. The complete relativity of both subject and object, indicating that the thing-in-itself, or the inner nature of the world, is to be sought not in them, but outside both them and every other thing that exists only relatively, still remained unknown. Just as though Kant had never existed, the principle of sufficient reason is for Fichte just what it was for all the scholastics, namely an *aeterna veritas.* Just as eternal fate reigned over the gods of the ancients, so over the God of the scholastics reigned those *aeternae veritates,* in other words, metaphysical, mathematical and metalogical truths, in the case of some even the validity of the moral law. These *veritates* alone depended on nothing, but through their necessity both God and the world existed. Therefore with Fichte, by virtue of the principle of sufficient reason as such a *veritas aeterna,* the ego is the ground of the world or of the non-ego, the object, which is just its consequent, its product. He has therefore taken good care not to examine further, or to check the principle of sufficient reason. But if I am to state the form of that principle, under the guidance of which Fichte makes the non-ego result from the ego as the web from the spider, I find that it is the principle of sufficient reason of being in space. For it is only in reference to this that those tortuous deductions of the way in which the ego produces and fabricates out of itself the non-ego, forming the subject-matter of the most senseless and consequently the most tedious book ever written, acquire a kind of sense and meaning. This philosophy of Fichte, not otherwise even worth mention, is therefore of interest to us only as the real opposite of the old and original materialism, making a belated appearance. Materialism was the most consistent system starting from the object, as this system was the most consistent starting from the subject.

Materialism overlooked the fact that, with the simplest object, it had at once posited the subject as well; so Fichte too overlooked the fact that with the subject (let him give it whatever title he likes) he posited the object, since no subject is thinkable without object. He also overlooked the fact that all deduction *a priori,* indeed all demonstration in general, rests on a necessity, and that all necessity is based simply and solely on the principle of sufficient reason, since to be necessary and to follow from a given ground or reason are convertible terms.[12] But the principle of sufficient reason is nothing but the universal form of the object as such; hence it presupposes the object, but is not valid before and outside it; it can first produce the object, and cause it to appear in accordance with its legislative force. Therefore, generally speaking, starting from the subject has in common with starting from the object the same defect as explained above, namely that it assumes in advance what it professes to deduce, that is to say, the necessary correlative of its point of departure.

Now our method of procedure is *toto genere* different from these two opposite misconceptions, since we start neither from the object nor from the subject, but from the *representation,* as the first fact of consciousness. The first, essential, fundamental form of this is the division into object and subject; again, the form of the object is the principle of sufficient reason in its different aspects. Each of these rules its own class of representations so much that, as has been shown, with the knowledge of that aspect or form the nature of the whole class is known also, since this (as representation) is nothing but this aspect or form itself. Thus time itself is nothing but the ground of being in it, i.e., succession; space is nothing but the principle of being in it, i.e., position; matter is nothing but causality; the concept (as will appear at once) is nothing but reference to the ground of knowledge. This complete and universal relativity of the world as representation according to its most general form (subject and object) as well as to the form that is subordinate thereto (principle of sufficient reason) suggests to us, as we have said, that we look for the inner nature of the world in quite another aspect of it which is *entirely different from the representation.* The next book will demonstrate this in a fact that is just as immediately certain to every living being.

However, there must first be considered that class of representations which belongs to man alone. The substance of these is the *concept,* and their subjective correlative is the faculty of *reason,* just

---

[12] On this see *The Fourfold Root of the Principle of Sufficient Reason,* second edition, § 49.

as the subjective correlatives of the representations so far considered were understanding and sensibility, which are also to be attributed to every animal.[13]

§ 8.

As from the direct light of the sun to the borrowed reflected light of the moon, so do we pass from the immediate representation of perception, which stands by itself and is its own warrant, to reflection, to the abstract, discursive concepts of reason (*Vernunft*), which have their whole content only from that knowledge of perception, and in relation to it. As long as our attitude is one of pure perception, all is clear, firm, and certain. For there are neither questions nor doubts nor errors; we do not wish to go farther, we cannot go farther; we have rest in perceiving, and satisfaction in the present moment. Perception by itself is enough; therefore what has sprung purely from it and has remained true to it, like the genuine work of art, can never be false, nor can it be refuted through any passing of time, for it gives us not opinion, but the thing itself. With abstract knowledge, with the faculty of reason, doubt and error have appeared in the theoretical, care and remorse in the practical. If in the representation of perception *illusion* does at moments distort reality, then in the representation of the abstract *error* can reign for thousands of years, impose its iron yoke on whole nations, stifle the noblest impulses of mankind; through its slaves and dupes it can enchain even the man it cannot deceive. It is the enemy against which the wisest minds of all times have kept up an unequal struggle, and only what these have won from it has become the property of mankind. Therefore it is a good thing to draw attention to it at once, since we are now treading the ground where its province lies. Although it has often been said that we ought to pursue truth, even when no use for it can be seen, since its use may be indirect and appear when not expected, I find I must add here that we should be just as anxious to discover and eradicate every error, even when no harm from it can be seen, because this harm may be very indirect, and appear one day when not expected;

---

[13] To these first seven paragraphs belong the first four chapters of the first book of supplements.

for every error carries a poison within itself. If it is the mind, if it is knowledge, that makes man lord of the earth, then no errors are harmless, still less venerable and holy. And for the consolation of those who devote their strength and life in any way or concern to the noble and difficult struggle against error, I cannot refrain from adding here that, so long as truth does not exist, error can play its game, just as owls and bats do at night. But we may sooner expect that owls and bats will drive the sun back into the east than that any truth that is known and expressed clearly and fully will again be supplanted, so that the old error may once more occupy its extensive position undisturbed. This is the power of truth, whose conquest is difficult and laborious; but when victory for it is once gained, it can never be wrested away again.

Besides the representations so far considered, namely those which according to their construction could be referred to time, space, and matter, if we see them with reference to the object, or to pure sensibility and understanding (i.e., knowledge of causality) if we see them with reference to the subject, yet another faculty of knowledge has appeared in man alone of all the inhabitants of the earth; an entirely new consciousness has arisen, which with very appropriate and significant accuracy is called *reflection*. For it is in fact a reflected appearance, a thing derived from this knowledge of perception, yet it has assumed a fundamentally different nature and character. It is not acquainted with the forms of perception, and in its regard even the principle of sufficient reason, which rules over every object, has an entirely different form. It is only this new consciousness at a higher potential, this abstract reflex of everything intuitive in the non-perceptive conception of reason, that endows man with that thoughtfulness which so completely distinguishes his consciousness from that of the animal, and through which his whole behaviour on earth turns out so differently from that of his irrational brothers. He far surpasses them in power and in suffering. They live in the present alone; he lives at the same time in the future and the past. They satisfy the need of the moment; he provides by the most ingenious preparations for his future, nay, even for times that he cannot live to see. They are given up entirely to the impression of the moment, to the effect of the motive of perception; he is determined by abstract concepts independent of the present moment. He therefore carries out considered plans, or acts in accordance with maxims, without regard to his surroundings, and to the accidental impressions of the moment. Thus, for example, he can with composure take cunning measures for his own death, dissemble to the point of inscrutableness, and take his secret with him to the grave.

Finally, he has an actual choice between several motives, for only *in abstracto* can such motives, simultaneously present in consciousness, afford knowledge with regard to themselves that the one excludes the other, and thus measure against one another their power over the will. Accordingly, the motive that prevails, in that it decides the matter, is the deliberate decision of the will, and it makes known as a sure indication the character of the will. The animal, on the contrary, is determined by the present impression; only the fear of present compulsion can restrain his desires, until at last this fear has become custom, and as such determines him; this is training. The animal feels and perceives; man, in addition, *thinks* and *knows*; both *will*. The animal communicates his feelings and moods by gesture and sound; man communicates thought to another, or conceals it from him, by language. Speech is the first product and the necessary instrument of his faculty of reason. Therefore in Greek and Italian speech and reason are expressed by the same word, ὁ λόγος, *il discorso*. *Vernunft* (reason) comes from *vernehmen*, which is not synonymous with hearing, but signifies the awareness of ideas communicated by words. Only by the aid of language does reason bring about its most important achievements, namely the harmonious and consistent action of several individuals, the planned cooperation of many thousands, civilization, the State; and then, science, the storing up of previous experience, the summarizing into one concept of what is common, the communication of truth, the spreading of error, thoughts and poems, dogmas and superstitions. The animal learns to know death only when he dies, but man consciously draws every hour nearer his death; and at times this makes life a precarious business, even to the man who has not already recognized this character of constant annihilation in the whole of life itself. Mainly on this account, man has philosophies and religions, though it is doubtful whether that which we rightly esteem above all else in his conduct, namely voluntary rectitude and nobility of feeling, have ever been the fruit of them. On the other hand, there are on this path, as certain creations belonging to them alone and as productions of reason, the strangest and oddest opinions of the philosophers of different schools, and the most extraordinary, and sometimes even cruel, customs of the priests of different religions.

It is the unanimous opinion of all times and of all nations that all these manifestations, so manifold and so far-reaching, spring from a common principle, from that special power of the mind which man possesses as distinct from the animal, and which has been called *Vernunft, reason,* ὁ λόγος, τὸ λογιστικόν, τὸ λόγικον, *ratio*. All men also know quite well how to recognize the manifestations of this faculty, and to say what is rational and what is irrational, where reason appears in contrast to man's other faculties and qualities, and finally what can never be expected even from the cleverest animal, on account of its lack of this faculty. The philosophers of all times speak on the whole with one voice about this universal knowledge of reason, and moreover stress some particularly important manifestations of it, such as the control of the emotions and passions, the capacity to make conclusions and to lay down general principles, even those that are certain prior to all experience, and so on. Nevertheless, all their explanations of the real nature of reason are irresolute, vague, not sharply defined, diffuse, without unity or a central point, stressing one or another manifestation, and hence often at variance among themselves. Besides this, many start from the contrast between reason and revelation, a contrast wholly foreign to philosophy, and serving only to add to the confusion. It is very remarkable that hitherto no philosopher has referred all these manifold expressions of reason strictly to one simple function which could be recognized in all of them, from which they could all be explained, and which would accordingly constitute the real inner nature of reason. It is true that the eminent Locke in his *Essay on the Human Understanding* (Book II, chap. xi, §§ 10 and 11) very rightly states that abstract, universal concepts are the characteristic that distinguishes animal from man, and that Leibniz in complete agreement repeats this in the *Nouveaux essais sur l'entendement humain* (Book II, chap. xi, §§ 10 and 11). But when Locke (Book IV, chap. xvii, §§ 2 and 3) comes to the real explanation of reason, he entirely loses sight of that simple main characteristic, and also falls into an irresolute, indefinite, incomplete account of piecemeal and derivative manifestations of it. In the corresponding passage of his work, Leibniz also behaves in just the same way, only with more confusion and vagueness. In the Appendix I have discussed in detail how much Kant confused and falsified the conception of the nature of reason. But he who will take the trouble to go through in this respect the mass of philosophical writings that have appeared since Kant, will recognize that, just as the mistakes of princes are expiated by whole nations, so do the errors of great minds extend their unwholesome influence over whole generations, centuries even, growing and propagating, and finally degenerating into monstrosities. All this can be deduced from the fact that, as Berkeley says, "Few men think; yet all will have opinions." [13A]

The understanding has one function alone, namely immediate knowledge of the relation of cause and effect; and perception of the

---

[13A] [*Three Dialogues between Hylas and Philonous*, no. 2, Tr.]

actual world, as well as all sagacity, good sense, and the inventive gift, however manifold their application may be, are quite obviously nothing but manifestations of that simple function. Reason also has one function, the formation of the concept, and from this single function are explained very easily and automatically all those phenomena, previously mentioned, that distinguish man's life from that of the animal. Everything that has been called rational or irrational everywhere and always points to the application or nonapplication of that function.[14]

§ 9.

The concepts form a peculiar class, existing only in the mind of man, and differing entirely from the representations of perception so far considered. Therefore we can never attain to a perceptive, a really evident knowledge of their nature, but only to an abstract and discursive one. It would therefore be absurd to demand that they should be demonstrated in experience, in so far as we understand by this the real external world that is simply representation of perception, or that they should be brought before the eyes or the imagination like objects of perception. They can only be conceived, not perceived, and only the effects that man produces through them are objects of experience proper. Such effects are language, deliberate and planned action and science, and what results from all these. As object of external experience, speech is obviously nothing but a very complete telegraph communicating arbitrary signs with the greatest rapidity and the finest difference of shades of meaning. But what do these signs mean? How are they. interpreted? While another person is speaking, do we at once translate his speech into pictures of the imagination that instantaneously flash upon us and are arranged, linked, formed, and coloured according to the words that stream forth, and to their grammatical inflexions? What a tumult there would be in our heads while we listened to a speech or read a book! This is not what happens at all. The meaning of the speech is immediately grasped, accurately and clearly apprehended, without as a rule any conceptions of fancy being mixed up with it.

---

[14] With this paragraph are to be compared §§ 26 and 27 of the second edition of the essay *On the Principle of Sufficient Reason*.

It is reason speaking to reason that keeps within its province, and what it communicates and receives are abstract concepts, non-perceptive representations, formed once for all and relatively few in number, but nevertheless embracing, containing, and representing all the innumerable objects of the actual world. From this alone is to be explained the fact that an animal can never speak and comprehend, although it has in common with us the organs of speech, and also the representations of perception. But just because words express this quite peculiar class of representations, whose subjective correlative is reason, they are for the animal without sense and meaning. Thus language, like every other phenomenon that we ascribe to reason, and like everything that distinguishes man from the animal, is to be explained by this one simple thing as its source, namely concepts, representations that are abstract not perceptive, universal not individual in time and space. Only in single cases do we pass from concepts to perception, or form phantasms as *representatives of concepts* in perception, to which, however, they are never adequate. These have been specially discussed in the essay *On the Principle of Sufficient Reason* (§28), and so I will not repeat this here. What is there said can be compared with what Hume says in the twelfth of his *Philosophical Essays* (p. 244), and Herder in the *Metacritic*—otherwise a bad book (Part I, p. 274). The Platonic Idea that becomes possible through the union of imagination and reason is the main subject of the third book of the present work.

Now although concepts are fundamentally different from representations of perception, they stand in a necessary relation to them, and without this they would be nothing. This relation consequently constitutes their whole nature and existence. Reflection is necessarily the copy or repetition of the originally presented world of perception, though a copy of quite a special kind in a completely heterogeneous material. Concepts, therefore, can quite appropriately be called representations of representations. Here too the principle of sufficient reason has a special form. The form under which the principle of sufficient reason rules in a class of representations also always constitutes and exhausts the whole nature of this class, in so far as they are representations, so that, as we have seen, time is throughout succession and nothing else, space is throughout position and nothing else, matter is throughout causality and nothing else. In the same way, the whole nature of concepts, or of the class of abstract representations, consists only in the relation expressed in them by the principle of sufficient reason. As this is the relation to the ground of knowledge, the abstract representation has its whole nature simply and solely in its relation to another representation that is its ground of knowledge. Now this of course can again be a concept or an abstract representation in the first instance, and even this again may have only such an abstract ground of knowledge. However, this does not go on *ad infinitum,* but the series of grounds of knowledge must end at last with a concept which has its ground in knowledge of perception. For the whole world of reflection rests on the world of perception as its ground of knowledge. Therefore the class of abstract representations is distinguished from the others, for in the latter the principle of sufficient reason always requires only a relation to another representation of the *same* class, but in the case of abstract representations it requires in the end a relation to a representation from *another* class.

Those concepts which, as just mentioned, are related to knowledge of perception not directly, but only through the medium of one or even several other concepts, have been called by preference *abstracta,* and on the other hand those which have their ground directly in the world of perception have been called *concreta.* This last name, however, fits the concepts denoted by it only in quite a figurative way, for even these too are always *abstracta,* and in no way representations of perception. These names have originated only from a very indistinct awareness of the difference they indicate; yet they can remain, with the explanation given here. Examples of the first kind, and hence *abstracta* in the fullest sense, are concepts such as "relation," "virtue," "investigation," "beginning," and so on. Examples of the latter kind, or those figuratively called *concreta,* are the concepts "man," "stone," "horse," and so on. If it were not somewhat too pictorial a simile, and thus one that verges on the facetious, the latter might very appropriately be called the ground floor and the former the upper storeys of the edifice of reflection.[15]

It is not, as is often said to be the case, an essential characteristic of a concept that it includes much under it, in other words, that many representations of perception, or even abstract representations, stand to it in the relation of ground of knowledge, that is to say, are thought through it. This is only a derived and secondary characteristic of a concept, and does not always exist in fact, although it must always do so potentially. This characteristic arises from the fact that the concept is a representation of a representation, in other words, has its whole nature only in its relation to another representation. But as it is not this representation itself, the latter indeed frequently belonging to quite a different class of representations, in other words, being of perception, it can have temporal, spatial, and other determinations, and in general many more relations that are

---

[15] Cf. chaps. 5 and 6 of volume 2.

not thought in the concept at all. Thus several representations differing in unessential points can be thought through the same concept, that is to say, subsumed under it. But this power of embracing several things is not an essential characteristic of the concept, but only an accidental one. Thus there can be concepts through which only a single real object is thought, but which are nevertheless abstract and general representations, and by no means particular representations of perception. Such, for example, is the concept one has of a definite town, known to one only from geography. Although this one town alone is thought through it, yet there might possibly be several towns differing in a few particulars, to all of which it is suited. Thus a concept has generality not because it is abstracted from several objects, but conversely because generality, that is to say, non-determination of the particular, is essential to the concept as abstract representation of reason; different things can be thought through the same concept.

From what has been said it follows that every concept, just because it is abstract representation, not representation of perception, and therefore not a completely definite representation, has what is called a range, an extension, or a sphere, even in the case where only a single real object corresponding to it exists. We usually find that the sphere of any concept has something in common with the spheres of others, that is to say, partly the same thing is thought in it which is thought in those others, and conversely in those others again partly the same thing is thought which is thought in the first concept; although, if they are really different concepts, each, or at any rate one of the two, contains something the other does not. In this relation every subject stands to its predicate. To recognize this relation means to *judge*. The presentation of these spheres by figures in space is an exceedingly happy idea. Gottfried Ploucquet, who had it first, used squares for the purpose. Lambert, after him, made use of simple lines placed one under another. Euler first carried out the idea completely with circles. On what this exact analogy between the relations of concepts and those of figures in space ultimately rests, I am unable to say. For logic, however, it is a very fortunate circumstance that all the relations of concepts can be made plain in perception, even according to their possibility, i.e., *a priori,* through such figures in the following way:

(1) The spheres of two concepts are equal in all respects, for example, the concept of necessity and the concept of following from a given ground or reason; in the same way, the concept of *Ruminantia* and that of *Bisulca* (ruminating and cloven-hoofed animals); like-

wise that of vertebrates and that of red-blooded animals (though there might be some objection to this by reason of the Annelida): these are convertible concepts. Such concepts, then, are represented by a single circle that indicates either the one or the other.

(2) The sphere of one concept wholly includes that of another:

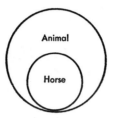

(3) A sphere includes two or several which exclude one another, and at the same time fill the sphere:

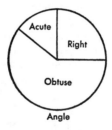

(4) Two spheres include each a part of the other:

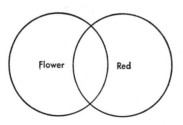

(5) Two spheres lie within a third, yet do not fill it:

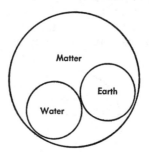

This last case applies to all concepts whose spheres have nothing immediately in common, for a third one, although often very wide, will include both.

All combinations of concepts may be referred to these cases, and from them can be derived the whole theory of judgements, of their conversion, contraposition, reciprocation, disjunction (this according to the third figure). From them may also be derived the properties of judgements, on which Kant based the pretended categories of the understanding, though with the exception of the hypothetical form, which is not a combination of mere concepts, but of judgements; and with the exception of modality, of which the Appendix gives a detailed account, as it does of all the properties of judgements that are the basis of the categories. Of the possible concept-combinations mentioned it has further to be remarked that they can also be combined with one another in many ways, e.g., the fourth figure with the second. Only if one sphere which wholly or partly contains another is in turn included wholly or partly within a third, do these together represent the syllogism in the first figure, that is to say, that combination of judgements by which it is known that a concept wholly or partly contained in another is also contained in a third, which in turn contains the first. Also the converse of this, the negation, whose pictorial representation can, of course, consist only in the two connected spheres not lying within a third sphere. If many spheres are brought together in this way, there arise long chains of syllogisms. This schematism of concepts, which has been fairly well explained in several textbooks, can be used as the basis of the theory of judgements, as also of the whole syllogistic theory, and in this way the discussion of both becomes very easy and simple. For all the rules of this theory can be seen from it according to their origin, and can be deduced and explained. But it is not necessary to load the memory with these rules, for logic can never be of practical use, but only of theoretical interest for philosophy. For although it might be said that logic is related to rational thinking as thorough-bass is to music, and also as ethics is to virtue, if we take it less precisely, or as aesthetics is to art, it must be borne in mind that no one ever became an artist by studying aesthetics, that a noble character was never formed by a study of ethics, that men composed correctly and beautifully long before Rameau, and that we do not need to be masters of thorough-bass in order to detect discords. Just as little do we need to know logic in order to avoid being deceived by false conclusions. But it must be conceded that thorough-bass is of great use in the practice of musical composition, although not for musical criticism. Aesthetics and ethics also, though in a much less degree, may have some use in practice, though a mainly negative one, and hence they too cannot be denied all practical value; but of logic not even this much can be conceded. It is merely knowing in the abstract what everyone knows in the concrete. Therefore we no more need to call in the aid of logical rules in order to construct a correct argument, than to do so to guard against agreeing with a false one. Even the most learned logician lays these rules altogether aside in his actual thinking. This is to be explained as follows. Every science consists of a system of general, and consequently abstract, truths, laws, and rules referring to some species of objects. The particular case which subsequently occurs under these laws is then determined each time in accordance with this universal knowledge that is valid once for all, because such application of the universal is infinitely easier than investigation from the very beginning of each individual case as it occurs. The universal abstract knowledge, once gained, is always nearer at hand than the empirical investigation of the particular thing. But with logic it is just the reverse. It is the universal knowledge of the reason's method of procedure, expressed in the form of rules. Such knowledge is reached by self-observation of the faculty of reason, and abstraction from all content. But that method of procedure is necessary and essential to reason; hence reason will not in any case depart from it, the moment it is left to itself. It is therefore easier and more certain to let reason proceed according to its nature in each particular case, than to hold before it knowledge of that case which is first abstracted from this procedure in the form of a foreign law given from outside. It is easier because, although in all the other sciences the universal rule is more within our reach than is the investigation of the particular case taken by itself, with the use of reason, on the contrary, its necessary procedure in the given case is always more within our reach than is the universal rule abstracted from it; for that which thinks within us is indeed this very faculty of reason itself. It is surer, because it is easier for an error to occur in such abstract knowledge or in its application than for a process of reason to take place which would run contrary to its essence and nature. Hence arises the strange fact that, whereas in other sciences we test the truth of the particular case by the rule, in logic, on the contrary, the rule must always be tested by the particular case. Even the most practised logician, if he notices that in a particular case he concludes otherwise than as stated by the rule, will always look for a mistake in the rule rather than in the conclusion he actually draws. To seek to make practical use of logic would therefore mean to seek to derive with unspeakable trouble from universal rules what is immediately known to us with the greatest certainty in the particular case. It is just as if a man were to consult mechanics with regard to his movements, or physiology with regard to his digestion; and one who has learnt logic for practical purposes is like a man who should seek to train a beaver to build its lodge. Logic is therefore without practical use; nevertheless it must be retained, because it has philosophical interest as special knowledge of the organization and action of the faculty of reason. It is rightly regarded as an exclusive, self-subsisting, self-contained, finished, and perfectly safe branch of knowledge, to be scientifically treated by itself alone and independently of everything else, and also to be taught at the universities. But it has its real value first in the continuity of philosophy as a whole with the consideration of knowledge, indeed of rational or abstract knowledge. Accordingly, the exposition of logic should not so much take the form of a science directed to what is practical, and should not contain merely bare rules laid down for the conversion of judgements, syllogisms, and so on, but should rather be directed to our knowing the nature of the faculty of reason and of the concept, and to our considering in detail the principle of sufficient reason of knowledge. For logic is a mere paraphrase of this principle, and is in fact really only for the case where the ground that gives truth to judgements is not empirical or metaphysical, but logical or metalogical. Therefore with the principle of sufficient reason of knowing must be mentioned the three remaining fundamental laws of thought, or judgements of metalogical truth, so closely related to it, out of which the whole technical science of the faculty of reason gradually grows. The nature of thought proper, that is to say, of the judgement and syllogism, can be shown from the combination of the concept-spheres according to the spatial schema in the way above mentioned, and from this all the rules of the judgement and syllogism can be deduced by construction. The only practical use we can make of logic is in an argument, when we do not so much demonstrate to our opponent his actual false conclusions as his intentionally false ones, through calling them by their technical names. By thus pushing the practical tendency into the background, and stressing the connexion of logic with the whole of philosophy as one of its chapters, knowledge of it should not become less prevalent than it is now. For at the present time everyone who does not wish to remain generally uncultured or to be reckoned one of the ignorant and dull mob, must have studied speculative philosophy. For this nineteenth century is a philosophical one; though by this we do not mean that it possesses philosophy or that philosophy prevails in it, but rather that it is ripe for philosophy and is therefore absolutely in need of it. This is a sign of a high degree of refinement, indeed a fixed point on the scale of the culture of the times.[16]

However little practical use logic may have, it cannot be denied that it was invented for practical purposes. I explain its origin in the following way. As the pleasure of debate developed more and more among the Eleatics, the Megarics, and the Sophists, and gradually became almost a passion, the confusion in which nearly every debate ended was bound to make them feel the necessity for a method of procedure as a guide, and for this a scientific dialectic had to be sought. The first thing that had to be observed was that the two disputing parties must always be agreed on some proposition to which the points in dispute were to be referred. The beginning of the methodical procedure consisted in formally stating as such these propositions jointly acknowledged, and putting them at the head of the inquiry. These propositions were at first concerned only with the material of the inquiry. It was soon observed that, even in the way in which the debaters went back to the jointly acknowledged truth, and sought to deduce their assertions from it, certain forms and laws were followed, about which, although without any previous agreement, there was never any dispute. From this it was seen that these must be the peculiar and essentially natural method of reason itself, the formal way of investigating. Now although this was not exposed to doubt and disagreement, some mind, systematic to the point of pedantry, nevertheless hit upon the idea that it would look fine, and would be the completion of methodical dialectic, if this formal part of all debating, this procedure of reason itself always conforming to law, were also expressed in abstract propositions. These would then be put at the head of the inquiry, just like those propositions jointly acknowledged and concerned with the material of the inquiry, as the

---

[16] Cf. chaps. 9 and 10 of volume 2.

fixed canon of debate, to which it would always be necessary to look back and to refer. In this way, what had hitherto been followed as if by tacit agreement or practised by instinct would be consciously recognized as law, and given formal expression. Gradually, more or less perfect expressions for logical principles were found, such as the principles of contradiction, of sufficient reason, of the excluded middle, the *dictum de omni et nullo,* and then the special rules of syllogistic reasoning, as for example *Ex meris particularibus aut negativis nihil sequitur; a rationato ad rationem non valet consequentia;*[17] and so on. That all this came about only slowly and very laboriously, and, until Aristotle, remained very incomplete, is seen in part from the awkward and tedious way in which logical truths are brought out in many of Plato's dialogues, and even better from what Sextus Empiricus tells us of the controversies of the Megarics concerning the easiest and simplest logical laws, and the laborious way in which they made such laws plain and intelligible (Sextus Empiricus, *Adversus Mathematicos,* 1. 8, p. 112 *seqq.*). Aristotle collected, arranged, and corrected all that had been previously discovered, and brought it to an incomparably higher state of perfection. If we thus consider how the course of Greek culture had prepared for and led up to Aristotle's work, we shall be little inclined to give credit to the statement of Persian authors reported to us by Sir William Jones, who was much prejudiced in their favour, namely that Callisthenes found among the Indians a finished system of logic which he sent to his uncle Aristotle (*Asiatic Researches,* Vol. IV, p. 163). It is easy to understand that in the dreary Middle Ages the Aristotelian logic was bound to be extremely welcome to the argumentative spirit of the scholastics, which, in the absence of real knowledge, feasted only on formulas and words. It is easy to see that this logic, even in its mutilated Arabic form, would be eagerly adopted, and soon elevated to the centre of all knowledge. Although it has since sunk from its position of authority, it has nevertheless retained up to our own time the credit of a self-contained, practical, and extremely necessary science. Even in our day the Kantian philosophy, which really took its foundation-stone from logic, has awakened a fresh interest in it. In this respect, that is to say, as a means to knowing the essential nature of reason, it certainly merits such interest.

Correct and exact conclusions are reached by our accurately observing the relation of the concept-spheres, and admitting that one sphere is wholly contained in a third only when a sphere is completely

---

[17] "From merely particular or negative premisses nothing follows." "A conclusion from the consequent to the ground is not valid." [Tr.]

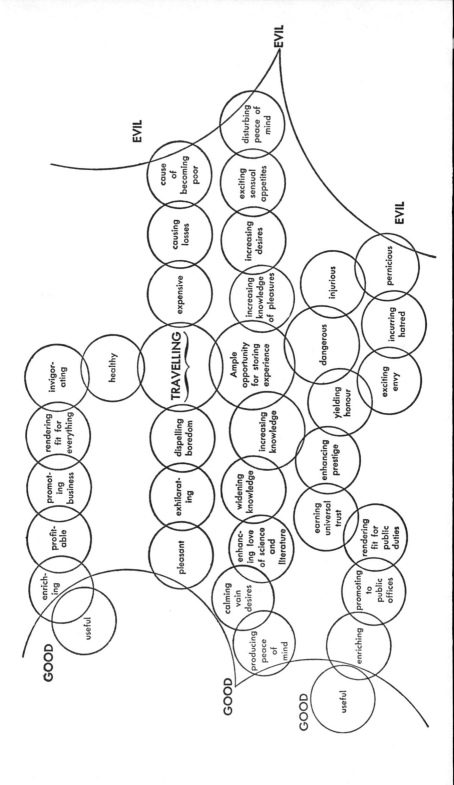

contained in another, which other is in turn wholly contained in the third. On the other hand, the *art of persuasion* depends on our subjecting the relations of the concept-spheres to a superficial consideration only, and then determining these only from one point of view, and in accordance with our intentions, mainly in the following way. If the sphere of a concept under consideration lies only partly in another sphere, and partly also in quite a different sphere, we declare it to be entirely in the first sphere or entirely in the second, according to our intentions. For example, when passion is spoken of, we can subsume this under the concept of the greatest force, of the mightiest agency in the world, or under the concept of irrationality, and this under the concept of powerlessness or weakness. We can continue this method, and apply it afresh with each concept to which the argument leads us. The sphere of a concept is almost invariably shared by several others, each of which contains a part of the province of the first sphere, while itself including something more besides. Of these latter concept-spheres we allow only that sphere to be elucidated under which we wish to subsume the first concept, leaving the rest unobserved, or keeping them concealed. On this trick all the arts of persuasion, all the more subtle sophisms, really depend; for the logical sophisms, such as *mentiens, velatus, cornutus,*[18] and so on, are obviously too clumsy for actual application. I am not aware that anyone hitherto has traced the nature of all sophistication and persuasion back to this ultimate ground of their possibility, and demonstrated this in the peculiar property of concepts, that is to say, the cognitive method of reason. As my discussion has led me to this, I will elucidate the matter, easy though it is to understand, by means of a schema in the accompanying diagram. This shows how the concept-spheres in many ways overlap one another, and thus enable us freely to pass arbitrarily from each concept to others in one direction or another. I do not want anyone to be led by this diagram into attaching more importance to this short incidental discussion than it has in its own right. I have chosen as an illustrative example the concept of *travelling*. Its sphere overlaps into the province of four others, to each of which the persuasive talker can pass at will. These again overlap into other spheres, several of them into two or more simultaneously; and through these the persuasive talker takes whichever way he likes, always as if it were the only way, and then ultimately arrives at good or evil, according to what his intention was. In going from one sphere to another, it is only necessary always to maintain direction from the centre (the given chief concept) to the circumference, and not go backwards. The manner of clothing such

---

[18] "lying, veiled, horned [dilemma]." [Tr.]

a sophistication in words can be continuous speech or even the strict syllogistic form, as the hearer's weak side may suggest. The nature of most scientific arguments, particularly of philosophical demonstrations, is not at bottom very different from this. Otherwise how would it be possible for so much at different periods to be not only erroneously assumed (for error itself has a different source), but demonstrated and proved, and then later found to be fundamentally false, such as, for example, the philosophy of Leibniz and Wolff, Ptolemaic astronomy, Stahl's chemistry, Newton's theory of colours, and so on? [19]

§ 10.

Through all this, the question becomes more and more pressing how *certainty* is to be attained, how *judgements are to be established,* in what *knowledge* and science consist; for, together with language and deliberate action, we extol these as the third great advantage conferred on us by the faculty of reason.

Reason is feminine in nature; it can give only after it has received. Of itself alone, it has nothing but the empty forms of its operation. There is absolutely no other perfectly pure rational knowledge than the four principles to which I have attributed metalogical truth, the principles of identity, of contradiction, of the excluded middle, and of sufficient reason of knowledge. For even the rest of logic is not perfectly pure rational knowledge, since it presupposes the relations and combinations of the spheres of concepts. But concepts in general exist only after previous representations of perception, and in the reference to these lies their whole nature; consequently, they presuppose these representations. As this assumption, however, does not extend to the definite content of concepts, but only to their general existence, logic can, on the whole, pass for a pure science of reason. In all the other sciences reason obtains its content from the representations of perception; in mathematics from the relations of space and time presented in intuition or perception prior to all experience; in pure natural science, that is to say, in what we know about the course of nature prior to all experience, the content of the science results from the pure understanding, i.e., from the *a priori* knowledge

_____
[19] Cf. chap. 11 of volume 2.

of the law of causality and of that law's connexion with those pure intuitions or perceptions of space and time. In all the other sciences everything that is not borrowed from the sources just mentioned belongs to experience. *To know* means generally to have within the power of the mind, ready to reproduce at will, such judgements as have their sufficient ground of knowledge in something outside them, in other words, such judgements as are *true*. Thus only abstract knowledge is rational knowledge (*Wissen*), and this is therefore conditioned by the faculty of reason, and, strictly speaking, we cannot say of the animals that they *rationally know* anything, although they have knowledge of perception, as well as recollection of it, and, on this very account, imagination; this, moreover, is proved by their dreaming. We attribute to them consciousness, and although the name (*Bewusstsein*) is derived from *wissen* (to know rationally), the concept of consciousness coincides with that of representation in general, of whatever kind it may be. Thus to the plant we attribute life, but not consciousness. *Rational knowledge* (*Wissen*) is therefore abstract consciousness, fixing in concepts of reason what is known generally in another way.

§ 11.

Now in this respect, the true opposite of *rational knowledge* (*Wissen*) is *feeling* (*Gefühl*), which we must therefore discuss at this point. The concept denoted by the word *feeling* has only a *negative* content, namely that something present in consciousness is *not a concept, not abstract knowledge of reason*. However, be it what it may, it comes under the concept of *feeling*. Thus the immeasurably wide sphere of this concept includes the most heterogeneous things, and we do not see how they come together so long as we have not recognized that they all agree in this negative respect of *not being abstract concepts*. For the most varied, indeed the most hostile, elements lie quietly side by side in this concept; e.g., religious feeling, feeling of sensual pleasure, moral feeling, bodily feeling such as touch, pain, feeling for colours, for sounds and their harmonies and discords, feeling of hatred, disgust, self-satisfaction, honour, disgrace, right and wrong, feeling of truth, aesthetic feeling, feeling of power, weakness, health, friendship, and so on. Between them there is absolutely nothing in common except the negative quality that they are not abstract knowledge of reason. But this becomes most striking when even *a priori* knowledge of perception of spatial relations, and moreover knowledge of the pure understanding, are brought under this concept, and generally when it is said of all knowledge, of all truth, of which we are at first conscious only intuitively, but which we have not yet formulated into abstract concepts, that we *feel* it. To make this clear, I will quote some examples from recent books, because they are striking proofs of my explanation. I remember having read in the introduction to a German translation of Euclid that we ought to make all beginners in geometry draw the figures first before proceeding to demonstrate, since they would then *feel* geometrical truth, before the demonstration brought them complete knowledge. In the same way F. Schleiermacher speaks in his *Kritik der Sittenlehre* of logical and mathematical feeling (p. 339), and also of the feeling of the sameness or difference of two formulas (p. 342). Further, in Tennemann's *Geschichte der Philosophie* (Vol. I, p. 361), it says: "It was *felt* that the false conclusions were not right, but yet the mistake could not be discovered." Now so long as we do not consider this concept of *feeling* from the right point of view, and do not recognize this one negative characteristic that alone is essential to it, that concept is always bound to give rise to misunderstandings and disputes on account of the excessive width of its sphere, and of its merely negative and very limited content, determined in an entirely one-sided way. As we have in German the almost synonymous word *Empfindung* (sensation), it would be useful to take over this for bodily feelings as a subspecies. Undoubtedly the origin of this concept of feeling, out of all proportion to the others, is the following. All concepts, and concepts only, are denoted by words; they exist only for the faculty of reason and proceed therefrom; hence with them we are already at a one-sided point of view. But from such a point of view, what is near appears distinct and is set down as positive; what is more distant coalesces, and is soon regarded only as negative. Thus each nation calls all others foreign; the Greeks called all other men barbarians. The Englishman calls everything that is not England or English *continent* and *continental;* the believer regards all others as heretics or heathens; the nobleman considers all others as *roturiers;* to the student all others are Philistines, and so on. Reason itself, strange as it may sound, renders itself guilty of the same one-sidedness, indeed, one may say of the same crude ignorance from pride, since it classifies under the one concept of *feeling* every modification of consciousness which does not belong directly to its own method of representation, in other words, which is *not abstract concept.* Hitherto it has had to atone for this by misunderstandings and confusions in its own province, because its own method of procedure had not become clear to it through thorough self-knowledge, for even a special faculty of feeling was put forward, and theories of it were constructed.

§ 12.

I have said that all abstract knowledge, i.e., all knowledge of reason, is *rational knowledge (Wissen)*, and I have just explained that the concept of feeling is the contradictory opposite of this. But, as reason always brings again before knowledge only what has been received in another way, it does not really extend our knowledge, but merely gives it another form. Thus it enables one to know in the abstract and in general what was known intuitively and in the concrete. But this is far more important than appears at first sight when thus expressed. For all safe preservation, all communicability, all sure and far-reaching application of knowledge to the practical, depend on its having become a rational knowledge *(Wissen)*, an abstract knowledge. Intuitive knowledge is always valid only of the particular case, extends only to what is nearest, and there stops, since sensibility and understanding can really comprehend only one object at a time. Therefore every continuous, coordinated, and planned activity must start from fundamental principles, i.e. from an abstract knowledge, and must be guided in accordance therewith. Thus, for example, knowledge which the understanding has of the relation of cause and effect is in itself much more complete, profound, and exhaustive than what can be thought of it in the abstract. The understanding alone knows from perception, directly and completely, the mode of operation of a lever, a block and tackle, a cog-wheel, the support of an arch, and so on. But on account of the property of intuitive knowledge just referred to, namely that it extends only to what is immediately present, the mere understanding is not sufficient for constructing machines and buildings. On the contrary, reason must put in an appearance here; it must replace intuitions and perceptions with abstract concepts, take those concepts as the guide of action, and, if they are right, success will be attained. In the same way, we know perfectly in pure perception the nature and conformity to law of a parabola, hyperbola, and spiral, but for this knowledge to be reliably applied in real life it must first have become abstract knowledge. Here, of course, it loses its character of intuition or perception, and acquires instead the certainty and definiteness of abstract knowledge. Thus the differential calculus does not really extend our knowledge of curves; it contains nothing more than what was already present in the mere pure perception of them. But it alters the kind of knowledge; it converts the intuitive into an abstract knowledge that is so extremely important for application. Here another peculiarity of our faculty of knowledge comes under discussion, and one that could not be observed previously, until the difference between knowledge of perception and abstract knowledge was made perfectly clear. It is that the relations of space cannot directly and as such be translated into abstract knowledge, but only temporal quantities, that is to say numbers, are capable of this. Numbers alone can be expressed in abstract concepts exactly corresponding to them; spatial quantities cannot. The concept thousand is just as different from the concept ten as are the two temporal quantities in perception. We think of a thousand as a definite multiple of ten into which we can resolve it at will for perception in time, in other words, we can count it. But between the abstract concept of a mile and that of a foot, without any representation from perception of either, and without the help of number, there is no exact distinction at all corresponding to these quantities themselves. In both we think only of a spatial quantity in general, and if they are to be adequately distinguished, we must either avail ourselves of intuition or perception in space, and hence leave the sphere of abstract knowledge, or we must think the difference in *numbers*. If, therefore, we want to have abstract knowledge of space-relations, we must first translate them into time-relations, that is, numbers. For this reason, arithmetic alone, and not geometry, is the universal theory of quantity, and geometry must be translated into arithmetic if it is to be communicable, precisely definite, and applicable in practice. It is true that a spatial relation as such may also be thought in the abstract, for example "The sine increases with the angle," but if the quantity of this relation is to be stated, number is required. This necessity for space with its three dimensions to be translated into time with only one dimension, if we wish to have an abstract knowledge (i.e., a rational knowledge, and no mere intuition or perception) of space-relations—this necessity it is that makes mathematics so difficult. This becomes very clear when we compare the perception of curves with their analytical calculation, or even merely the tables of the logarithms of trigonometrical functions with the perception of the changing relations of the parts of a triangle expressed by them. What vast tissues of figures, what laborious calculations, would be required to express in the abstract what perception here apprehends perfectly and with extreme accuracy at a glance, namely how the cosine diminishes while the sine increases, how the cosine of one angle is the sine of another, the inverse relation of the increase and decrease of the two angles, and so on! How time, we might say, with its one dimension must torture itself, in order to reproduce the three dimensions of space! But this was necessary if we wished to possess space-relations expressed in abstract concepts for the purpose of application. They could not go into abstract concepts directly, but only through the medium of the purely temporal quantity, number, which alone is directly connected to abstract knowledge. Yet it is remarkable that, as space is so well adapted to perception, and, by means of its three dimensions, even complicated relations can be taken in at a glance, whereas it defies abstract knowledge, time on the other hand passes easily into abstract concepts, but offers very little to perception. Our perception of numbers in their characteristic element, namely in mere time, without the addition of space, scarcely extends as far as ten. Beyond this we have only abstract concepts, and no longer perceptive knowledge of numbers. On the other hand, we connect with every numeral and with all algebraical signs precise and definite abstract concepts.

Incidentally, it may here be remarked that many minds find complete satisfaction only in what is known through perception. What they look for is reason or ground and consequent of being in space presented in perception. A Euclidean proof, or an arithmetical solution of spatial problems, makes no appeal to them. Other minds, on the contrary, want the abstract concepts of use solely for application and communication. They have patience and memory for abstract principles, formulas, demonstrations by long chains of reasoning, and calculations whose symbols represent the most complicated abstractions. The latter seek preciseness, the former intuitiveness. The difference is characteristic.

Rational or abstract knowledge has its greatest value in its communicability, and in its possibility of being fixed and retained; only through this does it become so invaluable for practice. Of the causal connexion of the changes and motions of natural bodies a man can have an immediate, perceptive knowledge in the mere understanding, and can find complete satisfaction in it, but it is capable of being communicated only after he has fixed it in concepts. Even knowledge of the first kind is sufficient for practice, as soon as a man puts it into execution entirely by himself, in fact when he carries it out in a practical action, while the knowledge from perception is still vivid. But such knowledge is not sufficient if a man requires the help of another, or if he needs to carry out on his own part some action manifested at different times and therefore needing a deliberate plan. Thus, for example, an experienced billiard-player can have a perfect knowledge of the laws of impact of elastic bodies on one another, merely in the understanding, merely for immediate perception, and with this he manages perfectly. Only the man who is versed in the science of mechanics, on the other hand, has a real rational knowledge of those laws, that is to say, a knowledge of them in the abstract. Even for the construction of machines such a merely intuitive knowledge of the understanding is sufficient, when the inventor of the machine himself executes the work, as is often seen in the case of talented workmen without any scientific knowledge. On the other hand, as soon as several men and their coordinated activity occurring at different times are necessary for carrying out a mechanical operation, for completing a machine or a building, then the man controlling it must have drafted the plan in the abstract, and such a cooperative activity is possible only through the assistance of the faculty of reason. But it is remarkable that, in the first kind of activity, where one man alone is supposed to execute something in an uninterrupted course of action, rational knowledge, the application of reason, reflection, may often be even a hindrance to him. For example, in the case of billiards-playing, fencing, tuning an instrument, or singing, knowledge of perception must directly guide activity; passage through reflection makes it uncertain, since it divides the attention, and confuses the executant. Therefore, savages and uneducated persons, not very accustomed to thinking, perform many bodily exercises, fight with animals, shoot with bows and arrows and the like, with a certainty and rapidity never reached by the reflecting European, just because his deliberation makes him hesitate and hang back. For instance, he tries to find the right spot or the right point of time from the mean between two false extremes, while the natural man hits it directly without reflecting on the wrong courses open to him. Likewise, it is of no use for me to be able to state in the abstract in degrees and minutes the angle at which I have to apply my razor, if I do not know it intuitively, in other words, if I do not know how to hold the razor. In like manner, the application of reason is also disturbing to the person who tries to understand physiognomy; this too must occur directly through the understanding. We say that the expression, the meaning of the features, can only be *felt,* that is to say, it cannot enter into abstract concepts. Every person has his own immediate intuitive method of physiognomy and pathognomy, yet one recognizes that *signatura rerum* more clearly than does another. But a science of physiognomy in the abstract cannot be brought into existence to be taught and learned, because in this field the shades of difference are so fine that the concept cannot reach them. Hence abstract rational knowledge is related to them as a mosaic is to a picture by a van der Werft or a Denner. However fine the mosaic may be, the edges of the stones always remain, so that no continuous transition from one tint to another is possible. In the same way, concepts, with their rigidity and sharp delineation, however finely they may be split by closer definition, are always incapable of reaching the fine modifications of perception, and this is the very point of the example I have taken here from physiognomy.[20]

This same property in concepts which makes them similar to the stones of a mosaic, and by virtue of which perception always remains their asymptote, is also the reason why nothing good is achieved through them in art. If the singer or virtuoso wishes to guide his recital by reflection, he remains lifeless. The same is true of the composer, the painter, and the poet. For art the concept always remains unproductive; in art it can guide only technique; its province is science. In the third book we shall inquire more closely into the reason why all genuine art proceeds from knowledge of perception, never from the concept. Even in regard to behaviour, to personal charm in mixing with people, the concept is only of negative value in restraining the uncouth outbursts of egoism and brutality, so that politeness is its commendable work. What is attractive, gracious, prepossessing in behaviour, what is affectionate and friendly, cannot have come from the concept, otherwise "We feel intention and are put out of tune." All dissimulation is the work of reflection, but it cannot be kept up permanently and without interruption; *nemo potest personam diu ferre fictam,*[21] says Seneca in his book *De Clementia;* for generally it is recognized, and loses its effect. Reason is necessary in the high stress of life where rapid decisions, bold action, quick and firm comprehension are needed, but if it gains the upper hand, if it confuses and hinders the intuitive, immediate discovery of what is

---

[20] I am therefore of the opinion that the science of physiognomy cannot go any further with certainty than to lay down a few quite general rules. For example, intellectual qualities are in the forehead and the eye; ethical qualities, manifestations of the will, are to be read in the mouth and the lower half of the face. Forehead and eye elucidate each other; either of them seen without the other can be only half understood. Genius is never without a high, broad, finely arched brow, but such a brow is often without genius. Intellect may be inferred from a clever appearance the more certainly, the uglier the face is, and stupidity the more certainly from a stupid appearance, the more beautiful a face is, because beauty, as fitness and appropriateness to the type of humanity, carries in and by itself the expression of mental clearness; the opposite is the case with ugliness, and so on.

[21] "No one can wear a mask for long." "Dissimulation soon reverts to its own nature." [Tr.]

right by the pure understanding, and at the same time prevents this from being grasped, and if it produces irresolution, then it can easily ruin everything.

Finally, virtue and holiness result not from reflection, but from the inner depth of the will, and from its relation to knowledge. This discussion belongs to an entirely different part of this work. Here I may observe only this much, that the dogmas relating to ethics can be the same in the reasoning faculty of whole nations, but the conduct of each individual different, and also the converse. Conduct, as we say, happens in accordance with *feelings,* that is to say, not precisely according to concepts, but to ethical worth and quality. Dogmas concern idle reason; conduct in the end pursues its own course independently of them, usually in accordance not with abstract, but with unspoken maxims, the expression of which is precisely the whole man himself. Therefore, however different the religious dogmas of nations may be, with all of them the good deed is accompanied by unspeakable satisfaction, and the bad by infinite dread. No mockery shakes the former; no father confessor's absolution delivers us from the latter. But it cannot be denied that the application of reason is necessary for the pursuit of a virtuous way of living; yet it is not the source of this, but its function is a subordinate one; to preserve resolutions once formed, to provide maxims for withstanding the weakness of the moment, and to give consistency to conduct. Ultimately, it achieves the same thing also in art, where it is not capable of anything in the principal matter, but assists in carrying it out, just because genius is not at a man's command every hour, and yet the work is to be completed in all its parts and rounded off to a whole.[22]

§ 13.

All these considerations of the advantages, as well as the disadvantages, of applying reason should help to make it clear that, although abstract rational knowledge is the reflex of the representation from perception, and is founded thereon, it is by no means so congruent with it that it could everywhere take its place; on the contrary, it never corresponds wholly to this representation. Hence, as we have seen, many human actions are performed by the aid of rea-

---

[22] Cf. chap. 7 of volume 2

son and deliberate method, yet some are better achieved without their application. This very incongruity of knowledge from perception and abstract knowledge, by virtue of which the latter always only approximates to the former as a mosaic approximates to a painting, is the cause of a very remarkable phenomenon. Like reason, this phenomenon is exclusively peculiar to human nature, and all the explanations of it which have so frequently been attempted up to now are insufficient. I refer to *laughter*. On account of this origin of the phenomenon, we cannot refrain from speaking about it here, although once more it interrupts the course of our discussion. In every case, *laughter* results from nothing but the suddenly perceived incongruity between a concept and the real objects that had been thought through it in some relation; and laughter itself is just the expression of this incongruity. It often occurs through two or more real objects being thought through one concept, and the identity of the concept being transferred to the objects. But then a complete difference of the objects in other respects makes it strikingly clear that the concept fitted them only from a one-sided point of view. It occurs just as often, however, that the incongruity between a single real object and the concept under which, on the one hand, it has been rightly subsumed, is suddenly felt. Now the more correct the subsumption of such actualities under the concept from one standpoint, and the greater and more glaring their incongruity with it from the other, the more powerful is the effect of the ludicrous which springs from this contrast. All laughter therefore is occasioned by a paradoxical, and hence unexpected, subsumption, it matters not whether this is expressed in words or in deeds. This in brief is the correct explanation of the ludicrous.

I shall not pause here to relate anecdotes as examples of this, for the purpose of illustrating my explanation; for this is so simple and easy to understand that it does not require them, and everything ludicrous that the reader calls to mind can likewise furnish a proof of it. But our explanation is at once confirmed and elucidated by setting forth two species of the ludicrous into which it is divided, and which result from this very explanation. Either we have previously known two or more very different real objects, representations of perception or intuition, and arbitrarily identified them through the unity of a concept embracing both; this species of the ludicrous is called *wit*. Or, conversely, the concept first of all exists in knowledge, and from it we pass to reality and to operation on reality, to action. Objects in other respects fundamentally different, but all thought in that concept, are now regarded and treated in the same way, until, to the astonishment of the person acting, their great difference in other respects stands out; this species of the ludicrous is called *folly*. Therefore everything ludicrous is either a flash of wit or a foolish action, according as one proceeded from the discrepancy of the objects to the identity of the concept, or the reverse; the former always arbitrary, the latter always unintentional and forced from without. Apparently to reverse the starting-point, and to mask wit as folly, is the art of the jester and clown. Such a person, well aware of the diversity of the objects, unites them with secret wit under one concept, and then, starting from this concept, obtains from the subsequently discovered diversity of the objects the surprise he had himself prepared. It follows from this short but adequate theory of the ludicrous that, setting aside the last case of the jester, wit must always show itself in words, folly usually in actions, though also in words when it merely expresses an intention instead of actually carrying it out, or again when it shows itself in mere judgements and opinions.

Pedantry also is a form of folly. It arises from a man's having little confidence in his own understanding, and therefore not liking to leave things to its discretion, to recognize directly what is right in the particular case. Accordingly, he puts his understanding entirely under the guardianship of his reason, and makes use thereof on all occasions; in other words, he wants always to start from general concepts, rules, and maxims, and to stick strictly to these in life, in art, and even in ethical good conduct. Hence that clinging to the form, the manner, the expression and the word that is peculiar to pedantry, and with it takes the place of the real essence of the matter. The incongruity between the concept and reality soon shows itself, as the former never descends to the particular case, and its universality and rigid definiteness can never accurately apply to reality's fine shades of difference and its innumerable modifications. Therefore the pedant with his general maxims almost always comes off badly in life, and shows himself foolish, absurd, and incompetent. In art, for which the concept is unproductive, he produces lifeless, stiff, abortive mannerisms. Even in regard to ethics, the intention to act rightly or nobly cannot be carried out in all cases in accordance with abstract maxims, since in many instances the infinitely nice distinctions in the nature of the circumstances necessitate a choice of right, proceeding directly from the character. For the application of merely abstract maxims sometimes gives false results, because they only half apply; sometimes it cannot be carried out, because such maxims are foreign to the individual character of the person acting, and this can never be entirely hidden; hence inconsistencies follow. We cannot entirely exonerate Kant from the reproach of causing moral pedantry, in so far as he makes it a condition of the moral worth of an action that it be done from purely rational abstract maxims without any inclination or momentary emotion. This reproach is also the meaning of Schiller's epigram *Gewissensskrupel*. When we speak, especially in political matters, of doctrinaires, theorists, savants, and so forth, we mean pedants, that is to say, persons who well know the things in the abstract, but not in the concrete. Abstraction consists in thinking away the closer and more detailed definitions, but it is precisely on these that very much depends in practice.

To complete the theory, we still have to mention a spurious kind of wit, the play upon words, the *calembour,* the pun, to which can be added the equivocation, *l'équivoque,* whose chief use is in the obscene (smut, filth). Just as wit forces two very different real objects under one concept, so the pun brings two different concepts under one word by the use of chance or accident. The same contrast again arises, but much more insipidly and superficially, because it springs not from the essential nature of things, but from the accident of nomenclature. In the case of wit, the identity is in the concept, the difference in the reality; but in the case of the pun, the difference is in the concepts and the identity in the reality to which the wording belongs. It would be a somewhat far-fetched comparison to say that the pun is related to wit as the hyperbola of the upper inverted cone is to that of the lower. But the misunderstanding of the word, or the *quid pro quo,* is the unintended *calembour,* and is related thereto exactly as folly is to wit. Hence even the man who is hard of hearing, as well as the fool, must afford material for laughter, and bad writers of comedy often use the former instead of the latter to raise a laugh.

I have here considered laughter merely from the psychical side; with regard to the physical side, I refer to the discussion on the subject in *Parerga* (vol. II, chap. 6, § 96), p. 134 (first edition).[23]

§ 14.

B_y all these various considerations it is hoped that the difference and the relation between the cognitive method of reason, rational knowledge, the concept, on the one hand, and the immediate knowledge in purely sensuous, mathematical perception or intuition and in apprehension by the understanding on the other,

---

[23] Cf. chap. 8 of volume 2.

has been brought out quite clearly. Further, there have been also the incidental discussions on feeling and laughter, to which we were almost inevitably led by a consideration of that remarkable relation of our modes of cognition. From all this I now return to a further discussion of science as being, together with speech and deliberate action, the third advantage which the faculty of reason confers on man. The general consideration of science which here devolves upon us will be concerned partly with its form, partly with the foundation of its judgements, and finally with its content.

We have seen that, with the exception of the basis of pure logic, all rational knowledge has its origin not in reason itself, but, having been otherwise gained as knowledge of perception, it is deposited in reason, since in this way it has passed into quite a different method of cognition, namely the abstract. All *rational knowledge,* that is to say, knowledge raised to consciousness in the abstract, is related to *science* proper as a part to the whole. Every person has obtained a rational knowledge about many different things through experience, through a consideration of the individual things presented to him; but only the person who sets himself the task of obtaining a complete knowledge in the abstract about some species of objects aspires to science. Only by a concept can he single out this species; therefore at the head of every science there is a concept through which the part is thought from the sum-total of all things, and of which that science promises a complete knowledge in the abstract. For example, the concept of spatial relations, or of the action of inorganic bodies on one another, or of the nature of plants and animals, or of the successive changes of the surface of the globe, or of the changes of the human race as a whole, or of the structure of a language, and so on. If science wished to obtain the knowledge of its theme by investigating every individual thing thought through the concept, till it had thus gradually learnt the whole, no human memory would suffice, and no certainty of completeness would be obtainable. It therefore makes use of that previously discussed property of concept-spheres of including one another, and it goes mainly to the wider spheres lying generally within the concept of its theme. When it has determined the relations of these spheres to one another, all that is thought in them is also determined in general, and can now be more and more accurately determined by separating out smaller and smaller concept-spheres. It thus becomes possible for a science to embrace its theme completely. This path to knowledge which it follows, namely that from the general to the particular, distinguishes it from ordinary rational knowledge. Systematic form is therefore an essential and characteristic feature of science. The combination of the most general concept-spheres of every science, in other words, the knowledge of its main principles, is the indispensable condition for mastering it. How far we want to go from these to the more special propositions is a matter of choice; it does not increase the thoroughness but the extent of learning. The number of the main principles to which all the rest are subordinated varies greatly as between the different sciences, so that in some there is more subordination, in others more coordination; and in this respect the former make greater claims on the power of judgement, the latter on memory. It was known even to the scholastics[24] that, because the syllogism requires two premises, no science can start from a single main principle that cannot be deduced further; on the contrary, it must have several, at least two, of these. The strictly classificatory sciences, such as zoology, botany, even physics and chemistry, in so far as these latter refer all inorganic action to a few fundamental forces, have the most subordination. History, on the other hand, has really none at all, for the universal in it consists merely in the survey of the principal periods. From these, however, the particular events cannot be deduced; they are subordinate to them only according to time, and are coordinate with them according to the concept. Therefore history, strictly speaking, is rational knowledge certainly, but not a science. In mathematics, according to Euclid's treatment, the axioms are the only indemonstrable first principles, and all demonstrations are in gradation strictly subordinate to them. This method of treatment, however, is not essential to mathematics, and in fact every proposition again begins a new spatial construction. In itself, this is independent of the previous constructions, and can actually be known from itself, quite independently of them, in the pure intuition of space, in which even the most complicated construction is just as directly evident as the axiom is. But this will be discussed in more detail later. Meanwhile, every mathematical proposition always remains a universal truth, valid for innumerable particular cases. A graduated process from the simple to the complicated propositions that are to be referred to them is also essential to mathematics; hence mathematics is in every respect a science. The completeness of a science as such, that is to say, according to form, consists in there being as much subordination and as little coordination of the principles as possible. Scientific talent in general, therefore, is the ability to subordinate the concept-spheres according to their different determinations, so that, as Plato repeatedly recommends, science may not be formed merely by something universal and an immense variety of things placed side by side directly under it, but that knowledge may step down gradually from

---

[24] Suarez, *Disputationes metaphysicae, disp.* III, *sect.* 3, *tit.* 3.

the most universal to the particular through intermediate concepts and divisions, made according to closer and closer definitions. According to Kant's expressions, this means complying equally with the law of homogeneity and with the law of specification. From the fact that this constitutes real scientific completeness, it follows that the aim of science is not greater certainty, for even the most disconnected single piece of knowledge can have just as much certainty; its aim is rather facility of rational knowledge through its form and the possibility, thus given, of completing such knowledge. It is for this reason a prevalent but perverted opinion that the scientific character of knowledge consists in greater certainty; and just as false is the assertion, following from this, that mathematics and logic alone are sciences in the proper sense, because only in them, on account of their wholly *a priori* nature, is there irrefutable certainty of knowledge. This last advantage cannot be denied them, but it does not give them a special claim to the nature of science. For that is to be found not in certainty, but in the systematic form of knowledge, established by the gradual descent from the universal to the particular. This way of knowledge from the universal to the particular, peculiar to the sciences, makes it necessary that in them much is established by deduction from previous propositions, that is by proofs. This has given rise to the old error that only what is demonstrated is perfectly true, and that every truth requires a proof. On the contrary, every proof or demonstration requires an undemonstrated truth, and this ultimately supports it or again its own proofs. Therefore a directly established truth is as preferable to a truth established by a proof as spring water is to piped water. Perception, partly pure *a priori,* as establishing mathematics, partly empirical *a posteriori,* as establishing all the other sciences, is the source of all truth and the basis of all science. (Logic alone is to be excepted, which is based not on knowledge of perception, but on reason's direct knowledge of its own laws.) Not the demonstrated judgements or their proofs, but judgements drawn directly from perception and founded thereon instead of on any proof, are in science what the sun is to the world. All light proceeds from them, and, illuminated thereby, the others in turn give light. To establish the truth of such primary judgements directly from perception, to raise such foundations of science from the immense number of real things, is the work of the *power of judgement.* This consists in the ability to carry over into abstract consciousness correctly and exactly what is known in perception; and judgement accordingly is the mediator between understanding and reason. Only outstanding and extraordinary strength of judgement in an individual can actually advance the sciences, but anyone who has merely a healthy faculty of reason is able to deduce propositions from propositions, to demonstrate, to draw conclusions. On the other hand, to lay down and fix in appropriate concepts for reflection what is known through perception, so that, firstly, what is common to many real objects is thought through *one* concept, and secondly, their points of difference are thought through just as many concepts; this is done by the *power of judgement*. From this what is different is known and thought as different, in spite of a partial agreement; and what is identical is known and thought as identical, in spite of a partial difference, all according to the purpose and consideration that actually exist in each case. This too is the work of judgement. Want of judgement is *silliness*. The silly person fails to recognize, now the partial or relative difference of what is in one respect identical, now the identity of what is relatively or partially different. Moreover, to this explanation of the power of judgement Kant's division of it into reflecting and subsuming judgement can be applied, according as it passes from the objects of perception to the concept, or from the concept to the objects of perception, in both cases always mediating between knowledge of the understanding through perception and reflective knowledge of reason. There can be no truth that could be brought out absolutely through syllogisms alone, but the necessity of establishing truth merely through syllogisms is always only relative, indeed subjective. As all proofs are syllogisms, we must first seek for a new truth not a proof, but direct evidence, and only so long as this is wanting is the proof to be furnished for the time being. No science can be capable of demonstration throughout any more than a building can stand in the air. All its proofs must refer to something perceived, and hence no longer capable of proof, for the whole world of reflection rests on, and is rooted in, the world of perception. All ultimate, i.e., original, *evidence* is one of *intuitive perception,* as the word already discloses. Accordingly, it is either empirical or based on the perception *a priori* of the conditions of possible experience. In both cases, therefore, it affords only immanent, not transcendent knowledge. Every concept has its value and its existence only in reference to a representation from perception, although such reference may be very indirect. What holds good of the concepts holds good also of the judgements constructed from them, and of all the sciences. Therefore it must be possible in some way to know directly, even without proofs and syllogisms, every truth that is found through syllogisms and communicated by proofs. This is most difficult certainly in the case of many complicated mathematical propositions which we reach only by chains of syllogisms; for example, the calculation of the chords and tangents to all arcs by means of deductions from the theorem of Pythagoras. But even such a truth cannot rest essentially and solely on abstract principles, and the spatial relations at the root of it must also be capable of being so displayed for pure intuition *a priori,* that their abstract expression is directly established. But shortly we shall discuss demonstration in mathematics in detail.

It may be that people often speak in a lofty tone about sciences which rest entirely on correct conclusions from sure premises, and are therefore incontestably true. But through purely logical chains of reasoning, however true the premises may be, we shall never obtain more than an elucidation and exposition of what already lies complete in the premises; thus we shall only *explicitly* expound what was already *implicitly* understood therein. By these esteemed sciences are meant especially the mathematical, in particular astronomy. But the certainty of astronomy arises from the fact that it has for its basis the intuition or perception of space, given *a priori,* and hence infallible. All spatial relations, however, follow from one another with a necessity (ground of being) that affords *a priori* certainty, and they can with safety be derived from one another. To these mathematical provisions is added only a single force of nature, namely gravity, operating exactly in proportion to the masses and to the square of the distance; and finally we have the law of inertia, *a priori* certain, because it follows from the law of causality, together with the empirical datum of the motion impressed on each of these masses once for all. This is the whole material of astronomy, which, by both its simplicity and its certainty, leads to definite results that are very interesting by virtue of the magnitude and importance of the objects. For example, if I know the mass of a planet and the distance from it of its satellite, I can infer with certainty the latter's period of revolution according to Kepler's second law. But the basis of this law is that at this distance only this velocity simultaneously chains the satellite to the planet, and prevents it from falling into it. Hence only on such a geometrical basis, that is to say, by means of an intuition or perception *a priori,* and moreover under the application of a law of nature, can we get very far with syllogisms, since here they are, so to speak, merely bridges from one perceptive apprehension to another. But it is not so with merely plain syllogisms on the exclusively logical path. The origin of the first fundamental truths of astronomy is really induction, in other words, the summarizing into one correct and directly founded judgement of what is given in many perceptions. From this judgement hypotheses are afterwards formed, and the confirmation of these by experience, as induction approaching completeness, gives the proof for that first judgement. For example, the apparent motion of the planets is known empirically; after many false hypotheses about the spatial connexion of this motion (planetary orbit), the correct one was at last found, then the laws followed by it (Kepler's laws), and finally the cause of these laws (universal gravitation). The empirically known agreement of all observed cases with the whole of the hypotheses and with their consequences, hence induction, gave them complete certainty. The discovery of the hypothesis was the business of the power of judgement which rightly comprehended the given fact, and expressed it accordingly; but induction, in other words perception of many kinds, confirmed its truth. But this truth could be established even directly through a single empirical perception, if we could freely pass through universal space, and had telescopic eyes. Consequently, even here syllogisms are not the essential and only source of knowledge, but are always in fact only a makeshift.

Finally, in order to furnish a third example from a different sphere, we will observe that even the so-called metaphysical truths, that is, such as are laid down by Kant in the *Metaphysical Rudiments of Natural Science,* do not owe their evidence to proofs. We know immediately what is *a priori* certain; this, as the form of all knowledge, is known to us with the greatest necessity. For instance, we know immediately as negative truth that matter persists, in other words, that it can neither come into being nor pass away. Our pure intuition or perception of space and time gives the possibility of motion; the understanding gives in the law of causality the possibility of change of form and quality, but we lack the forms for conceiving an origin or disappearance of matter. Therefore this truth has at all times been evident to all men everywhere, and has never been seriously doubted; and this could not be the case if its ground of knowledge were none other than the very difficult and hair-splitting proof of Kant. But in addition, I have found Kant's proof to be false (as explained in the Appendix), and I have shown above that the permanence of matter is to be deduced not from the share that time has in the possibility of experience, but from that which space has. The real foundation of all truths which in this sense are called metaphysical, that is, of abstract expressions of the necessary and universal forms of knowledge, can be found not in abstract principles, but only in the immediate consciousness of the forms of representation, manifesting itself through statements *a priori* that are apodictic and in fear of no refutation. But if we still want to furnish a proof of them, this can consist only in our showing that what is to be proved is already contained in some undoubted truth as a part or a presupposition of it. Thus, for example, I have shown that all empirical perception implies the application of the law of causality. Hence knowledge of this is a condition of all experience, and therefore cannot be given and conditioned through experience, as Hume asserted. Proofs are generally less for those who want to learn than for those who want to dispute. These latter obstinately deny directly established insight. Truth alone can be consistent in all directions; we must therefore show such persons that they admit under one form and indirectly what under another form and directly they deny, i.e. the logically necessary connexion between what is denied and what is admitted.

Moreover, it is a consequence of the scientific form, namely subordination of everything particular under something general, and then under something more and more general, that the truth of many propositions is established only logically, namely through their dependence on other propositions, and hence through syllogisms which appear simultaneously as proofs. But we should never forget that this entire form is a means only to facilitating knowledge, not to greater certainty. It is easier to know the nature of an animal from the species to which it belongs, and so on upwards from the genus, family, order, and class, than to examine the animal itself which is given to us on each occasion. But the truth of all propositions deduced by syllogisms is always only conditioned by, and ultimately dependent on, a truth that rests not on syllogisms, but on perception or intuition. If this perception were always as much within our reach as deduction through a syllogism is, it would be in every way preferable. For every deduction from concepts is exposed to many deceptions on account of the fact, previously demonstrated, that many different spheres are linked and interlocked, and again because their content is often ill-defined and uncertain. Examples of this are the many proofs of false doctrines and sophisms of every kind. Syllogisms are indeed perfectly certain as regards form, but very uncertain through their matter, namely the concepts. For on the one hand the spheres of these are often not defined with sufficient sharpness, and on the other they intersect one another in so many different ways, that one sphere is partly contained in many others, and therefore we can pass arbitrarily from it to one or another of these, and again to others, as we have already shown. Or, in other words, the minor and also the middle term can always be subordinated to different concepts, from which we choose at will the major term and the middle, whereupon the conclusion turns out differently. Consequently, immediate evidence is everywhere far preferable to demonstrated truth, and the latter is to be accepted only when the former is too remote, and not when it is just as near as, or even nearer than, the latter. Therefore we saw above that actually with logic, where in each individual case immediate knowledge lies nearer at hand than derived scientific knowledge, we always conduct our thinking only in accordance with immediate knowledge of the laws of thought, and leave logic unused.[25]

§ 15.

Now if with our conviction that perception is the first source of all evidence, that immediate or mediate reference to this alone is absolute truth, and further that the shortest way to this is always the surest, as every mediation through concepts exposes us to many deceptions; if, I say, we now turn with this conviction to *mathematics,* as it was laid down in the form of a science by Euclid, and has on the whole remained down to the present day, we cannot help finding the path followed by it strange and even perverted. We demand the reduction of every logical proof to one of perception. Mathematics, on the contrary, is at great pains deliberately to reject the evidence of perception peculiar to it and everywhere at hand, in order to substitute for it logical evidence. We must look upon this as being like a man who cuts off his legs in order to walk on crutches, or the prince in *Triumph der Empfindsamkeit* who flees from the beautiful reality of nature to enjoy a theatrical scene that imitates it. I must now call to mind what I said in the sixth chapter of the essay *On the Principle of Sufficient Reason,* which I assume to be quite fresh and present in the reader's memory. Here then I link my observations on to this without discussing afresh the difference between the mere ground of knowledge of a mathematical truth which can be given logically, and the ground of being, which is the immediate connexion of the parts of space and time, to be known only from perception. It is only insight into the ground of being which gives true satisfaction and thorough knowledge. The mere ground of knowledge, on the other hand, always remains on the surface, and can give us a rational knowledge *that* a thing is as it is, but no rational knowledge *why* it is so. Euclid chose this latter way to the obvious detriment of the science. For example, at the very beginning, he ought to show once for all how in the triangle angles and sides reciprocally determine one another, and are the reason or ground and consequent

[25] Cf. chap. 12 of volume 2.

of each other, in accordance with the form which the principle of sufficient reason has in mere space, and which there, as everywhere, provides the necessity that a thing is as it is, because another thing, quite different from it, is as it is. Instead of thus giving us a thorough insight into the nature of the triangle, he posits a few disconnected, arbitrarily chosen propositions about the triangle, and gives a logical ground of knowledge of them through a laborious logical proof furnished in accordance with the principle of contradiction. Instead of an exhaustive knowledge of these space-relations, we therefore obtain only a few arbitrarily communicated results from them, and are in the same position as the man to whom the different effects of an ingenious machine are shown, while its inner connexion and mechanism are withheld from him. We are forced by the principle of contradiction to admit that everything demonstrated by Euclid is so, but we do not get to know *why* it is so. We therefore have almost the uncomfortable feeling that we get after a conjuring trick, and in fact most of Euclid's proofs are remarkably like such a trick. The truth almost always comes in by the back door, since it follows *per accidens* from some minor circumstance. Frequently, an apagogic proof shuts all doors one after the other, and leaves open only one, through which merely for that reason we must now pass. Often, as in the theorem of Pythagoras, lines are drawn without our knowing why. It afterwards appears that they were traps, which shut unexpectedly and take prisoner the assent of the learner, who in astonishment has then to admit what remains wholly unintelligible to him in its inner connexion. This happens to such an extent that he can study the whole of Euclid throughout without gaining real insight into the laws of spatial relations, but instead of these, he learns by heart only a few of their results. This really empirical and unscientific knowledge is like that of the doctor who knows disease and remedy, but not the connexion between the two. But all this is what results when we capriciously reject the method of proof and evidence peculiar to one species of knowledge, and forcibly introduce instead of it a method that is foreign to its nature. In other respects, however, the way in which this is carried out by Euclid deserves all the admiration that for so many centuries has been bestowed on him. The method has been followed so far, that his treatment of mathematics has been declared to be the pattern for all scientific presentation. Men tried even to model all the other sciences on it, but later gave this up without really knowing why. In our view, however, this method of Euclid in mathematics can appear only as a very brilliant piece of perversity. When a great error concerning life or science is pursued intentionally and methodically, and is accompanied by universal assent, it is always possible to demonstrate the reason for this in the philosophy that prevails at the time. The Eleatics first discovered the difference, indeed more often the antagonism, between the perceived, φαινόμενον, and the conceived, νοούμενον,[26] and used it in many ways for their philosophemes, and also for sophisms.

They were followed later by the Megarics, Dialecticians, Sophists, New Academicians, and Sceptics; these drew attention to the illusion, that is, the deception of the senses, or rather of the understanding which converts the data of the senses into perception, and often causes us to see things to which the faculty of reason positively denies reality, for example, the stick broken in the water, and so on. It was recognized that perception through the senses was not to be trusted unconditionally, and it was hastily concluded that only rational logical thinking established truth, although Plato (in the *Parmenides*), the Megarics, Pyrrho, and the New Academicians showed by examples (in the way later adopted by Sextus Empiricus) how syllogisms and concepts were also misleading, how in fact they produced paralogisms and sophisms that arise much more easily, and are far harder to unravel, than the illusion in perception through the senses. But this rationalism, which arose in opposition to empiricism, kept the upper hand, and Euclid modelled mathematics in accordance with it. He was therefore necessarily compelled to found the axioms alone on the evidence of perception (φαινόμενον), and all the rest on syllogisms (νοούμενον). His method remained the prevailing one throughout all the centuries, and was bound so to remain, so long as there was no distinction between pure intuition or perception *a priori* and empirical perception. Indeed, Euclid's commentator Proclus appears to have fully recognized this distinction, as he shows in the passage translated by Kepler into Latin in his book *De Harmonia Mundi*. But Proclus did not attach enough weight to the matter; he raised it in too detached a manner, remained unnoticed, and achieved nothing. Therefore only after two thousand years will Kant's teaching, destined to bring about such great changes in all the knowledge, thought, and action of European nations, cause such a change in mathematics also. For only after we have learnt from this great mind that the intuitions or perceptions of space and time are quite different from empirical perception, entirely independent of any impression on the senses, conditioning this and not conditioned by it, i.e., are *a priori,* and hence not in any way exposed to sense-deception—only then can we see that Euclid's logical method of treating mathematics is a useless precaution, a crutch for sound legs.

---

[26] We must not think here of Kant's misuse of these Greek expressions which is condemned in the Appendix.

We see that such a method is like a wanderer who, mistaking at night a bright firm road for water, refrains from walking on it, and goes over the rough ground beside it, content to keep from point to point along the edge of the supposed water. Only now can we affirm with certainty that that which presents itself to us as necessary in the perception of a figure does not come from the figure on the paper, perhaps very imperfectly drawn, or from the abstract concept that we think with it, but immediately from the form of all knowledge, of which we are conscious *a priori*. This is everywhere the principle of sufficient reason; here, as form of perception, i.e., space, it is the principle of the ground of being; but the evidence and validity of this are just as great and immediate as that of the principle of the ground of knowledge, i.e., logical certainty. Thus we need not and should not leave the peculiar province of mathematics in order to trust merely logical certainty, and prove mathematics true in a province quite foreign to it, namely in the province of concepts. If we stick to the ground peculiar to mathematics, we gain the great advantage that in it the rational knowledge *that* something is so is one with the rational knowledge *why* it is so. The method of Euclid, on the other hand, entirely separates the two, and lets us know merely the first, not the second. Aristotle says admirably in the *Posterior Analytics* (I, 27): Ἀκριβεστέρα δ'ἐπιστήμη ἐπιστήμης καὶ προτέρα, τοῦ ἥτε τοῦ ὅτι καὶ τοῦ διότι ἡ αὐτή, ἀλλὰ μὴ χωρὶς ὅτι, τῆς τοῦ διότι. (*Subtilior autem et praestantior ea est scientia, quâ QUOD aliquid sit, et CUR sit una simulque intelligimus, non separatim QUOD, et CUR sit.*)[27] In physics we are satisfied only when the knowledge *that* something is thus is combined with the knowledge *why* it is thus. It is no use for us to know that the mercury in the Torricellian tube stands at a height of thirty inches, if we do not also know that it is kept at this height by the counterbalancing weight of the atmosphere. But are we in mathematics to be satisfied with the *qualitas occulta* of the circle that the segments of any two intersecting chords always form equal rectangles? That this is so is of course proved by Euclid in the 35th proposition of the third book, but *why* it is so remains uncertain. In the same way, the theorem of Pythagoras teaches us a *qualitas occulta* of the right-angled triangle; the stilted, and indeed subtle, proof of Euclid forsakes us at the *why,* and the accompanying simple figure, already known to us, gives at a glance far more insight into the matter, and firm inner

---

[27] "But more accurate and preferable to mere knowledge is that knowledge which not only says *that* something is, but also *why* it is so, and not that knowledge which teaches separately the *That* and the *Why*." [Tr.]

conviction of that necessity, and of the dependence of that property on the right angle, than is given by his proof.

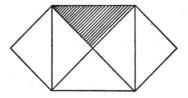

Even in the case when unequal sides contain the right angle, as generally with every possible geometrical truth, it must be possible to reach such a conviction based on perception, because its discovery always started from such a perceived necessity, and only afterwards was the proof thought out in addition. Thus we need only an analysis of the process of thought in the first discovery of a geometrical truth, in order to know its necessity intuitively or perceptively. It is generally the analytic method that I desire for the expounding of mathematics, instead of the synthetic method Euclid made use of. But of course with complicated mathematical truths this will entail very great, though not insuperable, difficulties. Here and there in Germany men are beginning to alter the exposition of mathematics, and to follow more this analytic path. The most positive work in this direction has been done by Herr Kosack, instructor in mathematics and physics at the Nordhausen Gymnasium, who added to the programme for the school examination of 6 April 1852 a detailed attempt to deal with geometry in accordance with my main principles.

To improve the method of mathematics, it is specially necessary to give up the prejudice that demonstrated truth has any advantage over truth known through perception or intuition, or that logical truth, resting on the principle of contradiction, has any advantage over metaphysical truth, which is immediately evident, and to which also belongs the pure intuition of space.

What is most certain yet everywhere inexplicable is the content of the principle of sufficient reason, for this principle in its different aspects expresses the universal form of all our representations and knowledge. All explanation is a tracing back to this principle, a demonstration in the particular case of the connexion of representations expressed generally through it. It is therefore the principle of all explanation, and hence is not itself capable of explanation; nor is it in need of one, for every explanation presupposes it, and only through it obtains any meaning. None of its forms is superior to another; it is equally certain and incapable of demonstration as principle of ground of being, or of becoming, or of acting, or of knowing. The relation of reason or ground to consequent is a necessary one in any one of its forms; indeed, it is in general the origin of the concept of necessity, as its one and only meaning. There is no other necessity than that of the consequent when the reason or ground is given; and there is no reason or ground that does not entail necessity of the consequent. Just as surely, then, as the consequent expressed in the conclusion flows from the ground of knowledge given in the premises, so does the ground of being in space condition its consequent in space. If I have recognized through perception the relation of these two, then this certainty is just as great as any logical certainty. But every geometrical proposition is just as good an expression of such a relation as is one of the twelve axioms. It is a metaphysical truth, and, as such, is just as immediately certain as is the principle of contradiction itself, which is a metalogical truth, and is the general foundation of all logical demonstration. Whoever denies the necessity, intuitively presented, of the space-relations expressed in any proposition, can with equal right deny the axioms, the following of the conclusion from the premises, or even the principle of contradiction itself, for all these relations are equally indemonstrable, immediately evident, and knowable *a priori*. Therefore, if anyone wishes to derive the necessity of space-relations, knowable in intuition or perception, from the principle of contradiction through a logical demonstration, it is just the same as if a stranger wished to enfeoff an estate to the immediate owner thereof. But this is what Euclid has done. Only his axioms is he compelled to leave resting on immediate evidence; all the following geometrical truths are logically proved, namely, under the presupposition of those axioms, from the agreement with the assumptions made in the proposition, or with an earlier proposition, or even from the contradiction between the opposite of the proposition and the assumptions, or the axioms, or the earlier propositions, or even itself. But the axioms themselves have no more immediate evidence than any other geometrical proposition has, but only greater simplicity by their smaller content.

When an accused person is examined, his statements are taken down in evidence, in order to judge of their truth from their agreement and consistency. But this is a mere makeshift, and we ought not to put up with it if we can investigate the truth of each of his statements directly and by itself, especially as he might consistently lie from the beginning. But it is by this first method that Euclid investigated space. He did indeed start from the correct assumption that nature must be consistent everywhere, and therefore also in space, its fundamental form. Therefore, since the parts of space stand to one another in the relation of reason or ground to consequent, no single determination of space can be other than it is without being in contradiction with all the others. But this is a very troublesome, unsatisfactory, and roundabout way, which prefers indirect knowledge to direct knowledge that is just as certain; which further separates the knowledge *that* something is from the knowledge *why* it is, to the great disadvantage of science; and which finally withholds entirely from the beginner insight into the laws of space, and indeed renders him unaccustomed to the proper investigation of the ground and inner connexion of things. Instead of this, it directs him to be satisfied with a mere historical knowledge *that a thing is as it is.* But the exercise of acuteness, mentioned so incessantly in praise of this method, consists merely in the fact that the pupil practises drawing conclusions, i.e., applying the principle of contradiction, but specially that he exerts his memory in order to retain all those data whose agreement and consistency are to be compared.

Moreover, it is worth noting that this method of proof was applied only to geometry and not to arithmetic. In arithmetic, on the contrary, truth is really allowed to become clear through perception alone, which there consists in mere counting. As the perception of numbers is in *time alone,* and therefore cannot be represented by a sensuous schema like the geometrical figure, the suspicion that perception was only empirical, and hence subject to illusion, disappeared in arithmetic. It was only this suspicion that was able to introduce the logical method of proof into geometry. Since time has only one dimension, counting is the only arithmetical operation, to which all others can be reduced. Yet this counting is nothing but intuition or perception *a priori,* to which we do not hesitate to refer, and by which alone everything else, every calculation, every equation, is ultimately verified. For example, we do not prove that $\dfrac{(7 + 9) \times 8 - 2}{3} = 42$, but refer to pure intuition in time, to counting; thus we make each individual proposition an axiom. Instead of the proofs that fill geometry, the whole content of arithmetic and algebra is thus a mere method for the abbreviation of counting. As mentioned above, our immediate perception of numbers in time does not extend to more than about ten. Beyond this an abstract concept of number, fixed by a word, must take the place of perception; thus perception is no longer actually carried out, but is only quite definitely indicated. Yet even so, through the important expedient of the order of ciphers, enabling larger numbers always to be represented by the same small ones, an intuitive or perceptive evidence of every sum or calculation is made possible, even where so much use is made of abstraction that not only the numbers, but indefinite quantities and whole operations are thought only in the abstract, and are indicated in this respect, such as $\sqrt{r^{-b}}$, so that they are no longer performed, but only symbolized.

With the same right and certainty we could enable truth to be established in geometry, just as in arithmetic, solely through pure intuition *a priori*. In fact, it is always this necessity, known from perception according to the principle of the ground or reason of being, which gives geometry its great evidence, and on which the certainty of its propositions rests in the consciousness of everyone. It is certainly not the stilted logical proof, which is always foreign to the matter, is generally soon forgotten without detriment to conviction, and could be dispensed with entirely, without diminishing the evidence of geometry. For geometry is quite independent of such proof, which always proves only what we are already through another kind of knowledge fully convinced of. To this extent it is like a cowardly soldier who gives another wound to an enemy killed by someone else, and then boasts that he himself killed him.[28]

As a result of all this, it is hoped there will be no doubt that the evidence of mathematics, which has become the pattern and symbol of all evidence, rests essentially not on proofs, but on immediate intuition or perception. Here, as everywhere, that is the ultimate ground and source of all truth. Yet the perception forming the basis of mathematics has a great advantage over every other perception, and hence over the empirical. Thus as it is *a priori,* and consequently independent of experience which is always given only partially and successively, everything is equally near to it, and we can start either from the reason or ground or from the consequent, as we please. Now this endows it with a complete certainty and infallibility, for in it the consequent is known from the ground or reason, and this knowledge alone has necessity. For example, the

---

[28] Spinoza, who always boasts of proceeding *more geometrico,* has actually done so more than he himself knew. For what to him was certain and settled from an immediate perceptive apprehension of the nature of the world, he tries to demonstrate logically and independently of this knowledge. But of course he arrives at the intended result predetermined by him, only by taking as the starting-point concepts arbitrarily made by him (*substantia, causa sui,* and so on), and by allowing himself in the demonstration all the freedom of choice for which the nature of the wide concept-spheres affords convenient opportunity. Therefore, what is true and excellent in his doctrine is in his case, as in that of geometry, quite independent of the proofs. Cf. chap. 13 of volume 2.

equality of the sides is known as established through the equality of the angles. On the other hand, all empirical perception and the greater part of all experience proceed only conversely from the consequent to the ground. This kind of knowledge is not infallible, for necessity belongs alone to the consequent in so far as the ground is given, and not to knowledge of the ground from the consequent, for the same consequent can spring from different grounds. This latter kind of knowledge is always only induction, i.e., from many consequents pointing to one ground, the ground is assumed as certain; but as all the cases can never be together, the truth here is never unconditionally certain. Yet all knowledge through sensuous perception and the great bulk of experience have only this kind of truth. The affection of a sense induces the understanding to infer the cause from the effect, but since the conclusion from what is established (the consequent) to the ground is never certain, illusion, which is deception of the senses, is possible, and often actual, as was said previously. Only when several or all of the five senses receive affections pointing to the same cause does the possibility of illusion become small. Even then it still exists, for in certain cases, such as with counterfeit coins, the whole sensitive faculty is deceived. All empirical knowledge, and consequently the whole of natural science, is in the same position, leaving aside its pure (or as Kant calls it metaphysical) part. Here also the causes are known from the effects; therefore all natural philosophy rests on hypotheses which are often false, and then gradually give way to others that are more correct. Only in the case of intentionally arranged experiments does knowledge proceed from the cause to the effect, in other words, does it go the sure and certain way; but these experiments are themselves undertaken only in consequence of hypotheses. For this reason, no branch of natural science, such as physics, or astronomy, or physiology, could be discovered all at once, as was possible with mathematics or logic, but it required and requires the collected and compared experiences of many centuries. Only empirical confirmation of many kinds brings the induction on which the hypothesis rests so near to completeness that in practice it takes the place of certainty. It is regarded as being no more detrimental to the hypothesis, its source, than is the incommensurability of straight and curved lines to the application of geometry, or perfect exactness of the logarithm, which is incapable of attainment, to arithmetic. For just as the squaring of the circle, and the logarithm, are brought infinitely near to correctness through infinite fractions, so also through manifold experience induction, i.e., knowledge of the ground from the consequents, is brought to mathematical evidence, i.e., to knowledge of the consequent from the ground, not indeed infinitely, but yet so close that the possibility of deception becomes so small that we can neglect it. But yet the possibility is there; for example, the conclusion from innumerable cases to all cases, i.e., in reality to the unknown ground on which all depend, is a conclusion of induction. Now what conclusion of this kind seems more certain than the one that all human beings have their heart on the left side? Yet there are extremely rare and quite isolated exceptions of persons whose heart is on the right side. Sense-perception and the science of experience have therefore the same kind of evidence. The advantage that mathematics, pure natural science, and logic as knowledge *a priori* have over them rests merely on the fact that the formal element of knowledge, on which all that is *a priori* is based, is given as a whole and at once. Here, therefore, we can always proceed from the ground to the consequent, but in the other kind of knowledge often only from the consequent to the ground. In other respects, the law of causality, or the principle of sufficient reason of becoming, which guides empirical knowledge, is in itself just as certain as are those other forms of the principle of sufficient reason followed by the above-mentioned sciences *a priori*. Logical proofs from concepts or syllogisms have the advantage of proceeding from the ground to the consequent, just as has knowledge through *a priori* perception; thus in themselves, that is to say, according to their form, they are infallible. This has been largely instrumental in bringing proofs generally into such great repute. But this infallibility of theirs is relative; they subsume merely under the main principles of science. It is these, however, that contain the whole material truth of science, and they cannot again be merely demonstrated, but must be founded on perception. In the few mentioned *a priori* sciences this perception is pure, but otherwise it is always empirical, and is raised to the universal only through induction. If, therefore, in the sciences of experience the particular is proved from the general, the general nevertheless has again obtained its truth only from the particular; it is only a granary of accumulated stocks, not a soil that is itself productive.

So much for the establishment of truth. Of the source and possibility of *error,* many explanations have been attempted since Plato's metaphorical solutions of the dovecot, where the wrong pigeon is caught, and so on (*Theaetetus* [197 ff.], p. 167 *et seqq.*). Kant's vague, indefinite explanation of the origin of error by means of the diagram of diagonal motion is found in the *Critique of Pure Reason* (p. 294 of the first edition, and p. 350 of the fifth). As truth is the relation of a judgement to its ground of knowledge, it is certainly a problem how the person judging can really believe he has such a ground and yet not have it, that is to say how error, the deception of the faculty of reason, is possible. I find this possibility wholly analogous to that of illusion, or deception of the understanding, previously explained. My opinion is (and this gives that explanation its place here) *that every error is a conclusion from the consequent to the ground,* which indeed is valid when we know that the consequent can have that ground and absolutely no other; otherwise it is not. The person making the error either assigns to the consequent a ground it cannot possibly have, wherein he shows actual want of understanding, i.e., deficiency in the ability to know immediately the connexion between cause and effect. Or, as is more often the case, he attributes to the consequent a ground that is indeed possible, yet he adds to the major proposition of his conclusion from the consequent to the ground that the aforesaid consequent arises *always* only from the ground mentioned by him. He could be justified in doing this only by a complete induction, which, however, he assumes without having made it. This "always" is therefore too wide a concept, and should be replaced by *sometimes* or *generally.* The conclusion would thus turn out to be problematical, and as such would not be erroneous. That the man who errs should proceed in the way mentioned is due either to haste or too limited a knowledge of what is possible, for which reason he does not know the necessity of the induction to be made. Error therefore is wholly analogous to illusion. Both are conclusions from the consequent to the ground; the illusion, brought about always according to the law of causality, by the mere understanding, and thus immediately, in perception itself; the error, brought about according to all the forms of the principle of sufficient reason, by our rational faculty, and thus in thought proper, yet most frequently according to the law of causality, as is proved by the three following examples, which may be regarded as types or representatives of the three kinds of error. (1) The illusion of the senses (deception of the understanding) gives rise to error (deception of reason); for example, if we mistake a painting for a high relief, and actually take it to be such; it happens through a conclusion from the following major premiss: "If dark grey here and there passes through all shades into white, the cause is *always* the light striking unequally projections and depressions, *ergo*—." (2) "If money is missing from my safe, the cause is *always* that my servant has a skeleton key, *ergo*—." (3) "If the solar image, broken through the prism, i.e., moved up or down, now appears elongated and coloured instead of round and white as previously, then the cause is always that in light there are differently coloured, and at the same time differently refrangible, homogeneous light-rays that, moved apart by their different refrangibility, now give an elongated, and at the same time variously coloured, image, *ergo—bibamus!"* It must be possible to trace every error to such a conclusion, drawn from a major premiss that is often only falsely generalized, hypothetical, and the result of assuming a ground to the consequent. Only some mistakes in calculation are to be excepted, which are not really errors, but mere mistakes. The operation stated by the concepts of the numbers has not been carried out in pure intuition or perception, in counting, but another operation instead.

As regards the *content* of the sciences generally, this is really always the relation of the phenomena of the world to one another according to the principle of sufficient reason, and on the guiding line of the *Why,* which has validity and meaning only through this principle. *Explanation* is the establishment of this relation. Therefore, explanation can never do more than show two representations standing to each other in the relation of that form of the principle of sufficient reason ruling in the class to which they belong. If it has achieved this, we cannot be further asked the question *why,* for the relation demonstrated is that which simply cannot be represented differently, in other words, it is the form of all knowledge. Therefore we do not ask why $2 + 2 = 4$, or why the equality of the angles in a triangle determines the equality of the sides, or why any given cause is followed by its effect, or why the truth of a conclusion is evident from the truth of the premisses. Every explanation not[29] leading back to such a relation of which no Why can further be demanded, stops at an accepted *qualitas occulta;* but this is also the character of every original force of nature. Every explanation of natural science must ultimately stop at such a *qualitas occulta,* and thus at something wholly obscure. It must therefore leave the inner nature of a stone just as unexplained as that of a human being; it can give as little account of the weight, cohesion, chemical properties, etc. of the former, as of the knowing and acting of the latter. Thus, for example, weight is a *qualitas occulta,* for it can be thought away, and hence it does not follow from the form of knowledge as something necessary. Again, this is the case with the law of inertia, which

---

[29] *Translator's note:* Dr Arthur Hübscher of the Schopenhauer Society of Germany is of the opinion that "not" should be deleted. In a letter he states that *"im Text selbst habe ich das 'nicht' nicht gestrichen. Es steht in allen von Schopenhauer besorgten Ausgaben. Die Handschrift besitzen wir nicht. Ich nehme an, dass es sich um einen Flüchtigkeitsfehler Schopenhauers handelt, wie sie öfter bei ihm vorkommen. . . . In diesem Falle scheint mir die Sache nicht ganz eindeutig entschieden zu sein, so dass ich in den Textbestand nicht eingreifen wollte."*

follows from the law of causality; hence a reference to this is a perfectly adequate explanation. Two things are absolutely inexplicable, in other words, do not lead back to the relation expressed by the principle of sufficient reason. The first of these is the principle of sufficient reason itself in all its four forms, because it is the principle of all explanation, which has meaning only in reference to it; the second is that which is not reached by this principle, but from which arises that original thing in all phenomena; it is the thing-in-itself, knowledge of which is in no wise subject to the principle of sufficient reason. Here for the present we must rest content not to understand this thing-in-itself, for it can be made intelligible only by the following book, where we shall also take up again this consideration of the possible achievements of the sciences. But there is a point where natural science, and indeed every science, leaves things as they are, since not only its explanation of them, but even the principle of this explanation, namely the principle of sufficient reason, does not go beyond this point. This is the real point where philosophy again takes up things and considers them in accordance with its method, which is entirely different from the method of science. In the essay *On the Principle of Sufficient Reason,* § 51, I have shown how in the different sciences the main guiding line is one form or another of this principle; in fact, the most appropriate classification of the sciences might perhaps be made in accordance therewith. But, as I have said, every explanation given in accordance with this guiding line is merely relative. It explains things in reference to one another, but it always leaves unexplained something that it presupposes. In mathematics, for example, this is space and time; in mechanics, physics, and chemistry, it is matter, qualities, original forces, laws of nature; in botany and zoology, it is the difference of species and life itself; in history, it is the human race with all its characteristics of thought and will. In all these it is the principle of sufficient reason in the form appropriate for application in each case. *Philosophy* has the peculiarity of presupposing absolutely nothing as known; everything to it is equally strange and a problem; not only the relations of phenomena, but also those phenomena themselves, and indeed the principle of sufficient reason itself, to which the other sciences are content to refer everything. In philosophy, however, nothing would be gained by such a reference, for one link of the series is just as foreign and strange to it as another. Moreover, that kind of connexion is itself just as much a problem for philosophy as what is joined together by that connexion, and this again is as much a problem after the combination thus explained as before it. For, as we have said, just what the sciences presuppose and lay down as the basis and limit of their explanation is precisely the real problem of philosophy, which consequently begins where the sciences leave off. Proofs cannot be its foundation, for these deduce unknown principles from others that are known; but to it everything is equally unknown and strange. There can be no principle in consequence of which the world with all its phenomena would first of all exist; therefore it is not possible, as Spinoza wished, to deduce a philosophy that demonstrates *ex firmis principiis*. Philosophy is also the most universal rational knowledge (*Wissen*), whose main principles, therefore, cannot be deductions from another principle still more universal. The principle of contradiction establishes merely the agreement of concepts, and does not itself give concepts. The principle of sufficient reason explains connexions and combinations of phenomena, not the phenomena themselves. Therefore, philosophy cannot start from these to look for a *causa efficiens* or a *causa finalis* of the whole world. The present philosophy, at any rate, by no means attempts to say *whence* or *for what purpose* the world exists, but merely *what* the world is. But here the *Why* is subordinated to the *What,* for it already belongs to the world, as it springs merely from the form of its phenomenon, the principle of sufficient reason, and only to this extent has it meaning and validity. Indeed, it might be said that everyone knows without further help what the world is, for he himself is the subject of knowing of which the world is representation, and so far this would be true. But this knowledge is a knowledge of perception, is in the concrete. The task of philosophy is to reproduce this in the abstract, to raise to a permanent rational knowledge successive, variable perceptions, and generally all that the wide concept of *feeling* embraces and describes merely negatively as not abstract, distinct, rational knowledge. Accordingly, it must be a statement in the abstract of the nature of the whole world, of the whole as well as of all the parts. However, in order not to be lost in an endless multitude of particular judgements, it must make use of abstraction, and think everything individual in the universal, and its differences also in the universal. It will therefore partly separate, partly unite, in order to present to rational knowledge the whole manifold of the world in general, according to its nature, condensed and summarized into a few abstract concepts. Yet through these concepts, in which it fixes the nature of the world, the whole individual as well as the universal must be known, and hence the knowledge of both must be closely bound up. Therefore, aptitude for philosophy consists precisely in what Plato put it in, namely in knowing the one in the many and the many in the one. Accordingly, philosophy will be a sum of very universal judgements, whose ground of knowledge is immediately the world itself in its entirety, without excluding anything, and hence everything to be found in human consciousness. It will be *a complete recapitulation, so to speak, a reflection of the world in abstract concepts,* and this is possible only by uniting the essentially identical into one concept, and by relegating the different and dissimilar to another. Bacon already set philosophy this task, when he said: *ea demum vera est philosophia, quae mundi ipsius voces fidelissime reddit, et veluti dictante mundo conscripta est, et nihil aliud est, quam ejusdem SIMULACRUM ET REFLEC-TIO, neque addit quidquam de proprio, sed tantum iterat et resonat* (*De Augmentis Scientiarum,* l. 2, c. 13).[30] However, we take this in a more extended sense than Bacon could conceive at that time.

The agreement which all aspects and parts of the world have with one another, just because they belong to one whole, must also be found again in this abstract copy of the world. Accordingly, in this sum-total of judgements one could to a certain extent be derived from another, and indeed always reciprocally. Yet in addition to this they must first exist, and therefore be previously laid down as immediately established through knowledge of the world in the concrete, the more so as all direct proofs are more certain than those that are indirect. Their harmony with one another, by virtue of which they flow together even into the unity of one thought, and which springs from the harmony and unity of the world of perception itself, their common ground of knowledge, will therefore not be used as the first thing for establishing them, but will be added only as confirmation of their truth. This problem itself can become perfectly clear only by its solution.[31]

§ 16.

After fully considering reason as a special faculty of knowledge peculiar to man alone, and the achievements and phenomena brought about by it and peculiar to human nature, it now remains for me to speak of reason in so far as it guides man's

---

[30] "That philosophy only is the true one which reproduces most faithfully the statements of nature, and is written down, as it were, from nature's dictation, so that it is nothing but a *copy and a reflection* of nature, and adds nothing of its own, but is merely a repetition and echo." [Tr.]

[31] Cf. chap. 17 of volume 2.

actions, and in this respect can be called *practical*. But what is here to be mentioned has for the most part found a place elsewhere, namely in the Appendix to this work, where I have had to dispute the existence of the so-called practical reason of Kant. This he represents (certainly very conveniently) as the immediate source of all virtue, and as the seat of an absolute (i.e., fallen from heaven) *imperative*. Later in the *Grundprobleme der Ethik* I have furnished the detailed and thorough refutation of this Kantian principle of morality. Here, therefore, I have but little to say about the actual influence of reason, in the true sense of the word, on conduct. At the beginning of our consideration of reason we remarked in general terms how the action and behaviour of man differ from those of the animal, and that this difference is to be regarded as solely the result of the presence of abstract concepts in consciousness. The influence of these on our whole existence is so decisive and significant that it places us to a certain extent in the same relation to the animals as that between animals that see and those without eyes (certain larvae, worms, and zoophytes). Animals without eyes know only by touch what is immediately present to them in space, what comes in contact with them. Animals that see, on the other hand, know a wide sphere of what is near and distant. In the same way, the absence of reason restricts the animals to representations of perception immediately present to them in time, in other words to real objects. We, on the other hand, by virtue of knowledge in the abstract, comprehend not only the narrow and actual present, but also the whole past and future together with the wide realm of possibility. We survey life freely in all directions, far beyond what is present and actual. Thus what the eye is in space and for sensuous knowledge, reason is, to a certain extent, in time and for inner knowledge. But just as the visibility of objects has value and meaning only by its informing us of their tangibility, so the whole value of abstract knowledge is always to be found in its reference to knowledge of perception. Therefore, the ordinary natural man always attaches far more value to what is known directly and through perception than to abstract concepts, to what is merely thought; he prefers empirical to logical knowledge. But those are of the opposite way of thinking who live more in words than in deeds, who have seen more on paper and in books than in the actual world, and who in their greatest degeneracy become pedants and lovers of the mere letter. Only from this is it conceivable how Leibniz, Wolff, and all their successors could go so far astray as to declare, after the example of Duns Scotus, knowledge of perception to be merely a confused abstract knowledge! To Spinoza's honour I must mention that his more accurate sense, on the contrary, declared all common concepts to have arisen from the confusion of what was known through perception (*Ethics* II, *prop.* 40, *schol.* 1). It is also a result of that perverted way of thinking that in mathematics the evidence peculiar to it was rejected, in order to accept and admit only logical evidence; that generally all knowledge that was not abstract was included under the broad name of feeling, and disparaged; finally, that the Kantian ethics declared the pure, good will, asserting itself on knowledge of the circumstances and leading to right and benevolent action, as mere feeling and emotion, to be worthless and without merit. Such ethics would concede moral worth only to actions arising from abstract maxims.

The universal survey of life as a whole, an advantage which man has over the animal through his faculty of reason, is also comparable to a geometrical, colourless, abstract, reduced plan of his way of life. He is therefore related to the animal as the navigator, who by means of chart, compass, and quadrant knows accurately at any moment his course and position on the sea, is related to the uneducated crew who see only the waves and skies. It is therefore worth noting, and indeed wonderful to see, how man, besides his life in the concrete, always lives a second life in the abstract. In the former he is abandoned to all the storms of reality and to the influence of the present; he must struggle, suffer, and die like the animal. But his life in the abstract, as it stands before his rational consciousness, is the calm reflection of his life in the concrete, and of the world in which he lives; it is precisely that reduced chart or plan previously mentioned. Here in the sphere of calm deliberation, what previously possessed him completely and moved him intensely appears to him cold, colourless, and, for the moment, foreign and strange; he is a mere spectator and observer. In respect of this withdrawal into reflection, he is like an actor who has played his part in one scene, and takes his place in the audience until he must appear again. In the audience he quietly looks on at whatever may happen, even though it be the preparation of his own death (in the play); but then he again goes on the stage, and acts and suffers as he must. From this double life proceeds that composure in man, so very different from the thoughtlessness of the animal. According to previous reflection, to a mind made up, or to a recognized necessity, a man with such composure suffers or carries out in cold blood what is of the greatest, and often most terrible, importance to him, such as suicide, execution, duels, hazardous enterprises of every kind fraught with danger to life, and generally things against which his whole animal nature rebels. We then see to what extent reason is master of the animal nature, and we exclaim to the strong: σιδήρειον νύ τοι ἦτορ! (*ferreum certe tibi cor!*) [*Iliad*, xxiv, 521.] [32] Here it can really be said that the faculty of reason manifests itself *practically,* and thus *practical reason* shows itself, wherever action is guided by reason, where motives are abstract concepts, wherever the determining factors are not individual representations of perception, or the impression of the moment which guides the animal. But I have explained at length in the Appendix, and illustrated by examples, that this is entirely different from, and independent of, the ethical worth of conduct; that rational action and virtuous action are two quite different things; that reason is just as well found with great wickedness as with great kindness, and by its assistance gives great effectiveness to the one as to the other; that it is equally ready and of service for carrying out methodically and consistently the noble resolution as well as the bad, the wise maxim as well as the imprudent. All this inevitably follows from the nature of reason, which is feminine, receptive, retentive, and not self-creative. What is said in the Appendix would be in its proper place here, yet on account of the polemic against Kant's so-called practical reason it had to be relegated to that Appendix, to which therefore I refer.

The most perfect development of *practical reason* in the true and genuine sense of the word, the highest point to which man can attain by the mere use of his faculty of reason, and in which his difference from the animal shows itself most clearly, is the ideal represented in the *Stoic sage*. For the Stoic ethics is originally and essentially not a doctrine of virtue, but merely a guide to the rational life, whose end and aim is happiness through peace of mind. Virtuous conduct appears in it, so to speak, only by accident, as means, not as end. Therefore the Stoic ethics is by its whole nature and point of view fundamentally different from the ethical systems that insist directly on virtue, such as the doctrines of the *Vedas,* of Plato, of Christianity, and of Kant. The aim of Stoic ethics is happiness: τέλος τὸ εὐδαιμονεῖν (*virtutes omnes finem habere beatitudinem*) it says in the description of the Stoa by Stobaeus (*Eclogae,* l. II, c. 7, p. 114, and also p. 138). Yet the Stoic ethics teaches that happiness is to be found with certainty only in inward calm and in peace of mind (ἀταραξία), and this again can be reached only through virtue. The expression that virtue is the highest good means just this. Now if of course the end is gradually lost sight of in the means, and virtue is commended in a way that betrays an interest entirely different from that of one's own happiness, in that it too clearly contradicts this, then this is one of the inconsistencies by which in every system the directly known truth, or, as they say,

---

[32] "Truly hast thou a heart of iron!" [Tr.]

the felt truth, leads us back on to the right path, violating all syllogistic argument. For instance, we clearly see this in the ethics of Spinoza, which deduces a pure doctrine of virtue from the egoistical *suum utile quaerere* through palpable sophisms. According to this, as I have understood the spirit of the Stoic ethics, its source lies in the thought whether reason, man's great prerogative, which, through planned action and its result, indirectly lightens the burdens of life so much for him, might not also be capable of withdrawing him at once and directly, i.e., through mere knowledge, either completely or nearly so, from the sorrows and miseries of every kind that fill his life. They held it to be not in keeping with the prerogative of reason that a being endowed with it and comprehending and surveying by it an infinity of things and conditions, should yet be exposed to such intense pain, such great anxiety and suffering, as arise from the tempestuous strain of desiring and shunning, through the present moment and the events that can be contained in the few years of a life so short, fleeting, and uncertain. It was thought that the proper application of reason was bound to raise man above them, and enable him to become invulnerable. Therefore Antisthenes said: Δεῖ κτᾶσθαι νοῦν, ἢ βρόχον (*aut mentem parandam, aut laqueum.* Plutarch, *De Stoicorum Repugnantia,* c. 14);[33] in other words, life is so full of troubles and vexations that we must either rise above it by means of corrected ideas, or leave it. It was seen that want and suffering did not result directly and necessarily from not having, but only from desiring to have and yet not having; that this desiring to have is therefore the necessary condition under which alone not having becomes privation and engenders pain. Οὐ πενία λύπην ἐργάζεται, ἀλλ' ἐπιθυμία (*non paupertas dolorem efficit, sed cupiditas*), Epictetus, *fragm.* 25.[34] Moreover, it was recognized from experience that it is merely the hope, the claim, which begets and nourishes the wish. Therefore neither the many unavoidable evils common to all, nor the unattainable blessings, disquiet and trouble us, but only the insignificant more or less of what for man is avoidable and attainable. Indeed, not only the absolutely unavoidable or unattainable, but also what is relatively so, leaves us quite calm; hence the evils that are once attached to our individuality, or the good things that must of necessity remain denied to it, are treated with indifference, and in consequence of this human characteristic every wish soon dies and so can beget no more pain, if no hope nourishes it. It follows from all this that all happiness depends on the proportion between what we claim and what we receive. It is

---

[33] "We must procure either understanding or a rope (for hanging ourselves)."
[34] "It is not poverty that pains, but strong desire." [Tr.]

immaterial how great or small the two quantities of this proportion are, and the proportion can be established just as well by diminishing the first quantity as by increasing the second. In the same way, it follows that all suffering really results from the want of proportion between what we demand and expect and what comes to us. But this want of proportion is to be found only in knowledge,[35] and through better insight it could be wholly abolished. Therefore Chrysippus said: δεῖ ζῆν κατ' ἐμπειρίαν τῶν φύσει συμβαινόντων (Stobaeus, *Eclogae*, 1. II, c. 7; [Ed. Heeren], p. 134),[36] in other words, we should live with due knowledge of the course of things in the world. For whenever a man in any way loses self-control, or is struck down by a misfortune, or grows angry, or loses heart, he shows in this way that he finds things different from what he expected, and consequently that he laboured under a mistake, did not know the world and life, did not know how at every step the will of the individual is crossed and thwarted by the chance of inanimate nature, by contrary aims and intentions, even by the malice inspired in others. Therefore either he has not used his reason to arrive at a general knowledge of this characteristic of life, or he lacks the power of judgement, when he does not again recognize in the particular what he knows in general, and when he is therefore surprised by it and loses his self-control.[37] Thus every keen pleasure is an error, an illusion, since no attained wish can permanently satisfy, and also because every possession and every happiness is only lent by chance for an indefinite time, and can therefore be demanded back in the next hour. But every pain rests on the disappearance of such an illusion; thus both originate from defective knowledge. Therefore the wise man always holds himself aloof from jubilation and sorrow, and no event disturbs his ἀταραξία.

In conformity with this spirit and aim of the Stoa, Epictetus begins with it and constantly returns to it as the kernel of his philosophy, that we should bear in mind and distinguish what depends on us and

---

[35] *Omnes perturbationes judicio censent fieri et opinione.* Cicero, *Tusc.*, iv, 6. ("All dejected moods, so they teach, rest on judgement and opinion." [Tr.])
Ταράσσει τοὺς ἀνθρώπους οὐ τὰ πράγματα, ἀλλὰ τὰ περὶ τῶν πραγμάτων δόγματα (*Perturbant homines non res ipsae, sed de rebus opiniones.*) Epictetus, c. V. ("It is not things that disturb men, but opinions about things." [Tr.])
[36] "We must live according to the experience of what usually happens in nature." [Tr.]
[37] Τοῦτο γάρ ἐστι τὸ αἴτιον τοῖς ἀνθρώποις πάντων τῶν κακῶν, τὸ τὰς προλήψεις τὰς κοινὰς μὴ δύνασθαι ἐφαρμόζειν ταῖς ἐπὶ μέρους. (*Haec est causa mortalibus omnium malorum, non posse communes notiones aptare singularibus.*) Epictetus, *Dissert.* III, 26. ("For this is the cause of all evil for men, namely that they are not able to apply universal concepts to particular cases." [Tr.])

what does not, and thus should not count on the latter at all. In this way we shall certainly remain free from all pain, suffering, and anxiety. Now what depends on us is the will alone, and here there gradually takes place a transition to a doctrine of virtue, since it is noticed that, as the external world that is independent of us determines good and bad fortune, so inner satisfaction or dissatisfaction with ourselves proceeds from the will. But later it was asked whether we should attribute the names *bonum et malum* to the two former or to the two latter. This was really arbitrary and a matter of choice, and made no difference. But yet the Stoics argued incessantly about this with the Peripatetics and Epicureans, and amused themselves with the inadmissible comparison of two wholly incommensurable quantities and with the contrary and paradoxical judgements arising therefrom, which they cast at one another. An interesting collection of these is afforded us from the Stoic side by the *Paradoxa* of Cicero.

Zeno, the founder, seems originally to have taken a somewhat different course. With him the starting-point was that a man, in order to attain the highest good, that is to say, bliss through peace of mind, should live in harmony with himself. (ὁμολογουμένως ζῆν· τοῦτο δ'ἔστι καθ' ἕνα λόγον καὶ σύμφωνον ζῆν.—*Consonanter vivere: hoc est secundum unam rationem et concordem sibi vivere.* Stobaeus, *Ecl.*, 1. II, c. 7, p. 132. Also: ἀρετὴν διάθεσιν εἶναι ψυχῆς σύμφωνον ἑαυτῇ περὶ ὅλον τὸν βίον. *Virtutem esse animi affectionem secum per totam vitam consentientem, ibid.*, p. 104).[38] Now this was possible only by a man determining himself entirely *rationally* according to concepts, not according to changing impressions and moods. But as only the maxims of our conduct, not the consequences or circumstances, are in our power, to be capable of always remaining consistent we must take as our object only the maxims, not the consequences and circumstances, and thus the doctrine of virtue is again introduced.

But the moral principle of Zeno—to live in harmony with oneself —seemed even to his immediate successors to be too formal and empty. They therefore gave it material content by the addition "to live in harmony with nature" (ὁμολογουμένως τῃ φυσεῖ ζῆν), which, as Stobaeus mentions *loc. cit.,* was first added by Cleanthes, and which greatly extended the matter through the wide sphere of the concept and the vagueness of the expression. For Cleanthes meant the whole of nature in general, but Chrysippus meant human nature in particular (Diogenes Laërtius, vii, 89). That which was alone adapted to

---

[38] "To live in harmony, i.e., according to one and the same principle and in harmony with oneself." [Tr.]
"Virtue consists in the agreement of the soul with itself during the whole of life." [Tr.]

the latter was then supposed to be virtue, just as the satisfaction of animal impulses was adapted to animal natures; and thus ethics was again forcibly united to a doctrine of virtue, and had to be established through physics by hook or by crook. For the Stoics everywhere aimed at unity of principle, as with them God and the world were not two different things.

Taken as a whole, Stoic ethics is in fact a very valuable and estimable attempt to use reason, man's great prerogative, for an important and salutary purpose, namely to raise him by a precept above the sufferings and pains to which all life is exposed:

> *"Qua ratione queas traducere leniter aevum:*
> *Ne te semper inops agitet vexetque cupido,*
> *Ne pavor et rerum mediocriter utilium spes."* [39]
> (Horace, *Epist.* I, xviii, 97.)

and in this way to make him partake in the highest degree of the dignity belonging to him as a rational being as distinct from the animal. We can certainly speak of a dignity in this sense, but not in any other. It is a consequence of my view of Stoic ethics that it had to be mentioned here with the description of what the faculty of *reason* is, and what it can achieve. But, however much this end is to a certain extent attainable through the application of reason and through a merely rational ethic, and although experience shows that the happiest are indeed those purely rational characters commonly called practical philosophers—and rightly so, because just as the real, i.e., theoretical, philosopher translates life into the concept, so they translate the concept into life—nevertheless we are still very far from being able to arrive at something perfect in this way, from being actually removed from all the burdens and sorrows of life, and led to the blissful state by the correct use of our reason. On the contrary, we find a complete contradiction in our wishing to live without suffering, a contradiction that is therefore implied by the frequently used phrase "blessed life." This will certainly be clear to the person who has fully grasped my discussion that follows. This contradiction is revealed in this ethic of pure reason itself by the fact that the Stoic is compelled to insert a recommendation of suicide in his guide to the blissful life (for this is what his ethics always remains). This is like the costly phial of poison to be found among the magnificent ornaments and apparel of oriental despots, and is for the case where the

---

[39] "That thou mayest be able to spend thy life smoothly, Let not ever-pressing desire torment and vex thee, Or fear or hope for things of little worth." [Tr.]

sufferings of the body, incapable of being philosophized away by any principles and syllogisms, are paramount and incurable. Thus its sole purpose, namely blessedness, is frustrated, and nothing remains as a means of escape from pain except death. But then death must be taken with unconcern, just as is any other medicine. Here a marked contrast is evident between the Stoic ethics and all those other ethical systems mentioned above. These ethical systems make virtue directly and in itself the aim and object, even with the most grievous sufferings, and will not allow a man to end his life in order to escape from suffering. But not one of them knew how to express the true reason for rejecting suicide, but they laboriously collected fictitious arguments of every kind. This true reason will appear in the fourth book in connexion with our discussion. But the above-mentioned contrast reveals and confirms just that essential difference to be found in the fundamental principle between the Stoa, really only a special form of eudaemonism, and the doctrines just mentioned, although both often agree in their results, and are apparently related. But the above-mentioned inner contradiction, with which the Stoic ethics is affected even in its fundamental idea, further shows itself in the fact that its ideal, the Stoic sage as represented by this ethical system, could never obtain life or inner poetical truth, but remains a wooden, stiff lay-figure with whom one can do nothing. He himself does not know where to go with his wisdom, and his perfect peace, contentment, and blessedness directly contradict the nature of mankind, and do not enable us to arrive at any perceptive representation thereof. Compared with him, how entirely different appear the overcomers of the world and voluntary penitents, who are revealed to us, and are actually produced, by the wisdom of India; how different even the Saviour of Christianity, that excellent form full of the depth of life, of the greatest poetical truth and highest significance, who stands before us with perfect virtue, holiness, and sublimity, yet in a state of supreme suffering.[40]

---

[40] Cf. chap. 16 of volume 2.

SECOND BOOK

THE WORLD AS WILL

FIRST ASPECT

The Objectification of the Will

Nos habitat, non tartara, sed nec sidera coeli:
Spiritus in nobis qui viget, illa facit.
[Agrippa von Nettesheim, *Epist.* v, 14.]

("He dwells in us, not in the nether world, not in the starry heavens.
The spirit living within us fashions all this." [Tr.])

§ 17.

In the first book we considered the representation only as such, and hence only according to the general form. It is true that, so far as the abstract representation, the concept, is concerned, we also obtained a knowledge of it according to its content, in so far as it has all content and meaning only through its relation to the representation of perception, without which it would be worthless and empty. Therefore, directing our attention entirely to the representation of perception, we shall endeavour to arrive at a knowledge of its content, its more precise determinations, and the forms it presents to us. It will be of special interest for us to obtain information about its real significance, that significance, otherwise merely felt, by virtue of which these pictures or images do not march past us strange and meaningless, as they would otherwise inevitably do, but speak to us directly, are understood, and acquire an interest that engrosses our whole nature.

We direct our attention to mathematics, natural science, and philosophy, each of which holds out the hope that it will furnish a part of the information desired. In the first place, we find philosophy to be a monster with many heads, each of which speaks a different language. Of course, they are not all at variance with one another on the point here mentioned, the significance of the representation of perception. For, with the exception of the Sceptics and Idealists, the others in the main speak fairly consistently of an *object* forming the *basis* of the representation. This object indeed is different in its whole being and nature from the representation, but yet is in all respects as like it as one egg is like another. But this does not help us, for we do not at all know how to distinguish that object from the representation. We find that the two are one and the same, for every object always and eternally presupposes a subject, and thus remains representation. We then recognize also that being-object belongs to the most universal form of the representation, which is precisely the division into object and subject. Further, the principle of sufficient reason, to which we here refer, is also for us only the form of the representation, namely the regular and orderly combination of one representation with another, and not the combination of the whole finite

[95]

or infinite series of representations with something which is not representation at all, and is therefore not capable of being in any way represented. We spoke above of the Sceptics and Idealists, when discussing the controversy about the reality of the external world.

Now if we look to mathematics for the desired more detailed knowledge of the representation of perception, which we have come to know only quite generally according to the mere form, then this science will tell us about these representations only in so far as they occupy time and space, in other words, only in so far as they are quantities. It will state with extreme accuracy the How-many and the How-large; but as this is always only relative, that is to say, a comparison of one representation with another, and even that only from the one-sided aspect of quantity, this too will not be the information for which principally we are looking.

Finally, if we look at the wide province of natural science, which is divided into many fields, we can first of all distinguish two main divisions. It is either a description of forms and shapes, which I call *Morphology;* or an explanation of changes, which I call *Etiology.* The former considers the permanent forms, the latter the changing matter, according to the laws of its transition from one form into another. Morphology is what we call natural history in its whole range, though not in the literal sense of the word. As botany and zoology especially, it teaches us about the various, permanent, organic, and thus definitely determined forms in spite of the incessant change of individuals; and these forms constitute a great part of the content of the perceptive representation. In natural history they are classified, separated, united, and arranged according to natural and artificial systems, and brought under concepts that render possible a survey and knowledge of them all. There is further demonstrated an infinitely fine and shaded analogy in the whole and in the parts of these forms which runs through them all (*unité de plan*),[1] by virtue of which they are like the many different variations on an unspecified theme. The passage of matter into those forms, in other words the origin of individuals, is not a main part of the consideration, for every individual springs from its like through generation, which everywhere is equally mysterious, and has so far baffled clear knowledge. But the little that is known of this finds its place in physiology, which belongs to etiological natural science. Mineralogy, especially where it becomes geology, though it belongs mainly to morphology, also inclines to this etiological science. Etiology proper includes all the branches of natural science in which the main concern everywhere is knowledge of cause and effect. These sciences teach how,

---

[1] "Unity of plan." [Tr.]

according to an invariable rule, one state of matter is necessarily followed by another definite state; how one definite change necessarily conditions and brings about another definite change; this demonstration is called *explanation*. Here we find principally mechanics, physics, chemistry, and physiology.

But if we devote ourselves to its teaching, we soon become aware that the information we are chiefly looking for no more comes to us from etiology than it does from morphology. The latter presents us with innumerable and infinitely varied forms that are nevertheless related by an unmistakable family likeness. For us they are representations that in this way remain eternally strange to us, and, when considered merely in this way, they stand before us like hieroglyphics that are not understood. On the other hand, etiology teaches us that, according to the law of cause and effect, this definite condition of matter produces that other condition, and with this it has explained it, and has done its part. At bottom, however, it does nothing more than show the orderly arrangement according to which the states or conditions appear in space and time, and teach for all cases what phenomenon must necessarily appear at this time and in this place. It therefore determines for them their position in time and space according to a law whose definite content has been taught by experience, yet whose universal form and necessity are known to us independently of experience. But in this way we do not obtain the slightest information about the inner nature of any one of these phenomena. This is called a *natural force,* and lies outside the province of etiological explanation, which calls the unalterable constancy with which the manifestation of such a force appears whenever its known conditions are present, a *law of nature.* But this law of nature, these conditions, this appearance in a definite place at a definite time, are all that it knows, or ever can know. The force itself that is manifested, the inner nature of the phenomena that appear in accordance with those laws, remain for it an eternal secret, something entirely strange and unknown, in the case of the simplest as well as of the most complicated phenomenon. For although etiology has so far achieved its aim most completely in mechanics, and least so in physiology, the force by virtue of which a stone falls to the ground, or one body repels another, is, in its inner nature, just as strange and mysterious as that which produces the movements and growth of an animal. Mechanics presupposes matter, weight, impenetrability, communicability of motion through impact, rigidity, and so on as unfathomable; it calls them forces of nature, and their necessary and regular appearance under certain conditions a law of nature. Only then does its explanation begin, and that consists in stating truly and with mathematical precision how, where, and when each force manifests itself, and referring to one of those forces every phenomenon that comes before it. Physics, chemistry, and physiology do the same in their province, only they presuppose much more and achieve less. Consequently, even the most perfect etiological explanation of the whole of nature would never be more in reality than a record of inexplicable forces, and a reliable statement of the rule by which their phenomena appear, succeed, and make way for one another in time and space. But the inner nature of the forces that thus appear was always bound to be left unexplained by etiology, which had to stop at the phenomenon and its arrangement, since the law followed by etiology does not go beyond this. In this respect it could be compared to a section of a piece of marble showing many different veins side by side, but not letting us know the course of these veins from the interior of the marble to the surface. Or, if I may be permitted a facetious comparison, because it is more striking, the philosophical investigator must always feel in regard to the complete etiology of the whole of nature like a man who, without knowing how, is brought into a company quite unknown to him, each member of which in turn presents to him another as his friend and cousin, and thus makes them sufficiently acquainted. The man himself, however, while assuring each person introduced of his pleasure at meeting him, always has on his lips the question: "But how the deuce do I stand to the whole company?"

Hence, about those phenomena known by us only as our representations, etiology can never give us the desired information that leads us beyond them. For after all its explanations, they still stand quite strange before us, as mere representations whose significance we do not understand. The causal connexion merely gives the rule and relative order of their appearance in space and time, but affords us no further knowledge of that which so appears. Moreover, the law of causality itself has validity only for representations, for objects of a definite class, and has meaning only when they are assumed. Hence, like these objects themselves, it always exists only in relation to the subject, and so conditionally. Thus it is just as well known when we start from the subject, i.e., *a priori,* as when we start from the object, i.e., *a posteriori,* as Kant has taught us.

But what now prompts us to make enquiries is that we are not satisfied with knowing that we have representations, that they are such and such, and that they are connected according to this or that law, whose general expression is always the principle of sufficient reason. We want to know the significance of those representations; we ask whether this world is nothing more than representation. In that case, it would inevitably pass by us like an empty dream, or a ghostly vision not worth our consideration. Or we ask whether it is something else, something in addition, and if so what that something is. This much is certain, namely that this something about which we are enquiring must be by its whole nature completely and fundamentally different from the representation; and so the forms and laws of the representation must be wholly foreign to it. We cannot, then, reach it from the representation under the guidance of those laws that merely combine objects, representations, with one another; these are the forms of the principle of sufficient reason.

Here we already see that we can never get at the inner nature of things *from without*. However much we may investigate, we obtain nothing but images and names. We are like a man who goes round a castle, looking in vain for an entrance, and sometimes sketching the façades. Yet this is the path that all philosophers before me have followed.

§ 18.

In fact, the meaning that I am looking for of the world that stands before me simply as my representation, or the transition from it as mere representation of the knowing subject to whatever it may be besides this, could never be found if the investigator himself were nothing more than the purely knowing subject (a winged cherub without a body). But he himself is rooted in that world; and thus he finds himself in it as an *individual,* in other words, his knowledge, which is the conditional supporter of the whole world as representation, is nevertheless given entirely through the medium of a body, and the affections of this body are, as we have shown, the starting-point for the understanding in its perception of this world. For the purely knowing subject as such, this body is a representation like any other, an object among objects. Its movements and actions are so far known to him in just the same way as the changes of all other objects of perception; and they would be equally strange and incomprehensible to him, if their meaning were not unravelled for him in an entirely different way. Otherwise, he would see his conduct follow on presented motives with the constancy of a law of nature, just as the changes of other objects follow upon causes, stimuli, and motives. But he would be no nearer to understanding the influence of the motives than he is to understanding the connexion with its cause of any other effect that appears before him. He would then also call the inner, to him incomprehensible, nature of those manifestations and actions of his body a force, a quality, or a character, just as he pleased, but he would have no further insight into it. All this, however, is not the case; on the contrary, the answer to the riddle is given to the subject of knowledge appearing as individual, and this answer is given in the word *Will*. This and this alone gives him the key to his own phenomenon, reveals to him the significance and shows him the inner mechanism of his being, his actions, his movements. To the subject of knowing, who appears as an individual only through his identity with the body, this body is given in two entirely different ways. It is given in intelligent perception as representation, as an object among objects, liable to the laws of these objects. But it is also given in quite a different way, namely as what is known immediately to everyone, and is denoted by the word *will*. Every true act of his will is also at once and inevitably a movement of his body; he cannot actually will the act without at the same time being aware that it appears as a movement of the body. The act of will and the action of the body are not two different states objectively known, connected by the bond of causality; they do not stand in the relation of cause and effect, but are one and the same thing, though given in two entirely different ways, first quite directly, and then in perception for the understanding. The action of the body is nothing but the act of will objectified, i.e., translated into perception. Later on we shall see that this applies to every movement of the body, not merely to movement following on motives, but also to involuntary movement following on mere stimuli; indeed, that the whole body is nothing but the objectified will, i.e., will that has become representation. All this will follow and become clear in the course of our discussion. Therefore the body, which in the previous book and in the essay *On the Principle of Sufficient Reason* I called the *immediate object,* according to the one-sided viewpoint deliberately taken there (namely that of the representation), will here from another point of view be called the *objectivity of the will.* Therefore, in a certain sense, it can also be said that the will is knowledge *a priori* of the body, and that the body is knowledge *a posteriori* of the will. Resolutions of the will relating to the future are mere deliberations of reason about what will be willed at some time, not real acts of will. Only the carrying out stamps the resolve; till then, it is always a mere intention that can be altered; it exists only in reason, in the abstract. Only in reflection are willing and acting different; in reality they are one. Every true, genuine, immediate act of the will is also at once and directly a manifest act of the body; and correspondingly, on the other hand, every impression on the body is also at once and directly an impression on the will. As such, it is called pain when it is contrary to the will, and gratification or pleasure when in accordance with the will. The gradations of the two are very different. However, we are quite wrong in calling pain and pleasure representations, for they are not these at all, but immediate affections of the will in its phenomenon, the body; an enforced, instantaneous willing or not-willing of the impression undergone by the body. There are only a certain few impressions on the body which do not rouse the will, and through these alone is the body an immediate object of knowledge; for, as perception in the understanding, the body is an indirect object like all other objects. These impressions are therefore to be regarded directly as mere representations, and hence to be excepted from what has just been said. Here are meant the affections of the purely objective senses of sight, hearing, and touch, although only in so far as their organs are affected in the specific natural way that is specially characteristic of them. This is such an exceedingly feeble stimulation of the enhanced and specifically modified sensibility of these parts that it does not affect the will, but, undisturbed by any excitement of the will, only furnishes for the understanding data from which perception arises. But every stronger or heterogeneous affection of these sense-organs is painful, in other words, is against the will; hence they too belong to its objectivity. Weakness of the nerves shows itself in the fact that the impressions which should have merely that degree of intensity that is sufficient to make them data for the understanding, reach the higher degree at which they stir the will, that is to say, excite pain or pleasure, though more often pain. This pain, however, is in part dull and inarticulate; thus it not merely causes us to feel painfully particular tones and intense light, but also gives rise generally to a morbid and hypochondriacal disposition without being distinctly recognized. The identity of the body and the will further shows itself, among other things, in the fact that every vehement and excessive movement of the will, in other words, every emotion, agitates the body and its inner workings directly and immediately, and disturbs the course of its vital functions. This is specially discussed in *The Will in Nature,* second edition, p. 27.

Finally, the knowledge I have of my will, although an immediate knowledge, cannot be separated from that of my body. I know my will not as a whole, not as a unity, not completely according to its nature, but only in its individual acts, and hence in time, which is the form of my body's appearing, as it is of every body. Therefore, the body is the condition of knowledge of my will. Accordingly, I cannot really imagine this will without my body. In the essay *On the Principle of Sufficient Reason* the will, or rather the subject of willing, is treated as a special class of representations or objects. But even there we saw this object coinciding with the subject, in other words, ceasing to be object. We then called this coincidence the miracle κατ' ἐξοχήν;[2] to a certain extent the whole of the present work is an explanation of this. In so far as I know my will really as object, I know it as body; but then I am again at the first class of representations laid down in that essay, that is, again at real objects. As we go on, we shall see more and more that the first class of representations finds its explanation, its solution, only in the fourth class enumerated in that essay, which could no longer be properly opposed to the subject as object; and that, accordingly, we must learn to understand the inner nature of the law of causality valid in the first class, and of what happens according to this law, from the law of motivation governing the fourth class.

The identity of the will and of the body, provisionally explained, can be demonstrated only as is done here, and that for the first time, and as will be done more and more in the further course of our discussion. In other words, it can be raised from immediate consciousness, from knowledge in the concrete, to rational knowledge of reason, or be carried over into knowledge in the abstract. On the other hand, by its nature it can never be demonstrated, that is to say, deduced as indirect knowledge from some other more direct knowledge, for the very reason that it is itself the most direct knowledge. If we do not apprehend it and stick to it as such, in vain shall we expect to obtain it again in some indirect way as derived knowledge. It is a knowledge of quite a peculiar nature, whose truth cannot therefore really be brought under one of the four headings by which I have divided all truth in the essay *On the Principle of Sufficient Reason,* § 29 *seqq.,* namely, logical, empirical, transcendental, and metalogical. For it is not, like all these, the reference of an abstract representation to another representation, or to the necessary form of intuitive or of abstract representing, but it is the reference of a judgement to the relation that a representation of perception, namely the body, has to that which is not a representation at all, but is *toto genere* different therefrom, namely will. I should therefore like to distinguish this truth from every other, and call it *philosophical truth* κατ' ἐξοχήν. We can turn the expression of this truth in different ways and say: My body and my will are one; or, What as representation of percep-

[2] *"par excellence."* [Tr.]

tion I call my body, I call my will in so far as I am conscious of it in an entirely different way comparable with no other; or, My body is the *objectivity of my will;* or, Apart from the fact that my body is my representation, it is still my will, and so on.[3]

§ 19.

Whereas in the first book we were reluctantly forced to declare our own body to be mere representation of the knowing subject, like all the other objects of this world of perception, it has now become clear to us that something in the consciousness of everyone distinguishes the representation of his own body from all others that are in other respects quite like it. This is that the body occurs in consciousness in quite another way, *toto genere* different, that is denoted by the word *will*. It is just this double knowledge of our own body which gives us information about that body itself, about its action and movement following on motives, as well as about its suffering through outside impressions, in a word, about what it is, not as representation, but as something over and above this, and hence what it is *in itself*. We do not have such immediate information about the nature, action, and suffering of any other real objects.

The knowing subject is an individual precisely by reason of this special relation to the one body which, considered apart from this, is for him only a representation like all other representations. But the relation by virtue of which the knowing subject is an *individual,* subsists for that very reason only between him and one particular representation among all his representations. He is therefore conscious of this particular representation not merely as such, but at the same time in a quite different way, namely as a will. But if he abstracts from that special relation, from that twofold and completely heterogeneous knowledge of one and the same thing, then that one thing, the body, is a representation like all others. Therefore, in order to understand where he is in this matter, the knowing individual must either assume that the distinctive feature of that one representation is to be found merely in the fact that his knowledge stands in this double reference only to that one representation; that only into this one object of perception is an insight in two ways at the same time open to him; and

[3] Cf. chap. 18 of volume 2.

that this is to be explained not by a difference of this object from all others, but only by a difference between the relation of his knowledge to this one object and its relation to all others. Or he must assume that this one object is essentially different from all others; that it alone among all objects is at the same time will and representation, the rest, on the other hand, being mere representation, i.e., mere phantoms. Thus, he must assume that his body is the only real individual in the world, i.e., the only phenomenon of will, and the only immediate object of the subject. That the other objects, considered as mere *representations,* are like his body, in other words, like this body fill space (itself perhaps existing only as representation), and also, like this body, operate in space—this, I say, is demonstrably certain from the law of causality, which is *a priori* certain for representations, and admits of no effect without a cause. But apart from the fact that we can infer from the effect only a cause in general, not a similar cause, we are still always in the realm of the mere representation, for which alone the law of causality is valid, and beyond which it can never lead us. But whether the objects known to the individual only as representations are yet, like his own body, phenomena of a will, is, as stated in the previous book, the proper meaning of the question as to the reality of the external world. To deny this is the meaning of *theoretical egoism,* which in this way regards as phantoms all phenomena outside its own will, just as practical egoism does in a practical respect; thus in it a man regards and treats only his own person as a real person, and all others as mere phantoms. Theoretical egoism, of course, can never be refuted by proofs, yet in philosophy it has never been positively used otherwise than as a sceptical sophism, i.e., for the sake of appearance. As a serious conviction, on the other hand, it could be found only in a madhouse; as such it would then need not so much a refutation as a cure. Therefore we do not go into it any further, but regard it as the last stronghold of scepticism, which is always polemical. Thus our knowledge, bound always to individuality and having its limitation in this very fact, necessarily means that everyone can *be* only one thing, whereas he can *know* everything else, and it is this very limitation that really creates the need for philosophy. Therefore we, who for this very reason are endeavouring to extend the limits of our knowledge through philosophy, shall regard this sceptical argument of theoretical egoism, which here confronts us, as a small frontier fortress. Admittedly the fortress is impregnable, but the garrison can never sally forth from it, and therefore we can pass it by and leave it in our rear without danger.

The double knowledge which we have of the nature and action of our own body, and which is given in two completely different ways, has now been clearly brought out. Accordingly, we shall use it further as a key to the inner being of every phenomenon in nature. We shall judge all objects which are not our own body, and therefore are given to our consciousness not in the double way, but only as representations, according to the analogy of this body. We shall therefore assume that as, on the one hand, they are representation, just like our body, and are in this respect homogeneous with it, so on the other hand, if we set aside their existence as the subject's representation, what still remains over must be, according to its inner nature, the same as what in ourselves we call *will*. For what other kind of existence or reality could we attribute to the rest of the material world? From what source could we take the elements out of which we construct such a world? Besides the will and the representation, there is absolutely nothing known or conceivable for us. If we wish to attribute the greatest known reality to the material world, which immediately exists only in our representation, then we give it that reality which our own body has for each of us, for to each of us this is the most real of things. But if now we analyse the reality of this body and its actions, then, beyond the fact that it is our representation, we find nothing in it but the will; with this even its reality is exhausted. Therefore we can nowhere find another kind of reality to attribute to the material world. If, therefore, the material world is to be something more than our mere representation, we must say that, besides being the representation, and hence in itself and of its inmost nature, it is what we find immediately in ourselves as will. I say 'of its inmost nature,' but we have first of all to get to know more intimately this inner nature of the will, so that we may know how to distinguish from it what belongs not to it itself, but to its phenomenon, which has many grades. Such, for example, is the circumstance of its being accompanied by knowledge, and the determination by motives which is conditioned by this knowledge. As we proceed, we shall see that this belongs not to the inner nature of the will, but merely to its most distinct phenomenon as animal and human being. Therefore, if I say that the force which attracts a stone to the earth is of its nature, in itself, and apart from all representation, will, then no one will attach to this proposition the absurd meaning that the stone moves itself according to a known motive, because it is thus that the will appears in man.[4] But we will now prove, establish, and develop to its

---

[4] Thus we cannot in any way agree with Bacon when he (*De Augmentis Scientiarum,* 1. 4 *in fine*) thinks that all mechanical and physical movements of bodies ensue only after a preceding perception in these bodies, although a glimmering of truth gave birth even to this false proposition. This is also the case with Kepler's statement, in his essay *De Planeta Martis,* that the planets

full extent, clearly and in more detail, what has hitherto been explained provisionally and generally.⁵

§ 20.

As the being-in-itself of our own body, as that which this body is besides being object of perception, namely representation, the *will,* as we have said, proclaims itself first of all in the voluntary movements of this body, in so far as these movements are nothing but the visibility of the individual acts of the will. These movements appear directly and simultaneously with those acts of will; they are one and the same thing with them, and are distinguished from them only by the form of perceptibility into which they have passed, that is to say, in which they have become representation.

But these acts of the will always have a ground or reason outside themselves in motives. Yet these motives never determine more than what I will at *this* time, in *this* place, in *these* circumstances, not *that* I will in general, or *what* I will in general, in other words, the maxim characterizing the whole of my willing. Therefore, the whole inner nature of my willing cannot be explained from the motives, but they determine merely its manifestation at a given point of time; they are merely the occasion on which my will shows itself. This will itself, on the other hand, lies outside the province of the law of motivation; only the phenomenon of the will at each point of time is determined by this law. Only on the presupposition of my empirical character is the motive a sufficient ground of explanation of my conduct. But if I abstract from my character, and then ask why in general I will this and not that, no answer is possible, because only the *appearance* or *phenomenon* of the will is subject to the principle of sufficient reason, not the will itself, which in this respect may be called *groundless.* Here I in part presuppose Kant's doctrine of the empirical and intelligible characters, as well as my remarks pertinent to this in the *Grundprobleme der Ethik,* pp. 48-58, and again p. 178 *seqq.* of the first edition (pp. 46-57 and 174 *seqq.* of the second). We shall have

---

must have knowledge in order to keep to their elliptical courses so accurately, and to regulate the velocity of their motion, so that the triangles of the plane of their course always remain proportional to the time in which they pass through their bases.

⁵ Cf. chap. 19 of volume 2.

to speak about this again in more detail in the fourth book. For the present, I have only to draw attention to the fact that one phenomenon being established by another, as in this case the deed by the motive, does not in the least conflict with the essence-in-itself of the deed being will. The will itself has no ground; the principle of sufficient reason in all its aspects is merely the form of knowledge, and hence its validity extends only to the representation, to the phenomenon, to the visibility of the will, not to the will itself that becomes visible.

Now if every action of my body is an appearance or phenomenon of an act of will in which my will itself in general and as a whole, and hence my character, again expresses itself under given motives, then phenomenon or appearance of the will must also be the indispensable condition and presupposition of every action. For the will's appearance cannot depend on something which does not exist directly and only through it, and would therefore be merely accidental for it, whereby the will's appearance itself would be only accidental. But that condition is the whole body itself. Therefore this body itself must be phenomenon of the will, and must be related to my will as a whole, that is to say, to my intelligible character, the phenomenon of which in time is my empirical character, in the same way as the particular action of the body is to the particular act of the will. Therefore the whole body must be nothing but my will become visible, must be my will itself, in so far as this is object of perception, representation of the first class. It has already been advanced in confirmation of this that every impression on my body also affects my will at once and immediately, and in this respect is called pain or pleasure, or in a lower degree, pleasant or unpleasant sensation. Conversely, it has also been advanced that every violent movement of the will, and hence every emotion and passion, convulses the body, and disturbs the course of its functions. Indeed an etiological, though very incomplete, account can be given of the origin of my body, and a somewhat better account of its development and preservation. Indeed this is physiology; but this explains its theme only in exactly the same way as motives explain action. Therefore the establishment of the individual action through the motive, and the necessary sequence of the action from the motive, do not conflict with the fact that action, in general and by its nature, is only phenomenon or appearance of a will that is in itself groundless. Just as little does the physiological explanation of the functions of the body detract from the philosophical truth that the whole existence of this body and the sum-total of its functions are only the objectification of that will which appears in this body's outward actions in accordance with motives. If, however,

physiology tries to refer even these outward actions, the immediate
voluntary movements, to causes in the organism, for example, to
explain the movement of a muscle from an affluxion of humours
("like the contraction of a cord that is wet," as Reil says in the
Archiv für Physiologie, Vol. VI, p. 153); supposing that it really did
come to a thorough explanation of this kind, this would never do
away with the immediately certain truth that every voluntary movement (*functiones animales*) is phenomenon of an act of will. Now,
just as little can the physiological explanation of vegetative life
(*functiones naturales, vitales*), however far it may be developed,
ever do away with the truth that this whole animal life, thus developing itself, is phenomenon of the will. Generally then, as already
stated, no etiological explanation can ever state more than the necessarily determined position in time and space of a particular phenomenon and its necessary appearance there according to a fixed rule. On
the other hand, the inner nature of everything that appears in this
way remains for ever unfathomable, and is presupposed by every
etiological explanation; it is merely expressed by the name force, or
law of nature, or, when we speak of actions, the name character or
will. Thus, although every particular action, under the presupposition
of the definite character, necessarily ensues with the presented motive,
and although growth, the process of nourishment, and all the changes
in the animal body take place according to necessarily acting causes
(stimuli), the whole series of actions, and consequently every individual act and likewise its condition, namely the whole body itself which
performs it, and therefore also the process through which and in
which the body exists, are nothing but the phenomenal appearance
of the will, its becoming visible, the *objectivity of the will*. On this
rests the perfect suitability of the human and animal body to the
human and animal will in general, resembling, but far surpassing, the
suitability of a purposely made instrument to the will of its maker,
and on this account appearing as fitness or appropriateness, i.e., the
teleological accountability of the body. Therefore the parts of the
body must correspond completely to the chief demands and desires
by which the will manifests itself; they must be the visible expression
of these desires. Teeth, gullet, and intestinal canal are objectified
hunger; the genitals are objectified sexual impulse; grasping hands
and nimble feet correspond to the more indirect strivings of the will
which they represent. Just as the general human form corresponds
to the general human will, so to the individually modified will, namely
the character of the individual, there corresponds the individual
bodily structure, which is therefore as a whole and in all its parts
characteristic and full of expression. It is very remarkable that even

Parmenides expressed this in the following verses, quoted by Aristotle (*Metaphysics,* iii, 5):

> Ὡς γὰρ ἕκαστος ἔχει κρᾶσιν μελέων πολυκάμπτων,
> Τὼς νόος ἀνθρώποισι παρέστηκεν τὸ γὰρ αὐτό
> Ἔστιν, ὅπερ φρονέει, μελέων φύσις ἀνθρώποισι,
> Καὶ πᾶσιν καὶ παντί· τὸ γὰρ πλέον ἐστὶ νόημα.

(*Ut enim cuique complexio membrorum flexibilium se habet, ita mens hominibus adest: idem namque est, quod sapit, membrorum natura hominibus, et omnibus et omni: quod enim plus est, intelligentia est.*)[6]

§ 21.

From all these considerations the reader has now gained in the abstract, and hence in clear and certain terms, a knowledge which everyone possesses directly in the concrete, namely as feeling. This is the knowledge that the inner nature of his own phenomenon, which manifests itself to him as representation both through his actions and through the permanent substratum of these his body, is his *will.* This will constitutes what is most immediate in his consciousness, but as such it has not wholly entered into the form of the representation, in which object and subject stand over against each other; on the contrary, it makes itself known in an immediate way in which subject and object are not quite clearly distinguished, yet it becomes known to the individual himself not as a whole, but only in its particular acts. The reader who with me has gained this conviction, will find that of itself it will become the key to the knowledge of the innermost being of the whole of nature, since he now transfers it to all those phenomena that are given to him, not like his own phenomenon both in direct and in indirect knowledge, but in the latter solely, and hence merely in a one-sided way, as *representation* alone. He will recognize that same will not

---

[6] "Just as everyone possesses the complex of flexible limbs, so does there dwell in men the mind in conformity with this. For everyone mind and complex of limbs are always the same; for intelligence is the criterion." [Tr.]

Cf. chap. 20 of volume 2; also my work *Über den Willen in der Natur,* under the heads "Physiology" and "Comparative Anatomy," where the subject, here merely alluded to, has received a full and thorough treatment.

only in those phenomena that are quite similar to his own, in men and animals, as their innermost nature, but continued reflection will lead him to recognize the force that shoots and vegetates in the plant, indeed the force by which the crystal is formed, the force that turns the magnet to the North Pole, the force whose shock he encounters from the contact of metals of different kinds, the force that appears in the elective affinities of matter as repulsion and attraction, separation and union, and finally even gravitation, which acts so powerfully in all matter, pulling the stone to the earth and the earth to the sun; all these he will recognize as different only in the phenomenon, but the same according to their inner nature. He will recognize them all as that which is immediately known to him so intimately and better than everything else, and where it appears most distinctly is called *will*. It is only this application of reflection which no longer lets us stop at the phenomenon, but leads us on to the *thing-in-itself*. Phenomenon means representation and nothing more. All representation, be it of whatever kind it may, all *object,* is *phenomenon.* But only the *will* is *thing-in-itself;* as such it is not representation at all, but *toto genere* different therefrom. It is that of which all representation, all object, is the phenomenon, the visibility, the *objectivity.* It is the innermost essence, the kernel, of every particular thing and also of the whole. It appears in every blindly acting force of nature, and also in the deliberate conduct of man, and the great difference between the two concerns only the degree of the manifestation, not the inner nature of what is manifested.

§ 22.

Now, if this *thing-in-itself* (we will retain the Kantian expression as a standing formula)—which as such is never object, since all object is its mere appearance or phenomenon, and not it itself—is to be thought of objectively, then we must borrow its name and concept from an object, from something in some way objectively given, and therefore from one of its phenomena. But in order to serve as a point of explanation, this can be none other than the most complete of all its phenomena, i.e., the most distinct, the most developed, the most directly enlightened by knowledge; but this is precisely man's *will.* We have to observe, however, that here of course we use only a *denominatio a potiori,* by which the concept of will therefore receives a greater extension than it has hitherto had. Knowledge of the identical in different phenomena and of the different in similar phenomena is, as Plato so often remarks, the condition for philosophy. But hitherto the identity of the inner essence of any striving and operating force in nature with the will has not been recognized, and therefore the many kinds of phenomena that are only different species of the same genus were not regarded as such; they were considered as being heterogeneous. Consequently, no word could exist to describe the concept of this genus. I therefore name the genus after its most important species, the direct knowledge of which lies nearest to us, and leads to the indirect knowledge of all the others. But anyone who is incapable of carrying out the required extension of the concept will remain involved in a permanent misunderstanding. For by the word *will,* he will always understand only that species of it hitherto exclusively described by the term, that is to say, the will guided by knowledge, strictly according to motives, indeed only to abstract motives, thus manifesting itself under the guidance of the faculty of reason. This, as we have said, is only the most distinct phenomenon or appearance of the will. We must now clearly separate out in our thoughts the innermost essence of this phenomenon, known to us directly, and then transfer it to all the weaker, less distinct phenomena of the same essence, and by so doing achieve the desired extension of the concept of will. From the opposite point of view, I should be misunderstood by anyone who thought that ultimately it was all the same whether we expressed this essence-in-itself of all phenomena by the word will or by any other word. This would be the case if this thing-in-itself were something whose existence we merely *inferred,* and thus knew only indirectly and merely in the abstract. Then certainly we could call it what we liked; the name would stand merely as the symbol of an unknown quantity. But the word *will, which,* like a magic word, is to reveal to us the innermost essence of everything in nature, by no means expresses an unknown quantity, something reached by inferences and syllogisms, but something known absolutely and immediately, and that so well that we know and understand what will is better than anything else, be it what it may. Hitherto, the concept of *will* has been subsumed under the concept of *force;* I, on the other hand, do exactly the reverse, and intend every force in nature to be conceived as will. We must not imagine that this is a dispute about words or a matter of no consequence; on the contrary, it is of the very highest significance and importance. For at the root of the concept of *force,* as of all other concepts, lies knowledge of the objective world through perception, in other words, the phenomenon, the representation, from which the concept is drawn. It is abstracted from the province where cause and effect reign, that is, from the representation of perception, and it signifies just the causal nature of the cause at the point where this causal nature is etiologically no longer explicable at all, but is the necessary presupposition of all etiological explanation. On the other hand, the concept of *will* is of all possible concepts the only one that has its origin *not* in the phenomenon, *not* in the mere representation of perception, but which comes from within, and proceeds from the most immediate consciousness of everyone. In this consciousness each one knows and at the same time is himself his own individuality according to its nature immediately, without any form, even the form of subject and object, for here knower and known coincide. Therefore, if we refer the concept of *force* to that of *will,* we have in fact referred something more unknown to something infinitely better known, indeed to the one thing really known to us immediately and completely; and we have very greatly extended our knowledge. If, on the other hand, we subsume the concept of *will* under that of *force,* as has been done hitherto, we renounce the only immediate knowledge of the inner nature of the world that we have, since we let it disappear in a concept abstracted from the phenomenon, with which therefore we can never pass beyond the phenomenon.

§ 23.

The *will* as thing-in-itself is quite different from its phenomenon, and is entirely free from all the forms of the phenomenon into which it first passes when it appears, and which therefore concern only its *objectivity,* and are foreign to the will itself. Even the most universal form of all representation, that of object for subject, does not concern it, still less the forms that are subordinate to this and collectively have their common expression in the principle of sufficient reason. As we know, time and space belong to this principle, and consequently plurality as well, which exists and has become possible only through them. In this last respect I shall call time and space the *principium individuationis,* an expression borrowed from the old scholasticism, and I beg the reader to bear this in mind once and for all. For it is only by means of time and space that something which is one and the same according to its nature and the concept appears as different, as a plurality of coexistent and successive things. Consequently, time and space are the *principium individuationis,* the subject of so many subtleties and disputes among the scholastics which are found collected in Suarez (*Disp. 5,* sect. 3). It is apparent from what has been said that the will as thing-in-itself lies outside the province of the principle of sufficient reason in all its forms, and is consequently completely groundless, although each of its phenomena is entirely subject to that principle. Further, it is free from all *plurality,* although its phenomena in time and space are innumerable. It is itself one, yet not as an object is one, for the unity of an object is known only in contrast to possible plurality. Again, the will is one not as a concept is one, for a concept originates only through abstraction from plurality; but it is one as that which lies outside time and space, outside the *principium individuationis,* that is to say, outside the possibility of plurality. Only when all this has become quite clear to us through the following consideration of phenomena and of the different manifestations of the will, can we fully understand the meaning of the Kantian doctrine that time, space, and causality do not belong to the thing-in-itself, but are only the forms of our knowing.

The groundlessness of the will has actually been recognized where it manifests itself most distinctly, that is, as the will of man; and this has been called free and independent. But as to the groundlessness of the will itself, the necessity to which its phenomenon is everywhere liable has been overlooked, and actions have been declared to be free, which they are not. For every individual action follows with strict necessity from the effect of the motive on the character. As we have already said, all necessity is the relation of the consequent to the ground, and nothing else whatever. The principle of sufficient reason is the universal form of every phenomenon, and man in his action, like every other phenomenon, must be subordinated to it. But because in self-consciousness the will is known directly and in itself, there also lies in this consciousness the consciousness of freedom. But the fact is overlooked that the individual, the person, is not will as thing-in-itself, but is *phenomenon* of the will, is as such determined, and has entered the form of the phenomenon, the principle of sufficient reason. Hence we get the strange fact that everyone considers himself to be *a priori* quite free, even in his individual actions, and imagines he can at any moment enter upon a different way of life, which is equivalent to saying that he can become a different person. But *a posteriori* through experience, he finds to his astonishment that he is not free, but liable to necessity; that notwithstanding all his resolutions and reflections he does not change his conduct, and that from the beginning to the end of his life he must bear the same character that he himself condemns, and, as it were, must play to the end the part he has taken upon himself. I cannot pursue this discussion any further here, for, being ethical, it belongs to another part of this work. Meanwhile, I wish to point out here only that the *phenomenon* of the will, in itself groundless, is yet subject as such to the law of necessity, that is to say, to the principle of sufficient reason, so that in the necessity with which the phenomena of nature ensue, we may not find anything to prevent us from recognizing in them the manifestations of the will.

Hitherto we have regarded as phenomena of the will only those changes that have no other ground than a motive, i.e., a representation. Therefore in nature a will has been attributed only to man, or at most to animals, because, as I have already mentioned elsewhere, knowing or representing is of course the genuine and exclusive characteristic of the animal kingdom. But we see at once from the instinct and mechanical skill of animals that the will is also active where it is not guided by any knowledge.[7] That they have representations and knowledge is of no account at all here, for the end towards which they work as definitely as if it were a known motive remains entirely unknown to them. Therefore, their action here takes place without motive, is not guided by the representation, and shows us first and most distinctly how the will is active even without any knowledge. The one-year-old bird has no notion of the eggs for which it builds a nest; the young spider has no idea of the prey for which it spins a web; the ant-lion has no notion of the ant for which it digs a cavity for the first time. The larva of the stag-beetle gnaws the hole in the wood, where it will undergo its metamorphosis, twice as large if it is to become a male beetle as if it is to become a female, in order in the former case to have room for the horns, though as yet it has no idea of these. In the actions of such animals the will is obviously at work as in the rest of their activities, but is in blind activity, which is accompanied, indeed, by knowledge, but not guided by it. Now if we have once gained insight into the fact that representation as motive is not a necessary and essential condition of the will's activity, we shall more easily recognize the action of the will in cases where it is less evident. For example, we shall no more ascribe the house of the snail to a will foreign to the snail itself but guided by knowledge, than we shall say that the house we ourselves build comes into existence through a will other than our

---

[7] This is specially dealt with in chap. 27 of volume 2.

own. On the contrary, we shall recognize both houses as works of the will objectifying itself in the two phenomena, working in us on the basis of motives, but in the snail blindly as formative impulse directed outwards. Even in us the same will in many ways acts blindly; as in all those functions of our body which are not guided by knowledge, in all its vital and vegetative processes, digestion, circulation, secretion, growth, and reproduction. Not only the actions of the body, but the whole body itself, as was shown above, is phenomenon of the will, objectified will, concrete will. All that occurs in it must therefore occur through will, though here this will is not guided by knowledge, not determined according to motives, but acts blindly according to causes, called in this case *stimuli*.

I call *cause* in the narrowest sense of the word that state or condition of matter which, while it brings about another state with necessity, itself suffers a change just as great as that which it causes. This is expressed by the rule "Action and reaction are equal." Further, in the case of a cause proper, the effect increases in exact proportion to the cause, and hence the counter-effect or reaction also. Thus, if once the mode of operation is known, the degree of the effect can be measured and calculated from the degree of intensity of the cause, and conversely. Such causes, properly so called, operate in all the phenomena of mechanics, chemistry, and so forth; in short, in all the changes of inorganic bodies. On the other hand, I call *stimulus* that cause which itself undergoes no reaction proportional to its effect, and whose intensity runs by no means parallel with the intensity of the effect according to degree; so that the effect cannot be measured from it. On the contrary, a small increase of the stimulus may cause a very large increase in the effect, or, conversely may entirely eliminate the previous effect, and so forth. Every effect on organized bodies as such is of this kind. Therefore all really organic and vegetative changes in the animal body take place from stimuli, not from mere causes. But the stimulus, like every cause and motive in general, never determines more than the point of entry of the manifestation of every force in time and space, not the inner nature of the force that manifests itself. According to our previous deduction, we recognize this inner nature to be will, and to this therefore we ascribe both the unconscious and the conscious changes of the body. The stimulus holds the mean, forms the transition, between the motive, which is causality that has passed through knowledge, and the cause in the narrowest sense. In particular cases it is sometimes nearer the motive, sometimes nearer the cause, yet it can always be distinguished from both. Thus, for example, the rising of the sap in plants occurs as a result of stimuli, and cannot be explained from mere causes in accordance with the laws of hydraulics or capillary tubes; yet it is certainly aided by these, and in general it approaches very closely to a purely causal change. On the other hand, the movements of *Hedysarum gyrans* and *Mimosa pudica,* though still following on mere stimuli, are very similar to those that follow on motives, and seem almost to want to make the transition. The contraction of the pupil of the eye with increased light occurs on stimulus, but passes over into movement on motive, for it takes place because too strong a light would affect the retina painfully, and to avoid this we contract the pupil. The occasion of an erection is a motive, as it is a representation; yet it operates with the necessity of a stimulus, in other words, it cannot be resisted, but must be put away in order to be made ineffective. This is also the case with disgusting objects which stimulate the desire to vomit. We have just considered the instinct of animals as an actual link of quite a different kind between movement on stimulus and action according to a known motive. We might be tempted to regard respiration as another link of this kind. It has been disputed whether it belongs to the voluntary or the involuntary movements, that is to say, whether it ensues on motive or on stimulus; accordingly, it might possibly be explained as something between the two. Marshall Hall (*On the Diseases of the Nervous System,* §§ 293 *seq.*) declares it to be a mixed function, for it is under the influence partly of the cerebral (voluntary), partly of the spinal (involuntary) nerves. However, we must class it ultimately with the manifestations of will following on motive, for other motives, i.e., mere representations, can determine the will to check or accelerate it, and, as with every other voluntary action, it seems that a man might abstain from breathing altogether and freely suffocate. In fact, this could be done the moment some other motive influenced the will so powerfully that it overcame the pressing need for air. According to some, Diogenes is supposed actually to have put an end to his life in this way (Diogenes Laërtius, VI, 76). Negroes also are said to have done this (F. B. Osiander, *Über den Selbstmord* [1813], pp. 170-180). We might have here a striking example of the influence of abstract motives, i.e., of the superior force of really rational over mere animal willing. That breathing is at any rate in part conditioned by cerebral activity is shown by the fact that prussic acid kills by first of all paralyzing the brain, and hence by indirectly stopping respiration. If, however, the breathing is artificially maintained until the narcotic effect has passed off, death does not occur at all. Incidentally, respiration gives us at the same time the most striking example of the fact that motives act with just as great a necessity as do stimuli and mere causes in the narrowest sense, and that they can be put out of action only by opposite motives, just as pressure is neutralized by counterpressure. For in the case of breathing, the illusion of being able to abstain is incomparably weaker than in the case of other movements that follow on motives, because with breathing the motive is very pressing, very near, its satisfaction is very easy on account of the untiring nature of the muscles that perform it, nothing as a rule opposes it, and the whole process is supported by the most inveterate habit on the part of the individual. And yet all motives really act with the same necessity. The knowledge that necessity is common to movements following on motives and to movements following on stimuli will make it easier for us to understand that even what takes place in the organic body on stimuli and in complete conformity to law is yet, according to its inner nature, will. This will, never of course in itself, but in all its phenomena, is subject to the principle of sufficient reason, in other words to necessity.[8] Accordingly, we shall not confine ourselves here to recognizing animals as phenomena of will in their actions as well as in their whole existence, bodily structure, and organization, but shall extend also to plants this immediate knowledge of the inner nature of things that is given to us alone. All the movements of plants follow on stimuli, for the absence of knowledge and of the movement on motives conditioned by such knowledge constitutes the only essential difference between animal and plant. Therefore what appears for the representation as plant, as mere vegetation, as blindly urging force, will be taken by us, according to its inner nature, to be will, and it will be recognized by us as that very thing which constitutes the basis of our own phenomenon, as it expresses itself in our actions, and also in the whole existence of our body itself.

It only remains for us to take the final step, namely that of extending our method of consideration to all those forces in nature which act according to universal, immutable laws, in conformity with which there take place the movements of all those bodies, such bodies being entirely without organs, and having no susceptibility to stimulus and no knowledge of motive. We must therefore also apply the key for an understanding of the inner nature of things, a key that only the immediate knowledge of our own inner nature could give us, to these phenomena of the inorganic world, which are the most remote of all from us. Now let us consider attentively and observe the

---

[8] This knowledge is fully established by my essay *On the Freedom of the Will*, in which therefore (pp. 30-44 of the *Grundprobleme der Ethik*, 2nd ed., pp. 29-41) the relation between *cause, stimulus,* and *motive* has been discussed in detail.

powerful, irresistible impulse with which masses of water rush downwards, the persistence and determination with which the magnet always turns back to the North Pole, the keen desire with which iron flies to the magnet, the vehemence with which the poles of the electric current strive for reunion, and which, like the vehemence of human desires, is increased by obstacles. Let us look at the crystal being rapidly and suddenly formed with such regularity of configuration; it is obvious that this is only a perfectly definite and precisely determined striving in different directions constrained and held firm by coagulation. Let us observe the choice with which bodies repel and attract one another, unite and separate, when set free in the fluid state and released from the bonds of rigidity. Finally, we feel directly and immediately how a burden, which hampers our body by its gravitation towards the earth, incessantly presses and squeezes this body in pursuit of its one tendency. If we observe all this, it will not cost us a great effort of the imagination to recognize once more our own inner nature, even at so great a distance. It is that which in us pursues its ends by the light of knowledge, but here, in the feeblest of its phenomena, only strives blindly in a dull, one-sided, and unalterable manner. Yet, because it is everywhere one and the same—just as the first morning dawn shares the name of sunlight with the rays of the full midday sun—it must in either case bear the name of *will*. For this word indicates that which is the being-in-itself of every thing in the world, and is the sole kernel of every phenomenon.

However, the remoteness, in fact the appearance of a complete difference between the phenomena of inorganic nature and the will, perceived by us as the inner reality of our own being, arises principally from the contrast between the wholly determined conformity to law in the one species of phenomenon, and the apparently irregular arbitrariness in the other. For in man individuality stands out powerfully; everyone has a character of his own, and hence the same motive does not have the same influence on all, and a thousand minor circumstances, finding scope in one individual's wide sphere of knowledge but remaining unknown to others, modify its effect. For this reason an action cannot be predetermined from the motive alone, since the other factor, namely an exact acquaintance with the individual character, and with the knowledge accompanying that character, is wanting. On the other hand, the phenomena of the forces of nature show the other extreme in this respect. They operate according to universal laws, without deviation, without individuality, in accordance with openly manifest circumstances, subject to the most precise predetermination; and the same force of nature manifests

itself in its million phenomena in exactly the same way. To explain
this point, to demonstrate the identity of the *one* and indivisible will
in all its very varied phenomena, in the feeblest as in the strongest,
we must first of all consider the relation between the will as thing-in-
itself and its phenomenon, i.e., between the world as will and
the world as representation. This will open up for us the best
way to a more thorough and searching investigation of the whole
subject dealt with in this second book.[9]

§ 24.

We have learnt from the great Kant that time,
space, and causality are present in our consciousness according to
their whole conformity to rule and the possibility of all their forms,
quite independently of the objects that appear in them and form
their content; or, in other words, they can be found just as well
when we start from the subject as when we start from the object.
Therefore we can with equal reason call them modes of perception
or intuition of the subject, or qualities of the object *in so far as it
is object* (with Kant, phenomenon, appearance), in other words,
representation. We can also regard these forms as the indivisible
boundary between object and subject. Therefore every object must of
course appear in them, but the subject, independently of the appearing object, also possesses and surveys them completely. Now if the
objects appearing in these forms are not to be empty phantoms, but
are to have a meaning, they must point to something, must be the
expression of something, which is not, like themselves, object,
representation, something existing merely relatively, namely for a
subject. On the contrary, they must point to something that exists
without such dependence on something that stands over against it
as its essential condition, and on its forms, in other words, must point
to something that is *not a representation,* but a *thing-in-itself.* Accordingly, it could at any rate be asked: Are those representations,
those objects, something more than and apart from representations,
objects of the subject? Then what would they be in this sense?

---

[9] Cf. chap. 23 of volume 2, and also in my work *Über den Willen in der
Natur* the chapter on "Physiology of Plants" and that on "Physical Astronomy," which is of the greatest importance for the kernel of my metaphysics.

What is that other side of them that is *toto genere* different from the representation? What is the thing-in-itself? Our answer has been *the will; but for the present I leave this answer aside.*

Whatever the thing-in-itself may be, Kant rightly concluded that time, space, and causality (which we later recognized as forms of the principle of sufficient reason, this principle being the universal expression of the forms of the phenomenon) could not be its properties, but could come to it only after, and in so far as, it had become representation, in other words, belonged only to its phenomenon or appearance, not to it itself. For as the subject completely knows and constructs them out of itself, independently of all object, they must adhere to *representation-existence* as such, not to that which becomes representation. They must be the form of the representation as such, but not qualities of what has assumed that form. They must be already given with the mere contrast of subject and object (not in the concept but in the fact); consequently, they must be only the closer determination of the form of knowledge in general, the most universal determination whereof is that very contrast. Now what in turn is conditioned in the phenomenon, in the object, by time, space, and causality, since it can be represented only by their means, namely *plurality* through coexistence and succession, *change and duration* through the law of causality, and *matter* which is capable of being represented only on the assumption of causality, and finally everything again that can be represented only by their means—all this as a whole does not really belong to *what* appears, to *what* has entered the form of the representation, but only to this form itself. Conversely, however, that which in the phenomenon is *not* conditioned by time, space, and causality, cannot be referred to them, and cannot be explained according to them, will be precisely that in which the thing that appears, the thing-in-itself, becomes immediately manifest. It follows from this that the most complete capacity for being known, in other words, the greatest clearness, distinctness, and susceptibility to exhaustive investigation, will necessarily belong to what is peculiar to knowledge *as such,* and hence to the *form* of knowledge, not to that which in itself is *not* representation, *not* object, but which has become knowable only by entering these forms, in other words, has become representation or object. Hence only that which depends solely on being known, on being representation in general and as such (not on what becomes known and has only become representation), and which therefore belongs without distinction to all that is known, and on that account is found just as well when we start from the subject as when we start from the object—this alone will be able to afford us without reserve a sufficient, exhaustive knowledge that is clear to the very foundation. But this consists in nothing but those forms of every phenomenon of which we are *a priori* conscious, and which can be commonly expressed as the principle of sufficient reason. The forms of this principle relating to knowledge through perception (with which exclusively we are here concerned) are time, space, and causality. The whole of pure mathematics and pure natural science *a priori* are based on these alone. Therefore in these sciences only does knowledge meet with no obscurity; in these it does not encounter the unfathomable (the groundless, i.e., the will), that which cannot be further deduced. It is in this respect that Kant wanted, as we have said, to call those branches of knowledge, together with logic, specially and exclusively science. On the other hand, these branches of knowledge show us nothing more than mere connexions, relations, of one representation to another, form without any content. All content received by them, every phenomenon that fills those forms, contains something no longer completely knowable according to its whole nature, something no longer entirely explicable by something else, and thus something groundless, whereby knowledge at once loses its evidence and complete lucidity. But this thing that withdraws from investigation is precisely the thing-in-itself, that which is essentially not representation, not object of knowledge; but only by entering that form has it become knowable. The form is originally foreign to it, and it can never become completely one therewith, can never be referred to the mere form, and, as this form is the principle of sufficient reason, can therefore never be completely *fathomed*. Therefore, although all mathematics gives us exhaustive knowledge of that which in phenomena is quantity, position, number, in short, spatial and temporal relation; although etiology tells us completely about the regular conditions under which phenomena, with all their determinations, appear in time and space, yet, in spite of all this, teaches us nothing more than why in each case every definite phenomenon must appear just at this time here and just at this place now, we can never with their assistance penetrate into the inner nature of things. There yet remains something on which no explanation can venture, but which it presupposes, namely the forces of nature, the definite mode of operation of things, the quality, the character of every phenomenon, the groundless, that which depends not on the form of the phenomenon, not on the principle of sufficient reason, that to which this form in itself is foreign, yet which has entered this form, and now appears according to its law. This law, however, determines only the appearing, not *that which* appears, only the *How*, not the *What* of the phenomenon, only its

form, not its content. Mechanics, physics, chemistry teach the rules
and laws by which the forces of impenetrability, gravitation, rigidity,
fluidity, cohesion, elasticity, heat, light, elective affinities, magnetism,
electricity, and so on operate, in other words, the law, the rule,
observed by these forces in regard to their entry into space and
time in each case. But whatever we may do, the forces themselves
remain *qualitates occultae*. For it is just the thing-in-itself which, by
appearing, exhibits those phenomena. It is entirely different from the
phenomena themselves, yet in its manifestation it is wholly subject
to the principle of sufficient reason as the form of the representation,
but it can never itself be referred to this form, and hence can never
be thoroughly explained etiologically, or completely and ultimately
fathomed. It is wholly comprehensible in so far as it has assumed
this form, in other words, in so far as it is phenomenon, but its
inner nature is not in the least explained by its thus being comprehensible. Therefore, the more necessity any knowledge carries with
it, the more there is in it of what cannot possibly be otherwise
thought or represented in perception—as, for example, space-
relations; hence the clearer and more satisfying it is, the less is its
purely objective content, or the less reality, properly so called, is
given in it. And conversely, the more there is in it that must be
conceived as purely accidental, the more it impresses us as given only
empirically, then the more that is properly objective and truly real
is there in such knowledge, and also at the same time the more that
is inexplicable, in other words, the more that cannot be further
derived from anything else.

Of course at all times an etiology, unmindful of its aim, has
striven to reduce all organized life to chemistry or electricity, all
chemistry, i.e., quality, in turn to mechanism (effect through the
shape of the atoms), and this again sometimes to the object of
phoronomy, i.e., time and space united for the possibility of motion,
sometimes to the object of mere geometry, i.e., position in space
(much in the same way as we rightly work out in a purely geometrical
way the diminution of an effect according to the square of the
distance and the theory of the lever). Finally, geometry can be
resolved into arithmetic, which by reason of its unity of dimension
is the most intelligible, comprehensible, and completely fathomable
form of the principle of sufficient reason. Proofs of the method
generally indicated here are the atoms of Democritus, the vortex
of Descartes, the mechanical physics of Lesage which, towards the
end of the eighteenth century, attempted to explain chemical affinities
as well as gravitation mechanically from impact and pressure, as may
be seen in detail from *Lucrèce Neutonien;* Reil's form and combina-

tion as the cause of animal life also tend in this direction. Finally, crude materialism, raked up once more in the middle of the nineteenth century and from ignorance fancying itself to be original, is entirely of this nature. First of all, stupidly denying vital force, it tries to explain the phenomena of life by physical and chemical forces, and these in turn by the mechanical operation of matter, the position, form, and motion of imagined atoms. Thus it would like to reduce all the forces of nature to thrust and counter-thrust as its "thing-in-itself." According to it, even light is supposed to be the mechanical vibration or undulation of an imaginary ether postulated for this purpose. When this ether reaches the retina, it beats on it, and, for example, four hundred and eighty-three thousand million beats a second give red, seven hundred and twenty-seven thousand million beats violet, and so on. So those who are colour-blind are those who cannot count the beats, I suppose! Such crass, mechanical, Democritean, ponderous, and truly clumsy theories are quite worthy of people who, fifty years after the appearance of Goethe's theory of colours, still believe in Newton's homogeneous light, and are not ashamed to say so. They will learn that what is condoned in the child (Democritus) will not be forgiven in the man. One day they might even come to an ignominious end, but then everyone would slink away and pretend he had had nothing to do with them. Soon we shall have more to say about this false reduction of original natural forces to each other; but for the moment this is enough. Suppose this were feasible, then of course everything would be explained and cleared up, and in fact would be reduced in the last resort to an arithmetical problem; and that would then be the holiest thing in the temple of wisdom, to which the principle of sufficient reason would at last have happily conducted us. But all content of the phenomenon would have vanished, and mere form would remain. The "what appears" would be referred to the "how it appears," and this "how" would be the *a priori* knowable, and so entirely dependent on the subject, and hence only for the subject, and so finally mere phantom, representation and form of the representation through and through; one could not ask for a thing-in-itself. Suppose this were feasible, then in actual fact the whole world would be derived from the subject, and that would be actually achieved which Fichte by his humbug sought to *seem* to achieve. But this will not do; phantasies, sophistications, castles in the air, have been brought into being in this way, but not science. The many and multifarious phenomena in nature have been successfully referred to particular original forces, and whenever this has been done, a real advance has been made. Several forces and qualities, at first regarded as different, have been derived from one another (e.g., magnetism from electricity), and thus their number has been reduced. Etiology will have attained its object when it has recognized and exhibited all the original forces of nature as such, and established their methods of operation, in other words, the rule by which, following the guidance of causality, their phenomena appear in time and space, and determine their position with regard to one another. But there will always remain over original forces; there will always remain, as an insoluble residuum, a content of the phenomenon which cannot be referred to its form, and which thus cannot be explained from something else in accordance with the principle of sufficient reason. For in everything in nature there is something to which no ground can ever be assigned, for which no explanation is possible, and no further cause is to be sought. This something is the specific mode of the thing's action, in other words, the very manner of its existence, its being or true essence. Of course, of each particular effect of the thing a cause can be demonstrated, from which it follows that it was bound to act at that particular time and place, but never a cause of its acting in general and precisely in the given way. If it has no other qualities, if it is a mote in a sunbeam, it still exhibits that unfathomable something, at any rate as weight and impenetrability. But this, I say, is to the mote what man's *will* is to a man; and, like the human will, it is in its inner nature not subject to explanation; indeed, it is in itself identical with this will. Of course, for every manifestation of the will, for every one of its individual acts at such a time and in such a place, a motive can be shown, upon which the act was necessarily bound to ensue on the presupposition of the man's character. But no reason can ever be stated for his having this character, for his willing in general, for the fact that, of several motives, just this one and no other, or indeed any motive, moves his will. That which for man is his unfathomable character, presupposed in every explanation of his actions from motives, is for every inorganic body precisely its essential quality, its manner of acting, whose manifestations are brought about by impressions from outside, while it itself, on the other hand, is determined by nothing outside it, and is thus inexplicable. Its particular manifestations, by which alone it becomes visible, are subject to the principle of sufficient reason; it itself is groundless. In essence this was correctly understood by the scholastics, who described it as *forma substantialis*. (Cf. Suárez, *Disputationes Metaphysicae, disp.* XV, sect. 1.)

It is an error as great as it is common that the most frequent, universal, and simple phenomena are those we best understand; on the contrary, they are just those phenomena which we are most accustomed to see, and about which we are most usually ignorant. For us it is just as inexplicable that a stone falls to the ground as that an animal moves itself. As mentioned above, it was supposed that, starting from the most universal forces of nature (e.g., gravitation, cohesion, impenetrability), we could explain from them those forces which operate more rarely and only under a combination of circumstances (e.g., chemical quality, electricity, magnetism), and finally from these could understand the organism and life of animals, and even the knowing and willing of man. Men tacitly resigned themselves to starting from mere *qualitates occultae,* whose elucidation was entirely given up, for the intention was to build upon them, not to undermine them. Such a thing, as we have said, cannot succeed; but apart from this, such a structure would always stand in the air. What is the use of explanations that ultimately lead back to something just as unknown as the first problem was? In the end, do we understand more about the inner nature of these natural forces than about the inner nature of an animal? Is not the one just as hidden and unexplored as the other? Unfathomable, because it is groundless, because it is the content, the *what* of the phenomenon, which can never be referred to the form of the phenomenon, to the *how,* to the principle of sufficient reason. But we, who are here aiming not at etiology but at philosophy, that is to say, not at relative but at unconditioned knowledge of the nature of the world, take the opposite course, and start from what is immediately and most completely known and absolutely familiar to us, from what lies nearest to us, in order to understand what is known to us only from a distance, one-sidedly, and indirectly. From the most powerful, most significant, and most distinct phenomenon we seek to learn to understand the weaker and less complete. With the exception of my own body, only *one* side of all things is known to me, namely that of the representation. Their inner nature remains sealed to me and is a profound secret, even when I know all the causes on which their changes ensue. Only from a comparison with what goes on within me when my body performs an action from a motive that moves me, with what is the inner nature of my own changes determined by external grounds or reasons, can I obtain an insight into the way in which those inanimate bodies change under the influence of causes, and thus understand what is their inner nature. Knowledge of the cause of this inner nature's manifestation tells me only the rule of its appearance in time and space, and nothing more. I can do this, because my body is the only object of which I know not merely the one side, that of the representation, but also the other, that is called *will.* Thus, instead of believing that I would better understand my own organization, and therefore my knowing and willing, and my movement on motives, if only I could refer them to movement from causes through electricity, chemistry, and mechanism, I must, in so far as I am looking for philosophy and not for etiology, first of all learn to understand from my own movement on motives the inner nature of the simplest and commonest movements of an inorganic body which I see ensuing on causes. I must recognize the inscrutable forces that manifest themselves in all the bodies of nature as identical in kind with what in me is the will, and as differing from it only in degree. This means that the fourth class of representations laid down in the essay *On the Principle of Sufficient Reason* must become for me the key to the knowledge of the inner nature of the first class, and from the law of motivation I must learn to understand the law of causality in its inner significance.

Spinoza (*Epist.* 62) says that if a stone projected through the air had consciousness, it would imagine it was flying of its own will. I add merely that the stone would be right. The impulse is for it what the motive is for me, and what in the case of the stone appears as cohesion, gravitation, rigidity in the assumed condition, is by its inner nature the same as what I recognize in myself as will, and which the stone also would recognize as will, if knowledge were added in its case also. In this passage Spinoza has his eye on the necessity with which the stone flies, and he rightly wants to transfer this to the necessity of a person's particular act of will. On the other hand, I consider the inner being that first imparts meaning and validity to all necessity (i.e., effect from cause) to be its presupposition. In the case of man, this is called character; in the case of the stone, it is called quality; but it is the same in both. Where it is immediately known, it is called *will,* and in the stone it has the weakest, and in man the strongest, degree of visibility, of objectivity. With the right touch, St. Augustine recognized in the tendency of all things this identity with our willing, and I cannot refrain from recording his naïve account of the matter: *Si pecora essemus, carnalem vitam et quod secundum sensum ejusdem est amaremus, idque esset sufficiens bonum nostrum, et secundum hoc si esset nobis bene, nihil aliud quaereremus. Item, si arbores essemus, nihil quidem sentientes motu amare possemus: verumtamen id quasi APPETERE videremur, quo feracius essemus, uberiusque fructuosae. Si essemus lapides, aut fluctus, aut ventus, aut flamma, vel quid ejusmodi, sine ullo quidem sensu atque vita, non tamen nobis deesset quasi quidam nostrorum locorum atque ordinis APPETITUS. Nam velut AMORES corporum momenta sunt ponderum, sive deorsum gravitate,*

sive sursum levitate nitantur: ita enim corpus pondere, sicut animus AMORE fertur quocunque fertur (*De Civitate Dei*, XI, 28).[10]

Further, it is worth noting that Euler saw that the inner nature of gravitation must ultimately be reduced to an "inclination and desire" (hence will) peculiar to bodies (in the 68th letter to the Princess). In fact, it is just this that makes him averse to the conception of gravitation as found in Newton, and he is inclined to try a modification of it in accordance with the earlier Cartesian theory, and thus to derive gravitation from the impact of an ether on bodies, as being "more rational and suitable for those who like clear and intelligible principles." He wants to see attraction banished from physics as a *qualitas occulta*. This is only in keeping with the dead view of nature which, as the correlative of the immaterial soul, prevailed in Euler's time. However, it is noteworthy in regard to the fundamental truth advanced by me, which even at that time this fine mind saw glimmering from a distance. He hastened to turn back in time, and then in his anxiety at seeing all the prevalent fundamental views endangered, sought refuge in old and already exploded absurdities.

§ 25.

We know that *plurality* in general is necessarily conditioned by time and space, and only in these is conceivable, and in this respect we call them the *principium individuationis*. But we have recognized time and space as forms of the principle of sufficient

---

[10] "If we were animals, we should love carnal life and what conforms to its meaning. For us this would be enough of a good, and accordingly we should demand nothing more, if all was well for us. Likewise, if we were trees, we should not feel or aspire to anything by movement, but yet we should seem to *desire* that by which we should be more fertile and bear more abundant fruits. If we were stones, or floods, or wind, or flame, or anything of the kind, without any consciousness and life, we should still not lack, so to speak, a certain *longing* for our position and order. For it is, so to speak, a *desire* that is decisive for the weight of bodies, whether by virtue of heaviness they tend downwards, or by virtue of lightness upwards. For the body is driven whither it is driven by its weight, precisely as the spirit is impelled by *desire*." [Tr.]

reason, and in this principle all our knowledge *a priori* is expressed. As explained above, however, this *a priori* knowledge, as such, applies only to the knowableness of things, not to the things themselves, i.e., it is only our form of knowledge, not a property of the thing-in-itself. The thing-in-itself, as such, is free from all forms of knowledge, even the most universal, namely that of being object for the subject; in other words, it is something entirely different from the representation. Now if this thing-in-itself, as I believe I have sufficiently proved and made clear, is the *will,* then, considered as such and apart from its phenomenon, it lies outside time and space, and accordingly knows no plurality, and consequently is *one.* Yet, as has been said already, it is not one as an individual or a concept is, but as something to which the condition of the possibility of plurality, that is, the *principium individuationis,* is foreign. Therefore, the plurality of things in space and time that together are the *objectivity* of the will, does not concern the will, which, in spite of such plurality, remains indivisible. It is not a case of there being a smaller part of will in the stone and a larger part in man, for the relation of part and whole belongs exclusively to space, and has no longer any meaning the moment we have departed from this form of intuition or perception. More and less concern only the phenomenon, that is to say, the visibility, the objectification. There is a higher degree of this objectification in the plant than in the stone, a higher degree in the animal than in the plant; indeed, the will's passage into visibility, its objectification, has gradations as endless as those between the feeblest twilight and the brightest sunlight, the loudest tone and the softest echo. Later on, we shall come back to a consideration of these degrees of visibility that belong to the objectification of the will, to the reflection of its inner nature. But as the gradations of its objectification do not directly concern the will itself, still less is it concerned by the plurality of the phenomena at these different grades, in other words, the multitude of individuals of each form, or the particular manifestations of each force. For this plurality is directly conditioned by time and space, into which the will itself never enters. The will reveals itself just as completely and just as much in *one* oak as in millions. Their number, their multiplication in space and time, has no meaning with regard to the will, but only with regard to the plurality of the individuals who know in space and time, and who are themselves multiplied and dispersed therein. But that same plurality of these individuals again applies not to the will, but only to its phenomenon. Therefore it could be asserted that if, *per impossible,* a single being, even the most insignificant, were

entirely annihilated, the whole world would inevitably be destroyed with it. The great mystic Angelus Silesius feels this when he says:

"I know God cannot live a moment without me;
If I should come to nought, He too must cease to be."
[*Cherubinischer Wandersmann*, i, 8].

Men have attempted in various ways to bring the immeasurable greatness of the universe nearer to the power of comprehension of each one of us, and have then seized the opportunity to make edifying observations. They have referred perhaps to the relative smallness of the earth, and indeed of man; then again, in contrast to this, they have spoken of the greatness of the mind of this man who is so small, a mind that can decipher, comprehend, and even measure the greatness of this universe, and so on. Now this is all very well, yet to me, when I consider the vastness of the world, the most important thing is that the essence in itself, the phenomenon whereof is the world—be it whatever else it may—cannot have its true self stretched out and dispersed in such fashion in boundless space, but that this endless extension belongs simply and solely to its phenomenon or appearance. On the other hand, the inner being itself is present whole and undivided in everything in nature, in every living being. Therefore we lose nothing if we stop at any particular thing, and true wisdom is not to be acquired by our measuring the boundless world, or, what would be more appropriate, by our personally floating through endless space. On the contrary, it is acquired by thoroughly investigating any individual thing, in that we try thus to know and understand perfectly its true and peculiar nature.

Accordingly, what follows, and this has already impressed itself as a matter of course on every student of Plato, will be in the next book the subject of a detailed discussion. Those different grades of the will's objectification, expressed in innumerable individuals, exist as the unattained patterns of these, or as the eternal forms of things. Not themselves entering into time and space, the medium of individuals, they remain fixed, subject to no change, always being, never having become. The particular things, however, arise and pass away; they are always becoming and never are. Now I say that these *grades of the objectification of the will* are nothing but *Plato's Ideas*. I mention this here for the moment, so that in future I can use the word *Idea* in this sense. Therefore with me the word is always to be understood in its genuine and original meaning, given to it by Plato; and in using it we must assuredly not think of those abstract productions of scholastic dogmatizing reason, to describe which Kant used the word wrongly as well as illegitimately, although Plato had already taken possession of it, and used it most appropriately. Therefore, by *Idea* I understand every definite and fixed *grade of the will's objectification,* in so far as it is thing-in-itself and is therefore foreign to plurality. These grades are certainly related to individual things as their eternal forms, or as their prototypes. Diogenes Laërtius (III, 12) gives us the shortest and most concise statement of this famous Platonic dogma: ὁ Πλάτων φησί, ἐν τῇ φύσει τὰς ἰδέας ἐστάναι, καθάπερ παραδείγματα· τὰ δ'ἄλλα ταύταις ἐοικέναι, τούτων ὁμοιώματα καθεστῶτα. (*Plato ideas in natura velut exemplaria dixit subsistere; cetera his esse similia, ad istarum similitudinem consistentia.*)[11] I take no further notice of the Kantian misuse of this word; the necessary remarks about it are in the Appendix.

§ 26.

The most universal forces of nature exhibit themselves as the lowest grade of the will's objectification. In part they appear in all matter without exception, as gravity and impenetrability, and in part have shared out among themselves the matter generally met with. Thus some forces rule over this piece of matter, others over that, and this constitutes their specific difference, as rigidity, fluidity, elasticity, electricity, magnetism, chemical properties, and qualities of every kind. In themselves they are immediate phenomena of the will, just as is the conduct of man; as such, they are groundless, just as is the character of man. Their particular phenomena alone are subject to the principle of sufficient reason, just as are the actions of men. On the other hand, they themselves can never be called either effect or cause, but are the prior and presupposed conditions of all causes and effects through which their own inner being is unfolded and revealed. It is therefore foolish to ask for a cause of gravity or of electricity; they are original forces, whose

---

[11] "Plato teaches that the Ideas exist in nature, so to speak, as patterns or prototypes, and that the remainder of things only resemble them, and exist as their copies." [Tr.]

manifestations certainly take place according to cause and effect, so that each of their particular phenomena has a cause. This cause itself, again, is just such a particular phenomenon, and determines that this force was bound to manifest itself here and to appear in time and space. But the force itself is by no means effect of a cause, or cause of an effect. It is therefore wrong to say that "gravity is the cause of a stone's falling"; the cause is rather the nearness of the earth, since it attracts the stone. Take away the earth, and the stone will not fall, although gravity remains. The force itself lies entirely outside the chain of causes and effects, which presupposes time, since it has meaning only in reference thereto; but the force lies also outside time. The individual change always has as its cause yet another change just as individual, and not the force of which it is the expression. For that which always endows a cause with efficacy, however innumerable the times of its appearance may be, is a force of nature. As such, it is groundless, i.e., it lies entirely outside the chain of causes, and generally outside the province of the principle of sufficient reason, and philosophically it is known as immediate objectivity of the will, and this is the in-itself of the whole of nature. In etiology, however, in this case physics, it is seen as an original force, i.e., a *qualitas occulta.*

At the higher grades of the will's objectivity, we see individuality standing out prominently, especially in man, as the great difference of individual characters, i.e., as complete personality, outwardly expressed by strongly marked individual physiognomy, which embraces the whole bodily form. No animal has this individuality in anything like such a degree; only the higher animals have a trace of it, but the character of the species completely predominates over it, and for this reason there is but little individual physiognomy. The farther down we go, the more completely is every trace of individual character lost in the general character of the species, and only the physiognomy of the species remains. We know the psychological character of the species, and from this know exactly what is to be expected from the individual. On the other hand, in the human species every individual has to be studied and fathomed by himself, and this is of the greatest difficulty, if we wish to determine beforehand with some degree of certainty his course of action, on account of the possibility of dissimulation which makes its first appearance with the faculty of reason. It is probably connected with this difference between the human species and all others, that the furrows and convolutions of the brain, entirely wanting in birds and still very weakly marked in rodents, are even in the higher animals far more symmetrical on both sides, and more constantly the same in each individual, than they are in man.[12] It is further to be regarded as a phenomenon of this peculiar individual character, distinguishing man from all the animals, that, in the case of the animals, the sexual impulse seeks its satisfaction without noticeable selection, whereas in the case of man this selection, in an instinctive manner independent of all reflection, is carried to such heights that it rises to a powerful passion. Therefore, while every person is to be regarded as a specially determined and characterized phenomenon of the will, and even to a certain extent as a special Idea, in the animals this individual character as a whole is lacking, since the species alone has a characteristic significance. This trace of the individual character fades away more and more, the farther we go from man. Finally, plants no longer have any individual characteristics save those that can be fully explained from the favourable or unfavourable external influences of soil, climate, and other contingencies. Finally, in the inorganic kingdom of nature all individuality completely disappears. Only the crystal can still to some extent be regarded as individual; it is a unity of the tendency in definite directions, arrested by coagulation, which makes the trace of this tendency permanent. At the same time, it is an aggregate from its central form, bound into unity by an Idea, just as the tree is an aggregate from the individual shooting fibre showing itself in every rib of the leaf, in every leaf, in every branch. It repeats itself, and to a certain extent makes each of these appear as a growth of its own, nourishing itself parasitically from the greater, so that the tree, resembling the crystal, is a systematic aggregate of small plants, although only the whole is the complete presentation of an indivisible Idea, in other words, of this definite grade of the will's objectification. But the individuals of the same species of crystal can have no other difference than what is produced by external contingencies; indeed we can even at will make any species crystallize into large or small crystals. But the individual as such, that is to say, with traces of an individual character, is certainly not to be found at all in inorganic nature. All its phenomena are manifestations of universal natural forces, in other words, of those grades of the will's objectification which certainly do not objectify themselves (as in organic nature) by means of the difference of individualities partially expressing the whole of the Idea, but exhibit themselves only in the species, and manifest this in each particular phenomenon absolutely without any deviation. As time, space, plural-

---

[12] Wenzel, *De Structura Cerebri Hominis et Brutorum* (1812), ch. 3; Cuvier, *Leçons d'anatomie comparée*, leçon 9, arts. 4 and 5; Vicq d'Azyr, *Histoire de l'Académie des Sciences de Paris* (1783), pp. 470 and 483.

ity, being-conditioned by cause do not belong to the will or to the Idea (the grade of the will's objectification), but only to their individual phenomena, such a force of nature as, e.g., gravity or electricity, must manifest itself as such in precisely the same way in all its millions of phenomena, and only the external circumstances can modify the phenomenon. This unity of its inner being in all its phenomena, this unchangeable constancy of its appearance, as soon as the conditions are present for this under the guidance of causality, is called a *law of nature*. If such a law is once known through experience, the phenomenon of that natural law whose character is expressed and laid down in it can be accurately predetermined and calculated. But it is just this conformity to law of the phenomena of the lower grades of the will's objectification which gives them an aspect so different from the phenomena of the same will at the higher grades of its objectification. These grades are more distinct, and we see them in animals, in men and their actions, where the stronger or weaker appearance of the individual character and susceptibility to motives, which often remain hidden from the observer because they reside in knowledge, have resulted in the identical aspect of the inner nature of both kinds of phenomena being until now entirely overlooked.

The infallibility of the laws of nature contains something astonishing, indeed at times almost terrible, when we start from knowledge of the individual thing, and not from that of the Idea. It might astonish us that nature does not even once forget her laws. For instance, when once it is according to a natural law that, if certain materials are brought together under definite conditions, a chemical combination will occur, gas will be evolved, or combustion will take place; then, if the conditions come about, either through our own agency or by pure chance, today just as much as a thousand years ago, the definite phenomenon appears at once and without delay. (In the case of pure chance, the promptness and accuracy are the more astonishing, because unexpected.) We are most vividly impressed by this marvellous fact in the case of rare phenomena which occur only in very complex circumstances, but whose occurrence in such circumstances has been previously foretold to us. For example, certain metals, arranged alternately in a fluid containing an acid, are brought into contact; silver leaf brought between the extremities of this series is inevitably consumed suddenly in green flames; or, under certain conditions, the hard diamond is transformed into carbonic acid. It is the ghostly omnipresence of natural forces which then astonishes us, and we notice here something that in the case of ordinary everyday phenomena no longer strikes us, namely how the connexion between cause and effect is really just as mysterious as that which we imagine between a magical formula and the spirit that necessarily appears when invoked thereby. On the other hand, if we have penetrated into the philosophical knowledge that a force of nature is a definite grade of the objectification of the will, in other words, a definite grade of what we recognize in ourselves as our innermost being; if we have attained to the knowledge that this will, in itself and apart from its phenomenon and the forms thereof, lies outside time and space, and thus that the plurality conditioned by these does not belong to it or directly to the grade of the will's objectification, i.e., to the Idea, but only to their phenomena; and if we remember that the law of causality has significance only in relation to time and space, since it determines the position therein of the many and varied phenomena of the different Ideas in which the will manifests itself, regulating the order in which they must appear; then, I say, the inner meaning of Kant's great doctrine has dawned on us in this knowledge. It is the doctrine that space, time, and causality belong not to the thing-in-itself, but only to the phenomenon, that they are only the forms of our knowledge, not qualities of the thing-in-itself. If we have grasped this, we shall see that this astonishment at the conformity to law and the accuracy of operation of a natural force, the complete sameness of all its millions of phenomena, and the infallibility of its appearance, is in fact like the astonishment of a child or of a savage who, looking for the first time at some flower through a many-faceted glass, marvels at the complete similarity of the innumerable flowers that he sees, and counts the leaves of each separately.

Therefore every universal, original force of nature is, in its inner essence, nothing but the objectification of the will at a low grade, and we call every such grade an eternal *Idea* in Plato's sense. But the *law of nature* is the relation of the Idea to the form of its phenomenon. This form is time, space, and causality, having a necessary and inseparable connexion and relation to one another. Through time and space the Idea multiplies itself into innumerable phenomena, but the order in which these enter into those forms of multiplicity is definitely determined by the law of causality. This law is, so to speak, the norm of the extreme points of those phenomena of different Ideas, according to which space, time, and matter are assigned to them. This norm is, therefore, necessarily related to the identity of the whole of existing matter which is the common substratum of all these different phenomena. If all these were not referred to that common matter, in the possession of which they have to be divided, there would be no need for such a law to determine their claims. They might all at once and together fill endless space throughout an endless time. Therefore only because all those phenomena of the eternal Ideas are referred to one and the same matter must there be a rule for their appearance and disappearance, otherwise one would not make way for another. Thus the law of causality is essentially bound up with that of the persistence of substance; each reciprocally obtains significance from the other. Again, space and time are related to them in just the same way. For time is the mere possibility of opposed states in the same matter; space is the mere possibility of the persistence of the same matter in all kinds of opposed states. Therefore in the previous book we declared matter to be the union of time and space, and this union shows itself as fluctuation of the accidents with persistence of the substance, the universal possibility of which is precisely causality or becoming. Therefore we said also that matter is through and through causality. We declared the understanding to be the subjective correlative of causality, and said that matter (and hence the whole world as representation) exists only for the understanding; the understanding is its condition, its supporter, as its necessary correlative. All this is here mentioned only in passing, to remind the reader of what was said in the first book. For a complete understanding of these two books, we are required to observe their inner agreement; for that which is inseparably united in the actual world as its two sides, namely will and representation, has been torn apart in these two books, so that we may recognize each of them more clearly in isolation.

Perhaps it may not be superfluous to make even clearer, by an example, how the law of causality has meaning only in relation to time and space, and to matter which consists in the union of the two. This law determines the limits according to which the phenomena of the forces of nature are distributed in the possession of matter. The original natural forces themselves, however, as immediate objectification of the will, that will as thing-in-itself not being subject to the principle of sufficient reason, lie outside those forms. Only within these forms has any etiological explanation validity and meaning, and for this reason it can never lead us to the inner reality of nature. For this purpose let us imagine some kind of machine constructed according to the laws of mechanics. Iron weights begin its movement by their gravity; copper wheels resist through their rigidity, thrust and raise one another and the levers by virtue of their impenetrability, and so on. Here gravity, rigidity, and impenetrability are original, unexplained forces; mechanics tells us merely the conditions under which, and the manner in which, they manifest themselves, appear, and govern a definite matter, time and place. Now a powerful magnet can affect the iron of the weights, and overcome gravity; the movement of the machine stops, and the matter is at once the scene of a quite different force of nature, namely magnetism, of which etiological explanation again tells us nothing more than the conditions of its appearance. Or let the copper discs of that machine be laid on zinc plates, and an acid solution be introduced between them. The same matter of the machine is at once subject to another original force, galvanism, which now governs it according to its own laws, and reveals itself in that matter through its phenomena. Again, etiology can tell us nothing more about these than the circumstances under which, and the laws by which, they manifest themselves. Now let us increase the temperature and add pure oxygen; the whole machine burns, in other words, once again an entirely different natural force, the chemical, has an irresistible claim to that matter at this time and in this place, and reveals itself in this matter as Idea, as a definite grade of the will's objectification. The resulting metallic oxide now combines with an acid, and a salt is produced; crystals are formed. These are the phenomenon of another Idea that in turn is itself quite unfathomable, whereas the appearance of its phenomenon depends on those conditions that etiology is able to state. The crystals disintegrate, mix with other materials, and a vegetation springs from them, a new phenomenon of will. And thus the same persistent matter could be followed *ad infinitum,* and we would see how first this and then that natural force obtained a right to it and inevitably seized it, in order to appear and reveal its own inner nature. The law of causality states the condition of this right, the point of time and space where it becomes valid, but the explanation based on this law goes only thus far. The force itself is phenomenon of the will, and, as such, is not subject to the forms of the principle of sufficient reason, that is to say, it is groundless. It lies outside all time, is omnipresent, and, so to speak, seems constantly to wait for the appearance of those circumstances under which it can manifest itself and take possession of a definite piece of matter, supplanting the forces that have hitherto governed it. All time exists only for the phenomenon of the force, and is without significance for the force itself. For thousands of years chemical forces slumber in matter, till contact with the reagents sets them free; then they appear, but time exists only for this phenomenon or appearance, not for the forces themselves. For thousands of years galvanism slumbers in copper and zinc, and they lie quietly beside silver, which must go up in flames as soon as all three come into contact under the required conditions. Even in the organic kingdom, we see a dry seed preserve the slumbering force for three thousand years, and with the ultimate appearance of favourable circumstances grow up as a plant.[13]

If from this discussion we now clearly understand the difference between the force of nature and all its phenomena; if we have clearly seen that the former is the will itself at this definite stage of its objectification, but that plurality comes to phenomena only through time and space, and that the law of causality is nothing but the determination in time and space of the position of the individual phenomena, then we shall also recognize the perfect truth and deep meaning of Malebranche's doctrine of occasional causes. It is well worth while to compare this doctrine of his, as he explains it in the *Recherches de la Vérité,* especially in the third chapter of the second part of the sixth book, and in the *éclaircissements*[14] appended to that chapter, with my present description, and to observe the perfect agreement of the two doctrines, in spite of so great a difference in the trains of thought. Indeed, I must admire how Malebranche, though completely involved in the positive dogmas inevitably forced on him by the men of his time, nevertheless, in such bonds and under such a burden, hit on the truth so happily, so correctly, and knew how to reconcile it with those very dogmas, at any rate in their language.

For the power of truth is incredibly great and of unutterable endurance. We find frequent traces of it again in all, even the most bizarre and absurd, dogmas of different times and countries, often

---

[13] On 16 September 1840, at a lecture on Egyptian Antiquities given at the Literary and Scientific Institute of London, Mr. Pettigrew exhibited some grains of wheat, found by Sir G. Wilkinson in a grave at Thebes, in which they must have been lying for three thousand years. They were found in a hermetically sealed vase. He had sown twelve grains, and from them had a plant which had grown to a height of five feet, whose seeds were now perfectly ripe. From *The Times,* 21 September 1840. In the same way, in 1830, Mr. Haulton produced at the Medical Botanical Society in London a bulbous root that had been found in the hand of an Egyptian mummy. It may have been put there from religious considerations, and was at least two thousand years old. He had planted it in a flower-pot, where it had at once grown up and was flourishing. This is quoted from the *Medical Journal* of 1830 in the *Journal of the Royal Institution of Great Britain,* October 1830, p. 196. "In the garden of Mr. Grimstone, of the Herbarium, Highgate, London, there is now a pea-plant, producing a full crop of peas, that came from a pea taken from a vase by Mr. Pettigrew and officials of the British Museum. This vase had been found in an Egyptian sarcophagus where it must have been lying for 2,844 years." From *The Times,* 16 August 1844. Indeed, the living toads found in limestone lead to the assumption that even animal life is capable of such a suspension for thousands of years, if this is initiated during hibernation and maintained through special circumstances.

[14] "Explanatory statements." [Tr.]

indeed in strange company, curiously mixed up but yet recognizable. It is then like a plant that germinates under a heap of large stones, but yet climbs up towards the light, working itself through with many deviations and windings, disfigured, bleached, stunted in growth—but yet towards the light.

In any case, Malebranche is right; every natural cause is only an occasional cause. It gives only the opportunity, the occasion, for the phenomenon of that one and indivisible will which is the in-itself of all things, and whose graduated objectification is this whole visible world. Only the appearing, the becoming visible, in such a place and at such a time, is brought about by the cause, and is to that extent dependent on it, but not the whole of the phenomenon, not its inner nature. This is the will itself, to which the principle of sufficient reason has no application, and which is therefore groundless. Nothing in the world has a cause of its existence absolutely and generally, but only a cause from which it exists precisely here and now. That a stone exhibits now gravity, now rigidity, now electricity, now chemical properties, depends on causes, on external impressions, and from these is to be explained. But those properties themselves, and hence the whole of its inner being which consists of them, and consequently manifests itself in all the ways mentioned, and thus in general that the stone is such as it is, that it exists generally—all this has no ground, but is the becoming visible of the groundless will. Thus every cause is an occasional cause. We have found it in nature-without-knowledge, but it is also precisely the same where motives, and not causes or stimuli, determine the point of entry of the phenomena, and hence in the actions of animals and of human beings. For in both cases it is one and the same will that appears, extremely different in the grades of its manifestation, multiplied in their phenomena, and, in regard to them, subject to the principle of sufficient reason, but in itself free from all this. Motives do not determine man's character, but only the phenomenon or appearance of that character, that is, the deeds and actions, the external form of the course of his life, not its inner significance and content. These proceed from the character which is the immediate phenomenon of the will, and is therefore groundless. That one man is wicked and another good does not depend on motives and external influences such as teaching and preaching; and in this sense the thing is absolutely inexplicable. But whether a wicked man shows his wickedness in petty injustices, cowardly tricks, and low villainy, practised by him in the narrow sphere of his surroundings, or as a conqueror oppresses nations, throws a world into misery and distress, and sheds the blood of millions, this is the outward form of his phenomenon or appearance, that which is inessential to it, and it depends on the circumstances in which fate has placed him, on the surroundings, on external influences, on motives. But his decision on these motives can never be explained from them; it proceeds from the will, whose phenomenon this man is. We shall speak of this in the fourth book. The way in which the character discloses its qualities can be fully compared with the way in which every body in nature-without-knowledge reveals its qualities. Water remains water with the qualities inherent in it. But whether as a calm lake it reflects its banks, or dashes in foam over rocks, or by artificial means spouts into the air in a tall jet, all this depends on external causes; the one is as natural to it as is the other. But it will always show one or the other according to the circumstances; it is equally ready for all, yet in every case it is true to its character, and always reveals that alone. So also will every human character reveal itself under all circumstances, but the phenomena proceeding from it will be in accordance with the circumstances.

§ 27.

If, from all the foregoing remarks on the forces of nature and their phenomena, we have come to see clearly how far explanation from causes can go, and where it must stop, unless it is to lapse into the foolish attempt to reduce the content of all phenomena to their mere form, when ultimately nothing but form would remain, we shall now be able to determine in general what is to be demanded of all etiology. It has to search for the causes of all phenomena in nature, in other words, for the circumstances under which they always appear. Then it has to refer the many different phenomena having various forms in various circumstances, to what operates in every phenomenon and is presupposed with the cause, namely to original forces of nature. It must correctly distinguish whether a difference of the phenomenon is due to a difference of the force, or only to a difference in the circumstances in which the force manifests itself. With equal care it must guard against regarding as phenomenon of different forces what is merely manifestation of one and the same force under different circumstances, and conversely against regarding as manifestations of one force what belongs originally to different forces. Now this directly requires the power of judgement; hence it is that so few are capable of broadening our insight into physics, but all are able to enlarge experience. Indolence and ignorance make us disposed to appeal too soon to original forces. This is seen with an exaggeration resembling irony in the entities and quiddities of the scholastics. Nothing is farther from my desire than to favour their reintroduction. We are as little permitted to appeal to the objectification of the will, instead of giving a physical explanation, as to appeal to the creative power of God. For physics demands causes, but the will is never a cause. Its relation to the phenomenon is certainly not in accordance with the principle of sufficient reason; but that which in itself is will, exists on the other hand as representation, that is to say, is phenomenon. As such, it follows the laws that constitute the form of the phenomenon. For example, although every movement is always phenomenon of will, it must nevertheless have a cause from which it is to be explained with reference to a definite time and place, in other words, not in general according to its inner nature, but as a *particular* phenomenon. In the case of the stone, this cause is mechanical; in the case of a man's movement, it is a motive; but it can never be absent. On the other hand, the universal, the common reality, of all phenomena of a definite kind, that which must be presupposed if explanation from the cause is to have sense or meaning, is the universal force of nature, which in physics must remain a *qualitas occulta,* just because etiological explanation here ends and the metaphysical begins. But the chain of causes and effects is never interrupted by an original force to which appeal has to be made. It does not run back to this force, as if it were the first link, but the nearest link of the chain, as well as the remotest, presupposes the original force, and could otherwise explain nothing. A series of causes and effects can be the phenomenon of the most various kinds of forces; the successive entry of such forces into visibility is conducted through the series, as I have illustrated above by the example of a metal machine. But the variety of these original forces, that cannot be derived from one another, in no way interrupts the unity of that chain of causes, and the connexion between all its links. The etiology and the philosophy of nature never interfere with each other; on the contrary, they go hand in hand, considering the same object from different points of view. Etiology gives an account of the causes which necessarily produce the particular phenomenon to be explained. It shows, as the basis of all its explanations, the universal forces that are active in all these causes and effects. It accurately determines these forces, their number, their differences, and then all the effects in which each force appears differently according to the difference of the circumstances, always in keeping with its own peculiar character. It discloses this character in accordance with an infallible rule that is called a *law of nature*. As soon as physics has achieved all this completely in every respect, it has attained perfection. In inorganic nature there is then no longer any force unknown, and there is no longer any effect which has not been shown to be the phenomenon of one of those forces under definite circumstances according to a law of nature. However, a law of nature remains merely the observed rule by which nature proceeds every time, as soon as certain definite circumstances arise. Therefore we can certainly define a law of nature as a fact generally expressed, *un fait généralisé.* Accordingly, a complete statement of all the laws of nature would be only a complete catalogue of facts. The consideration of the whole of nature is then completed by *morphology,* which enumerates, compares, and arranges all the enduring forms of organic nature. It has little to say about the cause of the appearance of individual beings, for this in the case of all is procreation, the theory of which is a separate matter; and in rare cases it is *generatio aequivoca.* But to this last belongs, strictly speaking, the way in which all the lower grades of the will's objectivity, that is, physical and chemical phenomena, appear in detail, and it is precisely the task of etiology to state the conditions for the appearance of these. On the other hand, philosophy everywhere, and hence in nature also, considers the universal alone. Here the original forces themselves are its object, and it recognizes in them the different grades of the objectification of the will that is the inner nature, the in-itself, of this world. When it regards the world apart from will, it declares it to be the mere representation of the subject. But if etiology, instead of paving the way for philosophy and supplying its doctrines with application by examples, imagines that its aim is rather to deny all original forces, except perhaps one, the most universal, e.g., impenetrability, which it imagines that it thoroughly understands, and to which it consequently tries to refer by force all the others, then it withdraws from its own foundation, and can only give us error instead of truth. The content of nature is now supplanted by the form; everything is ascribed to the circumstances working from outside, and nothing to the inner nature of things. If we could actually succeed in this way, then, as we have said already, an arithmetical sum would ultimately solve the riddle of the world. But this path is followed if, as already mentioned, it is thought that all physiological effects ought to be referred to form and combination, thus possibly to electricity, this again to chemical force, and chemical force to mechanism. The mistake of Descartes, for instance, and of all the Atomists, was of this last description. They referred the movement of heavenly bodies to the impact of a fluid, and the qualities to the connexion and form of the atoms. They endeavoured to explain all the phenomena of nature as mere phenomena of impenetrability and cohesion. Although this has been given up, the same thing is done in our day by the electrical, chemical, and mechanical physiologists who obstinately try to explain the whole of life and all the functions of the organism from the "form and combination" of its component parts. In Meckel's *Archiv für Physiologie*, 1820, Vol. V, p. 185, we still find it stated that the aim of physiological explanation is the reduction of organic life to the universal forces considered by physics. In his *Philosophie zoologique* (Vol. II, chap. 3) Lamarck also declares life to be a mere effect of heat and electricity: *le calorique et la matière électrique suffisent parfaitement pour composer ensemble cette cause essentielle de la vie* (p. 16).[15] Accordingly, heat and electricity would really be the thing-in-itself, and the animal and plant worlds its phenomenon. The absurdity of this opinion stands out glaringly on pages 306 *seqq.* of that work. It is well known that all those views, so often exploded, have again appeared with renewed audacity in recent times. If we examine the matter closely, then ultimately at the basis of these views is the presupposition that the organism is only an aggregate of phenomena of physical, chemical, and mechanical forces that have come together in it by chance, and have brought about the organism as a freak of nature without further significance. Accordingly, the organism of an animal or of a human being would be, philosophically considered, not the exhibition of a particular Idea, in other words, not itself immediate objectivity of the will at a definite higher grade, but there would appear in it only those Ideas that objectify the will in electricity, chemistry, and mechanism. Hence the organism would be just as fortuitously put together from the chance meeting of these forces as are the forms of men and animals in clouds or stalactites; and hence in itself it would be no more interesting. However, we shall see immediately to what extent this application of physical and chemical methods of explanation to the organism may still, within certain limits, be permissible and useful, for I shall explain that the vital force certainly avails itself of and uses the forces of inorganic nature. Yet these forces in no way constitute the vital force, any more than a hammer and an anvil constitute a blacksmith. Therefore, not even the simplest plant life can ever be explained from them, say from capillary attraction and endosmosis, much less animal life. The following observations will prepare for us the way to this somewhat difficult discussion.

---

[15] "Heat and electric matter are wholly sufficient to make up this essential cause of life." [Tr.]

From all that has been said, it follows that it is indeed a mistake of natural science for it to try to refer the higher grades of the will's objectivity to lower ones. Failing to recognize and denying original and self-existing natural forces is just as unsound as is the groundless assumption of characteristic forces, where what occurs is only a particular kind of manifestation of something already known. Therefore Kant is right when he says that it is absurd to hope for the Newton of a blade of grass, in other words, for the man who would reduce the blade of grass to phenomena of physical and chemical forces, of which it would be a chance concretion, and so a mere freak of nature. In such a freak no special and characteristic Idea would appear, that is to say, the will would not directly reveal itself in it at a higher and special grade, but only as in the phenomena of inorganic nature, and by chance in this form. The scholastics, who would certainly not have allowed such things, would have said quite rightly that it would be a complete denial of the *forma substantialis,* and a degrading of it to the mere *forma accidentalis.* For Aristotle's *forma substantialis* denotes exactly what I call the degree of the will's objectification in a thing. On the other hand, it must not be overlooked that in all Ideas, that is to say, in all the forces of inorganic and in all the forms of organic nature, it is *one and the same will* that reveals itself, i.e., enters the form of representation, enters *objectivity.* Therefore, its unity must make itself known also through an inner relationship between all its phenomena. Now this reveals itself at the higher grades of the will's objectivity, where the whole phenomenon is more distinct, and thus in the plant and animal kingdoms, through the universally prevailing analogy of all forms, namely the fundamental type recurring in all phenomena. This has therefore become the guiding principle of the admirable zoological systems begun by the French in the nineteenth century, and is most completely established in comparative anatomy as *l'unité de plan, l'uniformité de l'élément anatomique.*[16] To discover this fundamental type has been the main concern, or certainly at any rate the most laudable endeavour, of the natural philosophers of Schelling's school. In this respect they have much merit, although in many cases their hunting for analogies in nature degenerates into mere facetiousness. However, they have rightly shown the universal relationship and family likeness even in the Ideas of inorganic nature, for instance between electricity and magnetism, the identity of which was established later; between chemical attraction and gravitation, and so on. They drew special attention to the fact that *polarity,* that is to say, the sundering of a force into two qualitatively different and opposite activities striving for

[16] "Unity of plan, uniformity of the anatomical element." [Tr.]

reunion, a sundering which also frequently reveals itself spatially by a dispersion in opposite directions, is a fundamental type of almost all the phenomena of nature, from the magnet and the crystal up to man. Yet in China this knowledge has been current since the earliest times in the doctrine of the contrast of *Yin* and *Yang.* Indeed, since all things in the world are the objectivity of one and the same will, and consequently identical according to their inner nature, there must be between them that unmistakable analogy, and in everything less perfect there must be seen the trace, outline, and plan of the next more perfect thing. Moreover, since all these forms belong only to the world as *representation,* it can even be assumed that, in the .most universal forms of the representation, in this peculiar framework of the appearing phenomenal world, and thus in space and time, it is already possible to discover and establish the fundamental type, outline, and plan of all that fills the forms. It seems to have been an obscure discernment of this that was the origin of the Kabbala and of all the mathematical philosophy of the Pythagoreans, as well as of the Chinese in the *I Ching.* Also in the school of Schelling we find, among their many different efforts to bring to light the analogy between all the phenomena of nature, many attempts, although unfortunate ones, to derive laws of nature from the mere laws of space and time. However, we cannot know how far the mind of a genius will one day realize both endeavours.

Now the difference between phenomenon and thing-in-itself is never to be lost sight of, and therefore the identity of the will objectified in all Ideas (because it has definite grades of its objectivity) can never be distorted into an identity of the particular Ideas themselves in which the will appears; thus, for example, chemical or electrical attraction can never be reduced to attraction through gravitation, although their inner analogy is known, and the former can be regarded, so to speak, as higher powers of the latter. Just as little does the inner analogy in the structure of all animals justify us in mixing and identifying the species, and in declaring the more perfect to be variations of the less perfect. Finally, although the physiological functions are likewise never to be reduced to chemical or physical processes, yet, in justification of this method of procedure, we can, within certain limits, assume the following as highly probable.

If several of the phenomena of will at the lower grades of its objectification, that is, in inorganic nature, come into conflict with one another, because each under the guidance of causality wants to take possession of the existing matter, there arises from this conflict the phenomenon of a higher Idea. This higher Idea subdues all the less perfect phenomena previously existing, yet in such a way that it allows their essential nature to continue in a subordinate manner, since it takes up into itself an analogue of them. This process is intelligible only from the identity of the will apparent in all the Ideas, and from its striving for higher and higher objectification. Thus, for example, we see in the solidifying of bones an unmistakable analogy of crystallization, which originally controlled the lime, although ossification is never to be reduced to crystallization. This analogy appears more feebly in flesh becoming firm. The combination of humours in the animal body and secretion are also an analogue of chemical combination and separation. Indeed, the laws of chemistry continue to operate here, but are subordinated, much modified, and subdued by a higher Idea. Hence mere chemical forces outside the organism will never furnish such humours, but

> *Encheiresin naturae,* this Chemistry names,
> Nor knows how herself she banters and blames!
> Goethe [*Faust,* Part I].

The more perfect Idea, resulting from such a victory over several lower Ideas or objectifications of the will, gains an entirely new character just by taking up into itself from each of the subdued Ideas an analogue of higher power. The will is objectified in a new and more distinct way. There arise originally through *generatio aequivoca,* subsequently through assimilation to the existing germ, organic humour, plant, animal, man. Thus from the contest of lower phenomena the higher one arises, swallowing up all of them, but also realizing in the higher degree the tendency of them all. Accordingly, the law *Serpens, nisi serpentem comederit, non fit draco*[17] already applies here.

I wish it had been possible for me by clearness of explanation to dispel the obscurity that clings to the subject-matter of these thoughts. But I see quite well that the reader's own observation must help me a great deal, if I am not to remain uncomprehended or misunderstood. According to the view I have put forth, we shall certainly find in the organism traces of chemical and physical modes of operation, but we shall never explain the organism from these, because it is by no means a phenomenon brought about by the united operation of such forces, and therefore by accident, but a higher Idea that has subdued these lower ones through *overwhelming assimilation.* For the one will, that objectifies itself in all Ideas, strives for the highest possible objectification, and in this case gives up the low grades of its

---

[17] "The serpent can become the dragon only by swallowing the serpent." [Bacon, *Sermones Fideles* 38.—Tr.]

phenomenon after a conflict, in order to appear in a higher grade that is so much the more powerful. No victory without struggle; since the higher Idea or objectification of will can appear only by subduing the lower Ideas, it endures the opposition of these. Although these lower Ideas have been brought into subjection, they still constantly strive to reach an independent and complete expression of their inner nature. The magnet that has lifted a piece of iron keeps up a perpetual struggle with gravitation which, as the lowest objectification of the will, has a more original right to the matter of that iron. In this constant struggle, the magnet even grows stronger, since the resistance stimulates it, so to speak, to greater exertion. In the same way, every phenomenon of the will, and even that which manifests itself in the human organism, keeps up a permanent struggle against the many chemical and physical forces that, as lower Ideas, have a prior right to that matter. Thus a man's arm falls which he held upraised for a while by overcoming gravity. Hence the comfortable feeling of health which expresses the victory of the Idea of the organism, conscious of itself, over the physical and chemical laws which originally controlled the humours of the body. Yet this comfortable feeling is so often interrupted, and in fact is always accompanied by a greater or lesser amount of discomfort, resulting from the resistance of those forces; through such discomfort the vegetative part of our life is constantly associated with a slight pain. Thus digestion depresses all the animal functions, because it claims the whole vital force for overcoming by assimilation the chemical forces of nature. Hence also generally the burden of physical life, the necessity of sleep, and ultimately of death; for at last, favoured by circumstances, those subdued forces of nature win back from the organism, wearied even by constant victory, the matter snatched from them, and attain to the unimpeded expression of their being. It can therefore be said that every organism represents the Idea of which it is the image or copy, only after deduction of that part of its force which is expended in overcoming the lower Ideas that strive with it for the matter. This seems to have been present in the mind of Jacob Boehme, when he says somewhere that all the bodies of men and animals, and even all plants, are really half dead. Now, according as the organism succeeds more or less in subduing those natural forces that express the lower grades of the will's objectivity, it becomes the more or less perfect expression of its Idea, in other words, it stands nearer to or farther from the *Ideal* to which beauty in its species belongs.

Thus everywhere in nature we see contest, struggle, and the fluctuation of victory, and later on we shall recognize in this more distinctly that variance with itself essential to the will. Every grade of the will's objectification fights for the matter, the space, and the time of another. Persistent matter must constantly change the form, since, under the guidance of causality, mechanical, physical, chemical, and organic phenomena, eagerly striving to appear, snatch the matter from one another, for each wishes to reveal its own Idea. This contest can be followed through the whole of nature; indeed only through it does nature exist: εἰ γὰρ μὴ ἦν τὸ νεῖκος ἐν τοῖς πράγμασιν, ἓν ἂν ἦν ἅπαντα, ὥς φησίν 'Εμπεδοκλῆς. (*nam si non inesset in rebus contentio, unum omnia essent, ut ait Empedocles.* Aristotle, *Metaphysica,* ii, 5 [4]).[18] Yet this strife itself is only the revelation of that variance with itself that is essential to the will. This universal conflict is to be seen most clearly in the animal kingdom. Animals have the vegetable kingdom for their nourishment, and within the animal kingdom again every animal is the prey and food of some other. This means that the matter in which an animal's Idea manifests itself must stand aside for the manifestation of another Idea, since every animal can maintain its own existence only by the incessant elimination of another's. Thus the will-to-live generally feasts on itself, and is in different forms its own nourishment, till finally the human race, because it subdues all the others, regards nature as manufactured for its own use. Yet, as will be seen in the fourth book, this same human race reveals in itself with terrible clearness that conflict, that variance of the will with itself, and we get *homo homini lupus.*[19] However, we shall again recognize the same contest, the same subjugation, just as well at the low grades of the will's objectivity. Many insects (especially the ichneumon flies) lay their eggs on the skin, and even in the body, of the larvae of other insects, whose slow destruction is the first task of the newly hatched brood. The young hydra, growing out of the old one as a branch, and later separating itself therefrom, fights while it is still firmly attached to the old one for the prey that offers itself, so that the one tears it out of the mouth of the other (Trembley, *Poly-pod.* II, p. 110, and III, p. 165). But the most glaring example of this kind is afforded by the bulldog-ant of Australia, for when it is cut in two, a battle begins between the head and the tail. The head attacks the tail with its teeth, and the tail defends itself bravely by stinging the head. The contest usually lasts for half an hour, until they die or are dragged away by other ants. This takes place every time. (From a letter by Howitt in the *W. Journal,* reprinted in *Galignani's Messenger,* 17 November 1855.) On the banks of the Missouri one sometimes sees a mighty oak with its trunk and all its

---

[18] "For, as Empedocles says, if strife did not rule in things, then all would be a unity." [Tr.]

[19] "Man is a wolf for man." [Plautus, *Asinaria.*—Tr.]

branches so entwined, fettered, and interlaced by a gigantic wild vine, that it must wither as if choked. The same thing shows itself even at the lowest grades, for example where, through organic assimilation, water and carbon are converted into the sap of plants, plants or bread into blood; and so wherever, with the restriction of chemical forces to a subordinate mode of operation, animal secretion takes place. It also occurs in inorganic nature, when, for example, crystals in process of formation meet, cross, and disturb one another, so that they are unable to show the purely crystalline form; for almost every druse is the copy of such a conflict of the will at that low grade of its objectification. Or again, when a magnet forces magnetism on iron, in order to manifest its Idea in it; or when galvanism overcomes elective affinities, decomposes the closest combinations, and so entirely suspends the laws of chemistry that the acid of a salt, decomposed at the negative pole, must pass to the positive pole without combining with the alkalis through which it passes on its way, or without being able to turn red the litmus paper it touches. On a large scale, it shows itself in the relation between central body and planet; for although the planet is decidedly dependent, it always resists, just like the chemical forces in the organism. From this there results the constant tension between centripetal and centrifugal forces which keeps the globe in motion, and is itself an expression of that universal conflict which is essential to the phenomenon of the will, and which we are now considering. For, as every body must be regarded as the phenomenon of a will, which will necessarily manifests itself as a striving, the original condition or state of every heavenly body formed into a globe cannot be rest, but motion, a striving forward into endless space, without rest or aim. Neither the law of inertia nor that of causality is opposed to this. According to the law of inertia, matter as such is indifferent to rest and motion, and so its original condition can just as well be motion as rest. Therefore, if we first find it in motion, we are just as little entitled to assume that a state of rest preceded this, and to ask about the cause of the appearance of the motion, as conversely, if we found it at rest, we should be to assume a motion preceding this, and ask about the cause of its elimination. Therefore we cannot seek a first impulse for the centrifugal force, but in the case of the planets it is, according to the hypothesis of Kant and Laplace, the residue of the original rotation of the central body from which the planets were separated as it contracted. But to this central body itself motion is essential; it still always rotates, and at the same time sweeps along in endless space; or possibly it circulates round a greater central body invisible to us. This view agrees entirely with the conjecture of astronomers about a central sun, as well as with the observed advance of our whole solar system, and perhaps of the whole cluster of stars to which our sun belongs. From this we are led finally to infer a general advance of all fixed stars together with the central sun. Naturally this loses all meaning in endless space (for motion in absolute space does not differ from rest), and, as directly through striving and aimless flight, it thus becomes the expression of that nothingness, that lack of an ultimate purpose or object, which at the close of this book we shall have to attribute to the striving of the will in all its phenomena. Thus again, endless space and endless time must be the most universal and essential forms of the collective phenomenon of the will, which exists for the expression of its whole being. Finally, we can once more recognize the conflict we are considering of all the phenomena of the will with one another even in mere matter considered as such, namely in so far as the essential nature of its phenomenon is correctly expressed by Kant as repulsive and attractive force. Thus matter has its existence only in a struggle of conflicting forces. If we abstract from all chemical difference of matter, or if we think back so far in the chain of causes and effects that no chemical difference as yet exists, we are then left with mere matter, the world rounded into a globe. The life of this, i.e., objectification of the will, is now formed by the conflict between the force of attraction and that of repulsion. The former as gravitation presses from all sides towards the centre; the latter as impenetrability resists the former, either as rigidity or as elasticity. This constant pressure and resistance can be regarded as the objectivity of the will at the very lowest grade, and even there it expresses its character.

Here we see at the very lowest grade the will manifesting itself as a blind impulse, an obscure, dull urge, remote from all direct knowableness. It is the simplest and feeblest mode of its objectification. But it appears as such a blind urge and as a striving devoid of knowledge in the whole of inorganic nature, in all the original forces. It is the business of physics and chemistry to look for these forces and to become acquainted with their laws. Each of these forces manifests itself to us in millions of exactly similar and regular phenomena, showing no trace of individual character, but is merely multiplied through time and space, i.e., through the *principium individuationis,* just as a picture is multiplied through the facets of a glass.

Objectifying itself more distinctly from grade to grade, yet still completely without knowledge as an obscure driving force, the will acts in the plant kingdom. Here not causes proper, but stimuli, are the bond or its phenomena. Finally, it also acts in the vegetative part of the animal phenomenon, in the production and formation of every animal, and in the maintenance of its interior economy, where mere stimuli still always determine its phenomenon. The higher and higher grades of the will's objectivity lead ultimately to the point where the individual expressing the Idea could no longer obtain its food for assimilation through mere movement consequent on stimuli. Such a stimulus must be waited for; but here the food is of a kind that is more specially determined, and with the ever-growing multiplicity of the phenomena, the crowd and confusion have become so great that they disturb one another, and the chance event from which the individual moved by mere stimuli has to expect its food would be too unfavourable. The food must therefore be sought and selected, from the point where the animal has delivered itself from the egg or the womb in which it vegetated without knowledge. Thus movement consequent on motives and, because of this, knowledge, here become necessary; and hence knowledge enters as an expedient, μηχανή, required at this stage of the will's objectification for the preservation of the individual and the propagation of the species. It appears represented by the brain or a larger ganglion, just as every other effort or determination of the self-objectifying will is represented by an organ, in other words, is manifested for the representation as an organ.[20] But with this expedient, with this μηχανή, the *world as representation* now stands out at one stroke with all its forms, object and subject, time, space, plurality, and causality. The world now shows its second side; hitherto mere *will*, it is now at the same time *representation,* object of the knowing subject. The will, which hitherto followed its tendency in the dark with extreme certainty and infallibility, has at this stage kindled a light for itself. This was a means that became necessary for getting rid of the disadvantage which would result from the throng and the complicated nature of its phenomena, and would accrue precisely to the most perfect of them. The hitherto infallible certainty and regularity with which the will worked in inorganic and merely vegetative nature, rested on the fact that it alone in its original inner being was active as blind urge, as will, without assistance, but also without interruption, from a second and entirely different world, namely the world as representation. Indeed, such a world is only the copy of the will's own inner being, but yet it is of quite a different nature, and now intervenes in the sequence of phenomena of the

---

[20] Cf. chap. 22 of volume 2, also my work *Über den Willen in der Natur,* pp. 54 *seqq.* and 70-79 of the first edition, or pp. 46 *seqq.* and 63-72 of the second.

will. Thus their infallible certainty now comes to an end. Animals already are exposed to illusion, to deception; they, however, have merely representations from perception, no concepts, no reflection; they are therefore bound to the present, and cannot take the future into consideration. It appears as if this knowledge without reason was not in all cases sufficient for its purpose, and occasionally needed some assistance, as it were. For we have the very remarkable phenomenon that the blind working of the will and that enlightened by knowledge encroach in a most astonishing way on each other's spheres in two kinds of phenomena. In the one case we find, amid those actions of animals that are guided by knowledge of perception and its motives, one action that is carried out without these, and hence with the necessity of the blindly operating will. I refer to the mechanical instincts; these, not guided by any motive or knowledge, have the appearance of bringing about their operations from abstract rational motives. The other case, the opposite of this, is that where, on the contrary, the light of knowledge penetrates into the workshop of the blindly operating will, and illuminates the vegetative functions of the human organism. I refer to magnetic clairvoyance. Finally, where the will has attained to the highest degree of its objectification, knowledge of the understanding, which has dawned on the animals, for which the senses supply the data, and out of which arises mere perception or intuition bound to the present, no longer suffices. That complicated, many-sided, flexible being, man, who is extremely needy and exposed to innumerable shocks and injuries, had to be illuminated by a twofold knowledge in order to be able to exist. A higher power of knowledge of perception, so to speak, had to be added to this, a reflection of that knowledge of perception, namely reason as the faculty for forming abstract concepts. With this there came into existence thoughtfulness, surveying the future and the past, and, as a consequence thereof, deliberation, care, ability for premeditated action independent of the present, and finally the fully distinct consciousness of the decisions of one's own will as such. Now with the mere knowledge of perception there arises the possibility of illusion and deception, whereby the previous infallibility of the will acting without knowledge is abolished. Thus mechanical and other instincts, as manifestations of the will-without-knowledge, have to come to its aid, guided in the midst of manifestations from knowledge. Then with the appearance of reason, this certainty and infallibility of the will's manifestations (appearing at the other extreme in inorganic nature as strict conformity to law) are almost entirely lost. Instinct withdraws altogether; deliberation, now supposed to take the place of everything, begets (as was explained in the first book) irresolution and uncertainty. Error becomes possible, and in many cases obstructs the adequate objectification of the will through actions. For although the will has already taken in the character its definite and unalterable course, in accordance with which the willing itself invariably occurs on the occasion of motives, error can still falsify the manifestations of the will, since delusive motives, resembling the real ones, slip in and abolish these.[21] For example, when superstition foists on to a man imaginary motives that compel him to a course of action directly opposed to the way in which his will would otherwise manifest itself in the existing circumstances. Agamemnon slays his daughter; a miser dispenses alms out of pure egoism, in the hope of one day being repaid a hundredfold, and so on.

Thus knowledge in general, rational knowledge as well as mere knowledge from perception, proceeds originally from the will itself, belongs to the inner being of the higher grades of the will's objectifications as a mere μηχανή, a means for preserving the individual and the species, just like any organ of the body. Therefore, destined originally to serve the will for the achievement of its aims, knowledge remains almost throughout entirely subordinate to its service; this is the case with all animals and almost all men. However, we shall see in the third book how, in the case of individual persons, knowledge can withdraw from this subjection, throw off its yoke, and, free from all the aims of the will, exist purely for itself, simply as a clear mirror of the world; and this is the source of art. Finally, in the fourth book we shall see how, if this kind of knowledge reacts on the will, it can bring about the will's self-elimination, in other words, resignation. This is the ultimate goal, and indeed the innermost nature of all virtue and holiness, and is salvation from the world.

---

[21] The scholastics therefore said quite rightly: *Causa finalis movet non secundum suum esse reale, sed secundum esse cognitum.* See Suarez, *Disp. Metaph.,* disp. XXIII, sect. 7 *et* 8. ("The final cause operates not according to its real being, but only according to its being as that is known." [Tr.]

§ 28.

We have considered the great multiplicity and diversity of the phenomena in which the will objectifies itself; indeed, we have seen their endless and implacable struggle with one another. Yet, in pursuit of the whole of our discussion so far, the will itself, as thing-in-itself, is by no means included in that plurality, that change. The diversity of the (Platonic) Ideas, i.e., gradations of objectification, the multitude of individuals in which each of them manifests itself, the struggle of the forms for matter—all this does not concern it, but is only the manner of its objectification, and only through such objectification has all this an indirect relation to the will, by virtue of which it belongs to the expression of the inner nature of the will for the representation. Just as a magic lantern shows many different pictures, but it is only one and the same flame that makes them all visible, so in all the many different phenomena which together fill the world or supplant one another as successive events, it is only the *one will* that appears, and everything is its visibility, its objectivity; it remains unmoved in the midst of this change. It alone is the thing-in-itself; every object is phenomenon, to speak Kant's language, or appearance. Although in man, as (Platonic) Idea, the will finds its most distinct and perfect objectification, this alone could not express its true being. In order to appear in its proper significance, the Idea of man would need to manifest itself, not alone and torn apart, but accompanied by all the grades downwards through all the forms of animals, through the plant kingdom to the inorganic. They all supplement one another for the complete objectification of the will. They are as much presupposed by the Idea of man as the blossoms of the tree presuppose its leaves, branches, trunk, and root. They form a pyramid, of which the highest point is man. If we are fond of similes, we can also say that their appearance or phenomenon accompanies that of man as necessarily as the full light of day is accompanied by all the gradations of partial shadow through which it loses itself in darkness. Or we can also call them the echo of man, and say that animal and plant are the descending fifth and third of man, the inorganic kingdom being the lower octave. The full truth of this last simile will become clear to us only when, in the next book, we attempt to fathom the deep significance of music. There we shall see how the connected melody, progressing in high, light, and quick notes, is to be regarded in a certain sense as expressing the life and efforts of man, connected by reflection. The ripienos and the heavily moving bass, on the other hand, from which arises the harmony necessary for the perfection of the music, are a copy of the rest of animal nature and of nature-without-knowledge. But of this in its proper place, where it will no longer sound so paradoxical. But we also find that the *inner necessity* of the gradation of the will's phenomena, inseparable from the adequate objectivity of the will, is expressed by an *outer necessity* in the whole of these phenomena themselves. By virtue of such necessity, man needs the animals for his support, the animals in their grades need one another, and also the plants, which again need soil, water, chemical elements and their combinations, the planet, the sun, rotation and motion round the sun, the obliquity of the ecliptic, and so on. At bottom, this springs from the fact that the will must live on itself, since nothing exists besides it, and it is a hungry will. Hence arise pursuit, hunting, anxiety, and suffering.

Knowledge of the unity of the will as thing-in-itself, amid the endless diversity and multiplicity of the phenomena, alone affords us the true explanation of that wonderful, unmistakable analogy of all nature's productions, of that family likeness which enables us to regard them as variations on the same ungiven theme. In like measure, through the clearly and thoroughly comprehended knowledge of that harmony, of that essential connexion of all the parts of the world, of that necessity of their gradation that we have just been considering, there will be revealed to us a true and sufficient insight into the inner being and meaning of the undeniable *suitability or appropriateness* of all the organic productions of nature, which we even presupposed *a priori* when considering and investigating them.

This *suitability* is of a twofold nature; it is sometimes an *inner* one, that is to say, an agreement of all the parts of an individual organism so ordered that the maintenance of the individual and of its species results therefrom, and thus manifests itself as the purpose of that arrangement. But sometimes the suitability is an *external* one, namely a relation of inorganic to organic nature in general, or of the individual parts of organic nature to one another, which renders possible the maintenance of the whole of organic nature, or even of individual animal species, and thus presents itself to our judgement as the means to this end.

Inner suitability becomes connected with our discussion in the following way. If, according to what has so far been said, all variety of forms in nature and all plurality of individuals belong not to the will, but only to its objectivity and to the form thereof, it necessarily follows that the will is indivisible and is wholly present in every phenomenon, although the degrees of its objectification, the (Platonic) Ideas, are very different. For easier understanding, we may regard these different Ideas as individual, and in themselves simple, acts of will, in which its inner being expresses itself more or less. But the individuals again are phenomena of the Ideas, and hence of those acts, in time, space, and plurality. Now at the lowest grades of objectivity, such an act (or Idea) retains its unity even in the phenomenon; whereas, to appear at the higher grades, it requires a whole series of states and developments in time, all of which, taken together, first achieve the expression of its true being. Thus, for example, the Idea that reveals itself in some universal force of nature has always only a simple expression, although this presents itself differently according to the external relations; otherwise its identity could not be established at all, for this is done simply by abstracting the diversity that springs merely from the external relations. In the same way, the crystal has only one manifestation of life, namely its formation, which afterwards has its fully adequate and exhaustive expression in the coagulated form, in the corpse of that momentary life. The plant, however, does not express the Idea of which it is the phenomenon all at once and through a simple manifestation, but in a succession of developments of its organs in time. The animal develops its organism not only in the same way in a succession of forms often very different (metamorphosis), but this form itself, although objectivity of the will at this grade, does not reach the complete expression of its Idea. On the contrary, this is first completed through the animal's actions, in which its empirical character, the same in the whole species, expresses itself and is first the complete revelation of the Idea, and this presupposes the definite organism as fundamental condition. In the case of man, the empirical character is peculiar to every individual (indeed, as we shall see in the fourth book, even to the complete elimination of the character of the species, namely through the self-elimination of the whole will). That which is known as the empirical character, through the necessary development in time and the division into separate actions conditioned by time, is, with the abstraction of this temporal form of the phenomenon, the *intelligible character,* according to Kant's expression. In establishing this distinction and describing the relation between freedom and necessity, that is to say, between the will as thing-in-itself and its phenomenon, Kant brilliantly reveals his immortal merit.[22] Thus the intelligible character coincides with the Idea, or more properly with the original act of will that reveals itself in the Idea. Therefore to this extent, not only the empirical character of every person, but also that of every animal species, nay, of every plant species, and even of every original force of inorganic nature, is to be regarded as phenomenon or manifestation of an intelligible character, in other words, of an indivisible act of will that is outside time. Incidentally, I should like here to draw attention to the naïvety with which every plant expresses and lays open its whole character through its mere form, and reveals its whole being and willing. That is why the various physiognomies of plants are so interesting. On the other hand, to know an animal according to its Idea, we must observe its action and behaviour, and to know man, we must fully investigate and test him, for his faculty of reason makes him capable of a high degree of dissimulation. The animal is just as much more naïve than man as the plant is more naïve than the animal. In the animal we see the will-to-live more naked, as it were, than in man, where it is clothed in so much knowledge, and, more- over, is so veiled by the capacity for dissimulation that its true nature only comes to light almost by chance and in isolated cases. In the plant it shows itself quite nakedly, but also much more feebly, as mere blind impulse to exist without end and aim. For the plant re- veals its whole being at the first glance and with complete innocence. This does not suffer from the fact that it carries its genitals exposed to view on its upper surface, although with all animals these have been allotted to the most concealed place. This innocence on the part of the plant is due to its want of knowledge; guilt is to be found not in willing, but in willing with knowledge. Every plant tells us first of all about its native place, the climate found there, and the nature of the soil from which it has sprung. Therefore even the person with little experience easily knows whether an exotic plant belongs to the tropical or temperate zone, and whether it grows in water, in marshy country, on mountains or moorland. Moreover, every plant expresses the special will of its species, and says some- thing that cannot be expressed in any other language. But now let us apply what has been said to the teleological consideration of the organisms, in so far as it concerns their inner suitability. In inorganic nature the Idea, to be regarded everywhere as a single act of will,

---

[22] See *Critique of Pure Reason*, "Solution of the Cosmological Ideas of the Totality of the Deduction of World Events," pp. 560-586 of the fifth edition, and pp. 532 *seqǀ.* of the first edition; and *Critique of Practical Reason*, fourth edition, pp. 169-179; Rosenkranz's edition, pp. 224 *seqq.* Cf. my essay *On the Principle of Sufficient Reason*, § 43.

also reveals itself only in a particular and always similar manifestation, and thus it can be said that the empirical character here directly partakes of the unity of the intelligible. It coincides with it, so to speak, so that no inner suitability can show itself. On the other hand, all organisms express their Idea through a succession of developments one after another, conditioned by a multiplicity of coexisting parts. Hence the sum of the manifestations of their empirical character is first the collective expression of the intelligible character. Now this necessary coexistence of the parts and succession of development do not eliminate the unity of the appearing Idea, of the self-manifesting act of will. On the contrary, this unity now finds its expression in the necessary relation and concatenation of those parts and developments with one another, according to the law of causality. Since it is the one indivisible will, which for this reason is wholly in agreement with itself, and reveals itself in the whole Idea as in an act, its phenomenon, though broken up into a variety of different parts and conditions, must yet again show that unity in a thorough harmony of these. This takes place through a necessary relation and dependence of all the parts on one another, whereby the unity of the Idea is also re-established in the phenomenon. Accordingly, we now recognize those different parts and functions of the organism reciprocally as means and end of one another, and the organism itself as the ultimate end of all. Consequently, neither the breaking up of the Idea, in itself simple, into the plurality of the parts and conditions of the organism, on the one hand, nor, on the other, the re-establishment of its unity through the necessary connexion of those parts and functions arising from the fact that they are cause and effect, and hence means and end, of one another, is peculiar and essential to the appearing will as such, to the thing-in-itself, but only to its phenomenon in space, time, and causality (mere modes of the principle of sufficient reason, the form of the phenomenon). They belong to the world as representation, not to the world as will; they belong to the way in which the will becomes object, i.e., representation at this grade of its objectivity. Whoever has penetrated into the meaning of this rather difficult discussion, will now properly understand Kant's doctrine that both the suitability of the organic and the conformity to law of the inorganic are brought into nature first of all by our understanding; hence that both belong only to the phenomenon, not to the thing-in-itself. The above-mentioned admiration caused by the infallible constancy of the conformity to law in inorganic nature is essentially the same as that excited by the suitability in organic nature. For in both cases what surprises us is only the sight of the original unity of the Idea which for the phenomenon has assumed the form of plurality and diversity.[23]

Now, as regards the second kind of suitability, namely the *external,* to follow the division made above, this shows itself not in the inner economy of the organisms, but in the support and assistance they receive from outside, both from inorganic nature and from one another. This second kind finds its explanation in general in the discussion just given, since the whole world with all its phenomena is the objectivity of the one and indivisible will, the Idea, which is related to all the other Ideas as harmony is to the individual voices. Therefore that unity of the will must also show itself in the agreement of all its phenomena with one another. But we can raise this insight to very much greater clearness, if we go somewhat more closely into the phenomena of that outer suitability to and agreement with one another of the different parts of nature, a discussion that will at the same time throw light on the foregoing remarks. We shall best attain this end, however, by considering the following analogy.

The character of each individual man, in so far as it is thoroughly individual and not entirely included in that of the species, can be regarded as a special Idea, corresponding to a particular act of objectification of the will. This act itself would then be his intelligible character, and his empirical character would be its phenomenon. The empirical character is entirely determined by the intelligible that is groundless, that is to say, will as thing-in-itself, not subject to the principle of sufficient reason (the form of the phenomenon). The empirical character must in the course of a lifetime furnish a copy of the intelligible character, and cannot turn out differently from what is demanded by the latter's inner nature. But this disposition extends only to what is essential, not to what is inessential, in the course of the life that accordingly appears. To this inessential belongs the detailed determination of the events and actions which are the material in which the empirical character shows itself. These are determined by external circumstances, furnishing the motives on which the character reacts according to its nature. As they can be very different, the outward form of the empirical character's phenomenon, and so the definite actual or historical shape of the course of life, will have to adjust itself to their influence. Possibly this will turn out very differently, although the essential of this phenomenon, its content, remains the same. Thus, for example, it is not essential whether a man plays for nuts or for crowns; but whether in play a man cheats or goes about it honestly, this is what is essential.

[23] Cf. *Über den Willen in der Natur,* at the end of the section on "Comparative Anatomy."

The latter is determined by the intelligible character, the former by external influence. As the same theme can be presented in a hundred variations, so the same character can be expressed in a hundred very different courses of life. But however varied the outer influence may be, the empirical character, expressing itself in the course of life, must yet, however it may turn out, accurately objectify the intelligible character, since it adapts its objectification to the previously found material of actual circumstances. We have now to assume something analogous to that influence of outer circumstances on the course of life that is determined essentially by the character, if we wish to conceive how the will, in the original act of its objectification, determines the different Ideas in which it objectifies itself, in other words, the different forms of natural existence of every kind. It distributes its objectification among these forms, and these, therefore, must necessarily have in the phenomenon a relation to one another. We must assume that, between all these phenomena of the one will, there took place a universal and reciprocal adaptation and accommodation to one another. But here, as we shall soon see more clearly, all time-determination is to be left out, for the Idea lies outside time. Accordingly, every phenomenon has had to adapt itself to the environment into which it entered, but again the environment also has had to adapt itself to the phenomenon, although it occupies a much later position in time; and this *consensus naturae* we see everywhere. Therefore, every plant is well adapted to its soil and climate, every animal to its element and to the prey that is to become its food, that prey also being protected to a certain extent against its natural hunter. The eye is well adapted to light and its refrangibility, the lungs and the blood to air, the air-bladder of fishes to water, the eye of the seal to the change of its medium, the water-containing cells in the camel's stomach to the drought of the African desert, the sail of the nautilus to the wind that is to drive its tiny ship, and so on down to the most special and astonishing outward instances of suitability.[24] But we must abstract here from all time-relations, as these can concern only the phenomenon of the Idea, not the Idea itself. Accordingly, this kind of explanation is also to be used retrospectively, and it is not merely to be assumed that every species adapted itself to the circumstances previously found, but that these circumstances themselves, which preceded it in time, had just as much regard for the beings that at some future time were to arrive. For it is indeed one and the same will that objectifies itself in the whole world; it knows no time, for that form of the principle of sufficient reason does not belong to it, or to its

[24] See *Über den Willen in der Natur,* the section on "Comparative Anatomy."

original objectivity, namely the Ideas, but only to the way in which these are known by the individuals who are themselves transitory, in other words, to the phenomenon of the Ideas. Therefore as concerns our present discussion, time-sequence is entirely without significance for the way in which the objectification of the will is distributed among the Ideas. The Ideas, the *phenomena* of which entered the time-sequence earlier according to the law of causality to which they as such are subject, have thus no advantage over those whose phenomenon enters later. On the contrary, these last are precisely the most perfect objectifications of the will, to which the earlier phenomena had to adapt themselves, just as much as they had to adapt themselves to the earlier. Thus the course of the planets, the obliquity of the ecliptic, the rotation of the earth, the separation of dry land and sea, the atmosphere, light, heat, and all similar phenomena that are in nature what the ground bass is in harmony, accommodated themselves full of presentiment of the coming species of living beings, of which they were to become the supporter and sustainer. In the same way, the soil adapted itself to the nutrition of plants, plants to the nutrition of animals, animals to the nutrition of other animals, just as, conversely, all these again adapted themselves to the soil. All the parts of nature accommodate themselves to one another, since it is one will that appears in them all, but the time-sequence is quite foreign to its original and only *adequate objectivity,* namely the Ideas (the following book explains this expression). Even now, when the species have only to maintain themselves and no longer to come into existence, we see here and there such a foresight of nature, extending to the future and, so to speak, really abstracting from the time-sequence, a self-adaptation of what exists according to what is yet to come. Thus the bird builds the nest for the young it does not yet know; the beaver erects a dam, whose purpose is unknown to it; the ant, the marmot, and the bee collect stores for the winter that is unknown to them; the spider and the ant-lion build, as if with deliberate cunning, snares for the future prey unknown to them; insects lay their eggs where the future brood will find future nourishment. In the flowering season the female flower of the dioecian *Vallisneria* unwinds the spirals of its stem, by which it was hitherto held at the bottom of the water, and by that means rises to the surface. Just then the male flower, growing on a short stem at the bottom of the water, breaks away therefrom, and so, at the sacrifice of its life, reaches the surface, where it swims about in search of the female flower. The female, after fertilization, then withdraws to the bottom again by contracting its spirals, and there the fruit is developed.[25] Here I must refer once more to the larva of the male stag-beetle which gnaws the hole in the wood for its metamorphosis twice as large as does the female, in order to obtain room for its future horns. Therefore the instinct of animals generally gives us the best explanation for the remaining teleology of nature. For just as an instinct is an action, resembling one according to a concept of purpose, yet entirely without such concept, so are all formation and growth in nature like that which is according to a concept of purpose, and yet entirely without this. In outer as well as in inner teleology of nature, what we must think of as means and end is everywhere only *the phenomenon of the unity of the one will so far in agreement with itself*, which has broken up into space and time for our mode of cognition.

However, the reciprocal adaptation and adjustment of the phenomena springing from this unity cannot eradicate the inner antagonism described above, which appears in the universal conflict of nature, and is essential to the will. That harmony goes only so far as to render possible the *continuance* of the world and its beings, which without it would long since have perished. Therefore it extends only to the continuance of the species and of the general conditions of life, but not to that of individuals. Accordingly, as, by reason of that harmony and accommodation, the *species* in the organic, and the *universal natural forces* in the inorganic, continue to exist side by side and even mutually to support one another, so, on the other hand, the inner antagonism of the will, objectified through all those Ideas, shows itself in the never-ending war of extermination of the *individuals* of those species, and in the constant struggle of the *phenomena* of those natural forces with one another, as was stated above. The scene of action and the object of this conflict is matter that they strive to wrest from one another, as well as space and time, the union of which through the form of causality is really matter, as was explained in the first book.[26]

---

[25] Chatin, "Sur la Valisneria Spiralis," in the *Comptes Rendus de l'Académie des Sciences*, No. 13, 1855.
[26] Cf. chaps. 26 and 27 of volume 2.

§ 29.

Here I conclude the second main part of my discussion in the hope that, as far as is possible in the case of the very first communication of an idea that has never previously existed and therefore cannot be entirely free from those traces of individuality in which it originated, I have succeeded in conveying to the reader the clear certainty that this world in which we live and have our being is, by its whole nature, through and through *will,* and at the same time through and through *representation.* This representation as such already presupposes a form, namely object and subject; consequently it is relative; and if we ask what is left after the elimination of this form and of all the forms subordinate to it and expressed by the principle of sufficient reason, the answer is that, as something *toto genere* different from the representation, this cannot be anything but *will,* which is therefore the *thing-in-itself* proper. Everyone finds himself to be this will, in which the inner nature of the world consists, and he also finds himself to be the knowing subject, whose representation is the whole world; and this world has an existence only in reference to the knowing subject's consciousness as its necessary supporter. Thus everyone in this twofold regard is the whole world itself, the microcosm; he finds its two sides whole and complete within himself. And what he thus recognizes as his own inner being also exhausts the inner being of the whole world, of the macrocosm. Thus the whole world, like man himself, is through and through will and through and through representation, and beyond this there is nothing. So here we see that the philosophy of Thales, concerned with the macrocosm, and that of Socrates, concerned with the microcosm, coincide, since the object of both proves to be the same. But the whole of the knowledge communicated in the first and second books will gain greater completeness, and thus greater certainty, from the two books that follow. In these it is hoped that many a question that may have been raised distinctly or indistinctly in the course of our discussion so far, will find its adequate answer.

In the meantime, *one* such question may be particularly discussed, as, properly speaking, it can be raised only so long as we have not yet fully penetrated into the meaning of the foregoing discussion, and to this extent it can serve as an illustration thereof. It is the following. Every will is a will directed to something; it has an object, an aim of its willing; what then does it ultimately will, or what is that will which is shown to us as the being-in-itself of the world striving after? Like so many others, this question rests on the confusion of the thing-in-itself with the phenomenon. The principle of sufficient reason, of which the law of motivation is also a form, extends only to the phenomenon, not to the thing-in-itself. Everywhere a ground can be given only of phenomena as such, only of individual things, never of the will itself, or of the Idea in which it adequately objectifies itself. Thus of every particular movement, or generally of every change in nature, a cause, in other words, a condition or state that necessarily produced it, is to be sought, but never a cause of the natural force itself that is revealed in that phenomenon and in innumerable similar phenomena. Therefore it is really a misunder-, standing, arising from a want of thoughtfulness, to ask for a cause of gravity, of electricity, and so on. Only if it had been somehow shown that gravity and electricity were not original characteristic forces of nature, but only the modes of appearance of a more universal natural force already known, could one ask about the cause that makes this natural force produce the phenomenon of gravity or electricity in a given case. All this has been discussed in detail already. In the same way, every particular act of will on the part of a knowing individual (which itself is only phenomenon of the will as thing-in-itself) necessarily has a motive, without which that act would never take place. But just as the material cause contains merely the determination that at such a time, in such a place, and in such a matter, a manifestation of this or that natural force must take place, so also the motive determines only the act of will of a knowing being, at such a time, in such a place, and in such and such circumstances, as something quite individual; it by no means determines that that being wills in general and wills in this way. That is the expression of his intelligible character, which, as the will itself, the thing-in-itself, is groundless, for it lies outside the province of the principle of sufficient reason. Therefore every person invariably has purposes and motives by which he guides his conduct; and he is always able to give an account of his particular actions. But if he were asked why he wills generally, or why in general he wills to exist, he would have no answer; indeed, the question would seem to him absurd. This would really be the expression of his consciousness that he himself is nothing but will, and that the willing in general of this will is therefore a matter of course, and requires a more particular determination through motives only in its individual acts at each point of time.

In fact, absence of all aim, of all limits, belongs to the essential nature of the will in itself, which is an endless striving. This was touched on above, when centrifugal force was mentioned. It also reveals itself in the simplest form of the lowest grade of the will's objectivity, namely gravitation, the constant striving of which we see, although a final goal for it is obviously impossible. For if, according to its will, all existing matter were united into a lump, then within this lump gravity, ever striving towards the centre, would still always struggle with impenetrability as rigidity or elasticity. Therefore the striving of matter can always be impeded only, never fulfilled or satisfied. But this is precisely the case with the striving of all the will's phenomena. Every attained end is at the same time the beginning of a new course, and so on *ad infinitum*. The plant raises its phenomenon from the seed through stem and leaf to blossom and fruit, which is in turn only the beginning of a new seed, of a new individual, which once more runs through the old course, and so through endless time. Such also is the life course of the animal; procreation is its highest point, and after this has been attained, the life of the first individual quickly or slowly fades, while a new life guarantees to nature the maintenance of the species, and repeats the same phenomenon. Indeed, the constant renewal of the matter of every organism can also be regarded as the mere phenomenon of this continual pressure and change, and physiologists are now ceasing to regard such renewal as the necessary reparation of the substance consumed in movement. The possible wearing out of the machine cannot in any way be equivalent to the constant inflow through nourishment. Eternal becoming, endless flux, belong to the revelation of the essential nature of the will. Finally, the same thing is also seen in human endeavours and desires that buoy us up with the vain hope that their fulfilment is always the final goal of willing. But as soon as they are attained, they no longer look the same, and so are soon forgotten, become antiquated, and are really, although not admittedly, always laid aside as vanished illusions. It is fortunate enough when something to desire and to strive for still remains, so that the game may be kept up of the constant transition from desire to satisfaction, and from that to a fresh desire, the rapid course of which is called happiness, the slow course sorrow, and so that this game may not come to a standstill, showing itself as a fearful, life-destroying boredom, a lifeless longing without a definite object, a deadening languor. According to all this, the will always knows, when knowledge enlightens it, what it wills here and now, but never what it wills in general. Every individual act has a purpose or end; willing as a whole has no end in view. In the same way, every individual phenomenon of nature is determined by a sufficient cause as regards its appearance in such a place and at such a time, but the force manifesting itself in this phenomenon has in general no cause, for such a force is a stage of appearance of the thing-in-itself, of the groundless will. The sole self-knowledge of the will as a whole is the representation as a whole, the whole world of perception. It is the objectivity, the revelation, the mirror of the will. What it expresses in this capacity will be the subject of our further consideration.[27]

[27] Cf. chap. 28 of volume 2.

THIRD BOOK

THE WORLD AS REPRESENTATION

SECOND ASPECT

The Representation Independent of the Principle of Sufficient Reason:
The Platonic Idea: The Object of Art

τί τὸ ὂν μὲν ἀεί, γένεσιν δὲ οὐκ ἔχον; καὶ τὶ τὸ γιγνόμενον μὲν καὶ
ἀπολλύμενον, ὄντως δὲ οὐδέποτε ὄν; Plato [*Timaeus*, 27 D].

("What is that which eternally is, which has no origin? And what
is that which arises and passes away, but in truth never is?" [Tr.])

§ 30.

In the first book the world was shown to be mere representation, object for a subject. In the second book, we considered it from its other side, and found that this is *will*, which proved to be simply what this world is besides being representation. In accordance with this knowledge, we called the world as representation, both as a whole and in its parts, the *objectivity of the will*, which accordingly means the will become object, i.e., representation. Now we recall further that such objectification of the will had many but definite grades, at which, with gradually increasing distinctness and completeness, the inner nature of the will appeared in the representation, in other words, presented itself as object. In these grades we recognized the Platonic Ideas once more, namely in so far as such grades are just the definite species, or the original unchanging forms and properties of all natural bodies, whether organic or inorganic, as well as the universal forces that reveal themselves according to natural laws. Therefore these Ideas as a whole present themselves in innumerable individuals and in isolated details, and are related to them as the archetype is to its copies. The plurality of such individuals can be conceived only through time and space, their arising and passing away through causality. In all these forms we recognize only the different aspects of the principle of sufficient reason that is the ultimate principle of all finiteness, of all individuation, and the universal form of the representation as it comes to the knowledge of the individual as such. On the other hand, the Idea does not enter into that principle; hence neither plurality nor change belongs to it. While the individuals in which it expresses itself are innumerable and are incessantly coming into existence and passing away, it remains unchanged as one and the same, and the principle of sufficient reason has no meaning for it. But now, as this principle is the form under which all knowledge of the subject comes, in so far as the subject knows as an *individual,* the Ideas will also lie quite outside the sphere of its knowledge as such. Therefore, if the Ideas are to become object of knowledge, this can happen only by abolishing individuality in the knowing subject. The more definite and detailed explanation of this is what will now first concern us.

§ 31.

First of all, however, the following very essential remark. I hope that in the preceding book I have succeeded in producing the conviction that what in the Kantian philosophy is called the *thing-in-itself,* and appears therein as so significant but obscure and paradoxical a doctrine, is, if reached by the entirely different path we have taken, nothing but the *will* in the sphere of this concept, widened and defined in the way I have stated. It appears obscure and paradoxical in Kant especially through the way in which he introduced it, namely by inference from what is grounded to what is the ground, and it was considered to be a stumbling-block, in fact the weak side of his philosophy. Further, I hope that, after what has been said, there will be no hesitation in recognizing again in the definite grades of the objectification of that will, which forms the in-itself of the world, what Plato called the *eternal Ideas* or unchangeable forms (εἴδη). Acknowledged to be the principal, but at the same time the most obscure and paradoxical, dogma of his teaching, these Ideas have been a subject of reflection and controversy, of ridicule and reverence, for many and very differently endowed minds in the course of centuries.

Now if for us the will is the *thing-in-itself,* and the *Idea* is the immediate objectivity of that will at a definite grade, then we find Kant's thing-in-itself and Plato's Idea, for him the only ὄντως ὄν[1]—those two great and obscure paradoxes of the two greatest philosophers of the West—to be, not exactly identical, but yet very closely related, and distinguished by only a single modification. The two great paradoxes, just because, in spite of all inner harmony and relationship, they sound so very different by reason of the extraordinarily different individualities of their authors, are even the best commentary on each other, for they are like two entirely different paths leading to one goal. This can be made clear in a few words. What Kant says is in essence as follows: "Time, space, and causality are not determinations of the thing-in-itself, but belong only to its phenomenon, since they are nothing but forms of our knowledge.

---

[1] "Truly being." [Tr.]

Now as all plurality and all arising and passing away are possible only through time, space, and causality, it follows that they too adhere only to the phenomenon, and by no means to the thing-in-itself. But since our knowledge is conditioned by these forms, the whole of experience is only knowledge of the phenomenon, not of the thing-in-itself; hence also its laws cannot be made valid for the thing-in-itself. What has been said extends even to our own ego, and we know that only as phenomenon, not according to what it may be in itself." This is the meaning and content of Kant's teaching in the important respect we have considered. Now Plato says: "The things of this world, perceived by our senses, have no true being at all; *they are always becoming, but they never are.* They have only a relative being; they are together only in and through their relation to one another; hence their whole existence can just as well be called a non-being. Consequently, they are likewise not objects of a real knowledge (ἐπιστήμη), for there can be such a knowledge only of what exists in and for itself, and always in the same way. On the contrary, they are only the object of an opinion or way of thinking, brought about by sensation (δόξα μετ᾽ αἰσθήσεως ἀλόγου).[2] As long as we are confined to their perception, we are like persons sitting in a dark cave, and bound so fast that they cannot even turn their heads. They see nothing but the shadowy outlines of actual things that are led between them and a fire which burns behind them; and by the light of this fire these shadows appear on the wall in front of them. Even of themselves and of one another they see only the shadows on this wall. Their wisdom would consist in predicting the sequence of those shadows learned from experience. On the other hand, only the real archetypes of those shadowy outlines, the eternal Ideas, the original forms of all things, can be described as truly existing (ὄντως ὄν), since they *always are but never become and never pass away. No plurality* belongs to them; for each by its nature is only one, since it is the archetype itself, of which all the particular, transitory things of the same kind and name are copies or shadows. Also *no coming into existence and no passing away* belong to them, for they are truly being or existing, but are never becoming or vanishing like their fleeting copies. (But in these two negative definitions there is necessarily contained the presupposition that time, space, and causality have no significance or validity for these Ideas, and do not exist in them.) Thus only of them can there be a knowledge in the proper sense, for the object of such a knowledge can be only that which always and in every respect (and hence in-itself) is, not that which is and then again is not, according as we look at it." This is Plato's teaching. It is

---

[2] "A mere thinking by means of irrational sense perception." [Tr.]

obvious, and needs no further demonstration, that the inner meaning of both doctrines is wholly the same; that both declare the visible world to be a phenomenon which in itself is void and empty, and which has meaning and borrowed reality only through the thing that expresses itself in it (the thing-in-itself in the one case, the Idea in the other). To this latter, however, which truly is, all the forms of that phenomenon, even the most universal and essential, are, in the light of both doctrines, entirely foreign. In order to deny these forms, Kant has directly expressed them even in abstract terms, and has definitely deprived the thing-in-itself of time, space, and causality, as being mere forms of the phenomenon. On the other hand, Plato did not reach the highest expression, and only indirectly did he deprive his Ideas of those forms, in that he denied of the Ideas what is possible only through those forms, namely plurality of the homogeneous, origination and disappearance. Though it is superfluous, I wish to make this remarkable and important agreement clear by an example. Let us suppose an animal standing before us in the full activity of its life. Plato will say: "This animal has no true existence, but only an apparent one, a constant becoming, a relative existence that can just as well be called non-being as being. Only the Idea which is depicted in that animal is truly 'being' or the animal-in-itself (αὐτὸ τὸ θηρίον), which is dependent on nothing, but which is in and by itself (καθ' ἑαυτό, ἀεὶ ὡσαύτως);[3] it has not become, it is not passing away, but always is in the same way (ἀεὶ ὄν, καὶ μηδέποτε οὔτε γιγνόμενον, οὔτε ἀπολλύμενον).[4] Now, in so far as we recognize in this animal its Idea, it is all one and of no importance whether we now have before us this animal or its progenitor of a thousand years ago; also whether it is here or in a distant country; whether it presents itself in this manner, posture, or action, or in that; finally, whether it is this or any other individual of its species. All this is void and unreal, and concerns only the phenomenon; the Idea of the animal alone has true being, and is the object of real knowledge." Thus Plato. Kant would say something like this: "This animal is a phenomenon in time, space, and causality, which are collectively the conditions *a priori* of the possibility of experience residing in our faculty of knowledge, not determinations of the thing-in-itself. Therefore this animal, as we perceive it at this particular time, in this given place, as an individual that has come into existence and will just as necessarily pass away in the connexion of experience, in other words, in the chain of causes and effects, is not a thing-in-itself, but a phenomenon, valid only in reference to our knowledge. In order to know it according to what it

---

[3] "In itself always in the same way." [Tr.]
[4] "Always being, and never either arising or passing away." [Tr.]

may be in itself, and so independently of all determinations residing in time, space, and causality, a different kind of knowledge from that which is alone possible to us through the senses and understanding would be required."

In order to bring Kant's expression even closer to Plato's, we might also say that time, space, and causality are that arrangement of our intellect by virtue of which the *one* being of each kind that alone really exists, manifests itself to us as a plurality of homogeneous beings, always being originated anew and passing away in endless succession. The apprehension of things by means of and in accordance with this arrangement is *immanent;* on the other hand, that which is conscious of the true state of things is *transcendental.* We obtain this *in abstracto* through the *Critique of Pure Reason,* but in exceptional cases it can also appear intuitively. This last point is my own addition, which I am endeavouring to explain in the present third book.

If Kant's teaching, and, since Kant's time, that of Plato, had ever been properly understood and grasped; if men had truly and earnestly reflected on the inner meaning and content of the teachings of the two great masters, instead of lavishly using the technical expressions of the one and parodying the style of the other, they could not have failed long ago to discover how much the two great sages agree, and that the true significance, the aim, of both teachings is absolutely the same. Not only would they have refrained from constantly comparing Plato with Leibniz, on whom his spirit certainly did not rest, or even with a well-known gentleman still living,[5] as if they wanted to mock at the manes of the great thinker of antiquity, but in general they would have gone much farther than they did, or rather would not have fallen behind so shamefully as they have done in the last forty years. They would not have allowed themselves to be led by the nose, today by one braggart tomorrow by another, and would not have opened with philosophical farces the nineteenth century that announced itself so importantly in Germany. These were performed over Kant's grave (just as was done sometimes by the ancients at the funeral rites of their dead), and occasioned the well-merited ridicule of other nations, for such things least suit the serious and even solid German. But so small is the real public of genuine philosophers, that even followers who understand are brought to them only sparingly by the centuries. Εἰσὶ δὴ ναρθηκοφόροι μὲν πολλοί, βάκχοι δέ γε παῦροι. (*Thyrsigeri quidem multi, Bacchi vero pauci.*) Ἡ ἀτιμία φιλοσοφίᾳ διὰ ταῦτα προσπέπτωκεν, ὅτι οὐ κατ' ἀξίαν αὐτῆς ἅπτονται· οὐ γὰρ νόθους ἔδει ἅπτεσθαι, ἀλλὰ γνησίους. (*Eam ob rem philosophia in infamiam incidit, quod non pro*

---

[5] F. H. Jacobi.

dignitate ipsam attingunt: neque enim a spuriis, sed a legitimis erat attrectanda,) Plato [*Republic*, 535 C].[6]

Men followed words, such words as "representations *a priori*," "forms of perceiving and thinking known independently of experience," "primary concepts of the pure understanding," and so on. They now asked whether Plato's Ideas, which were also primary concepts and which, moreover, were supposed to be reminiscences from a prenatal perception of truly existing things, were in some way the same thing as Kant's forms of intuition and thought, residing *a priori* in our consciousness. As there was a slight resemblance in the expression of these two entirely different doctrines, the Kantian doctrine of forms, limiting the knowledge of the individual to the phenomenon, and the Platonic doctrine of Ideas, the knowledge of which expressly denies those very forms, these doctrines, in this respect diametrically opposite, were carefully compared, and men deliberated and disputed over their identity. Ultimately, they found that they were not the same, and concluded that Plato's doctrine of Ideas and Kant's critique of reason had no agreement at all. But enough of this.[7]

§ 32.

It follows from our observations so far that, in spite of all the inner agreement between Kant and Plato, and of the identity of the aim that was in the mind of each, or of the world-view that inspired and led them to philosophize, Idea and thing-in-itself are not for us absolutely one and the same. On the contrary, for us the Idea is only the immediate, and therefore adequate, objectivity of the thing-in-itself, which itself, however, is the *will*—the will in so far as it is not yet objectified, has not yet become representation. For, precisely according to Kant, the thing-in-itself is supposed to be free from all the forms that adhere to knowledge as such. It is merely an error of Kant (as is shown in the Appendix) that he did not

[6] "Many are rod-bearers, yet few become Bacchantes." [Tr.] "Philosophy has fallen into contempt, because people are not engaged in it to the extent that it merits; for not spurious, but genuine, philosophers should devote themselves to it." [Tr.]

[7] See, for example, *Immanuel Kant, ein Denkmal*, by Fr. Bouterweck, p. 49; and Buhle's *Geschichte der Philosophie*, Vol. 6, pp. 802-815, and 823.

reckon among these forms, before all others, that of being-object-
for-a-subject; for this very form is the first and most universal of all
phenomenon, i.e., of all representation. He should therefore have
expressly denied being-object to his thing-in-itself, for this would have
protected him from that great inconsistency which was soon discovered. On the other hand, the Platonic Idea is necessarily object,
something known, a representation, and precisely, but only, in this
respect is it different from the thing-in-itself. It has laid aside merely
the subordinate forms of the phenomenon, all of which we include
under the principle of sufficient reason; or rather it has not yet entered into them. But it has retained the first and most universal
form, namely that of the representation in general, that of being
object for a subject. It is the forms subordinate to this (the general
expression of which is the principle of sufficient reason) which mul-
tiply the Idea in particular and fleeting individuals, whose number
in respect of the Idea is a matter of complete indifference. Therefore
the principle of sufficient reason is again the form into which the Idea
enters, since the Idea comes into the knowledge of the subject as
individual. The particular thing, appearing in accordance with the
principle of sufficient reason, is therefore only an indirect objectification of the thing-in-itself (which is the will). Between it and the
thing-in-itself the Idea still stands as the only direct objectivity of the
will, since it has not assumed any other form peculiar to knowledge
as such, except that of the representation in general, i.e., that of being
object for a subject. Therefore, it alone is the most *adequate objectivity* possible of the will or of the thing-in-itself; indeed it is even the
whole thing-in-itself, only under the form of the representation. Here
lies the ground of the great agreement between Plato and Kant,
although in strict accuracy that of which they both speak is not the
same. The particular things, however, are not an entirely adequate
objectivity of the will, but this is obscured in them by those forms,
whose common expression is the principle of sufficient reason, but
which are the condition of knowledge such as is possible to the individual as such. If it is permitted to infer from an impossible presupposition, we should in fact no longer know particular things, or
events, or change, or plurality, but apprehend only Ideas, only the
grades of objectification of that one will, of the true thing-in-itself, in
pure unclouded knowledge. Consequently, our world would be a
nunc stans,[8] if we were not, as subject of knowledge, at the same
time individuals, in other words, if our perception did not come about
through the medium of a body, from whose affections it starts. This
body itself is only concrete willing, objectivity of will; hence it is an

---

[8] "Persisting in the present." [Tr.]

object among objects, and as such comes into the knowing consciousness in the only way it can, namely in the forms of the principle of sufficient reason. Consequently, it presupposes and thus introduces time and all the other forms expressed by that principle. Time is merely the spread-out and piecemeal view that an individual being has of the Ideas. These are outside time, and consequently *eternal*. Therefore Plato says that time is the moving image of eternity: αἰῶνος εἰκὼν κινητὴ ὁ χρόνος. [*Timaeus,* 37 D.][9]

§ 33.

Now since as individuals we have no other knowledge than that which is subject to the principle of sufficient reason, this form, however, excluding knowledge of the Ideas, it is certain that, if it is possible for us to raise ourselves from knowledge of particular things to that of the Ideas, this can happen only by a change taking place in the subject. Such a change is analogous and corresponds to that great change of the whole nature of the object, and by virtue of it the subject, in so far as it knows an Idea, is no longer individual.

We remember from the previous book that knowledge in general itself belongs to the objectification of the will at its higher grades. Sensibility, nerves, brain, just like other parts of the organic being, are only an expression of the will at this grade of its objectivity; hence the representation that arises through them is also destined to serve the will as a means (μηχανή) for the attainment of its now complicated (πολυτελέστερα) ends, for the maintenance of a being with many different needs. Thus, originally and by its nature, knowledge is completely the servant of the will, and, like the immediate object which, by the application of the law of causality, becomes the starting-point of knowledge, is only objectified will. And so all knowledge which follows the principle of sufficient reason remains in a nearer or remoter relation to the will. For the individual finds his body as an object among objects, to all of which it has many different relations and connexions according to the principle of sufficient reason. Hence a consideration of these always leads back, by a shorter

[9] Cf. chap. 29 of volume 2.

or longer path, to his body, and thus to his will. As it is the principle of sufficient reason that places the objects in this relation to the body and so to the will, the sole endeavour of knowledge, serving this will, will be to get to know concerning objects just those relations that are laid down by the principle of sufficient reason, and thus to follow their many different connexions in space, time, and causality. For only through these is the object *interesting* to the individual, in other words, has it a relation to the will. Therefore, knowledge that serves the will really knows nothing more about objects than their relations, knows the objects only in so far as they exist at such a time, in such a place, in such and such circumstances, from such and such causes, and in such and such effects—in a word, as particular things. If all these relations were eliminated, the objects also would have disappeared for knowledge, just because it did not recognize in them anything else. We must also not conceal the fact that what the sciences consider in things is also essentially nothing more than all this, namely their relations, the connexions of time and space, the causes of natural changes, the comparison of forms, the motives of events, and thus merely relations. What distinguishes science from ordinary knowledge is merely its form, the systematic, the facilitating of knowledge by summarizing everything particular in the universal by means of the subordination of concepts, and the completeness of knowledge thus attained. All relation has itself only a relative existence; for example, all being in time is also a non-being, for time is just that by which opposite determinations can belong to the same thing. Therefore every phenomenon in time again is not, for what separates its beginning from its end is simply time, essentially an evanescent, unstable, and relative thing, here called duration. But time is the most universal form of all objects of this knowledge that is in the service of the will, and is the prototype of the remaining forms of such knowledge.

Now as a rule, knowledge remains subordinate to the service of the will, as indeed it came into being for this service; in fact, it sprang from the will, so to speak, as the head from the trunk. With the animals, this subjection of knowledge to the will can never be eliminated. With human beings, such elimination appears only as an exception, as will shortly be considered in more detail. This distinction between man and animal is outwardly expressed by the difference in the relation of head to trunk. In the lower animals both are still deformed; in all, the head is directed to the ground, where the objects of the will lie. Even in the higher animals, head and trunk are still far more one than in man, whose head seems freely set on to the body, only carried by the body and not serving it. This human superiority is exhibited in the highest degree by the Apollo Belvedere. The head of the god of the Muses, with eyes looking far afield, stands so freely on the shoulders that it seems to be wholly delivered from the body, and no longer subject to its cares.

§ 34.

As we have said, the transition that is possible, but to be regarded only as an exception, from the common knowledge of particular things to knowledge of the Idea takes place suddenly, since knowledge tears itself free from the service of the will precisely by the subject's ceasing to be merely individual, and being now a pure will-less subject of knowledge. Such a subject of knowledge no longer follows relations in accordance with the principle of sufficient reason; on the contrary, it rests in fixed contemplation of the object presented to it out of its connexion with any other, and rises into this.

To be made clear, this needs a detailed discussion, and the reader must suspend his surprise at it for a while, until it has vanished automatically after he has grasped the whole thought to be expressed in this work.

Raised up by the power of the mind, we relinquish the ordinary way of considering things, and cease to follow under the guidance of the forms of the principle of sufficient reason merely their relations to one another, whose final goal is always the relation to our own will. Thus we no longer consider the where, the when, the why, and the whither in things, but simply and solely the *what*. Further, we do not let abstract thought, the concepts of reason, take possession of our consciousness, but, instead of all this, devote the whole power of our mind to perception, sink ourselves completely therein, and let our whole consciousness be filled by the calm contemplation of the natural object actually present, whether it be a landscape, a tree, a rock, a crag, a building, or anything else. We *lose* ourselves entirely in this object, to use a pregnant expression; in other words, we forget our individuality, our will, and continue to exist only as pure subject, as clear mirror of the object, so that it is as though the object alone existed without anyone to perceive it, and thus we are no longer able to separate the perceiver from the perception, but the two have become one, since the entire consciousness is filled and occupied by a single image of perception. If, therefore, the object has to such an extent passed out of all relation to something outside it, and the subject has passed out of all relation to the will, what is thus known is no longer the individual thing as such, but the *Idea,* the eternal form, the immediate objectivity of the will at this grade. Thus at the same time, the person who is involved in this perception is no longer an individual, for in such perception the individual has lost himself; he is *pure will-less, painless, timeless subject of knowledge.* This, which for the moment is so remarkable (which I well know confirms the saying, attributed to Thomas Paine, that *du sublime au ridicule il n'y a qu'un pas*),[10] will gradually become clearer and less surprising through what follows. It was this that was in Spinoza's mind when he wrote: *Mens aeterna est, quatenus res sub aeternitatis specie concipit* (*Ethics,* V, prop. 31, schol.).[11] Now in such contemplation, the particular thing at one stroke becomes the *Idea* of its species, and the perceiving individual becomes the *pure subject of knowing.* The individual, as such, knows only particular things; the pure subject of knowledge knows only Ideas. For the individual is the subject of knowledge in its relation to a definite particular phenomenon of will and in subjection thereto. This particular phenomenon of will is, as such, subordinate to the principle of sufficient reason in all its forms; therefore all knowledge which relates itself to this, also follows the principle of sufficient reason, and no other knowledge than this is fit to be of any use to the will; it always has only relations to the object. The knowing individual as such and the particular thing known by him are always in a particular place, at a particular time, and are links in the chain of causes and effects. The pure subject of knowledge and its correlative, the Idea, have passed out of all these forms of the principle of sufficient reason. Time, place, the individual that knows, and the individual that is known, have no meaning for them. First of all, a knowing individual raises himself in the manner described to the pure subject of knowing, and at the same time raises the contemplated object to the Idea; the *world as representation* then stands out whole and pure, and the complete objectification of the will takes place, for only the Idea is the *adequate objectivity* of the will. In itself, the Idea includes object and subject in like manner,

---

[10] "From the sublime to the ridiculous is but a step." [Tr.]

[11] "The mind is eternal in so far as it conceives things from the standpoint of eternity." [Tr.]

I also recommend what he says *ibid.,* l. II, prop. 40, schol. 2, and l. V, prop. 25-38, about the *cognitio tertii generis, sive intuitiva,* in illustration of the method of cognition we are here considering, and most particularly prop. 29, schol.; prop. 36, schol.; and prop. 38 demonstr. et schol.

for these are its sole form. In it, however, both are of entirely equal weight; and as the object also is here nothing but the representation of the subject, so the subject, by passing entirely into the perceived object, has also become that object itself, since the entire consciousness is nothing more than its most distinct image. This consciousness really constitutes the whole *world as representation,* since we picture to ourselves the whole of the Ideas, or grades of the will's objectivity, passing through it successively. The particular things of all particular times and spaces are nothing but the Ideas multiplied through the principle of sufficient reason (the form of knowledge of the individuals as such), and thus obscured in their pure objectivity. When the Idea appears, subject and object can no longer be distinguished in it, because the Idea, the adequate objectivity of the will, the real world as representation, arises only when subject and object reciprocally fill and penetrate each other completely. In just the same way the knowing and the known individual, as things-in-themselves, are likewise not different. For if we look entirely away from that true *world as representation,* there is nothing left but the *world as will.*

The will is the "in-itself" of the Idea that completely objectifies it; it is also the "in-itself" of the particular thing and of the individual that knows it, and these two objectify it incompletely. As will, outside the representation and all its forms, it is one and the same in the contemplated object and in the individual who soars aloft in this contemplation, who becomes conscious of himself as pure subject. Therefore in themselves these two are not different; for in themselves they are the will that here knows itself. Plurality and difference exist only as the way in which this knowledge comes to the will, that is to say, only in the phenomenon, by virtue of its form, the principle of sufficient reason. Without the object, without the representation, I am not knowing subject, but mere, blind will; in just the same way, without me as subject of knowledge, the thing known is not object, but mere will, blind impulse. In itself, that is to say outside the representation, this will is one and the same with mine; only in the world as representation, the form of which is always at least subject and object, are we separated out as known and knowing individual. As soon as knowledge, the world as representation, is abolished, nothing in general is left but mere will, blind impulse. That it should obtain objectivity, should become representation, immediately supposes subject as well as object; but that this objectivity should be pure, complete, adequate objectivity of the will, supposes the object as Idea, free from the forms of the principle of sufficient reason, and the subject as pure subject of knowledge, free from individuality and from servitude to the will.

Now whoever has, in the manner stated, become so absorbed and lost in the perception of nature that he exists only as purely knowing subject, becomes in this way immediately aware that, as such, he is the condition, and hence the supporter, of the world and of all objective existence, for this now shows itself as dependent on his existence. He therefore draws nature into himself, so that he feels it to be only an accident of his own being. In this sense Byron says:

Are not the mountains, waves and skies, a part
Of me and of my soul, as I of them? [12]

But how could the person who feels this regard himself as absolutely perishable in contrast to imperishable nature? Rather will he be moved by the consciousness of what the *Upanishad* of the Veda expresses: *Hae omnes creaturae in totum ego sum, et praeter me aliud (ens) non est. (Oupnek'hat* [ed. Anquetil Duperron, 2 vols., Paris, 1801-2], I, 122.)[13]

§ 35.

In order to reach a deeper insight into the nature of the world, it is absolutely necessary for us to learn to distinguish the will as thing-in-itself from its adequate objectivity, and then to distinguish the different grades at which this objectivity appears more distinctly and fully, i.e., the Ideas themselves, from the mere phenomenon of the Ideas in the forms of the principle of sufficient reason, the restricted method of knowledge of individuals. We shall then agree with Plato, when he attributes actual being to the Ideas alone, and only an apparent, dreamlike existence to the things in space and time, to this world that is real for the individual. We shall then see how one and the same Idea reveals itself in so many phenomena, and presents its nature to knowing individuals only piecemeal, one side after another. Then we shall also distinguish the Idea itself from the way in which its phenomenon comes into the observation of the individual, and shall recognize the former as essential, and the latter

---

[12] [*Childe Harold's Pilgrimage*, III, lxxv.—Tr.]
[13] "I am all this creation collectively, and besides me there exists no other being." [Tr.] Cf. chap. 30 of volume 2.

as inessential. We intend to consider this by way of example on the smallest scale, and then on the largest. When clouds move, the figures they form are not essential, but indifferent to them. But that as elastic vapour they are pressed together, driven off, spread out, and torn apart by the force of the wind, this is their nature, this is the essence of the forces that are objectified in them, this is the Idea. The figures in each case are only for the individual observer. To the brook which rolls downwards over the stones, the eddies, waves, and foam-forms exhibited by it are indifferent and inessential; but that it follows gravity, and behaves as an inelastic, perfectly mobile, formless, and transparent fluid, this is its essential nature, this, *if known through perception,* is the Idea. Those foam-forms exist only for us so long as we know as individuals. The ice on the window-pane is formed into crystals according to the laws of crystallization, which reveal the essence of the natural force here appearing, which exhibit the Idea. But the trees and flowers formed by the ice on the window-pane are inessential, and exist only for us. What appears in clouds, brook, and crystal is the feeblest echo of that will which appears more completely in the plant, still more completely in the animal, and most completely in man. But only the *essential* in all these grades of the will's objectification constitutes the *Idea;* on the other hand, its unfolding or development, because drawn apart in the forms of the principle of sufficient reason into a multiplicity of many-sided phenomena, is inessential to the Idea; it lies merely in the individual's mode of cognition, and has reality only for that individual. Now the same thing necessarily holds good of the unfolding of that Idea which is the most complete objectivity of the will. Consequently, the history of the human race, the throng of events, the change of times, the many varying forms of human life in different countries and centuries, all this is only the accidental form of the phenomenon of the Idea. All this does not belong to the Idea itself, in which alone lies the adequate objectivity of the will, but only to the phenomenon. The phenomenon comes into the knowledge of the individual, and is just as foreign, inessential, and indifferent to the Idea itself as the figures they depict are to the clouds, the shape of its eddies and foam-forms to the brook, and the trees and flowers to the ice.

To the man who has properly grasped this, and is able to distinguish the will from the Idea, and the Idea from its phenomenon, the events of the world will have significance only in so far as they are the letters from which the Idea of man can be read, and not in and by themselves. He will not believe with the general public that time may produce something actually new and significant; that through it or in it something positively real may attain to existence, or indeed that time itself as a whole has beginning and end, plan and development, and in some way has for its final goal the highest perfection (according to their conceptions) of the latest generation that lives for thirty years. Therefore just as little will he, with Homer, set up a whole Olympus full of gods to guide the events of time, as he will, with Ossian, regard the figures of the clouds as individual beings. For, as we have said, both have just as much significance with regard to the Idea appearing in them. In the many different forms and aspects of human life, and in the interminable change of events, he will consider only the Idea as the abiding and essential, in which the will-to-live has its most perfect objectivity, and which shows its different sides in the qualities, passions, errors, and excellences of the human race, in selfishness, hatred, love, fear, boldness, frivolity, stupidity, slyness, wit, genius, and so on. All of these, running and congealing together into a thousand different forms and shapes (individuals), continually produce the history of the great and the small worlds, where in itself it is immaterial whether they are set in motion by nuts or by crowns. Finally, he will find that in the world it is the same as in the dramas of Gozzi, in all of which the same persons always appear with the same purpose and the same fate. The motives and incidents certainly are different in each piece, but the spirit of the incidents is the same. The persons of one piece know nothing of the events of another, in which, of course, they themselves performed. Therefore, after all the experiences of the earlier pieces, Pantaloon has become no more agile or generous, Tartaglia no more conscientious, Brighella no more courageous, and Columbine no more modest.

Suppose we were permitted for once to have a clear glance into the realm of possibility, and over all the chains of causes and effects, then the earth-spirit would appear and show us in a picture the most eminent individuals, world-enlighteners, and heroes, destroyed by chance before they were ripe for their work. We should then be shown the great events that would have altered the history of the world, and brought about periods of the highest culture and enlightenment, but which the blindest chance, the most insignificant accident, prevented at their beginning. Finally, we should see the splendid powers of great individuals who would have enriched whole world-epochs, but who, misled through error or passion, or compelled by necessity, squandered them uselessly on unworthy or unprofitable objects, or even dissipated them in play. If we saw all this, we should shudder and lament at the thought of the lost treasures of whole periods of the world. But the earth-spirit would smile and say: "The source from which the individuals and their powers flow is inexhaustible, and is as boundless as are time and space; for, just like these forms of every phenomenon, they too are only phenomenon, visibility of the will. No finite measure can exhaust that infinite source; therefore undiminished infinity is still always open for the return of any event or work that was nipped in the bud. In this world of the phenomenon, true loss is as little possible as is true gain. The will alone is; it is the thing-in-itself, the source of all those phenomena. Its self-knowledge and its affirmation or denial that is then decided on, is the only event in-itself." [14]

§ 36.

History follows the thread of events; it is pragmatic in so far as it deduces them according to the law of motivation, a law that determines the appearing will where that will is illuminated by knowledge. At the lower grades of its objectivity, where it still acts without knowledge, natural science as etiology considers the laws of the changes of its phenomena, and as morphology considers what is permanent in them. This almost endless theme is facilitated by the aid of concepts that comprehend the general, in order to deduce from it the particular. Finally, mathematics considers the mere forms, that is, time and space, in which the Ideas appear drawn apart into plurality for the knowledge of the subject as individual. All these, the common name of which is science, therefore follow the principle of sufficient reason in its different forms, and their theme remains the phenomenon, its laws, connexion, and the relations resulting from these. But now, what kind of knowledge is it that considers what continues to exist outside and independently of all relations, but which alone is really essential to the world, the true content of its phenomena, that which is subject to no change, and is therefore known with equal truth for all time, in a word, the *Ideas* that are the immediate and adequate objectivity of the thing-in-itself, of the will? It is *art*, the work of genius. It repeats the eternal Ideas apprehended through pure contemplation, the essential and abiding element in all the phenomena of the world. According to the material in which it repeats, it is sculpture, painting, poetry, or music. Its only source is

---

[14] This last sentence cannot be understood without some acquaintance with the following book.

knowledge of the Ideas; its sole aim is communication of this knowledge. Whilst science, following the restless and unstable stream of the fourfold forms of reasons or grounds and consequents, is with every end it attains again and again directed farther, and can never find an ultimate goal or complete satisfaction, any more than by running we can reach the point where the clouds touch the horizon; art, on the contrary, is everywhere at its goal. For it plucks the object of its contemplation from the stream of the world's course, and holds it isolated before it. This particular thing, which in that stream was an infinitesimal part, becomes for art a representative of the whole, an equivalent of the infinitely many in space and time. It therefore pauses at this particular thing; it stops the wheel of time; for it the relations vanish; its object is only the essential, the Idea. We can therefore define it accurately as *the way of considering things independently of the principle of sufficient reason,* in contrast to the way of considering them which proceeds in exact accordance with this principle, and is the way of science and experience. This latter method of consideration can be compared to an endless line running horizontally, and the former to a vertical line cutting the horizontal at any point. The method of consideration that follows the principle of sufficient reason is the rational method, and it alone is valid and useful in practical life and in science. The method of consideration that looks away from the content of this principle is the method of genius, which is valid and useful in art alone. The first is Aristotle's method; the second is, on the whole, Plato's. The first is like the mighty storm, rushing along without beginning or aim, bending, agitating, and carrying everything away with it; the second is like the silent sunbeam, cutting through the path of the storm, and quite unmoved by it. The first is like the innumerable violently agitated drops of the waterfall, constantly changing and never for a moment at rest; the second is like the rainbow silently resting on this raging torrent. Only through the pure contemplation described above, which becomes absorbed entirely in the object, are the Ideas comprehended; and the nature of *genius* consists precisely in the preeminent ability for such contemplation. Now as this demands a complete forgetting of our own person and of its relations and connexions, the *gift of genius* is nothing but the most complete *objectivity,* i.e., the objective tendency of the mind, as opposed to the subjective directed to our own person, i.e., to the will. Accordingly, genius is the capacity to remain in a state of pure perception, to lose oneself in perception, to remove from the service of the will the knowledge which originally existed only for this service. In other words, genius is the ability to leave entirely out of sight our own

interest, our willing, and our aims, and consequently to discard
entirely our own personality for a time, in order to remain *pure
knowing subject,* the clear eye of the world; and this not merely for
moments, but with the necessary continuity and conscious thought
to enable us to repeat by deliberate art what has been apprehended,
and "what in wavering apparition gleams fix in its place with thoughts
that stand for ever!"[15] For genius to appear in an individual, it is as if a
measure of the power of knowledge must have fallen to his lot far exceeding that required for the service of an individual will; and this
superfluity of knowledge having become free, now becomes the subject purified of will, the clear mirror of the inner nature of the world.
This explains the animation, amounting to disquietude, in men of
genius, since the present can seldom satisfy them, because it does
not fill their consciousness. This gives them that restless zealous
nature, that constant search for new objects worthy of contemplation, and also that longing, hardly ever satisfied, for men of like
nature and stature to whom they may open their hearts. The common
mortal, on the other hand, entirely filled and satisfied by the common
present, is absorbed in it, and, finding everywhere his like, has that
special ease and comfort in daily life which are denied to the man
of genius. Imagination has been rightly recognized as an essential
element of genius; indeed, it has sometimes been regarded as identical
with genius, but this is not correct. The objects of genius as such are
the eternal Ideas, the persistent, essential forms of the world and
of all its phenomena; but knowledge of the Idea is necessarily knowledge through perception, and is not abstract. Thus the knowledge of
the genius would be restricted to the Ideas of objects actually
present to his own person, and would be dependent on the concatenation of circumstances that brought them to him, did not
imagination extend his horizon far beyond the reality of his personal
experience, and enable him to construct all the rest out of the little
that has come into his own actual apperception, and thus to let
almost all the possible scenes of life pass by within himself. Moreover, the actual objects are almost always only very imperfect copies
of the Idea that manifests itself in them. Therefore the man of
genius requires imagination, in order to see in things not what
nature has actually formed, but what she endeavoured to form, yet
did not bring about, because of the conflict of her forms with one
another which was referred to in the previous book. We shall
return to this later, when considering sculpture. Thus imagination
extends the mental horizon of the genius beyond the objects that

---

[15] Goethe's *Faust,* Bayard Taylor's translation. [Tr.]

actually present themselves to his person, as regards both quality and quantity. For this reason, unusual strength of imagination is a companion, indeed a condition, of genius. But the converse is not the case, for strength of imagination is not evidence of genius; on the contrary, even men with little or no touch of genius may have much imagination. For we can consider an actual object in two opposite ways, purely objectively, the way of genius grasping the Idea of the object, or in the common way, merely in its relations to other objects according to the principle of sufficient reason, and in its relations to our own will. In a similar manner, we can also perceive an imaginary object in these two ways. Considered in the first way, it is a means to knowledge of the Idea, the communication of which is the work of art. In the second case, the imaginary object is used to build castles in the air, congenial to selfishness and to one's own whim, which for the moment delude and delight; thus only the relations of the phantasms so connected are really ever known. The man who indulges in this game is a dreamer; he will easily mingle with reality the pictures that delight his solitude, and will thus become unfit for real life. Perhaps he will write down the delusions of his imagination, and these will give us the ordinary novels of all kinds which entertain those like him and the public at large, since the readers fancy themselves in the position of the hero, and then find the description very "nice." [16]

As we have said, the common, ordinary man, that manufactured article of nature which she daily produces in thousands, is not capable, at any rate continuously, of a consideration of things wholly disinterested in every sense, such as is contemplation proper. He can direct his attention to things only in so far as they have some relation to his will, although that relation may be only very indirect. As in this reference that always demands only knowledge of the relations, the abstract concept of the thing is sufficient and often even more appropriate, the ordinary man does not linger long over the mere perception, does not fix his eye on an object for long, but, in everything that presents itself to him, quickly looks merely for the concept under which it is to be brought, just as the lazy man looks for a chair, which then no longer interests him. Therefore he is very soon finished with everything, with works of art, with beautiful natural objects, and with that contemplation of life in all its scenes which is really of significance everywhere. He does not linger; he seeks only his way in life, or at most all that might at any time become his way. Thus he makes topographical notes in the widest

---

[16] The word used by Schopenhauer is *"gemütlich."* [Tr.]

sense, but on the consideration of life itself as such he wastes no time. On the other hand, the man of genius, whose power of knowledge is, through its excess, withdrawn for a part of his time from the service of his will, dwells on the consideration of life itself, strives to grasp the Idea of each thing, not its relations to other things. In doing this, he frequently neglects a consideration of his own path in life, and therefore often pursues this with insufficient skill. Whereas to the ordinary man his faculty of knowledge is a lamp that lights his path, to the man of genius it is the sun that reveals the world. This great difference in their way of looking at life soon becomes visible even in the outward appearance of them both. The glance of the man in whom genius lives and works readily distinguishes him; it is both vivid and firm and bears the character of thoughtfulness, of contemplation. We can see this in the portraits of the few men of genius which nature has produced here and there among countless millions. On the other hand, the real opposite of contemplation, namely spying or prying, can be readily seen in the glance of others, if indeed it is not dull and vacant, as is often the case. Consequently a face's "expression of genius" consists in the fact that a decided predominance of knowing over willing is visible in it, and hence that there is manifested in it a knowledge without any relation to a will, in other words, a *pure knowing*. On the other hand, in the case of faces that follow the rule, the expression of the will predominates, and we see that knowledge comes into activity only on the impulse of the will, and so is directed only to motives.

As the knowledge of the genius, or knowledge of the Idea, is that which does not follow the principle of sufficient reason, so, on the other hand, the knowledge that does follow this principle gives us prudence and rationality in life, and brings about the sciences. Thus individuals of genius will be affected with the defects entailed in the neglect of the latter kind of knowledge. Here, however, a limitation must be observed, that what I shall state in this regard concerns them only in so far as, and while, they are actually engaged with the kind of knowledge peculiar to the genius. Now this is by no means the case at every moment of their lives, for the great though spontaneous exertion required for the will-free comprehension of the Ideas necessarily relaxes again, and there are long intervals during which men of genius stand in very much the same position as ordinary persons, both as regards merits and defects. On this account, the action of genius has always been regarded as an inspiration, as indeed the name itself indicates, as the action of a superhuman being different from the individual himself, which takes possession of him only periodically. The disinclination of men of genius to direct their attention to the content of the principle of sufficient reason will show itself first in regard to the ground of being, as a disinclination for mathematics. The consideration of mathematics proceeds on the most universal forms of the phenomenon, space and time, which are themselves only modes or aspects of the principle of sufficient reason; and it is therefore the very opposite of that consideration that seeks only the content of the phenomenon, namely the Idea expressing itself in the phenomenon apart from all relations. Moreover, the logical procedure of mathematics will be repugnant to genius, for it obscures real insight and does not satisfy it; it presents a mere concatenation of conclusions according to the principle of the ground of knowing. Of all the mental powers, it makes the greatest claim on memory, so that one may have before oneself all the earlier propositions to which reference is made. Experience has also confirmed that men of great artistic genius have no aptitude for mathematics; no man was ever very distinguished in both at the same time. Alfieri relates that he was never able to understand even the fourth proposition of Euclid. Goethe was reproached enough with his want of mathematical knowledge by the ignorant opponents of his colour theory. Here, where it was naturally not a question of calculation and measurement according to hypothetical data, but one of direct knowledge by understanding cause and effect, this reproach was so utterly absurd and out of place, that they revealed their total lack of judgement just as much by such a reproach as by the rest of their Midas-utterances. The fact that even today, nearly half a century after the appearance of Goethe's colour theory, the Newtonian fallacies still remain in undisturbed possession of the professorial chair even in Germany, and that people continue to talk quite seriously about the seven homogeneous rays of light and their differing refrangibility, will one day be numbered among the great intellectual peculiarities of mankind in general, and of the Germans in particular. From the same above-mentioned cause may be explained the equally well-known fact that, conversely, distinguished mathematicians have little susceptibility to works of fine art. This is expressed with particular naïvety in the well-known anecdote of that French mathematician who, after reading Racine's *Iphigenia*, shrugged his shoulders and asked: *Qu'est-ce que cela prouve?* [17] Further, as keen comprehension of relations according to the laws of causality and motivation really constitutes prudence or sagacity, whereas the knowledge of genius is not directed to relations, a prudent man will not be a genius insofar as and while he is prudent,

---

[17] "What does all that prove?" [Tr.]

and a genius will not be prudent insofar as and while he is a genius. Finally, knowledge of perception generally, in the province of which the Idea entirely lies, is directly opposed to rational or abstract knowledge which is guided by the principle of the ground of knowing. It is also well known that we seldom find great genius united with preeminent reasonableness; on the contrary, men of genius are often subject to violent emotions and irrational passions. But the cause of this is not weakness of the faculty of reason, but partly unusual energy of that whole phenomenon of will, the individual genius. This phenomenon manifests itself through vehemence of all his acts of will. The cause is also partly a preponderance of knowledge from perception through the senses and the understanding over abstract knowledge, in other words, a decided tendency to the perceptive. In such men the extremely energetic impression of the perceptive outshines the colourless concepts so much that conduct is no longer guided by the latter, but by the former, and on this very account becomes irrational. Accordingly, the impression of the present moment on them is very strong, and carries them away into thoughtless actions, into emotion and passion. Moreover, since their knowledge has generally been withdrawn in part from the service of the will, they will not in conversation think so much of the person with whom they are speaking as of the thing they are speaking about, which is vividly present in their minds. Therefore they will judge or narrate too objectively for their own interests; they will not conceal what it would be more prudent to keep concealed, and so on. Finally, they are inclined to soliloquize, and in general may exhibit several weaknesses that actually are closely akin to madness. It is often remarked that genius and madness have a side where they touch and even pass over into each other, and even poetic inspiration has been called a kind of madness; *amabilis insania,* as Horace calls it (*Odes,* iii, 4); and in the introduction to *Oberon* Wieland speaks of "amiable madness." Even Aristotle, as quoted by Seneca (*De Tranquillitate Animi,* xv, 16 [xvii, 10]), is supposed to have said: *Nullum magnum ingenium sine mixtura dementiae fuit.*[18] Plato expresses it in the above mentioned myth of the dark cave (*Republic,* Bk. 7) by saying that those who outside the cave have seen the true sunlight and the things that actually are (the Ideas), cannot afterwards see within the cave any more, because their eyes have grown unaccustomed to the darkness; they no longer recognize the shadow-forms correctly. They are therefore ridiculed for their mistakes by those others who have never left that

---

[18] "There has been no great mind without an admixture of madness." [Tr.]

cave and those shadow-forms. Also in the *Phaedrus* (245 A), he distinctly says that without a certain madness there can be no genuine poet, in fact (249 D) that everyone appears mad who recognizes the eternal Ideas in fleeting things. Cicero also states: *Negat enim sine furore Democritus quemquam poetam magnum esse posse; quod idem dicit Plato* (*De Divinatione,* i, 37).[19] And finally, Pope says:

> "Great wits to madness sure are near allied,
> And thin partitions do their bounds divide." [20]

Particularly instructive in this respect is Goethe's *Torquato Tasso,* in which he brings before our eyes not only suffering, the essential martyrdom of genius as such, but also its constant transition into madness. Finally, the fact of direct contact between genius and madness is established partly by the biographies of great men of genius, such as Rousseau, Byron, and Alfieri, and by anecdotes from the lives of others. On the other hand, I must mention having found, in frequent visits to lunatic asylums, individual subjects endowed with unmistakably great gifts. Their genius appeared distinctly through their madness which had completely gained the upper hand. Now this cannot be ascribed to chance, for on the one hand the number of mad persons is relatively very small, while on the other a man of genius is a phenomenon rare beyond all ordinary estimation, and appearing in nature only as the greatest exception. We may be convinced of this from the mere fact that we can compare the number of the really great men of genius produced by the whole of civilized Europe in ancient and modern times, with the two hundred and fifty millions who are always living in Europe and renew themselves every thirty years. Among men of genius, however, can be reckoned only those who have furnished works that have retained through all time an enduring value for mankind. Indeed, I will not refrain from mentioning that I have known some men of decided, though not remarkable, mental superiority who at the same time betrayed a slight touch of insanity. Accordingly, it might appear that every advance of the intellect beyond the usual amount, as an abnormality, already disposes to madness. Meanwhile, however, I will give as briefly as possible my opinion about the purely intellectual ground of the kinship between genius and

---

[19] "For Democritus asserts that there can be no great poet without madness; and Plato says the same thing." [Tr.]
[20] From Dryden's *Absalom and Achitophel,* I, 163; not from Pope as attributed by Schopenhauer. [Tr.]

madness, for this discussion will certainly contribute to the explanation of the real nature of genius, in other words, of that quality of the mind which is alone capable of producing genuine works of art. But this necessitates a brief discussion of madness itself.[21]

A clear and complete insight into the nature of madness, a correct and distinct conception of what really distinguishes the sane from the insane, has, so far as I know, never yet been found. Neither the faculty of reason nor understanding can be denied to the mad, for they talk and understand, and often draw very accurate conclusions. They also, as a rule, perceive quite correctly what is present, and see the connexion between cause and effect. Visions, like the fancies of an overwrought brain, are no ordinary symptom of madness; delirium falsifies perception, madness the thoughts. For the most part, mad people do not generally err in the knowledge of what is immediately *present;* but their mad talk relates always to what is *absent* and *past,* and only through these to its connexion with what is present. Therefore, it seems to me that their malady specially concerns the *memory.* It is not, indeed, a case of memory failing them entirely, for many of them know a great deal by heart, and sometimes recognize persons whom they have not seen for a long time. Rather is it a case of the thread of memory being broken, its continuous connexion being abolished, and of the impossibility of a uniformly coherent recollection of the past. Individual scenes of the past stand out correctly, just like the individual present; but there are gaps in their recollection that they fill up with fictions. These are either always the same, and so become fixed ideas; it is then a fixed mania or melancholy; or they are different each time, momentary fancies; it is then called folly, *fatuitas.* This is the reason why it is so difficult to question a mad person about his previous life-history when he enters an asylum. In his memory the true is for ever mixed up with the false. Although the immediate present is correctly known, it is falsified through a fictitious connexion with an imaginary past. Mad people therefore consider themselves and others as identical with persons who live merely in their fictitious past. Many acquaintances they do not recognize at all, and, in spite of a correct representation or mental picture of the individual actually present, they have only false relations of this to what is absent. If the madness reaches a high degree, the result is a complete absence of memory; the mad person is then wholly incapable of any reference to what is absent or past, but is determined solely by the whim of the moment in combination with fictions that in his head fill up the

---

[21] Cf. chap. 31 of volume 2.

past. In such a case, we are then not safe for one moment from ill-treatment or murder, unless we constantly and visibly remind the insane person of superior force. The mad person's knowledge has in common with the animal's the fact that both are restricted to the present; but what distinguishes them is that the animal has really no notion at all of the past as such, although the past acts on it through the medium of custom. Thus, for instance, the dog recognizes his former master even after years, that is to say, it receives the accustomed impression at the sight of him; but the dog has no recollection of the time that has since elapsed. On the other hand, the madman always carries about in his faculty of reason a past in the abstract, but it is a false past that exists for him alone, and that either all the time or merely for the moment. The influence of this false past then prevents the use of the correctly known present which the animal makes. The fact that violent mental suffering or unexpected and terrible events are frequently the cause of madness, I explain as follows. Every such suffering is as an actual event always confined to the present; hence it is only transitory, and to that extent is never excessively heavy. It becomes insufferably great only in so far as it is a lasting pain, but as such it is again only a thought, and therefore resides in the *memory*. Now if such a sorrow, such painful knowledge or reflection, is so harrowing that it becomes positively unbearable, and the individual would succumb to it, then nature, alarmed in this way, seizes on *madness* as the last means of saving life. The mind, tormented so greatly, destroys, as it were, the thread of its memory, fills up the gaps with fictions, and thus seeks refuge in madness from the mental suffering that exceeds its strength, just as a limb affected by mortification is cut off and replaced with a wooden one. As examples, we may consider the raving Ajax, King Lear, and Ophelia; for the creations of the genuine genius, to which alone we can here refer, as being generally known, are equal in truth to real persons; moreover, frequent actual experience in this respect shows the same thing. A faint analogy of this kind of transition from pain to madness is to be found in the way in which we all frequently try, as it were, mechanically, to banish a tormenting memory that suddenly occurs to us by some loud exclamation or movement, to turn ourselves from it, to distract ourselves by force.

Now, from what we have stated, we see that the madman correctly knows the individual present as well as many particulars of the past, but that he fails to recognize the connexion, the relations, and therefore goes astray and talks nonsense. Just this is his point of contact with the genius; for he too leaves out of sight knowledge of the connexion of things, as he neglects that knowledge of relations which is knowledge according to the principle of sufficient reason, in order to see in things only their Ideas, and to try to grasp their real inner nature which expresses itself to perception, in regard to which *one* thing represents its whole species, and hence, as Goethe says, one case is valid for a thousand. The individual object of his contemplation, or the present which he apprehends with excessive vividness, appears in so strong a light that the remaining links of the chain, so to speak, to which they belong, withdraw into obscurity, and this gives us phenomena that have long been recognized as akin to those of madness. That which exists in the actual individual thing, only imperfectly and weakened by modifications, is enhanced to perfection, to the Idea of it, by the method of contemplation used by the genius. Therefore he everywhere sees extremes, and on this account his own actions tend to extremes. He does not know how to strike the mean; he lacks cool-headedness, and the result is as we have said. He knows the Ideas perfectly, but not the individuals. Therefore it has been observed that a poet may know *man* profoundly and thoroughly, but *men* very badly; he is easily duped, and is a plaything in the hands of the cunning and crafty.[22]

§ 37.

Now according to our explanation, genius consists in the ability to know, independently of the principle of sufficient reason, not individual things which have their existence only in the relation, but the Ideas of such things, and in the ability to be, in face of these, the correlative of the Idea, and hence no longer individual, but pure subject of knowing. Yet this ability must be inherent in all men in a lesser and different degree, as otherwise they would be just as incapable of enjoying works of art as of producing them. Generally they would have no susceptibility at all to the beautiful and to the sublime; indeed, these words could have no meaning for them. We must therefore assume as existing in all men that power of recognizing in things their Ideas, of divesting themselves for a moment of their personality, unless indeed there are

---

[22] Cf. chap. 32 of volume 2.

some who are not capable of any aesthetic pleasure at all. The man of genius excels them only in the far higher degree and more continuous duration of this kind of knowledge. These enable him to retain that thoughtful contemplation necessary for him to repeat what is thus known in a voluntary and intentional work, such repetition being the work of art. Through this he communicates to others the Idea he has grasped. Therefore this Idea remains unchanged and the same, and hence aesthetic pleasure is essentially one and the same, whether it be called forth by a work of art, or directly by the contemplation of nature and of life. The work of art is merely a means of facilitating that knowledge in which this pleasure consists. That the Idea comes to us more easily from the work of art than directly from nature and from reality, arises solely from the fact that the artist, who knew only the Idea and not reality, clearly repeated in his work only the Idea, separated it out from reality, and omitted all disturbing contingencies. The artist lets us peer into the world through his eyes. That he has these eyes, that he knows the essential in things which lies outside all relations, is the gift of genius and is inborn; but that he is able to lend us this gift, to let us see with his eyes, is acquired, and is the technical side of art. Therefore, after the account I have given in the foregoing remarks of the inner essence of the aesthetic way of knowing in its most general outline, the following more detailed philosophical consideration of the beautiful and the sublime will explain both simultaneously, in nature and in art, without separating them further. We shall first consider what takes place in a man when he is affected by the beautiful and the sublime. Whether he draws this emotion directly from nature, from life, or partakes of it only through the medium of art, makes no essential difference, but only an outward one.

§ 38.

In the aesthetic method of consideration we found *two inseparable constituent parts:* namely, knowledge of the object not as individual thing, but as Platonic *Idea,* in other words, as persistent form of this whole species of things; and the self-consciousness of the knower, not as individual, but as *pure, will-less subject of knowledge.* The condition under which the two constituent parts appear always united was the abandonment of the method of knowledge that is bound to the principle of sufficient reason, a knowledge that, on the contrary, is the only appropriate kind for serving the will and also for science. Moreover, we shall see that the *pleasure* produced by contemplation of the beautiful arises from those two constituent parts, sometimes more from the one than from the other, according to what the object of aesthetic contemplation may be.

All *willing* springs from lack, from deficiency, and thus from suffering. Fulfilment brings this to an end; yet for one wish that is fulfilled there remain at least ten that are denied. Further, desiring lasts a long time, demands and requests go on to infinity; fulfilment is short and meted out sparingly. But even the final satisfaction itself is only apparent; the wish fulfilled at once makes way for a new one; the former is a known delusion, the latter a delusion not as yet known. No attained object of willing can give a satisfaction that lasts and no longer declines; but it is always like the alms thrown to a beggar, which reprieves him today so that his misery may be prolonged till tomorrow. Therefore, so long as our consciousness is filled by our will, so long as we are given up to the throng of desires with its constant hopes and fears, so long as we are the subject of willing, we never obtain lasting happiness or peace. Essentially, it is all the same whether we pursue or flee, fear harm or aspire to enjoyment; care for the constantly demanding will, no matter in what form, continually fills and moves consciousness; but without peace and calm, true well-being is absolutely impossible. Thus the subject of willing is constantly lying on the revolving wheel of Ixion, is always drawing water in the sieve of the Danaids, and is the eternally thirsting Tantalus.

When, however, an external cause or inward disposition suddenly raises us out of the endless stream of willing, and snatches knowledge from the thraldom of the will, the attention is now no longer directed to the motives of willing, but comprehends things free from their relation to the will. Thus it considers things without interest, without subjectivity, purely objectively; it is entirely given up to them in so far as they are merely representations, and not motives. Then all at once the peace, always sought but always escaping us on that first path of willing, comes to us of its own accord, and all is well with us. It is the painless state, prized by Epicurus as the highest good and as the state of the gods; for that moment we are delivered from the miserable pressure of the will. We celebrate the Sabbath of the penal servitude of willing; the wheel of Ixion stands still.

But this is just the state that I described above as necessary for knowledge of the Idea, as pure contemplation, absorption in perception, being lost in the object, forgetting all individuality, abolishing the kind of knowledge which follows the principle of sufficient reason, and comprehends only relations. It is the state where, simultaneously and inseparably, the perceived individual thing is raised to the Idea of its species, and the knowing individual to the pure subject of will-less knowing, and now the two, as such, no longer stand in the stream of time and of all other relations. It is then all the same whether we see the setting sun from a prison or from a palace.

Inward disposition, predominance of knowing over willing, can bring about this state in any environment. This is shown by those admirable Dutchmen who directed such purely objective perception to the most insignificant objects, and set up a lasting monument of their objectivity and spiritual peace in paintings of *still life.* The aesthetic beholder does not contemplate this without emotion, for it graphically describes to him the calm, tranquil, will-free frame of mind of the artist which was necessary for contemplating such insignificant things so objectively, considering them so attentively, and repeating this perception with such thought. Since the picture invites the beholder to participate in this state, his emotion is often enhanced by the contrast between it and his own restless state of mind, disturbed by vehement willing, in which he happens to be. In the same spirit landscape painters, especially Ruysdael, have often painted extremely insignificant landscape objects, and have thus produced the same effect even more delightfully.

So much is achieved simply and solely by the inner force of an artistic disposition; but that purely objective frame of mind is facilitated and favoured from without by accommodating objects, by the abundance of natural beauty that invites contemplation, and even presses itself on us. Whenever it presents itself to our gaze all at once, it almost always succeeds in snatching us, although only for a few moments, from subjectivity, from the thraldom of the will, and transferring us into the state of pure knowledge. This is why the man tormented by passions, want, or care, is so suddenly revived, cheered, and comforted by a single, free glance into nature. The storm of passions, the pressure of desire and fear, and all the miseries of willing are then at once calmed and appeased in a marvellous way. For at the moment when, torn from the will, we have given ourselves up to pure, will-less knowing, we have stepped into another world, so to speak, where everything that moves our will, and thus violently agitates us, no longer exists. This liberation of knowledge lifts us as wholly and completely above all this as do sleep and dreams. Happiness and unhappiness have vanished;

we are no longer the individual; that is forgotten; we are only pure
subject of knowledge. We are only that *one* eye of the world which
looks out from all knowing creatures, but which in man alone can be
wholly free from serving the will. In this way, all difference of
individuality disappears so completely that it is all the same whether
the perceiving eye belongs to a mighty monarch or to a stricken
beggar; for beyond that boundary neither happiness nor misery is
taken with us. There always lies so near to us a realm in which
we have escaped entirely from all our affliction; but who has the
strength to remain in it for long? As soon as any relation to our will,
to our person, even of those objects of pure contemplation, again
enters consciousness, the magic is at an end. We fall back into
knowledge governed by the principle of sufficient reason; we now
no longer know the Idea, but the individual thing, the link of a
chain to which we also belong, and we are again abandoned to all
our woe. Most men are almost always at this standpoint, because
they entirely lack objectivity, i.e., genius. Therefore they do not
like to be alone with nature; they need company, or at any rate
a book, for their knowledge remains subject to the will. Therefore
in objects they seek only some relation to their will, and with
everything that has not such a relation there sounds within them, as
it were like a ground-bass, the constant, inconsolable lament, "It
is of no use to me." Thus in solitude even the most beautiful surroundings have for them a desolate, dark, strange, and hostile
appearance.

Finally, it is also that blessedness of will-less perception which
spreads so wonderful a charm over the past and the distant, and
by a self-deception presents them to us in so flattering a light. For
by our conjuring up in our minds days long past spent in a distant
place, it is only the objects recalled by our imagination, not the
subject of will, that carried around its incurable sorrows with it just
as much then as it does now. But these are forgotten, because since
then they have frequently made way for others. Now in what is
remembered, objective perception is just as effective as it would be
in what is present, if we allowed it to have influence over us, if, free
from will, we surrendered ourselves to it. Hence it happens that,
especially when we are more than usually disturbed by some want,
the sudden recollection of past and distant scenes flits across our
minds like a lost paradise. The imagination recalls merely what was
objective, not what was individually subjective, and we imagine that
that something objective stood before us then just as pure and undisturbed by any relation to the will as its image now stands in the
imagination; but the relation of objects to our will caused us just as

much affliction then as it does now. We can withdraw from all
suffering just as well through present as through distant objects,
whenever we raise ourselves to a purely objective contemplation of
them, and are thus able to produce the illusion that only those
objects are present, not we ourselves. Then, as pure subject of
knowing, delivered from the miserable self, we become entirely one
with those objects, and foreign as our want is to them, it is at such
moments just as foreign to us. Then the world as representation
alone remains; the world as will has disappeared.

In all these remarks, I have sought to make clear the nature and
extent of the share which the subjective condition has in aesthetic
pleasure, namely the deliverance of knowledge from the service of
the will, the forgetting of oneself as individual, and the enhancement
of consciousness to the pure, will-less, timeless subject of knowing
that is independent of all relations. With this subjective side of
aesthetic contemplation there always appears at the same time as
necessary correlative its objective side, the intuitive apprehension of
the Platonic Idea. But before we turn to a closer consideration of
this and to the achievements of art in reference to it, it is better
to stop for a while at the subjective side of aesthetic pleasure, in
order to complete our consideration of this by discussing the impression of the *sublime,* which depends solely on it, and arises through a
modification of it. After this, our investigation of aesthetic pleasure
will be completed by a consideration of its objective side.

But first of all, the following remarks appertain to what has so far
been said. Light is most pleasant and delightful; it has become the
symbol of all that is good and salutary. In all religions it indicates
eternal salvation, while darkness symbolizes damnation. Ormuzd
dwells in the purest light, Ahriman in eternal night. Dante's Paradise
looks somewhat like Vauxhall in London, since all the blessed spirits
appear there as points of light that arrange themselves in regular
figures. The absence of light immediately makes us sad, and its
return makes us feel happy. Colours directly excite a keen delight,
which reaches its highest degree when they are translucent. All this
is due to the fact that light is the correlative and condition of the
most perfect kind of knowledge through perception, of the only
knowledge that in no way directly affects the will. For sight, unlike
the affections of the other senses, is in itself, directly, and by its
sensuous effect, quite incapable of pleasantness or unpleasantness of
sensation in the organ; in other words, it has no direct connexion
with the will. Only perception arising in the understanding can have
such a connexion, which then lies in the relation of the object to
the will. In the case of hearing, this is different; tones can excite pain

immediately, and can also be directly agreeable sensuously without reference to harmony or melody. Touch, as being one with the feeling of the whole body, is still more subject to this direct influence on the will; and yet there is a touch devoid of pain and pleasure. Odours, however, are always pleasant or unpleasant, and tastes even more so. Thus the last two senses are most closely related to the will, and hence are always the most ignoble, and have been called by Kant the subjective senses. Therefore the pleasure from light is in fact the pleasure from the objective possibility of the purest and most perfect kind of knowledge from perception. As such it can be deduced from the fact that pure knowing, freed and delivered from all willing, is extremely gratifying, and, as such, has a large share in aesthetic enjoyment. Again, the incredible beauty that we associate with the reflection of objects in water can be deduced from this view of light. That lightest, quickest, and finest species of the effect of bodies on one another, that to which we owe also by far the most perfect and pure of our perceptions, namely the impression by means of reflected light-rays, is here brought before our eyes quite distinctly, clearly, and completely, in cause and effect, and indeed on a large scale. Hence our aesthetic delight from it, which in the main is entirely rooted in the subjective ground of aesthetic pleasure, and is delight from pure knowledge and its ways.[23]

§ 39.

All these considerations are intended to stress the subjective part of aesthetic pleasure, namely, that pleasure in so far as it is delight in the mere knowledge of perception as such, in contrast to the will. Now directly connected with all this is the following explanation of that frame of mind which has been called the feeling of the *sublime*.

It has already been observed that transition into the state of pure perception occurs most easily when the objects accommodate themselves to it, in other words, when by their manifold and at the same time definite and distinct form they easily become representatives of their Ideas, in which beauty, in the objective sense, consists.

---

[23] Cf. chap. 33 of volume 2.

Above all, natural beauty has this quality, and even the most stolid and apathetic person obtains therefrom at least a fleeting, aesthetic pleasure. Indeed, it is remarkable how the plant world in particular invites one to aesthetic contemplation, and, as it were, obtrudes itself thereon. It might be said that such accommodation was connected with the fact that these organic beings themselves, unlike animal bodies, are not immediate object of knowledge. They therefore need the foreign intelligent individual in order to come from the world of blind willing into the world of the representation. Thus they yearn for this entrance, so to speak, in order to attain at any rate indirectly what directly is denied to them. For the rest, I leave entirely undecided this bold and venturesome idea that perhaps borders on the visionary, for only a very intimate and devoted contemplation of nature can excite or justify it.[24] Now so long as it is this accommodation of nature, the significance and distinctness of its forms, from which the Ideas individualized in them readily speak to us; so long as it is this which moves us from knowledge of mere relations serving the will into aesthetic contemplation, and thus raises us to the will-free subject of knowing, so long is it merely the *beautiful* that affects us, and the feeling of beauty that is excited. But these very objects, whose significant forms invite us to a pure contemplation of them, may have a hostile relation to the human will in general, as manifested in its objectivity, the human body. They may be opposed to it; they may threaten it by their might that eliminates all resistance, or their immeasurable greatness may reduce it to nought. Nevertheless, the beholder may not direct his attention to this relation to his will which is so pressing and hostile, but, although he perceives and acknowledges it, he may consciously turn away from it, forcibly tear himself from his will and its relations, and, giving himself up entirely to knowledge, may quietly contemplate, as pure, will-less subject of knowing, those very objects so terrible to the will. He may comprehend only their Idea that is foreign to all relation, gladly linger over its contemplation, and consequently be elevated precisely in this way above himself, his person, his willing, and all willing. In that case, he is then filled with the feeling of the *sublime;* he is in the state of exaltation, and

---

[24] I am now all the more delighted and surprised, forty years after advancing this thought so timidly and hesitatingly, to discover that St. Augustine had already expressed it: *Arbusta formas suas varias, quibus mundi hujus visibilis structura formosa est, sentiendas sensibus praebent; ut, pro eo quod NOSSE non possunt, quasi INNOTESCERE velle videantur.* (*De Civitate Dei,* xi, 27.)

"The trees offer to the senses for perception the many different forms by which the structure of this visible world is adorned, so that, because they are unable to *know*, they may appear, as it were, to want to *be known.*" [Tr.]

therefore the object that causes such a state is called *sublime*. Thus what distinguishes the feeling of the sublime from that of the beautiful is that, with the beautiful, pure knowledge has gained the upper hand without a struggle, since the beauty of the object, in other words that quality of it which facilitates knowledge of its Idea, has removed from consciousness, without resistance and hence imperceptibly, the will and knowledge of relations that slavishly serve this will. What is then left is pure subject of knowing, and not even a recollection of the will remains. On the other hand, with the sublime, that state of pure knowing is obtained first of all by a conscious and violent tearing away from the relations of the same object to the will which are recognized as unfavourable, by a free exaltation, accompanied by consciousness, beyond the will and the knowledge related to it. This exaltation must not only be won with consciousness, but also be maintained, and it is therefore accompanied by a constant recollection of the will, yet not of a single individual willing, such as fear or desire, but of human willing in general, in so far as it is expressed universally through its objectivity, the human body. If a single, real act of will were to enter consciousness through actual personal affliction and danger from the object, the individual will, thus actually affected, would at once gain the upper hand. The peace of contemplation would become impossible, the impression of the sublime would be lost, because it had yielded to anxiety, in which the effort of the individual to save himself supplanted every other thought. A few examples will contribute a great deal to making clear this theory of the aesthetically sublime, and removing any doubt about it. At the same time they will show the difference in the degrees of this feeling of the sublime. For in the main it is identical with the feeling of the beautiful, with pure will-less knowing, and with the knowledge, which necessarily appears therewith, of the Ideas out of all relation that is determined by the principle of sufficient reason. The feeling of the sublime is distinguished from that of the beautiful only by the addition, namely the exaltation beyond the known hostile relation of the contemplated object to the will in general. Thus there result several degrees of the sublime, in fact transitions from the beautiful to the sublime, according as this addition is strong, clamorous, urgent, and near, or only feeble, remote, and merely suggested. I regard it as more appropriate to the discussion to adduce first of all in examples these transitions, and generally the weaker degrees of the impression of the sublime, although those whose aesthetic susceptibility in general is not very great, and whose imagination is not vivid, will understand only the examples, given later, of the higher and more distinct degrees of that impression. They should therefore confine themselves to these, and should ignore the examples of the very weak degree of the above-mentioned impression, which are to be spoken of first.

Just as man is simultaneously impetuous and dark impulse of willing (indicated by the pole of the genitals as its focal point), and eternal, free, serene subject of pure knowing (indicated by the pole of the brain), so, in keeping with this antithesis, the sun is simultaneously the source of *light,* the condition for the most perfect kind, of knowledge, and therefore of the most delightful of things; and the source of *heat,* the first condition of all life, in other words, of every phenomenon of the will at its higher grades. Therefore what heat is for the will, light is for knowledge. For this reason, light is the largest diamond in the crown of beauty, and has the most decided influence on the knowledge of every beautiful object. Its presence generally is an indispensable condition; its favourable arrangement enhances even the beauty of the beautiful. But above all else, the beautiful in architecture is enhanced by the favour of light, and through it even the most insignificant thing becomes a beautiful object. Now if in the depth of winter, when the whole of nature is frozen and stiff, we see the rays of the setting sun reflected by masses of stone, where they illuminate without warming, and are thus favourable only to the purest kind of knowledge, not to the will, then contemplation of the beautiful effect of light on these masses moves us into the state of pure knowing, as all beauty does. Yet here, through the faint recollection of the lack of warmth from those rays, in other words, of the absence of the principle of life, a certain transcending of the interest of the will is required. There is a slight challenge to abide in pure knowledge, to turn away from all willing, and precisely in this way we have a transition from the feeling of the beautiful to that of the sublime. It is the faintest trace of the sublime in the beautiful, and beauty itself appears here only in a slight degree. The following is an example almost as weak.

Let us transport ourselves to a very lonely region of boundless horizons, under a perfectly cloudless sky, trees and plants in the perfectly motionless air, no animals, no human beings, no moving masses of water, the profoundest silence. Such surroundings are as it were a summons to seriousness, to contemplation, with complete emancipation from all willing and its cravings; but it is just this that gives to such a scene of mere solitude and profound peace a touch of the sublime. For, since it affords no objects, either favourable or unfavourable, to the will that is always in need of strife and attainment, there is left only the state of pure contemplation, and whoever is incapable of this is abandoned with shameful ignominy to the emptiness of unoccupied will, to the torture and misery of boredom. To this extent it affords us a measure of our own intellectual worth, and for this generally the degree of our ability to endure solitude, or our love of it, is a good criterion. The surroundings just described, therefore, give us an instance of the sublime in a low degree, for in them with the state of pure knowing in its peace and all-sufficiency there is mingled, as a contrast, a recollection of the dependence and wretchedness of the will in need of constant activity. This is the species of the sublime for which the sight of the boundless prairies of the interior of North America is renowned.

Now let us imagine such a region denuded of plants and showing only bare rocks; the will is at once filled with alarm through the total absence of that which is organic and necessary for our subsistence. The desert takes on a fearful character; our mood becomes more tragic. The exaltation to pure knowledge comes about with a more decided emancipation from the interest of the will, and by our persisting in the state of pure knowledge, the feeling of the sublime distinctly appears.

The following environment can cause this in an even higher degree. Nature in turbulent and tempestuous motion; semi-darkness through threatening black thunder-clouds; immense, bare, overhanging cliffs shutting out the view by their interlacing; rushing, foaming masses of water; complete desert; the wail of the wind sweeping through the ravines. Our dependence, our struggle with hostile nature, our will that is broken in this, now appear clearly before our eyes. Yet as long as personal affliction does not gain the upper hand, but we remain in aesthetic contemplation, the pure subject of knowing gazes through this struggle of nature, through this picture of the broken will, and comprehends calmly, unshaken and unconcerned, the Ideas in those very objects that are threatening and terrible to the will. In this contrast is to be found the feeling of the sublime.

But the impression becomes even stronger, when we have before our eyes the struggle of the agitated forces of nature on a large scale, when in these surroundings the roaring of a falling stream deprives us of the possibility of hearing our own voices. Or when we are abroad in the storm of tempestuous seas; mountainous waves rise and fall, are dashed violently against steep cliffs, and shoot their spray high into the air. The storm howls, the sea roars, the lightning flashes from black clouds, and thunder-claps drown the noise of storm and sea. Then in the unmoved beholder of this scene the twofold nature of his consciousness reaches the highest distinctness. Simultaneously, he feels himself as individual, as the feeble phenomenon of will, which the slightest touch of these forces can annihilate, helpless against powerful nature, dependent, abandoned to chance, a vanishing nothing in face of stupendous forces; and he also feels himself as the eternal, serene subject of knowing, who as the condition of every object is the supporter of this whole world, the fearful struggle of nature being only his mental picture or representation; he himself is free from, and foreign to, all willing and all needs, in the quiet comprehension of the Ideas. This is the full impression of the sublime. Here it is caused by the sight of a power beyond all comparison superior to the individual, and threatening him with annihilation.

The impression of the sublime can arise in quite a different way by our imagining a mere magnitude in space and time, whose immensity reduces the individual to nought. By retaining Kant's terms and his correct division, we can call the first kind the dynamically sublime, and the second the mathematically sublime, although we differ from him entirely in the explanation of the inner nature of that impression, and can concede no share in this either to moral reflections or to hypostases from scholastic philosophy.

If we lose ourselves in contemplation of the infinite greatness of the universe in space and time, meditate on the past millennia and on those to come; or if the heavens at night actually bring innumerable worlds before our eyes, and so impress on our consciousness the immensity of the universe, we feel ourselves reduced to nothing; we feel ourselves as individuals, as living bodies, as transient phenomena of will, like drops in the ocean, dwindling and dissolving into nothing. But against such a ghost of our own nothingness, against such a lying impossibility, there arises the immediate consciousness that all these worlds exist only in our representation, only as modifications of the eternal subject of pure knowing. This we find ourselves to be, as soon as we forget individuality; it is the necessary, conditional supporter of all worlds and of all periods of time. The vastness of the world, which previously disturbed our peace of mind, now rests within us; our dependence on it is now annulled by its dependence on us. All this, however, does not come into reflection at once, but shows itself as a consciousness, merely felt, that in some sense or other (made clear only by philosophy) we are one with the world, and are therefore not oppressed but exalted by its immensity. It is the felt consciousness of what the Upanishads of the Vedas express repeatedly in so many different ways, but most admirably in the saying already quoted: *Hae omnes creaturae in totum ego sum, et praeter me aliud (ens) non est* (*Oupnek'hat,*

Vol. I, p. 122).[25] It is an exaltation beyond our own individuality, a feeling of the sublime.

We receive this impression of the mathematically sublime in quite a direct way through a space which is small indeed as compared with the universe, but which, by becoming directly and wholly perceptible to us, affects us with its whole magnitude in all three dimensions, and is sufficient to render the size of our own body almost infinitely small. This can never be done by a space that is empty for perception, and therefore never by an open space, but only by one that is directly perceivable in all its dimensions through delimitation, and so by a very high and large dome, like that of St. Peter's in Rome or of St. Paul's in London. The feeling of the sublime arises here through our being aware of the vanishing nothingness of our own body in the presence of a greatness which itself, on the other hand, resides only in our representation, and of which we, as knowing subject, are the supporter. Therefore, here as everywhere, it arises through the contrast between the insignificance and dependence of ourselves as individuals, as phenomena of will, and the consciousness of ourselves as pure subject of knowing. Even the vault of the starry heavens, if contemplated without reflection, has only the same effect as that vault of stone, and acts not with its true, but only with its apparent, greatness. Many objects of our perception excite the impression of the sublime; by virtue both of their spatial magnitude and of their great antiquity, and therefore of their duration in time, we feel ourselves reduced to nought in their presence, and yet revel in the pleasure of beholding them. Of this kind are very high mountains, the Egyptian pyramids, and colossal ruins of great antiquity.

Our explanation of the sublime can indeed be extended to cover the ethical, namely what is described as the sublime character. Such a character springs from the fact that the will is not excited here by objects certainly well calculated to excite it, but that knowledge retains the upper hand. Such a character will accordingly consider men in a purely objective way, and not according to the relations they might have to his will. For example, he will observe their faults, and even their hatred and injustice to himself, without being thereby stirred to hatred on his own part. He will contemplate their happiness without feeling envy, recognize their good qualities without desiring closer association with them, perceive the beauty of women without hankering after them. His personal happiness or unhappiness will

[25] "I am all this creation collectively, and besides me there exists no other being." [Tr.]

not violently affect him; he will be rather as Hamlet describes Horatio:

> / for thou hast been
> As one, in suffering all, that suffers nothing;
> A man, that fortune's buffets and rewards
> Hast ta'en with equal thanks, *etc.*
>
> (Act III, Sc. 2.)

For, in the course of his own life and in its misfortunes, he will look less at his own individual lot than at the lot of mankind as a whole, and accordingly will conduct himself in this respect rather as a knower than as a sufferer.

§ 40.

Since opposites throw light on each other, it may here be in place to remark that the real opposite of the sublime is something that is not at first sight recognized as such, namely the *charming or attractive.* By this I understand that which excites the will by directly presenting to it satisfaction, fulfilment. The feeling of the sublime arose from the fact that something positively unfavourable to the will becomes object of pure contemplation. This contemplation is then maintained only by a constant turning away from the will and exaltation above its interests; and this constitutes the sublimity of the disposition. On the other hand, the charming or attractive draws the beholder down from pure contemplation, demanded by every apprehension of the beautiful, since it necessarily stirs his will by objects that directly appeal to it. Thus the beholder no longer remains pure subject of knowing, but becomes the needy and dependent subject of willing. That every beautiful thing of a cheering nature is usually called charming or attractive is due to a concept too widely comprehended through want of correct discrimination, and I must put it entirely on one side, and even object to it. But in the sense already stated and explained, I find in the province of art only two species of the charming, and both are unworthy of it. The one species, a very low one, is found in the still life painting of the Dutch, when they err by depicting edible objects. By their deceptive appearance these necessarily excite the appetite, and this is just a stimulation of the will which puts an end to any aesthetic contemplation of the object. Painted fruit, however, is, admissible, for it exhibits itself as a further development of the flower, and as a beautiful product of nature through form and colour, without our being positively forced to think of its edibility. But unfortunately we often find, depicted with deceptive naturalness, prepared and served-up dishes, oysters, herrings, crabs, bread and butter, beer, wine, and so on, all of which is wholly objectionable. In historical painting and in sculpture the charming consists in nude figures, the position, semi-drapery, and whole treatment of which are calculated to excite lustful feeling in the beholder. Purely aesthetic contemplation is at once abolished, and the purpose of art thus defeated. This mistake is wholly in keeping with what was just censured when speaking of the Dutch. In the case of all beauty and complete nakedness of form, the ancients are almost always free from this fault, since the artist himself created them with a purely objective spirit filled with ideal beauty, not in the spirit of subjective, base sensuality. The charming, therefore, is everywhere to be avoided in art.

There is also a negatively charming, even more objectionable than the positively charming just discussed, and that is the disgusting or offensive. Just like the charming in the proper sense, it rouses the will of the beholder, and therefore disturbs purely aesthetic contemplation. But it is a violent non-willing, a repugnance, that it excites; it rouses the will by holding before it objects that are abhorrent. It has therefore always been recognized as absolutely inadmissible in art, where even the ugly can be tolerated in its proper place so long as it is not disgusting, as we shall see later.

§ 41.

The course of our remarks has made it necessary to insert here a discussion of the sublime, when the treatment of the beautiful has been only half completed, merely from one side, the subjective. For it is only a special modification of this subjective side which distinguishes the sublime from the beautiful. The difference between the beautiful and the sublime depends on whether the state of pure, will-less knowing, presupposed and demanded by any aesthetic contemplation, appears of itself, without opposition, by the mere disappearance of the will from consciousness, since the object invites and attracts us to it; or whether this state is reached only by free, conscious exaltation above the will, to which the contemplated object itself has an unfavourable, hostile relation, a relation that would do away with contemplation if we gave ourselves up to it. This is the distinction between the beautiful and the sublime. In the object the two are not essentially different, for in every case the object of aesthetic contemplation is not the individual thing, but the Idea in it striving for revelation, in other words, the adequate objectivity of the will at a definite grade. Its necessary correlative, withdrawn like itself from the principle of sufficient reason, is the pure subject of knowing, just as the correlative of the particular thing is the knowing individual, both of which lie within the province of the principle of sufficient reason.

By calling an object *beautiful*, we thereby assert that it is an object of our aesthetic contemplation, and this implies two different things. On the one hand, the sight of the thing makes us *objective*, that is to say, in contemplating it we are no longer conscious of ourselves as individuals, but as pure, will-less subjects of knowing. On the other hand, we recognize in the object not the individual thing, but an Idea; and this can happen only in so far as our contemplation of the object is not given up to the principle of sufficient reason, does not follow the relation of the object to something outside it (which is ultimately always connected with relations to our own willing), but rests on the object itself. For the Idea and the pure subject of knowing always appear simultaneously in consciousness as necessary correlatives, and with this appearance all distinction of time at once vanishes, as both are wholly foreign to the principle of sufficient reason in all its forms. Both lie outside the relations laid down by this principle; they can be compared to the rainbow and the sun that take no part in the constant movement and succession of the falling drops. Therefore if, for example, I contemplate a tree aesthetically, i.e., with artistic eyes, and thus recognize not it but its Idea, it is immediately of no importance whether it is this tree or its ancestor that flourished a thousand years ago, and whether the contemplator is this individual, or any other living anywhere and at any time. The particular thing and the knowing individual are abolished with the principle of sufficient reason, and nothing remains but the Idea and the pure subject of knowing, which together constitute the adequate objectivity of the will at this grade. And the Idea is released not only from time but also from space; for the Idea is not really this spatial form which floats before me, but its expression, its pure significance, its innermost being, disclosing itself and appealing to me; and it can be wholly the same, in spite of great difference in the spatial relations of the form.

Now since, on the one hand, every existing thing can be observed purely objectively and outside all relation, and, on the other, the will appears in everything at some grade of its objectivity, and this thing is accordingly the expression of an Idea, everything is also *beautiful.* That even the most insignificant thing admits of purely objective and will-less contemplation and thus proves itself to be beautiful, is testified by the still life paintings of the Dutch, already mentioned in this connexion in para. 38. But one thing is more beautiful than another because it facilitates this purely objective contemplation, goes out to meet it, and, so to speak, even compels it, and then we call the thing very beautiful. This is the case partly because, as individual thing, it expresses purely the Idea of its species through the very distinct, clearly defined, and thoroughly significant relation of its parts. It also completely reveals that Idea through the completeness, united in it, of all the manifestations possible to its species, so that it greatly facilitates for the beholder the transition from the individual thing to the Idea, and thus also the state of pure contemplation. Sometimes that eminent quality of special beauty in an object is to be found in the fact that the Idea itself, appealing to us from the object, is a high grade of the will's objectivity, and is therefore most significant and suggestive. For this reason, man is more beautiful than all other objects, and the revelation of his inner nature is the highest aim of art. Human form and human expression are the most important object of plastic art, just as human conduct is the most important object of poetry. Yet each thing has its own characteristic beauty, not only everything organic that manifests itself in the unity of an individuality, but also everything inorganic and formless, and even every manufactured article. For all these reveal the Ideas through which the will objectifies itself at the lowest grades; they sound, as it were, the deepest, lingering bass-notes of nature. Gravity, rigidity, fluidity, light, and so on, are the Ideas that express themselves in rocks, buildings, and masses of water. Landscape-gardening and architecture can do no more than help them to unfold their qualities distinctly, perfectly, and comprehensively. They give them the opportunity to express themselves clearly, and in this way invite and facilitate aesthetic contemplation. On the other hand, this is achieved in a slight degree, or not at all, by inferior buildings and localities neglected by nature or spoiled by art. Yet these universal basic Ideas of nature do not entirely disappear even from them. Here too they address themselves to the observer who looks for them, and even bad buildings and the like are still capable of being aesthetically contemplated; the Ideas of the most universal properties of their material are still recognizable in them. The artificial form given to them, however, is a means not of facilitating, but rather of hindering, aesthetic contemplation. Manufactured articles also help the expression of Ideas, though here it is not the Idea of the manufactured articles that speaks from them, but the Idea of the material to which this artificial form has been given. In the language of the scholastics this can be very conveniently expressed in two words; thus in the manufactured article is expressed the Idea of its *forma substantialis*, not that of its *forma accidentalis*; the latter leads to no Idea, but only to a human conception from which it has come. It goes without saying that by manufactured article we expressly do not mean any work of plastic art. Moreover, by *forma substantialis* the scholastics in fact understood what I call the grade of the will's objectification in a thing. We shall return once more to the Idea of the material when we consider architecture. Consequently, from our point of view, we cannot agree with Plato when he asserts (*Republic*, X [596 ff.], pp. 284-285, and *Parmenides* [130 ff.], p. 79, *ed. Bip.*) that table and chair express the Ideas of table and chair, but we say that they express the Ideas already expressed in their mere material as such. However, according to Aristotle (*Metaphysics*, xii, chap. 3), Plato himself would have allowed Ideas only of natural beings and entities: ὁ Πλάτων ἔφη, ὅτι εἴδη ἐστὶν ὁπόσα φύσει (*Plato dixit, quod ideae eorum sunt, quae natura sunt*),[26] and in chapter 5 it is said that, according to the Platonists, there are no Ideas of house and ring. In any case, Plato's earliest disciples, as Alcinous informs us (*Introductio in Platonicam philosophiam*, chap. 9), denied that there were Ideas of manufactured articles. Thus he says: Ὁρίζονται δὲ τὴν ἰδέαν, παράδειγμα τῶν κατὰ φύσιν αἰώνιον. Οὔτε γὰρ τοῖς πλείστοις τῶν ἀπὸ Πλάτωνος ἀρέσκει, τῶν τεχνικῶν εἶναι ἰδέας, οἷον ἄσπιδος ἢ λύρας, οὔτε μὴν τῶν παρὰ φύσιν, οἷον πυρετοῦ καὶ χολέρας, οὔτε τῶν κατὰ μέρος, οἷον Σωκράτους καὶ Πλάτωνος, ἀλλ᾽ οὔτε τῶν εὐτελῶν τινός, οἷον ῥύπου καὶ κάρφους, οὔτε τῶν πρός τι, οἷον μείζονος καὶ ὑπερέχοντος· εἶναι γὰρ τὰς ἰδέας νοήσεις θεοῦ αἰωνίους τε καὶ αὐτοτελεῖς.—(*Definiunt autem IDEAM exemplar aeternum eorum quae secundum naturam existunt. Nam plurimis ex iis, qui Platonem secuti sunt, minime placuit, arte factorum ideas esse, ut clypei atque lyrae; neque rursus eorum, quae praeter naturam, ut febris et cholerae; neque particularium, ceu Socratis et Platonis; neque etiam rerum vilium, veluti sordium et festucae; neque relationum, ut majoris et excedentis: esse namque ideas intellectiones dei*

---

aeternas, ac seipsis perfectas.)[27] We may take this opportunity to mention yet another point in which our theory of Ideas differs widely from that of Plato. Thus he teaches (*Republic,* X [601], p. 288) that the object which art aims at expressing, the prototype of painting and poetry, is not the Idea, but the individual thing. The whole of our discussion so far maintains the very opposite, and Plato's opinion is the less likely to lead us astray, as it is the source of one of the greatest and best known errors of that great man, namely of his disdain and rejection of art, especially of poetry. His false judgement of this is directly associated with the passage quoted.

§ 42.

I return to our discussion of the aesthetic impression. Knowledge of the beautiful always supposes, simultaneously and inseparably, a purely knowing subject and a known Idea as object. But yet the source of aesthetic enjoyment will lie sometimes rather in the apprehension of the known Idea, sometimes rather in the bliss and peace of mind of pure knowledge free from all willing, and thus from all individuality and the pain that results therefrom. And in fact, this predominance of the one or the other constituent element of aesthetic enjoyment will depend on whether the intuitively grasped Idea is a higher or a lower grade of the will's objectivity. Thus with aesthetic contemplation (in real life or through the medium of art) of natural beauty in the inorganic and vegetable kingdoms and of the works of architecture, the enjoyment of pure, will-less knowing will predominate, because the Ideas here apprehended are only low grades of the will's objectivity, and therefore are not phenomena of deep significance and suggestive content. On the other hand, if animals and human beings are the object of aesthetic contemplation or presentation, the enjoyment will consist rather in the objective apprehension of these Ideas that are the most distinct revelations of the will. For

---

[27] "But they define *Idea* as a timeless prototype of natural things. For most of Plato's followers do not admit that there are Ideas of products of art, e.g., of shields or lyres, or of things opposed to nature like fever or cholera, or even of individuals like Socrates and Plato, or even of trifling things like bits and chips, or of relations such as being greater or being taller; for the Ideas are the eternal thoughts of God which are in themselves complete." [Tr.]

these exhibit the greatest variety of forms, a wealth and deep significance of phenomena; they reveal to us most completely the essence of the will, whether in its violence, its terribleness, its satisfaction, or its being broken (this last in tragic situations), finally even in its change or self-surrender, which is the particular theme of Christian painting. Historical painting and the drama generally have as object the Idea of the will enlightened by full knowledge. We will now go over the arts one by one, and in this way the theory of the beautiful that we put forward will gain in completeness and distinctness.

§ 43.

Matter as such cannot be the expression of an Idea. For, as we found in the first book, it is causality through and through; its being is simply its acting. But causality is a form of the principle of sufficient reason; knowledge of the Idea, on the other hand, essentially excludes the content of this principle. In the second book we also found matter to be the common substratum of all individual phenomena of the Ideas, and consequently the connecting link between the Idea and the phenomenon or the individual thing. Therefore, for both these reasons, matter cannot by itself express an Idea. This is confirmed *a posteriori* by the fact that of matter as such absolutely no representation from perception is possible, but only an abstract concept. In the representation of perception are exhibited only the forms and qualities, the supporter of which is matter, and in all of which Ideas reveal themselves. This is also in keeping with the fact that causality (the whole essence of matter) cannot by itself be exhibited in perception, but only a definite causal connexion. On the other hand, every *phenomenon* of an Idea, because, as such, it has entered into the form of the principle of sufficient reason, or the *principium individuationis,* must exhibit itself in matter as a quality thereof. Therefore, as we have said, matter is to this extent the connecting link between the Idea and the *principium individuationis,* which is the individual's form of knowledge, or the principle of sufficient reason. Therefore Plato was quite right, for after the Idea and its phenomenon, namely the individual thing, both of which include generally all the things of the world, he put forward matter only as a third thing different from these two (*Timaeus* [48-9], p. 345). The individual, as phenomenon of the Idea, is always matter. Every quality of matter is also always phenomenon of an Idea, and as such is also susceptible of aesthetic contemplation, i.e., of knowledge of the Idea that expresses itself in it. Now this holds good even of the most universal qualities of matter, without which it never exists, and the Ideas of which are the weakest objectivity of the will. Such are gravity, cohesion, rigidity, fluidity, reaction to light, and so on.

Now if we consider *architecture* merely as a fine art and apart from its provision for useful purposes, in which it serves the will and not pure knowledge, and thus is no longer art in our sense, we can assign it no purpose other than that of bringing to clearer perceptiveness some of those Ideas that are the lowest grades of the will's objectivity. Such Ideas are gravity, cohesion, rigidity, hardness, those universal qualities of stone, those first, simplest, and dullest visibilities of the will, the fundamental bass-notes of nature; and along with these, light, which is in many respects their opposite. Even at this low stage of the will's objectivity, we see its inner nature revealing itself in discord; for, properly speaking, the conflict between gravity and rigidity is the sole aesthetic material of architecture; its problem is to make this conflict appear with perfect distinctness in many different ways. It solves this problem by depriving these indestructible forces of the shortest path to their satisfaction, and keeping them in suspense through a circuitous path; the conflict is thus prolonged, and the inexhaustible efforts of the two forces become visible in many different ways. The whole mass of the building, if left to its original tendency, would exhibit a mere heap or lump, bound to the earth as firmly as possible, to which gravity, the form in which the will here appears, presses incessantly, whereas rigidity, also objectivity of the will, resists. But this very tendency, this effort, is thwarted in its immediate satisfaction by architecture, and only an indirect satisfaction by roundabout ways is granted to it. The joists and beams, for example, can press the earth only by means of the column; the arch must support itself, and only through the medium of the pillars can it satisfy its tendency towards the earth, and so on. By just these enforced digressions, by these very hindrances, those forces inherent in the crude mass of stone unfold themselves in the most distinct and varied manner; and the purely aesthetic purpose of architecture can go no farther. Therefore the beauty of a building is certainly to be found in the evident and obvious suitability of every part, not to the outward arbitrary purpose of man (to this extent the work belongs to practical architecture), but directly to the stability of the whole. The position, size, and form of every part must have so necessary a relation to this stability that if it were possible to remove some part, the whole would inevitably collapse. For only by each part bearing as much as it conveniently can, and each being supported exactly where it ought to be and to exactly the necessary extent, does this play of opposition, this conflict between rigidity and gravity, that constitutes the life of the stone and the manifestations of its will, unfold itself in the most complete visibility. These lowest grades of the will's objectivity distinctly reveal themselves. In just the same way, the form of each part must be determined not arbitrarily, but by its purpose and its relation to the whole. The column is the simplest form of support, determined merely by the purpose or intention. The twisted column is tasteless; the four-cornered pillar is in fact less simple than the round column, though it happens to be more easily made. Also the forms of frieze, joist, arch, vault, dome are determined entirely by their immediate purpose, and are self-explanatory therefrom. Ornamental work on capitals, etc., belongs to sculpture and not to architecture, and is merely tolerated as an additional embellishment, which might be dispensed with. From what has been said, it is absolutely necessary for an understanding and aesthetic enjoyment of a work of architecture to have direct knowledge through perception of its matter as regards its weight, rigidity, and cohesion. Our pleasure in such a work would suddenly be greatly diminished by the disclosure that the building material was pumice-stone, for then it would strike us as a kind of sham building. We should be affected in almost the same way if we were told that it was only of wood, when we had assumed it to be stone, just because this alters and shifts the relation between rigidity and gravity, and thus the significance and necessity of all the parts; for those natural forces reveal themselves much more feebly in a wooden building. Therefore, no architectural work as fine art can really be made of timber, however many forms this may assume; this can be explained simply and solely by our theory. If we were told clearly that the building, the sight of which pleased us, consisted of entirely different materials of very unequal weight and consistency, but not distinguishable by the eye, the whole building would become as incapable of affording us pleasure as would a poem in an unknown language. All this proves that architecture affects us not only mathematically, but dynamically, and that what speaks to us through it is not mere form and symmetry, but rather those fundamental forces of nature, those primary Ideas, those lowest grades of the will's objectivity. The regularity of the building and its parts is produced to some extent by the direct adaptation of each member to the stability of the whole; to some extent it serves to facilitate a survey and comprehension of the whole. Finally regular figures contribute to the beauty by revealing the conformity to law of space as such. All this, however, is only of subordinate value and necessity, and is by no means the principal thing, for symmetry is not invariably demanded, as even ruins are still beautiful.

Now architectural works have a quite special relation to light; in full sunshine with the blue sky as a background they gain a twofold beauty; and by moonlight again they reveal quite a different effect. Therefore when a fine work of architecture is erected, special consideration is always given to the effects of light and to the climate. The reason for all this is to be found principally in the fact that only a bright strong illumination makes all the parts and their relations clearly visible. Moreover, I am of the opinion that architecture is destined to reveal not only gravity and rigidity, but at the same time the nature of light, which is their very opposite. The light is intercepted, impeded, and reflected by the large, opaque, sharply contoured and variously formed masses of stone, and thus unfolds its nature and qualities in the purest and clearest way, to the great delight of the beholder; for light is the most agreeable of things as the condition and objective correlative of the most perfect kind of knowledge through perception.

Now since the Ideas, brought to clear perception by architecture, are the lowest grades of the will's objectivity, and since, in consequence, the objective significance of what architecture reveals to us is relatively small, the aesthetic pleasure of looking at a fine and favourably illuminated building will lie not so much in the apprehension of the Idea as in the subjective correlative thereof which accompanies this apprehension. Hence this pleasure will consist preeminently in the fact that, at the sight of this building, the beholder is emancipated from the kind of knowledge possessed by the individual, which serves the will and follows the principle of sufficient reason, and is raised to that of the pure, will-free subject of knowing. Thus it will consist in pure contemplation itself, freed from all the suffering of will and of individuality. In this respect, the opposite of architecture, and the other extreme in the series of fine arts, is the drama, which brings to knowledge the most significant of all the Ideas; hence in the aesthetic enjoyment of it the objective side is predominant throughout.

Architecture is distinguished from the plastic arts and poetry by the fact that it gives us not a copy, but the thing itself. Unlike those arts, it does not repeat the known Idea, whereby the artist lends his eyes to the beholder. But in it the artist simply presents the object to the beholder, and makes the apprehension of the Idea easy for him by bringing the actual individual object to a clear and complete expression of its nature.

Unlike the works of the other fine arts, those of architecture are very rarely executed for purely aesthetic purposes. On the contrary, they are subordinated to other, practical ends that are foreign to art itself. Thus the great merit of the architect consists in his achieving and attaining purely aesthetic ends, in spite of their subordination to other ends foreign to them. This he does by skilfully adapting them in many different ways to the arbitrary ends in each case, and by correctly judging what aesthetically architectural beauty is consistent and compatible with a temple, a palace, a prison, and so on. The more a harsh climate increases those demands of necessity and utility, definitely determines them, and inevitably prescribes them, the less scope is there for the beautiful in architecture. In the mild climate of India, Egypt, Greece, and Rome, where the demands of necessity were fewer and less definite, architecture was able to pursue its aesthetic ends with the greatest freedom. Under a northern sky these are greatly curtailed for architecture; here, where the requirements were coffers, pointed roofs, and towers, it could unfold its beauty only within very narrow limits, and had to make amends all the more by making use of embellishments borrowed from sculpture, as can be seen in Gothic architecture.

In this way architecture is bound to suffer great restrictions through the demands of necessity and utility. On the other hand, it has in these a very powerful support, for with the range and expense of its works and with the narrow sphere of its aesthetic effect, it certainly could not maintain itself merely as a fine art unless it had at the same time, as a useful and necessary profession, a firm and honourable place among men's occupations. It is the lack of this that prevents another art from standing beside architecture as a sister art, although, in an aesthetic respect, this can be quite properly coordinated with architecture as its companion; I am referring to the artistic arrangement of water. For what architecture achieves for the Idea of gravity where this appears associated with rigidity, is the same as what this other art achieves for the same Idea where this Idea is associated with fluidity, in other words, with formlessness, maximum mobility, and transparency. Waterfalls tumbling, dashing, and foaming over rocks, cataracts softly dispersed into spray, springs gushing up as high columns of water, and clear reflecting lakes reveal the Ideas of fluid heavy matter in exactly the same way as the works of architecture unfold the Ideas of rigid matter. Hydraulics as a fine art finds no support in practical hydraulics, for as a rule the ends of the one cannot be combined with those of the other. Only by way of an exception does this come about, for example, in the *Cascata di Trevi* in Rome.[28]

§ 44.

W hat the two arts just mentioned achieve for these lowest grades of the will's objectivity is achieved to a certain extent for the higher grade of vegetable nature by artistic horticulture. The landscape-beauty of a spot depends for the most part on the multiplicity of the natural objects found together in it, and on the fact that they are clearly separated, appear distinctly, and yet exhibit themselves in fitting association and succession. It is these two conditions that are assisted by artistic horticulture; yet this art is not nearly such a master of its material as architecture is of its, and so its effect is limited. The beauty displayed by it belongs almost entirely to nature; the art itself does little for it. On the other hand, this art can also do very little against the inclemency of nature, and where nature works not for but against it, its achievements are insignificant.

Therefore, in so far as the plant world, which offers itself to aesthetic enjoyment everywhere without the medium of art, is an object of art, it belongs principally to landscape-painting, and in the province of this is to be found along with it all the rest of nature-devoid-of-knowledge. In paintings of still life and of mere architecture, ruins, church interiors, and so on, the subjective side of aesthetic pleasure is predominant, in other words, our delight does not reside mainly in the immediate apprehension of the manifested Ideas, but rather in the subjective correlative of this apprehension, in pure will-less knowing. For since the painter lets us see the things through his eyes, we here obtain at the same time a sympathetic

---

[28] Cf. chap. 35 of volume 2.

and reflected feeling of the profound spiritual peace and the complete silence of the will, which were necessary for plunging knowledge so deeply into those inanimate objects, and for comprehending them with such affection, in other words with such a degree of objectivity. Now the effect of landscape-painting proper is on the whole also of this kind; but because the Ideas manifested, as higher grades of the will's objectivity, are more significant and suggestive, the objective side of aesthetic pleasure comes more to the front, and balances the subjective. Pure knowing as such is no longer entirely the main thing, but the known Idea, the world as representation at an important grade of the will's objectification, operates with equal force.

But an even much higher grade is revealed by animal painting and animal sculpture. Of the latter we have important antique remains, for example, the horses in Venice, on Monte Cavallo, in the Elgin Marbles, also in Florence in bronze and marble; in the same place the ancient wild boar, the howling wolves; also the lions in the Venice Arsenal; in the Vatican there is a whole hall almost filled with ancient animals and other objects. In these presentations the objective side of aesthetic pleasure obtains a decided predominance over the subjective. The peace of the subject who knows these Ideas, who has silenced his own will, is present, as indeed it is in any aesthetic contemplation, but its effect is not felt, for we are occupied with the restlessness and impetuosity of the depicted will. It is that willing, which also constitutes our own inner nature, that here appears before us in forms and figures. In these the phenomenon of will is not, as in us, controlled and tempered by thoughtfulness, but is exhibited in stronger traits and with a distinctness verging on the grotesque and monstrous. On the other hand, this phenomenon manifests itself without dissimulation, naïvely and openly, freely and evidently, and precisely on this rests our interest in animals. The characteristic of the species already appeared in the presentation of plants, yet it showed itself only in the forms; here it becomes much more significant, and expresses itself not only in the form, but in the action, position, and deportment, though always only as the character of the species, not of the individual. This knowledge of the Ideas at higher grades, which we receive in painting through the agency of another person, can also be directly shared by us through the purely contemplative perception of plants, and by the observation of animals, and indeed of the latter in their free, natural, and easy state. The objective contemplation of their many different and marvellous forms, and of their actions and behaviour, is an instructive lesson from the great book of nature; it is the deciphering of the true *signatura rerum*.[29] We see in it the manifold grades and modes of manifestation of the will that is one and the same in all beings and everywhere wills the same thing. This will objectifies itself as life, as existence, in such endless succession and variety, in such different forms, all of which are accommodations to the various external conditions, and can be compared to many variations on the same theme. But if we had to convey to the beholder, for reflection and in a word, the explanation and information about their inner nature, it would be best for us to use the Sanskrit formula which occurs so often in the sacred books of the Hindus, and is called *Mahavakya*, i.e., the great word: *"Tat tvam asi,"* which means "This living thing art thou."

§ 45.

Finally, the great problem of historical painting and of sculpture is to present, immediately and for perception, the Idea in which the will reaches the highest degree of its objectification. The objective side of pleasure in the beautiful is here wholly predominant, and the subjective is now in the background. Further, it is to be observed that at the next grade below this, in other words, in animal painting, the characteristic is wholly one with the beautiful; the most characteristic lion, wolf, horse, sheep, or ox is always the most beautiful. The reason for this is that animals have only the character of the species, not an individual character. But in the manifestation of man the character of the species is separated from the character of the individual. The former is now called beauty (wholly in the objective sense), but the latter retains the name of character or expression, and the new difficulty arises

---

[29] Jacob Böhme in his book *De Signatura Rerum,* chap. I, §§ 15, 16, 17, says: "And there is no thing in nature that does not reveal its inner form outwardly as well; for the internal continually works towards revelation . . . Each thing has its mouth for revelation. And this is the language of nature in which each thing speaks out of its own property, and always reveals and manifests itself . . . For each thing reveals its mother, who therefore gives the *essence and the will* to the form."

of completely presenting both at the same time in the same individual. *Human beauty* is an objective expression that denotes the will's most complete objectification at the highest grade at which this is knowable, namely the Idea of man in general, completely and fully expressed in the perceived form. But however much the objective side of the beautiful appears here, the subjective still always remains its constant companion. No object transports us so rapidly into purely aesthetic contemplation as the most beautiful human countenance and form, at the sight of which we are instantly seized by an inexpressible satisfaction and lifted above ourselves and all that torments us. This is possible only because of the fact that this most distinct and purest perceptibility of the will raises us most easily and rapidly into the state of pure knowing in which our personality, our willing with its constant pain, disappears, as long as the purely aesthetic pleasure lasts. Therefore, Goethe says that "Whoever beholds human beauty cannot be infected with evil; he feels in harmony with himself and the world." Now, that nature succeeds in producing a beautiful human form must be explained by saying that the will at this highest grade objectifies itself in an individual, and thus, through fortunate circumstances and by its own power, completely overcomes all the obstacles and opposition presented to it by phenomena of the lower grades. Such are the forces of nature from which the will must always wrest and win back the matter that belongs to them all. Further, the phenomenon of the will at the higher grades always has multiplicity in its form. The tree is only a systematic aggregate of innumerably repeated sprouting fibres. This combination increases more and more the higher we go, and the human body is a highly complex system of quite different parts, each of which has its *vita propria*, a life subordinate to the whole, yet characteristic. That all these parts are precisely and appropriately subordinated to the whole and coordinated with one another; that they conspire harmoniously to the presentation of the whole, and there is nothing excessive or stunted; all these are the rare conditions, the result of which is beauty, the completely impressed character of the species. Thus nature: but how is it with art? It is imagined that this is done by imitating nature. But how is the artist to recognize the perfect work to be imitated, and how is he to discover it from among the failures, unless he anticipates the beautiful *prior to experience?* Moreover, has nature ever produced a human being perfectly beautiful in all his parts? It has been supposed that the artist must gather the beautiful parts separately distributed among many human beings, and construct a beautiful whole from them; an absurd and meaningless opinion. Once again, it is asked, how is he to know that just these forms and not others are beautiful? We also see how far the old German painters arrived at beauty by imitating nature. Let us consider their nude figures. No knowledge of the beautiful is at all possible purely *a posteriori* and from mere experience. It is always, at least partly, *a priori*, though of quite a different kind from the forms of the principle of sufficient reason, of which we are *a priori* conscious. These concern the universal form of the phenomenon as such, as it establishes the possibility of knowledge in general, the universal *how* of appearance without exception, and from this knowledge proceed mathematics and pure natural science. On the other hand, that other kind of knowledge *a priori*, which makes it possible to present the beautiful, concerns the content of phenomena instead of the form, the *what* of the appearance instead of the *how*. We all recognize human beauty when we see it, but in the genuine artist this takes place with such clearness that he shows it as he has never seen it, and in his presentation he surpasses nature. Now this is possible only because *we ourselves* are the will, whose adequate objectification at its highest grade is here to be judged and discovered. In fact, only in this way have we an anticipation of what nature (which is in fact just the will constituting our own inner being) endeavours to present. In the true genius this anticipation is accompanied by a high degree of thoughtful intelligence, so that, by recognizing in the individual thing its *Idea*, he, so to speak, *understands nature's half-spoken words*. He expresses clearly what she merely stammers. He impresses on the hard marble the beauty of the form which nature failed to achieve in a thousand attempts, and he places it before her, exclaiming as it were, "This is what you desired to say!" And from the man who knows comes the echoing reply, "Yes, that is it!" Only in this way was the Greek genius able to discover the prototype of the human form, and to set it up as the canon for the school of sculpture. Only by virtue of such an anticipation also is it possible for all of us to recognize the beautiful where nature has actually succeeded in the particular case. This anticipation is the *Ideal;* it is the *Idea* in so far as it is known *a priori*, or at any rate half-known; and it becomes practical for art by accommodating and supplementing as such what is given *a posteriori* through nature. The possibility of such anticipation of the beautiful *a priori* in the artist, as well as of its recognition *a posteriori* by the connoisseur, is to be found in the fact that artist and connoisseur are themselves the "in-itself" of nature, the will objectifying itself. For, as Empedocles said, like can be recognized only by like; only nature can understand herself; only nature will fathom herself; but also only by the mind is the mind comprehended.[30]

The opinion is absurd, although expressed by Xenophon's Socrates (Stobaeus, *Florilegium,* ii, p. 384), that the Greeks discovered the established ideal of human beauty wholly empirically by collecting separate beautiful parts, uncovering and noting here a knee, and there an arm. It has its exact parallel in regard to the art of poetry, namely the assumption that Shakespeare, for example, noted, and then reproduced from his own experience of life, the innumerable and varied characters in his dramas, so true, so sustained, so thoroughly and profoundly worked out. The impossibility and absurdity of such an assumption need not be discussed. It is obvious that the man of genius produces the works of poetic art only by an anticipation of what is characteristic, just as he produces the works of plastic and pictorial art only by a prophetic anticipation of the beautiful, though both require experience as a schema or model. In this alone is that something of which they are dimly aware *a priori,* called into distinctness, and the possibility of thoughtful and intelligent presentation appears.

Human beauty was declared above to be the most complete objectification of the will at the highest grade of its knowability. It expresses itself through the form, and this resides in space alone, and has no necessary connexion with time, as movement for example has. To this extent we can say that the adequate objectification of the will through a merely spatial phenomenon is beauty, in the objective sense. The plant is nothing but such a merely spatial phenomenon of the will; for no movement, and consequently no relation to time (apart from its development), belong to the expression of its nature. Its mere form expresses and openly displays its whole inner being. Animal and man, however, still need for the complete revelation of the will appearing in them a series of actions, and thus that phenomenon in them obtains a direct relation to time. All this has already been discussed in the previous book; it is connected with our present remarks in the following way. As the merely spatial phenomenon of the will can objectify that will perfectly or imperfectly at each definite grade—and it is just this that constitutes beauty or ugliness

---

[30] The last sentence is the translation of *il n'y a que l'esprit qui sente l'esprit* of Helvetius. There was no need to mention this in the first edition. But since then, the times have become so degraded and crude through the stupefying influence of Hegel's sham wisdom, that many might well imagine here an allusion to the antithesis between "spirit and nature." I am therefore compelled to guard myself expressly against the interpolation of such vulgar philosophemes.

—so also can the temporal objectification of the will, i.e., the action, and indeed the direct action, and hence the movement, correspond purely and perfectly to the will which objectifies itself in it, without foreign admixture, without superfluity, without deficiency, expressing only the exact act of will determined in each case; or the converse of all this may occur. In the first case, the movement occurs with *grace;* in the second, without it. Thus as beauty is the adequate and suitable manifestation of the will in general, through its merely spatial phenomenon, so *grace* is the adequate manifestation of the will through its temporal phenomenon, in other words, the perfectly correct and appropriate expression of each act of will through the movement and position that objectifies it. As movement and position presuppose the body, Winckelmann's expression is very true and to the point when he says: "Grace is the peculiar relation of the acting person to the action." (*Werke,* Vol. I, p. 258.) It follows automatically that beauty can be attributed to plants, but not grace, unless in a figurative sense; to animals and human beings, both beauty and grace. In accordance with what has been said, grace consists in every movement being performed and every position taken up in the easiest, most appropriate, and most convenient way, and consequently in being the purely adequate expression of its intention or of the act of will, without any superfluity that shows itself as unsuitable meaningless bustle or absurd posture; without any deficiency that shows itself as wooden stiffness. Grace presupposes a correct proportion in all the limbs, a symmetrical, harmonious structure of the body, as only by means of these are perfect ease and evident appropriateness in all postures and movements possible. Therefore grace is never without a certain degree of beauty of the body. The two, complete and united, are the most distinct phenomenon of the will at the highest grade of its objectification.

As mentioned above, it is one of the distinguishing features of mankind that therein the character of the species and that of the individual are separated so that, as was said in the previous book, each person exhibits to a certain extent an Idea that is wholly characteristic of him. Therefore the arts, aiming at a presentation of the Idea of mankind, have as their problem both beauty as the character of the species, and the character of the individual, which is called *character par excellence.* Again, they have this only in so far as this character is to be regarded not as something accidental and quite peculiar to the man as a single individual, but as a side of the Idea of mankind, specially appearing in this particular individual; and thus the presentation of this individual serves to reveal this Idea. Therefore the character, although individual as such, must be comprehended and expressed ideally, in other words, with emphasis on its significance in regard to the Idea of mankind in general (to the objectifying of which it contributes in its own way). Moreover, the presentation is a portrait, a repetition of the individual as such, with all his accidental qualities. And as Winckelmann says, even the portrait should be the ideal of the individual.

That *character,* to be comprehended ideally, which is the emphasis of a particular and peculiar side of the Idea of mankind, now manifests itself visibly, partly through permanent physiognomy and bodily form, partly through fleeting emotion and passion, the reciprocal modification of knowing and willing through each other; and all this is expressed in mien and movement. The individual always belongs to humanity; on the other hand, humanity always reveals itself in the individual, and that with the peculiar ideal significance of this individual; therefore beauty cannot be abolished by character, or character by beauty. For the abolition of the character of the species by that of the individual would give us caricature, and the abolition of the character of the individual by that of the species would result in meaninglessness. Therefore, the presentation that aims at beauty, as is done mainly by sculpture, will always modify this (i.e., the character of the species) in some respect by the individual character, and will always express the Idea of mankind in a definite individual way, emphasizing a particular side of it. For the human individual as such has, to a certain extent, the dignity of an Idea of his own; and it is essential to the Idea of mankind that it manifest itself in individuals of characteristic significance. Therefore we find in the works of the ancients that the beauty distinctly apprehended by them is expressed not by a single form, but by many forms bearing various characters. It is always grasped, so to speak, from a different side, and is accordingly presented in one manner in Apollo, in another in Bacchus, in another in Hercules, and in yet another in Antinous. In fact, the characteristic can limit the beautiful, and finally can appear even as ugliness, in the drunken Silenus, in the Faun, and so on. But if the characteristic goes so far as actually to abolish the character of the species, that is, if it extends to the unnatural, it becomes caricature. But far less than beauty can grace be interfered with by what is characteristic, for the expression of the character also demands graceful position and movement; yet it must be achieved in a way that is most fitting, appropriate, and easy for the person. This will be observed not only by the sculptor and painter, but also by every good actor, otherwise caricature appears here also as grimace or distortion.

In sculpture beauty and grace remain the principal matter. The real character of the mind, appearing in emotion, passion, alternations of knowing and willing, which can be depicted only by the expression of the face and countenance, is preeminently the province of *painting.* For although eyes and colour, lying outside the sphere of sculpture, contribute a great deal to beauty, they are far more essential for the character. Further, beauty unfolds itself more completely to contemplation from several points of view; on the other hand, the expression, the character, can be completely apprehended from a single viewpoint.

Since beauty is obviously the chief aim of sculpture, Lessing tried to explain the fact that the Laocoön *does not cry out* by saying that crying out is incompatible with beauty. This subject became for Lessing the theme, or at any rate the starting-point, of a book of his own, and a great deal has been written on the subject both before and after him. I may therefore be permitted incidentally to express my opinion about it here, although such a special discussion does not really belong to the sequence of our argument, which throughout is directed to what is general.

§ 46.

It is obvious that, in the famous group, Laocoön is not crying out, and the universal and ever-recurring surprise at this must be attributable to the fact that we should all cry out in his place. Nature also demands this; for in the case of the most acute physical pain and the sudden appearance of the greatest bodily fear, all reflection that might induce silent endurance is entirely expelled from consciousness, and nature relieves itself by crying out, thus expressing pain and fear at the same time, summoning the deliverer and terrifying the assailant. Therefore Winckelmann regretted the absence of the expression of crying out; but as he tried to justify the artist, he really made Laocoön into a Stoic who considered it beneath his dignity to cry out *secundum naturam,*[31] but added to his pain the useless constraint of stifling its expression. Winckelmann therefore sees in him "the tried spirit of a great man writhing in agony, and trying to suppress the expression of feeling and to lock it up in himself. He does not break out into a loud shriek, as in Virgil, but only

---

[31] "In accordance with nature." [Tr.]

anxious sighs escape him," and so on. (*Werke*, Vol. vii, p. 98; the same in more detail in Vol. vi, pp. 104 *seq.*) This opinion of Winckelmann was criticized by Lessing in his Laocoön, and improved by him in the way mentioned above. In place of the psychological reason, he gave the purely aesthetic one that beauty, the principle of ancient art, does not admit the expression of crying out. Another argument he gives is that a wholly fleeting state, incapable of any duration, should not be depicted in a motionless work of art. This has against it a hundred examples of excellent figures that are fixed in wholly fleeting movements, dancing, wrestling, catching, and so on. Indeed, Goethe, in the essay on the Laocoön which opens the *Propyläen* (p. 8) considers the choice of such a wholly fleeting moment to be absolutely necessary. In our day, Hirt (*Horae*, 1797, tenth St.), reducing everything to the highest truth of the expression, decided the matter by saying that Laocoön does not cry out because he is no longer able to, as he is on the point of dying from suffocation. Finally, Fernow (*Römische Studien*, Vol. I, pp. 426 *seq.*) weighed and discussed all these three opinions; he did not, however, add a new one of his own, but reconciled and amalgamated all three.

I cannot help being surprised that such thoughtful and acute men laboriously bring in far-fetched and inadequate reasons, and resort to psychological and even physiological arguments, in order to explain a matter the reason of which is quite near at hand, and to the unprejudiced is immediately obvious. I am particularly surprised that Lessing, who came so near to the correct explanation, completely missed the point.

Before all psychological and physiological investigation as to whether Laocoön in his position would cry out or not (and I affirm that he certainly would), it has to be decided as regards the group that crying out ought not to be expressed in it, for the simple reason that the presentation of this lies entirely outside the province of sculpture. A shrieking Laocoön could not be produced in marble, but only one with the mouth wide open fruitlessly endeavouring to shriek, a Laocoön whose voice was stuck in his throat, *vox faucibus haesit*.[32] The essence of shrieking, and consequently its effect on the onlooker, lies entirely in the sound, not in the gaping mouth. This latter phenomenon that necessarily accompanies the shriek must be motivated and justified first through the sound produced by it; it is then permissible and indeed necessary, as characteristic of the action, although it is detrimental to beauty. But in plastic art, to which the presentation of shrieking is quite foreign and impossible, it would be

---

[32] Virgil, *Aeneid*, xii, 868. [Tr.]

really foolish to exhibit the violent medium of shrieking, namely the gaping mouth, which disturbs all the features and the rest of the expression, since we should then have before us the means, which moreover demands many sacrifices, whilst its end, the shrieking itself together with its effect on our feelings, would fail to appear. Moreover there would be produced each time the ridiculous spectacle of a permanent exertion without effect. This could actually be compared to the wag who, for a joke, stopped up with wax the horn of the sleeping night watchman, and then woke him up with the cry of fire, and amused himself watching the man's fruitless efforts to blow. On the other hand, where the expression of shrieking lies in the province of dramatic art, it is quite admissible, because it serves truth, in other words, the complete expression of the Idea. So in poetry, which claims for perceptive presentation the imagination of the reader. Therefore in Virgil Laocoön cries out like an ox that has broken loose after being struck by an axe. Homer (*Iliad,* xx, 48-53) represents Ares and Athene as shrieking horribly without detracting from their divine dignity or beauty. In just the same way with acting; on the stage Laocoön would certainly have to cry out. Sophocles also represents Philoctetes as shrieking, and on the ancient stage he would certainly have done so. In quite a similar case, I remember having seen in London the famous actor Kemble in a piece called *Pizarro,* translated from the German. He played the part of the American, a half-savage, but of very noble character. Yet when he was wounded, he cried out loudly and violently, and this was of great and admirable effect, since it was highly characteristic and contributed a great deal to the truth. On the other hand, a painted or voiceless shrieker in stone would be much more ridiculous than the painted music that is censured in Goethe's *Propyläen.* For shrieking is much more detrimental to the rest of the expression and to beauty than music is; for at most this concerns only hands and arms, and is to be looked upon as an action characterizing the person. Indeed, to this extent it can be quite rightly painted, so long as it does not require any violent movement of the body or distortion of the mouth; thus for example, St. Cecilia at the organ, Raphael's violinist in the Sciarra Gallery in Rome, and many others. Now since, on account of the limitations of the art, the pain of Laocoön could not be expressed by shrieking, the artist had to set in motion every other expression of pain. This he achieved to perfection, as is ably described by Winckelmann (*Werke,* Vol. vi, pp. 104 *seq.*), whose admirable account therefore retains its full value and truth as soon as we abstract from the stoical sentiment underlying it.[33]

---

[33] This episode has its supplement in chap. 36 of volume 2.

§ 47.

Because beauty with grace is the principal subject of sculpture, it likes the nude, and tolerates clothing only in so far as this does not conceal the form. It makes use of drapery, not as a covering, but as an indirect presentation of the form. This method of presentation greatly engrosses the understanding, since the understanding reaches the perception of the cause, namely the form of the body, only through the one directly given effect, that is to say, the arrangement of the drapery. Therefore in sculpture drapery is to some extent what foreshortening is in painting. Both are suggestions, yet not symbolical, but such that, if they succeed, they force the understanding immediately to perceive what is suggested, just as if it were actually given.

Here I may be permitted in passing to insert a comparison relating to the rhetorical arts. Just as the beautiful bodily form can be seen to the best advantage with the lightest clothing, or even no clothing at all, and thus a very handsome man, if at the same time he had taste and could follow it, would prefer to walk about almost naked, clothed only after the manner of the ancients; so will every fine mind rich in ideas express itself always in the most natural, candid, and simple way, concerned if it be possible to communicate its thoughts to others, and thus to relieve the loneliness that one is bound to feel in a world such as this. Conversely, poverty of mind, confusion and perversity of thought will clothe themselves in the most far-fetched expressions and obscure forms of speech, in order to cloak in difficult and pompous phrases small, trifling, insipid, or commonplace ideas. It is like the man who lacks the majesty of beauty, and wishes to make up for this deficiency by clothing; he attempts to cover up the insignificance or ugliness of his person under barbaric finery, tinsel, feathers, ruffles, cuffs, and mantles. Thus many an author, if compelled to translate his pompous and obscure book into its little clear content, would be as embarrassed as that man would be if he were to go about naked.

§ 48.

*H*istorical *painting* has, besides beauty and grace, character as its principal object; by character is to be understood in general the manifestation of the will at the highest grade of its objectification. Here the individual, as emphasizing a particular side of the Idea of mankind, has peculiar significance, and makes this known not by mere form alone; on the contrary, he renders it visible in mien and countenance by action of every kind, and by the modifications of knowing and willing which occasion and accompany it. Since the Idea of mankind is to be exhibited in this sphere, the unfolding of its many-sidedness must be brought before our eyes in significant individuals, and these again can be made visible in their significance only through many different scenes, events, and actions. Now this endless problem is solved by historical painting, for it brings before our eyes scenes from life of every kind, of great or trifling significance. No individual and no action can be without significance; in all and through all, the Idea of mankind unfolds itself more and more. Therefore no event in the life of man can possibly be excluded from painting. Consequently, a great injustice is done to the eminent painters of the Dutch school, when their technical skill alone is esteemed, and in other respects they are looked down on with disdain, because they generally depict objects from everyday life, whereas only events from world or biblical history are regarded as significant. We should first of all bear in mind that the inward significance of an action is quite different from the outward, and that the two often proceed in separation from each other. The outward significance is the importance of an action in relation to its consequences for and in the actual world, and hence according to the principle of sufficient reason. The inward significance is the depth of insight into the Idea of mankind which it discloses, in that it brings to light sides of that Idea which rarely appear. This it does by causing individualities, expressing themselves distinctly and decidedly, to unfold their peculiar characteristics by means of appropriately arranged circumstances. In art only the inward significance is of importance; in history the outward. The two are wholly independent of each other; they can appear together, but they can also appear alone. An action of the highest significance for history can in its inner significance be very common and ordinary. Conversely, a scene from everyday life can be of great inward significance, if human individuals and the innermost recesses of human action and will appear in it in a clear and distinct light. Even in spite of very different outward significance, the inward can be the same; thus, for example, it is all the same as regards inward significance whether ministers dispute about countries and nations over a map, or boors in a beer-house choose to wrangle over cards and dice; just as it is all the same whether we play chess with pieces of gold or of wood. Moreover, the scenes and events that make up the life of so many millions of human beings, their actions, their sorrows, and their joys, are on that account important enough to be the object of art, and by their rich variety must afford material enough to unfold the many-sided Idea of mankind. Even the fleeting nature of the moment, which art has fixed in such a picture (nowadays called *genre painting*), excites a slight, peculiar feeling of emotion. For to fix the fleeting world, which is for ever transforming itself, in the enduring picture of particular events that nevertheless represent the whole, is an achievement of the art of painting by which it appears to bring time itself to a standstill, since it raises the individual to the Idea of its species. Finally, the historical and outwardly significant subjects of painting often have the disadvantage that the very thing that is significant in them cannot be presented in perception, but must be added in thought. In this respect the nominal significance of the picture must generally be distinguished from the real. The former is the outward significance, to be added, however, only as concept; the latter is that side of the Idea of mankind which becomes evident for perception through the picture. For example, Moses found by the Egyptian princess may be the nominal significance of a picture, an extremely important moment for history; on the other hand, the real significance, that which is actually given to perception, is a foundling rescued from its floating cradle by a great lady, an incident that may have happened more than once. The costume alone can here make known to the cultured person the definite historical case; but the costume is of importance only for the nominal significance; for the real significance it is a matter of indifference, for the latter knows only the human being as such, not the arbitrary forms. Subjects taken from history have no advantage over those which are taken from mere possibility, and are thus to be called not individual, but only general. For what is really significant in the former is not the individual, not the particular event as such, but the universal in it, the side of the Idea of mankind that is expressed through it. On the other hand, definite historical subjects are not on any account to be rejected; only the really artistic view of such subjects, both in the painter and in the beholder, concerns never the individual particulars in them, which properly constitute the historical, but the universal that is expressed in them, namely the Idea. Only those historical subjects are to be chosen in which the main thing can actually be shown, and has not to be merely added in thought; otherwise the nominal significance is too remote from the real. What is merely thought in connexion with the picture becomes of the greatest importance, and interferes with what is perceived. If, even on the stage, it is not right for the main incident to take place behind the scenes (as in French tragedy), it is obviously a far greater fault in the picture. Historical subjects have a decidedly detrimental effect only when they restrict the painter to a field chosen arbitrarily, and not for artistic but for other purposes. This is particularly the case when this field is poor in picturesque and significant objects, when, for example, it is the history of a small, isolated, capricious, hierarchical (i.e., ruled by false notions), obscure people, like the Jews, despised by the great contemporary nations of the East and of the West. Since the great migration of peoples lies between us and all the ancient nations, just as between the present surface of the earth and the surface whose organisms appear only as fossil remains there lies the former change of the bed of the ocean, it is to be regarded generally as a great misfortune that the people whose former culture was to serve mainly as the basis of our own were not, say, the Indians or the Greeks, or even the Romans, but just these Jews. But it was a particularly unlucky star for the Italian painters of genius in the fifteenth and sixteenth centuries that, in the narrow sphere to which they were arbitrarily referred for the choice of subjects, they had to resort to miserable wretches of every kind. For the New Testament, as regards its historical part, is almost more unfavourable to painting than is the Old, and the subsequent history of martyrs and doctors of the Church is a very unfortunate subject. Yet we have to distinguish very carefully between those pictures whose subject is the historical or mythological one of Judaism and Christianity, and those in which the real, i.e., the ethical, spirit of Christianity is revealed for perception by the presentation of persons full of this spirit. These presentations are in fact the highest and most admirable achievements of the art of painting, and only the greatest masters of this art succeeded in producing them, in particular Raphael and Correggio, the latter especially in his earlier pictures. Paintings of this kind are really not to be numbered among the historical, for often they do not depict any event or action, but are mere groups of saints with the Saviour himself, often still as a child with his mother, angels, and so on. In their countenances, especially in their eyes, we see the expression, the reflection, of the most perfect knowledge, that knowledge namely which is not directed to particular things, but which has fully grasped the Ideas, and hence the whole inner nature of the world and of life. This knowledge in them, reacting on the will, does not, like that other knowledge, furnish *motives* for the will, but on the contrary has become a *quieter* of all willing. From this has resulted perfect resignation, which is the innermost spirit of Christianity as of Indian wisdom, the giving up of all willing, turning back, abolition of the will and with it of the whole inner being of this world, and hence salvation. Therefore, those eternally praiseworthy masters of art expressed the highest wisdom perceptibly in their works. Here is the summit of all art that has followed the will in its adequate objectivity, namely in the Ideas, through all the grades, from the lowest where it is affected, and its nature is unfolded, by causes, then where it is similarly affected by stimuli, and finally by motives. And now art ends by presenting the free self-abolition of the will through the one great quieter that dawns on it from the most perfect knowledge of its own nature.[34]

§ 49.

The truth which lies at the foundation of all the remarks we have so far made on art is that the object of art, the depiction of which is the aim of the artist, and the knowledge of which must consequently precede his work as its germ and source, is an *Idea* in Plato's sense, and absolutely nothing else; not the particular thing, the object of common apprehension, and not the concept, the object of rational thought and of science. Although Idea and concept have something in common, in that both as unities represent a plurality of actual things, the great difference between the two will have become sufficiently clear and evident from what was said in the first book about the concept, and what has been said in the present book about the Idea. I certainly do not mean to assert that Plato grasped this difference clearly; indeed many of his examples of Ideas and his discussions of them are applicable only to concepts. How-

---

[34] This passage presupposes for its comprehension the whole of the following book.

ever, we leave this aside, and go our way, glad whenever we come across traces of a great and noble mind, yet pursuing not his footsteps, but our own aim. The *concept* is abstract, discursive, wholly undetermined within its sphere, determined only by its limits, attainable and intelligible only to him who has the faculty of reason, communicable by words without further assistance, entirely exhausted by its definition. The *Idea*, on the other hand, definable perhaps as the adequate representative of the concept, is absolutely perceptive, and, although representing an infinite number of individual things, is yet thoroughly definite. It is never known by the individual as such, but only by him who has raised himself above all willing and all individuality to the pure subject of knowing. Thus it is attainable only by the man of genius, and by him who, mostly with the assistance of works of genius, has raised his power of pure knowledge, and is now in the frame of mind of the genius. Therefore it is communicable not absolutely, but only conditionally, since the Idea, apprehended and repeated in the work of art, appeals to everyone only according to the measure of his own intellectual worth. For this reason the most excellent works of any art, the noblest productions of genius, must eternally remain sealed books to the dull majority of men, and are inaccessible to them. They are separated from them by a wide gulf, just as the society of princes is inaccessible to the common people. It is true that even the dullest of them accept on authority works which are acknowledged to be great, in order not to betray their own weakness. But they always remain in silence, ready to express their condemnation the moment they are allowed to hope that they can do so without running the risk of exposure. Then their long-restrained hatred of all that is great and beautiful and of the authors thereof readily relieves itself; for such things never appealed to them, and so humiliated them. For in order to acknowledge, and freely and willingly to admit, the worth of another, a man must generally have some worth of his own. On this is based the necessity for modesty in spite of all merit, as also for the disproportionately loud praise of this virtue, which alone of all its sisters is always included in the eulogy of anyone who ventures to praise a man distinguished in some way, in order to conciliate and appease the wrath of worthlessness. For what is modesty but hypocritical humility, by means of which, in a world swelling with vile envy, a man seeks to beg pardon for his excellences and merits from those who have none? For whoever attributes no merits to himself because he really has none, is not modest, but merely honest.

The *Idea* is the unity that has fallen into plurality by virtue of the temporal and spatial form of our intuitive apprehension. The *concept,*

on the other hand, is the unity once more produced out of plurality by means of abstraction through our faculty of reason; the latter can be described as *unitas post rem,* and the former as *unitas ante rem.* Finally, we can express the distinction between concept and Idea figuratively, by saying that the *concept is like a dead receptacle in which whatever has been put actually lies side by side, but from which no more can be taken out (by analytical judgements) than has been put in (by synthetical reflection).* The *Idea,* on the other hand, develops in him who has grasped it representations that are new as regards the concept of the same name; it is like a living organism, developing itself and endowed with generative force, which brings forth that which was not previously put into it.
Now it follows from all that has been said that the concept, useful as it is in life, serviceable, necessary, and productive as it is in science, is eternally barren and unproductive in art. The apprehended Idea, on the contrary, is the true and only source of every genuine work of art. In its powerful originality it is drawn only from life itself, from nature, from the world, and only by the genuine genius, or by him whose momentary inspiration reaches the point of genius. Genuine works bearing immortal life arise only from such immediate apprehension. Just because the Idea is and remains perceptive, the artist is not conscious *in abstracto* of the intention and aim of his work. Not a concept but an Idea is present in his mind; hence he cannot give an account of his actions. He works, as people say, from mere feeling and unconsciously, indeed instinctively. On the other hand, imitators, mannerists, *imitatores, servum pecus,*[35] in art start from the concept. They note what pleases and affects in genuine works, make this clear to themselves, fix it in the concept, and hence in the abstract, and then imitate it, openly or in disguise, with skill and intention. Like parasitic plants, they suck their nourishment from the works of others; and like polyps, take on the colour of their nourishment. Indeed, we could even carry the comparison farther, and assert that they are like machines which mince very fine and mix up what is put into them, but can never digest it, so that the constituent elements of others can always be found again, and picked out and separated from the mixture. Only the genius, on the other hand, is like the organic body that assimilates, transforms, and produces. For he is, indeed, educated and cultured by his predecessors and their works; but only by life and the world itself is he made directly productive through the impression of what is perceived; therefore the highest culture never interferes with his originality. All imi-

---

[35] "Imitators, the slavish mob." [Tr.]

tators, all mannerists apprehend in the concept the essential nature of the exemplary achievements of others; but they can never impart inner life to a work. The generation, in other words the dull multitude of any time, itself knows only concepts and sticks to them; it therefore accepts mannered works with ready and loud applause. After a few years, however, these works become unpalatable, because the spirit of the times, in other words the prevailing concepts, in which alone those works could take root, has changed. Only the genuine works that are drawn directly from nature and life remain eternally young and strong, like nature and life itself. For they belong to no age, but to mankind; and for this reason they are received with indifference by their own age to which they disdained to conform; and because they indirectly and negatively exposed the errors of the age, they were recognized tardily and reluctantly. On the other hand, they do not grow old, but even down to the latest times always make an ever new and fresh appeal to us. They are then no longer exposed to neglect and misunderstanding; for they now stand crowned and sanctioned by the approbation of the few minds capable of judging. These appear singly and sparingly in the course of centuries,[36] and cast their votes, the slowly increasing number of which establishes the authority, the only judgement-seat that is meant when an appeal is made to posterity. It is these successively appearing individuals alone; for the mass and multitude of posterity will always be and remain just as perverse and dull as the mass and multitude of contemporaries always were and always are. Let us read the complaints of the great minds of every century about their contemporaries; they always sound as if they were of today, since the human race is always the same. In every age and in every art affectation takes the place of the spirit, which always is only the property of individuals. Affectation, however, is the old, cast-off garment of the phenomenon of the spirit which last existed and was recognized. In view of all this, the approbation of posterity is earned as a rule only at the expense of the approbation of one's contemporaries, and *vice versa*.[37]

---

[36] *Apparent rari, nantes in gurgite vasto.* ("Singly they appear, swimming by in the vast waste of waves." Virgil, *Aeneid*, i, 118. [Tr.])

[37] Cf. chap. 34 of volume 2.

§ 50.

Now, if the purpose of all art is the communication of the apprehended Idea, and this Idea is then grasped by the man of weaker susceptibility and no productive capacity through the medium of the artist's mind, in which it appears isolated and purged of everything foreign; further, if starting from the concept is objectionable in art, then we shall not be able to approve, when a work of art is intentionally and avowedly chosen to express a concept; this is the case in *allegory*. An allegory is a work of art signifying something different from what it depicts. But that which is perceptive, and consequently the Idea as well, expresses itself immediately and completely, and does not require the medium of another thing through which it is outlined or suggested. Therefore that which is suggested and represented in this way by something quite different is always a concept, because it cannot itself be brought before perception. Hence through the allegory a concept is always to be signified, and consequently the mind of the beholder has to be turned aside from the depicted representation of perception to one that is quite different, abstract, and not perceptive, and lies entirely outside the work of art. Here, therefore, the picture or statue is supposed to achieve what a written work achieves far more perfectly. Now what we declare to be the aim of art, namely presentation of the Idea to be apprehended only through perception, is not the aim here. But certainly no great perfection in the work of art is demanded for what is here intended; on the contrary, it is enough if we see what the thing is supposed to be; for as soon as this is found, the end is reached, and the mind is then led on to quite a different kind of representation, to an abstract concept which was the end in view. Allegories in plastic and pictorial art are consequently nothing but *hieroglyphics*; the artistic value they may have as expressions of perception does not belong to them as allegories, but otherwise. That the *Night* of Correggio, the *Genius of Fame* of Annibale Carracci, and the *Goddesses of the Seasons* of Poussin are very beautiful pictures is to be kept quite apart from the fact that they are allegories. As allegories, they do not achieve more than an inscription, in fact rather less. Here we are again reminded of the above-mentioned distinction between the real and the nominal significance of a picture. Here the nominal is just the allegorical as such, for example, the *Genius of Fame.* The real is what is actually depicted, namely a beautiful winged youth with beautiful boys flying round him; this expresses an Idea. This real significance, however, is effective only so long as we forget the nominal, allegorical significance. If we think of the latter, we forsake perception, and an abstract concept occupies the mind; but the transition from the Idea to the concept is always a descent. In fact, that nominal significance, that allegorical intention, often detracts from the real significance, from the truth of perception. For example, the unnatural light in Correggio's *Night,* which, although beautifully executed, has yet a merely allegorical motive and is in reality impossible. When, therefore, an allegorical picture has also artistic value, that is quite separate from and independent of what it achieves as allegory. Such a work of art serves two purposes simultaneously, namely the expression of a concept and the expression of an Idea. Only the latter can be an aim of art; the other is a foreign aim, namely the trifling amusement of causing a picture to serve at the same time as an inscription, as a hieroglyphic, invented for the benefit of those to whom the real nature of art can never appeal. It is the same as when a work of art is at the same time a useful implement, where it also serves two purposes; for example, a statue that is at the same time a candelabrum or a caryatid; or a bas-relief that is at the same time the shield of Achilles. Pure lovers of art will not approve either the one or the other. It is true that an allegorical picture can in just this quality produce a vivid impression on the mind and feelings; but under the same circumstances even an inscription would have the same effect. For instance, if the desire for fame is firmly and permanently rooted in a man's mind, since he regards fame as his rightful possession, withheld from him only so long as he has not yet produced the documents of its ownership; and if he now stands before the *Genius of Fame* with its laurel crowns, then his whole mind is thus excited, and his powers are called into activity. But the same thing would also happen if he suddenly saw the word "fame" in large clear letters on the wall. Or if a person has proclaimed a truth that is important either as a maxim for practical life or as an insight for science, but has not met with any belief in it, then an allegorical picture depicting time as it lifts the veil and reveals the naked truth will affect him powerfully. But the same thing would be achieved by the motto *"Le temps découvre la vérité."* [38] For what really produces the effect in this case is always only the abstract thought, not what is perceived.

---

[38] "Time discloses the truth." [Tr.]

If, then, in accordance with the foregoing, allegory in plastic and pictorial art is a mistaken effort, serving a purpose entirely foreign to art, it becomes wholly intolerable when it leads one so far astray that the depicting of forced and violently far-fetched subtleties degenerates into the silly and absurd. Such, for example, is a tortoise to suggest feminine seclusion; the downward glance of Nemesis into the drapery of her bosom, indicating that she sees what is hidden; Bellori's explanation that Annibale Carracci clothed voluptuousness in a yellow robe because he wished to indicate that her pleasures soon fade and become as yellow as straw. Now, if there is absolutely no connexion between what is depicted and the concept indicated by it, a connexion based on subsumption under that concept or on association of Ideas, but the sign and the thing signified are connected quite conventionally by positive fixed rule casually introduced, I call this degenerate kind of allegory *symbolism*. Thus the rose is the symbol of secrecy, the laurel the symbol of fame, the palm the symbol of victory, the mussel-shell the symbol of pilgrimage, the cross the symbol of the Christian religion. To this class also belong all indications through mere colours, such as yellow as the colour of falseness and blue the colour of fidelity. Symbols of this kind may often be of use in life, but their value is foreign to art. They are to be regarded entirely as hieroglyphics, or like Chinese calligraphy, and are really in the same class as armorial bearings, the bush that indicates a tavern, the key by which chamberlains are recognized, or the leather signifying mountaineers. Finally, if certain historical or mythical persons or personified conceptions are made known by symbols fixed on once for all, these are properly called *emblems*. Such are the animals of the Evangelists, the owl of Minerva, the apple of Paris, the anchor of hope, and so on. But by emblems we often understand those symbolical, simple presentations elucidated by a motto which are supposed to illustrate a moral truth, of which there are large collections by J. Camerarius, Alciati, and others. They form the transition to poetical allegory, of which we shall speak later. Greek sculpture appeals to perception, and is therefore *aesthetic*; Indian sculpture appeals to the concept, and is therefore *symbolical*.

This opinion of allegory, based on our consideration of the inner nature of art and quite consistent with it, is directly opposed to Winckelmann's view. Far from explaining allegory, as we do, as something quite foreign to the aim of art and often interfering with it, he speaks everywhere in favour of it; indeed (*Werke,* Vol. i, pp. 55 *seq.*), he places art's highest aim in the "presentation of universal concepts and non-sensuous things." It is left to everyone to assent either to one view or to the other. With these and similar views of

Winckelmann concerning the real metaphysics of the beautiful, the truth became very clear to me that a man can have the greatest susceptibility to artistic beauty and the most correct opinion with regard to it, without his being in a position to give an abstract and really philosophical account of the nature of the beautiful and of art. In the same way, a man can be very noble and virtuous, and can have a very tender conscience that weighs decisions accurately in particular cases, without being on that account in a position to ascertain philosophically, and explain in the abstract, the ethical significance of actions.

But allegory has an entirely different relation to *poetry* from that which it has to plastic and pictorial art; and although it is objectionable in the latter, it is quite admissible and very effective in the former. For in plastic and pictorial art allegory leads away from what is given in perception, from the real object of all art, to abstract thoughts; but in poetry the relation is reversed. Here the concept is what is directly given in words, and the first aim is to lead from this to the perceptive, the depiction of which must be undertaken by the imagination of the hearer. If in plastic and pictorial art we are led from what is immediately given to something else, this must always be a concept, because here only the abstract cannot be immediately given. But a concept can never be the source, and its communication can never be the aim, of a work of art. On the other hand, in poetry the concept is the material, the immediately given, and we can therefore very well leave it, in order to bring about something perceptive which is entirely different, and in which the end is attained. Many a concept or abstract thought may be indispensable in the sequence and connexion of a poem, while in itself and immediately it is quite incapable of being perceived. It is then often brought to perception by some example to be subsumed under it. This occurs in every figurative expression, in every metaphor, simile, parable, and allegory, all of which differ only by the length and completeness of their expression. Therefore similes and allegories are of striking effect in the rhetorical arts. How beautifully Cervantes says of sleep, in order to express that it withdraws us from all bodily and mental suffering: "It is the mantle that covers the whole person." How beautifully Kleist expresses allegorically the thought that philosophers and men of science enlighten the human race, in the verse [*Der Frühling*]:

"Those whose nocturnal lamp illumines all the globe."

How strongly and graphically Homer describes the fatal and pernicious Ate, when he says: "She has tender feet, for she walks not on the hard ground, but only on the heads of men." (*Iliad*, xix, 91.)

How very effective the fable of Menenius Agrippa about the stomach and limbs was when it was addressed to the Roman people who had quitted their country! How beautifully is a highly abstract philosophical dogma expressed by Plato's allegory of the cave at the beginning of the seventh book of the *Republic,* which we have already mentioned. The fable of Persephone is also to be regarded as a profound allegory of philosophical tendency, for she falls into the underworld through tasting a pomegranate. This becomes particularly illuminating in the treatment of this fable which Goethe introduced as an episode in the *Triumph der Empfindsamkeit,* which is beyond all praise. Three fairly long allegorical works are known to me; one open and avowed, is the incomparable *Criticón* of Balthasar Gracián. It consists of a great rich web of connected and highly ingenious allegories, serving here as bright clothing for moral truths, and to these he thus imparts the greatest perceptiveness, and astonishes us with the wealth of his inventions. Two, however, are concealed allegories, *Don Quixote* and *Gulliver's Travels.* The first is an allegory of the life of every man who, unlike others, will not be careful merely for his own personal welfare, but pursues an objective, ideal end that has taken possession of his thinking and willing; and then, of course, in this world he looks queer and odd. In the case of Gulliver, we need only take everything physical as spiritual or intellectual, in order to observe what the "satirical rogue," as Hamlet would have called him, meant by it. Therefore, since the concept is always what is given in the poetical allegory, and tries to make this perceptive through a picture, it may sometimes be expressed or supported by a painted picture. Such a picture is not for this reason regarded as a work of pictorial art, but only as an expressive hieroglyph, and it makes no claims to pictorial, but only to poetic, worth. Of such a kind is that beautiful allegorical vignette of Lavater, which must have so heartening an effect on every champion of truth: a hand holding a light is stung by a wasp, while in the flame above, gnats are being burnt; underneath is the motto:

> "And though it singes the wing of the gnat,
> Destroys its skull and scatters all its little brains;
> Light remains light!
> And although I am stung by the angriest of wasps,
> I will not let it go."

To this class belongs also the gravestone with the blown-out, smoking candle and the encircling inscription:

> "When it is out, it becomes clear
> Whether the candle be tallow or wax."

Finally, of this kind is an old German genealogical tree on which the last descendant of a very ancient family expressed the determination to live his life to the end in complete continence and chastity, and thus to let his race die out. This he did by depicting himself at the root of the tree of many branches, clipping it above himself with a pair of shears. In general, the above-mentioned symbols, usually called emblems, which might also be described as short painted fables with an expressed moral, belong to this class. Allegories of this kind are always to be reckoned among the poetical and not the pictorial, and as being justified in precisely this way. Here the pictorial execution also is always a matter of secondary importance, and no more is demanded of it than that it depict the thing conspicuously. But in poetry, as in plastic and pictorial art, the allegory passes over into the symbol, if there is none but an arbitrary connexion between what is presented in perception and what is expressed by this in the abstract. Since everything symbolical rests at bottom on a stipulated agreement, the symbol has this disadvantage among others, that its significance is forgotten in the course of time, and it then becomes dumb. Indeed, who would guess why the fish is the symbol of Christianity, if he did not know? Only a Champollion, for it is a phonetic hieroglyphic through and through. Therefore as a poetical allegory the *Revelation* of John stands roughly in the same position as the reliefs with *Magnus Deus sol Mithra,* which are still always being explained.[39]

§ 51.

If with the foregoing observations on art in general we turn from the plastic and pictorial arts to *poetry,* we shall have no doubt that its aim is also to reveal the Ideas, the grades of the will's objectification, and to communicate them to the hearer with that distinctness and vividness in which they were apprehended by the poetical mind. Ideas are essentially perceptive; therefore, if in poetry only abstract concepts are directly communicated by words,

[39] Cf. chap. 36 of volume 2.

yet it is obviously the intention to let the hearer perceive the Ideas of life in the representatives of these concepts; and this can take place only by the assistance of his own imagination. But in order to set this imagination in motion in accordance with the end in view, the abstract concepts that are the direct material of poetry, as of the driest prose, must be so arranged that their spheres intersect one another, so that none can continue in its abstract universality, but instead of it a perceptive representative appears before the imagination, and this is then modified further and further by the words of the poet according to his intention. Just as the chemist obtains solid precipitates by combining perfectly clear and transparent fluids, so does the poet know how to precipitate, as it were, the concrete, the individual, the representation of perception, out of the abstract, transparent universality of the concepts by the way in which he combines them. For the Idea can be known only through perception, but knowledge of the Idea is the aim of all art. The skill of a master in poetry as in chemistry enables one always to obtain the precise precipitate that was intended. The many epithets in poetry serve this purpose, and through them the universality of every concept is restricted more and more till perceptibility is reached. To almost every noun Homer adds an adjective, the concept of which cuts, and at once considerably diminishes, the sphere of the first concept, whereby it is brought so very much nearer to perception; for example:

ʼΕν δʼέπεσʼ ʼΩκεανῷ λαμπρὸν φάος ἠελίοιο,
῞Ελκον νύκτα μέλαιναν ἐπὶ ζείδωρον ἄρουραν.

(Occidit vero in Oceanum splendidum lumen solis,
Trahens noctem nigram super alman terram.)[40]

And

"Where gentle breezes from the blue heavens sigh,
There stands the myrtle still, the laurel high,"
[Goethe, *Mignon*]

precipitates from a few concepts before the imagination the delight of the southern climate.

Rhythm and rhyme are quite special aids to poetry. I can give no other explanation of their incredibly powerful effect than that our powers of representation have received from time, to which they are

[40] "Into the ocean sank the sun's glittering orb, drawing dark night over the bountiful earth." *Iliad,* viii, 485-6 [Tr.]

essentially bound, some special characteristic, by virtue of which we inwardly follow and, as it were, consent to each regularly recurring sound. In this way rhythm and rhyme become a means partly of holding our attention, since we more willingly follow the poem when read; and partly through them there arises in us a blind consent to what is read, prior to any judgement, and this gives the poem a certain emphatic power of conviction, independent of all reason or argument.

In virtue of the universality of the material, and hence of the concepts of which poetry makes use to communicate the Ideas, the range of its province is very great. The whole of nature, the Ideas of all grades, can be expressed by it, since it proceeds, according to the Idea to be communicated, to express these sometimes in a descriptive, sometimes in a narrative, and sometimes in a directly dramatic way. But if, in the presentation of the lower grades of the will's objectivity, plastic and pictorial art often surpasses poetry, because inanimate, and also merely animal, nature reveals almost the whole of its inner being in a single well-conceived moment; man, on the other hand, in so far as he expresses himself not through the mere form and expression of his features and countenance, but through a chain of actions and of the accompanying thoughts and emotions, is the principal subject of poetry. In this respect no other art can compete with poetry, for it has the benefit of progress and movement which the plastic and pictorial arts lack.

Revelation of that Idea which is the highest grade of the will's objectivity, namely the presentation of man in the connected series of his efforts and actions, is thus the great subject of poetry. It is true that experience and history teach us to know man, yet more often *men* rather than *man;* in other words, they give us empirical notes about the behaviour of men towards one another. From these we obtain rules for our own conduct rather than a deep insight into the inner nature of man. This latter, however, is by no means ruled out; yet, whenever the inner nature of mankind itself is disclosed to us in history or in our own experience, we have apprehended this experience poetically, and the historian has apprehended history with artistic eyes, in other words, according to the Idea, not to the phenomenon; according to its inner nature, not to the relations. Our own experience is the indispensable condition for understanding poetry as well as history, for it is, so to speak, the dictionary of the language spoken by both. But history is related to poetry as portrait-painting to historical painting; the former gives us the true in the individual, the latter the true in the universal; the former has the truth of the phenomenon and can verify it therefrom; the latter has the truth of the Idea, to be found in no particular phenomenon, yet speaking from them all. The poet from deliberate choice presents us with significant characters in significant situations; the historian takes both as they come. In fact, he has to regard and select the events and persons not according to their inner genuine significance expressing the Idea, but according to the outward, apparent, and relatively important significance in reference to the connexion and to the consequences. He cannot consider anything in and by itself according to its essential character and expression, but must look at everything according to its relation, its concatenation, its influence on what follows, and especially on its own times. Therefore he will not pass over a king's action, in itself quite common and of little significance, for it has consequences and influence. On the other hand, extremely significant actions of very distinguished individuals are not to be mentioned by him if they have no consequences and no influence. For his considerations proceed in accordance with the principle of sufficient reason, and apprehend the phenomenon of which this principle is the form. The poet, however, apprehends the Idea, the inner being of mankind outside all relation and all time, the adequate objectivity of the thing-in-itself at its highest grade. Even in that method of treatment necessary to the historian, the inner nature, the significance of phenomena, the kernel of all those shells, can never be entirely lost, and can still be found and recognized by the person who looks for it. Yet that which is significant in itself, not in the relation, namely the real unfolding of the Idea, is found to be far more accurate and clear in poetry than in history; therefore, paradoxical as it may sound, far more real, genuine, inner truth is to be attributed to poetry than to history. For the historian should accurately follow the individual event according to life as this event is developed in time in the manifold tortuous and complicated chains of reasons or grounds and consequents. But he cannot possibly possess all the data for this; he cannot have seen all and ascertained everything. At every moment he is forsaken by the original of his picture, or a false picture is substituted for it; and this happens so frequently, that I think I can assume that in all history the false outweighs the true. On the other hand, the poet has apprehended the Idea of mankind from some definite side to be described; thus it is the nature of his own self that is objectified in it for him. His knowledge, as was said above in connexion with sculpture, is half a priori; his ideal is before his mind, firm, clear, brightly illuminated, and it cannot forsake him. He therefore shows us in the mirror of his mind the Idea purely and distinctly,

and his description down to the last detail is as true as life itself.[41]
The great ancient historians are therefore poets in the particulars
where data forsake them, e.g., in the speeches of their heroes; indeed,
the whole way in which they handle their material approaches the
epic. But this gives their presentations unity, and enables them to
retain inner truth, even where outer truth was not accessible to them,
or was in fact falsified. If just now we compared history to portrait-
painting, in contrast to poetry that corresponded to historical painting, we find Winckelmann's maxim, that the portrait should be the
ideal of the individual, also followed by the ancient historians, for
they depict the individual in such a way that the side of the Idea of
mankind expressed in it makes its appearance. On the other hand,
modern historians, with few exceptions, generally give us only "an
offal-barrel and a lumber-garret, or at the best a Punch-and-Judy
play." [42] Therefore, he who seeks to know mankind according to its
inner nature which is identical in all its phenomena and developments, and thus according to its Idea, will find that the works of the
great, immortal poets present him with a much truer and clearer picture than the historians can ever give. For even the best of them are
as poets far from being the first, and also their hands are not free.
In this respect we can illustrate the relation between historian and
poet by the following comparison. The mere, pure historian, working

---

[41] It goes without saying that everywhere I speak exclusively of the great and
genuine poet, who is so rare. I mean no one else; least of all that dull and
shallow race of mediocre poets, rhymesters, and devisers of fables which
flourishes so luxuriantly, especially in Germany at the present time; but we
ought to shout incessantly in their ears from all sides:

Mediocribus esse poetis
Non homines, non Di, non concessere columnae.

["Neither gods, nor men, nor even advertising pillars permit the poet to be a
mediocrity." Horace, *Ars Poetica*, 372-3. Tr.] It is worth serious consideration
how great an amount of time—their own and other people's—and of paper is
wasted by this swarm of mediocre poets, and how injurious their influence is.
For the public always seizes on what is new, and shows even more inclination
to what is perverse and dull, as being akin to its own nature. These works of
the mediocre, therefore, draw the public away and hold it back from genuine
masterpieces, and from the education they afford. Thus they work directly
against the benign influence of genius, ruin taste more and more, and so arrest
the progress of the age. Therefore criticism and satire should scourge mediocre
poets without pity or sympathy, until they are induced for their own good to
apply their muse rather to read what is good than to write what is bad. For if
the bungling of the meddlers put even the god of the Muses in such a rage that
he could flay Marsyas, I do not see on what mediocre poetry would base its
claims to tolerance.
[42] From Goethe's *Faust*, Bayard Taylor's translation. [Tr.]

only according to data, is like a man who, without any knowledge of mathematics, investigates by measurement the proportions of figures previously found by accident, and therefore the statement of these measurements found empirically is subject to all the errors of the figure as drawn. The poet, on the contrary, is like the mathematician who constructs these ratios *a priori* in pure intuition or perception, and expresses them not as they actually are in the drawn figure, but as they are in the Idea that the drawing is supposed to render perceptible. Therefore Schiller [*An die Freunde*] says:

> "What has never anywhere come to pass,
> That alone never grows old."

In regard to knowledge of the inner nature of mankind, I must concede a greater value to biographies, and particularly to autobiographies, than to history proper, at any rate to history as it is usually treated. This is partly because, in the former, the data can be brought together more accurately and completely than in the latter; partly because, in history proper, it is not so much men that act as nations and armies, and the individuals who do appear seem to be so far off, surrounded by such pomp and circumstance, clothed in the stiff robes of State, or in heavy and inflexible armour, that it is really very difficult to recognize human movement through it all. On the other hand, the truly depicted life of the individual in a narrow sphere shows the conduct of men in all its nuances and forms, the excellence, the virtue, and even the holiness of individuals, the perversity, meanness, and malice of most, the profligacy of many. Indeed, from the point of view we are here considering, namely in regard to the inner significance of what appears, it is quite immaterial whether the objects on which the action hinges are, relatively considered, trifling or important, farmhouses or kingdoms. For all these things are without significance in themselves, and obtain it only in so far as the will is moved by them. The motive has significance merely through its relation to the will; on the other hand, the relation that it has as a thing to other such things does not concern us at all. Just as a circle of one inch in diameter and one of forty million miles in diameter have absolutely the same geometrical properties, so the events and the history of a village and of a kingdom are essentially the same; and we can study and learn to know mankind just as well in the one as in the other. It is also wrong to suppose that autobiographies are full of deceit and dissimulation; on the contrary, lying, though possible everywhere, is perhaps more difficult there than anywhere else. Dissimulation is easiest in mere conversation;

indeed, paradoxical as it may sound, it is fundamentally more difficult in a letter, since here a man, left to his own devices, looks into
himself and not outwards. The strange and remote are with difficulty
brought near to him, and he does not have before his eyes the measure of the impression made on another. The other person, on the
contrary, peruses the letter calmly, in a mood that is foreign to the
writer, reads it repeatedly and at different times, and thus easily finds
out the concealed intention. We also get to know an author as a man
most easily from his book, since all those conditions have there an
even stronger and more lasting effect; and in an autobiography it is so
difficult to dissimulate, that there is perhaps not a single one that is
not on the whole truer than any history ever written. The man who
records his life surveys it as a whole; the individual thing becomes
small, the near becomes distant, the distant again becomes near,
motives shrink and contract. He is sitting at the confessional, and is
doing so of his own free will. Here the spirit of lying does not seize
him so readily, for there is to be found in every man an inclination
to truth which has first to be overcome in the case of every lie, and
has here taken up an unusually strong position. The relation between
biography and the history of nations can be made clear to perception
by the following comparison. History shows us mankind just as a
view from a high mountain shows us nature. We see a great deal at
a time, wide stretches, great masses, but nothing is distinct or recognizable according to the whole of its real nature. On the other hand,
the depicted life of the individual shows us the person, just as we
know nature when we walk about among her trees, plants, rocks, and
stretches of water. Through landscape-painting, in which the artist
lets us see nature through his eyes, the knowledge of her Ideas and
the condition of pure, will-less knowing required for this are made
easy for us. In the same way, poetry is far superior to history and
biography for expressing the Ideas that we are able to seek in both.
For here also genius holds up before us the illuminating glass in
which everything essential and significant is gathered together and
placed in the brightest light; but everything accidental and foreign is
eliminated.[43]

The expression of the Idea of mankind, which devolves on the
poet, can now be carried out in such a way that the depicted is also
at the same time the depicter. This occurs in lyric poetry, in the song
proper, where the poet vividly perceives and describes only his own
state; hence through the object, a certain subjectivity is essential to
poetry of this kind. Or again, the depicter is entirely different from

---

[43] Cf. chap. 38 of volume 2.

what is to be depicted, as is the case with all other kinds of poetry. Here the depicter more or less conceals himself behind what is depicted, and finally altogether disappears. In the ballad the depicter still expresses to some extent his own state through the tone and proportion of the whole; therefore, though much more objective than the song, it still has something subjective in it. This fades away more in the idyll, still more in the romance, almost entirely in the epic proper, and finally to the last vestige in the drama, which is the most objective, and in more than one respect the most complete, and also the most difficult, form of poetry. The lyric form is therefore the easiest, and if in other respects art belongs only to the true genius who is so rare, even the man who is on the whole not very eminent can produce a beautiful song, when in fact, through strong excitement from outside, some inspiration enhances his mental powers. For this needs only a vivid perception of his own state at the moment of excitement. This is proved by many single songs written by individuals who have otherwise remained unknown, in particular by the German national songs, of which we have an excellent collection in the *Wunderhorn,* and also by innumerable love-songs and other popular songs in all languages. For to seize the mood of the moment, and embody it in the song, is the whole achievement of poetry of this kind. Yet in the lyrics of genuine poets is reflected the inner nature of the whole of mankind; and all that millions of past, present, and future human beings have found and will find in the same constantly recurring situations, finds in them its corresponding expression. Since these situations, by constant recurrence, exist as permanently as humanity itself, and always call up the same sensations, the lyrical productions of genuine poets remain true, effective, and fresh for thousands of years. If, however, the poet is the universal man, then all that has ever moved a human heart, and all that human nature produces from itself in any situation, all that dwells and broods in any human breast—all these are his theme and material, and with these all the rest of nature as well. Therefore the poet can just as well sing of voluptuousness as of mysticism, be Anacreon or Angelus Silesius, write tragedies or comedies, express the sublime or the common sentiment, according to his mood and disposition. Accordingly, no one can prescribe to the poet that he should be noble and sublime, moral, pious, Christian, or anything else, still less reproach him for being this and not that. He is the mirror of mankind, and brings to its consciousness what it feels and does.

Now if we consider more closely the nature of the lyric proper, and take as examples exquisite and at the same time pure models, not those in any way approximating to another kind of poetry, such as the ballad, the elegy, the hymn, the epigram, and so on, we shall find that the characteristic nature of the song in the narrowest sense is as follows. It is the subject of the will, in other words, the singer's own willing, that fills his consciousness, often as a released and satisfied willing (joy), but even more often as an impeded willing (sorrow), always as emotion, passion, an agitated state of mind. Besides this, however, and simultaneously with it, the singer, through the sight of surrounding nature, becomes conscious of himself as the subject of pure, will-less knowing, whose unshakable, blissful peace now appears in contrast to the stress of willing that is always restricted and needy. The feeling of this contrast, this alternate play, is really what is expressed in the whole of the song, and what in general constitutes the lyrical state. In this state pure knowing comes to us, so to speak, in order to deliver us from willing and its stress. We follow, yet only for a few moments; willing, desire, the recollection of our own personal aims, always tears us anew from peaceful contemplation; but yet again and again the next beautiful environment, in which pure, will-less knowledge presents itself to us, entices us away from willing. Therefore in the song and in the lyrical mood, willing (the personal interest of the aims) and pure perception of the environment that presents itself are wonderfully blended with each other. Relations between the two are sought and imagined; the subjective disposition, the affection of the will, imparts its hue to the perceived environment, and this environment again imparts in the reflex its colour to that disposition. The genuine song is the expression or copy of the whole of this mingled and divided state of mind. In order to make clear in examples this abstract analysis of a state that is very far from all abstraction, we can take up any of the immortal songs of Goethe. As specially marked out for this purpose I will recommend only a few; *The Shepherd's Lament, Welcome and Farewell, To the Moon, On the Lake, Autumnal Feelings;* further the real songs in the *Wunderhorn* are excellent examples, especially the one that begins: "O Bremen, I must leave you now." As a comical and really striking parody of the lyric character, a song by Voss strikes me as remarkable. In it he describes the feelings of a drunken plumber, falling from a tower, who in passing observes that the clock on the tower is at half past eleven, a remark quite foreign to his condition, and hence belonging to will-free knowledge. Whoever shares with me the view expressed of the lyrical state of mind will also admit that this is really the perceptive and poetical knowledge of that principle, which I advanced in my essay *On the Principle of Sufficient Reason,* and which I have also mentioned in this work, namely that the identity of the subject of knowing with the subject of willing can be called the miracle κατ᾽ ἐξοχήν,[44] so that the poetical effect of the song really rests ultimately on the truth of that principle. In the course of life, these two subjects, or in popular language head and heart, grow more and more apart; men are always separating more and more their subjective feeling from their objective knowledge. In the child the two are still fully blended; it hardly knows how to distinguish itself from its surroundings; it is merged into them. In the youth all perception in the first place affects feeling and mood, and even mingles with these, as is very beautifully expressed by Byron:

> "I live not in myself, but I become
> Portion of that around me; and to me
> High mountains are a feeling."
> [*Childe Harold's Pilgrimage,* III, lxxii.]

This is why the youth clings so much to the perceptive and outward side of things; this is why he is fit only for lyrical poetry, and only the mature man for dramatic poetry. We can think of the old man as at most an epic poet, like Ossian or Homer, for narration is characteristic of the old.

In the more objective kinds of poetry, especially in the romance, the epic, and the drama, the end, the revelation of the Idea of mankind, is attained especially by two means, namely by true and profound presentation of significant characters, and by the invention of pregnant situations in which they disclose themselves. For it is incumbent on the chemist not only to exhibit purely and genuinely the simple elements and their principal compounds, but also to expose them to the influence of those reagents in which their peculiar properties become clearly and strikingly visible. In just the same way, it is incumbent on the poet not only to present to us significant characters as truly and faithfully as does nature herself, but, so that we may get to know them, he must place them in those situations in which their peculiar qualities are completely unfolded, and in which they are presented distinctly in sharp outline; in situations that are therefore called significant. In real life and in history, situations of this nature are only rarely brought about by chance; they exist there alone, lost and hidden in the mass of insignificant detail. The universal significance of the situations should distinguish the romance, the epic, and the drama from real life just as much as do the arrangement and selection of the significant characters. In both, however, the strictest truth is an indispensable condition of their effect, and want of unity in the characters,

---

[44] "*Par excellence.*" [Tr.]

contradiction of themselves or of the essential nature of mankind in general, as well as impossibility of the events or improbability amounting almost to impossibility, even though it is only in minor circumstances, offend just as much in poetry as do badly drawn figures, false perspective, or defective lighting in painting. For in both poetry and painting we demand a faithful mirror of life, of mankind, of the world, only rendered clear by the presentation, and made significant by the arrangement. As the purpose of all the arts is merely the expression and presentation of the Ideas, and as their essential difference lies only in what grade of the will's objectification the Idea is that we are to express, by which again the material of expression is determined, even those arts that are most widely separated can by comparison throw light on one another. For example, to grasp completely the Ideas expressing themselves in water, it is not sufficient to see it in the quiet pond or in the evenly-flowing stream, but those Ideas completely unfold themselves only when the water appears under all circumstances and obstacles. The effect of these on it causes it to manifest completely all its properties. We therefore find it beautiful when it rushes down, roars, and foams, or leaps into the air, or falls in a cataract of spray, or finally, when artificially forced, it springs up as a fountain. Thus, exhibiting itself differently in different circumstances, it always asserts its character faithfully; it is just as natural for it to spirt upwards as to lie in glassy stillness; it is as ready for the one as for the other, as soon as the circumstances appear. Now what the hydraulic engineer achieves in the fluid matter of water, the architect achieves in the rigid matter of stone; and this is just what is achieved by the epic or dramatic poet in the Idea of mankind. The common aim of all the arts is the unfolding and elucidation of the Idea expressing itself in the object of every art, of the will objectifying itself at each grade. The life of man, as often seen in the world of reality, is like the water as seen often in pond and river; but in the epic, the romance, and the tragedy, selected characters are placed in those circumstances in which all their characteristics are unfolded, the depths of the human mind are revealed and become visible in extraordinary and significant actions. Thus poetry objectifies the Idea of man, an Idea which has the peculiarity of expressing itself in highly individual characters.

Tragedy is to be regarded, and is recognized, as the summit of poetic art, both as regards the greatness of the effect and the difficulty of the achievement. For the whole of our discussion, it is very significant and worth noting that the purpose of this highest poetical achievement is the description of the terrible side of life.

The unspeakable pain, the wretchedness and misery of mankind, the triumph of wickedness, the scornful mastery of chance, and the irretrievable fall of the just and the innocent are all here presented to us; and here is to be found a significant hint as to the nature of the world and of existence. It is the antagonism of the will with itself which is here most completely unfolded at the highest grade of its objectivity, and which comes into fearful prominence. It becomes visible in the suffering of mankind which is produced partly by chance and error; and these stand forth as the rulers of the world, personified as fate through their insidiousness which appears almost like purpose and intention. In part it proceeds from mankind itself through the self-mortifying efforts of will on the part of individuals, through the wickedness and perversity of most. It is one and the same will, living and appearing in them all, whose phenomena fight with one another and tear one another to pieces. In one individual it appears powerfully, in another more feebly. Here and there it reaches thoughtfulness and is softened more or less by the light of knowledge, until at last in the individual case this knowledge is purified and enhanced by suffering itself. It then reaches the point where the phenomenon, the veil of Maya, no longer deceives it. It sees through the form of the phenomenon, the *principium individuationis;* the egoism resting on this expires with it. The *motives* that were previously so powerful now lose their force, and instead of them, the complete knowledge of the real nature of the world, acting as a *quieter* of the will, produces resignation, the giving up not merely of life, but of the whole will-to-live itself. Thus we see in tragedy the noblest men, after a long conflict and suffering, finally renounce for ever all the pleasures of life and the aims till then pursued so keenly, or cheerfully and willingly give up life itself. Thus the steadfast prince of Calderón, Gretchen in *Faust,* Hamlet whom his friend Horatio would gladly follow, but who enjoins him to remain for a while in this harsh world and to breathe in pain in order to throw light on Hamlet's fate and clear his memory; also the *Maid of Orleans,* the *Bride of Messina.* They all die purified by suffering, in other words after the will-to-live has already expired in them. In Voltaire's *Mohammed* this is actually expressed in the concluding words addressed to Mohammed by the dying Palmira: "The world is for tyrants: live!" On the other hand, the demand for so-called poetic justice rests on an entire misconception of the nature of tragedy, indeed of the nature of the world. It boldly appears in all its dulness in the criticisms that Dr. Samuel Johnson made of individual plays of Shakespeare, since he very naïvely laments the complete disregard of it; and this disregard certainly exists, for what wrong have the Ophelias, the Desdemonas, and the Cordelias done? But only a dull, insipid, optimistic, Protestant-rationalistic, or really Jewish view of the world will make the demand for poetic justice, and find its own satisfaction in that of the demand. The true sense of the tragedy is the deeper insight that what the hero atones for is not his own particular sins, but original sin, in other words, the guilt of existence itself:

> *Pues el delito mayor*
> *Del hombre es haber nacido.*
>
> ("For man's greatest offence
> Is that he has been born,")

as Calderón [*La Vida es Sueño*] frankly expresses it.

I will allow myself only one observation more closely concerning the treatment of tragedy. The presentation of a great misfortune is alone essential to tragedy. But the many different ways in which it is produced by the poet can be brought under three typical characteristics. It can be done through the extraordinary wickedness of a character, touching the extreme bounds of possibility, who becomes the author of the misfortune. Examples of this kind are *Richard III,* Iago in *Othello,* Shylock in *The Merchant of Venice,* Franz Moor, the *Phaedra* of Euripides, Creon in the *Antigone,* and others. Again, it can happen through blind fate, i.e., chance or error; a true model of this kind is the *King Oedipus* of Sophocles, also the *Trachiniae;* and in general most of the tragedies of the ancients belong to this class. Examples among modern tragedies are *Romeo and Juliet,* Voltaire's *Tancred,* and *The Bride of Messina.* Finally, the misfortune can be brought about also by the mere attitude of the persons to one another through their relations. Thus there is no need either of a colossal error, or of an unheard-of accident, or even of a character reaching the bounds of human possibility in wickedness, but characters as they usually are in a moral regard in circumstances that frequently occur, are so situated with regard to one another that their position forces them, knowingly and with their eyes open, to do one another the greatest injury, without any one of them being entirely in the wrong. This last kind of tragedy seems to me far preferable to the other two; for it shows us the greatest misfortune not as an exception, not as something brought about by rare circumstances or by monstrous characters, but as something that arises easily and spontaneously out of the actions and characters of men, as something almost essential to them, and in this way it is brought terribly near to us. In the other two kinds of tragedy, we look on the prodigious fate and the frightful wickedness as terrible powers threatening us only from a distance, from which we ourselves might well escape without taking refuge in renunciation. The last kind of tragedy, however, shows us those powers that destroy happiness and life, and in such a way that the path to them is at any moment open even to us. We see the greatest suffering brought about by entanglements whose essence could be assumed even by our own fate, and by actions that perhaps even we might be capable of committing, and so we cannot complain of injustice. Then, shuddering, we feel ourselves already in the midst of hell. In this last kind of tragedy the working out is of the greatest difficulty; for the greatest effect has to be produced in it with the least use of means and occasions for movement, merely by their position and distribution. Therefore even in many of the best tragedies this difficulty is evaded. One play, however, can be mentioned as a perfect model of this kind, a tragedy that in other respects is far surpassed by several others of the same great master; it is *Clavigo*. To a certain extent *Hamlet* belongs to this class, if, that is to say, we look merely at his relation to Laërtes and to Ophelia. *Wallenstein* also has this merit. *Faust* is entirely of this kind, if we consider merely the event connected with Gretchen and her brother as the main action; also the *Cid* of Corneille, only that this lacks the tragic conclusion, while, on the other hand, the analogous relation of Max to Thecla has it.[45]

§ 52.

W̄e have now considered all the fine arts in the general way suitable to our point of view. We began with architecture, whose aim as such is to elucidate the objectification of the will at the lowest grade of its visibility, where it shows itself as the dumb striving of the mass, devoid of knowledge and conforming to law; yet it already reveals discord with itself and conflict, namely that between gravity and rigidity. Our observations ended with tragedy, which presents to us in terrible magnitude and distinctness at the highest grade of the will's objectification that very conflict of the will with itself. After this, we find that there is yet another fine art that

---

[45] Cf. chap. 37 of volume 2.

remains excluded, and was bound to be excluded, from our considera-tion, for in the systematic connexion of our discussion there was no fitting place for it; this art is *music*. It stands quite apart from all the others. In it we do not recognize the copy, the repetition, of any Idea of the inner nature of the world. Yet it is such a great and exceedingly fine art, its effect on man's innermost nature is so powerful, and it is so completely and profoundly understood by him in his innermost being as an entirely universal language, whose distinctness surpasses even that of the world of perception itself, that in it we certainly have to look for more than that *exercitium arithmeticae occultum nescientis se numerare animi* which Leibniz took it to be.[46] Yet he was quite right, in so far as he considered only its immediate and outward significance, its exterior. But if it were nothing more, the satisfaction afforded by it would inevitably be similar to that which we feel when a sum in arithmetic comes out right, and could not be that profound pleasure with which we see the deepest recesses of our nature find expression. Therefore, from our standpoint, where the aesthetic effect is the thing we have in mind, we must attribute to music a far more serious and profound signifi-cance that refers to the innermost being of the world and of our own self. In this regard the numerical ratios into which it can be resolved are related not as the thing signified, but only as the sign. That in some sense music must be related to the world as the depiction to the thing depicted, as the copy to the original, we can infer from the analogy with the remaining arts, to all of which this character is peculiar; from their effect on us, it can be inferred that that of music is on the whole of the same nature, only stronger, more rapid, more necessary and infallible. Further, its imitative reference to the world must be very profound, infinitely true, and really striking, since it is instantly understood by everyone, and presents a certain infallibility by the fact that its form can be reduced to quite definite rules expressible in numbers, from which it cannot possibly depart without entirely ceasing to be music. Yet the point of comparison between music and the world, the regard in which it stands to the world in the relation of a copy or a repetition, is very obscure. Men have practised music at all times without being able to give an account of this; content to understand it immediately, they renounce any abstract conception of this direct understanding itself.

I have devoted my mind entirely to the impression of music in its many different forms; and then I have returned again to reflection

---

[46] Leibniz' *Letters,* Kortholt's edition, *ep.* 154. "An unconscious exercise in arithmetic in which the mind does not know it is counting." [Tr.]

and to the train of my thought expounded in the present work, and have arrived at an explanation of the inner essence of music, and the nature of its imitative relation to the world, necessarily to be presupposed from analogy. This explanation is quite sufficient for me, and satisfactory for my investigation, and will be just as illuminating also to the man who has followed me thus far, and has agreed with my view of the world. I recognize, however, that it is essentially impossible to demonstrate this explanation, for it assumes and establishes a relation of music as a representation to that which of its essence can never be representation, and claims to regard music as the copy of an original that can itself never be directly represented. Therefore, I can do no more than state here at the end of this third book, devoted mainly to a consideration of the arts, this explanation of the wonderful art of tones which is sufficient for me. I must leave the acceptance or denial of my view to the effect that both music and the whole thought communicated in this work have on each reader. Moreover, I regard it as necessary, in order that a man may assent with genuine conviction to the explanation of the significance of music here to be given, that he should often listen to music with constant reflection on this; and this again requires that he should be already very familiar with the whole thought which I expound.

The (Platonic) Ideas are the adequate objectification of the will. To stimulate the knowledge of these by depicting individual things (for works of art are themselves always such) is the aim of all the other arts (and is possible with a corresponding change in the knowing subject). Hence all of them objectify the will only indirectly, in other words, by means of the Ideas. As our world is nothing but the phenomenon or appearance of the Ideas in plurality through entrance into the *principium individuationis* (the form of knowledge possible to the individual as such), music, since it passes over the Ideas, is also quite independent of the phenomenal world, positively ignores it, and, to a certain extent, could still exist even if there were no world at all, which cannot be said of the other arts. Thus music is as *immediate* an objectification and copy of the whole *will* as the world itself is, indeed as the Ideas are, the multiplied phenomenon of which constitutes the world of individual things. Therefore music is by no means like the other arts, namely a copy of the Ideas, but a *copy of the will itself*, the objectivity of which are the Ideas. For this reason the effect of music is so very much more powerful and penetrating than is that of the other arts, for these others speak only of the shadow, but music of the essence. However, as it is the same will that objectifies itself both in the Ideas and in music, though in quite a different way in each, there must be, not indeed an absolutely direct likeness, but yet a parallel, an analogy, between music and the Ideas, the phenomenon of which in plurality and in incompleteness is the visible world. The demonstration of this analogy will make easier, as an illustration, an understanding of this explanation, which is difficult because of the obscurity of the subject.

I recognize in the deepest tones of harmony, in the ground-bass, the lowest grades of the will's objectification, inorganic nature, the mass of the planet. It is well known that all the high notes, light, tremulous, and dying away more rapidly, may be regarded as resulting from the simultaneous vibrations of the deep bass-note. With the sounding of the low note, the high notes always sound faintly at the same time, and it is a law of harmony that a bass-note may be accompanied only by those high notes that actually sound automatically and simultaneously with it (its *sons harmoniques*)[47] through the accompanying vibrations. Now this is analogous to the fact that all the bodies and organizations of nature must be regarded as having come into existence through gradual development out of the mass of the planet. This is both their supporter and their source, and the high notes have the same relation to the ground-bass. There is a limit to the depth, beyond which no sound is any longer audible. This corresponds to the fact that no matter is perceivable without form and quality, in other words, without the manifestation of a force incapable of further explanation, in which an Idea expresses itself, and, more generally, that no matter can be entirely without will. Therefore, just as a certain degree of pitch is inseparable from the tone as such, so a certain grade of the will's manifestation is inseparable from matter. Therefore, for us the ground-bass is in harmony what inorganic nature, the crudest mass on which everything rests and from which everything originates and develops, is in the world. Further, in the whole of the ripienos that produce the harmony, between the bass and the leading voice singing the melody, I recognize the whole gradation of the Ideas in which the will objectifies itself. Those nearer to the bass are the lower of those grades, namely the still inorganic bodies manifesting themselves, however, in many ways. Those that are higher represent to me the plant and animal worlds. The definite intervals of the scale are parallel to the definite grades of the will's objectification, the definite species in nature. The departure from the arithmetical correctness of the intervals through some temperament, or produced by the selected key, is analogous to the departure of the individual from

---

[47] "Harmonics." [Tr.]

the type of the species. In fact, the impure discords, giving no definite interval, can be compared to the monstrous abortions between two species of animals, or between man and animal. But all these bass-notes and ripienos that constitute the *harmony,* lack that sequence and continuity of progress which belong only to the upper voice that sings the *melody.* This voice alone moves rapidly and lightly in modulations and runs, while all the others have only a slower movement without a connexion existing in each by itself. The deep bass moves most ponderously, the representative of the crudest mass; its rising and falling occur only in large intervals, in thirds, fourths, fifths, never by *one* tone, unless it be a bass transposed by double counterpoint. This slow movement is also physically essential to it; a quick run or trill in the low notes cannot even be imagined. The higher ripienos, running parallel to the animal world, move more rapidly, yet without melodious connexion and significant progress. The disconnected course of the ripienos and their determination by laws are analogous to the fact that in the whole irrational world, from the crystal to the most perfect animal, no being has a really connected consciousness that would make its life into a significant whole. No being experiences a succession of mental developments, none perfects itself by training or instruction, but at any time everything exists uniformly according to its nature, determined by a fixed law. Finally, in the *melody,* in the high, singing, principal voice, leading the whole and progressing with unrestrained freedom, in the uninterrupted significant connexion of *one* thought from beginning to end, and expressing a whole, I recognize the highest grade of the will's objectification, the intellectual life and endeavour of man. He alone, because endowed with the faculty of reason, is always looking before and after on the path of his actual life and of its innumerable possibilities, and so achieves a course of life that is intellectual, and is thus connected as a whole. In keeping with this, *melody* alone has significant and intentional connexion from beginning to end. Consequently, it relates the story of the intellectually enlightened will, the copy or impression whereof in actual life is the series of its deeds. Melody, however, says more; it relates the most secret history of the intellectually enlightened will, portrays every agitation, every effort, every movement of the will, everything which the faculty of reason summarizes under the wide and negative concept of feeling, and which cannot be further taken up into the abstractions of reason. Hence it has always been said that music is the language of feeling and of passion, just as words are the language of reason. Plato explains it as ἡ τῶν μελῶν κίνησις μεμιμημένη, ἐν τοῖς παθήμασιν ὅταν ψυχὴ γίνηται (*melodiarum motus, animi affectus imitans*),[48] *Laws,* VIII [812c]; and Aristotle also says: διὰ τί οἱ ῥυθμοὶ καὶ τὰ μέλη, φωνὴ οὖσα, ἤθεσιν ἔοικε; (*Cur numeri musici et modi, qui voces sunt, moribus similes sese exhibent?*), *Problemata,* c. 19.[49]

Now the nature of man consists in the fact that his will strives, is satisfied, strives anew, and so on and on; in fact his happiness and well-being consist only in the transition from desire to satisfaction, and from this to a fresh desire, such transition going forward rapidly. For the non-appearance of satisfaction is suffering; the empty longing for a new desire is languor, boredom. Thus, corresponding to this, the nature of melody is a constant digression and deviation from the keynote in a thousand ways, not only to the harmonious intervals, the third and dominant, but to every tone, to the dissonant seventh, and to the extreme intervals; yet there always follows a final return to the keynote. In all these ways, melody expresses the many different forms of the will's efforts, but also its satisfaction by ultimately finding again a harmonious interval, and still more the keynote. The invention of melody, the disclosure in it of all the deepest secrets of human willing and feeling, is the work of genius, whose effect is more apparent here than anywhere else, is far removed from all reflection and conscious intention, and might be called an inspiration. Here, as everywhere in art, the concept is unproductive. The composer reveals the innermost nature of the world, and expresses the profoundest wisdom in a language that his reasoning faculty does not understand, just as a magnetic somnambulist gives information about things of which she has no conception when she is awake. Therefore in the composer, more than in any other artist, the man is entirely separate and distinct from the artist. Even in the explanation of this wonderful art, the concept shows its inadequacy and its limits; however, I will try to carry out our analogy. Now, as rapid transition from wish to satisfaction and from this to a new wish are happiness and well-being, so rapid melodies without great deviations are cheerful. Slow melodies that strike painful discords and wind back to the keynote only through many bars, are sad, on the analogy of delayed and hard-won satisfaction. Delay in the new excitement of the will, namely languor, could have no other expression than the sustained keynote, the effect of which would soon be intolerable; very monotonous and meaningless melodies approximate to this. The short, intelligible phrases of rapid dance music seem

---

[48] "The movement of the melody which it imitates, when the soul is stirred by passions." [Tr.]

[49] "How is it that rhythms and melodies, although only sound, resemble states of the soul?" [Tr.]

to speak only of ordinary happiness which is easy of attainment. On the other hand, the *allegro maestoso* in great phrases, long passages, and wide deviations expresses a greater, nobler effort towards a distant goal, and its final attainment. The *adagio* speaks of the suffering of a great and noble endeavour that disdains all trifling happiness. But how marvellous is the effect of *minor* and *major!* How astonishing that the change of half a tone, the entrance of a minor third instead of a major, at once and inevitably forces on us an anxious and painful feeling, from which we are again delivered just as instantaneously by the major! The *adagio* in the minor key reaches the expression of the keenest pain, and becomes the most convulsive lament. Dance music in the minor key seems to express the failure of the trifling happiness that we ought rather to disdain; it appears to speak of the attainment of a low end with toil and trouble. The inexhaustibleness of possible melodies corresponds to the inexhaustibleness of nature in the difference of individuals, physiognomies, and courses of life. The transition from one key into quite a different one, since it entirely abolishes the connexion with what went before, is like death inasmuch as the individual ends in it. Yet the will that appeared in this individual lives on just the same as before, appearing in other individuals, whose consciousness, however, has no connexion with that of the first.

But we must never forget when referring to all these analogies I have brought forward, that music has no direct relation to them, but only an indirect one; for it never expresses the phenomenon, but only the inner nature, the in-itself, of every phenomenon, the will itself. Therefore music does not express this or that particular and definite pleasure, this or that affliction, pain, sorrow, horror, gaiety, merriment, or peace of mind, but joy, pain, sorrow, horror, gaiety, merriment, peace of mind *themselves,* to a certain extent in the abstract, their essential nature, without any accessories, and so also without the motives for them. Nevertheless, we understand them perfectly in this extracted quintessence. Hence it arises that our imagination is so easily stirred by music, and tries to shape that invisible, yet vividly aroused, spirit-world that speaks to us directly, to clothe it with flesh and bone, and thus to embody it in an analogous example. This is the origin of the song with words, and finally of the opera. For this reason they should never forsake that subordinate position in order to make themselves the chief thing, and the music a mere means of expressing the song, since this is a great misconception and an utter absurdity. Everywhere music expresses only the quintessence of life and of its events, never these themselves, and therefore their differences do not always influence it.

It is just this universality that belongs uniquely to music, together with the most precise distinctness, that gives it that high value as the panacea of all our sorrows. Therefore, if music tries to stick too closely to the words, and to mould itself according to the events, it is endeavouring to speak a language not its own. No one has kept so free from this mistake as Rossini; hence his music speaks its *own* language so distinctly and purely that it requires no words at all, and therefore produces its full effect even when rendered by instruments alone.

As a result of all this, we can regard the phenomenal world, or nature, and music as two different expressions of the same thing; and this thing itself is therefore the only medium of their analogy, a knowledge of which is required if we are to understand that analogy. Accordingly, music, if regarded as an expression of the world, is in the highest degree a universal language that is related to the universality of concepts much as these are related to the particular things. Yet its universality is by no means that empty universality of abstraction, but is of quite a different kind; it is united with thorough and unmistakable distinctness. In this respect it is like geometrical figures and numbers, which are the universal forms of all possible objects of experience and are *a priori* applicable to them all, and yet are not abstract, but perceptible and thoroughly definite. All possible efforts, stirrings, and manifestations of the will, all the events that occur within man himself and are included by the reasoning faculty in the wide, negative concept of feeling, can be expressed by the infinite number of possible melodies, but always in the universality of mere form without the material, always only according to the in-itself, not to the phenomenon, as it were the innermost soul of the phenomenon without the body. This close relation that music has to the true nature of all things can also explain the fact that, when music suitable to any scene, action, event, or environment is played, it seems to disclose to us its most secret meaning, and appears to be the most accurate and distinct commentary on it. Moreover, to the man who gives himself up entirely to the impression of a symphony, it is as if he saw all the possible events of life and of the world passing by within himself. Yet if he reflects, he cannot assert any likeness between that piece of music and the things that passed through his mind. For, as we have said, music differs from all the other arts by the fact that it is not a copy of the phenomenon, or, more exactly, of the will's adequate objectivity, but is directly a copy of the will itself, and therefore expresses the metaphysical to everything physical in the world, the thing-in-itself to every phenomenon. Accordingly, we could just as

well call the world embodied music as embodied will; this is the
reason why music makes every picture, indeed every scene from
real life and from the world, at once appear in enhanced significance,
and this is, of course, all the greater, the more analogous its melody
is to the inner spirit of the given phenomenon. It is due to this that
we are able to set a poem to music as a song, or a perceptive
presentation as a pantomime, or both as an opera. Such individual
pictures of human life, set to the universal language of music, are
never bound to it or correspond to it with absolute necessity, but
stand to it only in the relation of an example, chosen at random, to
a universal concept. They express in the distinctness of reality what
music asserts in the universality of mere form. For, to a certain
extent, melodies are, like universal concepts, an abstraction from
reality. This reality, and hence the world of particular things,
furnishes what is perceptive, special, and individual, the particular
case, both to the universality of the concepts and to that of the
melodies. These two universalities, however, are in a certain respect
opposed to each other, since the concepts contain only the forms,
first of all abstracted from perception, so to speak the stripped-off
outer shell of things; hence they are quite properly *abstracta*. Music,
on the other hand, gives the innermost kernel preceding all form, or
the heart of things. This relation could very well be expressed in the
language of the scholastics by saying that the concepts are the
universalia post rem, but music gives the *universalia ante rem*, and
reality the *universalia in re*. Even other examples, just as arbitrarily
chosen, of the universal expressed in a poem could correspond in the
same degree to the general significance of the melody assigned to this
poem; and so the same composition is suitable to many verses;
hence also the *vaudeville*. But that generally a relation between a
composition and a perceptive expression is possible is due, as we
have said, to the fact that the two are simply quite different
expressions of the same inner nature of the world. Now when in the
particular case such a relation actually exists, thus when the composer
has known how to express in the universal language of music the
stirrings of will that constitute the kernel of an event, then the melody
of the song, the music of the opera, is expressive. But the analogy
discovered by the composer between these two must have come from
the immediate knowledge of the inner nature of the world unknown
to his faculty of reason; it cannot be an imitation brought about
with conscious intention by means of concepts, otherwise the music
does not ·express the inner nature of the will itself, but merely
imitates its phenomenon inadequately. All really imitative music
does this; for example, *The Seasons* by Haydn, also many passages

of his *Creation,* where phenomena of the world of perception are directly imitated; also in all battle pieces. All this is to be entirely rejected.

The inexpressible depth of all music, by virtue of which it floats past us as a paradise quite familiar and yet eternally remote, and is so easy to understand and yet so inexplicable, is due to the fact that it reproduces all the emotions of our innermost being, but entirely without reality and remote from its pain. In the same way, the seriousness essential to it and wholly excluding the ludicrous from its direct and peculiar province is to be explained from the fact that its object is not the representation, in regard to which deception and ridiculousness alone are possible, but that this object is directly the will; and this is essentially the most serious of all things, as being that on which all depends. How full of meaning and significance the language of music is we see from the repetition signs, as well as from the *Da capo* which would be intolerable in the case of works composed in the language of words. In music, however, they are very appropriate and beneficial; for to comprehend it fully, we must hear it twice.

In the whole of this discussion on music I have been trying to make it clear that music expresses in an exceedingly universal language, in a homogeneous material, that is, in mere tones, and with the greatest distinctness and truth, the inner being, the in-itself, of the world, which we think of under the concept of will, according to its most distinct manifestation. Further, according to my view and contention, philosophy is nothing but a complete and accurate repetition and expression of the inner nature of the world in very general concepts, for only in these is it possible to obtain a view of that entire inner nature which is everywhere adequate and applicable. Thus whoever has followed me and has entered into my way of thinking will not find it so very paradoxical when I say that, supposing we succeeded in giving a perfectly accurate and complete explanation of music which goes into detail, and thus a detailed repetition in concepts of what it expresses, this would also be at once a sufficient repetition and explanation of the world in concepts, or one wholly corresponding thereto, and hence the true philosophy. Consequently, we can parody in the following way the above-mentioned saying of Leibniz, in the sense of our higher view of music, for it is quite correct from a lower point of view: *Musica est exercitium metaphysices occultum nescientis se philosophari animi.*[50] For *scire,* to know, always means to have couched in abstract

---

[50] "Music is an unconscious exercise in metaphysics in which the mind does not know it is philosophizing." [Tr.]

concepts. But further, in virtue of the truth of the saying of Leibniz, corroborated in many ways, music, apart from its aesthetic or inner significance, and considered merely externally and purely empirically, is nothing but the means of grasping, immediately and in the concrete, larger numbers and more complex numerical ratios that we can otherwise know only indirectly by comprehension in concepts. Therefore, by the union of these two very different yet correct views of music, we can now arrive at a conception of the possibility of a philosophy of numbers, like that of Pythagoras and of the Chinese in the *I Ching*, and then interpret in this sense that saying of the Pythagoreans quoted by Sextus Empiricus (*Adversus Mathematicos*, Bk. vii [§ 94]): τῷ ἀριθμῷ δὲ τὰ πάντ᾽ ἐπέοικεν (*numero cuncta assimilantur*).[51] And if, finally, we apply this view to our above-mentioned interpretation of harmony and melody, we shall find a mere moral philosophy without an explanation of nature, such as Socrates tried to introduce, to be wholly analogous to a melody without harmony, desired exclusively by Rousseau; and in contrast to this, mere physics and metaphysics without ethics will correspond to mere harmony without melody. Allow me to add to these occasional observations a few more remarks concerning the analogy of music with the phenomenal world. We found in the previous book that the highest grade of the will's objectification, namely man, could not appear alone and isolated, but that this presupposed the grades under him, and these again presupposed lower and lower grades. Now music, which, like the world, immediately objectifies the will, is also perfect only in complete harmony. In order to produce its full impression, the high leading voice of melody requires the accompaniment of all the other voices down to the lowest bass which is to be regarded as the origin of all. The melody itself intervenes as an integral part in the harmony, as the harmony does in the melody, and only thus, in the full-toned whole, does music express what it intends to express. Thus the one will outside time finds its complete objectification only in the complete union of all the grades that reveal its inner nature in the innumerable degrees of enhanced distinctness. The following analogy is also remarkable. In the previous book we saw that, notwithstanding the self-adaptation of all the phenomena of the will to one another as regards the species, which gives rise to the teleological view, there yet remains an unending conflict between those phenomena as individuals. It is visible at all grades of individuals, and makes the world a permanent battle-field of all those phenomena of one and the same will; and in this

---

[51] "All things are similar to number." [Tr.]

way the will's inner contradiction with itself becomes visible. In music there is also something corresponding to this; thus a perfectly pure harmonious system of tones is impossible not only physically, but even arithmetically. The numbers themselves, by which the tones can be expressed, have insoluble irrationalities. No scale can ever be computed within which every fifth would be related to the keynote as 2 to 3, every major third as 4 to 5, every minor third as 5 to 6, and so on. For if the tones are correctly related to the keynote, they no longer are so to one another, because, for example, the fifth would have to be the minor third to the third, and so on. For the notes of the scale can be compared to actors, who have to play now one part, now another. Therefore a perfectly correct music cannot even be conceived, much less worked out; and for this reason all possible music deviates from perfect purity. It can merely conceal the discords essential to it by dividing these among all the notes, i.e., by temperament. On this see Chladni's *Akustik,* § 30, and his *Kurze Übersicht der Schall- und Klanglehre,* p. 12.[52]

I might still have much to add on the way in which music is perceived, namely in and through time alone, with absolute exclusion of space, even without the influence of the knowledge of causality, and thus of the understanding. For the tones make the aesthetic impression as effect, and this without our going back to their causes, as in the case of perception. But I do not wish to make these remarks still more lengthy, as I have perhaps already gone too much into detail with regard to many things in this third book, or have dwelt too much on particulars. However, my aim made it necessary, and will be the less disapproved of, if the importance and high value of art, seldom sufficiently recognized, are realized. According to our view, the whole of the visible world is only the objectification, the mirror, of the will, accompanying it to knowledge of itself, and indeed, as we shall soon see, to the possibility of its salvation. At the same time, the world as representation, if we consider it in isolation, by tearing ourselves from willing, and letting it alone take possession of our consciousness, is the most delightful, and the only innocent, side of life. We have to regard art as the greater enhancement, the more perfect development, of all this; for essentially it achieves just the same thing as is achieved by the visible world itself, only with greater concentration, perfection, intention, and intelligence; and therefore, in the full sense of the word, it may be called the flower of life. If the whole world as representation is only the visibility of the will, then art is the elucidation of this visibility, the *camera obscura*

<hr />

[52] Cf. chap. 39 of volume 2.

which shows the objects more purely, and enables us to survey and comprehend them better. It is the play within the play, the stage on the stage in *Hamlet*.

The pleasure of everything beautiful, the consolation afforded by art, the enthusiasm of the artist which enables him to forget the cares of life, this one advantage of the genius over other men alone compensating him for the suffering that is heightened in proportion to the clearness of consciousness, and for the desert loneliness among a different race of men, all this is due to the fact that, as we shall see later on, the in-itself of life, the will, existence itself, is a constant suffering, and is partly woeful, partly fearful. The same thing, on the other hand, as representation alone, purely contemplated, or repeated through art, free from pain, presents us with a significant spectacle. This purely knowable side of the world and its repetition in any art is the element of the artist. He is captivated by a consideration of the spectacle of the will's objectification. He sticks to this, and does not get tired of contemplating it, and of repeating it in his descriptions. Meanwhile, he himself bears the cost of producing that play; in other words, he himself is the will objectifying itself and remaining in constant suffering. That pure, true, and profound knowledge of the inner nature of the world now becomes for him an end in itself; at it he stops. Therefore it does not become for him a quieter of the will, as we shall see in the following book in the case of the saint who has attained resignation; it does not deliver him from life for ever, but only for a few moments. For him it is not the way out of life, but only an occasional consolation in it, until his power, enhanced by this contemplation, finally becomes tired of the spectacle, and seizes the serious side of things. The St. Cecilia of Raphael can be regarded as a symbol of this transition. Therefore we will now in the following book turn to the serious side.

FOURTH BOOK

THE WORLD AS WILL

SECOND ASPECT

With the Attainment of Self-Knowledge, Affirmation and Denial of the Will-to-Live

Tempore quo cognitio simul advenit, amor e medio supersurrexit.
Oupnek'hat, studio Anquetil Duperron, Vol. ii. p. 216.

("The moment knowledge appeared on the scene, thence arose desire." [Tr.])

§ 53.

The last part of our discussion proclaims itself as the most serious, for it concerns the actions of men, the subject of direct interest to everyone, and one which can be foreign or indifferent to none. Indeed, to refer everything else to action is so characteristic of man's nature that, in every systematic investigation, he will always consider that part of it which relates to action as the result of its whole content, at any rate in so far as this interests him, and he will therefore devote his most serious attention to this part, even if to no other. In this respect, the part of our discussion which follows would, according to the ordinary method of expression, be called practical philosophy in contrast to the theoretical dealt with up to now. In my opinion, however, all philosophy is always theoretical, since it is essential to it always to maintain a purely contemplative attitude, whatever be the immediate object of investigation; to inquire, not to prescribe. But to become practical, to guide conduct, to transform character, are old claims which with mature insight it ought finally to abandon. For here, where it is a question of the worth or worthlessness of existence, of salvation or damnation, not the dead concepts of philosophy decide the matter, but the innermost nature of man himself, the daemon which guides him and has not chosen him, but has been chosen by him, as Plato would say; his intelligible character, as Kant puts it. Virtue is as little taught as is genius; indeed, the concept is just as unfruitful for it as it is for art, and in the case of both can be used only as an instrument. We should therefore be just as foolish to expect that our moral systems and ethics would create virtuous, noble, and holy men, as that our aesthetics would produce poets, painters, and musicians.

Philosophy can never do more than interpret and explain what is present and at hand; it can never do more than bring to the distinct, abstract knowledge of the faculty of reason the inner nature of the world which expresses itself intelligibly to everyone in the concrete, that is, as feeling. It does this, however, in every possible relation and connexion and from every point of view. Now just as in the three previous books the attempt has been made to achieve the same thing with the generality proper to philosophy, from different points of view, so in the present book man's conduct will be considered in the same way. This side of the world might prove to be the most important of all, not only, as I remarked above, from a subjective, but also from an objective point of view. Here I shall remain absolutely faithful to the method of consideration we have hitherto followed, and shall support myself by assuming what has been stated up to now. Indeed, there is really only one thought that forms the content of this whole work, and as I have developed it hitherto as regards other subjects, I shall now develop it in the conduct of man. I shall thus do the last thing I am able to do for communicating this thought as fully and completely as possible.

The point of view given and the method of treatment announced suggest that in this ethical book no precepts, no doctrine of duty are to be expected; still less will there be set forth a universal moral principle, a universal recipe, so to speak, for producing all the virtues. Also we shall not speak of an *"unconditioned ought,"* since this involves a contradiction, as is explained in the Appendix; or of a "law for freedom," which is in the same position. Generally we shall not speak of "ought" at all, for we speak in this way to children and to peoples still in their infancy, but not to those who have appropriated to themselves all the culture of a mature age. It is indeed a palpable contradiction to call the will free and yet to prescribe for it laws by which it is to will. "Ought to will!" wooden-iron![1] But in the light of our whole view, the will is not only free, but even almighty; from it comes not only its action, but also its world; and as the will is, so does its action appear, so does its world appear; both are its self-knowledge and nothing more. The will determines itself, and therewith its action and its world also; for besides it there is nothing, and these are the will itself. Only thus is the will truly autonomous, and from every other point of view it is heteronomous. Our philosophical attempts can go only so far as to interpret and explain man's action, and the very different and even opposite maxims of which it is the living expression, according to their innermost nature and content. This is done in connexion with our previous discussion, and in precisely the same way in which we have attempted hitherto to interpret the remaining phenomena of the world, and to bring their innermost nature to distinct, abstract knowledge. Our philosophy will affirm the same *immanence* here as in all that we have considered hitherto. It will not, in opposition to Kant's great teaching, attempt to use as a jumping-pole the forms of

---

[1] Cf. Book i, p. 30. [Tr.]

the phenomenon, whose general expression is the principle of sufficient reason, in order to leap over the phenomenon itself,] which alone gives those forms meaning, and to land in the boundless sphere of empty fictions. This actual world of what is knowable, in which we are and which is in us, remains both the material and the limit of our consideration. It is a world so rich in content that not even the profoundest investigation of which the human mind is capable could exhaust it. Now since the real, knowable world will never fail to afford material and reality to our ethical observations any more than it will to our previous observations, nothing will be less necessary than for us to take refuge in negative concepts devoid of content, and then somehow to make even ourselves believe that we were saying something when we spoke with raised eyebrows about the "absolute," the "infinite," the "supersensuous," and whatever other mere negations of the sort there may be (οὐδέν ἐστι, ἢ τὸ τῆς στερήσεως ὄνομα, μετὰ ἀμυδρᾶς ἐπινοίας. *Nihil est, nisi negationis nomen, cum obscura notione.* Julian, *Oratio 5.*)[2] Instead of this, we could call it more briefly cloud-cuckoo-land (νεφελοκοκκυγία).[3] We shall not need to serve up covered, empty dishes of this sort. Finally, no more here than in the previous books shall we relate histories and give them out as philosophy. For we are of opinion that anyone who imagines that the inner nature of the world can be *historically* comprehended, however finely glossed over it may be, is still infinitely far from a philosophical knowledge of the world. But this is the case as soon as a *becoming,* or a *having-become,* or a *will-become* enters into his view of the inner nature of the world; whenever an earlier or a later has the least significance; and consequently whenever points of beginning and of ending in the world, together with a path between the two, are sought and found, and the philosophizing individual even recognizes his own position on this path. Such *historical philosophizing* in most cases furnishes a cosmogony admitting of many varieties, or else a system of emanations, a doctrine of diminutions, or finally, when driven in despair over the fruitless attempts of those paths to the last path, it furnishes, conversely, a doctrine of a constant becoming, springing up, arising, coming to light out of darkness, out of the obscure ground, primary ground, groundlessness, or some other drivel of this kind. But all this is most briefly disposed of by remarking that a whole eternity, in other words an endless time, has already elapsed up to the present moment,

---

[2] "It is nothing but a mere negation, united with an obscure notion." [Tr.]
[3] From *The Birds* of Aristophanes. [Tr.]

and therefore everything that can or should become must have become already. For all such historical philosophy, whatever airs it may assume, regards *time,* just as though Kant had never existed, as a determination of things-in-themselves, and therefore stops at what Kant calls the phenomenon in opposition to the thing-in-itself, and what Plato calls the becoming never the being in opposition to the being never the becoming, or finally what is called by the Indians the web of Maya. It is just the knowledge belonging to the principle of sufficient reason, with which we never reach the inner nature of things, but endlessly pursue phenomena only, moving without end or aim like a squirrel in its wheel, until in the end we are tired out, and stop still at some arbitrarily chosen point, and then wish to extort respect for this from others as well. The genuine method of considering the world philosophically, in other words, that consideration which acquaints us with the inner nature of the world and thus takes us beyond the phenomenon, is precisely the method that does not ask about the whence, whither, and why of the world, but always and everywhere about the *what* alone. Thus it is the method that considers things not according to any relation, not as becoming and passing away, in short not according to one of the four forms of the principle of sufficient reason. On the contrary, it is precisely what is still left over after we eliminate the whole of this method of consideration that follows the principle of sufficient reason; thus it is the inner nature of the world, always appearing the same in all relations, but itself never amenable to them, in other words the Ideas of the world, that forms the object of our method of philosophy. From such knowledge we get philosophy as well as art; in fact, we shall find in this book that we can also reach that disposition of mind which alone leads to true holiness and to salvation from the world.

§ 54.

The first three books will, it is hoped, have produced the distinct and certain knowledge that the mirror of the will has appeared to it in the world as representation. In this mirror the will knows itself in increasing degrees of distinctness and completeness, the highest of which is man. Man's inner nature, however, receives its complete expression above all through the connected series of his actions. The self-conscious connexion of these actions is rendered possible by the faculty of reason, which enables him to survey the whole in the abstract.

The will, considered purely in itself, is devoid of knowledge, and is only a blind, irresistible urge, as we see it appear in inorganic and vegetable nature and in their laws, and also in the vegetative part of our own life. Through the addition of the world as representation, developed for its service, the will obtains knowledge of its own willing and what it wills, namely that this is nothing but this world, life, precisely as it exists. We have therefore called the phenomenal world the mirror, the objectivity, of the will; and as what the will wills is always life, just because this is nothing but the presentation of that willing for the representation, it is immaterial and a mere pleonasm if, instead of simply saying "the will," we say "the will-to-live."

As the will is the thing-in-itself, the inner content, the essence of the world, but life, the visible world, the phenomenon, is only the mirror of the will, this world will accompany the will as inseparably as a body is accompanied by its shadow; and if will exists, then life, the world, will exist. Therefore life is certain to the will-to-live, and as long as we are filled with the will-to-live we need not be apprehensive for our existence, even at the sight of death. It is true that we see the individual come into being and pass away; but the individual is only phenomenon, exists only for knowledge involved in the principle of sufficient reason, in the *principium individuationis*. Naturally, for this knowledge, the individual receives his life as a gift, rises out of nothing, and then suffers the loss of this gift through death, and returns to nothing. We, however, wish to consider life philosophically, that is to say, according to its Ideas, and then we shall find that neither the will, the thing-in-itself in all phenomena, nor the subject of knowing, the spectator of all phenomena, is in any way affected by birth and death. Birth and death belong only to the phenomenon of the will, and hence to life; and it is essential to this that it manifest itself in individuals that come into being and pass away, as fleeting phenomena, appearing in the form of time, of that which in itself knows no time, but must be manifested precisely in the way aforesaid in order to objectify its real nature. Birth and death belong equally to life, and hold the balance as mutual conditions of each other, or, if the expression be preferred, as poles of the whole phenomenon of life. The wisest of all mythologies, the Indian, expresses this by giving to the very god who symbolizes destruction and death (just as

Brahma, the most sinful and lowest god of the Trimurti, symbolizes generation, origination, and Vishnu preservation), by giving, I say, to Shiva as an attribute not only the necklace of skulls, but also the lingam, that symbol of generation which appears as the counterpart of death. In this way it is intimated that generation and death are essential correlatives which reciprocally neutralize and eliminate each other. It was precisely the same sentiment that prompted the Greeks and Romans to adorn the costly sarcophagi, just as we still see them, with feasts, dances, marriages, hunts, fights between wild beasts, bacchanalia, that is with presentations of life's most powerful urge. This they present to us not only through such diversions and merriments, but even in sensual groups, to the point of showing us the sexual intercourse between satyrs and goats. The object was obviously to indicate with the greatest emphasis from the death of the mourned individual the immortal life of nature, and thus to intimate, although without abstract knowledge, that the whole of nature is the phenomenon, and also the fulfilment, of the will-to-live. The form of this phenomenon is time, space, and causality, and through these individuation, which requires that the individual must come into being and pass away. But this no more disturbs the will-to-live—the individual being only a particular example or specimen, so to speak, of the phenomenon of this will—than does the death of an individual injure the whole of nature. For it is not the individual that nature cares for, but only the species; and in all seriousness she urges the preservation of the species, since she provides for this so lavishly through the immense surplus of the seed and the great strength of the fructifying impulse. The individual, on the contrary, has no value for nature, and can have none, for infinite time, infinite space, and the infinite number of possible individuals therein are her kingdom. Therefore nature is always ready to let the individual fall, and the individual is accordingly not only exposed to destruction in a thousand ways from the most insignificant accidents, but is even destined for this and is led towards it by nature herself, from the moment that individual has served the maintenance of the species. In this way, nature quite openly expresses the great truth that only the Ideas, not individuals, have reality proper, in other words are a complete objectivity of the will. Now man is nature herself, and indeed nature at the highest grade of her self-consciousness, but nature is only the objectified will-to-live; the person who has grasped and retained this point of view may certainly and justly console himself for his own death and for that of his friends by looking back on the immortal life of nature, which he himself is. Consequently, Shiva with the lingam is to be understood in this way, and so are those ancient sarcophagi that with their pictures of glowing life exclaim to the lamenting beholder: *Natura non contristatur.*[4]

That generation and death are to be regarded as something belonging to life, and essential to this phenomenon of the will, arises also from the fact that they both exhibit themselves merely as the higher powers of expression of that in which all the rest of life consists. This is everywhere nothing but a constant change of matter under a fixed permanence of form; and this is precisely the transitoriness of the individuals with the imperishableness of the species. Constant nourishment and renewal differ from generation only in degree, and only in degree does constant excretion differ from death. The former shows itself most simply and distinctly in the plant, which is throughout only the constant repetition of the same impulse of its simplest fibre grouping itself into leaf and branch. It is a systematic aggregate of homogeneous plants supporting one another, and their constant reproduction is its simple impulse. It ascends to the complete satisfaction of this impulse by means of the gradation of metamorphosis, finally to the blossom and the fruit, that compendium of its existence and effort in which it attains in a shorter way what is its sole aim. It now produces at one stroke a thousandfold what till then it effected in the particular case, namely the repetition of itself. Its growth up to the fruit is related to that fruit as writing is to printing. In the case of the animal, it is obviously exactly the same. The process of nourishment is a constant generation; the process of generation is a higher power of nourishment. The pleasure that accompanies procreation is a higher power of the agreeableness of the feeling of life. On the other hand, excretion, the constant exhalation and throwing off of matter, is the same as what at a higher power is death, namely the opposite of procreation. Now, if here we are always content to retain the form without lamenting the discarded matter, we must behave in the same way when in death the same thing happens at a higher potential and to the whole, as occurs every day and hour in a partial way with excretion. Just as we are indifferent to the one, so we should not recoil at the other. Therefore, from this point of view, it seems just as absurd to desire the continuance of our individuality, which is replaced by other individuals, as to desire the permanence of the matter of our body, which is constantly replaced by fresh matter. It appears just as foolish to embalm corpses as it would be carefully to preserve our excreta. As for the individual consciousness bound to the individual body, it is completely interrupted every day by sleep.

---

[4] "Nature is not grieved." [Tr.]

Deep sleep, while it lasts, is in no way different from death, into which it constantly passes, for example in the case of freezing to death, differing only as to the future, namely with regard to the awakening. Death is a sleep in which individuality is forgotten; everything else awakens again, or rather has remained awake.[5]

Above all, we must clearly recognize that the form of the phenomenon of the will, and hence the form of life or of reality, is really only the *present,* not the future or the past. Future and past are only in the concept, exist only in the connexion and continuity of knowledge in so far as this follows the principle of sufficient reason. No man has lived in the past, and none will ever live in the future; the *present* alone is the form of all life, but it is also life's sure possession which can never be torn from it. The present always exists together with its content; both stand firm without wavering, like the rainbow over the waterfall. For life is sure and certain to the will, and the present is sure and certain to life. Of course, if we think back to the thousands of years that have passed, to the millions of men and women who lived in them, we ask, What were they? What has become of them? But, on the other hand, we need recall only the past of our own life, and vividly renew its scenes in our imagination, and then ask again, What was all this? What has become of it? As it is with our life, so is it with the life of those millions. Or should we suppose that the past took on a new existence by its being sealed through death? Our own past, even the most recent, even the previous day, is only an empty dream of the imagination, and the past of all those millions is the same. What was? What is? The will, whose mirror is life, and will-free knowledge beholding the will clearly in that mirror. He who has not already recognized this, or will not recognize it, must add to the above question as to the fate of past generations this ques-

---

[5] The following remark can also help the person for whom it is not too subtle to understand clearly that the individual is only the phenomenon, not the thing-in-itself. On the one hand, every individual is the subject of knowing, in other words, the supplementary condition of the possibility of the whole objective world, and, on the other, a particular phenomenon of the will, of that will which objectifies itself in each thing. But this double character of our inner being does not rest on a self-existent unity, otherwise it would be possible for us to be conscious of ourselves *in ourselves and independently of the objects of knowing and willing.* Now we simply cannot do this, but as soon as we enter into ourselves in order to attempt it, and wish for once to know ourselves fully by directing our knowledge inwards, we lose ourselves in a bottomless void; we find ourselves like a hollow glass globe, from the emptiness of which a voice speaks. But the cause of this voice is not to be found in the globe, and since we want to comprehend ourselves, we grasp with a shudder nothing but a wavering and unstable phantom.

tion as well: Why precisely is he, the questioner, so lucky as to possess this precious, perishable, and only real present, while those hundreds of generations of men, even the heroes and sages of former times, have sunk into the night of the past, and have thus become nothing, while he, his insignificant ego, actually exists? Or, more briefly, although strangely: Why is this now, his now, precisely now and *was* not long ago? Since he asks such strange questions, he regards his existence and his time as independent of each other, and the former as projected into the latter. He really assumes two nows, one belonging to the object and the other to the subject, and marvels at the happy accident of their coincidence. Actually, however, only the point of contact of the object, the form of which is time, with the subject that has no mode of the principle of sufficient reason as its form, constitutes the present (as is shown in the essay *On the Principle of Sufficient Reason*). But all object is the will, in so far as the will has become representation, and the subject is the necessary correlative of all object; only in the present, however, are there real objects. Past and future contain mere concepts and phantasms; hence the present is the essential form of the phenomenon of the will, and is inseparable from that form. The present alone is that which always exists and stands firm and immovable. That which, empirically apprehended, is the most fleeting of all, manifests itself to the metaphysical glance that sees beyond the forms of empirical perception as that which alone endures, as the *nunc stans* of the scholastics. The source and supporter of its content is the will-to-live, or the thing-in-itself— which we are. That which constantly becomes and passes away, in that it either has been already or is still to come, belongs to the phenomenon as such by virtue of its forms which render coming into being and passing away possible. Accordingly, let us think: *Quid fuit? Quod est. Quid erit? Quod fuit,*[6] and take it in the strict sense of the words, understanding not *simile* but *idem*. For life is certain to the will, and the present is certain to life. Therefore everyone can also say: "I am once for all lord and master of the present, and through all eternity it will accompany me as my shadow; accordingly, I do not wonder where it comes from, and how it is that it is precisely now." We can compare time to an endlessly revolving sphere; the half that is always sinking would be the past, and the half that is always rising would be the future; but at the top, the indivisible point that touches the tangent would be the extensionless present. Just as the tangent does not continue rolling with the sphere, so also the present, the point of contact of the object whose form is time, does

---

[6] "What was? That which is. What will be? That which was." [Tr.]

not roll on with the subject that has no form, since it does not belong to the knowable, but is the condition of all that is knowable. Or time is like an irresistible stream, and the present like a rock on which the stream breaks, but which it does not carry away. The will, as thing-in-itself, is as little subordinate to the principle of sufficient reason as is the subject of knowledge which is ultimately in a certain regard the will itself or its manifestation; and just as life, the will's own phenomenon, is certain to the will, so also is the present, the sole form of actual life. Accordingly, we have not to investigate the past before life or the future after death; rather have we to know the *present* as the only form in which the will manifests itself.[7] It will not run away from the will, nor the will from it. Therefore whoever is satisfied with life as it is, whoever affirms it in every way, can confidently regard it as endless, and can banish the fear of death as a delusion. This delusion inspires him with the foolish dread that he can ever be deprived of the present, and deceives him about a time without a present in it. This is a delusion which in regard to time is like that other in regard to space, in virtue of which everyone imagines the precise position occupied by him on the globe as above, and all the rest as below. In just the same way, everyone connects the present with his own individuality, and imagines that all present becomes extinguished therewith; that past and future are then without a present. But just as on the globe everywhere is above, so the form of all life is the *present;* and to fear death because it robs us of the present is no wiser than to fear that we can slip down from the round globe on the top of which we are now fortunately standing. The form of the present is essential to the objectification of the will. As an extensionless point, it cuts time which extends infinitely in both directions, and stands firm and immovable, like an everlasting midday without a cool evening, just as the actual sun burns without intermission, while only apparently does it sink into the bosom of the night. If, therefore, a person fears death as his annihilation, it is just as if he were to think that the sun can lament in the evening and say: "Woe is me! I am going down into eternal night."[8] Conversely, who-

---

[7] *Scholastici docuerunt quod aeternitas non sit temporis sine fine aut principio successio, sed NUNC STANS; i.e. idem nobis NUNC esse, quod erat NUNC Adamo: i.e. inter NUNC et TUNC nullam esse differentiam.* Hobbes, *Leviathan* [Latin ed., 1841], c. 46.

("The scholastics taught that eternity is not a succession without beginning and end, but a permanent *Now;* in other words, that we possess the same *Now* which existed for Adam; that is to say, that there is no difference between the *Now* and the *Then.*" [Tr.])

[8] In Eckermann's *Gespräche mit Goethe* (second edition, Vol. I, p. 154), Goethe says: "Our spirit is a being of a quite indestructible nature; it acts

ever is oppressed by the burdens of life, whoever loves life and affirms it, but abhors its torments, and in particular can no longer endure the hard lot that has fallen to just him, cannot hope for deliverance from death, and cannot save himself through suicide. Only by a false illusion does the cool shade of Orcus allure him as a haven of rest. The earth rolls on from day into night; the individual dies; but the sun itself burns without intermission, an eternal noon. Life is certain to the will-to-live; the form of life is the endless present; it matters not how individuals, the phenomena of the Idea, arise and pass away in time, like fleeting dreams. Therefore suicide already appears to us to be a vain and therefore foolish action; when we have gone farther in our discussion, it will appear to us in an even less favourable light.

Dogmas change and our knowledge is deceptive, but nature does not err; her action is sure and certain, and she does not conceal it. Everything is entirely in nature, and she is entirely in everything. She has her centre in every animal; the animal has certainly found its way into existence just as it will certainly find its way out of it. Meanwhile, it lives fearlessly and heedlessly in the presence of annihilation, supported by the consciousness that it is nature herself and is as imperishable as she. Man alone carries about with him in abstract concepts the certainty of his own death, yet this can frighten him only very rarely and at particular moments, when some occasion calls it up to the imagination. Against the mighty voice of nature reflection can do little. In man, as in the animal that does not think, there prevails as a lasting state of mind the certainty, springing from innermost consciousness, that he is nature, the world itself. By virtue of this, no one is noticeably disturbed by the thought of certain and never-distant death, but everyone lives on as though he is bound to live for ever. Indeed, this is true to the extent that it might be said that no one has a really lively conviction of the certainty of his death, as otherwise there could not be a very great difference between his frame of mind and that of the condemned criminal. Everyone recog-

---

continuously from eternity to eternity. It is similar to the sun which seems to set only to our earthly eyes, but which really never sets; it shines on incessantly." Goethe took the simile from me, not I from him. He undoubtedly uses it in this conversation of 1824 in consequence of a (possibly unconscious) reminiscence of the above passage, for it appears in the first edition, p. 401, in the same words as here, and also occurs there again on p. 528, and here at the end of § 65. The first edition was sent to him in December 1818, and in March 1819 he sent me in Naples, where I then was, a letter of congratulation through my sister. He had enclosed a piece of paper on which he had noted the numbers of some pages that had specially pleased him. So he had read my book.

nizes that certainty in the abstract and theoretically, but lays it on one side, like other theoretical truths that are not applicable in practice, without taking it into his vivid consciousness. Whoever carefully considers this peculiarity of the human way of thinking, will see that the psychological methods of explaining it from habit and acquiescence in the inevitable are by no means sufficient, but that the reason for it is the deeper one that we state. The same thing can also explain why at all times and among all peoples dogmas of some kind, dealing with the individual's continued existence after death, exist and are highly esteemed, although the proofs in support of them must always be extremely inadequate, whereas those which support the contrary are bound to be powerful and numerous. This is really in no need of any proof, but is recognized by the healthy understanding as a fact; it is confirmed as such by the confidence that nature no more lies than errs, but openly exhibits her action and her essence, and even expresses these naïvely. It is only we ourselves who obscure these by erroneous views, in order to explain from them what is agreeable to our limited view.

But we have now brought into clear consciousness the fact that, although the individual phenomenon of the will begins and ends in time, the will itself, as thing-in-itself, is not affected thereby, nor is the correlative of every object, namely the knowing but never known subject, and that life is always certain to the will-to-live. This is not to be numbered among those doctrines of immortality. For permanence no more belongs to the will, considered as thing-in-itself, or to the pure subject of knowing, to the eternal eye of the world, than does transitoriness, since passing away and transitoriness are determinations valid in time alone, whereas the will and the pure subject of knowing lie outside time. Therefore the egoism of the individual (this particular phenomenon of the will enlightened by the subject of knowing) can as little extract nourishment and consolation for his wish to assert himself through endless time from the view we express, as he could from the knowledge that, after his death, the rest of the external world will continue to exist in time; but this is only the expression of just the same view considered objectively, and so temporally. For it is true that everyone is transitory only as phenomenon; on the other hand, as thing-in-itself he is timeless, and so endless. But also only as phenomenon is the individual different from the other things of the world; as thing-in-itself, he is the will that appears in everything, and death does away with the illusion that separates his consciousness from that of the rest; this is future existence or immortality. His exemption from death, which belongs to him only as thing-in-itself, coincides for the phenomenon with the continued existence of the rest of the external world.[9] Hence it also comes about that the inward and merely felt consciousness of what we have just raised to distinct knowledge does, as we have said, prevent the thought of death from poisoning the life of the rational being. For such consciousness is the basis of that courage to face life which maintains every living thing and enables it to live on cheerfully, as if there were no death, so long as it is face to face with life and is directed thereto. However, the individual is not prevented in this way from being seized with the fear of death, and from trying in every way to escape from it, when it presents itself to him in real life in a particular case, or even only in his imagination, and he then has to face it. For as long as his knowledge was directed to life as such, he was bound to recognize imperishableness in it; and so when death is brought before his eyes, he is bound to recognize it as what it is, namely the temporal end of the particular temporal phenomenon. What we fear in death is by no means the pain, for that obviously lies on this side of death; moreover, we often take refuge in death from pain, just as, conversely, we sometimes endure the most fearful pain merely in order to escape death for a while, although it would be quick and easy. Therefore we distinguish pain and death as two entirely different evils. What we fear in death is in fact the extinction and end of the individual, which it openly proclaims itself to be, and as the individual is the will-to-live itself in a particular objectification, its whole nature struggles against death. Now when feeling leaves us helpless to such an extent, our faculty of reason can nevertheless appear and for the most part overcome influences adverse to it, since it places us at a higher standpoint from which we now view the whole instead of the particular. Therefore, a philosophical knowledge of the nature of the world which had reached the point we are now considering, but went no farther, could, even at this point of view, overcome the terrors of death according as reflection had power over direct feeling in the given individual. A man who had assimilated firmly into his way of thinking the truths so far advanced, but at the same time had not come to know, through his own experience or through a deeper insight, that constant suffering is essential to all life; who found satisfaction in life and took perfect delight in it; who desired, in spite of calm deliberation, that the course of his life as he had hitherto experi-

---

[9] In the *Veda* this is expressed by saying that, when a man dies, his visual faculty becomes one with the sun, his smell with the earth, his taste with water, his hearing with the air, his speech with fire, and so on (*Oupnek'hat,* Vol. I, pp. 249 *seqq.*); as also by the fact that, in a special ceremony, the dying person entrusts his senses and all his faculties one by one to his son, in whom they are then supposed to continue to live. (*Ibid.,* Vol. II, pp. 82 *seqq.*)

enced it should be of endless duration or of constant recurrence; and whose courage to face life was so great that, in return for life's pleasures, he would willingly and gladly put up with all the hardships and miseries to which it is subject; such a man would stand "with firm, strong bones on the well-grounded, enduring earth," [10] and would have nothing to fear. Armed with the knowledge we confer on him, he would look with indifference at death hastening towards him on the wings of time. He would consider it as a false illusion, an impotent spectre, frightening to the weak but having no power over him who knows that he himself is that will of which the whole world is the objectification or copy, to which therefore life and also the present always remain certain and sure. The present is the only real form of the phenomenon of the will. Therefore no endless past or future in which he will not exist can frighten him, for he regards these as an empty mirage and the web of Maya. Thus he would no more have to fear death than the sun would the night. In the *Bhagavad-Gita* Krishna puts his young pupil Arjuna in this position, when, seized with grief at the sight of the armies ready for battle (somewhat after the manner of Xerxes), Arjuna loses heart and wishes to give up the fight, to avert the destruction of so many thousands. Krishna brings him to this point of view, and the death of those thousands can no longer hold him back; he gives the sign for battle. This point of view is also expressed by Goethe's *Prometheus,* especially when he says:

> "Here sit I, form men
> In my own image,
> A race that is like me,
> To suffer, to weep,
> To enjoy and to rejoice,
> And to heed you not,
> As I!"

The philosophy of Bruno and that of Spinoza might also bring to this standpoint the person whose conviction was not shaken or weakened by their errors and imperfections. Bruno's philosophy has no real ethics, and the ethics in Spinoza's philosophy does not in the least proceed from the inner nature of his teaching, but is attached to it merely by means of weak and palpable sophisms, though in itself it is praiseworthy and fine. Finally, many men would occupy the standpoint here set forth, if their knowledge kept pace with their willing, in other words if they were in a position, free from every erroneous

---

[10] From Goethe's *Gränzen der Menschheit.* [Tr.]

idea, to become clearly and distinctly themselves. This is for knowledge the viewpoint of the complete *affirmation of the will-to-live.*

The will affirms itself; this means that while in its objectivity, that is to say, in the world and in life, its own inner nature is completely and distinctly given to it as representation, this knowledge does not in any way impede its willing. It means that just this life thus known is now willed as such by the will with knowledge, consciously and deliberately, just as hitherto the will willed it without knowledge and as a blind impulse. The opposite of this, the *denial of the will-to-live,* shows itself when willing ends with that knowledge, since the particular phenomena known then no longer act as *motives* of willing, but the whole knowledge of the inner nature of the world that mirrors the will, knowledge that has grown up through apprehension of the Ideas, becomes the *quieter* of the will, and thus the will freely abolishes itself. It is hoped that these conceptions, quite unfamiliar and difficult to understand in this general expression, will become clear through the discussion, which will shortly follow, of the phenomena, namely the modes of conduct, in which is expressed affirmation in its different degrees on the one hand, and denial on the other. For both start from *knowledge,* though not from an abstract knowledge expressing itself in words, but from living knowledge expressing itself in deed and conduct alone. Such living knowledge remains independent of the dogmas that here, as abstract knowledge, concern the faculty of reason. To exhibit both and to bring them to the distinct knowledge of the faculty of reason can be my only aim, and not to prescribe or recommend the one or the other, which would be as foolish as it would be pointless. The will in itself is absolutely free and entirely self-determining, and for it there is no law. First of all, however, before we embark on the aforesaid discussion, we must explain and define more precisely this *freedom* and its relation to necessity. Then we must insert a few general remarks, relating to the will and its objects, as regards life, the affirmation and denial whereof are our problem. Through all this, we shall facilitate for ourselves the intended knowledge of the ethical significance of modes of conduct according to their innermost nature.

Since, as I have said, this whole work is only the unfolding of a single thought, it follows therefrom that all its parts have the most intimate connexion with one another. Not only does each part stand in a necessary relation to that which immediately precedes it, and thus presuppose it as within the reader's memory, as is the case with all philosophies consisting merely of a series of inferences, but every part of the whole work is related to every other part, and presupposes it. For this reason, it is required that the reader should remember not only what has just been said, but also every previous remark, so that he is able to connect it with what he is reading at any moment, however much else there may have been between the two. Plato has also made this exacting demand on his reader through the tortuous and complicated digressions of his dialogues which take up the main idea again only after long episodes; but precisely in this way is it made more clear. With us this demand is necessary, for the analysis of our one and only thought into many aspects is indeed the only means of communicating it, though it is not a form essential to the thought itself, but only an artificial form. The separation of the four principal points of view into four books, and the most careful connexion of what is related and homogeneous, help to render the discussion and its comprehension easier. But the subject-matter does not by any means admit of an advance in a straight line, like the progress of history, but renders a more complicated discussion necessary. This also makes necessary a repeated study of the book; only thus does the connexion of every part with every other become evident, and then all together elucidate one another and become clear.[11]

§ 55.

That the will as such is *free*, follows already from the fact that, according to our view, it is the thing-in-itself, the content of all phenomena. The phenomenon, on the other hand, we recognize as absolutely subordinate to the principle of sufficient reason in its four forms. As we know that necessity is absolutely identical with consequent from a given ground, and that the two are convertible concepts, all that belongs to the phenomenon, in other words all that is object for the subject that knows as an individual, is on the one hand ground or reason, on the other consequent, and in this last capacity is determined with absolute necessity; thus it cannot be in any respect other than it is. The whole content of nature, the sum-total of her phenomena, is absolutely necessary, and the necessity of every part, every phenomenon, every event, can always be demonstrated, since it must be possible to find the ground or reason

---

[11] Cf. chaps. 41-44 of volume 2.

on which it depends as consequent. This admits of no exception; it follows from the unrestricted and absolute validity of the principle of sufficient reason. But on the other hand, this same world in all its phenomena is for us objectivity of the will. As the will itself is not phenomenon, not representation or object, but thing-in-itself, it is also not subordinate to the principle of sufficient reason, the form of all object. Thus it is not determined as consequent by a reason or ground, and so it knows no necessity; in other words, it is *free*. The concept of freedom is therefore really a negative one, since its content is merely the denial of necessity, in other words, the denial of the relation of consequent to its ground according to the principle of sufficient reason. Now here we have before us most clearly the point of unity of that great contrast, namely the union of freedom with necessity, which in recent times has often been discussed, yet never, so far as I know, clearly and adequately. Everything as phenomenon, as object, is absolutely necessary; *in itself* it is will, and this is perfectly free to all eternity. The phenomenon, the object, is necessarily and unalterably determined in the concatenation of grounds and consequents which cannot have any discontinuity. But the existence of this object in general and the manner of its existing, that is to say, the Idea which reveals itself in it, or in other words its character, is directly phenomenon of the will. Hence, in conformity with the freedom of this will, the object might not exist at all, or might be something originally and essentially quite different. In that case, however, the whole chain of which the object is a link, and which is itself phenomenon of the same will, would also be quite different. But once there and existent, the object has entered the series of grounds and consequents, is always necessarily determined therein, and accordingly cannot either become another thing, i.e., change itself, or withdraw from the series, i.e., vanish. Like every other part of nature, man is objectivity of the will; therefore all that we have said holds good of him also. Just as everything in nature has its forces and qualities that definitely react to a definite impression, and constitute its character, so man also has his *character,* from which the motives call forth his actions with necessity. In this way of acting his empirical character reveals itself, but in this again is revealed his intelligible character, i.e., the will in itself, of which he is the determined phenomenon. Man, however, is the most complete phenomenon of the will, and, as was shown in the second book, in order to exist, this phenomenon had to be illuminated by so high a degree of knowledge that even a perfectly adequate repetition of the inner nature of the world under the form of the representation became possible in it. This is the apprehension of the Ideas, the pure

mirror of the world, as we have come to know them in the third
book. Therefore in man the will can reach full self-consciousness,
distinct and exhaustive knowledge of its own inner nature, as reflected
in the whole world. As we saw in the preceding book, art results from
the actual presence and existence of this degree of knowledge. At the
end of our whole discussion it will also be seen that, through the same
knowledge, an elimination and self-denial of the will in its most perfect phenomenon is possible, by the will's relating such knowledge to
itself. Thus the freedom which in other respects, as belonging to the
thing-in-itself, can never show itself in the phenomenon, in such a
case appears in this phenomenon; and by abolishing the essential
nature at the root of the phenomenon, whilst the phenomenon itself
still continues to exist in time, it brings about a contradiction of the
phenomenon with itself. In just this way, it exhibits the phenomena of
holiness and self-denial. All this, however, will be fully understood
only at the end of this book. Meanwhile, all this indicates only in a
general way how man is distinguished from all the other phenomena
of the will by the fact that freedom, i.e., independence of the principle of sufficient reason, which belongs only to the will as thing-in-
itself and contradicts the phenomenon, may yet in his case possibly
appear even in the phenomenon, where it is then, however, necessarily
exhibited as a contradiction of the phenomenon with itself. In this
sense not only the will in itself, but even man can certainly be called
free, and can thus be distinguished from all other beings. But how
this is to be understood can become clear only through all that follows, and for the present we must wholly disregard it. For in the first
place we must beware of making the mistake of thinking that the
action of the particular, definite man is not subject to any necessity,
in other words that the force of the motive is less certain than the
force of the cause, or than the following of the conclusion from the
premisses. If we leave aside the above-mentioned case, which, as we
have said, relates only to an exception, the freedom of the will as
thing-in-itself by no means extends directly to its phenomenon, not
even where this reaches the highest grade of visibility, namely in the
rational animal with individual character, in other words, the man.
This man is never free, although he is the phenomenon of a free will,
for he is the already determined phenomenon of this will's free willing; and since he enters into the form of all objects, the principle of
sufficient reason, he develops the unity of that will into a plurality of
actions. But since the unity of that will in itself lies outside time,
this plurality exhibits itself with the conformity to law of a force of
nature. Since, however, it is that free willing which becomes visible
in the man and in his whole conduct, and is related to this as the

concept to the definition, every particular deed of the man is to be ascribed to the free will, and directly proclaims itself as such to consciousness. Therefore, as we said in the second book, everyone considers himself *a priori* (i.e., according to his original feeling) free, even in his particular actions, in the sense that in every given case any action is possible to him, and only *a posteriori,* from experience and reflection thereon, does he recognize that his conduct follows with absolute necessity from the coincidence of the character with the motives. Hence it arises that any coarse and uncultured person, following his feelings, most vigorously defends complete freedom in individual actions, whereas the great thinkers of all ages, and the more profound religious teachings, have denied it. But the person who has come to see clearly that man's whole inner nature is will, and that man himself is only phenomenon of this will, but that such phenomenon has the principle of sufficient reason as its necessary form, knowable even from the subject, and appearing in this case as the law of motivation; to such a person a doubt as to the inevitability of the deed, when the motive is presented to the given character, seems like doubting that the three angles of a triangle are equal to two right angles. In his *Doctrine of Philosophical Necessity,* Priestley has very adequately demonstrated the necessity of the individual action. Kant, however, whose merit in this regard is specially great, was the first to demonstrate the coexistence of this necessity with the freedom of the will in itself, i.e., outside the phenomenon, for he established the difference between the intelligible and empirical characters.[12] I wholly support this distinction, for the former is the will as thing-in-itself, in so far as it appears in a definite individual in a definite degree, while the latter is this phenomenon itself as it manifests itself in the mode of action according to time, and in the physical structure according to space. To make the relation between the two clear, the best expression is that already used in the introductory essay, namely that the intelligible character of every man is to be regarded as an act of will outside time, and thus indivisible and unalterable. The phenomenon of this act of will, developed and drawn out in time, space, and all the forms of the principle of sufficient reason, is the empirical character as it exhibits itself for experience in the man's whole manner of action and course of life. The whole tree is only the constantly repeated phenomenon of one and the same impulse that manifests itself most simply in the fibre, and is repeated and easily recognizable in the construction of leaf, stem, branch, and trunk. In the same way,

---

[12] *Critique of Pure Reason,* first edition, pp. 532-558; fifth edition, pp. 560-586; and *Critique of Practical Reason,* fourth edition, pp. 169-179; Rosenkranz's edition, pp. 224-231.

all man's deeds are only the constantly repeated manifestation, varying somewhat in form, of his intelligible character, and the induction resulting from the sum of these gives us his empirical character. However, I shall not repeat Kant's masterly exposition here, but shall presuppose that it is already known.

In 1840 I dealt thoroughly and in detail with the important chapter on the freedom of the will, in my crowned prize-essay on this subject. In particular, I exposed the reason for the delusion in consequence of which people imagined they found an empirically given, absolute freedom of the will, and hence a *liberum arbitrium indifferentiae,*[13] in self-consciousness as a fact thereof; for with great insight the question set for the essay was directed to this very point. I therefore refer the reader to that work, and likewise to para. 10 of the prize-essay *On the Basis of Morality,* which was published along with it under the title *Die Beiden Grundprobleme der Ethik,* and I omit the discussion on the necessity of the acts of will which was inserted here in the first edition, and was still incomplete. Instead of this, I will explain the delusion above mentioned in a brief discussion which is presupposed by the nineteenth chapter of our second volume, and which therefore could not be given in the essay above mentioned.

Apart from the fact that the will, as the true thing-in-itself, is something actually original and independent, and that in self-consciousness the feeling of originality and arbitrariness must accompany its acts, though these are already determined; apart from this, there arises the semblance of an empirical freedom of the will (instead of the transcendental freedom which alone is to be attributed to it). Thus there arises the appearance of a freedom of the individual acts from the attitude of the intellect towards the will which is explained, separated out, and subordinated in the nineteenth chapter of the second volume, under No. 3. The intellect gets to know the conclusions of the will only *a posteriori* and empirically. Accordingly, where a choice is presented to it, it has no datum as to how the will is going to decide. For the intelligible character, by virtue of which with the given motives only *one* decision is possible, which is accordingly a necessary decision, the intelligible character, I say, does not come into the knowledge of the intellect; the empirical character only is successively known to it through its individual acts. Therefore it seems to the knowing consciousness (intellect) that two opposite decisions are equally possible to the will in a given case. But this is just the same as if we were to say in the case of a vertical pole, thrown off its balance and hesitating which way to fall, that "it can

---

[13] "The free decision of the will not influenced in any direction." [Tr.]

topple over to the right or to the left." Yet this *"can"* has only a subjective significance, and really means "in view of the data known to us." For objectively, the direction of the fall is necessarily determined as soon as the hesitation takes place. Accordingly, the decision of one's own will is undetermined only for its spectator, one's own intellect, and therefore only relatively and subjectively, namely for the subject of knowing. In itself and objectively, on the other hand, the decision is at once determined and necessary in the case of every choice presented to it. But this determination enters consciousness only through the ensuing decision. We even have an empirical proof of this when some difficult and important choice lies before us, yet only under a condition that has not yet appeared but is merely awaited, so that for the time being we can do nothing, but must maintain a passive attitude. We then reflect on how we shall decide when the circumstances that allow us freedom of activity and decision have made their appearance. It is often the case that far-seeing, rational deliberation speaks rather in support of one of the resolves, while direct inclination leans rather to the other. As long as we remain passive and under compulsion, the side of reason apparently tries to keep the upper hand, but we see in advance how strongly the other side will draw us when the opportunity for action comes. Till then, we are eagerly concerned to place the motives of the two sides in the clearest light by coolly meditating on the *pro et contra,* so that each motive can influence the will with all its force when the moment arrives, and so that some mistake on the part of the intellect will not mislead the will into deciding otherwise than it would do if everything exerted an equal influence. This distinct unfolding of the motives on both sides is all that the intellect can do in connexion with the choice. It awaits the real decision just as passively and with the same excited curiosity as it would that of a foreign will. Therefore, from its point of view, both decisions must seem to it equally possible. Now it is just this that is the semblance of the will's empirical freedom. Of course, the decision enters the sphere of the intellect quite empirically as the final conclusion of the matter. Yet this decision proceeded from the inner nature, the intelligible character, of the individual will in its conflict with given motives, and hence came about with complete necessity. The intellect can do nothing more here than clearly examine the nature of the motives from every point of view. It is unable to determine the will itself, for the will is wholly inaccessible to it, and, as we have seen, is for it inscrutable and impenetrable.

If, under the same conditions, a man could act now in one way, now in another, then in the meantime his will itself would have had to be changed, and thus would have to reside in time, for only in time is change possible. But then either the will would have to be a mere phenomenon, or time would have to be a determination of the thing-in-itself. Accordingly, the dispute as to the freedom of the individual action, as to the *liberum arbitrium indifferentiae,* really turns on the question whether the will resides in time or not. If, as Kant's teaching as well as the whole of my system makes necessary, the will as thing-in-itself is outside time and outside every form of the principle of sufficient reason, then not only must the individual act in the same way in the same situation, and not only must every bad deed be the sure guarantee of innumerable others that the individual *must* do and *cannot* leave undone, but, as Kant says, if only the empirical character and the motives were completely given, a man's future actions could be calculated like an eclipse of the sun or moon. Just as nature is consistent, so also is the character; every individual action must come about in accordance with the character, just as every phenomenon comes about in accordance with a law of nature. The cause in the latter case and the motive in the former are only the occasional causes, as was shown in the second book. The will, whose phenomenon is the whole being and life of man, cannot deny itself in the particular case, and the man also will always will in the particular what he wills on the whole.

The maintenance of an empirical freedom of will, a *liberum arbitrium indifferentiae,* is very closely connected with the assertion that places man's inner nature in a *soul* that is originally a *knowing,* indeed really an abstract *thinking* entity, and only in consequence thereof a *willing* entity. Such a view, therefore, regarded the will as of a secondary nature, instead of knowledge, which is really secondary. The will was even regarded as an act of thought, and was identified with the judgement, especially by Descartes and Spinoza. According to this, every man would have become what he is only in consequence of his *knowledge.* He would come into the world as a moral cipher, would know the things in it, and would then determine to be this or that, to act in this or that way. He could, in consequence of new knowledge, choose a new course of action, and thus become another person. Further, he would then first know a thing to be *good,* and in consequence will it, instead of first *willing* it, and in consequence calling it *good.* According to the whole of my fundamental view, all this is a reversal of the true relation. The will is first and original; knowledge is merely added to it as an instrument belonging to the phenomenon of the will. Therefore every man is what he is through his will, and his character is original, for willing is the basis of his inner being. Through the knowledge added to it, he gets to know in the course of experience *what* he is; in other words, he becomes acquainted with his character. Therefore he *knows* himself in consequence of, and in accordance with, the nature of his will, instead of *willing* in consequence of, and according to, his knowing, as in the old view. According to this view, he need only consider *how* he would best like to be, and he would be so; this is its freedom of the will. It therefore consists in man's being his own work in the light of knowledge. I, on the other hand, say that he is his own work prior to all knowledge, and knowledge is merely added to illuminate it. Therefore he cannot decide to be this or that; also he cannot become another person, but he *is* once for all, and subsequently knows *what* he is. With those other thinkers, he *wills* what he knows; with me he *knows* what he wills.

The Greeks called the character ἦθος, and its expressions, i.e., morals, ἤθη. But this word comes from ἔθος, custom; they chose it in order to express metaphorically constancy of character through constancy of custom. Τὸ γὰρ ἦθος ἀπὸ τοῦ ἔθους ἔχει τὴν ἐπωνυμίαν. ἠθικὴ γὰρ καλεῖται διὰ τὸ ἐθίζεσθαι (*a voce* ἔθος, *i.e., consuetudo,* ἦθος *est appellatum: ethica ergo dicta est* ἀπὸ τοῦ ἐθίζεσθαι, *sive ab assuescendo*) says Aristotle[14] (*Ethica Magna,* I, 6, p. 1186 [Berlin ed.], and *Ethica Eudemica,* p. 1220, and *Ethica Nicomachaea,* p. 1103). Stobaeus, II, chap. 7, quotes: οἱ δὲ κατὰ Ζήνωνα τροπικῶς· ἦθος ἐστι πηγὴ βίου, ἀφ' ἧς αἱ κατὰ μέρος πράξεις ῥέουσι. (*Stoici autem, Zenonis castra sequentes, metaphorice ethos definiunt vitae fontem, e quo singulae manant actiones.*)[15] In the Christian teaching we find the dogma of predestination in consequence of election and non-election by grace (Rom. ix, 11-24), obviously springing from the view that man does not change, but his life and conduct, in other words his empirical character, are only the unfolding of the intelligible character, the development of decided and unalterable tendencies already recognizable in the child. Therefore his conduct is, so to speak, fixed and settled even at his birth, and remains essentially the same to the very end. We too agree with this, but of course the consequences which resulted from the union of this perfectly correct view with the dogmas previously found in Jewish theology, and which gave rise to the greatest of all difficulties, namely to the eternally insoluble Gordian knot on which most of the controversies of the Church turn; these I do not undertake to defend. For even the

---

[14] "For the word ἦθος (character) has its name from ἔθος (custom); for ethics has its name from being customary." [Tr.]

[15] "The followers of Zeno declare figuratively that ethos is the source of life from which individual acts spring." [Tr.]

Apostle Paul himself scarcely succeeded in doing this by his parable of the potter, invented for this purpose, for ultimately the result was in fact none other than this:

> "Let the human race
> Fear the gods!
> They hold the dominion
> In eternal hands:
> And they can use it
> As it pleases them."
> Goethe, *Iphigenia* [IV, 5].

But such considerations are really foreign to our subject. However, some observations on the relation between the character and the knowledge in which all its motives reside will here be appropriate.

The motives determining the phenomenon or appearance of the character, or determining conduct, influence the character through the medium of knowledge. Knowledge, however, is changeable, and often vacillates between error and truth; yet, as a rule, in the course of life it is rectified more and more, naturally in very different degrees. Thus a man's manner of acting can be noticeably changed without our being justified in inferring from this a change in his character. What the man really and generally wills, the tendency of his innermost nature, and the goal he pursues in accordance therewith—these we can never change by influencing him from without, by instructing him, otherwise we should be able to create him anew. Seneca says admirably: *velle non discitur;*[16] in this he prefers truth to his Stoic philosophers, who taught: διδακτὴν εἶναι τὴν ἀρετήν (*doceri posse virtutem*).[17] From without, the will can be affected only by motives; but these can never change the will itself, for they have power over it only on the presupposition that it is precisely such as it is. All that the motives can do, therefore, is to alter the direction of the will's effort, in other words to make it possible for it to seek what it invariably seeks by a path different from the one it previously followed. Therefore instruction, improved knowledge, and thus influence from without, can indeed teach the will that it erred in the means it employed. Accordingly, outside influence can bring it about that the will pursues the goal to which it aspires once for all in accordance with its inner nature, by quite a different path, and even in an entirely different object, from what it did previously. But such an influence can never bring it about that the will wills

---

[16] "Willing cannot be taught." [*Epist.* 81, 14. Tr.]
[17] "Virtue can be taught." [Diogenes Laërtius, VII, 91. Tr.]

something actually different from what it has willed hitherto. This remains unalterable, for the will is precisely this willing itself, which would otherwise have to be abolished. However, the former, the ability to modify knowledge, and through this to modify action, goes so far that the will seeks to attain its ever unalterable end, for example, Mohammed's paradise, at one time in the world of reality, at another in the world of imagination, adapting the means thereto, and so applying prudence, force, and fraud in the one case, abstinence, justice, righteousness, alms, and pilgrimage to Mecca in the other. But the tendency and endeavour of the will have not themselves been changed on that account, still less the will itself. Therefore, although its action certainly manifests itself differently at different times, its willing has nevertheless remained exactly the same. *Velle non discitur.*

For motives to be effective, it is necessary for them to be not only present but known; for according to a very good saying of the scholastics, which we have already mentioned, *causa finalis movet non secundum suum esse reale, sed secundum esse cognitum.*[18] For example, in order that the relation which exists in a given man between egoism and sympathy may appear, it is not enough that he possesses some wealth and sees the misery of others; he must also know what can be done with wealth both for himself and for others. Not only must another's suffering present itself to him, but he must also know what suffering is, and indeed what pleasure is. Perhaps on a first occasion he did not know all this so well as on a second; and if now on a similar occasion he acts differently, this is due simply to the circumstances being really different, namely as regards that part of them which depends on his knowledge of them, although they appear to be the same. Just as not to know actually existing circumstances deprives them of their effectiveness, so, on the other hand, entirely imaginary circumstances can act like real ones, not only in the case of a particular deception, but also in general and for some length of time. For example, if a man is firmly persuaded that every good deed is repaid to him a hundredfold in a future life, then such a conviction is valid and effective in precisely the same way as a safe bill of exchange at a very long date, and he can give from egoism just as, from another point of view, he would take from egoism. He himself has not changed: *velle non discitur.* In virtue of this great influence of knowledge on conduct, with an unalterable will, it comes about that the character develops and its different features appear only gradually. It therefore appears different at each

---

[18] "The final cause operates not according to its real being, but only according to its being as that is known." [Tr.]

period of life, and an impetuous, wild youth can be followed by a staid, sober, manly age. In particular, what is bad in the character will come out more and more powerfully with time; but sometimes passions to which a man gave way in his youth are later voluntarily restrained, merely because the opposite motives have only then come into knowledge. Hence we are all innocent to begin with, and this merely means that neither we nor others know the evil of our own nature. This appears only in the motives, and only in the course of time do the motives appear in knowledge. Ultimately we become acquainted with ourselves as quite different from what *a priori* we considered ourselves to be; and then we are often alarmed at ourselves.

Repentance never results from the fact that the will has changed —this is impossible—but from a change of knowledge. I must still continue to will the essential and real element of what I have always willed; for I am myself this will, that lies outside time and change. Therefore I can never repent of what I have willed, though I can repent of what I have done, when, guided by false concepts, I did something different from what was in accordance with my will. *Repentance* is the insight into this with more accurate knowledge. It extends not merely to worldly wisdom, the choice of means, and judging the appropriateness of the end to my will proper, but also to what is properly ethical. Thus, for example, it is possible for me to have acted more egoistically than is in accordance with my character, carried away by exaggerated notions of the need in which I myself stood, or even by the cunning, falseness, and wickedness of others, or again by the fact that I was in too much of a hurry; in other words, I acted without deliberation, determined not by motives distinctly known in the abstract, but by motives of mere perception, the impression of the present moment, and the emotion it excited. This emotion was so strong that I really did not have the use of my faculty of reason. But here also the return of reflection is only corrected knowledge, and from this repentance can result, which always proclaims itself by making amends for what has happened, so far as that is possible. But it is to be noted that, in order to deceive themselves, men prearrange apparent instances of precipitancy which are really secretly considered actions. For by such fine tricks we deceive and flatter no one but ourselves. The reverse case to what we have mentioned can also occur. I can be misled by too great confidence in others, or by not knowing the relative value of the good things of life, or by some abstract dogma in which I have now lost faith. Thus I act less egoistically than is in accordance with my character, and in this way prepare for myself repentance of another kind. Thus repentance is always corrected knowledge of the relation of the deed to the real intention. In so far as the will reveals its Ideas in space alone, that is to say, through mere form, the matter already controlled and ruled by other Ideas, in this case natural forces, resists the will, and seldom allows the form that was striving for visibility to appear in perfect purity and distinctness, i.e., in perfect beauty. This will, revealing itself in time alone, i.e., through actions, finds an analogous hindrance in the knowledge that rarely gives it the data quite correctly; and in this way the deed does not turn out wholly and entirely in keeping with the will, and therefore leads to repentance. Thus repentance always results from corrected knowledge, not from change in the will, which is impossible. Pangs of conscience over past deeds are anything but repentance; they are pain at the knowledge of oneself in one's own nature, in other words, as will. They rest precisely on the certainty that we always have the same will. If the will were changed, and thus the pangs of conscience were mere repentance, these would be abolished; for then the past could no longer cause any distress, as it would exhibit the manifestations of a will that was no longer that of the repentant person. We shall discuss in detail the significance of pangs of conscience later on.

The influence exerted by knowledge as the medium of motives, not indeed on the will itself, but on its manifestation in actions, is also the basis of the chief difference between the actions of men and those of animals, since the methods of cognition of the two are different. The animal has only knowledge of perception, but man through the faculty of reason has also abstract representations, concepts. Now, although animal and man are determined by motives with equal necessity, man nevertheless has the advantage over the animal of a complete *elective decision* (*Wahlentscheidung*). This has often been regarded as a freedom of the will in individual actions, although it is nothing but the possibility of a conflict, thoroughly fought out, between several motives, the strongest of which then determines the will with necessity. For this purpose the motives must have assumed the form of abstract thoughts, since only by means of these is real deliberation, in other words, a weighing of opposed grounds for conduct, possible. With the animal a choice can take place only between motives of perception actually present; hence this choice is restricted to the narrow sphere of its present apprehension of perception. Therefore the necessity of the determination of the will by motives, like that of the effect by the cause, can be exhibited in perception and directly only in the case of the animals, since here the spectator has the motives just as directly before his eyes as he has their effect. In the case of man, however, the motives are almost always abstract representations; these are not shared by the spectator, and the necessity of their effect is concealed behind their conflict even from the person himself who acts. For only *in abstracto* can several representations lie beside one another in consciousness as judgements and chains of conclusions, and then, free from all determination of time, work against one another, until the strongest overpowers the rest, and determines the will. This is the complete *elective decision* or faculty of deliberation which man has as an advantage over the animal, and on account of which freedom of will has been attributed to him, in the belief that his willing was a mere result of the operations of his intellect, without a definite tendency to serve as its basis. The truth is, however, that motivation works only on the basis and assumption of his definite tendency, that is in his case individual, in other words, a character. A more detailed discussion of this power of deliberation and of the difference between human and animal free choice brought about by it, is to be found in *Die Beiden Grundprobleme der Ethik* (first edition, pp. 35 *seqq.*, second edition, pp. 33 *seqq.*), to which therefore I refer. Moreover, this faculty for deliberation which man possesses is also one of the things that make his existence so very much more harrowing than the animal's. For generally our greatest sufferings do not lie in the present as representations of perception or as immediate feeling, but in our faculty of reason as abstract concepts, tormenting thoughts, from which the animal is completely free, living as it does in the present, and thus in enviable ease and unconcern.

It seems to have been the dependence, described by us, of the human power of deliberation on the faculty of thinking in the abstract, and hence also of judging and inferring, which led both Descartes and Spinoza to identify the decisions of the will with the faculty of affirmation and denial (power of judgement). From this Descartes deduced that the will, according to him indifferently free, was to blame even for all theoretical error. On the other hand, Spinoza deduced that the will was necessarily determined by the motives, just as the judgement is by grounds or reasons.[19] However, this latter deduction is quite right, though it appears as a true conclusion from false premises.

The distinction which we have demonstrated between the ways in which the animal and man are each moved by motives has a very far-reaching influence on the nature of both, and contributes most to the complete and obvious difference in the existence of the two. Thus while the animal is always motivated only by a representa-

---

[19] Descartes, *Meditations*, 4; Spinoza, *Ethics*, part II, props. 48 and 49, *caet.*

tion of perception, man endeavours entirely to exclude this kind of motivation, and to let himself be determined only by abstract representations. In this way he uses his prerogative of reason to the greatest possible advantage, and, independent of the present moment, neither chooses nor avoids the passing pleasure or pain, but ponders over the consequences of both. In most cases, apart from quite insignificant actions, we are determined by abstract, considered motives, not by present impressions. Therefore, any particular privation for the moment is fairly light for us, but any renunciation is terribly hard. The former concerns only the fleeting present, but the latter concerns the future, and therefore includes in itself innumerable privations of which it is the equivalent. The cause of our pain as of our pleasure, therefore, lies for the most part not in the real present, but merely in abstract thoughts. It is these that are often unbearable to us, and inflict torments in comparison with which all the sufferings of the animal kingdom are very small; for even our own physical pain is often not felt at all when they are in question. Indeed, in the case of intense mental suffering, we cause ourselves physical suffering in order in this way to divert our attention from the former to the latter. Therefore in the greatest mental suffering men tear out their hair, beat their breasts, lacerate their faces, roll on the ground, for all these are really only powerful means of distraction from an unbearable thought. Just because mental pain, being much greater, makes one insensible to physical pain, suicide becomes very easy for the person in despair or consumed by morbid depression, even when previously, in comfortable circumstances, he recoiled from the thought of it. In the same way, care and passion, and thus the play of thought, wear out the body oftener and more than physical hardships do. In accordance with this, Epictetus rightly says: Ταράσσει τοὺς ἀνθρώπους οὐ τὰ πράγματα, ἀλλὰ τὰ περὶ τῶν πραγμάτων δόγματα (*Perturbant homines non res ipsae, sed de rebus decreta*) (*Enchiridion*, V)[20] and Seneca: *Plura sunt, quae nos terrent, quam quae premunt, et saepius opinione quam re laboramus* (*Ep.* 5).[21] Eulenspiegel also admirably satirized human nature, since when going uphill he laughed, but going downhill he wept. Indeed, children who have hurt themselves often cry not at the pain, but only at the thought of the pain, which is aroused when anyone condoles with them. Such great differences in conduct and suffering result from the diversity between the animal and human

---

[20] "It is not things that disturb men, but opinions about things." [Tr.]

[21] "There are more things that terrify us than there are that oppress us, and we suffer more often in opinion than in reality." [The correct reference is to Seneca, *Ep.*, 13, 4. Tr.]

ways of knowing. Further, the appearance of the distinct and decided individual character that mainly distinguishes man from the animal, having scarcely more than the character of the species, is likewise conditioned by the choice between several motives, which is possible only by means of abstract concepts. For only after a precedent choice are the resolutions, which came about differently in different individuals, an indication of their individual character which is a different one in each case. On the other hand, the action of the animal depends only on the presence or absence of the impression, assuming that this is in general a motive for its species. Finally, therefore, in the case of man only the resolve, and not the mere wish, is a valid indication of his character for himself and for others. But for himself as for others the resolve becomes a certainty only through the deed. The wish is merely the necessary consequence of the present impression, whether of the external stimulus or of the inner passing mood, and is therefore as directly necessary and without deliberation as is the action of animals. Therefore, just like that action, it expresses merely the character of the species, not that of the individual, in other words, it indicates merely what *man in general,* not what the *individual* who feels the wish, would be capable of doing. The deed alone, because as human action it always requires a certain deliberation, and because as a rule man has command of his faculty of reason, and hence is thoughtful, in other words, decides according to considered abstract motives, is the expression of the intelligible maxims of his conduct, the result of his innermost willing. It is related as a letter is to the word that expresses his empirical character, this character itself being only the temporal expression of his intelligible character. Therefore in a healthy mind only deeds, not desires and thoughts, weigh heavily on the conscience; for only our deeds hold up before us the mirror of our will. The deed above mentioned, which is committed entirely without any thought and actually in blind emotion, is to a certain extent something between the mere wish and the resolve. Therefore through true repentance, which also shows itself in a deed, it can be obliterated as a falsely drawn line from the picture of our will, which our course of life is. Moreover, as a unique comparison, we may insert here the remark that the relation between wish and deed has an entirely accidental but accurate analogy to that between electrical accumulation and electrical discharge.

As a result of all this discussion on the freedom of the will and what relates to it, we find that, although the will in itself and apart from the phenomenon can be called free and even omnipotent, in its individual phenomena, illuminated by knowledge, and thus in persons and animals, it is determined by motives to which the character in each case regularly and necessarily always reacts in the same way. We see that, in virtue of the addition of abstract or rational knowledge, man has the advantage over the animal of an *elective decision,* which, however, simply makes him the scene of a conflict of motives, without withdrawing him from their control. Therefore this elective decision is certainly the condition of the possibility of the individual character's complete expression, but it is by no means to be regarded as freedom of the individual willing, in other words, as independence of the law of causality, whose necessity extends to man as to every other phenomenon. Thus the difference produced between human and animal willing by the faculty of reason or knowledge by means of concepts extends as far as the point mentioned, and no farther. But, what is quite a different thing, there can arise a phenomenon of the human will which is impossible in the animal kingdom, namely when man abandons all knowledge of individual things as such, which is subordinate to the principle of sufficient reason, and, by means of knowledge of the Ideas, sees through the *principium individuationis.* An actual appearance of the real freedom of the will as thing-in-itself then becomes possible, by which the phenomenon comes into a certain contradiction with itself, as is expressed by the word self-renunciation, in fact the in-itself of its real nature ultimately abolishes itself. This sole and immediate manifestation proper of the freedom of the will in itself even in the phenomenon cannot as yet be clearly explained here, but will be the subject at the very end of our discussion.

After clearly seeing, by virtue of the present arguments, the unalterable nature of the empirical character which is the mere unfolding of the intelligible character that resides outside time, and also the necessity with which actions result from its contact with motives, we have first of all to clear away an inference that might very easily be drawn from this in favour of unwarrantable tendencies. Our character is to be regarded as the temporal unfolding of an extratemporal, and so indivisible and unalterable, act of will, or of an intelligible character. Through this, all that is essential in our conduct of life, in other words its ethical content, is invariably determined, and must express itself accordingly in its phenomenon, the empirical character. On the other hand, only the inessential of this phenomenon, the external form of our course of life, depends on the forms in which the motives present themselves. Thus it might be inferred that for us to work at improving our character, or at resisting the power of evil tendencies, would be labour in vain; that it would therefore be more advisable to submit to the inevitable and unalterable, and to gratify at once every inclination, even if it is bad. But this is precisely the same case as that of the theory of inevitable fate, and of the inference drawn therefrom, which is called ἀργὸς λόγος,[22] and in more recent times Turkish or Mohammedan faith. Its correct refutation, as Chrysippus is supposed to have given it, is described by Cicero in his book *De Fato,* ch. 12, 13.

Although everything can be regarded as irrevocably predetermined by fate, it is so only by means of the chain of causes. Therefore in no case can it be determined that an effect should appear without its cause. Thus it is not simply the event that is predetermined, but the event as the result of preceding causes; and hence it is not the result alone, but also the means as the result of which it is destined to appear, that are settled by fate. Accordingly, if the means do not appear, the result also certainly does not appear; the two always exist according to the determination of fate, but it is always only afterwards that we come to know this.

Just as events always come about in accordance with fate, in other words, according to the endless concatenation of causes, so do our deeds always come about according to our intelligible character. But just as we do not know the former in advance, so also are we given no *a priori* insight into the latter; only *a posteriori* through experience do we come to know ourselves as we come to know others. If the intelligible character made it inevitable that we could form a good resolution only after a long conflict with a bad disposition, this conflict would have to come first and to be waited for. Reflection on the unalterable nature of the character, on the unity of the source from which all our deeds flow, should not mislead us into forestalling the decision of the character in favour of one side or the other. In the ensuing resolve we shall see what kind of men we are, and in our deeds we shall mirror ourselves. From this very fact is explained the satisfaction or agony of mind with which we look back on the course of our life. Neither of these results from past deeds still having an existence. These deeds are past; they have been, and now are no more, but their great importance to us comes from their significance, from the fact that such deeds are the impression or copy of the character, the mirror of the will; and, looking into this mirror, we recognize our innermost self, the kernel of our will. Because we experience this not before but only after, it is proper for us to fight and strive in time, simply in order that the picture we produce through our deeds may so turn out

---

[22] "Indolent reason," which is quietened by the fact that everything is necessarily predetermined. [Tr.]

that the sight of it will cause us the greatest possible peace of mind, and not uneasiness or anxiety. The significance of such peace or agony of mind will, as we have said, be further investigated later. But the following discussion, standing by itself, belongs here.

Besides the intelligible and empirical characters, we have still to mention a third which is different from these two, namely the *acquired character*. We obtain this only in life, through contact with the world, and it is this we speak of when anyone is praised as a person who has character, or censured as one without character. It might of course be supposed that, since the empirical character, as the phenomenon of the intelligible, is unalterable, and, like every natural phenomenon, is in itself consistent, man also for this very reason would have to appear always like himself and consistent, and would therefore not need to acquire a character for himself artificially through experience and reflection. But the case is otherwise, and although a man is always the same, he does not always understand himself, but often fails to recognize himself until he has acquired some degree of real self-knowledge. As a mere natural tendency, the empirical character is in itself irrational; indeed its expressions are in addition disturbed by the faculty of reason, and in fact the more so, the more intellect and power of thought the man has. For these always keep before him what belongs to *man in general* as the character of the species, and what is possible for him both in willing and in doing. In this way, an insight into that which alone of all he wills and is able to do by dint of his individuality, is made difficult for him. He finds in himself the tendencies to all the various human aspirations and abilities, but the different degrees of these in his individuality do not become clear to him without experience. Now if he resorts to those pursuits that alone conform to his character, he feels, especially at particular moments and in particular moods, the impulse to the very opposite pursuits that are incompatible with them; and if he wishes to follow the former pursuits undisturbed, the latter must be entirely suppressed. For, as our physical path on earth is always a line and not a surface, we must in life, if we wish to grasp and possess one thing, renounce and leave aside innumerable others that lie to the right and to the left. If we cannot decide to do this, but, like children at a fair, snatch at everything that fascinates us in passing, this is the perverted attempt to change the line of our path into a surface. We then run a zigzag path, wander like a will-o'-the-wisp, and arrive at nothing. Or, to use another comparison, according to Hobbes's doctrine of law, everyone originally has a right to everything, but an exclusive right to nothing; but he can obtain an exclusive right to individual things by renouncing his right to all the rest, while the others do the same thing with regard to what was chosen by him. It is precisely the same in life, where we can follow some definite pursuit, whether it be of pleasure, honour, wealth, science, art, or virtue, seriously and successfully only when we give up all claims foreign to it, and renounce everything else. Therefore mere willing and mere ability to do are not enough of themselves, but a man must also *know* what he wills, and *know* what he can do. Only thus will he display character, and only then can he achieve anything solid. Until he reaches this, he is still without character, in spite of the natural consistency of the empirical character. Although, on the whole, he must remain true to himself and run his course drawn by his daemon, he will not describe a straight line, but a wavering and uneven one. He will hesitate, deviate, turn back, and prepare for himself repentance and pain. All this because, in great things and in small, he sees before him as much as is possible and attainable for man, and yet does not know what part of all this is alone suitable and feasible for him, or even merely capable of being enjoyed by him. Therefore he will envy many on account of a position and circumstances which yet are suitable only to their character, not to his, in which he would feel unhappy, and which he might be unable to endure. For just as a fish is happy only in water, a bird only in the air, and a mole only under the earth, so every man is happy only in an atmosphere suitable to him. For example, not everyone can breathe the atmosphere of a court. From lack of moderate insight into all this, many a man will make all kinds of abortive attempts; he will do violence to his character in particulars, and yet on the whole will have to yield to it again. What he thus laboriously attains contrary to his nature will give him no pleasure; what he learns in this way will remain dead. Even from an ethical point of view, a deed too noble for his character, which has sprung not from pure, direct impulse, but from a concept, a dogma, will lose all merit even in his own eyes through a subsequent egoistical repentance. *Velle non discitur.* Only through experience do we become aware of the inflexibility of other people's characters, and till then we childishly believe that we could succeed by representations of reason, by entreaties and prayers, by example and noble-mindedness, in making a man abandon his own way, change his mode of conduct, depart from his way of thinking, or even increase his abilities; it is the same, too, with ourselves. We must first learn from experience what we will and what we can do; till then we do not know this, are without character, and must often be driven back on to our own path by hard blows from outside. But if we have finally learnt it, we have then obtained what in the world is called character, the *acquired character,* which, accordingly, is nothing but the most complete possible knowledge of our own individuality. It is the abstract, and consequently distinct, knowledge of the unalterable qualities of our own empirical character, and of the measure and direction of our mental and bodily powers, and so of the whole strength and weakness of our own individuality. This puts us in a position to carry out, deliberately and methodically, the unalterable role of our own person, and to fill up the gaps caused in it by whims or weaknesses, under the guidance of fixed concepts. This role is in itself unchangeable once for all, but previously we allowed it to follow its natural course without any rule. We have now brought to clearly conscious maxims that are always present to us, the manner of acting necessarily determined by our individual nature. In accordance with these, we carry it out as deliberately as though it were one that had been learnt, without ever being led astray by the fleeting influence of the mood or impression of the present moment, without being checked by the bitterness or sweetness of a particular thing we meet with on the way, without wavering, without hesitation, without inconsistencies. Now we shall no longer, as novices, wait, attempt, and grope about, in order to see what we really desire and are able to do; we know this once for all, and with every choice we have only to apply general principles to particular cases, and at once reach a decision. We know our will in general, and do not allow ourselves to be misled by a mood, or by entreaty from outside, into arriving at a decision in the particular case which is contrary to the will as a whole. We also know the nature and measure of our powers and weaknesses, and shall thus spare ourselves much pain and suffering. For there is really no other pleasure than in the use and feeling of our own powers, and the greatest pain is when we are aware of a deficiency of our powers where they are needed. Now if we have found out where our strong and weak points lie, we shall attempt to develop, employ, and use in every way those talents that are naturally prominent in us. We shall always turn to where these talents are useful and of value, and shall avoid entirely and with self-restraint those pursuits for which we have little natural aptitude. We shall guard against attempting that in which we do not succeed. Only the man who has reached this will always be entirely himself with complete awareness, and will never fail himself at the critical moment, because he has always known what he could expect from himself. He will then often partake of the pleasure of feeling his strength, and will rarely experience the pain of being reminded of his weaknesses. The latter is humiliation, which perhaps causes the greatest of mental suffering. Therefore we are far better able to endure the clear sight of our ill-luck than that of our incapacity. Now if we are thus fully acquainted with our strength and weakness, we shall not attempt to display powers we do not possess; we shall not play with false coin, because such dissimulation in the end misses its mark. For as the whole man is only the phenomenon of his will, nothing can be more absurd than for him, starting from reflection, to want to be something different from what he is; for this is an immediate contradiction of the will itself. Imitating the qualities and idiosyncrasies of others is much more outrageous than wearing others' clothes, for it is the judgement we ourselves pronounce on our own worthlessness. Knowledge of our own mind and of our capabilities of every kind, and of their unalterable limits, is in this respect the surest way to the attainment of the greatest possible contentment with ourselves. For it holds good of inner as of outer circumstances that there is no more effective consolation for us than the complete certainty of unalterable necessity. No evil that has befallen us torments us so much as the thought of the circumstances by which it could have been warded off. Therefore nothing is more effective for our consolation than a consideration of what has happened from the point of view of necessity, from which all accidents appear as tools of a governing fate; so that we recognize the evil that has come about as inevitably produced by the conflict of inner and outer circumstances, that is, fatalism. We really wail or rage only so long as we hope either to affect others in this way, or to stimulate ourselves to unheard-of efforts. But children and adults know quite well how to yield and to be satisfied, as soon as they see clearly that things are absolutely no different;

θυμὸν ἐνὶ στήθεσσι φίλον δαμάσαντες ἀνάγκῃ.

(*Animo in pectoribus nostro domito necessitate.*)[23]

We are like entrapped elephants, which rage and struggle fearfully for many days, until they see that it is fruitless, and then suddenly offer their necks calmly to the yoke, tamed for ever. We are like King David who, so long as his son was still alive, incessantly implored Jehovah with prayers, and behaved as if in despair; but as soon as his son was dead, he thought no more about him. Hence we see that innumerable permanent evils, such as lameness, poverty, humble position, ugliness, unpleasant dwelling-place, are endured with

---

[23] "Curbing with restraint the grudge nurtured within the breast." [*Iliad,* XVIII. 113. Tr.]

complete indifference, and no longer felt at all by innumerable persons, just like wounds that have turned to scars. This is merely because they know that inner or outer necessity leaves them nothing here that could be altered. On the other hand, more fortunate people do not see how such things can be endured. Now as with outer necessity so with inner, nothing reconciles so firmly as a distinct knowledge of it. If we have clearly recognized once for all our good qualities and strong points as well as our defects and weaknesses; if we have fixed our aim accordingly, and rest content about the unattainable, we thus escape in the surest way, as far as our individuality allows, that bitterest of all sufferings, dissatisfaction with ourselves, which is the inevitable consequence of ignorance of our own individuality, of false conceit, and of the audacity and presumption that arise therefrom. Ovid's verses admit of admirable application to the bitter chapter of self-knowledge that is here recommended:

> *Optimus ille animi vindex laedentia pectus*
> *Vincula qui rupit, dedoluitque semel.*[24]

So much as regards the *acquired character,* that is of importance not so much for ethics proper as for life in the world. But a discussion of it was related to that of the intelligible and empirical characters, and we had to enter into a somewhat detailed consideration of it in order to see clearly how the will in all its phenomena is subject to necessity, while in itself it can be called free and even omnipotent.

§ 56.

This freedom, this omnipotence, as the manifestation and copy of which the whole visible world, the phenomenon of this omnipotence, exists and progressively develops according to laws necessitated by the form of knowledge, can now express itself anew, and that indeed where, in its most perfect phenomenon, the completely adequate knowledge of its own inner nature has dawned on it. Thus either it wills here, at the summit of mental endowment

---

[24] "He helps the mind best who once for all breaks the tormenting bonds that ensnare and entangle the heart." [*Remedia Amoris,* 293. Tr.]

and self-consciousness, the same thing that it willed blindly and without knowledge of itself; and then knowledge always remains *motive* for it, in the whole as well as in the particular. Or, conversely, this knowledge becomes for it a *quieter,* silencing and suppressing all willing. This is the affirmation and denial of the will-to-live already stated previously in general terms. As a general, not a particular, manifestation of will in regard to the conduct of the individual, it does not disturb and modify the development of the character, nor does it find its expression in particular actions; but either by an ever more marked appearance of the whole previous mode of action, or conversely, by its suppression, it vividly expresses the maxims that the will has freely adopted in accordance with the knowledge now obtained. The clearer development of all this, the main subject of this last book, is now facilitated and prepared for us to some extent by the considerations on freedom, necessity, and character which have been set forth. This will be even more so after we have postponed it once again, and have first turned our attention to life itself, the willing or not willing of which is the great question; indeed we shall attempt to know in general what will really come to the will itself, which everywhere is the innermost nature of this life, through its affirmation, in what way and to what extent this affirmation satisfies the will or indeed can satisfy it. In short, we shall try to find out what is generally and essentially to be regarded as its state or condition in this world which is its own, and which belongs to it in every respect.

In the first place, I wish the reader here to recall those remarks with which we concluded the second book, and which were occasioned by the question there raised as to the will's aim and object. Instead of the answer to this question, we clearly saw how, at all grades of its phenomenon from the lowest to the highest, the will dispenses entirely with an ultimate aim and object. It always strives, because striving is its sole nature, to which no attained goal can put an end. Such striving is therefore incapable of final satisfaction; it can be checked only by hindrance, but in itself it goes on for ever. We saw this in the simplest of all natural phenomena, namely gravity, which does not cease to strive and press towards an extensionless central point, whose attainment would be the annihilation of itself and of matter; it would not cease, even if the whole universe were already rolled into a ball. We see it in other simple natural phenomena. The solid tends to fluidity, either by melting or dissolving, and only then do its chemical forces become free: rigidity is the imprisonment in which they are held by cold. The fluid tends to the gaseous form, into which it passes at once as soon as it is freed from all pressure. No body is without relationship, i.e., without striving, or without longing and desire, as Jacob Boehme would say. Electricity transmits its inner self-discord to infinity, although the mass of the earth absorbs the effect. Galvanism, so long as the pile lasts, is also an aimlessly and ceaselessly repeated act of self-discord and reconciliation. The existence of the plant is just such a restless, never satisfied striving, a ceaseless activity through higher and higher forms, till the final point, the seed, becomes anew a starting-point; and this is repeated *ad infinitum;* nowhere is there a goal, nowhere a final satisfaction, nowhere a point of rest. At the same time, we recall from the second book that everywhere the many different forces of nature and organic forms contest with one another for the matter in which they desire to appear, since each possesses only what it has wrested from another. Thus a constant struggle is carried on between life and death, the main result whereof is the resistance by which that striving which constitutes the innermost nature of everything is everywhere impeded. It presses and urges in vain; yet, by reason of its inner nature, it cannot cease; it toils on laboriously until this phenomenon perishes, and then others eagerly seize its place and its matter.

We have long since recognized this striving, that constitutes the kernel and in-itself of everything, as the same thing that in us, where it manifests itself most distinctly in the light of the fullest consciousness, is called *will*. We call its hindrance through an obstacle placed between it and its temporary goal, *suffering;* its attainment of the goal, on the other hand, we call *satisfaction,* well-being, happiness. We can also transfer these names to those phenomena of the world-without-knowledge which, though weaker in degree, are identical in essence. We then see these involved in constant suffering and without any lasting happiness. For all striving springs from want or deficiency, from dissatisfaction with one's own state or condition, and is therefore suffering so long as it is not satisfied. No satisfaction, however, is lasting; on the contrary, it is always merely the starting-point of a fresh striving. We see striving everywhere impeded in many ways, everywhere struggling and fighting, and hence always as suffering. Thus that there is no ultimate aim of striving means that there is no measure or end of suffering.

But what we thus discover in nature-without-knowledge only by sharpened observation, and with an effort, presents itself to us distinctly in nature-with-knowledge, in the life of the animal kingdom, the constant suffering whereof is easily demonstrable. But without dwelling on these intermediate stages, we will turn to the life of man, where everything appears most distinctly and is illuminated by the clearest knowledge. For as the phenomenon of the will becomes more complete, the suffering becomes more and more evident. In the plant there is as yet no sensibility, and hence no pain. A certain very small degree of both dwells in the lowest animals, in infusoria and radiata; even in insects the capacity to feel and suffer is still limited. It first appears in a high degree with the complete nervous system of the vertebrate animals, and in an ever higher degree, the more intelligence is developed. Therefore, in proportion as knowledge attains to distinctness, consciousness is enhanced, pain also increases, and consequently reaches its highest degree in man; and all the more, the more distinctly he knows, and the more intelligent he is. The person in whom genius is to be found suffers most of all. In this sense, namely in reference to the degree of knowledge generally, not to mere abstract knowledge, I understand and here use that saying in Ecclesiastes: *Qui auget scientiam, auget et dolorem.*[25] This precise relation between the degree of consciousness and that of suffering has been beautifully expressed in perceptive and visible delineation in a drawing by Tischbein, that philosophical painter or painting philosopher. The upper half of his drawing represents women from whom their children are being snatched away, and who by different groupings and attitudes express in many ways deep maternal pain, anguish, and despair. The lower half of the drawing shows, in exactly the same order and grouping, sheep whose lambs are being taken from them. In the lower half of the drawing an animal analogy corresponds to each human head, to each human attitude, in the upper half. We thus see clearly how the pain possible in the dull animal consciousness is related to the violent grief that becomes possible only through distinctness of knowledge, through clearness of consciousness.

For this reason, we wish to consider in *human existence* the inner and essential destiny of the will. Everyone will readily find the same thing once more in the life of the animal, only more feebly expressed in various degrees. He can also sufficiently convince himself in the suffering animal world how essentially *all life is suffering.*

---

[25] "He that increaseth knowledge increaseth sorrow." [Ecclesiastes, i, 18. Tr.]

§ 57.

At every stage illuminated by knowledge, the will appears as individual. The human individual finds himself in endless space and time as finite, and consequently as a vanishing quantity compared with these. He is projected into them, and on account of their boundlessness has always only a relative, never an absolute, *when* and *where* of his existence; for his place and duration are finite parts of what is infinite and boundless. His real existence is only in the present, whose unimpeded flight into the past is a constant transition into death, a constant dying. For his past life, apart from its eventual consequences for the present, and also apart from the testimony regarding his will that is impressed in it, is entirely finished and done with, dead, and no longer anything. Therefore, as a matter of reason, it must be indifferent to him whether the contents of that past were pains or pleasures. But the present in his hands is constantly becoming the past; the future is quite uncertain and always short. Thus his existence, even considered from the formal side alone, is a continual rushing of the present into the dead past, a constant dying. And if we look at it also from the physical side, it is evident that, just as we know our walking to be only a constantly prevented falling, so is the life of our body only a constantly prevented dying, an ever-deferred death. Finally, the alertness and activity of our mind are also a continuously postponed boredom. Every breath we draw wards off the death that constantly impinges on us. In this way, we struggle with it every second, and again at longer intervals through every meal we eat, every sleep we take, every time we warm ourselves, and so on. Ultimately death must triumph, for by birth it has already become our lot, and it plays with its prey only for a while before swallowing it up. However, we continue our life with great interest and much solicitude as long as possible, just as we blow out a soap-bubble as long and as large as possible, although with the perfect certainty that it will burst.

We have already seen in nature-without-knowledge her inner being as a constant striving without aim and without rest, and this stands out much more distinctly when we consider the animal or man. Willing and striving are its whole essence, and can be fully compared to an unquenchable thirst. The basis of all willing, however, is need, lack, and hence pain, and by its very nature and origin it is therefore destined to pain. If, on the other hand, it lacks objects of willing, because it is at once deprived of them again by too easy a satisfaction, a fearful emptiness and boredom come over it; in other words, its being and its existence itself become an intolerable burden for it. Hence its life swings like a pendulum to and fro between pain and boredom, and these two are in fact its ultimate constituents. This has been expressed very quaintly by saying that, after man had placed all pains and torments in hell, there was nothing left for heaven but boredom.

But the constant striving, which constitutes the inner nature of every phenomenon of the will, obtains at the higher grades of objectification its first and most universal foundation from the fact that the will here appears as a living body with the iron command to nourish it. What gives force to this command is just that this body is nothing but the objectified will-to-live itself. Man, as the most complete objectification of this will, is accordingly the most necessitous of all beings. He is concrete willing and needing through and through; he is a concretion of a thousand wants and needs. With these he stands on the earth, left to his own devices, in uncertainty about everything except his own need and misery. Accordingly, care for the maintenance of this existence, in the face of demands that are so heavy and proclaim themselves anew every day, occupies, as a rule, the whole of human life. With this is directly connected the second demand, that for the propagation of the race. At the same time dangers of the most varied kinds threaten him from all sides, and to escape from them calls for constant vigilance. With cautious step and anxious glance around he pursues his path, for a thousand accidents and a thousand enemies lie in wait for him. Thus he went in the savage state, and thus he goes in civilized life; there is no security for him:

> *Qualibus in tenebris vitae, quantisque periclis*
> *Degitur hocc' aevi, quodcunque est!*[26]
>   Lucretius, ii, 15.

The life of the great majority is only a constant struggle for this same existence, with the certainty of ultimately losing it. What enables them to endure this wearisome battle is not so much the

---

[26] "In what gloom of existence, in what great perils, this life is spent as long as it endures!" [Tr.]

love of life as the fear of death, which nevertheless stands in the background as inevitable, and which may come on the scene at any moment. Life itself is a sea full of rocks and whirlpools that man avoids with the greatest caution and care, although he knows that, even when he succeeds with all his efforts and ingenuity in struggling through, at every step he comes nearer to the greatest, the total, the inevitable and irremediable shipwreck, indeed even steers right on to it, namely death. This is the final goal of the wearisome voyage, and is worse for him than all the rocks that he has avoided.

Now it is at once well worth noting that, on the one hand, the sufferings and afflictions of life can easily grow to such an extent that even death, in the flight from which the whole of life consists, becomes desirable, and a man voluntarily hastens to it. Again, on the other hand, it is worth noting that, as soon as want and suffering give man a relaxation, boredom is at once so near that he necessarily requires diversion and amusement. The striving after existence is what occupies all living things, and keeps them in motion. When existence is assured to them, they do not know what to do with it. Therefore the second thing that sets them in motion is the effort to get rid of the burden of existence, to make it no longer felt, "to kill time," in other words, to escape from boredom. Accordingly we see that almost all men, secure from want and cares, are now a burden to themselves, after having finally cast off all other burdens. They regard as a gain every hour that is got through, and hence every deduction from that very life, whose maintenance as long as possible has till then been the object of all their efforts. Boredom is anything but an evil to be thought of lightly; ultimately it depicts on the countenance real despair. It causes beings who love one another as little as men do, to seek one another so much, and thus becomes the source of sociability. From political prudence public measures are taken against it everywhere, as against other universal calamities, since this evil, like its opposite extreme, famine, can drive people to the greatest excesses and anarchy; the people need *panem et circenses*. The strict penitentiary system of Philadelphia makes mere boredom ·an instrument of punishment through loneliness and idleness. It is so terrible an instrument, that it has brought convicts to suicide. Just as need and want are the constant scourge of the people, so is boredom that of the world of fashion. In middle-class life boredom is represented by the Sunday, just as want is represented by the six weekdays.

Now absolutely every human life continues to flow on between willing and attainment. Of its nature the wish is pain; attainment quickly begets satiety. The goal was only apparent; possession takes away its charm. The wish, the need, appears again on the scene under a new form; if it does not, then dreariness, emptiness, and boredom follow, the struggle against which is just as painful as is that against want. For desire and satisfaction to follow each other at not too short and not too long intervals, reduces the suffering occasioned by both to the smallest amount, and constitutes the happiest life. What might otherwise be called the finest part of life, its purest joy, just because it lifts us out of real existence, and transforms us into disinterested spectators of it, is pure knowledge which remains foreign to all willing, pleasure in the beautiful, genuine delight in art. But because this requires rare talents, it is granted only to extremely few, and even to those only as a fleeting dream. Then again higher intellectual power makes those very few susceptible to much greater sufferings than duller men can ever feel. Moreover, it makes them feel lonely among beings that are noticeably different from them, and in this way also matters are made even. But purely intellectual pleasures are not accessible to the vast majority of men. They are almost wholly incapable of the pleasure to be found in pure knowledge; they are entirely given over to willing. Therefore, if anything is to win their sympathy, to be *interesting* to them, it must (and this is to be found already in the meaning of the word) in some way excite their *will*, even if it be only through a remote relation to it which is merely within the bounds of possibility. The will must never be left entirely out of question, since their existence lies far more in willing than in knowing; action and reaction are their only element. The naïve expressions of this quality can be seen in trifles and everyday phenomena; thus, for example, they write their names up at places worth seeing which they visit, in order thus to react on, to affect the place, since it does not affect them. Further, they cannot easily just contemplate a rare and strange animal, but must excite it, tease it, play with it, just to experience action and reaction. But this need for exciting the will shows itself particularly in the invention and maintenance of card-playing, which is in the truest sense an expression of the wretched side of humanity.

But whatever nature and good fortune may have done, whoever a person may be and whatever he may possess, the pain essential to life cannot be thrown off:

‘Πηλείδης δ᾽ᾤμωξεν, ἰδὼν εἰς οὐρανὸν εὐρύν.

(*Pelides autem ejulavit, intuitus in coelum latum*).[27]

---

[27] "Peleus' son was wailing and lamenting, looking up to the broad heaven." [*Iliad,* xxi, 272. Tr.]

And again:

> Ζηνὸς μὲν πᾶις ἦα Κρονίονος, αὐτὰρ ὀϊζύν
> Εἶχον ἀπειρεσίην.
>
> (*Jovis quidem filius eram Saturnii; verum aerumnam Habebam infinitam.*) [28]

The ceaseless efforts to banish suffering achieve nothing more than a change in its form. This is essentially want, lack, care for the maintenance of life. If, which is very difficult, we have succeeded in removing pain in this form, it at once appears on the scene in a thousand others, varying according to age and circumstances, such as sexual impulse, passionate love, jealousy, envy, hatred, anxiety, ambition, avarice, sickness, and so on. Finally, if it cannot find entry in any other shape, it comes in the sad, grey garment of weariness, satiety, and boredom, against which many different attempts are made. Even if we ultimately succeed in driving these away, it will hardly be done without letting pain in again in one of the previous forms, and thus starting the dance once more at the beginning; for every human life is tossed backwards and forwards between pain and boredom. Depressing as this discussion is, I will, however, draw attention in passing to one aspect of it from which a consolation can be derived, and perhaps even a stoical indifference to our own present ills may be attained. For our impatience at these arises for the most part from the fact that we recognize them as accidental, as brought about by a chain of causes that might easily be different. We are not usually distressed at evils that are inescapably necessary and quite universal, for example, the necessity of old age and death, and of many daily inconveniences. It is rather a consideration of the accidental nature of the circumstances that have brought suffering precisely on us which gives this suffering its sting. Now we have recognized that pain as such is inevitable and essential to life; that nothing but the mere form in which it manifests itself depends on chance; that therefore our present suffering fills a place which without it would be at once occupied by some other suffering which the one now present excludes; and that, accordingly, fate can affect us little in what is essential. If such a reflection were to become a living conviction, it might produce a considerable degree of stoical equanimity, and greatly reduce our anxious concern about our own welfare. But such a powerful control of the faculty of reason over directly felt suffering is seldom or never found in fact.

---

[28] "I was the son of Zeus, of Kronos, and yet I endured unspeakable afflictions." [*Odyssey,* xi, 620. Tr.]

Moreover, through this consideration of the inevitability of pain, of the supplanting of one pain by another, of the dragging in of a fresh pain by the departure of the preceding one, we might be led to the paradoxical but not absurd hypothesis that in every individual the measure of the pain essential to him has been determined once for all by his nature, a measure that could not remain empty or be filled to excess, however much the form of the suffering might change. Accordingly, his suffering and well-being would not be determined at all from without, but only by that measure, that disposition, which might in fact through the physical condition experience some increase and decrease at different times, but which on the whole would remain the same, and would be nothing but what is called his temperament. More accurately, this is called the degree in which he might be εὔκολος or δύσκολος, as Plato puts it in the first book of the *Republic,* in other words, of an easy or difficult nature. In support of this hypothesis is the well-known experience that great sufferings render lesser ones quite incapable of being felt, and conversely, that in the absence of great sufferings even the smallest vexations and annoyances torment us, and put us in a bad mood. But experience also teaches us that if a great misfortune, at the mere thought of which we shuddered, has now actually happened, our frame of mind remains on the whole much the same as soon as we have overcome the first pain. Conversely, experience also teaches us that, after the appearance of a long-desired happiness, we do not feel ourselves on the whole and permanently much better off or more comfortable than before. Only the moment of appearance of these changes moves us with unusual strength, as deep distress or shouts of joy; but both of these soon disappear, because they rested on illusion. For they do not spring from the immediately present pleasure or pain, but only from the opening up of a new future that is anticipated in them. Only by pain or pleasure borrowing from the future could they be heightened so abnormally, and consequently not for any length of time. The following remarks may be put in evidence in support of the hypothesis we advanced, by which, in knowing as well as in feeling suffering or well-being, a very large part would be subjective and determined *a priori.* Human cheerfulness or dejection is obviously not determined by external circumstances, by wealth or position, for we come across at least as many cheerful faces among the poor as among the rich. Further, the motives that induce suicide are so very different, that we cannot mention any misfortune which would be great enough to bring it about in any character with a high degree of probability, and few that would be so small that those like them would not at some time have caused it. Now although the degree of our cheerfulness or sadness is not at all times the same, yet in consequence of this view we shall attribute it not to the change of external circumstances, but to that of the internal state, the physical condition. For when an actual, though always only temporary, enhancement of our cheerfulness takes place, even to the extent of joy, it usually appears without any external occasion. It is true that we often see our pain result only from a definite external relation, and that we are visibly oppressed and saddened merely by this. We then believe that, if only this were removed, the greatest contentment would necessarily ensue. But this is a delusion. The measure of our pain and our well-being is, on the whole, subjectively determined for each point of time according to our hypothesis; and in reference to this, that external motive for sadness is only what a blister is for the body, to which are drawn all the bad humours that would otherwise be spread throughout it. The pain to be found in our nature for this period of time, which therefore cannot be shaken off, would be distributed at a hundred points were it not for that definite external cause of our suffering. It would appear in the form of a hundred little annoyances and worries over things we now entirely overlook, because our capacity for pain is already filled up by that principal evil that has concentrated at a point all the suffering otherwise dispersed. In keeping with this is also the observation that, if a great and pressing care is finally lifted from our breast by a fortunate issue, another immediately takes its place. The whole material of this already existed previously, yet it could not enter consciousness as care, because the consciousness had no capacity left for it. This material for care, therefore, remained merely as a dark and unobserved misty form on the extreme horizon of consciousness. But now, as there is room, this ready material at once comes forward and occupies the throne of the reigning care of the day (πρυτανεύουσα). If so far as its matter is concerned it is very much lighter than the material of the care that has vanished, it knows how to blow itself out, so that it apparently equals it in size, and thus, as the chief care of the day, completely fills the throne.

Excessive joy and very severe pain occur always only in the same person, for they reciprocally condition each other, and are also conditioned in common by great mental activity. As we have just now found, both are brought about not by what is actually present, but by anticipation of the future. But as pain is essential to life, and is also determined as regards its degree by the nature of the subject, sudden changes, since they are always external, cannot really change its degree. Thus an error and delusion are at the root of immoderate joy or pain; consequently, these two excessive strains of the mind could be avoided by insight. Every immoderate joy (*exultatio, insolens laetitia*) always rests on the delusion that we have found something in life that is not to be met with at all, namely permanent satisfaction of the tormenting desires or cares that constantly breed new ones. From each particular delusion of this kind we must inevitably later be brought back; and then, when it vanishes, we must pay for it with pains just as bitter as the joy caused by its entry was keen. To this extent it is exactly like a height from which we can descend again only by a fall; we should therefore avoid them; and every sudden, excessive grief is just a fall from such a height, the vanishing of such a delusion, and is thus conditioned by it. Consequently, we could avoid both, if we could bring ourselves always to survey things with perfect clearness as a whole and in their connexion, and resolutely to guard against actually lending them the colour we should like them to have. The Stoic ethics aimed principally at freeing the mind from all such delusion and its consequences, and at giving it an unshakable equanimity instead. Horace is imbued with this insight in the well-known ode:

> *Aequam memento rebus in arduis*
> *Servare mentem, non secus in bonis*
> *Ab insolenti temperatam*
> *Laetitia.*—[29]

But we frequently shut our eyes to the truth, comparable to a bitter medicine, that suffering is essential to life, and therefore does not flow in upon us from outside, but that everyone carries around within himself its perennial source. On the contrary, we are constantly looking for a particular external cause, as it were a pretext for the pain that never leaves us, just as the free man makes for himself an idol, in order to have a master. For we untiringly strive from desire to desire, and although every attained satisfaction, however much it promised, does not really satisfy us, but often stands before us as a mortifying error, we still do not see that we are drawing water with the vessel of the Danaides, and we hasten to ever fresh desires:

> *Sed, dum abest quod avemus, id exsuperare videtur*
> *Caetera; post aliud, quum contigit illud, avemus;*
> *Et sitis aequa tenet vitai semper hiantes.*[30]
> （Lucretius, iii, 1082.）

---

[29] "Remember always to preserve equanimity when in adversity, and guard against overweening joy when in luck." [*Odes* II, iii, 1. Tr.]

[30] "For so long as we lack what we desire, it seems to us to surpass everything in value; but when it is acquired, it at once appears like something different; and a similar longing always holds us fast, as we thirst and hanker after life." [Tr.]

Thus it goes on either *ad infinitum,* or, what is rarer and already presupposes a certain strength of character, till we come to a wish that is not fulfilled, and yet cannot be given up. We then have, so to speak, what we were looking for, namely something that we can denounce at any moment, instead of our own inner nature, as the source of our sufferings. Thus, although at variance with our fate, we become reconciled to our existence in return for this, since the knowledge that suffering is essential to this existence itself and that true satisfaction is impossible, is again withdrawn from us. The consequence of this last kind of development is a somewhat melancholy disposition, the constant bearing of a single, great pain, and the resultant disdain for all lesser joys and sorrows. This is in consequence a worthier phenomenon than the constant hunting for ever different deceptive forms which is much more usual.

§ 58.

Alll satisfaction, or what is commonly called happiness, is really and essentially always *negative* only, and never positive. It is not a gratification which comes to us originally and of itself, but it must always be the satisfaction of a wish. For desire, that is to say, want, is the precedent condition of every pleasure; but with the satisfaction, the desire and therefore the pleasure cease; and so the satisfaction or gratification can never be more than deliverance from a pain, from a want. Such is not only every actual and evident suffering, but also every desire whose importunity disturbs our peace, and indeed even the deadening boredom that makes existence a burden to us. But it is so difficult to attain and carry through anything; difficulties and troubles without end oppose every plan, and at every step obstacles are heaped up. But when everything is finally overcome and attained, nothing can ever be gained but deliverance from some suffering or desire; consequently, we are only in the same position as we were before this suffering or desire appeared. What is immediately given to us is always only the want, i.e., the pain. The satisfaction and pleasure can be known only indirectly by remembering the preceding suffering and privation that ceased on their entry. Hence it comes about that we are in no way aware of the blessings and advantages we actually possess; we do not value them, but simply imagine that they must be so, for they make us happy only negatively by preventing suffering. Only after we have lost them do we become sensible of their value, for the want, the privation, the suffering is what is positive, and proclaims itself immediately. Thus also we are pleased at remembering need, sickness, want, and so on which have been overcome, because such remembrance is the only means of enjoying present blessings. It is also undeniable that in this respect, and from this standpoint of egoism, which is the form of the will-to-live, the sight or description of another's sufferings affords us satisfaction and pleasure, just as Lucretius beautifully and frankly expresses it at the beginning of his second book:

> Suave, mari magno, turbantibus aequora ventis,
> E terra magnum alterius spectare laborem:
> Non, quia vexari quemquam est jucunda voluptas;
> Sed, quibus ipse malis careas, quia cernere suave est.[31]

Yet later on we shall see that this kind of pleasure, through knowledge of our own well-being obtained in this way, lies very near the source of real, positive wickedness.

In art, especially in poetry, that true mirror of the real nature of the world and of life, we also find evidence of the fact that all happiness is only of a negative, not a positive nature, and that for this reason it cannot be lasting satisfaction and gratification, but always delivers us only from a pain or want that must be followed either by a new pain or by languor, empty longing, and boredom. Every epic or dramatic poem can always present to us only a strife, an effort, and a struggle for happiness, never enduring and complete happiness itself. It conducts its heroes to their goal through a thousand difficulties and dangers; as soon as the goal is reached, it quickly lets the curtain fall. For there would be nothing left for it but to show that the glittering goal, in which the hero imagined he could find happiness, had merely mocked him, and that he was no better after its attainment than before. Since a genuine, lasting happiness is not possible, it cannot be a subject of art. It is true that the real purpose of the idyll is the description of such a happiness, but we also see that the idyll as such cannot endure. In the hands of the poet it always becomes an epic, and is then only a very insignificant epic made up of trifling sorrows, trifling joys, and trifling efforts; this is the com-

---

[31] "It is a pleasure to stand on the seashore when the tempestuous winds whip up the sea, and to behold the great toils another is enduring. Not that it pleases us to watch another being tormented, but that it is a joy to us to observe evils from which we ourselves are free." [*De Rerum Natura*, II. 1 *seqq.* —Tr.]

monest case. Or it becomes a merely descriptive poem, depicting the beauty of nature, in other words, really pure, will-free knowing, which is of course the only pure happiness which is not preceded either by suffering or need, or yet followed by repentance, suffering, emptiness, or satiety. This happiness, however, cannot fill the whole of life, but only moments of it. What we see in poetry we find again in music, in the melodies of which we again recognize the universally expressed, innermost story of the will conscious of itself, the most secret living, longing, suffering, and enjoying, the ebb and flow of the human heart. Melody is always a deviation from the keynote through a thousand crotchety wanderings up to the most painful discord. After this, it at last finds the keynote again, which expresses the satisfaction and composure of the will, but with which nothing more can then be done, and the continuation of which would be only a wearisome and meaningless monotony corresponding to boredom.

All that these remarks are intended to make clear, namely the impossibility of attaining lasting satisfaction and the negative nature of all happiness, finds its explanation in what is shown at the end of the second book, namely that the will, whose objectification is human life like every phenomenon, is a striving without aim or end. We find the stamp of this endlessness imprinted on all the parts of the will's phenomenon as a whole, from its most universal form, namely endless time and space, up to the most perfect of all phenomena, the life and efforts of man. We can in theory assume three extremes of human life, and consider them as elements of actual human life. Firstly, powerful and vehement willing, the great passions (Raja-Guna); it appears in great historical characters, and is described in the epic and the drama. It can also show itself, however, in the small world, for the size of the objects is here measured only according to the degree in which they excite the will, not to their external relations. Then secondly, pure knowing, the comprehension of the Ideas, conditioned by freeing knowledge from the service of the will: the life of the genius (Sattva-Guna). Thirdly and lastly, the greatest lethargy of the will and also of the knowledge attached to it, namely empty longing, life-benumbing boredom (Tama-Guna). The life of the individual, far from remaining fixed in one of these extremes, touches them only rarely, and is often only a weak and wavering approximation to one side or the other, a needy desiring of trifling objects, always recurring and thus running away from boredom. It is really incredible how meaningless and insignificant when seen from without, and how dull and senseless when felt from within, is the course of life of the great majority of men. It is weary longing and worrying, a dreamlike staggering through the four ages of life to death, accompanied by a series of trivial thoughts. They are like clockwork that is wound up and goes without knowing why. Every time a man is begotten and born the clock of human life is wound up anew, to repeat once more its same old tune that has already been played innumerable times, movement by movement and measure by measure, with insignificant variations. Every individual, every human apparition and its course of life, is only one more short dream of the endless spirit of nature, of the persistent will-to-live, is only one more fleeting form, playfully sketched by it on its infinite page, space and time; it is allowed to exist for a short while that is infinitesimal compared with these, and is then effaced, to make new room. Yet, and here is to be found the serious side of life, each of these fleeting forms, these empty fancies, must be paid for by the whole will-to-live in all its intensity with many deep sorrows, and finally with a bitter death, long feared and finally made manifest. It is for this reason that the sight of a corpse suddenly makes us serious.

The life of every individual, viewed as a whole and in general, and when only its most significant features are emphasized, is really a tragedy; but gone through in detail it has the character of a comedy. For the doings and worries of the day, the restless mockeries of the moment, the desires and fears of the week, the mishaps of every hour, are all brought about by chance that is always bent on some mischievous trick; they are nothing but scenes from a comedy. The never-fulfilled wishes, the frustrated efforts, the hopes mercilessly blighted by fate, the unfortunate mistakes of the whole life, with increasing suffering and death at the end, always give us a tragedy. Thus, as if fate wished to add mockery to the misery of our existence, our life must contain all the woes of tragedy, and yet we cannot even assert the dignity of tragic characters, but, in the broad detail of life, are inevitably the foolish characters of a comedy.

Now however much great and small worries fill up human life, and keep it in constant agitation and restlessness, they are unable to mask life's inadequacy to satisfy the spirit; they cannot conceal the emptiness and superficiality of existence, or exclude boredom which is always ready to fill up every pause granted by care. The result of this is that the human mind, still not content with the cares, anxieties, and preoccupations laid upon it by the actual world, creates for itself an imaginary world in the shape of a thousand different superstitions. Then it sets itself to work with this in all kinds of ways, and wastes time and strength on it, as soon as the real world is willing to grant it the peace and quiet to which it is not in the least responsive. Hence this is at bottom most often the case with those peoples for whom life is made easy by the mildness of the climate and of the soil, above all the Hindus, then the Greeks and Romans, and later the Italians, Spaniards, and others. Man creates for himself in his own image demons, gods, and saints; then to these must be incessantly offered sacrifices, prayers, temple decorations, vows and their fulfilment, pilgrimages, salutations, adornment of images and so on. Their service is everywhere closely interwoven with reality, and indeed obscures it. Every event in life is then accepted as the counter-effect of these beings. Intercourse with them fills up half the time of life, constantly sustains hope, and, by the charm of delusion, often becomes more interesting than intercourse with real beings. It is the expression and the symptom of man's double need, partly for help and support, partly for occupation and diversion. While it often works in direct opposition to the first need, in that, with the occurrence of accidents and dangers, valuable time and strength, instead of averting them, are uselessly wasted on prayers and sacrifices, then, by way of compensation, it serves the second need all the better by that imaginary conversation with a visionary spirit-world; and this is the advantage of all superstitions, which is by no means to be despised.

§ 59.

Now if we have so far convinced ourselves *a priori* by the most universal of all considerations, by investigation of the first, elementary features of human life, that such a life, by its whole tendency and disposition, is not capable of any true bliss or happiness, but is essentially suffering in many forms and a tragic state in every way, we might now awaken this conviction much more vividly within us, if, by proceeding more *a posteriori,* we turned to more definite instances, brought pictures to the imagination, and described by examples the unspeakable misery presented by experience and history, wherever we look, and whatever avenue we explore. But the chapter would be without end, and would carry us far from the standpoint of universality which is essential to philosophy. Moreover, such a description might easily be regarded as a mere declamation on human misery, such as has often been made already, and as such it might be charged with one-sidedness, because it started from particular facts. From such reproach and suspicion our perfectly cold and philosophical demonstration of the inevitable suffering at the very foundation of the nature of life is free; for it starts from the universal and is conducted *a priori*. However, confirmation *a posteriori* can easily be obtained everywhere. Anyone who has awakened from the first dreams of youth; who has considered his own and others' experience; who has looked at life in the history of the past and of his own time, and finally in the works of the great poets, will certainly acknowledge the result, if his judgement is not paralysed by some indelibly imprinted prejudice, that this world of humanity is the kingdom of chance and error. These rule in it without mercy in great things as in small; and along with them folly and wickedness also wield the scourge. Hence arises the fact that everything better struggles through only with difficulty; what is noble and wise very rarely makes its appearance, becomes effective, or meets with a hearing, but the absurd and perverse in the realm of thought, the dull and tasteless in the sphere of art, and the wicked and fraudulent in the sphere of action, really assert a supremacy that is disturbed only by brief interruptions. On the other hand, everything excellent or admirable is always only an exception, one case in millions; therefore, if it has shown itself in a lasting work, this subsequently exists in isolation, after it has outlived the rancour of its contemporaries. It is preserved like a meteorite, sprung from an order of things different from that which prevails here. But as regards the life of the individual, every life-history is a history of suffering, for, as a rule, every life is a continual series of mishaps great and small, concealed as much as possible by everyone, because he knows that others are almost always bound to feel satisfaction at the spectacle of annoyances from which they are for the moment exempt; rarely will they feel sympathy or compassion. But perhaps at the end of his life, no man, if he be sincere and at the same time in possession of his faculties, will ever wish to go through it again. Rather than this, he will much prefer to choose complete non-existence. The essential purport of the world-famous monologue in *Hamlet* is, in condensed form, that our state is so wretched that complete non-existence would be decidedly preferable to it. Now if suicide actually offered us this, so that the alternative "to be or not to be" lay before us in the full sense of the words, it could be chosen unconditionally as a highly desirable termination ("a consummation devoutly to be wish'd").[32] There is something in us, however, which tells us that this is not so, that this is not the end of things, that death is not an absolute annihilation. Similarly, what has been said by the father of history (Herodotus, vii, 46) has not since been refuted, namely that no person has existed who has not wished more than once that he had not to live through

---

[32] *Hamlet*, Act III, Sc. I. [Tr.]

the following day. Accordingly, the shortness of life, so often lamented, may perhaps be the very best thing about it. If, finally, we were to bring to the sight of everyone the terrible sufferings and afflictions to which his life is constantly exposed, he would be seized with horror. If we were to conduct the most hardened and callous optimist through hospitals, infirmaries, operating theatres, through prisons, torture-chambers, and slave-hovels, over battlefields and to places of execution; if we were to open to him all the dark abodes of misery, where it shuns the gaze of cold curiosity, and finally were to allow him to glance into the dungeon of Ugolino where prisoners starved to death, he too would certainly see in the end what kind of a world is this *meilleur des mondes possibles.*[33] For whence did Dante get the material for his hell, if not from this actual world of ours? And indeed he made a downright hell of it. On the other hand, when he came to the task of describing heaven and its delights, he had an insuperable difficulty before him, just because our world affords absolutely no materials for anything of the kind. Therefore, instead of describing the delights of paradise, there was nothing left for him but to repeat to us the instruction imparted to him there by his ancestor, by his Beatrice, and by various saints. But it is clear enough from this what kind of a world this is. Certainly human life, like all inferior goods, is covered on the outside with a false glitter; what suffers always conceals itself. On the other hand, everyone parades whatever pomp and splendour he can obtain by effort, and the more he is wanting in inner contentment, the more he desires to stand out as a lucky and fortunate person in the opinion of others. Folly goes to such lengths, and the opinion of others is a principal aim of the efforts of everyone, although the complete futility of this is expressed by the fact that in almost all languages vanity, *vanitas,* originally signifies emptiness and nothingness. But even under all this deception, the miseries of life can very easily increase to such an extent—and this happens every day—that death, which is otherwise feared more than everything, is eagerly resorted to. In fact, if fate wants to show the whole of its malice, even this refuge can be barred to the sufferer, and in the hands of enraged enemies he may remain exposed to merciless and slow tortures without escape. In vain does the tortured person then call on his gods for help; he remains abandoned to his fate without mercy. But this hopeless and irretrievable state is precisely the mirror of the invincible and indomitable nature of his will, the objectivity of which is his person. An external power is little able to change or suppress this will, and any strange and unknown power is just as little able to deliver him from the miseries

---

[33] Best of all possible worlds." [Tr.]

resulting from the life that is the phenomenon of this will. As in everything, so in the principal matter, a man is always referred back to himself. In vain does he make gods for himself, in order to get from them by prayers and flattery what can be brought about only by his own will-power. While the Old Testament made the world and man the work of a God, the New saw itself compelled to represent that God as becoming man, in order to teach that holiness and salvation from the misery of this world can come only from the world itself. It is and remains the will of man on which everything depends for him. Sannyasis, martyrs, saints of every faith and name, have voluntarily and gladly endured every torture, because the will-to-live had suppressed itself in them; and then even the slow destruction of the phenomenon of the will was welcome to them. But I will not anticipate the further discussion. For the rest, I cannot here withhold the statement that *optimism,* where it is not merely the thoughtless talk of those who harbour nothing but words under their shallow foreheads, seems to me to be not merely an absurd, but also a really *wicked,* way of thinking, a bitter mockery of the unspeakable sufferings of mankind. Let no one imagine that the Christian teaching is favourable to optimism; on the contrary, in the Gospels world and evil are used almost as synonymous expressions.[34]

§ 60.

We have now completed the two discussions whose insertion was necessary; namely that about the freedom of the will in itself simultaneously with the necessity of its phenomenon; and that about its fate in the world that reflects its inner nature, on the knowledge of which it has to affirm or deny itself. We can now bring to greater clearness this affirmation and denial, which above we expressed and stated only in general terms. This we can do by describing the modes of conduct in which alone they find their expression, and considering them according to their inner significance.

The affirmation of the will is the persistent willing itself, undisturbed by any knowledge, as it fills the life of man in general. For the body of man is already the objectivity of the will, as it appears at this grade and in this individual; and thus his willing that develops in

---

[34] Cf. chap. 46 of volume 2.

time is, so to speak, the paraphrase of the body, the elucidation of the meaning of the whole and of its parts. It is another way of exhibiting the same thing-in-itself of which the body is already the phenomenon. Therefore, instead of affirmation of the will, we can also say affirmation of the body. The fundamental theme of all the many different acts of will is the satisfaction of the needs inseparable from the body's existence in health; they have their expression in it, and can be reduced to the maintenance of the individual and the propagation of the race. But indirectly, motives of the most various kinds in this way obtain power over the will, and bring about acts of will of the most various kinds. Each of these is only a pattern, an example, of the will which appears here in general. The nature of this example, and what form the motive may have and impart to it, are not essential; the important points are only that there is a willing in general, and the degree of intensity of this willing. The will can become visible only in the motives, just as the eye manifests its visual faculty only in light. The motive in general stands before the will in protean forms; it always promises complete satisfaction, the quenching of the thirst of will. But if this is attained, it at once appears in a different form, and therein moves the will afresh, always according to the degree of the will's intensity and to its relation to knowledge, which in these very patterns and examples are revealed as empirical character.

From the first appearance of his consciousness, man finds himself to be a willing being, and his knowledge, as a rule, remains in constant relation to his will. He tries to become thoroughly acquainted only with the objects of his willing, and then with the means to attain these. Now he knows what he has to do, and does not, as a rule, aim at other knowledge. He proceeds and acts; consciousness keeps him always working steadfastly and actively in accordance with the aim of his willing; his thinking is concerned with the choice of means. This is the life of almost all men; they will, they know what they will, and they strive after this with enough success to protect them from despair, and enough failure to preserve them from boredom and its consequences. From this results a certain serenity, or at any rate composure, that cannot really be changed by wealth or poverty; for the rich and the poor enjoy, not what they have, since, as we have shown, this acts only negatively, but what they hope to obtain by their efforts. They press forward with much seriousness and indeed with an air of importance; children also pursue their play in this way. It is always an exception, when such a life suffers an interruption through the fact that either the aesthetic demand for contemplation or the ethical demand for renunciation proceeds from a knowledge independent of the service of the will, and directed to the inner nature of the world in general. Most men are pursued by want throughout their lives, without being allowed to come to their senses. On the other hand, the will is often inflamed to a degree far exceeding the affirmation of the body. This degree is then revealed by violent emotions and powerful passions in which the individual not merely affirms his own existence, but denies and seeks to suppress that of others, when it stands in his way.

The maintenance of the body by its own powers is so small a degree of the will's affirmation that, if it voluntarily stopped at this, we might assume that, with the death of this body, the will that appeared in it would also be extinguished. But the satisfaction of the sexual impulse goes beyond the affirmation of one's own existence that fills so short a time; it affirms life for an indefinite time beyond the death of the individual. Nature, always true and consistent, here even naïve, exhibits to us quite openly the inner significance of the act of procreation. Our own consciousness, the intensity of the impulse, teaches us that in this act is expressed the most decided *affirmation of the will-to-live,* pure and without further addition (say of the denial of other and foreign individuals). Now, as the consequence of the act, a new life appears in time and the causal series, i.e., in nature. The begotten appears before the begetter, different from him in the phenomenon, but in himself, or according to the Idea, identical with him. It is therefore by this act that every species of living thing is bound to a whole and perpetuated as such. In reference to the begetter, procreation is only the expression, the symptom, of his decided affirmation of the will-to-live. In reference to the begotten, procreation is not the ground or reason of the will that appears in him, for the will in itself knows neither reason nor consequent; but, like every cause, this procreation is only the occasional cause of this will's phenomenon, at a given time and in a given place. As thing-in-itself, the will of the begetter is not different from that of the begotten, for only the phenomenon, not the thing-in-itself, is subordinate to the *principium individuationis*. With that affirmation beyond one's own body to the production of a new body, suffering and death, as belonging to the phenomenon of life, are also affirmed anew, and the possibility of salvation, brought about by the most complete faculty of knowledge, is for this time declared to be fruitless. Here is to be seen the profound reason for the shame connected with the business of procreation. This view is mythically expressed in the dogma of the Christian teaching that we all share the sin of Adam (which is obviously only the satisfaction of sexual passion), and through it are guilty of suffering and death. In this respect, religious teaching goes beyond the consideration of things according to the principle of sufficient reason; it recognizes the Idea of man. The unity of this Idea is re-established out of its dispersion into innumerable individuals through the bond of procreation that holds them all together. According to this, religious teaching regards every individual, on the one hand, as identical with Adam, with the representative of the affirmation of life, and to this extent as fallen into sin (original sin), suffering, and death. On the other hand, knowledge of the Idea also shows it every individual as identical with the Saviour, with the representative of the denial of the will-to-live, and to this extent as partaking of his self-sacrifice, redeemed by his merit, and rescued from the bonds of sin and death, i.e., of the world (Rom. v, 12-21).

Another mythical description of our view of sexual satisfaction as the affirmation of the will-to-live beyond the individual life, as a falling into life first brought about in this way, or, so to speak, as a renewed assignment to life, is the Greek myth of Proserpine. A return from the nether world was still possible for her, so long as she had not tasted the fruits of the lower world; but she was wholly buried there through eating the pomegranate. The meaning of this is very clearly expressed in Goethe's incomparable telling of this myth, especially when, immediately after she has tasted the pomegranate, the invisible chorus of the three Parcae joins in and says:

> "You are ours!
> Fasting you could return:
> The bite of the apple makes you ours!"
> [*Triumph der Empfindsamkeit*, IV]

It is noteworthy that Clement of Alexandria (*Stromata*, iii, c. 15) describes the matter through the same image and expression: Οἱ μὲν εὐνουχίσαντες ἑαυτοὺς ἀπὸ πάσης ἁμαρτίας, διὰ τὴν βασιλείαν τῶν οὐρανῶν, μακάριοι οὗτοί εἰσιν, οἱ τοῦ κόσμου νηστεύοντες. (*Qui se castrarunt ab omni peccato propter regnum coelorum, ii sunt beati, A MUNDO JEJUNANTES.*)[35]

The sexual impulse is proved to be the decided and strongest affirmation of life by the fact that for man in the natural state, as for the animal, it is his life's final end and highest goal. Self-preservation and maintenance are his first aim, and as soon as he has provided for that, he aims only at the propagation of the race; as a merely natural being, he cannot aspire to anything more. Nature

---

[35] "Those who have castrated themselves from all sin for the sake of the kingdom of heaven, are blessed; *they abstain from the world.*" [Tr.]

too, the inner being of which is the will-to-live itself, with all her force impels both man and the animal to propagate. After this she has attained her end with the individual, and is quite indifferent to its destruction; for, as the will-to-live, she is concerned only with the preservation of the species; the individual is nothing to her. Because the inner being of nature, the will-to-live, expresses itself most strongly in the sexual impulse, the ancient poets and philosophers—Hesiod and Parmenides—said very significantly that *Eros* is the first, that which creates, the principle from which all things emerge. (See Aristotle, *Metaphysica*, i, 4.) Pherecydes said: Εἰς ἔρωτα μεταβεβλῆσθαι τὸν Δία, μέλλοντα δημιουργεῖν. (*Jovem, cum mundum fabricare vellet, in cupidinem sese transformasse.*)[36] Proclus *ad Platonis Timaeum,* Bk. iii. We have recently had from G. F. Schoemann, *De Cupidine Cosmogonico,* 1852, a detailed treatment of this subject. The Maya of the Indians, the work and fabric of which are the whole world of illusion, is paraphrased by *amor.*

Far more than any other external member of the body, the genitals are subject merely to the will, and not at all to knowledge. Here, in fact, the will shows itself almost as independent of knowledge as it does in those parts which, on the occasion of mere stimuli, serve vegetative life, reproduction, and in which the will operates blindly as it does in nature-without-knowledge. For generation is only reproduction passing over to a new individual, reproduction at the second power so to speak, just as death is only excretion at the second power. By reason of all this, the genitals are the real *focus* of the will, and are therefore the opposite pole to the brain, the representative of knowledge, i.e., to the other side of the world, the world as representation. The genitals are the life-preserving principle assuring to time endless life. In this capacity they were worshipped by the Greeks in the *phallus,* and by the Hindus in the *lingam,* which are therefore the symbol of the affirmation of the will. On the other hand, knowledge affords the possibility of the suppression of willing, of salvation through freedom, of overcoming and annihilating the world.

At the beginning of this fourth book, we considered in detail how the will-to-live in its affirmation has to regard its relation to death. We saw that it is not troubled by death, because death exists as something already included in and belonging to life. Its opposite, namely generation, completely balances it, and, in spite of the death of the individual, ensures and guarantees life for all time to the will-to-live. To express this, the Indians gave the *lingam* as an

---

[36] "Zeus transformed himself into Eros, when he wished to create the world." [Tr.]

attribute to Shiva, the god of death. We also explained there how the man who has perfect awareness and occupies the standpoint of a decided affirmation of life, faces death fearlessly. Therefore nothing more will be said about this here. Without clear awareness, most people occupy this standpoint, and continue to affirm life. The world stands out as the mirror of this affirmation, with innumerable individuals in endless time, and endless space, and endless suffering, between generation and death without end. Yet no further complaint of this can be made from any direction, for the will performs the great tragedy and comedy at its own expense, and is also its own spectator. The world is precisely as it is, because the will, whose phenomenon is the world, is such a will as it is, because it wills in such a way. The justification for suffering is the fact that the will affirms itself even in this phenomenon; and this affirmation is justified and balanced by the fact that the will bears the suffering. Here we have a glimpse of *eternal justice* in general; later on we shall also recognize it more clearly and distinctly in the particular. We must first, however, speak of temporal or human justice.[37]

§ 61.

We recall from the second book that in the whole of nature, at all grades of the will's objectification, there was necessarily a constant struggle between the individuals of every species, and that precisely in this way was expressed an inner antagonism of the will-to-live with itself. At the highest grade of objectification, this phenomenon, like everything else, will manifest itself in enhanced distinctness, and can be further unravelled. For this purpose we will first of all trace to its source *egoism* as the starting-point of all conflict.

We have called time and space the *principium individuationis,* because only through them and in them is plurality of the homogeneous possible. They are the essential forms of natural knowledge, in other words, knowledge that has sprung from the will. Therefore, the will will everywhere manifest itself in the plurality of individuals. This plurality, however, does not concern the will as

---

[37] Cf. chap. 45 of volume 2.

thing-in-itself, but only its phenomena. The will is present, whole and undivided, in each of these, and perceives around it the innumerably repeated image of its own inner being; but this inner nature itself, and hence what is actually real, it finds immediately only in its inner self. Therefore everyone wants everything for himself, wants to possess, or at least control, everything, and would like to destroy whatever opposes him. In addition, there is in the case of knowing beings the fact that the individual is the bearer of the knowing subject, and this knowing subject is the bearer of the world. This is equivalent to saying that the whole of nature outside the knowing subject, and so all remaining individuals, exist only in his representation; that he is conscious of them always only as his representation, and so merely indirectly, and as something dependent on his own inner being and existence. With his consciousness the world also necessarily ceases to exist for him, in other words, its being and non-being become synonymous and indistinguishable. Every knowing individual is therefore in truth, and finds himself as, the whole will-to-live, or as the in-itself of the world itself, and also as the complementary condition of the world as representation, consequently as a microcosm to be valued equally with the macrocosm. Nature herself, always and everywhere truthful, gives him, originally and independently of all reflection, this knowledge with simplicity and immediate certainty. Now from the two necessary determinations we have mentioned is explained the fact that every individual, completely vanishing and reduced to nothing in a boundless world, nevertheless makes himself the centre of the world, and considers his own existence and well-being before everything else. In fact, from the natural standpoint, he is ready for this to sacrifice everything else; he is ready to annihilate the world, in order to maintain his own self, that drop in the ocean, a little longer. This disposition is *egoism,* which is essential to everything in nature. But it is precisely through egoism that the will's inner conflict with itself attains to such fearful revelation; for this egoism has its continuance and being in that opposition of the microcosm and macrocosm, or in the fact that the objectification of the will has for its form the *principium individuationis,* and thus the will manifests itself in innumerable individuals in the same way, and moreover in each of these entirely and completely in both aspects (will and representation). Therefore, whereas each individual is immediately given to himself as the whole will and the entire representer, all others are given to him in the first instance only as his representations. Hence for him his own inner being and its preservation come before all others taken together. Everyone looks on his own death as the end of the world, whereas he hears about the death of his acquaintances as a matter of comparative indifference, unless he is in some way personally concerned in it. In the consciousness that has reached the highest degree, that is, human consciousness, egoism, like knowledge, pain, and pleasure, must also have reached the highest degree, and the conflict of individuals conditioned by it must appear in the most terrible form. Indeed, we see this everywhere before our eyes, in small things as in great. At one time we see it from its dreadful side in the lives of great tyrants and evildoers, and in world-devastating wars. On another occasion we see its ludicrous side, where it is the theme of comedy, and shows itself particularly in self-conceit and vanity. La Rochefoucauld understood this better than anyone else, and presented it in the abstract. We see it in the history of the world and in our own experience. But it appears most distinctly as soon as any mob is released from all law and order; we then see at once in the most distinct form the *bellum omnium contra omnes*[38] which Hobbes admirably described in the first chapter of his *De Cive*. We see not only how everyone tries to snatch from another what he himself wants, but how one often even destroys another's whole happiness or life, in order to increase by an insignificant amount his own well-being. This is the highest expression of egoism, the phenomena of which in this respect are surpassed only by those of real wickedness that seeks, quite disinterestedly, the pain and injury of others without any advantage to itself; we shall shortly speak about this. With this disclosure of the source of egoism the reader should compare my description of it in my essay *On the Basis of Morality,* § 14.

A principal source of the suffering that we found above to be essential and inevitable to all life, is, when it actually appears in a definite form, that *Eris,* the strife of all individuals, the expression of the contradiction with which the will-to-live is affected in its inner self, and which attains visibility through the *principium individuationis.* Wild-beast fights are the barbarous means of making it directly and strikingly clear. In this original discord is to be found a perennial source of suffering, in spite of the precautions that have been taken against it; we shall now consider it more closely.

---

[38] "War of all against all." [Tr.]

§ 62.

It has already been explained that the first and simplest affirmation of the will-to-live is only affirmation of one's own body, in other words, manifestation of the will through acts in time, in so far as the body, in its form and suitability, exhibits the same will spatially, and no farther. This affirmation shows itself as maintenance and preservation of the body by means of the application of its own powers. With it is directly connected the satisfaction of the sexual impulse; indeed, this belongs to it in so far as the genitals belong to the body. Hence *voluntary* renunciation of the satisfaction of that impulse, such renunciation being set at work by no *motive* at all, is already a degree of denial of the will-to-live; it is a voluntary self-suppression of it on the appearance of knowledge acting as a *quieter*. Accordingly, such denial of one's own body exhibits itself as a contradiction by the will of its own phenomenon. For although here also the body objectifies in the genitals the will to propagate, yet propagation is not willed. Just because such renunciation is a denial or abolition of the will-to-live, it is a difficult and painful self-conquest; but we shall discuss this later. Now since the will manifests that *self-affirmation* of one's own body in innumerable individuals beside one another, in one individual, by virtue of the egoism peculiar to all, it very easily goes beyond this affirmation to the *denial* of the same will appearing in another individual. The will of the first breaks through the boundary of another's affirmation of will, since the individual either destroys or injures this other body itself, or compels the powers of that other body to serve *his* will, instead of serving the will that appears in that other body. Thus if from the will, appearing as the body of another, he takes away the powers of this body, and thereby increases the power serving *his* will beyond that of his own body, he in consequence affirms his own will beyond his own body by denying the will that appears in the body of another. This breaking through the boundary of another's affirmation of will has at all times been distinctly recognized, and its concept has been denoted by the word *wrong* (*Unrecht*). For both parties instantly recognize the fact, not indeed as we do here in distinct abstraction, but as feeling.

The sufferer of the wrong feels the transgression into his own body's sphere of affirmation through the denial of this by another individual, as an immediate and mental pain. This is entirely separate and different from the physical suffering through the deed or annoyance at the loss, which is felt simultaneously with it. On the other hand, to the perpetrator of wrong the knowledge presents itself that in himself he is the same will which appears also in that body, and affirms itself in the one phenomenon with such vehemence that, transgressing the limits of its own body and its powers, it becomes the denial of this very will in the other phenomenon. Consequently, regarded as will in itself, it struggles with itself through its vehemence and tears itself to pieces. I say that this knowledge presents itself to him instantly, not in the abstract, but as an obscure feeling. This is called remorse, the sting of conscience, or more accurately in this case, the feeling of *wrong committed*.

Wrong, the concept of which we have analysed here in its most universal abstraction, is most completely, peculiarly, and palpably expressed in cannibalism. This is its most distinct and obvious type, the terrible picture of the greatest conflict of the will with itself at the highest grade of its objectification which is man. After this, we have murder, the commission of which is therefore instantly followed with fearful distinctness by the sting of conscience, whose significance we have just stated dryly in the abstract. It inflicts on our peace of mind a wound that a lifetime cannot heal. Our horror at a murder committed, and our shrinking from committing it, correspond to the boundless attachment to life with which every living thing is permeated, precisely as phenomenon of the will-to-live. (Later on, however, we shall analyse still more fully, and raise to the distinctness of a concept, that feeling which accompanies the doing of wrong and evil, in other words, the pangs of conscience.) Intentional mutilation or mere injury of the body of another, indeed every blow, is to be regarded essentially as of the same nature as murder, and as differing therefrom only in degree. Moreover, wrong manifests itself in the subjugation of another individual, in forcing him into slavery, and finally in seizing the property of another, which, in so far as that property is considered as the fruit of his labour, is essentially the same thing as slavery, and is related thereto as mere injury is to murder.

For *property*, that is not taken from a person *without wrong*, can, in view of our explanation of wrong, be only what is made by his own powers. Therefore by taking this, we take the powers of his body from the will objectified in it, in order to make them serve the will objectified in another body. For only in this way does the wrongdoer, by seizing not another's body, but an inanimate thing entirely different from it, break into the sphere of another's affirmation of will, since the powers, the work of another's body, are, so to speak, incorporated in, and identified with, this thing. It follows from this that all genuine, i.e., moral, right to property is originally based simply and solely on elaboration and adaptation, as was pretty generally assumed even before Kant, indeed as the oldest of all the codes of law clearly and finely expresses it: "Wise men who know olden times declare that a cultivated field is the property of him who cut down the wood and cleared and ploughed the land, just as an antelope belongs to the first hunter who mortally wounds it." (*Laws of Manu*, ix, 44.) Kant's whole theory of law is a strange tangle of errors, one leading to another, and he attempts to establish the right to property through first occupation. I can explain this only by Kant's feebleness through old age. For how could the mere declaration of my will to exclude others from the use of a thing give me at once a *right* to it? Obviously the declaration itself requires a foundation of right, instead of Kant's assumption that it is one. How could the person act wrongly or unjustly in himself, i.e., morally, who paid no regard to those claims to the sole possession of a thing which were based on nothing but his own declaration? How would his conscience trouble him about it? For it is so clear and easy to see that there can be absolutely no *just and lawful seizure* of a thing, but only a lawful *appropriation or acquired possession* of it, through our originally applying our own powers to it. A thing may be developed, improved, protected, and preserved from mishaps by the efforts and exertions of some other person, however small these may be; in fact, they might be only the plucking or picking up from the ground fruit that has grown wild. The person who seizes such a thing obviously deprives the other of the result of his labour expended on it. He makes the body of the other serve *his* will instead of the other's will; he affirms his own will beyond its phenomenon to the denial of the other's will; in other words, he does wrong or injustice.[39] On the other hand, the mere enjoyment of a thing, without any cultivation or preservation of it from destruction, gives us just as little right

---

[39] Therefore the establishment of the natural right to property does not require the assumption of two grounds of right side by side with each other, namely that based on *detention* with that based on *formation*, but the latter is always sufficient. But the name *formation* is not really suitable, for the expenditure of effort on a thing need not always be a fashioning or shaping of it.

to it as does the declaration of our will to its sole possession. Therefore, although a family has hunted over a district alone even for a century without having done anything to improve it, it cannot without moral injustice prevent a newcomer from hunting there, if he wants to. Thus morally the so-called right of preoccupation is entirely without foundation; according to it, for the mere past enjoyment of a thing, a man demands a reward into the bargain, namely the exclusive right to enjoy it further. To the man who rests merely on this right, the newcomer might retort with much better right: "Just because you have already enjoyed it for so long, it is right for others also to enjoy it now." There is no morally grounded sole possession of anything that is absolutely incapable of development by improvement or preservation from mishaps, unless it be through voluntary surrender on the part of all others, possibly as a reward for some other service. This, however, in itself presupposes a community or commonwealth ruled by convention, namely the State. The morally established right to property, as deduced above, by its nature gives the possessor of a thing a power over it just as unlimited as that which he has over his own body. From this it follows that he can hand over his property to others by exchange or donation, and those others then possess the thing with the same moral right as he did.

As regards the *doing* of wrong generally, it occurs either through *violence* or through *cunning;* it is immaterial as regards what is morally essential. First, in the case of murder, it is morally immaterial whether I make use of a dagger or of poison; and the case of every bodily injury is analogous. The other cases of wrong can all be reduced to the fact that I, as the wrongdoer, compel the other individual to serve my will instead of his own, or to act according to my will instead of to his. On the path of violence, I attain this through physical causality; but on the path of cunning by means of motivation, in other words, of causality that has passed through knowledge. Through cunning I place before the other man's will *fictitious motives,* on the strength of which he follows *my* will, while believing that he follows *his* own. As knowledge is the medium in which the motives are to be found, I can achieve this only by falsifying his knowledge, and this is the *lie.* The lie always aims at influencing another's will, not at influencing his knowledge alone by itself and as such, but merely as means, namely in so far as it determines his will. For my lying itself, as coming from my will, requires a motive; but only the will of another can be such a motive, not his knowledge in and by itself. As such, his knowledge can never have an influence on *my* will, and hence can never move it, can never be a motive of its aims; only the willing and doing of another can be such a motive, and his knowledge through these, and consequently only indirectly. This holds good not only of all lies that arise from obvious selfishness, but also of those that arise from pure wickedness which wishes to delight in the painful consequences of another person's error that it has caused. Even mere boasting aims at influencing the will and action of others more or less by means of enhanced respect or improved opinion on their part. The mere refusal of a truth, i.e., of a statement in general, is in itself no wrong; but every imposing of a lie is a wrong. The person who refuses to show the right path to the wanderer who has lost his way, does not do him any wrong; but whoever directs him on to a false path certainly does. From what has been said, it follows that every *lie,* like every act of violence, is as such *wrong,* since it has, as such, the purpose of extending the authority of my will over other individuals, of affirming my will by denying theirs, just as violence has. The most complete lie, however, is the *broken contract,* since all the stipulations mentioned are here found completely and clearly together. For, by my entering into a contract, the promised performance of the other person is immediately and admittedly the motive for my performance now taking place. The promises are deliberately and formally exchanged; it is assumed that the truth of the statement made in the contract is in the power of each of the parties. If the other breaks the contract, he has deceived me, and, by substituting merely fictitious motives in my knowledge, he has directed my will in accordance with his intention, has extended the authority of his will to another individual, and has thus committed a distinct and complete wrong. On this are based the moral legality and validity of *contracts.*

Wrong through violence is not so *ignominious* for the perpetrator as wrong through *cunning,* because the former is evidence of physical strength, which in all circumstances powerfully impresses the human race. The latter, on the other hand, by using the crooked way, betrays weakness, and at the same time degrades the perpetrator as a physical and moral being. Moreover, lying and deception can succeed only through the fact that the person who practises them is at the same time compelled to express horror and contempt of them, in order to gain confidence; and his triumph rests on the fact that he is credited with an honesty he does not possess. The deep horror everywhere excited by cunning, perfidy, and treachery, rests on the fact that faithfulness and honesty are the bond which once more binds into a unity from outside the will that is split up into the plurality of individuals, and thus puts a limit to the consequences that arise from that dispersion. Faithlessness and treachery break this last, outer bond, and thus afford boundless scope for the consequences of egoism.

In connexion with our method of discussion, we have found the content of the concept of *wrong* to be that quality of an individual's conduct in which he extends the affirmation of the will that appears in his own body so far that it becomes the denial of the will that appears in the bodies of others. We have also indicated by quite general examples the boundary where the province of wrong begins, in that we determined at the same time its gradations from the highest degree to the lowest by a few main concepts. According to this, the concept of *wrong* is the original and positive; the opposite concept of *right* is the derivative and negative, for we must keep to the concepts, and not to the words. Indeed, there would be no talk of *right* if there were no wrong. The concept of *right* contains merely the negation of wrong, and under it is subsumed every action which is not an overstepping of the boundary above described, in other words, is not a denial of another's will for the stronger affirmation of one's own. This boundary, therefore, divides, as regards a purely *moral* definition, the whole province of possible actions into those that are wrong and those that are right. An action is not wrong the moment it does not encroach, in the way explained above, on the sphere of another's affirmation of will and deny this. Thus, for example, the refusal to help another in dire distress, the calm contemplation of another's death from starvation while we have more than enough, are certainly cruel and diabolical, but are not wrong. It can, however, be said with complete certainty that whoever is capable of carrying uncharitableness and hardness to such lengths, will quite certainly commit any wrong the moment his desires demand it, and no compulsion prevents it.

The concept of *right,* however, as the negation of wrong, finds its principal application, and doubtless also its first origin, in those cases where an attempted wrong by violence is warded off. This warding off cannot itself be wrong, and consequently is right, although the violent action committed in connexion with it, and considered merely in itself and in isolation, would be wrong. It is justified here only by its motive, in other words, it becomes right. If an individual goes so far in the affirmation of his own will that he encroaches on the sphere of the will-affirmation essential to my person as such, and denies this, then my warding off of that encroachment is only the denial of that denial, and to this extent is nothing more on my part than the affirmation of the will appearing essentially and originally in my body, and implicitly expressed by the mere phenomenon of this body; consequently it is not wrong and is therefore right. This means, then, that I have a *right* to deny that other person's denial with what force is necessary to suppress it; and it is easy to see that this may extend even to the killing of the other person whose encroachment as pressing external violence can be warded off with a counteraction somewhat stronger than this, without any wrong, consequently with right. For everything that happens on my part lies always only in the sphere of will-affirmation essential to my person as such, and already expressed by it (which is the scene of the conflict); it does not encroach on that of another, and is therefore only negation of the negation, and hence affirmation, not itself negation. Thus, if the will of another denies my will, as this appears in my body and in the use of its powers for its preservation without denying anyone else's will that observes a like limitation, then I can *compel it without wrong* to desist from this denial, in other words, I have to this extent a *right of compulsion*.

In all cases in which I have a right of compulsion, a perfect right to use *violence* against others, I can, according to the circumstances, just as well oppose another's violence with *cunning* without doing wrong, and consequently I have an actual *right to lie precisely to the extent that I have a right to compulsion*. Therefore, anyone acts with perfect right who assures a highway robber who is searching him that he has nothing more on him. In just the same way, a person acts rightly who by a lie induces a burglar at night to enter a cellar, and there locks him up. A person who is carried off in captivity by robbers, pirates for example, has the right to kill them not only by violence, but even by cunning, in order to gain his freedom. For this reason also, a promise is in no way binding when it has been extorted by a direct bodily act of violence, since the person who suffers such compulsion can with absolute right free himself by killing, not to mention deceiving, his oppressors. Whoever cannot recover his stolen property by violence, commits no wrong if he obtains it by cunning. Indeed, if anyone gambles with me for money stolen from me, I have the right to use false dice against him, since everything I win from him belongs to me already. If anyone should deny this, he would have still more to deny the legality of any ruse adopted in war, of stratagem; this is just the lie founded on fact, and is a proof of the saying of Queen Christina of Sweden that "The words of men are to be esteemed as nothing; hardly are their deeds to be trusted." So sharply does the limit of right border on that of wrong. But I regard it as superfluous to show that all this agrees entirely with what was said above about the illegality of the lie as well as of violence. It can also serve to explain the strange theories of the white lie (*Notlüge*).[40]

Therefore, by all that has so far been said, right and wrong are merely *moral* determinations, i.e., such as have validity with regard to the consideration of human conduct as such, and in reference to the *inner significance of this conduct in itself.* This announces itself directly in consciousness by the fact that, on the one hand, the wrongdoing is accompanied by an inner pain, and this is the merely felt consciousness of the wrongdoer of the excessive strength of will-affirmation in himself which reaches the degree of denial of another's phenomenon of will, as also the fact that, as phenomenon, he is different from the sufferer of wrong, but is yet in himself identical with him. The further explanation of this inner significance of all the pangs of conscience cannot follow until later. On the other hand, the sufferer of wrong is painfully aware of the denial of his will, as it is expressed through his body and its natural wants, for whose satisfaction nature refers him to the powers of this body. At the same time he is also aware that, without doing wrong, he could ward off that denial by every means, unless he lacked the power. This purely moral significance is the only one which right and wrong have for men as men, not as citizens of the State, and which would, in consequence, remain even in the state of nature, without any positive law. It constitutes the basis and content of all that has for this reason been called *natural right,* but might better be called moral right; for its validity does not extend to the suffering, to the external reality, but only to the action and the self-knowledge of the man's individual will which arises in him from this action, and is called *conscience.* However, in a state of nature, it cannot assert itself in every case on other individuals even from outside, and cannot prevent might from reigning instead of right. In the state of nature, it depends on everyone merely in every case to *do* no wrong, but by no means in every case to *suffer* no wrong, which depends on his accidental, external power. Therefore, the concepts of right and wrong, even for the state of nature, are indeed valid and by no means conventional; but they are valid there merely as *moral* concepts, for the self-knowledge of the will in each of us. They are, on the scale of the extremely different degrees of strength with which the will-to-live affirms itself in human individuals, a fixed point like the freezing-point on the thermometer; namely the point

---

[40] The further explanation of the doctrine of right here laid down will be found in my essay *On the Basis of Morality,* § 17, pp. 221-230 of the first edition (pp. 216-226 of the second).

where the affirmation of one's own will becomes the denial of another's, in other words, specifies through wrongdoing the degree of its intensity combined with the degree in which knowledge is involved in the *principium individuationis* (which is the form of knowledge wholly in the service of the will). Now whoever wishes to set aside the purely moral consideration of human conduct, or to deny it, and to consider conduct merely according to its external effect and the result thereof, can certainly, with Hobbes, declare right and wrong to be conventional determinations arbitrarily assumed, and thus not existing at all outside positive law; and we can never explain to him through external experience what does not belong to external experience. Hobbes characterizes his completely empirical way of thinking very remarkably by the fact that, in his book *De Principiis Geometrarum,* he denies the whole of really pure mathematics, and obstinately asserts that the point has extension and the line breadth. Yet we cannot show him a point without extension or a line without breadth; hence we can just as little explain to him the *a priori* nature of mathematics as the *a priori* nature of right, because he pays no heed to any knowledge that is not empirical.

The pure *doctrine of right* is therefore a chapter of *morality,* and is directly related merely to *doing,* not to *suffering;* for the former alone is manifestation of the will, and only this is considered by ethics. Suffering is mere occurrence; morality can have regard to suffering only indirectly, namely to show merely that what is done simply in order not to suffer any wrong, is not wrongdoing. The working out of this chapter of morality would contain the exact definition of the limit to which an individual could go in the affirmation of the will already objectified in his own body, without this becoming the denial of that very will in so far as it appeared in another individual. It would contain also a definition of the actions that transgress this limit, and are consequently wrong, and which can therefore in turn be warded off without wrong. Hence one's own *action* would always remain the object of consideration.

Now *the suffering of wrong* appears as an event in external experience, and, as we have said, there is manifested in it more distinctly than anywhere else the phenomenon of the conflict of the will-to-live with itself, arising from the plurality of individuals and from egoism, both of which are conditioned by the *principium individuationis* which is the form of the world as representation for the knowledge of the individual. We also saw above that a very great part of the suffering essential to human life has its constantly flowing source in the conflict of individuals.

The faculty of reason that is common to all these individuals, and enables them to know not merely the particular case, as the animals do, but also the whole abstractly in its connexion, has taught them to discern the source of that suffering. It has made them mindful of the means of diminishing, or if possible suppressing, this suffering by a common sacrifice which is, however, outweighed by the common advantage resulting therefrom. However agreeable wrongdoing is to the egoism of the individual in particular cases, it still has a necessary correlative in another individual's suffering of wrong, for whom this is a great pain. Now since the faculty of reason, surveying the whole in thought, left the one-sided standpoint of the individual to which it belongs, and for the moment freed itself from attachment thereto, it saw the pleasure of wrongdoing in an individual always outweighed by a relatively greater pain in the other's suffering of wrong. This faculty of reason also found that, because everything was here left to chance, everyone was bound to fear that the pleasures of occasional wrongdoing would much more rarely fall to his lot than would the pain of suffering wrong. Reason recognized from this that, to diminish the suffering spread over all, as well as to distribute it as uniformly as possible, the best and only means was to spare all men the pain of suffering wrong by all men's renouncing the pleasure to be obtained from doing wrong. This means is the *State contract* or the *law*. It is readily devised and gradually perfected by egoism which, by using the faculty of reason, proceeds methodically, and forsakes its one-sided point of view. The origin of the State and of the law, as I have here mentioned, was described by Plato in the *Republic*. Indeed, this origin is essentially the only one, and is determined by the nature of the case. Moreover, in no land can the State have ever had a different origin, just because this mode of origination alone, this aim, makes it into a State. But it is immaterial whether in each definite nation the condition that preceded it was that of a horde of savages independent of one another (anarchy), or that of a horde of slaves arbitrarily ruled by the stronger (despotism). In neither case did any State as yet exist; it first arises through that common agreement, and according as this agreement is more or less unalloyed with anarchy or despotism, the State is more or less perfect. Republics tend to anarchy, monarchies to despotism; the mean of constitutional monarchy, devised on this account, tends to government by factions. In order to found a perfect State, we must begin by producing beings whose nature permits them generally to sacrifice their own good to that of the public. Till then, however, something can be attained by there being *one* family whose welfare is quite inseparable from that of the country, so that, at any rate in the principal matters, it can never advance the one without the other. On this rest the power and advantage of hereditary monarchy.

Now if morality is concerned exclusively with the *doing* of right and wrong, and can accurately define the limits of his conduct for the man who is resolved to do no wrong, political science, the theory of legislation, on the other hand, is concerned solely with the *suffering* of wrong. It would never trouble itself about the *doing* of wrong, were it not on account of its ever-necessary correlative, the suffering of wrong, which is kept in view by legislation as the enemy against which it works. Indeed, if it were possible to conceive a wrongdoing unconnected with the suffering of wrong by another party, then, consistently, the State would not prohibit it at all. Further, since in *morality* the will, the disposition, is the object of consideration and the only real thing, the firm will to commit wrong, restrained and rendered ineffective only by external force, and the actually committed wrong, are for it exactly the same, and at its tribunal it condemns as unjust the person who wills this. On the other hand, will and disposition, merely as such, do not concern the State at all; the *deed* alone does so (whether it be merely attempted or carried out), on account of its correlative, namely the *suffering* of the other party. Thus for the State the deed, the occurrence, is the only real thing; the disposition, the intention, is investigated only in so far as from it the significance of the deed becomes known. Therefore, the State will not forbid anyone constantly carrying about in his head the thought of murder and poison against another, so long as it knows for certain that the fear of sword and wheel will always restrain the effects of that willing. The State also has by no means to eradicate the foolish plan, the inclination to wrongdoing, the evil disposition, but only to place beside every possible motive for committing a wrong a more powerful motive for leaving it undone, in the inescapable punishment. Accordingly, the criminal code is as complete a register as possible of counter-motives to all the criminal actions that can possibly be imagined,—both in the abstract, in order to make concrete application of any case that occurs. Political science or legislation will borrow for this purpose from morality that chapter which is the doctrine of right, and which, besides the inner significance of right and wrong, determines the exact limit between the two, yet simply and solely in order to use the reverse side of it, and to consider from that other side all the limits which morality states are not to be transgressed, if we wish to *do* no wrong, as the limits we must not allow another to transgress, if we wish to *suffer* no wrong, and from which we therefore have a *right* to drive others back.

Therefore these limits are barricaded by laws as much as possible from the passive side. It follows that, as a historian has very wittily been called an inverted prophet, the professor of law is the inverted moralist, and therefore even jurisprudence in the proper sense, i.e., the doctrine of the *rights* that may be asserted, is inverted morality, in the chapter where it teaches the rights that are not to be violated. The concept of wrong and of its negation, right, which is originally *moral,* becomes *juridical* by shifting the starting-point from the active to the passive side, and hence by inversion. This, together with Kant's theory of law, which very falsely derives from his categorical imperative the foundation of the State as a moral duty, has even in quite recent times occasionally been the cause of that very strange error, that the State is an institution for promoting morality, that it results from the endeavour to achieve this, and that it is accordingly directed against egoism. As if the inner disposition, to which alone morality or immorality belongs, the eternally free will, could be modified from outside, and changed by impression or influence! Still more preposterous is the theorem that the State is the condition of freedom in the moral sense, and thus the condition of morality; for freedom lies beyond the phenomenon, to say nothing of human institutions. As we have said, the State is so little directed against egoism in general and as such, that, on the contrary, it is precisely from egoism that it has sprung, and it exists merely to serve it. This egoism well understands itself, proceeds methodically, and goes from the one-sided to the universal point of view, and thus by summation is the common egoism of all. The State is set up on the correct assumption that pure morality, i.e., right conduct from moral grounds, is not to be expected; otherwise it itself would be superfluous. Thus the State, aiming at well-being, is by no means directed against egoism, but only against the injurious consequences of egoism arising out of the plurality of egoistic individuals, reciprocally affecting them, and disturbing their well-being. Therefore, even Aristotle says (*Politics,* iii, 9): Τέλος μὲν οὖν πόλεως τὸ εὖ ζῆν· τοῦτο δ'ἔστιν τὸ ζῆν εὐδαιμόνως καὶ καλῶς. (*Finis civitatis est bene vivere, hoc autem est beate et pulchre vivere.*)[41] Hobbes has also quite correctly and admirably explained this origin and object of the State; the old fundamental principle of all State law and order, *salus publica prima lex esto,*[42] indicates the same thing. If the State attains its object completely, it will produce the same phenomenon as if perfect justice of disposition everywhere prevailed; but the inner

---

[41] "The object of the State is that men may live well, that is, pleasantly and happily." [Tr.]

[42] "Universal welfare must be the first law." [Cicero, *De Legibus,* iii. Tr.]

nature and origin of both phenomena will be the reverse. Thus in the latter case, it would be that no one wished to *do* wrong, but in the former that no one wished to *suffer* wrong, and the means appropriate to this end would be fully employed. Thus the same line can be drawn from opposite directions, and a carnivorous animal with a muzzle is as harmless as a grass-eating animal. But the State cannot go beyond this point; hence it cannot exhibit a phenomenon like that which would spring from universal mutual benevolence and affection. For we found that, by its nature, the State would not forbid a wrongdoing to which corresponded absolutely no suffering of wrong by the other party; and, simply because this is impossible, it prohibits all wrongdoing. So, conversely, in accordance with its tendency directed to the well-being of all, the State would gladly see to it that everyone *experienced* benevolence and works of every kind of human affection, were it not that these also have an inevitable correlative in the *performance* of benevolent deeds and of works of affection. But then every citizen of the State would want to assume the passive, and none the active role, and there would be no reason for exacting the latter from one citizen rather than from another. Accordingly, only the negative, which is just the *right*, not the positive, which is understood by the name of charitable duties, or incomplete obligations, can be *enforced*.

As we have said, legislation borrows the pure doctrine of right, or the theory of the nature and limits of right and wrong, from morality, in order to apply this from the reverse side to its own ends which are foreign to morality, and accordingly to set up positive legislation and the means for maintaining it, in other words the State. Positive legislation is therefore the purely moral doctrine of right applied from the reverse side. This application can be made with reference to the peculiar relations and circumstances of a given people. But only if positive legislation is essentially determined throughout in accordance with the guidance of the pure doctrine of right, and a reason for each of its laws can be indicated in the pure theory of right, is the resultant legislation really a *positive* right, and the State a *legal and just* association, a *State* in the proper sense of the word, a morally admissible, not an immoral, institution. In the opposite case, positive legislation is the establishment of a *positive wrong;* it is a publicly avowed enforced wrong. Such is every despotism, the constitution of most Mohammedan kingdoms; and several parts of many constitutions are of the same kind, as, for example, serfdom, villeinage, and so on. The pure theory of right or natural right, better moral right, though always by inversion, is the basis of every just positive legislation, as pure mathematics is the basis of every branch of applied. The most important points of the pure doctrine of right, as philosophy has to hand it on to legislation for that purpose, are the following: (1) Explanation of the inner and real significance and the origin of the concepts of wrong and right, and of their application and position in morality. (2) The derivation of the right to property. (3) The derivation of the moral validity of contracts, for this is the moral basis of the contract of the State. (4) The explanation of the origin and object of the State, of the relation of this object to morality, and of the appropriate transference of the moral doctrine of right by inversion to legislation, in consequence of this relation. (5) The derivation of the right to punish. The remaining contents of the doctrine of right are mere applications of those principles, a closer definition of the limits of right and wrong in all possible circumstances of life, which are therefore united and arranged under certain aspects and titles. In these particular theories the text-books of pure law are all in fair agreement; only in the principles are they worded very differently, since the principles are always connected with some philosophical system. After having discussed briefly and generally, yet definitely and distinctly, the first four of these main points in accordance with our own system, we have still to speak of the right to punish.

Kant makes the fundamentally false assertion that, apart from the State, there would be no perfect right to property. According to the deduction we have just made, there is property even in the state of nature with perfect natural, i.e., moral, right, which cannot be encroached on without wrong, and without wrong can be defended to the uttermost. On the other hand it is certain that, apart from the State, there is no right to punish. All right to punish is established by positive law alone, which has determined *before* the offence a punishment therefor, and the threat of such punishment should, as countermotive, outweigh all possible motives for that offence. This positive law is to be regarded as sanctioned and acknowledged by all the citizens of the State. Thus it is based on a common contract that the members of the State are in duty bound to fulfil in all circumstances, and hence to inflict the punishment on the one hand, and to endure it on the other; therefore the endurance is with right enforceable. Consequently, the immediate *object of punishment* in the particular case is *fulfilment of the law as a contract;* but the sole object of the *law* is to *deter* from encroachment on the rights of others. For, in order that each may be protected from suffering wrong, all have combined into the State, renounced wrongdoing, and taken upon themselves the burdens of maintaining the State. Thus the law and its fulfilment, namely punishment, are directed essentially to the *future,* not to the *past.* This distinguishes *punishment* from *revenge,,* for revenge is motivated simply by what has happened, and hence by the past as such. All retaliation for wrong by inflicting a pain without any object for the future is revenge, and can have no other purpose than consolation for the suffering one has endured by the sight of the suffering one has caused in another. Such a thing is wickedness and cruelty, and cannot be ethically justified. Wrong inflicted on me by someone does not in any way entitle me to inflict wrong on him. Retaliation of evil for evil without any further purpose cannot be justified, either morally or otherwise, by any ground of reason, and the *jus talionis,* set up as an independent, ultimate principle of the right to punish, is meaningless. Therefore, Kant's theory of punishment as mere requital for requital's sake is a thoroughly groundless and perverse view. Yet it still haunts the writings of many professors of law under all kinds of fine phrases which amount to nothing but empty verbiage; as that, for example, through the punishment the crime is expiated or neutralized and abolished, and many others of the same kind. But no person has the authority or power to set himself up as a purely moral judge and avenger, to punish the misdeeds of another with pains he inflicts on him, and thus to impose penance on him for these misdeeds. On the contrary, this would be a most impudent presumption; therefore the Bible says: "Vengeance is mine; I will repay, saith the Lord." Yet man has the right to provide for the safety of society; but this can be done only by interdicting all those actions denoted by the word "criminal," in order to prevent them by means of countermotives, which are the threatened punishments. This threat can be effective only by carrying out the punishment when the case occurs in spite of it. Therefore that the object of punishment, or more precisely of the penal law, is deterrence from crime is a truth so generally recognized, and indeed self-evident, that in England it is expressed even in the very old form of indictment still made use of in criminal cases by counsel for the Crown, since it ends with the words: "If this be proved, you, the said N.N., ought to be punished with pains of law, to deter others from the like crimes in all time coming." If a prince desires to pardon a criminal who has been justly condemned, his minister will represent to him that the crime will soon be repeated. Object and purpose for the future distinguish punishment from revenge, and punishment has this object only when it is inflicted *in fulfilment of a law.* Only in this way does it proclaim itself to be inevitable and infallible for every future case; and thus it obtains for the law the power to deter; and it is precisely in this that the object of the law consists. Now a Kantian would infallibly reply here that, according to this view, the criminal punished would be used "merely as a *means*." This proposition, repeated so indefatigably by all the Kantians, namely that "Man must always be treated only as an end, never as a means," certainly sounds important, and is therefore very suitable for all those who like to have a formula that relieves them of all further thinking. Closely examined, however, it is an extremely vague, indefinite assertion which reaches its aim quite indirectly; it needs for every case of its application a special explanation, definition, and modification, but, taken generally, it is inadequate, says little, and moreover is problematical. The murderer who is condemned to death according to the law must, it is true, be now used as a mere *means,* and with complete right. For public security, which is the principal object of the State, is disturbed by him; indeed it is abolished if the law remains unfulfilled. The murderer, his life, his person, must be the *means* of fulfilling the law, and thus of re-establishing public security. He is made this with every right for the carrying out of the State contract, into which he also entered in so far as he was a citizen of the State. Accordingly, in order to enjoy security for his life, his freedom, and his property, he had pledged his life, his freedom, and his property for the security of all, and this pledge is now forfeit.

The theory of punishment here advanced, and immediately obvious to sound reason, is certainly in the main no new idea, but only one that was well-nigh supplanted by new errors; and to this extent its very clear statement was necessary. The same thing is contained essentially in what Pufendorf says about it in *De Officio Hominis et Civis* (Book II, chap. 13). Hobbes also agrees with it (*Leviathan,* chaps. 15 and 28). It is well known that Feuerbach has upheld it in our own day. Indeed, it is already found in the utterances of the philosophers of antiquity. Plato clearly expounds it in the *Protagoras* (p. 114, *edit. Bip.*), also in the *Gorgias* (p. 168), and finally in the eleventh book of the *Laws* (p. 165). Seneca perfectly expresses Plato's opinion and the theory of all punishment in the short sentence: *"Nemo prudens punit, quia peccatum est; sed ne peccetur"* (*De Ira,* I, 19).[43]

We have thus learnt to recognize in the State the means by which egoism, endowed with the faculty of reason, seeks to avoid its own evil consequences that turn against itself; and then each promotes the well-being of all, because he sees his own well-being bound up therewith. If the State attained its end completely, then, since it is able to make the rest of nature more and more serviceable by the human

---

[43] "No sensible person punishes because a wrong has been done, but in order that a wrong may not be done." [Tr.]

forces united in it, something approaching a Utopia might finally be brought about to some extent by the removal of all kinds of evil. But up to now the State has always remained very far from this goal; and even with its attainment, innumerable evils, absolutely essential to life, would still always keep it in suffering. Finally, even if all these evils were removed, boredom would at once occupy the place vacated by the other evils. Moreover, even the dissension and discord of individuals can never be wholly eliminated by the State, for they irritate and annoy in trifles where they are prohibited in great things. Finally, Eris, happily expelled from within, at last turns outwards; as the conflict of individuals, she is banished by the institution of the State, but she enters again from without as war between nations, and demands in bulk and all at once, as an accumulated debt, the bloody sacrifices that singly had been withheld from her by wise precaution. Even supposing all this were finally overcome and removed by prudence based on the experience of thousands of years, the result in the end would be the actual over-population of the whole planet, the terrible evil of which only a bold imagination can conjure up in the mind.[44]

§ 63.

We have learnt to recognize *temporal justice,* which has its seat in the State, as requiting or punishing, and have seen that this becomes justice with regard only to the *future.* For without such regard, all punishing and requital of an outrage would remain without justification, would indeed be a mere addition of a second evil to that which had happened, without sense or significance. But it is quite different with *eternal justice,* which has been previously mentioned, and which rules not the State but the world; this is not dependent on human institutions, not subject to chance and deception, not uncertain, wavering, and erring, but infallible, firm, and certain. The concept of retaliation implies time, therefore *eternal justice* cannot be a retributive justice, and hence cannot, like that, admit respite and reprieve, and require time in order to succeed, balancing the evil deed against the evil consequence only by means of time.

---

[44] Cf. chap. 47 of volume 2.

Here the punishment must be so linked with the offence that the two are one.

> Δοκεῖτε πηδᾶν τ'ἀδικήματ' εἰς θεούς
> Πτεροῖσι κἄπειτ' ἐν Διὸς δέλτου πτυχαῖς
> Γράφειν τιν' αὐτά, Ζῆνα δ'εἰσορῶντά νιν
> Θνητοῖς δικάζειν; Οὐδ' ὁ πᾶς ἂν οὐρανός,
> Διὸς γράφοντος τὰς βροτῶν ἁμαρτίας,
> Ἐξαρκέσειεν, οὐδ' ἐκεῖνος ἂν σκοπῶν
> Πέμπειν ἑκάστῳ ζημίαν· ἀλλ' ἡ Δίκη
> Ἐνταῦθά που 'στὶν ἐγγύς, εἰ βούλεσθ' ὁρᾶν.
>   Euripides, *Apud Stobaeus,* Eclog., I, c. 4.
>
> (*Volare pennis scelera ad aetherias domus*
> *Putatis, illic in Jovis tabularia*
> *Scripto referri; tum Jovem lectis super*
> *Sententiam proferre? sed mortalium*
> *Facinora coeli, quantaquanta est, regia*
> *Nequit tenere: nec legendis Juppiter*
> *Et puniendis par est. Est tamen ultio,*
> *Et, si intuemur, illa nos habitat prope.*)[45]

Now that such an eternal justice is actually to be found in the inner nature of the world will soon become perfectly clear to the reader who has grasped in its entirety the thought that we have so far developed.

The phenomenon, the objectivity of the one will-to-live, is the world in all the plurality of its parts and forms. Existence itself, and the kind of existence, in the totality as well as in every part, is only from the will. The will is free; it is almighty. The will appears in everything, precisely as it determines itself in itself and outside time. The world is only the mirror of this willing; and all finiteness, all suffering, all miseries that it contains, belong to the expression of what the will wills, are as they are because the will so wills. Accordingly, with the strictest right, every being supports existence in general, and the existence of its species and of its characteristic individuality, entirely as it is and in surroundings as they are, in a world such as it is, swayed by chance and error, fleeting, transient, always suffering; and in all that happens or indeed can happen to the individual, justice is always done to it. For the will belongs to it; and as

---

[45] "Do you think that crimes ascend to the gods on wings, and then someone has to record them there on the tablet of Jove, and that Jove looks at them and pronounces judgement on men? The whole of heaven would not be great enough to contain the sins of men, were Jove to record them all, nor would he to review them and assign to each his punishment. No! the punishment is already here, if only you will see it." [Tr.]

the will is, so is the world. Only this world itself—no other—can bear the responsibility for its existence and its nature; for how could anyone else have assumed this responsibility? If we want to know what human beings, morally considered, are worth as a whole and in general, let us consider their fate as a whole and in general. This fate is want, wretchedness, misery, lamentation, and death. Eternal justice prevails; if they were not as a whole contemptible, their fate as a whole would not be so melancholy. In this sense we can say that the world itself is the tribunal of the world. If we could lay all the misery of the world in one pan of the scales, and all its guilt in the other, the pointer would certainly show them to be in equilibrium.

But of course the world does not exhibit itself to knowledge which has sprung from the will to serve it, and which comes to the individual as such in the same way as it finally discloses itself to the inquirer, namely as the objectivity of the one and only will-to-live, which he himself is. On the contrary, the eyes of the uncultured individual are clouded, as the Indians say, by the veil of Maya. To him is revealed not the thing-in-itself, but only the phenomenon in time and space, in the *principium individuationis,* and in the remaining forms of the principle of sufficient reason. In this form of his limited knowledge he sees not the inner nature of things, which is one, but its phenomena as separated, detached, innumerable, very different, and indeed opposed. For pleasure appears to him as one thing, and pain as quite another; one man as tormentor and murderer, another as martyr and victim; wickedness as one thing, evil as another. He sees one person living in pleasure, abundance, and delights, and at the same time another dying in agony of want and cold at the former's very door. He then asks where retribution is to be found. He himself in the vehement pressure of will, which is his origin and inner nature, grasps the pleasures and enjoyments of life, embraces them firmly, and does not know that, by this very act of his will, he seizes and hugs all the pains and miseries of life, at the sight of which he shudders. He sees the evil, he sees the wickedness in the world; but, far from recognizing that the two are but different aspects of the phenomenon of the one will-to-live, he regards them as very different, indeed as quite opposed. He often tries to escape by wickedness, in other words, by causing another's suffering, from the evil, from the suffering of his own individuality, involved as he is in the *principium individuationis,* deluded by the veil of Maya. Just as the boatman sits in his small boat, trusting his frail craft in a stormy sea that is boundless in every direction, rising and falling with the howling, mountainous waves, so in the midst of a world full of suffering and misery the individual man calmly sits, supported by and trusting the *principium individuationis,* or the way in which the individual knows things as phenomenon. The boundless world, everywhere full of suffering in the infinite past, in the infinite future, is strange to him, is indeed a fiction. His vanishing person, his extensionless present, his momentary gratification, these alone have reality for him; and he does everything to maintain them, so long as his eyes are not opened by a better knowledge. Till then, there lives only in the innermost depths of his consciousness the wholly obscure presentiment that all this is indeed not really so strange to him, but has a connexion with him from which the *principium individuationis* cannot protect him. From this presentiment arises that ineradicable *dread,* common to all human beings (and possibly even to the more intelligent animals), which suddenly seizes them, when by any chance they become puzzled over the *principium individuationis,* in that the principle of sufficient reason in one or other of its forms seems to undergo an exception. For example, when it appears that some change has occurred without a cause, or a deceased person exists again; or when in any other way the past or the future is present, or the distant is near. The fearful terror at anything of this kind is based on the fact that they suddenly become puzzled over the forms of knowledge of the phenomenon which alone hold their own individuality separate from the rest of the world. This separation, however, lies only in the phenomenon and not in the thing-in-itself; and precisely on this rests eternal justice. In fact, all temporal happiness stands, and all prudence proceeds, on undermined ground. They protect the person from accidents, and supply it with pleasures, but the person is mere phenomenon, and its difference from other individuals, and exemption from the sufferings they bear, rest merely on the form of the phenomenon, on the *principium individuationis.* According to the true nature of things, everyone has all the sufferings of the world as his own; indeed, he has to look upon all merely possible sufferings as actual for him, so long as he is the firm and constant will-to-live, in other words, affirms life with all his strength. For the knowledge that sees through the *principium individuationis,* a happy life in time, given by chance or won from it by shrewdness, amid the sufferings of innumerable others, is only a beggar's dream, in which he is a king, but from which he must awake, in order to realize that only a fleeting illusion had separated him from the suffering of his life.

Eternal justice is withdrawn from the view that is involved in knowledge following the principle of sufficient reason, in the *principium individuationis;* such a view altogether misses it, unless it vindicates it in some way by fictions. It sees the wicked man, after misdeeds and cruelties of every kind, live a life of pleasure, and quit

the world undisturbed. It sees the oppressed person drag out to the
end a life full of suffering without the appearance of an avenger or
vindicator. But eternal justice will be grasped and comprehended
only by the man who rises above that knowledge which proceeds on
the guiding line of the principle of sufficient reason and is bound to
individual things, who recognizes the Ideas, who sees through the
principium individuationis, and who is aware that the forms of the
phenomenon do not apply to the thing-in-itself. Moreover, it is this
man alone who, by dint of the same knowledge, can understand the
true nature of virtue, as will soon be disclosed to us in connexion
with the present discussion, although for the practice of virtue this
knowledge in the abstract is by no means required. Therefore, it becomes clear to the man who has reached the knowledge referred to,
that, since the will is the in-itself of every phenomenon, the misery
inflicted on others and that experienced by himself, the bad and the
evil, always concern the one and the same inner being, although the
phenomena in which the one and the other exhibit themselves stand
out as quite different individuals, and are separated even by wide
intervals of time and space. He sees that the difference between the
inflicter of suffering and he who must endure it is only phenomenon,
and does not concern the thing-in-itself which is the will that lives in
both. Deceived by the knowledge bound to its service, the will here
fails to recognize itself; seeking enhanced well-being in *one* of its
phenomena, it produces great suffering in *another.* Thus in the fierceness and intensity of its desire it buries its teeth in its own flesh, not
knowing that it always injures only itself, revealing in this form
through the medium of individuation the conflict with itself which it
bears in its inner nature. Tormentor and tormented are one. The
former is mistaken in thinking he does not share the torment, the
latter in thinking he does not share the guilt. If the eyes of both were
opened, the inflicter of the suffering would recognize that he lives in
everything that suffers pain in the whole wide world, and, if endowed
with the faculty of reason, ponders in vain over why it was called
into existence for such great suffering, whose cause and guilt it does
not perceive. On the other hand, the tormented person would see
that all the wickedness that is or ever was perpetrated in the world
proceeds from that will which constitutes also *his* own inner being,
and appears also in *him.* He would see that, through this phenomenon
and its affirmation, he has taken upon himself all the sufferings resulting from such a will, and rightly endures them so long as he is this
will. In *Life a Dream* the prophetic poet Calderón speaks from this
knowledge:

Pues el delito mayor
Del hombre es haber nacido.

(For man's greatest offence
Is that he has been born.)

How could it fail to be an offence, as death comes after it in accordance with an eternal law? In that verse Calderón has merely expressed the Christian dogma of original sin.

The vivid knowledge of eternal justice, of the balance inseparably uniting the *malum culpae* with the *malum poenae,* demands the complete elevation above individuality and the principle of its possibility. It will therefore always remain inaccessible to the majority of men, as also will the pure and distinct knowledge of the real nature of all virtue which is akin to it, and which we are about to discuss. Hence the wise ancestors of the Indian people have directly expressed it in the *Vedas,* permitted only to the three twice-born castes, or in the esoteric teaching, namely in so far as concept and language comprehend it, and in so far as their method of presentation, always pictorial and even rhapsodical, allows it. But in the religion of the people, or in exoteric teaching, they have communicated it only mythically. We find the direct presentation in the *Vedas,* the fruit of the highest human knowledge and wisdom, the kernel of which has finally come to us in the *Upanishads* as the greatest gift to the nineteenth century. It is expressed in various ways, but especially by the fact that all beings of the world, living and lifeless, are led past in succession in the presence of the novice, and that over each of them is pronounced the word which has become a formula, and as such has been called the *Mahavakya: Tatoumes,* or more correctly, *tat tvam asi,* which means "This art thou." [46] For the people, however, that great truth, in so far as it was possible for them to comprehend it with their limited mental capacity, was translated into the way of knowledge following the principle of sufficient reason. From its nature, this way of knowledge is indeed quite incapable of assimilating that truth purely and in itself; indeed it is even in direct contradiction with it; yet in the form of a myth, it received a substitute for it which was sufficient as a guide to conduct. For the myth makes intelligible the ethical significance of conduct through figurative description in the method of knowledge according to the principle of sufficient reason, which is eternally foreign to this significance. This is the object of religious teachings, since these are all the mythical garments of the truth which is inaccessible to the crude human intellect. In this sense,

---

[46] *Oupnek'hat,* Vol. I, pp. 60 *seqq.*

that myth might be called in Kant's language a postulate of practical reason (*Vernunft*), but, considered as such, it has the great advantage of containing absolutely no elements but those which lie before our eyes in the realm of reality, and thus of being able to support all its concepts with perceptions. What is here meant is the myth of the transmigration of souls. This teaches that all sufferings inflicted in life by man on other beings must be expiated in a following life in this world by precisely the same sufferings. It goes to the length of teaching that a person who kills only an animal, will be born as just such an animal at some point in endless time, and will suffer the same death. It teaches that wicked conduct entails a future life in suffering and despised creatures in this world; that a person is accordingly born again in lower castes, or as a woman, or as an animal, as a pariah or Chandala, as a leper, a crocodile, and so on. All the torments threatened by the myth are supported by it with perceptions from the world of reality, through suffering creatures that do not know how they have merited the punishment of their misery; and it does not need to call in the assistance of any other hell. On the other hand, it promises as reward rebirth in better and nobler forms, as Brahmans, sages, or saints. The highest reward awaiting the noblest deeds and most complete resignation, which comes also to the woman who in seven successive lives has voluntarily died on the funeral pile of her husband, and no less to the person whose pure mouth has never uttered a single lie—such a reward can be expressed by the myth only negatively in the language of this world, namely by the promise, so often occurring, of not being reborn any more: *non adsumes iterum existentiam apparentem;*[47] or as the Buddhists, admitting neither *Vedas* nor castes, express it: "You shall attain to Nirvana, in other words, to a state or condition in which there are not four things, namely birth, old age, disease, and death."

Never has a myth been, and never will one be, more closely associated with a philosophical truth accessible to so few, than this very ancient teaching of the noblest and oldest of peoples. Degenerate as this race may now be in many respects, this truth still prevails with it as the universal creed of the people, and it has a decided influence on life today, as it had four thousand years ago. Therefore Pythagoras and Plato grasped with admiration that *non plus ultra* of mythical expression, took it over from India or Egypt, revered it, applied it, and themselves believed it, to what extent we know not. We, on the contrary, now send to the Brahmans English clergymen and evangelical linen-weavers, in order out of sympathy to put them right, and to point out to them that they are created out of nothing, and that

---

[47] "You will not again assume phenomenal existence." [Tr.]

they ought to be grateful and pleased about it. But it is just the same as if we fired a bullet at a cliff. In India our religions will never at any time take root; the ancient wisdom of the human race will not be supplanted by the events in Galilee. On the contrary, Indian wisdom flows back to Europe, and will produce a fundamental change in our knowledge and thought.

§ 64.

From our description of eternal justice, which is not mythical but philosophical, we will now proceed to the kindred consideration of the ethical significance of conduct, and of conscience, which is merely the felt knowledge of that significance. Here, however, I wish first of all to draw attention to two characteristics of human nature which may help to make clear how the essential nature of that eternal justice and the unity and identity of the will in all its phenomena, on which that justice rests, are known to everyone, at least as an obscure feeling.

After a wicked deed has been done, it affords satisfaction not only to the injured party, who is often filled with a desire for revenge, but also to the completely indifferent spectator, to see that the person who caused pain to another suffers in turn exactly the same measure of pain; and this quite independently of the object (which we have demonstrated) of the State in punishing, which is the basis of criminal law. It seems to me that nothing is expressed here but consciousness of that eternal justice, which, however, is at once misunderstood and falsified by the unpurified mind. Such a mind, involved in the *principium individuationis,* commits an amphiboly of the concepts, and demands of the phenomenon what belongs only to the thing-in-itself. It does not see to what extent the offender and the offended are in themselves one, and that it is the same inner nature which, not recognizing itself in its own phenomenon, bears both the pain and the guilt. On the contrary, it longs to see again the pain in the same individual to whom the guilt belongs. A man might have a very high degree of wickedness, which yet might be found in many others, though not matched with other qualities such as are found in him, namely one who was far superior to others through unusual mental powers, and who, accordingly, inflicted unspeakable sufferings on millions of others—a world conqueror, for instance. Most people would like to demand that such a man should at some time and in some place atone for all those sufferings by an equal amount of pain; for they do not recognize how the tormentor and tormented are in themselves one, and that it is the same will by which these latter exist and live, which appears in the former, and precisely through him attains to the most distinct revelation of its inner nature. This will likewise suffers both in the oppressed and in the oppressor, and in the latter indeed all the more, in proportion as the consciousness has greater clearness and distinctness, and the will a greater vehemence. But Christian ethics testifies to the fact that the deeper knowledge, no longer involved in the *principium individuationis,* a knowledge from which all virtue and nobleness of mind proceed, no longer cherishes feelings demanding retaliation. Such ethics positively forbids all retaliation of evil for evil, and lets eternal justice rule in the province of the thing-in-itself which is different from that of the phenomenon ("Vengeance is mine; I will repay, saith the Lord." Rom. xii, 19).

A much more striking, but likewise much rarer, characteristic of human nature, which expresses that desire to draw eternal justice into the province of experience, i.e., of individuation, and at the same time indicates a felt consciousness that, as I put it above, the will-to-live acts out the great tragedy and comedy at its own expense, and that the same one will lives in all phenomena—such a characteristic, I say, is the following. Sometimes we see a man so profoundly indignant at a great outrage, which he has experienced or perhaps only witnessed, that he deliberately and irretrievably stakes his own life in order to take vengeance on the perpetrator of that outrage. We see him search for years for some mighty oppressor, finally murder him, and then himself die on the scaffold, as he had foreseen. Indeed, often he did not attempt in any way to avoid this, since his life was of value to him only as a means for revenge. Such instances are found especially among the Spaniards.[48] Now if we carefully consider the spirit of that mania for retaliation, we find it to be very different from common revenge, which desires to mitigate suffering endured by the sight of suffering caused; indeed, we find that what it aims at deserves to be called not so much revenge as punishment. For in it there is really to be found the intention of an effect on the future through the example, and without any selfish aim either for the avenging individual, who perishes in the attempt, or for a society

---

[48] That Spanish bishop, who in the last war simultaneously poisoned himself and the French generals at his table, is an instance of this; as also are various facts of that war. Examples are also found in Montaigne, Book 2, chap. 12.

that secures its own safety through laws. This punishment is carried out by the individual, not by the State; nor is it in fulfilment of a law; on the contrary, it always concerns a deed which the State would not or could not punish, and whose punishment it condemns. It seems to me that the wrath which drives such a man so far beyond the limits of all self-love, springs from the deepest consciousness that he himself is the whole will-to-live that appears in all creatures through all periods of time, and that therefore the most distant future, like the present, belongs to him in the same way, and cannot be a matter of indifference to him. Affirming this will, he nevertheless desires that in the drama that presents its inner nature no such monstrous outrage shall ever appear again; and he wishes to frighten every future evildoer by the example of a revenge against which there is no wall of defence, as the fear of death does not deter the avenger. The will-to-live, though it still affirms itself here, no longer depends on the individual phenomenon, on the individual person, but embraces the Idea of man. It desires to keep the phenomenon of this Idea pure from such a monstrous and revolting outrage. It is a rare, significant, and even sublime trait of character by which the individual sacrifices himself, in that he strives to make himself the arm of eternal justice, whose true inner nature he still fails to recognize.

§ 65.

In all the observations on human conduct hitherto made, we have been preparing for the final discussion, and have greatly facilitated the task of raising to abstract and philosophical clearness, and of demonstrating as a branch of our main idea, the real ethical significance of conduct which in life is described by the words *good* and *bad,* and is thus made perfectly intelligible.

First of all, however, I wish to trace back to their proper meaning these concepts of *good* and *bad,* which are treated by the philosophical writers of our times in a very odd way as simple concepts, that is, as concepts incapable of any analysis. I will do this so that the reader shall not remain involved in some hazy and obscure notion that they contain more than is actually the case, and that they state in and by themselves all that is here necessary. I am able to do this because in ethics I myself am as little disposed to take refuge behind the word *good* as I was earlier to hide behind the words *beautiful* and *true,* in order that, by an added "-ness," supposed nowadays to have a special σεμνότης (solemnity), and hence to be of help in various cases, and by a solemn demeanour, I might persuade people that by uttering three such words I had done more than express three concepts which are very wide and abstract, which therefore contain nothing at all, and are of very different origin and significance. Who is there indeed, who has made himself acquainted with the writings of our times, and has not finally become sick of those three words, admirable as are the things to which they originally refer, after he has been made to see a thousand times how those least capable of thinking believe they need only utter these three words with open mouth and the air of infatuated sheep, in order to have spoken great wisdom?

The explanation of the concept *true* is already given in the essay *On the Principle of Sufficient Reason,* chap. V, §§ 29 *seqq.* The content of the concept *beautiful* received for the first time its proper explanation in the whole of our third book. We will now trace the meaning of the concept *good;* this can be done with very little trouble. This concept is essentially relative, and denotes the *fitness or suitableness of an object to any definite effort of the will.* Therefore everything agreeable to the will in any one of its manifestations, and fulfilling the will's purpose, is thought of through the concept *good,* however different in other respects such things may be. We therefore speak of good eating, good roads, good weather, good weapons, good auguries, and so on; in short, we call everything good that is just as we want it to be. Hence a thing can be good to one person, and the very opposite to another. The concept of good is divided into two subspecies, that of the directly present satisfaction of the will in each case, and that of its merely indirect satisfaction concerning the future, in other words, the agreeable and the useful. The concept of the opposite, so long as we are speaking of beings without knowledge, is expressed by the word *bad,* more rarely and abstractly by the word *evil,* which therefore denotes everything that is not agreeable to the striving of the will in each case. Like all other beings that can come into relation with the will, persons who favour, promote, and befriend aims that happen to be desired are called *good,* with the same meaning, and always with the retention of the relative that is seen, for example, in the expression: "This is good for me, but not for you." Those, however, whose character induces them generally not to hinder another's efforts of will as such, but rather to promote them, and who are therefore consistently helpful, benevolent, friendly, and charitable, are called *good,* on account of this relation of their mode of conduct to the will of others in general. In the case of beings with knowledge (animals and human beings), the opposite concept is denoted in German, and has been for about a hundred years in French also, by a word different from that used in the case of beings without knowledge, namely *böse, méchant* (spiteful, malicious, unkind); whereas in almost all other languages this distinction does not occur. *Malus,* κακός, *cattivo, bad,* are used both of human beings and of inanimate things which are opposed to the aims of a definite individual will. Thus, having started entirely from the passive side of the good, the discussion could only later pass to the active side, and investigate the mode of conduct of the man called *good,* in reference no longer to others, but to himself. It could then specially set itself the task of explaining the purely objective esteem produced in others by such conduct, as well as the characteristic contentment with himself obviously engendered in the person, for he purchases this even with sacrifices of another kind. On the other hand, it could also explain the inner pain that accompanies the evil disposition, however many advantages it may bring to the man who cherishes it. Now from this sprang the ethical systems, both the philosophical and those supported by religious teachings. Both always attempt to associate happiness in some way with virtue, the former either by the principle of contradiction, or even by that of sufficient reason, and thus to make happiness either identical with, or the consequence of, virtue, always sophistically; but the latter by asserting the existence of worlds other than the one that can be known to experience.[49] On the other hand, from

---

[49] Incidentally, it should be observed that what gives every positive religious doctrine its great strength, the essential point by which it takes firm possession of souls, is wholly its ethical side; though not directly as such, but as it appears firmly united and interwoven with the rest of the mythical dogma that is characteristic of every religious teaching, and as explicable only through this. So much is this the case that, although the ethical significance of actions cannot possibly be explained in accordance with the principle of sufficient reason, but every myth follows this principle, believers nevertheless consider the ethical significance of conduct and its myth to be quite inseparable, indeed as positively one, and regard every attack on the myth as an attack on right and virtue. This reaches such lengths that, in monotheistic nations, atheism or godlessness has become the synonym for absence of all morality. To priests such confusions of concepts are welcome, and only in consequence of them could that fearful monster, fanaticism, arise and govern not merely single individuals who are exceedingly perverse and wicked, but whole nations, and finally embody itself in the West as the Inquisition, a thing that, to the honour of mankind, has happened only once in its history. According to the latest and most authentic reports, in Madrid alone (whilst in the rest of Spain there were also many such ecclesiastical dens of murderers) the Inquisition in three hundred years put three hundred thousand human beings

our discussion, the inner nature of virtue will show itself as a striving in quite the opposite direction to that of happiness, which is that of well-being and life.

It follows from the above remarks that the *good* is according to its concept τῶν πρὸς τί,[50] hence every good is essentially relative; for it has its essential nature only in its relation to a desiring will. Accordingly, *absolute good* is a contradiction; highest good, *summum bonum,* signifies the same thing, namely in reality a final satisfaction of the will, after which no fresh willing would occur; a last motive, the attainment of which would give the will an imperishable satisfaction. According to the discussion so far carried on in this fourth book, such a thing cannot be conceived. The will can just as little through some satisfaction cease to will always afresh, as time can end or begin; for the will there is no permanent fulfilment which completely and for ever satisfies its craving. It is the vessel of the Danaides; there is no highest good, no absolute good, for it, but always a temporary good only. However, if we wish to give an honorary, or so to speak an emeritus, position to an old expression that from custom we do not like entirely to discard, we may, metaphorically and figuratively, call the complete self-effacement and denial of the will, true will-lessness, which alone stills and silences for ever the craving of the will; which alone gives that contentment that cannot again be disturbed; which alone is world-redeeming; and which we shall now consider at the conclusion of our whole discussion; the absolute good, the *summum bonum;* and we may regard it as the only radical cure for the disease against which all other good things, such as all fulfilled wishes and all attained happiness, are only palliatives, anodynes. In this sense, the Greek τέλος and also *finis bonorum* meet the case even better. So much for the words *good* and *bad;* now to the matter itself.

If a person is always inclined to do *wrong* the moment the inducement is there and no external power restrains him, we call him *bad.* In accordance with our explanation of wrong, this means that such a man not only affirms the will-to-live as it appears in his own body, but in this affirmation goes so far as to deny the will that appears in other individuals. This is shown by the fact that he demands their powers for the service of his own will, and tries to destroy their existence when they stand in the way of the efforts of his will. The ultimate source of this is a high degree of egoism, the

---

to a painful death at the stake, on account of matters of faith. All fanatics and zealots should be at once reminded of this whenever they want to make themselves heard.

[50] "Something belonging to the relative." [Tr.]

nature of which has already been explained. Two different things are at once clear here; *firstly,* that in such a person an excessively vehement will-to-live, going far beyond the affirmation of his own body, expresses itself; and *secondly,* that this knowledge, devoted entirely to the principle of sufficient reason and involved in the *principium individuationis,* definitely confines itself to the complete difference, established by this latter principle, between his own person and all others. He therefore seeks only his own well-being, and is completely indifferent to that of all others. On the contrary, their existence is wholly foreign to him, separated from his by a wide gulf; indeed, he really regards them only as masks without any reality. And these two qualities are the fundamental elements of the bad character.

This great intensity of willing is in and by itself and directly a constant source of suffering, firstly because all willing as such springs from want, and hence from suffering. (Therefore, as will be remembered from the third book, the momentary silencing of all willing, which comes about whenever as pure will-less subject of knowing, the correlative of the Idea, we are devoted to aesthetic contemplation, is a principal element of pleasure in the beautiful.) Secondly because, through the causal connexion of things, most desires must remain unfulfilled, and the will is much more often crossed than satisfied. Consequently, much intense willing always entails much intense suffering. For all suffering is simply nothing but unfulfilled and thwarted willing, and even the pain of the body, when this is injured or destroyed, is as such possible only by the fact that the body is nothing but the will itself become object. Now, for the reason that much intense suffering is inseparable from much intense willing, the facial expression of very bad people already bears the stamp of inward suffering. Even when they have obtained every external happiness, they always look unhappy, whenever they are not transported by momentary exultation, or are not pretending. From this inward torment, absolutely and directly essential to them, there finally results even that delight at the suffering of another which has not sprung from egoism, but is disinterested; this is *wickedness* proper, and rises to the pitch of *cruelty.* For this the suffering of another is no longer a means for attaining the ends of its own will, but an end in itself. The following is a more detailed explanation of this phenomenon. Since man is phenomenon of the will illuminated by the clearest knowledge, he is always measuring and comparing the actual and felt satisfaction of his will with the merely possible satisfaction put before him by knowledge. From this springs envy; every privation is infinitely aggravated by the pleasure of others, and relieved by the knowledge that others also endure the same privation. The evils that are common to all and inseparable from human life do not trouble us much, just as little as do those that belong to the climate and to the whole country. The calling to mind of sufferings greater than our own stills their pain; the sight of another's sufferings alleviates our own. Now a person filled with an extremely intense pressure of will wants with burning eagerness to accumulate everything, in order to slake the thirst of egoism. As is inevitable, he is bound to see that all satisfaction is only apparent, and that the attained object never fulfils the promise held out by the desired object, namely the final appeasement of the excessive pressure of will. He sees that, with fulfilment, the wish changes only its form, and now torments under another form; indeed, when at last all wishes are exhausted, the pressure of will itself remains, even without any recognized motive, and makes itself known with terrible pain as a feeling of the most frightful desolation and emptiness. If from all this, which with ordinary degrees of willing is felt only in a smaller measure, and produces only the ordinary degree of dejection, there necessarily arise an excessive inner torment, an eternal unrest, an incurable pain in the case of a person who is the phenomenon of the will reaching to extreme wickedness, he then seeks indirectly the alleviation of which he is incapable directly, in other words, he tries to mitigate his own suffering by the sight of another's, and at the same time recognizes this as an expression of his power. The suffering of another becomes for him an end in itself; it is a spectacle over which he gloats; and so arises the phenomenon of cruelty proper, of bloodthirstiness, so often revealed by history in the Neros and Domitians, in the African Deys, in Robespierre and others.

The thirst for revenge is closely related to wickedness. It repays evil with evil, not from regard for the future, which is the character of punishment, but merely on account of what has happened and is past as such, and thus disinterestedly, not as means but as end, in order to gloat over the offender's affliction caused by the avenger himself. What distinguishes revenge from pure wickedness, and to some extent excuses it, is an appearance of right, in so far as the same act that is now revenge, if ordered by law, in other words, according to a previously determined and known rule and in a society that has sanctioned such a rule, would be punishment, and hence justice or right.

Besides the suffering described, and inseparable from wickedness, as having sprung from a single root, namely a very intense will, there is associated with wickedness another particular pain quite different from this. This pain is felt in the case of every bad action, whether it be mere injustice arising out of egoism, or pure wickedness; and according to the length of its duration it is called the *sting of conscience* or the *pangs of conscience.* Now he who remembers, and has present in his mind, the foregoing contents of this fourth book, especially the truth explained at its beginning, namely that life itself is always sure and certain to the will-to-live as its mere copy or mirror, and also the discussion on eternal justice, will find that, in accordance with those remarks, the sting of conscience can have no other meaning than the following; in other words, its content, expressed in the abstract, is as follows, in which two parts are distinguished, but again these entirely coincide, and must be thought of as wholly united.

However densely the veil of Maya envelops the mind of the bad person, in other words, however firmly involved he is in the *principium individuationis,* according to which he regards his person as absolutely different from every other and separated from it by a wide gulf, a knowledge to which he adheres with all his might, since it alone suits and supports his egoism, so that knowledge is almost always corrupted by the will, there is nevertheless roused in the innermost depths of his consciousness the secret presentiment that such an order of things is only phenomenon, but that, in themselves, things are quite different. He has a presentiment that, however much time and space separate him from other individuals and the innumerable miseries they suffer, indeed suffer through him; however much time and space present these as quite foreign to him, yet in themselves and apart from the representation and its forms, it is the one will-to-live appearing in them all which, failing to recognize itself here, turns its weapons against itself, and, by seeking increased well-being in one of its phenomena, imposes the greatest suffering on another. He dimly sees that he, the bad person, is precisely this whole will; that in consequence he is not only the tormentor but also the tormented, from whose suffering he is separated and kept free only by a delusive dream, whose form is space and time. But this dream vanishes, and he sees that in reality he must pay for the pleasure with the pain, and that all suffering which he knows only as possible actually concerns him as the will-to-live, since possibility and actuality, near and remote in time and space, are different only for the knowledge of the individual, only by means of the *principium individuationis,* and not in themselves. It is this truth which mythically, in other words, adapted to the principle of sufficient reason, is expressed by the transmigration of souls, and is thus translated into the form of the phenomenon. Nevertheless it has its purest expression, free from all admixture, precisely in that obscurely felt but inconsolable misery called the pangs of conscience. But this also springs from a *second* immediate knowledge closely associated with the first, namely knowledge of the strength with which the will-to-live affirms itself in the wicked individual, extending as it does far beyond his individual phenomenon to the complete denial of the same will as it appears in individuals foreign to him. Consequently, the wicked man's inward alarm at his own deed, which he tries to conceal from himself, contains that presentiment of the nothingness and mere delusiveness of the *principium individuationis,* and of the distinction established by this principle between him and others. At the same time it contains the knowledge of the vehemence of his own will, of the strength with which he has grasped life and attached himself firmly to it, this very life whose terrible side he sees before him in the misery of those he oppresses, and with which he is nevertheless so firmly entwined that, precisely in this way, the most terrible things come from himself as a means to the fuller affirmation of his own will. He recognizes himself as the concentrated phenomenon of the will-to-live; he feels to what degree he is given up to life, and therewith also to the innumerable sufferings essential to it, for it has infinite time and infinite space to abolish the distinction between possibility and actuality, and to change all the sufferings as yet merely *known* by him into those *felt and experienced* by him. The millions of years of constant rebirth certainly continue merely in conception, just as the whole of the past and future exists only in conception. Occupied time, the form of the phenomenon of the will, is only the present, and time for the individual is always new; he always finds himself as newly sprung into existence. For life is inseparable from the will-to-live, and its form is only the Now. Death (the repetition of the comparison must be excused) is like the setting of the sun, which is only apparently engulfed by the night, but actually, itself the source of all light, burns without intermission, brings new days to new worlds, and is always rising and always setting. Beginning and end concern only the individual by means of time, of the form of this phenomenon for the representation. Outside time lie only the will, Kant's thing-in-itself, and its adequate objectivity, namely Plato's Idea. Suicide, therefore, affords no escape; what everyone *wills* in his innermost being, that must he *be;* and what everyone *is,* is just what he *wills.* Therefore, besides the merely felt knowledge of the delusiveness and nothingness of the forms of the representation that separate individuals, it is the self-knowledge of one's own will and of its degree that gives conscience its sting. The course of life brings out the picture of the empirical character, whose original is the intelligible character, and the wicked person is horrified at this picture. It is immaterial whether the picture is produced in large characters, so that the world shares his horror, or in characters so small that he alone sees it; for it directly concerns him alone. The past would be a matter of indifference as mere phenomenon, and could not disturb or alarm the conscience, did not the character feel itself free from all time and incapable of alteration by it, so long as it does not deny itself. For this reason, things that happened long ago still continue to weigh heavily on the conscience. The prayer, "Lead me not into temptation" means "Let me not see who I am." In the strength with which the wicked person affirms life, and which is exhibited to him in the suffering he perpetrates on others, he estimates how far he is from the surrender and denial of that very will, from the only possible deliverance from the world and its miseries. He sees to what extent he belongs to the world, and how firmly he is bound to it. The *known* suffering of others has not been able to move him; he is given up to life and to *felt or experienced* suffering. It remains doubtful whether this will ever break and overcome the vehemence of his will.

This explanation of the significance and inner nature of the *bad,* which as mere feeling, i.e., *not* as distinct, abstract knowledge, is the content of the *pangs of conscience,* will gain even more clarity and completeness from a consideration of the *good* carried out in precisely the same way. This will consider the *good* as a quality of the human will, and finally of complete resignation and holiness that result from this quality, when it has reached the highest degree. For opposites always elucidate each other, and the day simultaneously reveals both itself and the night, as Spinoza has admirably said.

§ 66.

Morality without argumentation and reasoning, that is, mere moralizing, cannot have any effect, because it does not motivate. But a morality that *does* motivate can do so only by acting on self-love. Now what springs from this has no moral worth. From this it follows that no genuine virtue can be brought about through morality and abstract knowledge in general, but that such virtue must spring from the intuitive knowledge that recognizes in another's individuality the same inner nature as in one's own.

For virtue does indeed result from knowledge, but not from abstract knowledge communicable through words. If this were so, virtue could be taught, and by expressing here in the abstract its real nature and the knowledge at its foundation, we should have ethically improved everyone who comprehended this. But this is by no means the case. On the contrary, we are as little able to produce a virtuous person by ethical discourses or sermons as all the systems of aesthetics from Aristotle's downwards have ever been able to produce a poet. For the concept is unfruitful for the real inner nature of virtue, just as it is for art; and only in a wholly subordinate position can it serve as an instrument in elaborating and preserving what has been ascertained and inferred in other ways. *Velle non discitur.*[51] In fact, abstract dogmas are without influence on virtue, i.e., on goodness of disposition; false dogmas do not disturb it, and true ones hardly support it. Actually it would be a bad business if the principal thing in a man's life, his ethical worth that counts for eternity, depended on something whose attainment was so very much subject to chance as are dogmas, religious teachings, and philosophical arguments. For morality dogmas have merely the value that the man who is virtuous from another kind of knowledge shortly to be discussed has in them a scheme or formula. According to this, he renders to his own faculty of reason an account, for the most part only fictitious, of his non-egoistical actions, the nature of which it, in other words he himself, does not *comprehend*. With such an account he has been accustomed to rest content.

Dogmas can of course have a powerful influence on *conduct,* on outward actions, and so can custom and example (the latter, because the ordinary man does not trust his judgement, of whose weakness he is conscious, but follows only his own or someone else's experience); but the disposition is not altered in this way.[52] All abstract knowledge gives only motives, but, as was shown above, motives can alter only the direction of the will, never the will itself. But all communicable knowledge can affect the will as motive only; therefore, however the will is guided by dogmas, what a person really and generally wills still always remains the same. He has obtained different ideas merely of the ways in which it is to be attained, and imaginary motives guide him like real ones. Thus, for instance, it is immaterial, as regards his ethical worth, whether he makes donations

---

[51] "Willing cannot be taught." [Tr.]

[52] The Church would say they are mere *opera operata,* that are of no avail unless grace gives the faith leading to regeneration; but of this later on.

to the destitute, firmly persuaded that he will receive everything back tenfold in a future life, or spends the same sum on improving an estate that will bear interest, late certainly, but all the more secure and substantial. And the man who, for the sake of orthodoxy, commits the heretic to the flames, is just as much a murderer as the bandit who earns a reward by killing; indeed, as regards inner circumstances, so also is he who massacres the Turks in the Promised Land, if, like the burner of heretics, he really does it because he imagines he will thus earn a place in heaven. For these are anxious only about themselves, about their egoism, just like the bandit, from whom they differ only in the absurdity of their means. As we have already said, the will can be reached from outside only through motives; but these alter merely the way in which it manifests itself, never the will itself. *Velle non discitur* (Willing cannot be taught).

In the case of good deeds, however, the doer of which appeals to dogmas, we must always distinguish whether these dogmas are really the motive for them, or whether, as I said above, they are nothing more than the delusive account by which he tries to satisfy his own faculty of reason about a good deed that flows from quite a different source. He performs such a deed because he is *good,* but he does not understand how to explain it properly, since he is not a philosopher, and yet he would like to think something with regard to it. But the distinction is very hard to find, since it lies in the very depths of our inner nature. Therefore we can hardly ever pronounce a correct moral judgement on the actions of others, and rarely on our own. The deeds and ways of acting of the individual and of a nation can be very much modified by dogmas, example, and custom. In themselves, however, all deeds (*opera operata*) are merely empty figures, and only the disposition that leads to them gives them moral significance. But this disposition can be actually quite the same, in spite of a very different external phenomenon. With an equal degree of wickedness one person can die on the wheel, and another peacefully in the bosom of his family. It can be the same degree of wickedness that expresses itself in one nation in the crude characteristics of murder and cannibalism, and in another finely and delicately in miniature, in court intrigues, oppressions, and subtle machinations of every kind; the inner nature remains the same. It is conceivable that a perfect State, or even perhaps a complete dogma of rewards and punishments after death firmly believed in, might prevent every crime. Politically much would be gained in this way; morally, absolutely nothing; on the contrary, only the mirroring of the will through life would be checked.

Genuine goodness of disposition, disinterested virtue, and pure nobleness of mind, therefore, do not come from abstract knowledge; yet they do come from knowledge. But it is a direct and intuitive knowledge that cannot be reasoned away or arrived at by reasoning; a knowledge that, just because it is not abstract, cannot be communicated, but must dawn on each of us. It therefore finds its real and adequate expression not in words, but simply and solely in deeds, in conduct, in the course of a man's life. We who are here looking for the theory of virtue, and who thus have to express in abstract terms the inner nature of the knowledge lying at its foundation, shall nevertheless be unable to furnish that knowledge itself in this expression, but only the concept of that knowledge. We thus always start from conduct, in which alone it becomes visible, and refer to such conduct as its only adequate expression. We only interpret and explain this expression, in other words, express in the abstract what really takes place in it.

Now before we speak of the *good* proper, in contrast to the *bad* that has been described, we must touch on the mere negation of the bad as an intermediate stage; this is *justice*. We have adequately explained above what right and wrong are; therefore we can briefly say here that the man who voluntarily recognizes and accepts that merely moral boundary between wrong and right, even where no State or other authority guarantees it, and who consequently, according to our explanation, never in the affirmation of his own will goes to the length of denying the will that manifests itself in another individual, is *just*. Therefore, in order to increase his own well-being, he will not inflict suffering on others; that is to say, he will not commit any crime; he will respect the rights and property of everyone. We now see that for such a just man the *principium individuationis* is no longer an absolute partition as it is for the bad; that he does not, like the bad man, affirm merely his own phenomenon of will and deny all others; that others are not for him mere masks, whose inner nature is quite different from his. On the contrary, he shows by his way of acting that he *again recognizes* his own inner being, namely the will-to-live as thing-in-itself, in the phenomenon of another given to him merely as representation. Thus he finds himself again in that phenomenon up to a certain degree, namely that of doing no wrong, i.e., of not injuring. Now in precisely this degree he sees through the *principium individuationis,* the veil of Maya. To this extent he treats the inner being outside himself like his own; he does not injure it.

If we examine the innermost nature of this justice, there is to be found in it the intention not to go so far in the affirmation of one's own will as to deny the phenomena of will in others by compelling them to serve one's own will. We shall therefore want to provide for others just as much as we benefit from them. The highest degree of this justice of disposition, which, however, is always associated with goodness proper, the character of this last being no longer merely negative, extends so far that a person questions his right to inherited property, desires to support his body only by his own powers, mental and physical, feels every service rendered by others, every luxury, as a reproach, and finally resorts to voluntary poverty. Thus we see how Pascal would not allow the performance of any more services when he turned to asceticism, although he had servants enough. In spite of his constant bad health, he made his own bed, fetched his own food from the kitchen, and so on. (*Vie de Pascal,* by his Sister, p. 19.) Quite in keeping with this, it is reported that many Hindus, even rajas, with great wealth, use it merely to support and maintain their families, their courts, and their establishment of servants, and follow with strict scrupulousness the maxim of eating nothing but what they have sown and reaped with their own hands. Yet at the bottom of this there lies a certain misunderstanding, for just because the individual is rich and powerful, he is able to render such important services to the whole of human society that they counterbalance inherited wealth, for the security of which he is indebted to society. In reality, that excessive justice of such Hindus is more than justice, indeed actual renunciation, denial of the will-to-live, asceticism, about which we shall speak last of all. On the other hand, pure idleness and living through the exertions of others with inherited property, without achieving anything, can indeed be regarded as morally wrong, even though it must remain right according to positive laws.

We have found that voluntary justice has its innermost origin in a certain degree of seeing through the *principium individuationis,* while the unjust man remains entirely involved in this principle. This seeing through can take place not only in the degree required for justice, but also in the higher degree that urges a man to positive benevolence and well-doing, to philanthropy. Moreover, this can happen however strong and energetic the will that appears in such an individual may be in itself. Knowledge can always counterbalance it, can teach a man to resist the temptation to do wrong, and can even produce every degree of goodness, indeed of resignation. Therefore the good man is in no way to be regarded as an originally weaker phenomenon of will than the bad, but it is knowledge that masters in him the blind craving of will. Certainly there are individuals who merely seem to be good-natured on account of the weakness of the will that appears in them; but what they are soon shows itself in the fact that they are not capable of any considerable self-conquest, in order to perform a just or good deed.

Now if, as a rare exception, we come across a man who possesses a considerable income, but uses only a little of it for himself, and gives all the rest to persons in distress, whilst he himself forgoes many pleasures and comforts, and we try to make clear to ourselves the action of this man, we shall find, quite apart from the dogmas by which he himself will make his action intelligible to his faculty of reason, the simplest general expression and the essential character of his way of acting to be that he *makes less distinction than is usually made between himself and others.* This very distinction is in the eyes of many so great, that the suffering of another is a direct pleasure for the wicked, and a welcome means to their own well-being for the unjust. The merely just person is content not to cause it; and generally most people know and are acquainted with innumerable sufferings of others in their vicinity, but do not decide to alleviate them, because to do so they would have to undergo some privation. Thus a strong distinction seems to prevail in each of all these between his own ego and another's. On the other hand, to the noble person, whom we have in mind, this distinction is not so significant. The *principium individuationis,* the form of the phenomenon, no longer holds him so firmly in its grasp, but the suffering he sees in others touches him almost as closely as does his own. He therefore tries to strike a balance between the two, denies himself pleasures, undergoes privations, in order to alleviate another's suffering. He perceives that the distinction between himself and others, which to the wicked man is so great a gulf, belongs only to a fleeting, deceptive phenomenon. He recognizes immediately, and without reasons or arguments, that the in-itself of his own phenomenon is also that of others, namely that will-to-live which constitutes the inner nature of everything, and lives in all; in fact, he recognizes that this extends even to the animals and to the whole of nature; he will therefore not cause suffering even to an animal.[53]

[53] Man's right over the life and power of animals rests on the fact that, since with the enhanced clearness of consciousness suffering increases in like measure, the pain that the animal suffers through death or work is still not so great as that which man would suffer through merely being deprived of the animal's flesh or strength. Therefore in the affirmation of his own existence, man can go so far as to deny the existence of the animal. In this way, the will-to-live as a whole endures less suffering than if the opposite course were adopted. At the same time, this determines the extent to which man may, without wrong, make use of the powers of animals. This limit, however, is often exceeded, especially in the case of beasts of burden, and of hounds used in hunting. The activities of societies for the prevention of

He is now just as little able to let others starve, while he himself has enough and to spare, as anyone would one day be on short commons, in order on the following day to have more than he can enjoy. For the veil of Maya has become transparent for the person who performs works of love, and the deception of the *principium individuationis* has left him. Himself, his will, he recognizes in every creature, and hence in the sufferer also. He is free from the perversity with which the will-to-live, failing to recognize itself, here in one individual enjoys fleeting and delusive pleasures, and there in another individual suffers and starves in return for these. Thus this will inflicts misery and endures misery, not knowing that, like Thyestes, it is eagerly devouring its own flesh. Then it here laments its unmerited suffering, and there commits an outrage without the least fear of Nemesis, always merely because it fails to recognize itself in the phenomenon of another, and thus does not perceive eternal justice, involved as it is in the *principium individuationis,* and so generally in that kind of knowledge which is governed by the principle of sufficient reason. To be cured of this delusion and deception of Maya and to do works of love are one and the same thing; but the latter is the inevitable and infallible symptom of that knowledge.

The opposite of the sting of conscience, whose origin and significance were explained above, is the *good conscience,* the satisfaction we feel after every disinterested deed. It springs from the fact that such a deed, as arising from the direct recognition of our own inner being-in-itself in the phenomenon of another, again affords us the verification of this knowledge, of the knowledge that our true self exists not only in our own person, in this particular phenomenon, but in everything that lives. In this way, the heart feels itself enlarged, just as by egoism it feels contracted. For just as egoism concentrates our interest on the particular phenomenon of our own individuality, and then knowledge always presents us with the innumerable perils that continually threaten this phenomenon, whereby anxiety and care become the keynote of our disposition, so the knowledge that every living thing is just as much our own inner being-in-itself as is our own person, extends our interest to all that lives; and in this way the heart is enlarged. Thus through the reduced interest in our own self, the anxious care for that self is attacked and restricted at its root; hence the calm and confident serenity afforded

---

cruelty to animals are therefore directed especially against these. In my opinion, that right does not extend to vivisection, particularly of the higher animals. On the other hand, the insect does not suffer through its death as much as man suffers through its sting. The Hindus do not see this.

by a virtuous disposition and a good conscience, and the more distinct appearance of this with every good deed, since this proves to ourselves the depth of that disposition. The egoist feels himself surrounded by strange and hostile phenomena, and all his hope rests on his own well-being. The good person lives in a world of friendly phenomena; the well-being of any of these is his own well-being. Therefore, although the knowledge of the lot of man generally does not make his disposition a cheerful one, the permanent knowledge of his own inner nature in everything that lives nevertheless gives him a certain uniformity and even serenity of disposition. For the interest extended over innumerable phenomena cannot cause such anxiety as that which is concentrated on one phenomenon. The accidents that concern the totality of individuals equalize themselves, while those that befall the individual entail good or bad fortune.

Therefore, although others have laid down moral principles which they gave out as precepts for virtue and laws necessarily to be observed, I cannot do this, as I have said already, because I have no "ought" or law to hold before the eternally free will. On the other hand, in reference to my discussion, what corresponds and is analogous to that undertaking is that purely theoretical truth, and the whole of my argument can be regarded as a mere elaboration thereof, namely that the will is the in-itself of every phenomenon, but itself as such is free from the forms of that phenomenon, and so from plurality. In reference to conduct, I do not know how this truth can be more worthily expressed than by the formula of the *Veda* already quoted: *Tat tvam asi* ("This art thou!"). Whoever is able to declare this to himself with clear knowledge and firm inward conviction about every creature with whom he comes in contact, is certain of all virtue and bliss, and is on the direct path to salvation.

Now before I go farther, and show, as the last item in my discussion, how love, whose origin and nature we know to be seeing through the *principium individuationis,* leads to salvation, that is, to the entire surrender of the will-to-live, i.e., of all willing, and also how another path, less smooth yet more frequented, brings man to the same goal, a paradoxical sentence must first be here stated and explained. This is not because it is paradoxical, but because it is true, and is necessary for the completeness of the thought I have to express. It is this: "All love (ἀγάπη, *caritas*) is compassion or sympathy."

§ 67.

We have seen how, from seeing through the *principium individuationis*, in the lesser degree justice arises, and in the higher degree real goodness of disposition, a goodness that shows itself as pure, i.e., disinterested, affection towards others. Now where this becomes complete, the individuality and fate of others are treated entirely like one's own. It can never go farther, for no reason exists for preferring another's individuality to one's own. Yet the great number of the other individuals whose whole well-being or life is in danger can outweigh the regard for one's own particular well-being. In such a case, the character that has reached the highest goodness and perfect magnanimity will sacrifice its well-being and its life completely for the well-being of many others. So died Codrus, Leonidas, Regulus, Decius Mus, and Arnold von Winkelried; so does everyone die who voluntarily and consciously goes to certain death for his friends, or for his native land. And everyone also stands at this level who willingly takes suffering and death upon himself for the maintenance of what conduces and rightfully belongs to the welfare of all mankind, in other words, for universal, important truths, and for the eradication of great errors. So died Socrates and Giordano Bruno; and so did many a hero of truth meet his death at the stake at the hands of the priests.

Now with reference to the paradox above expressed, I must call to mind the fact that we previously found suffering to be essential to, and inseparable from, life as a whole, and that we saw how every desire springs from a need, a want, a suffering, and that every satisfaction is therefore only a pain removed, not a positive happiness brought. We saw that the joys certainly lie to the desire in stating that they are a positive good, but that in truth they are only of a negative nature, and only the end of an evil. Therefore, whatever goodness, affection, and magnanimity do for others is always only an alleviation of their sufferings; and consequently what can move them to good deeds and to works of affection is always only *knowledge of the suffering of others,* directly intelligible from one's own suffering, and put on a level therewith. It follows from this, however, that pure affection (ἀγάπη, *caritas*) is of its nature sympathy or compassion. The suffering alleviated by it, to which every unsatisfied desire belongs, may be great or small. We shall therefore have no hesitation in saying that the mere concept is as unfruitful for genuine virtue as it is for genuine art; that all true and pure affection is sympathy or compassion, and all love that is not sympathy is selfishness. All this will be in direct contradiction to Kant, who recognizes all true goodness and all virtue as such, only if they have resulted from abstract reflection, and in fact from the concept of duty and the categorical imperative, and who declares felt sympathy to be weakness, and by no means virtue. Selfishness is ἔρως, sympathy or compassion is ἀγάπη. Combinations of the two occur frequently; even genuine friendship is always a mixture of selfishness and sympathy. Selfishness lies in the pleasure in the presence of the friend, whose individuality corresponds to our own, and it almost invariably constitutes the greatest part; sympathy shows itself in a sincere participation in the friend's weal and woe, and in the disinterested sacrifices made for the latter. Even Spinoza says: *Benevolentia nihil aliud est, quam cupiditas ex commiseratione orta*[54] (*Ethics,* iii, pr. 27, cor. 3 schol.). As confirmation of our paradoxical sentence, it may be observed that the tone and words of the language and the caresses of pure love entirely coincide with the tone of sympathy or compassion. Incidentally, it may be observed also that sympathy and pure love are expressed in Italian by the same word, *pietà*.

This is also the place to discuss one of the most striking peculiarities of human nature, *weeping,* which, like laughter, belongs to the manifestations that distinguish man from the animal. Weeping is by no means a positive manifestation of pain, for it occurs where pains are least. In my opinion, we never weep directly over pain that is felt, but always only over its repetition in reflection. Thus we pass from the felt pain, even when it is physical, to a mere mental picture or representation of it; we then find our own state so deserving of sympathy that, if another were the sufferer, we are firmly and sincerely convinced that we would be full of sympathy and love to help him. Now we ourselves are the object of our own sincere sympathy; with the most charitable disposition, we ourselves are most in need of help. We feel that we endure more than we could see another endure, and in this peculiarly involved frame of mind, in which the directly felt suffering comes to perception only in a doubly indirect way, pictured as the suffering of another and sympathized with as such, and then suddenly perceived again as directly our own; in such a frame of mind nature finds relief through

---

[54] "Benevolence is nothing but a desire sprung from compassion." [Tr.]

that curious physical convulsion. Accordingly, *weeping is sympathy with ourselves,* or sympathy thrown back to its starting-point. It is therefore conditioned by the capacity for affection and sympathy, and by the imagination. Therefore people who are either hard-hearted or without imagination do not readily weep; indeed weeping is always regarded as a sign of a certain degree of goodness of character, and it disarms anger. This is because it is felt that who-ever is still able to weep must also necessarily be capable of affec-tion, i.e., of sympathy towards others, for this enters in the way described into that mood that leads to weeping. The description which Petrarch gives of the rising of his own tears, naïvely and truly expressing his feeling, is entirely in accordance with the explana-tion that has been given:

> *I' vo pensando: e nel pensar m'assale*
> *Una pietà si forte di me stesso,*
> *Che mi conduce spesso*
> *Ad alto lagrimar, ch' i' non soleva.*[55]

What has been said is also confirmed by the fact that children who have been hurt generally cry only when they are pitied, and hence not on account of the pain, but on account of the conception of it. That we are moved to tears not by our own sufferings, but by those of others, happens in the following way; either in imagina-tion we put ourselves vividly in the sufferer's place, or we see in his fate the lot of the whole of humanity, and consequently above all our own fate. Thus in a very roundabout way, we always weep about ourselves; we feel sympathy with ourselves. This seems also to be a main reason for the universal, and hence natural, weeping in cases of death. It is not the mourner's loss over which he weeps; he would be ashamed of such egoistical tears, instead of sometimes being ashamed of not weeping. In the first place, of course, he weeps over the fate of the deceased; yet he weeps also when for the de-ceased death was a desirable deliverance after long, grave, and in-curable sufferings. In the main, therefore, he is seized with sym-pathy over the lot of the whole of mankind that is given over to finiteness. In consequence of this, every life, however ambitious and often rich in deeds, must become extinct and nothing. In this lot of mankind, however, the mourner sees first of all his own lot, and this the more, the more closely he was related to the deceased, and

---

[55] "As I wander deep in thought, so strong a *sympathy with myself* comes over me, that I must often weep aloud, a thing I am otherwise not accustomed to do." [Tr.]

most of all therefore when the deceased was his father. Although to this father life was a misery through age and sickness, and through his helplessness a heavy burden to the son, the son nevertheless weeps bitterly over the death of his father for the reason already stated.[56]

§ 68.

After this digression on the identity of pure love with sympathy, the turning back of sympathy on to our own individuality having as its symptom the phenomenon of weeping, I take up again the thread of our discussion of the ethical significance of conduct, to show how, from the same source from which all goodness, affection, virtue, and nobility of character spring, there ultimately arises also what I call denial of the will-to-live.

Just as previously we saw hatred and wickedness conditioned by egoism, and this depending on knowledge being entangled in the *principium individuationis,* so we found as the source and essence of justice, and, when carried farther to the highest degrees, of love and magnanimity, that penetration of the *principium individuationis.* This penetration alone, by abolishing the distinction between our own individuality and that of others, makes possible and explains perfect goodness of disposition, extending to the most disinterested love, and the most generous self-sacrifice for others.

Now, if seeing through the *principium individuationis,* if this direct knowledge of the identity of the will in all its phenomena, is present in a high degree of distinctness, it will at once show an influence on the will which goes still farther. If that veil of Maya, the *principium individuationis,* is lifted from the eyes of a man to such an extent that he no longer makes the egoistical distinction between himself and the person of others, but takes as much interest in the sufferings of other individuals as in his own, and thus is not only benevolent

---

[56] Cf. chap. 47 of volume 2. It is scarcely necessary to remind the reader that the whole of the ethics given in outline in §§ 61-67 has received a more detailed and complete description in my essay *On the Basis of Morality.*

and charitable in the highest degree, but even ready to sacrifice his own individuality whenever several others can be saved thereby, then it follows automatically that such a man, recognizing in all beings his own true and innermost self, must also regard the endless sufferings of all that lives as his own, and thus take upon himself the pain of the whole world. No suffering is any longer strange or foreign to him. All the miseries of others, which he sees and is so seldom able to alleviate, all the miseries of which he has indirect knowledge, and even those he recognizes merely as possible, affect his mind just as do his own. It is no longer the changing weal and woe of his person that he has in view, as is the case with the man still involved in egoism, but, as he sees through the *principium individuationis,* everything lies equally near to him. He knows the whole, comprehends its inner nature, and finds it involved in a constant passing away, a vain striving, an inward conflict, and a continual suffering. Wherever he looks, he sees suffering humanity and the suffering animal world, and a world that passes away. Now all this lies just as near to him as only his own person lies to the egoist. Now how could he, with such knowledge of the world, affirm this very life through constant acts of will, and precisely in this way bind himself more and more firmly to it, press himself to it more and more closely? Thus, whoever is still involved in the *principium individuationis,* in egoism, knows only particular things and their relation to his own person, and these then become ever renewed *motives* of his willing. On the other hand, that knowledge of the whole, of the inner nature of the thing-in-itself, which has been described, becomes the *quieter* of all and every willing. The will now turns away from life; it shudders at the pleasures in which it recognizes the affirmation of life. Man attains to the state of voluntary renunciation, resignation, true composure, and complete willlessness. At times, in the hard experience of our own sufferings or in the vividly recognized suffering of others, knowledge of the vanity and bitterness of life comes close to us who are still enveloped in the veil of Maya. We would like to deprive desires of their sting, close the entry to all suffering, purify and sanctify ourselves by complete and final resignation. But the illusion of the phenomenon soon ensnares us again, and its motives set the will in motion once more; we cannot tear ourselves free. The allurements of hope, the flattery of the present, the sweetness of pleasures, the well-being that falls to the lot of our person amid the lamentations of a suffering world governed by chance and error, all these draw us back to it, and rivet the bonds anew. Therefore Jesus says: "It is easier for a camel to go through the eye of a needle, than for a rich man to enter into the Kingdom of God." [57]

If we compare life to a circular path of red-hot coals having a few cool places, a path that we have to run over incessantly, then the man entangled in delusion is comforted by the cool place on which he is just now standing, or which he sees near him, and sets out to run over the path. But the man who sees through the *principium individuationis,* and recognizes the true nature of things-in-themselves, and thus the whole, is no longer susceptible of such consolation; he sees himself in all places simultaneously, and withdraws. His will turns about; it no longer affirms its own inner nature, mirrored in the phenomenon, but denies it. The phenomenon by which this becomes manifest is the transition from virtue to *asceticism.* In other words, it is no longer enough for him to love others like himself, and to do as much for them as for himself, but there arises in him a strong aversion to the inner nature whose expression is his own phenomenon, to the will-to-live, the kernel and essence of that world recognized as full of misery. He therefore renounces precisely this inner nature, which appears in him and is expressed already by his body, and his action gives the lie to his phenomenon, and appears in open contradiction thereto. Essentially nothing but phenomenon of the will, he ceases to will anything, guards against attaching his will to anything, tries to establish firmly in himself the greatest indifference to all things. His body, healthy and strong, expresses the sexual impulse through the genitals, but he denies the will, and gives the lie to the body; he desires no sexual satisfaction on any condition. Voluntary and complete chastity is the first step in asceticism or the denial of the will-to-live. It thereby denies the affirmation of the will which goes beyond the individual life, and thus announces that the will, whose phenomenon is the body, ceases with the life of this body. Nature, always true and naïve, asserts that, if this maxim became universal, the human race would die out; and after what was said in the second book about the connexion of all phenomena of will, I think I can assume that, with the highest phenomenon of will, the weaker reflection of it, namely the animal world, would also be abolished, just as the half-shades vanish with the full light of day. With the complete abolition of knowledge the rest of the world would of itself also vanish into nothing, for there can be no object without a subject. Here I would like to refer to a passage in the *Veda* where it says: "As in this world hungry children press round their mother, so do all beings await the holy obla-

---

[57] Matthew xix, 24. [Tr.]

tion." (*Asiatic Researches,* Vol. viii; Colebrooke, *On the Vedas, Epitome of the Sama Veda; idem, Miscellaneous Essays,* Vol. i, p. 88.)[58] Sacrifice signifies resignation generally, and the rest of nature has to expect its salvation from man who is at the same time priest and sacrifice. In fact, it is worth mentioning as extremely remarkable that this thought has also been expressed by the admirable and immeasurably profound Angelus Silesius in the little poem entitled "Man brings all to God"; it runs:

> "Man! all love you; great is the throng around you:
> All flock to you that they may attain to God."

But an even greater mystic, Meister Eckhart, whose wonderful writings have at last (1857) become accessible to us through the edition of Franz Pfeiffer, says (p. 459) wholly in the sense here discussed: "I confirm this with Christ, for he says: 'I, if I be lifted up from the earth, will draw all things [men] unto me' (John xii, 32). So shall the good man draw all things up to God, to the source whence they first came. The masters certify to us that all creatures are made for the sake of man. This is proved in all creatures by the fact that one creature makes use of another; the ox makes use of the grass, the fish of the water, the bird of the air, the animals of the forest. Thus all creatures come to the profit of the good man. A good man bears to God one creature in the other." He means that because, in and with himself, man also saves the animals, he makes use of them in this life. It seems to me indeed that that difficult passage in the Bible, Rom. viii, 21-24, is to be interpreted in this sense.

Even in Buddhism there is no lack of expressions of this matter; for example, when the Buddha, while still a Bodhisattva, has his horse saddled for the last time, for the flight from his father's house into the wilderness, he says to the horse in verse: "Long have you existed in life and in death, but now you shall cease to carry and to draw. Bear me away from here just this once, O Kantakana, and when I have attained the Law (have become Buddha), I shall not forget you." (*Foe Koue Ki,* trans. by Abel Rémusat, p. 233.)

Asceticism shows itself further in voluntary and intentional poverty, which arises not only *per accidens,* since property is given away to alleviate the sufferings of others, but which is here an end in itself; it is to serve as a constant mortification of the will, so that

---

[58] The passage is taken from the *Chandogya Upanishad,* V, 24, 5, and in literal translation is: "Just as hungry children here sit round their mother, so do all beings sit round the agnihotram" (the fire-sacrifice offered by the knower of Brahman). [Tr.]

satisfaction of desires, the sweets of life, may not again stir the will, of which self-knowledge has conceived a horror. He who has reached this point still always feels, as living body, as concrete phenomenon of will, the natural tendency to every kind of willing; but he deliberately suppresses it, since he compels himself to refrain from doing all that he would like to do, and on the other hand to do all that he would not like to do, even if this has no further purpose than that of serving to mortify the will. As he himself denies the will that appears in his own person, he will not resist when another does the same thing, in other words, inflicts wrong on him. Therefore, every suffering that comes to him from outside through chance or the wickedness of others is welcome to him; every injury, every ignominy, every outrage. He gladly accepts them as the opportunity for giving himself the certainty that he no longer affirms the will, but gladly sides with every enemy of the will's phenomenon that is his own person. He therefore endures such ignominy and suffering with inexhaustible patience and gentleness, returns good for all evil without ostentation, and allows the fire of anger to rise again within him as little as he does the fire of desires. Just as he mortifies the will itself, so does he mortify its visibility, its objectivity, the body. He nourishes it sparingly, lest its vigorous flourishing and thriving should animate afresh and excite more strongly the will, of which it is the mere expression and mirror. Thus he resorts to fasting, and even to self-castigation and self-torture, in order that, by constant privation and suffering, he may more and more break down and kill the will that he recognizes and abhors as the source of his own suffering existence and of the world's. Finally, if death comes, which breaks up the phenomenon of this will, the essence of such will having long since expired through free denial of itself except for the feeble residue which appears as the vitality of this body, then it is most welcome, and is cheerfully accepted as a longed-for deliverance. It is not merely the phenomenon, as in the case of others, that comes to an end with death, but the inner being itself that is abolished; this had a feeble existence merely in the phenomenon.[59] This last slender bond is now severed; for him who ends thus, the world has at the same time ended.

---

[59] This idea is expressed by a fine simile in the ancient Sanskrit philosophical work *Sankhya Karika:* "Yet the soul remains for a time clothed with the body, just as the potter's wheel continues to spin after the pot has been finished, in consequence of the impulse previously given to it. Only when the inspired soul separates itself from the body and nature ceases for it, does its complete salvation take place." Colebrooke, "On the Philosophy of the Hindus": *Miscellaneous Essays,* Vol. I, p. 259. Also in the *Sankhya Carica* by Horace Wilson, § 67, p. 184.

And what I have described here with feeble tongue, and only in general terms, is not some philosophical fable, invented by myself and only of today. No, it was the enviable life of so many saints and great souls among the Christians, and even more among the Hindus and Buddhists, and also among the believers of other religions. Different as were the dogmas that were impressed on their faculty of reason, the inner, direct, and intuitive knowledge from which alone all virtue and holiness can come is nevertheless expressed in precisely the same way in the conduct of life. For here also is seen the great distinction between intuitive and abstract knowledge, a distinction of such importance and of general application in the whole of our discussion, and one which hitherto has received too little notice. Between the two is a wide gulf; and, in regard to knowledge of the inner nature of the world, this gulf can be crossed only by philosophy. Intuitively, or *in concreto,* every man is really conscious of all philosophical truths; but to bring them into his abstract knowledge, into reflection, is the business of the philosopher, who neither ought to nor can do more than this.

Thus it may be that the inner nature of holiness, of self-renunciation, of mortification of one's own will, of asceticism, is here for the first time expressed in abstract terms and free from everything mythical, as *denial of the will-to-live,* which appears after the complete knowledge of its own inner being has become for it the quieter of all willing. On the other hand, it has been known directly and expressed in deed by all those saints and ascetics who, in spite of the same inner knowledge, used very different language according to the dogmas which their faculty of reason had accepted, and in consequence of which an Indian, a Christian, or a Lamaist saint must each give a very different account of his own conduct; but this is of no importance at all as regards the fact. A saint may be full of the most absurd superstition, or, on the other hand, may be a philosopher; it is all the same. His conduct alone is evidence that he is a saint; for, in a moral regard, it springs not from abstract knowledge, but from intuitively apprehended, immediate knowledge of the world and of its inner nature, and is expressed by him through some dogma only for the satisfaction of his faculty of reason. It is therefore just as little necessary for the saint to be a philosopher as for the philosopher to be a saint; just as it is not necessary for a perfectly beautiful person to be a great sculptor, or for a great sculptor to be himself a beautiful person. In general, it is a strange demand on a moralist that he should commend no other virtue than that which he himself possesses. To repeat abstractly, universally, and distinctly in concepts the whole inner nature of the world, and thus to deposit it as a reflected image in permanent concepts always ready for the faculty of reason, this and nothing else is philosophy. I recall the passage from Bacon quoted in the first book.

But my description, given above, of the denial of the will-to-live, or of the conduct of a beautiful soul, of a resigned and voluntarily expiating saint, is only abstract and general, and therefore cold. As the knowledge from which results the denial of the will is intuitive and not abstract, it finds its complete expression not in abstract concepts, but only in the deed and in conduct. Therefore, in order to understand more fully what we express philosophically as denial of the will-to-live, we have to learn to know examples from experience and reality. Naturally we shall not come across them in daily experience: *nam omnia praeclara tam difficilia quam rara sunt,*[60] as Spinoza admirably says. Therefore, unless we are made eyewitnesses by a specially favourable fate, we shall have to content ourselves with the biographies of such persons. Indian literature, as we see from the little that is so far known to us through translations, is very rich in descriptions of the lives of saints, penitents, Samanas, Sannyasis, and so on. Even the well-known *Mythologie des Indous* of Madame de Polier, although by no means praiseworthy in every respect, contains many excellent examples of this kind (especially in Vol. 2, chapter 13). Among Christians there is also no lack of examples affording us the illustrations that we have in mind. Let us see the biographies, often badly written, of those persons sometimes called saintly souls, sometimes pietists, quietists, pious enthusiasts, and so on. Collections of such biographies have been made at various times, such as Tersteegen's *Leben heiliger Seelen,* Reiz's *Geschichte der Wiedergeborenen* in our own day, a collection by Kanne which, with much that is bad, yet contains some good, especially the *Leben der Beata Sturmin.* To this category very properly belongs the life of St. Francis of Assisi, that true personification of asceticism and prototype of all mendicant friars. His life, described by his younger contemporary St. Bonaventure, also famous as a scholastic, has recently been republished: *Vita S. Francisci a S. Bonaventura concinnata* (Soest, 1847), shortly after the appearance in France of an accurate and detailed biography which utilizes all the sources: *Histoire de S. François d'Assise,* by Chavin de Mallan (1845). As an oriental parallel to these monastic writings, we have the book of Spence Hardy: *Eastern Monachism, An Account of the Order of Mendicants founded by Gotama Budha* (1850), which is very well worth reading. It shows us the same thing under a

---

[60] "For all that is excellent and eminent is as difficult as it is rare." [*Ethics,* v, prop. 42 schol. Tr.]

different cloak. We also see how immaterial it is whether it proceeds from a theistic or from an atheistic religion. But as a special and extremely full example and actual illustration of the conceptions I advance, I can particularly recommend the *Autobiography* of Madame de Guyon. To become acquainted with that great and beautiful soul, whose remembrance always fills me with reverence, and to do justice to the excellence of her disposition while making allowances for the superstition of her faculty of reason, must be gratifying to every person of the better sort, just as with common thinkers, in other words the majority, that book will always stand in bad repute. For everyone, always and everywhere, can appreciate only that which is to some extent analogous to him, and for which he has at any rate a feeble gift; this holds good of the ethical as well as of the intellectual. To a certain extent we might regard even the well-known French biography of Spinoza as a case in point, if we use as the key to it that excellent introduction to his very inadequate essay, *De Emendatione Intellectus*. At the same time, I can recommend this passage as the most effective means known to me of stilling the storm of the passions. Finally, even the great Goethe, Greek as he was, did not regard it as beneath his dignity to show us this most beautiful side of humanity in the elucidating mirror of the poetic art, since he presented to us in an idealized form the life of Fräulein Klettenberg in the *Confessions of a Beautiful Soul,* and later, in his own biography, gave us also a historical account of it. Besides this, he twice narrated the life of St. Philip Neri. The history of the world will, and indeed must, always keep silence about the persons whose conduct is the best and only adequate illustration of this important point of our investigation. For the material of world-history is quite different therefrom, and indeed opposed to it; thus it is not the denial and giving up of the will-to-live, but its affirmation and manifestation in innumerable individuals in which its dissension with itself at the highest point of its objectification appears with perfect distinctness, and brings before our eyes, now the superior strength of the individual through his shrewdness, now the might of the many through their mass, now the ascendancy of chance personified as fate, always the vanity and futility of the whole striving and effort. But we do not follow here the thread of phenomena in time, but, as philosophers, try to investigate the ethical significance of actions, and take this as the only criterion of what is significant and important for us. No fear of the always permanent majority of vulgarity and shallowness will prevent us from acknowledging that the greatest, the most important, and the most significant phenomenon that the world can show is not the conqueror of the world, but the overcomer of the world, and so really nothing but the quiet and unobserved conduct in the life of such a man. On this man has dawned the knowledge in consequence of which he gives up and denies that will-to-live that fills everything, and strives and strains in all. The freedom of this will first appears here in him alone, and by it his actions now become the very opposite of the ordinary. For the philosopher, therefore, in this respect those accounts of the lives of saintly, self-denying persons, badly written as they generally are, and mixed up with superstition and nonsense, are through the importance of the material incomparably more instructive and important than even Plutarch and Livy.

Further, a more detailed and complete knowledge of what we express in abstraction and generality through our method of presentation as denial of the will-to-live, will be very greatly facilitated by a consideration of the ethical precepts given in this sense and by people who were full of this spirit. These will at the same time show how old our view is, however new its purely philosophical expression may be. In the first place, Christianity is nearest at hand, the ethics of which is entirely in the spirit we have mentioned, and leads not only to the highest degrees of charity and human kindness, but also to renunciation. The germ of this last side is certainly distinctly present in the writings of the Apostles, yet only later is it fully developed and explicitly expressed. We find commanded by the Apostles love for our neighbour as for ourselves, returning of hatred with love and good actions, patience, meekness, endurance of all possible affronts and injuries without resistance, moderation in eating and drinking for suppressing desire, resistance to the sexual impulse, even complete if possible for us. Here we see the first stages of asceticism or of real denial of the will; this last expression denotes what is called in the Gospels denying the self and taking of the cross upon oneself. (Matt. xvi, 24, 25; Mark viii, 34, 35; Luke ix, 23, 24; xiv, 26, 27, 33.) This tendency was soon developed more and more, and was the origin of penitents, anchorites, and monasticism, an origin that in itself was pure and holy, but, for this very reason, quite unsuitable to the great majority of people. Therefore what developed out of it could be only hypocrisy and infamy, for *abusus optimi pessimus*.[61] In more developed Christianity, we see that seed of asceticism unfold into full flower in the writings of the Christian saints and mystics. Besides the purest love,

---

[61] "The worst is the abuse of the best." [Tr.]

these preach also complete resignation, voluntary and absolute poverty, true composure, complete indifference to all worldly things, death to one's own will and regeneration in God, entire forgetting of one's own person and absorption in the contemplation of God. A complete description of this is to be found in Fénélon's *Explication des maximes des Saints sur la vie intérieure*. But the spirit of this development of Christianity is certainly nowhere so perfectly and powerfully expressed as in the writings of the German mystics, e.g. those of Meister Eckhart, and the justly famous book *Theologia Germanica*. In the introduction to this last which Luther wrote, he says of it that, with the exception of the Bible and St. Augustine, he had learnt more from it of what God, Christ, and man are than from any other book. Yet only in the year 1851 did we acquire its genuine and unadulterated text in the Stuttgart edition of Pfeiffer. The precepts and doctrines given in it are the most perfect explanation, springing from deep inward conviction, of what I have described as the denial of the will-to-live. One has therefore to make a closer study of it before dogmatizing about it with Jewish-Protestant assurance. Tauler's *Nachfolgung des armen Leben Christi,* together with his *Medulla Animae,* are written in the same admirable spirit, although not quite equal in value to that work. In my opinion, the teachings of these genuine Christian mystics are related to those of the New Testament as alcohol is to wine; in other words, what becomes visible to us in the New Testament as if through a veil and mist, stands before us in the works of the mystics without cloak or disguise, in full clearness and distinctness. Finally, we might also regard the New Testament as the first initiation, the mystics as the second, σμικρὰ καὶ μεγάλα μυστήρια.[62]

But we find what we have called denial of the will-to-live still further developed, more variously expressed, and more vividly presented in the ancient works in the Sanskrit language than could be the case in the Christian Church and the Western world. That this important ethical view of life could attain here to a more far-reaching development and a more decided expression, is perhaps to be ascribed mainly to the fact that it was not restricted by an element quite foreign to it, as the Jewish doctrine of faith is in Christianity. The sublime founder of Christianity had necessarily to adapt and accommodate himself, partly consciously, partly, it may be, unconsciously, to this doctrine; and so Christianity is composed of two very heterogeneous elements. Of these I should like to call the

---

[62] "Small and great mysteries" [the former celebrated by the Athenians in March, the latter in October. Tr.].

purely ethical element preferably, indeed exclusively, the Christian, and to distinguish it from the Jewish dogmatism with which it is found. If, as has often been feared, and especially at the present time, that excellent and salutary religion should completely decline, then I would look for the reason for this simply in the fact that it does not consist of one simple element, but of two originally heterogeneous elements, brought into combination only by means of world events. In such a case, dissolution would necessarily result through the break-up of these elements, which arises from their different relationship and reaction to the advanced spirit of the times. Yet after this dissolution, the purely ethical part would still be bound always to remain intact, because it is indestructible. However imperfect our knowledge of Hindu literature still is, as we now find it most variously and powerfully expressed in the ethics of the Hindus, in the *Vedas, Puranas,* poetical works, myths, legends of their saints, in aphorisms, maxims, and rules of conduct,[63] we see that it ordains love of one's neighbour with complete denial of all self-love; love in general, not limited to the human race, but embracing all that lives; charitableness even to the giving away of one's hard-won daily earnings; boundless patience towards all offenders; return of all evil, however bad it may be, with goodness and love; voluntary and cheerful endurance of every insult and ignominy; abstinence from all animal food; perfect chastity and renunciation of all sensual pleasure for him who aspires to real holiness; the throwing away of all property; the forsaking of every dwelling-place and of all kinsfolk; deep unbroken solitude spent in silent contemplation with voluntary penance and terrible slow self-torture for the complete mortification of the will, ultimately going as far as voluntary death by starvation, or facing crocodiles, or jumping over the consecrated precipice in the Himalaya, or being buried alive, or flinging oneself under the wheels of the huge car that drives round with the images of the gods amid the singing, shouting, and dancing of bayaderes. These precepts, whose origin reaches back more than four thousand years, are still lived up to by individuals even to the utmost ex-

---

[63] See, for example, *Oupnek'hat,* studio Anquetil du Perron, Vol. II. Nos. 138, 144, 145, 146; *Mythologie des Indous,* by Madame de Polier, Vol. II, chaps. 13, 14, 15, 16, 17; *Asiatisches Magazin,* by Klaproth, in the first volume; *Ueber die Fo-Religion, also Bhaguat-Geeta oder Gespräche zwischen Kreeshna und Arjoon;* in the second volume, *'Moha-Mudgava;* then *Institutes of Hindu Law, or the Ordinances of Manu,* from the Sanskrit by Sir William Jones (German by Hüttner, 1797); especially the sixth and twelfth chapters. Finally, many passages in the *Asiatic Researches.* (In the last forty years Indian literature has grown so much in Europe, that if I now wished to complete this note to the first edition, it would fill several pages.)

treme,[64] degenerate as that race is in many respects. That which has remained in practice for so long in a nation embracing so many millions, while it imposes the heaviest sacrifices, cannot be an arbitrarily invented freak, but must have its foundation in the very nature of mankind. But besides this, we cannot sufficiently wonder at the harmony we find, when we read the life of a Christian penitent or saint and that of an Indian. In spite of such fundamentally different dogmas, customs, and circumstances, the endeavour and the inner life of both are absolutely the same; and it is also the same with the precepts for both. For example, Tauler speaks of the complete poverty which one should seek, and which consists in giving away and divesting oneself entirely of everything from which one might draw some comfort or worldly pleasure, clearly because all this always affords new nourishment to the will, whose complete mortification is intended. As the Indian counterpart of this, we see in the precepts of Fo that the Sannyasi, who is supposed to be without dwelling and entirely without property, is finally enjoined not to lie down too often under the same tree, lest he acquire a preference or inclination for it. The Christian mystics and the teachers of the Vedanta philosophy agree also in regarding all outward works and religious practices as superfluous for the man who has attained perfection. So much agreement, in spite of such different ages and races, is a practical proof that here is expressed not an eccentricity and craziness of the mind, as optimistic shallowness and dulness like to assert, but an essential side of human nature which appears rarely only because of its superior quality.

I have now mentioned the sources from which we can obtain a direct knowledge, drawn from life, of the phenomena in which the denial of the will-to-live exhibits itself. To a certain extent, this is the most important point of our whole discussion; yet I have explained it only quite generally, for it is better to refer to those who speak from direct experience, than to increase the size of this book unnecessarily by repeating more feebly what they say.

I wish to add only a little more to the general description of their state. We saw above that the wicked man, by the vehemence of his willing, suffers constant, consuming, inner torment, and finally that, when all the objects of willing are exhausted, he quenches the fiery thirst of his wilfulness by the sight of others' pain. On the other hand, the man in whom the denial of the will-to-live has dawned, however poor, cheerless, and full of privation his state may be when

---

[64] At the procession of Jagganath in June 1840, eleven Hindus threw themselves under the car, and were instantly killed. (Letter from an East Indian landowner in *The Times* of 30 December, 1840.)

looked at from outside, is full of inner cheerfulness and true heavenly peace. It is not the restless and turbulent pressure of life, the jubilant delight that has keen suffering as its preceding or succeeding condition, such as constitute the conduct of the man attached to life, but it is an unshakable peace, a deep calm and inward serenity, a state that we cannot behold without the greatest longing, when it is brought before our eyes or imagination, since we at once recognize it as that which alone is right, infinitely outweighing everything else, at which our better spirit cries to us the great *sapere aude*.[65] We then feel that every fulfilment of our wishes won from the world is only like the alms that keep the beggar alive today so that he may starve again tomorrow. Resignation, on the other hand, is like the inherited estate; it frees its owner from all care and anxiety for ever.

It will be remembered from the third book that aesthetic pleasure in the beautiful consists, to a large extent, in the fact that, when we enter the state of pure contemplation, we are raised for the moment above all willing, above all desires and cares; we are, so to speak, rid of ourselves. We are no longer the individual that knows in the interest of its constant willing, the correlative of the particular thing to which objects become motives, but the eternal subject of knowing purified of the will, the correlative of the Idea. And we know that these moments, when, delivered from the fierce pressure of the will, we emerge, as it were, from the heavy atmosphere of the earth, are the most blissful that we experience. From this we can infer how blessed must be the life of a man whose will is silenced not for a few moments, as in the enjoyment of the beautiful, but for ever, indeed completely extinguished, except for the last glimmering spark that maintains the body and is extinguished with it. Such a man who, after many bitter struggles with his own nature, has at last completely conquered, is then left only as pure knowing being, as the undimmed mirror of the world. Nothing can distress or alarm him any more; nothing can any longer move him; for he has cut all the thousand threads of willing which hold us bound to the world, and which as craving, fear, envy, and anger drag us here and there in constant pain. He now looks back calmly and with a smile on the phantasmagoria of this world which was once able to move and agonize even his mind, but now stands before him as indifferently as chess-men at the end of a game, or as fancy dress cast off in the morning, the form and figure of which taunted and disquieted us on the carnival night. Life and its forms merely float

---

[65] "Bring yourself to be reasonable!" [Tr.]

before him as a fleeting phenomenon, as a light morning dream to one half-awake, through which reality already shines, and which can no longer deceive; and, like this morning dream, they too finally vanish without any violent transition. From these considerations we can learn to understand what Madame Guyon means when, towards the end of her *Autobiography,* she often expresses herself thus: "Everything is indifferent to me; I *cannot* will anything more; often I do not know whether I exist or not." In order to express how, after the dying-away of the will, the death of the body (which is indeed only the phenomenon of the will, and thus with the abolition of the will loses all meaning) can no longer have anything bitter, but is very welcome, I may be permitted to record here that holy penitent's own words, although they are not very elegantly turned: *"Midi de la gloire; jour où il n'y a plus de nuit; vie qui ne craint plus la mort, dans la mort même: parceque la mort a vaincu la mort, et que celui qui a souffert la première mort, ne goûtera plus la seconde mort."* (*Vie de Madame de Guion* [Cologne, 1720], Vol. II, p. 13.)[66]

However, we must not imagine that, after the denial of the will-to-live has once appeared through knowledge that has become a quieter of the will, such denial no longer wavers or falters, and that we can rest on it as on an inherited property. On the contrary, it must always be achieved afresh by constant struggle. For as the body is the will itself only in the form of objectivity, or as phenomenon in the world as representation, that whole will-to-live exists potentially so long as the body lives, and is always striving to reach actuality and to burn afresh with all its intensity. We therefore find in the lives of saintly persons that peace and bliss we have described, only as the blossom resulting from the constant overcoming of the will; and we see the constant struggle with the will-to-live as the soil from which it shoots up; for on earth no one can have lasting peace. We therefore see the histories of the inner life of saints full of spiritual conflicts, temptations, and desertion from grace, in other words, from that kind of knowledge which, by rendering all motives ineffectual, as a universal quieter silences all willing, gives the deepest peace, and opens the gate to freedom. Therefore we see also those who have once attained to denial of the will, strive with all their might to keep to this path by self-imposed renunciations of every kind, by a penitent and hard way of life, and by looking for

---

[66] "The noonday of glory; a day no longer followed by night; a life that no longer fears death, even in death itself, because death has overcome death, and because whoever has suffered the first death will no longer feel the second." [Tr.]

what is disagreeable to them; all this in order to suppress the will that is constantly springing up afresh. Finally, therefore, because they already know the value of salvation, their anxious care for the retention of the hard-won blessing, their scruples of conscience in the case of every innocent enjoyment or with every little excitement of their vanity; this is also the last thing to die, the most indestructible, the most active, and the most foolish of all man's inclinations. By the expression *asceticism,* which I have already used so often, I understand in the narrower sense this *deliberate* breaking of the will by refusing the agreeable and looking for the disagreeable, the voluntarily chosen way of life of penance and self-chastisement, for the constant mortification of the will.

Now, if we see this practised by persons who have already attained to denial of the will, in order that they may keep to it, then suffering in general, as it is inflicted by fate, is also a second way (δεύτερος πλοῦς)* of attaining to that denial. Indeed, we may assume that most men can reach it only in this way, and that it is the suffering personally felt, not the suffering merely known, which most frequently produces complete resignation, often only at the approach of death. For only in the case of a few is mere knowledge sufficient to bring about the denial of the will, the knowledge namely that sees through the *principium individuationis,* first producing perfect goodness of disposition and universal love of mankind, and finally enabling them to recognize as their own all the sufferings of the world. Even in the case of the individual who approaches this point, the tolerable condition of his own person, the flattery of the moment, the allurement of hope, and the satisfaction of the will offering itself again and again, i.e., the satisfaction of desire, are almost invariably a constant obstacle to the denial of the will, and a constant temptation to a renewed affirmation of it. For this reason, all those allurements have in this respect been personified as the devil. Therefore in most cases the will must be broken by the greatest personal suffering before its self-denial appears. We then see the man suddenly retire into himself, after he is brought to the verge of despair through all the stages of increasing affliction with the most violent resistance. We see him know himself and the world, change his whole nature, rise above himself and above all suffering, as if purified and sanctified by it, in inviolable peace, bliss, and sublimity, willingly renounce

---

* On δεύτερος πλοῦς cf. Stobaeus, *Florilegium,* Vol. II, p. 374. [Footnotes indicated by an asterisk represent additions made by Schopenhauer in his interleaved copy of the third edition of 1859. He died in 1860, and so there are very few of these. Tr.]

everything he formerly desired with the greatest vehemence, and gladly welcome death. It is the gleam of silver that suddenly appears from the purifying flame of suffering, the gleam of the denial of the will-to-live, of salvation. Occasionally we see even those who were very wicked purified to this degree by the deepest grief and sorrow; they have become different, and are completely converted. Therefore, their previous misdeeds no longer trouble their consciences, yet they gladly pay for such misdeeds with death, and willingly see the end of the phenomenon of that will that is now foreign to and abhorred by them. The great Goethe has given us a distinct and visible description of this denial of the will, brought about by great misfortune and by the despair of all deliverance, in his immortal masterpiece *Faust*, in the story of the sufferings of Gretchen. I know of no other description in poetry. It is a perfect specimen of the second path, which leads to the denial of the will not, like the first, through the mere knowledge of the suffering of a whole world which one acquires voluntarily, but through the excessive pain felt in one's own person. It is true that very many tragedies bring their violently willing heroes ultimately to this point of complete resignation, and then the will-to-live and its phenomenon usually end at the same time. But no description known to me brings to us the essential point of that conversion so distinctly and so free from everything extraneous as the one mentioned in *Faust*.

In real life we see those unfortunate persons who have to drink to the dregs the greatest measure of suffering, face a shameful, violent, and often painful death on the scaffold with complete mental vigour, after they are deprived of all hope; and very often we see them converted in this way. We should not, of course, assume that there is so great a difference between their character and that of most men as their fate seems to suggest; we have to ascribe the latter for the most part to circumstances; yet they are guilty and, to a considerable degree, bad. But we see many of them converted in the way mentioned, after the appearance of complete hopelessness. They now show actual goodness and purity of disposition, true abhorrence of committing any deed in the least degree wicked or uncharitable. They forgive their enemies, even those through whom they innocently suffered; and not merely in words and from a kind of hypocritical fear of the judges of the nether world, but in reality and with inward earnestness, and with no wish for revenge. Indeed, their suffering and dying in the end become agreeable to them, for the denial of the will-to-live has made its appearance. They often decline the deliverance offered them, and die willingly, peacefully, and blissfully. The last secret of life has revealed itself to them in the excess of pain, the secret, namely, that evil and wickedness, suffering and hatred, the tormented and the tormentor, different as they may appear to knowledge that follows the principle of sufficient reason, are in themselves one, phenomenon of the one will-to-live that objectifies its conflict with itself by means of the *principium individuationis*. They have learned to know both sides in full measure, the wickedness and the evil; and since they ultimately see the identity of the two, they reject them both at the same time; they deny the will-to-live. As we have said, it is a matter of complete indifference by what myths and dogmas they account to their faculty of reason for this intuitive and immediate knowledge, and for their conversion.

Matthias Claudius was undoubtedly a witness to a change of mind of this sort, when he wrote the remarkable essay which appears in the *Wandsbecker Bote* (Pt. I, p. 115) under the title *Bekehrungs-geschichte des* . . . ("History of the Conversion of . . .") which has the following ending: "Man's way of thinking can pass over from a point of the periphery to the opposite point, and back again to the previous point, if circumstances trace out for him the curved path to it. And these changes are not really anything great and interesting in man. But that *remarkable, catholic, transcendental change,* where the whole circle is irreparably torn up and all the laws of psychology become vain and empty, where the coat of skins is taken off, or at any rate turned inside out, and man's eyes are opened, is such that everyone who is conscious to some extent of the breath in his nostrils, forsakes father and mother, if he can hear and experience something certain about it."

The approach of death and hopelessness, however, are not absolutely necessary for such a purification through suffering. Even without them, the knowledge of the contradiction of the will-to-live with itself can, through great misfortune and suffering, violently force itself on us, and the vanity of all endeavour can be perceived. Hence men who have led a very adventurous life under the pressure of passions, men such as kings, heroes, or adventurers, have often been seen suddenly to change, resort to resignation and penance, and become hermits and monks. To this class belong all genuine accounts of conversion, for instance that of Raymond Lull, who had long wooed a beautiful woman, was at last admitted to her chamber, and was looking forward to the fulfilment of all his desires, when, opening her dress, she showed him her bosom terribly eaten away with cancer. From that moment, as if he had looked into hell, he was converted; leaving the court of the King of Majorca, he went into the wilderness to do penance.[67] This story of conversion is very similar to that of the Abbé de Rancé which I have briefly related in chapter 48 of volume two. If we consider how, in both cases, the transition from the pleasure to the horror of life was the occasion, this gives us an explanation of the remarkable fact that it is the French nation, the most cheerful, merry, gay, sensual, and frivolous in Europe, in which by far the strictest of all monastic orders, namely the Trappist, arose, was re-established by Rancé after its decline, and maintains itself even to the present day in all its purity and fearful strictness, in spite of revolutions, changes in the Church, and the encroachments of infidelity.

However, a knowledge of the above-mentioned kind of the nature of this existence may depart again simultaneously with its occasion, and the will-to-live, and with it the previous character, may reappear. Thus we see that the passionate Benvenuto Cellini was converted in such a way, once in prison and again during a serious illness, but relapsed into his old state after the suffering had disappeared. In general, the denial of the will by no means results from suffering with the necessity of effect from cause; on the contrary, the will remains free. For here is just the one and only point where its freedom enters directly into the phenomenon; hence the astonishment so strongly expressed by Asmus about the "transcendental change." For every case of suffering, a will can be conceived which surpasses it in intensity, and is unconquered by it. Therefore, Plato speaks in the *Phaedo* [116 E] of persons who, up to the moment of their execution, feast, carouse, drink, indulge in sexual pleasures, affirming life right up to the death. Shakespeare in Cardinal Beaufort[68] presents to us the fearful end of a wicked ruffian who dies full of despair, since no suffering or death can break his will that is vehement to the extreme point of wickedness.

The more intense the will, the more glaring the phenomenon of its conflict, and hence the greater the suffering. A world that was the phenomenon of an incomparably more intense will-to-live than the present one is, would exhibit so much the greater suffering; thus it would be a *hell*.

Since all suffering is a mortification and a call to resignation, it has potentially a sanctifying force. By this is explained the fact that great misfortune and deep sorrow in themselves inspire one with a certain awe. But the sufferer becomes wholly an object of reverence to us only when, surveying the course of his life as a chain of sorrows, or mourning a great and incurable pain, he does not really

---

[67] Brucker, *Hist. Philos.*, Tom. IV, pars I, p. 10.

[68] *Henry VI, Part II, Act 3, Scene 3.*

look at the concatenation of circumstances which plunged just his life into mourning; he does not stop at that particular great misfortune that befell him. For up till then, his knowledge still follows the principle of sufficient reason, and clings to the particular phenomenon; he still continues to will life, only not on the conditions that have happened to him. He is really worthy of reverence only when his glance has been raised from the particular to the universal, and when he regards his own suffering merely as an example of the whole and for him; for in an ethical respect he becomes inspired with genius, one case holds good for a thousand, so that the whole of life, conceived as essential suffering, then brings him to resignation. For this reason it is worthy of reverence when in Goethe's *Torquato Tasso* the princess speaks of how her own life and that of her relations have always been sad and cheerless, and here her regard is wholly towards the universal.

We always picture a very noble character to ourselves as having a certain trace of silent sadness that is anything but constant peevishness over daily annoyances (that would be an ignoble trait, and might lead us to fear a bad disposition). It is a consciousness that has resulted from knowledge of the vanity of all possessions and of the suffering of all life, not merely of one's own. Such knowledge, however, may first of all be awakened by suffering personally experienced, especially by a single great suffering, just as a single wish incapable of fulfilment brought Petrarch to that resigned sadness concerning the whole of life which appeals to us so pathetically in his works; for the Daphne he pursued had to vanish from his hands, in order to leave behind for him the immortal laurel instead of herself. If the will is to a certain extent broken by such a great and irrevocable denial of fate, then practically nothing more is desired, and the character shows itself as mild, sad, noble, and resigned. Finally, when grief no longer has any definite object, but is extended over the whole of life, it is then to a certain extent a self-communion, a withdrawal, a gradual disappearance of the will, the visibility of which, namely the body, is imperceptibly but inwardly undermined by it, so that the person feels a certain loosening of his bonds, a mild foretaste of the death that proclaims itself to be the dissolution of the body and of the will at the same time. A secret joy therefore accompanies this grief; and I believe it is this that the most melancholy of all nations has called "the joy of grief." Here, however, lies the danger of *sentimentality,* both in life itself and in its description in poetry; namely when a person is always mourning and wailing without standing up courageously and rising to resignation. In this way heaven and earth are both lost, and only a watery sentimentality is retained. Only when suffering assumes the form of pure knowledge, and then this knowledge, as a *quieter of the will,* produces true resignation, is it the path to salvation, and thus worthy of reverence. But in this respect, we feel on seeing any very unfortunate person a certain esteem akin to that which virtue and nobility of character force from us; at the same time, our own fortunate condition seems like a reproach. We cannot help but regard every suffering, both those felt by ourselves and those felt by others, as at least a possible advance towards virtue and holiness, and pleasures and worldly satisfactions, on the other hand, as a departure therefrom. This goes so far that every man who undergoes great bodily or mental suffering, indeed everyone who performs a physical labour demanding the greatest exertion in the sweat of his brow and with evident exhaustion, yet does all this with patience and without grumbling, appears, when we consider him with close attention, somewhat like a sick man who applies a painful cure. Willingly, and even with satisfaction, he endures the pain caused by the cure, since he knows that the more he suffers, the more is the substance of the disease destroyed; and thus the present pain is the measure of his cure.

It follows from all that has been said, that the denial of the will-to-live, which is the same as what is called complete resignation or holiness, always proceeds from that quieter of the will; and this is the knowledge of its inner conflict and its essential vanity, expressing themselves in the suffering of all that lives. The difference, that we have described as two paths, is whether that knowledge is called forth by suffering which is merely and simply *known* and freely appropriated by our seeing through the *principium individuationis,* or by suffering immediately felt by ourselves. True salvation, deliverance from life and suffering, cannot even be imagined without complete denial of the will. Till then, everyone is nothing but this will itself, whose phenomenon is an evanescent existence, an always vain and constantly frustrated striving, and the world full of suffering as we have described it. All belong to this irrevocably and in like manner. For we found previously that life is always certain to the will-to-live, and its sole actual form is the present from which they never escape, since birth and death rule in the phenomenon. The Indian myth expresses this by saying that "they are born again." The great ethical difference of characters means that the bad man is infinitely remote from attaining that knowledge, whose result is the denial of the will, and is therefore in truth *actually* abandoned to all the miseries which appear in life as *possible.* For even the present fortunate state of his person is only a phenomenon brought about by the *principium individuationis,* and the illusion of Maya, the happy dream of a beggar. The sufferings that in the vehemence and passion of his pressing will he inflicts on others are the measure of the sufferings, the experience of which in his own person cannot break his will and lead to final denial. On the other hand, all true and pure affection, and even all free justice, result from seeing through the *principium individuationis;* when this penetration occurs in all its force, it produces perfect sanctification and salvation, the phenomenon of which are the state of resignation previously described, the unshakable peace accompanying this, and the highest joy and delight in death.[69]

§ 69.

*S*uicide, the arbitrary doing away with the individual phenomenon, differs most widely from the denial of the will-to-live, which is the only act of its freedom to appear in the phenomenon, and hence, as Asmus calls it, the transcendental change. The denial of the will has now been adequately discussed within the limits of our method of consideration. Far from being denial of the will, suicide is a phenomenon of the will's strong affirmation. For denial has its essential nature in the fact that the pleasures of life, not its sorrows, are shunned. The suicide wills life, and is dissatisfied merely with the conditions on which it has come to him. Therefore he gives up by no means the will-to-live, but merely life, since he destroys the individual phenomenon. He wills life, wills the unchecked existence and affirmation of the body; but the combination of circumstances does not allow of these, and the result for him is great suffering. The will-to-live finds itself so hampered in this particular phenomenon, that it cannot develop and display its efforts. It therefore decides in accordance with its own inner nature, which lies outside the forms of the principle of sufficient reason, and to which every individual phenomenon is therefore indifferent, in that it remains itself untouched by all arising and passing away, and is the inner core of the life of all things. For that same firm, inner assurance, which enables all of us to live without the constant dread of death, the assurance that the will can never

---

[69] Cf. chap. 48 of volume 2.

lack its phenomenon, supports the deed even in the case of suicide. Thus the will-to-live appears just as much in this suicide (Shiva) as in the ease and comfort of self-preservation (Vishnu), and the sensual pleasure of procreation (Brahma). This is the inner meaning of the *unity of the Trimurti* which every human being entirely is, although in time it raises now one, now another of its three heads. As the individual thing is related to the Idea, so is suicide to the denial of the will. The suicide denies merely the individual, not the species. We have already found that, since life is always certain to the will-to-live, and suffering is essential to life, suicide, or the arbitrary destruction of an individual phenomenon, is a quite futile and foolish act, for the thing-in-itself remains unaffected by it, just as the rainbow remains unmoved, however rapidly the drops may change which sustain it for the moment. But in addition to this, it is also the masterpiece of Maya as the most blatant expression of the contradiction of the will-to-live with itself. Just as we have recognized this contradiction in the lowest phenomena of the will in the constant struggle of all the manifestations of natural forces and of all organic individuals for matter, time, and space, and as we saw that conflict stand out more and more with terrible distinctness on the ascending grades of the will's objectification; so at last at the highest stage, the Idea of man, it reaches that degree where not only the individuals exhibiting the same Idea exterminate one another, but even the one individual declares war on itself. The vehemence with which it wills life and revolts against what hinders it, namely suffering, brings it to the point of destroying itself, so that the individual will by an act of will eliminates the body that is merely the will's own becoming visible, rather than that suffering should break the will. Just because the suicide cannot cease willing, he ceases to live; and the will affirms itself here even through the cessation of its own phenomenon, because it can no longer affirm itself otherwise. But as it was just the suffering it thus shunned which, as mortification of the will, could have led it to the denial of itself and to salvation, so in this respect the suicide is like a sick man who, after the beginning of a painful operation that could completely cure him, will not allow it to be completed, but prefers to retain his illness. Suffering approaches and, as such, offers the possibility of a denial of the will; but he rejects it by destroying the will's phenomenon, the body, so that the will may remain unbroken. This is the reason why almost all ethical systems, philosophical as well as religious, condemn suicide, though they themselves cannot state anything but strange and sophistical arguments for so doing. But if ever a man was kept from suicide by purely moral incentive, the innermost meaning of this self-conquest (whatever the concepts in which his faculty of reason may have clothed it) was as follows: "I do not want to avoid suffering, because it can help to put an end to the will-to-live, whose phenomenon is so full of misery, by so strengthening the knowledge of the real nature of the world now already dawning on me, that such knowledge may become the final quieter of the will, and release me for ever."

It is well known that, from time to time, cases repeatedly occur where suicide extends to the children; the father kills the children of whom he is very fond, and then himself. If we bear in mind that conscience, religion, and all traditional ideas teach him to recognize murder as the gravest crime, but yet in the hour of his own death he commits this, and indeed without his having any possible ego-istical motive for it, then the deed can be explained only in the following way. The will of the individual again recognizes itself im-mediately in the children, although it is involved in the delusion of regarding the phenomenon as the being-in-itself. At the same time, he is deeply moved by the knowledge of the misery of all life; he imagines that with the phenomenon he abolishes the inner nature itself, and therefore wants to deliver from existence and its misery both himself and his children in whom he directly sees himself living again. It would be an error wholly analogous to this to suppose that one can reach the same end as is attained by voluntary chastity by frustrating the aims of nature in fecundation, or even by men, in consideration of the inevitable suffering of life, countenancing the death of the new-born child, instead of rather doing everything to ensure life to every being that is pressing into it. For if the will-to-live exists, it cannot, as that which alone is metaphysical or the thing-in-itself, be broken by any force, but that force can destroy only its phenomenon in such a place and at such a time. The will itself cannot be abolished by anything except *knowledge*. Therefore the only path to salvation is that the will should appear freely and with-out hindrance, in order that it can *recognize or know* its own inner nature in this phenomenon. Only in consequence of this knowledge can the will abolish itself, and thus end the suffering that is insepara-ble from its phenomenon. This, however, is not possible through physical force, such as the destruction of the seed or germ, the killing of the new-born child, or suicide. Nature leads the will to the light, just because only in the light can it find its salvation. Therefore the purposes of nature are to be promoted in every way, as soon as the will-to-live, that is her inner being, has determined itself.

There appears to be a special kind of suicide, quite different from the ordinary, which has perhaps not yet been adequately verified.

This is voluntarily chosen death by starvation at the highest degree of asceticism. Its manifestation, however, has always been accompanied, and thus rendered vague and obscure, by much religious fanaticism and even superstition. Yet it seems that the complete denial of the will can reach that degree where even the necessary will to maintain the vegetative life of the body, by the assimilation of nourishment, ceases to exist. This kind of suicide is so far from being the result of the will-to-live, that such a completely resigned ascetic ceases to live merely because he has completely ceased to will. No other death than that by starvation is here conceivable (unless it resulted from a special superstition), since the intention to cut short the agony would actually be a degree of affirmation of the will. The dogmas that satisfy the faculty of reason of such a penitent delude him with the idea that a being of a higher nature has ordered for him the fasting to which his inner tendency urges him. Old instances of this can be found in the *Breslauer Sammlung von Natur- und Medicin-Geschichten,* September 1719, p. 363 *seq.;* in Bayle's *Nouvelles de la république des lettres,* February 1685, p. 189 *seq.;* in Zimmermann, *Ueber die Einsamkeit,* Vol. I, p. 182; in the *Histoire de l'Académie des Sciences* of 1764, an account by Houttuyn; the same account is repeated in the *Sammlung für praktische Aerzte,* Vol. I, p. 69. Later reports are to be found in Hufeland's *Journal für praktische Heilkunde,* Vol. X, p. 181, and Vol. XLVIII, p. 95; also in Nasse's *Zeitschrift für psychische Aerzte,* 1819, Part III, p. 460; in the *Edinburgh Medical and Surgical Journal,* 1809, Vol. V, p. 319. In the year 1833, all the papers reported that the English historian, Dr. Lingard, had died of voluntary starvation at Dover in January; according to later accounts it was not Lingard himself but a kinsman of his who died. But in these accounts the individuals are for the most part described as mad, and it is no longer possible to ascertain how far this may have been the case. But I will here give a more recent account of this kind, if only to ensure the preservation of one of the rare instances of the striking and extraordinary phenomenon of human nature just mentioned, which, at any rate, apparently belongs to where I should like to assign it, and could hardly be explained in any other way. This recent account is to be found in the *Nürnberger Korrespondent* of 29 July 1813, in the following words:

"It is reported from Bern that in a dense forest near Thurnen a small hut was discovered in which was lying the decomposed corpse of a man who had been dead for about a month. His clothes gave little information about his social position. Two very fine shirts lay beside him. The most important thing was a Bible, interleaved with blank pages, which had been partly written on by the deceased. In it he announced the day of his departure from home (but it did not mention where his home was). He then said that he was driven into the wilderness by the spirit of God to pray and fast. On his journey to that spot, he had already fasted for seven days, and had then eaten again. After settling down here, he began to fast again, and indeed fasted for as many days. Every day was now indicated by a stroke, of which there were five, after which the pilgrim had presumably died. There was also found a letter to a clergyman about a sermon that the deceased had heard him preach; but the address was missing." Between this voluntary death springing from the extreme of asceticism and that resulting from despair there may be many different intermediate stages and combinations, which are indeed hard to explain; but human nature has depths, obscurities, and intricacies, whose elucidation and unfolding are of the very greatest difficulty.

§ 70.

We might perhaps regard the whole of our discussion (now concluded) of what I call the denial of the will as inconsistent with the previous explanation of necessity, that appertains just as much to motivation as to every other form of the principle of sufficient reason. As a result of that necessity, motives, like all causes, are only occasional causes on which the character unfolds its nature, and reveals it with the necessity of a natural law. For this reason we positively denied freedom as *liberum arbitrium indifferentiae*. Yet far from suppressing this here, I call it to mind. In truth, real freedom, in other words, independence of the principle of sufficient reason, belongs to the will as thing-in-itself, not to its phenomenon, whose essential form is everywhere this principle of sufficient reason, the element of necessity. But the only case where that freedom can become immediately visible in the phenomenon is the one where it makes an end of what appears, and because the mere phenomenon, in so far as it is a link in the chain of causes, namely the living body, still continues to exist in time that contains only phenomena, the will, manifesting itself through this phenomenon, is then in contradiction with it, since it denies what the phenomenon expresses. In such a case the genitals, for example, as the visibility of the sexual impulse, are there and in health; but yet in the innermost consciousness no sexual satisfaction is desired. The whole body is the visible expression of the will-to-live, yet the motives corresponding to this will no longer act; indeed the dissolution of the body, the end of the individual, and thus the greatest suppression of the natural will, is welcome and desired. Now the contradiction between our assertions, on the one hand, of the necessity of the will's determinations through motives according to the character, and our assertions, on the other, of the possibilty of the whole suppression of the will, whereby motives become powerless, is only the repetition in the reflection of philosophy of this *real* contradiction that arises from the direct encroachment of the freedom of the will-in-itself, knowing no necessity, on the necessity of its phenomenon. But the key to the reconciliation of these contradictions lies in the fact that the state in which the character is withdrawn from the power of motives does not proceed directly from the will, but from a changed form of knowledge. Thus, so long as the knowledge is only that which is involved in the *principium individuationis,* and which positively follows the principle of sufficent reason, the power of the motives is irresistible. But when the *principium individuationis* is seen through, when the Ideas, and indeed the inner nature of the thing-in-itself, are immediately recognized as the same will in all, and the result of this knowledge is a universal quieter of willing, then the individual motives become ineffective, because the kind of knowledge that corresponds to them is obscured and pushed into the background by knowledge of quite a different kind. Therefore the character can never partially change, but must, with the consistency of a law of nature, realize in the particular individual the will whose phenomenon it is in general and as a whole. But this whole, the character itself, can be entirely eliminated by the abovementioned change of knowledge. It is this elimination or suppression at which Asmus marvels, as said above, and which he describes as the "catholic, transcendental change." It is also that which in the Christian Church is very appropriately called *new birth* or *regeneration,* and the knowledge from which it springs, the *effect of divine grace.* Therefore, it is not a question of a change, but of an entire suppression of the character; and so it happens that, however different the characters that arrived at that suppression were before it, they nevertheless show after it a great similarity in their mode of conduct, although each *speaks* very differently according to his concepts and dogmas.

Therefore, in this sense, the old philosophical argument about the freedom of the will, constantly contested and constantly maintained, is not without ground, and the Church dogma of the effect of grace and the new birth is also not without meaning and significance. But now we unexpectedly see both coincide into one, and can understand in what sense the admirable Malebranche could say: *"La liberté est un mystère"*;[70] and he was right. For just what the Christian mystics call the *effect of grace* and the *new birth,* is for us the only direct expression of the *freedom of the will*. It appears only when the will, after arriving at the knowledge of its own inner nature, obtains from this a *quieter,* and is thus removed from the effect of *motives* which lies in the province of a different kind of knowledge, whose objects are only phenomena. The possibility of the freedom that thus manifests itself is man's greatest prerogative, which is for ever wanting in the animal, because the condition for it is the deliberation of the faculty of reason, enabling him to survey the whole of life independently of the impression of the present moment. The animal is without any possibility of freedom, as indeed it is without the possibility of a real, and hence deliberate, elective decision after a previous complete conflict of motives, which for this purpose would have to be abstract representations. Therefore the hungry wolf buries its teeth in the flesh of the deer with the same necessity with which the stone falls to the ground, without the possibility of the knowledge that it is the mauled as well as the mauler. *Necessity is the kingdom of nature; freedom is the kingdom of grace.*

Now since, as we have seen, that *self-suppression of the will* comes from knowledge, but all knowledge and insight as such are independent of free choice, that denial of willing, that entrance into freedom, is not to be forcibly arrived at by intention or design, but comes from the innermost relation of knowing and willing in man; hence it comes suddenly, as if flying in from without. Therefore, the Church calls it the *effect of grace;* but just as she still represents it as depending on the acceptance of grace, so too the effect of the quieter is ultimately an act of the freedom of the will. In consequence of such an effect of grace, man's whole inner nature is fundamentally changed and reversed, so that he no longer wills anything of all that he previously willed so intensely; thus a new man, so to speak, actually takes the place of the old. For this reason, the Church calls this consequence of the effect of grace *new birth* or *regeneration.* For what she calls the *natural man,* to whom she denies all capacity

---

[70] "Freedom is a mystery." [Tr.]

for good, is that very will-to-live that must be denied if salvation is to be attained from an existence like ours. Behind our existence lies something else that becomes accessible to us only by our shaking off the world.

Considering not the individuals according to the principle of sufficient reason, but the Idea of man in its unity, the Christian teaching symbolizes *nature,* the *affirmation of the will-to-live, in Adam.* His sin bequeathed to us, in other words, our unity with him in the Idea, which manifests itself in time through the bond of generation, causes us all to partake of suffering and eternal death. On the other hand, the Christian teaching symbolizes *grace,* the *denial of the will, salvation,* in the God become man. As he is free from all sinfulness, in other words, from all willing of life, he cannot, like us, have resulted from the most decided affirmation of the will; nor can he, like us, have a body that is through and through only concrete will, phenomenon of the will, but, born of a pure virgin, he has only a phantom body. This last is what was taught by the Docetae, certain Fathers of the Church, who in this respect are very consistent. It was taught especially by Apelles, against whom and his followers Tertullian revolted. But even Augustine comments on the passage, Rom. viii, 3, "God sending his Son in the likeness of sinful flesh," and says: *"Non enim caro peccati erat, quae non de carnali delectatione nata erat: sed tamen inerat ei similitudo carnis peccati, quia mortalis caro erat"* (*Liber 83 Quaestionum, qu.* 66).[71] He also teaches in his work entitled *Opus Imperfectum,* i, 47, that original sin is sin and punishment at the same time. It is already to be found in new-born children, but shows itself only when they grow up. Nevertheless the origin of this sin is to be inferred from the will of the sinner. This sinner was Adam, but we all existed in him; Adam became miserable, and in him we have all become miserable. The doctrine of original sin (affirmation of the will) and of salvation (denial of the will) is really the great truth which constitutes the kernel of Christianity, while the rest is in the main only clothing and covering, or something accessory. Accordingly, we should interpret Jesus Christ always in the universal, as the symbol or personification of the denial of the will-to-live, but not in the individual, whether according to his mythical history in the Gospels, or according to the probably true history lying at the root thereof. For neither the one nor the other will easily satisfy us entirely. It is merely the vehicle of that first interpretation for the people, who

---

[71] "For it was not a sinful flesh, as it was not born of carnal desire; but yet the form of sinful flesh was in it, because it was a mortal flesh." [Tr.]

always demand something founded on fact. That Christianity has recently forgotten its true significance, and has degenerated into shallow optimism, does not concern us here.

It is further an original and evangelical doctrine of Christianity, which Augustine, with the consent of the heads of the Church, defended against the platitudes of the Pelagians; and to purify this of errors and re-establish it was the principal aim of Luther's efforts, as is expressly declared in his book *De Servo Arbitrio;* namely the doctrine that the *will is not free,* but is originally subject to a propensity for evil. Therefore the works of the will are always sinful and imperfect, and can never satisfy justice; finally, these works can never save us, but faith alone can do this. Yet this faith itself does not originate from resolution and free will, but through the *effect of grace* without our participation, like something coming to us from outside. Not only the dogmas previously mentioned, but also this last genuinely evangelical dogma is among those that an ignorant and dull opinion at the present day rejects as absurd or conceals, since, in spite of Augustine and Luther, this opinion adheres to the Pelagian plain common sense, which is just what present-day rationalism is. It treats as antiquated precisely those profound dogmas that are peculiar and essential to Christianity in the narrowest sense. On the other hand, it clings to, and regards as the principal thing, only the dogma originating in and retained from Judaism, and connected with Christianity only in a historical way.[72] We, however,

---

[72] How much this is the case is seen from the fact that all the contradictions and inconceivable mysteries contained in the Christian dogmatics and consistently systematized by Augustine, which have led precisely to the opposite Pelagian insipidity, vanish, as soon as we abstract from the fundamental Jewish dogma, and recognize that man is not the work of another, but of his own will. Then all is at once clear and correct; then there is no need of a freedom in the *operari,* for it lies in the *esse;* and here also lies the sin as original sin. The effect of grace, however, is our own. With the present-day rationalistic view, on the other hand, many doctrines of the Augustinian dogmatics, established in the New Testament, appear absolutely untenable and even revolting, for example predestination. Accordingly, what is really Christian is then rejected, and a return is made to crude Judaism. But the miscalculation or primary defect of Christian dogmatics lies where it is never sought, namely in what is withdrawn from all investigation as settled and certain. Take this away, and the whole of dogmatics is rational; for that dogma ruins theology, as it does all the other sciences. Thus, if we study the Augustinian theology in the books *De Civitate Dei* (especially in the fourteenth book), we experience something analogous to the case when we try to make a body stand, whose centre of gravity falls outside it; however we may turn and place it, it always topples over again. So also here, in spite of all the efforts and sophisms of Augustine, the guilt of the world and its misery always fall back on God, who made everything and everything that is

recognize in the above-mentioned doctrine the truth that is in complete agreement with our own investigations. Thus we see that genuine virtue and saintliness of disposition have their first origin not in deliberate free choice (works), but in knowledge (faith), precisely as we developed it also from our principal idea. If it were works, springing from motives and deliberate intention, that led to the blissful state, then, however we may turn it, virtue would always be only a prudent, methodical, far-seeing egoism. But the faith to which the Christian Church promises salvation is this: that as through the fall of the first man we all partake of sin, and are subject to death and perdition, we are also all saved through grace and by the divine mediator taking upon himself our awful guilt, and this indeed entirely without any merit of our own (of the person). For what can result from the intentional (motive-determined) action of the person, namely works, can never justify us, by its very nature, just because it is *intentional* action brought about by motives, and hence *opus operatum*. Thus in this faith it is implied first of all that our state is originally and essentially an incurable one, and that we need *deliverance* from it; then that we ourselves belong essentially to evil, and are so firmly bound to it that our works according to law and precept, i.e., according to motives, can never satisfy justice or save us, but salvation is to be gained only through faith, in other words, through a changed way of knowledge. This faith can come only through grace, and hence as from without. This means that salvation is something quite foreign to our person, and points to a denial and surrender of this very person being necessary for salvation. Works, the observance of the law as such, can never justify, because they are always an action from motives. Luther requires (in his book *De Libertate Christiana*) that, after faith has made its appearance, good works shall result from it entirely of themselves, as

in everything, and who also knew how things would turn out. I have already shown in my essay *On the Freedom of the Will* (chap. 4, pp. 66-68 of the first edition) that Augustine himself was aware of the difficulty, and was puzzled by it. In the same way, the contradiction between the goodness of God and the misery of the world, as also that between the freedom of the will and the foreknowledge of God, is the inexhaustible theme of a controversy, lasting nearly a hundred years, between the Cartesians, Malebranche, Leibniz, Bayle, Clarke, Arnauld, and many others. The only dogma fixed for the disputants is the existence of God together with his attributes, and they all incessantly turn in a circle, since they try to bring these things into harmony, in other words, to solve an arithmetical sum which never comes right, but the remainder of which appears now in one place, now in another, after it has been concealed elsewhere. But it does not 'occur to anyone that the source of the dilemma is to be looked for in the fundamental assumption, although it palpably obtrudes itself. Bayle alone shows that he notices this.

its symptoms, its fruits; certainly not as something which in itself pretends to merit, justification, or reward, but occurs quite arbitrarily and gratuitously. We also represented, as resulting from an ever clearer discernment of the *principium individuationis,* first of all merely free justice, then affection extending to the complete surrender of egoism, and finally resignation or denial of the will.

Here I have introduced these dogmas of Christian theology, in themselves foreign to philosophy, merely in order to show that the ethics which results from the whole of our discussion, and is in complete agreement and connexion with all its parts, although possibly new and unprecedented according to the expression, is by no means so in essence. On the contrary, this system of ethics fully agrees with the Christian dogmas proper, and, according to its essentials, was contained and present even in these very dogmas. It is also just as much in agreement with the doctrines and ethical precepts of the sacred books of India, which again are presented in quite different forms. At the same time, the calling to mind of the dogmas of the Christian Church served to explain and elucidate the apparent contradiction between the *necessity* of all the manifestations of the character with the presentation of motives (kingdom of nature) on the one hand, and the *freedom* of the will-in-itself to deny itself and to abolish the character, on the other, together with all the necessity of the motives which is based on this character (kingdom of grace).

§ 71.

In now bringing to a conclusion the main points of ethics, and with these the whole development of that one idea the imparting of which was my object, I do not wish by any means to conceal an objection concerning this last part of the discussion. On the contrary, I want to show that this objection lies in the nature of the case, and that it is quite impossible to remedy it. This objection is that, after our observations have finally brought us to the point where we have before our eyes in perfect saintliness the denial and surrender of all willing, and thus a deliverance from a world whose whole existence presented itself to us as suffering, this now appears to us as a transition into empty *nothingness*.

On this I must first of all observe that the concept of *nothing* is essentially relative, and always refers to a definite something that it negates. This quality has been attributed (especially by Kant) merely to the *nihil privativum* indicated by − in contrast to +. This negative sign (−) from the opposite point of view might become +, and, in opposition to this *nihil privativum,* the *nihil negativum* has been set up, which would in every respect be nothing. For this purpose, the logical contradiction that does away with itself has been used as an example. But considered more closely, an absolute nothing, a really proper *nihil negativum,* is not even conceivable, but everything of this kind, considered from a higher standpoint or subsumed under a wider concept, is always only a *nihil privativum.* Every nothing is thought of as such only in relation to something else; it presupposes this relation, and thus that other thing also. Even a logical contradiction is only a relative nothing; it is no thought of our faculty of reason; yet it is not on that account an absolute nothing. For it is a word-combination; it is an example of the unthinkable which is necessarily required in logic to demonstrate the laws of thought. Therefore, if for this purpose we look for such an example, we shall stick to the nonsense as the positive we are just looking for, and skip the sense as the negative. Thus every *nihil negativum* or absolute nothing, if subordinated to a higher concept, will appear as a mere *nihil privativum* or relative nothing, which can always change signs with what it negates, so that that would then be thought of as negation, but it itself as affirmation. This also agrees with the result of the difficult dialectical investigation on the conception of nothing which is given by Plato in the *Sophist* [258 D] (pp. 277-287, *Bip.*): Τὴν τοῦ ἑτέρου φύσιν ἀποδείξαντες οὖσάν τε, καὶ κατακεκερματισμένην ἐπὶ πάντα τὰ ὄντα πρὸς ἄλληλα, τὸ πρὸς τὸ ὄν ἑκάστου μόριον αὐτῆς ἀντιτιθέμενον, ἐτολμήσαμεν εἰπεῖν, ὡς αὐτὸ τοῦτό ἐστιν ὄντως τὸ μὴ ὄν. (*Cum enim ostenderemus, ALTERIUS ipsius naturam esse, perque omnia entia divisam atque dispersam INVICEM; tunc partem ejus oppositam ei, quod cujusque ens est, esse ipsum revera NON ENS asseruimus.*)[73]

What is universally assumed as positive, what we call *being,* the negation of which is expressed by the concept *nothing* in its most

---

[73] "It is the nature of *being different,* of which we have demonstrated that it exists and is dispersed piecemeal over all being in *mutual relationship,* and since we opposed to being every single particle of this nature, we have ventured to assert that precisely this is in truth *non-being.*" [Tr.]

general significance, is exactly the world as representation, which I have shown to be the objectivity, the mirror, of the will. We ourselves are also this will and this world, and to it belongs the representation in general as one aspect of it. The form of this representation is space and time; and so, for this point of view, everything that exists must be in some place and at some time. Then the concept, the material of philosophy, and finally the word, the sign of the concept, also belong to the representation. Denial, abolition, turning of the will are also abolition and disappearance of the world, of its mirror. If we no longer perceive the will in this mirror, we ask in vain in what direction it has turned, and then, because it no longer has any *where* and any *when,* we complain that it is lost in nothingness.

If a contrary point of view were possible for us, it would cause the signs to be changed, and would show what exists for us as nothing, and this nothing as that which exists. But so long as we ourselves are the will-to-live, this last, namely the nothing as that which exists, can be known and expressed by us only negatively, since the old saying of Empedocles, that like can be known only by like, deprives us here of all knowledge, just as, conversely, on it ultimately rests the possibility of all our actual knowledge, in other words, the world as representation, or the objectivity of the will; for the world is the self-knowledge of the will.

If, however, it should be absolutely insisted on that somehow a positive knowledge is to be acquired of what philosophy can express only negatively as denial of the will, nothing would be left but to refer to that state which is experienced by all who have attained to complete denial of the will, and which is denoted by the names ecstasy, rapture, illumination, union with God, and so on. But such a state cannot really be called knowledge, since it no longer has the form of subject and object; moreover, it is accessible only to one's own experience that cannot be further communicated.

We, however, who consistently occupy the standpoint of philosophy, must be satisfied here with negative knowledge, content to have reached the final landmark of the positive. If, therefore, we have recognized the inner nature of the world as will, and have seen in all its phenomena only the objectivity of the will; and if we have followed these from the unconscious impulse of obscure natural forces up to the most conscious action of man, we shall by no means evade the consequence that, with the free denial, the surrender, of the will, all those phenomena also are now abolished. That constant pressure and effort, without aim and without rest, at all grades of objectivity in which and through which the world exists; the multifarious forms succeeding one another in gradation; the whole phenomenon of the will; finally, the universal forms of this phenomenon, time and space, and also the last fundamental form of these, subject and object; all these are abolished with the will. No will: no representation, no world.

Before us there is certainly left only nothing; but that which struggles against this flowing away into nothing, namely our nature, is indeed just the will-to-live which we ourselves are, just as it is our world. That we abhor nothingness so much is simply another way of saying that we will life so much, and that we are nothing but this will and know nothing but it alone. But we now turn our glance from our own needy and perplexed nature to those who have overcome the world, in whom the will, having reached complete self-knowledge, has found itself again in everything, and then freely denied itself, and who then merely wait to see the last trace of the will vanish with the body that is animated by that trace. Then, instead of the restless pressure and effort; instead of the constant transition from desire to apprehension and from joy to sorrow; instead of the never-satisfied and never-dying hope that constitutes the life-dream of the man who wills, we see that peace that is higher than all reason, that ocean-like calmness of the spirit, that deep tranquillity, that unshakable confidence and serenity, whose mere reflection in the countenance, as depicted by Raphael and Correggio, is a complete and certain gospel. Only knowledge remains; the will has vanished. We then look with deep and painful yearning at that state, beside which the miserable and desperate nature of our own appears in the clearest light by the contrast. Yet this consideration is the only one that can permanently console us, when, on the one hand, we have recognized incurable suffering and endless misery as essential to the phenomenon of the will, to the world, and on the other see the world melt away with the abolished will, and retain before us only empty nothingness. In this way, therefore, by contemplating the life and conduct of saints, to meet with whom is of course rarely granted to us in our own experience, but who are brought to our notice by their recorded history, and, vouched for with the stamp of truth by art, we have to banish the dark impression of that nothingness, which as the final goal hovers behind all virtue and holiness, and which we fear as children fear darkness. We must not even evade it, as the Indians do, by myths and meaningless words, such as reabsorption in *Brahman,* or the *Nirvana* of the Buddhists. On the contrary, we freely acknowledge that what remains after the complete abolition of the will is, for all who are still full of the will, assuredly nothing. But also conversely, to those in whom the will has turned and denied itself, this very real world of ours with all its suns and galaxies, is—nothing.*

* This is also the Prajna-Paramita of the Buddhists, the "beyond all knowledge," in other words, the point where subject and object no longer exist. See I. J. Schmidt, *Ueber das Mahajana und Pradschna-Paramita.*

APPENDIX

CRITICISM OF THE KANTIAN PHILOSOPHY

C'est le privilège du vrai génie, et surtout du génie qui ouvre une carrière, de faire impunément de grandes fautes.

Voltaire [*Siècle de Louis XIV*, ch. 32]

["It is the privilege of true genius, and especially of the genius who opens up a new path, to make great mistakes with impunity." Tr.]

¹It is much easier to point out the faults and errors in the work of a great mind than to give a clear and complete exposition of its value. For the faults are something particular and finite, which can therefore be taken in fully at a glance. On the other hand, the very stamp that genius impresses on its works is that their excellence is unfathomable and inexhaustible, and therefore they do not become obsolete, but are the instructors of many succeeding centuries. The perfected masterpiece of a truly great mind will always have a profound and vigorous effect on the whole human race, so much so that it is impossible to calculate to what distant centuries and countries its enlightening influence may reach. This is always the case, since, however accomplished and rich the age might be in which the masterpiece itself arose, genius always rises like a palm-tree above the soil in which it is rooted.

A far-reaching, deep, and widespread effect of this kind cannot, however, take place suddenly, on account of the great difference between the genius and ordinary mankind. The knowledge this one man in a lifetime drew directly from life and the world, won, and presented to others as acquired and finished, cannot at once become the property of mankind, since men have not so much strength to receive as the genius has to give. But even after a successful struggle with unworthy opponents, who contest the life of what is immortal at its very birth, and would like to nip in the bud the salvation of mankind (like the serpent in Hercules' cradle), that knowledge must first wander through the circuitous paths of innumerable false interpretations and distorted applications; it must overcome the attempts to unite it with old errors, and thus live in conflict, until a new and unprejudiced generation grows up to meet it. Even in youth this generation gradually receives some of the contents of that source from a thousand different channels, assimilates it by degrees, and

---

¹ *Translator's Note:* In this criticism of Kant's philosophy, Schopenhauer frequently uses the words *Vernunft* and *Grund. Vernunft* means "reason" in the sense of the mental faculty, possessed by man alone, of forming concepts from individually perceived things, and thus of erecting the vast and intricate structure of language and logic. *Grund* means "reason" in the sense of a ground of explanation, as in the expressions "the principle of sufficient reason," "the reason for this." In the translation the German word is inserted in brackets where it is thought that the correct meaning of the word "reason" may not be obvious.

thus shares in the benefit that was to flow from that great mind to mankind. So slow is the advance in the education of the human race, that feeble, and at the same time refractory, pupil of genius. Thus the whole strength and importance of Kant's teaching will become evident only in the course of time, when the spirit of the age, itself gradually reformed and altered in the most important and essential respect by the influence of that teaching, furnishes living evidence of the power of that giant mind. However, I will certainly not take upon myself the thankless role of Calchas and Cassandra by presumptuously anticipating the spirit of the age. Only I may be allowed, in agreement with what has been said, to regard Kant's works as still very new, whereas many at the present day look upon them as already antiquated. Indeed, they have discarded them as settled and done with, or, as they put it, have left them behind. Others, emboldened by this, ignore them altogether, and with brazen effrontery continue to philosophize about God and the soul on the assumptions of the old realistic dogmatism and its scholastic philosophy. This is as if we wished to introduce into modern chemistry the theories of the alchemists. Kant's works, however, do not need my feeble eulogy, but will themselves externally extol their master, and will always live on earth, though perhaps not in the letter, yet in the spirit.

But, of course, if we look back at the first result of his doctrines, and the efforts and events in the sphere of philosophy during the period that has since elapsed, we see the corroboration of a very depressing saying of Goethe: "Just as the water displaced by a ship immediately flows in again behind it, so, when eminent minds have pushed error on one side and made room for themselves, it naturally closes in behind them again very rapidly." (*Poetry and Truth,* Pt. 3, [Book 15], p. 521.) This period, however, has been only an episode that is to be reckoned as part of the above-mentioned fate of all new and great knowledge, an episode now unmistakably near its end, since the bubble so steadily blown out is at last bursting. People generally are beginning to be conscious that real and serious philosophy still stands where Kant left it. In any case, I cannot see that anything has been done in philosophy between him and me; I therefore take my departure direct from him.

What I have in view in this Appendix to my work is really only a vindication of the teaching I have set forth in it, in so far as in many points it does not agree with the Kantian philosophy, but actually contradicts it. Yet a discussion thereof is necessary, for evidently my line of thought, different as its content is from the Kantian, is completely under its influence, and necessarily presupposes and starts from it; and I confess that, next to the impression of the world of perception, I owe what is best in my own development to the impression made by Kant's works, the sacred writings of the Hindus, and Plato. But I can justify the disagreements with Kant that are nevertheless to be found in my work, only by accusing him of error in the same points, and exposing mistakes he made. In this Appendix I must therefore deal with Kant in a thoroughly polemical manner, and seriously and with every effort; for only thus can the error that clings to Kant's teaching be burnished away, and the truth of that teaching shine all the more brightly, and endure more positively. Therefore it must not be expected that my sincere and deep reverence for Kant will also extend to his weaknesses and mistakes, and hence that I should expose them only with the most cautious indulgence, for thus my language would of necessity become feeble and flat through circumlocutions. Towards a living person such indulgence is needed, since human frailty cannot endure even the most just refutation of an error, unless it is tempered by soothing and flattery, and hardly even then; and a teacher of the ages and benefactor of mankind deserves at least that his human frailty shall also be treated with indulgence, so that he may not be caused any pain. But the man who is dead has cast this weakness aside; his merit stands firm; time will purify it more and more of all overestimation and detraction. His mistakes must be separated from it, rendered harmless, and then given over to oblivion. Therefore in the polemic I am about to institute against Kant, I have only his mistakes and weaknesses in view. I face them with hostility, and wage a relentless war of extermination upon them, always mindful not to conceal them with indulgence, but rather to place them in the brightest light, the more surely to reduce them to nought. For the reasons above-mentioned, I am not aware here of either injustice or ingratitude to Kant. But in order that, even in the eyes of others, every appearance of malignancy may be removed, I will first of all bring out clearly my deeply-felt veneration for and gratitude to Kant by stating briefly what in my eyes appears to be his principal merit. I will do this from so general a standpoint that it will not be necessary for me to touch on those points in which I must later contradict him.

* * *

Kant's greatest merit is the distinction of the phenomenon from the thing-in-itself, based on the proof that between things and us there always stands the *intellect,* and that on this account they cannot be known according to what they may be in themselves. He was led on to this path by Locke (see *Prolegomena to every Metaphysic,* § 13, note 2). Locke had shown that the secondary qualities of things, such as sound, odour, colour, hardness, softness, smoothness, and the like, founded on the affections of the senses, do not belong to the objective body, the thing-in-itself. To this, on the contrary, he attributed only the primary qualities, i.e., those that presuppose merely space and impenetrability, and so extension, shape, solidity, number, mobility. But this Lockean distinction, which was easy to find, and keeps only to the surface of things, was, so to speak, merely a youthful prelude to the Kantian. Thus, starting from an incomparably higher standpoint, Kant explains all that Locke had admitted as *qualitates primariae,* that is, as qualities of the thing-in-itself, as also belonging merely to its phenomenon in our faculty of perception or apprehension, and this just because the conditions of this faculty, namely space, time, and causality, are known by us *a priori.* Thus Locke had abstracted from the thing-in-itself the share that the sense-organs have in its phenomenon; but Kant further abstracted the share of the brain-functions (although not under this name). In this way the distinction between the phenomenon and the thing-in-itself obtained an infinitely greater significance, and a very much deeper meaning. For this purpose he had to take in hand the great separation of our *a priori* from our *a posteriori* knowledge, which before him had never been made with proper precision and completeness or with clear and conscious knowledge. Accordingly, this then became the principal subject of his profound investigations. We wish here to observe at once that Kant's philosophy has a three-fold relation to that of his predecessors; firstly, as we have seen, a relation to Locke's philosophy, confirming and extending it; secondly, a relation to Hume's, correcting and employing it, a relation that we find most distinctly expressed in the preface to the *Prolegomena* (that finest and most comprehensible of all Kant's principal works, which is far too little read, for it immensely facilitates the study of his philosophy); thirdly, a decidedly polemical and destructive relation to the philosophy of Leibniz and Wolff. We should know all three doctrines before proceeding to the study of the Kantian philosophy. Now if, in accordance with the above, the distinction of the phenomenon from the thing-in-itself, and hence the doctrine of the complete diversity of the ideal from the real, is the fundamental characteristic of the Kantian philosophy, then the assertion of the absolute identity of these two, which appeared soon afterwards, affords a melancholy proof of the saying of Goethe previously quoted. This is all the more the case, inasmuch as that identity rested on nothing but the vapouring of intellectual intuition. Accordingly, it was only a return to the crudeness of the common view, masked under the imposing impression of an air of importance, under bombast and nonsense. It became the worthy starting-point of the even grosser nonsense of the ponderous and witless Hegel. Now as Kant's separation of the phenomenon from the thing-in-itself, arrived at in the manner previously explained, far surpassed in the profundity and thoughtfulness of its argument all that had ever existed, it was infinitely important in its results. For in it he propounded, quite originally and in an entirely new way, the same truth, found from a new aspect and on a new path, which Plato untiringly repeats, and generally expresses in his language as follows. This world that appears to the senses has no true being, but only a ceaseless becoming; it is, and it also is not; and its comprehension is not so much a knowledge as an illusion. This is what he expresses in a myth at the beginning of the seventh book of the *Republic,* the most important passage in all his works, which has been mentioned already in the third book of the present work. He says that men, firmly chained in a dark cave, see neither the genuine original light nor actual things, but only the inadequate light of the fire in the cave, and the shadows of actual things passing by the fire behind their backs. Yet they imagine that the shadows are the reality, and that determining the succession of these shadows is true wisdom. The same truth, though presented quite differently, is also a principal teaching of the *Vedas* and *Puranas,* namely the doctrine of Maya, by which is understood nothing but what Kant calls the phenomenon as opposed to the thing-in-itself. For the work of Maya is stated to be precisely this visible world in which we are, a magic effect called into being, an unstable and inconstant illusion without substance, comparable to the optical illusion and the dream, a veil enveloping human consciousness, a something of which it is equally false and equally true to say that it is and that it is not. Now Kant not only expressed the same doctrine in an entirely new and original way, but made of it a proved and incontestable truth through the most calm and dispassionate presentation. Plato and the Indians, on the other hand, had based their contentions merely on a universal perception of the world; they produced them as the direct utterance of their consciousness, and presented them mythically and poetically rather than philosophically and distinctly. In this respect they are related to Kant as are the Pythagoreans Hicetas, Philolaus, and Aristarchus, who asserted the motion of the earth round the stationary sun, to Copernicus. Such clear knowledge and calm, deliberate presentation of this dreamlike quality of the whole world is really the basis of the whole Kantian philosophy; it is its soul and its greatest merit. He achieved it by taking to pieces the whole machinery of our cognitive faculty, by means of which the phantasmagoria of the objective world is brought about, and presenting it piecemeal with marvellous insight and ability. All previous Western philosophy, appearing unspeakably clumsy when compared with the Kantian, had failed to recognize that truth, and had therefore in reality always spoken as if in a dream. Kant first suddenly wakened it from this dream; therefore the last sleepers (Mendelssohn) called him the all-pulverizer. He showed that the laws which rule with inviolable necessity in existence, i.e., in experience generally, are not to be applied to deduce and explain *existence itself;* that their validity is therefore only relative, in other words, begins only after existence, the world of experience generally, is already settled and established; that in consequence these laws cannot be our guiding line when we come to the explanation of the existence of the world and of ourselves. All previous Western philosophers had imagined that these laws, according to which all phenomena are connected to one another, and all of which—time and space as well as causality and inference—I comprehend under the expression the principle of sufficient reason, were absolute laws conditioned by nothing at all, *aeternae veritates;* that the world itself existed only in consequence of and in conformity with them; and that under their guidance the whole riddle of the world must therefore be capable of solution. The assumptions made for this purpose, which Kant criticizes under the name of the Ideas of reason (*Vernunft*), really served only to raise the mere phenomenon, the work of Maya, the shadow-world of Plato, to the one highest reality, to put it in the place of the innermost and true essence of things, and thus to render the real knowledge thereof impossible, in a word, to send the dreamers still more soundly to sleep. Kant showed that those laws, and consequently the world itself, are conditioned by the subject's manner of knowing. From this it followed that, however far one might investigate and infer under the guidance of these laws, in the principal matter, i.e., in knowledge of the inner nature of the world in itself and outside the representation, no step forward was made, but one moved merely like a squirrel in his wheel. We therefore compare all the dogmatists to people who imagine that, if only they go straight forward long enough, they will come to the end of the world; but Kant had then circumnavigated the globe, and had shown that, because it is round, we cannot get out of it by horizontal movement, but that by perpendicular movement it is perhaps not impossible to do so. It can also be said that Kant's teaching gives the insight that the beginning and end of the world are to be sought not without us, but rather within.

Now all this rests on the fundamental distinction between dogmatic and *critical or transcendental philosophy*. He who wishes to be clear about this, and to realize it by means of an example, can do so quite briefly if he reads, as a specimen of dogmatic philosophy, an essay by Leibniz, entitled *De Rerum Originatione Radicali,* printed for the first time in the edition of Leibniz's philosophical works by Erdmann, vol. i, p. 147. Here the origin and excellent nature of the world are demonstrated *a priori* so thoroughly in the realistic-dogmatic manner with the aid of the ontological and cosmological proofs, and on the ground of the *veritates aeternae*. It is admitted once, by the way, that experience shows the very opposite of the excellence of the world here demonstrated, whereupon experience is then told that it does not understand anything about it, and ought to hold its tongue when philosophy has spoken *a priori*. With Kant the *critical philosophy* appeared as the opponent of this entire method. It makes its problem just those *veritates aeternae* that serve as the foundation of every such dogmatic structure, investigates their origin, and then finds this to be in man's head. Here they spring from the forms properly belonging to it, which it carries in itself for the purpose of perceiving and apprehending an objective world. Thus here in the brain is the quarry furnishing the material for that proud, dogmatic structure. Now because the critical philosophy, in order to reach this result, had to go *beyond* the *veritates aeternae,* on which all the previous dogmatism was based, so as to make these truths themselves the subject of investigation, it became *transcendental* philosophy. From this it follows also that the objective world as we know it does not belong to the true being of things-in-themselves, but is its mere *phenomenon,* conditioned by those very forms that lie *a priori* in the human intellect (i.e., the brain); hence the world cannot contain anything but phenomena.

It is true that Kant did not arrive at the knowledge that the phenomenon is the world as representation and that the thing-in-itself is the will. He showed, however, that the phenomenal world is conditioned just as much by the subject as by the object, and by isolating the most universal forms of its phenomenon, i.e., of the representation, he demonstrated that we know these forms and survey them according to their whole constitutional nature not only by starting from the object, but just as well by starting from the subject, since they are really the limit between object and subject and are common to both. He concluded that, by pursuing this limit, we do not penetrate into the inner nature of the object or the subject, and consequently that we never know the essential nature of the world, namely the thing-in-itself.

He did not deduce the thing-in-itself in the right way, as I shall soon show, but by means of an inconsistency; and he had to pay the penalty for this in the frequent and irresistible attacks on this principal part of his teaching. He did not recognize the thing-in-itself directly in the will, but made a great and original step towards this knowledge, since he demonstrated the undeniable moral significance of human conduct to be quite different from, and not dependent on, the laws of the phenomenon, to be not even capable of explanation according to them, but to be something directly touching the thing-in-itself. This is the second main point of view for assessing his merit.

We can regard as the third point the complete overthrow of the scholastic philosophy. By this term I propose to denote generally the whole period beginning with Augustine, the Church Father, and ending just before Kant. For the chief characteristic of scholasticism is indeed that which is very correctly stated by Tennemann, namely the guardianship of the prevailing national religion over philosophy, for which there was in reality nothing left but to prove and embellish the principal dogmas religion prescribed for it. The scholastics proper down to Suarez confess this openly and without reserve; the succeeding philosophers do so more unconsciously, or at any rate not avowedly. It is held that the scholastic philosophy extends only to about a hundred years before Descartes, and that with him there begins an entirely new epoch of free investigation, independent of all positive theological doctrine. Such an investigation, however, cannot in fact be attributed to Descartes and his successors,[2] but only

---

[2] Here Bruno and Spinoza are to be entirely excepted. Each stands by himself and alone; and they do not belong either to their age or to their part of the globe, which rewarded the one with death, and the other with persecution and ignominy. Their miserable existence and death in this Western world are like that of a tropical plant in Europe. The banks of the sacred Ganges were their true spiritual home; there they would have led a peaceful and honoured life among men of like mind. In the following verses, with which Bruno opens his book *Della Causa Principio ed Uno,* for which he was brought to the stake, he expresses clearly and beautifully how lonely he felt in his day; and at the same time he reveals a presentiment of his fate which caused him to hesitate before stating his case, until that tendency prevailed to communicate what is known to be true, a tendency that is so strong in noble minds:

> *Ad partum properare tuum, mens aegra, quid obstat;*
> *Seclo haec indigno sint tribuenda licet?*
> *Umbrarum fluctu terras mergente, cacumen*
> *Adtolle in clarum, noster Olympe, Jovem.*

an appearance of it, and in any case only an attempt at it. Descartes was an extremely great man, and, if we take into consideration the age in which he lived, he achieved very much. But if we set this consideration aside, and measure him according to the emancipation of thought from all fetters and to the beginning of a new period of impartial and original investigation with which he has been credited, we are obliged to find that, with his scepticism still lacking in true earnestness, and thus abating and passing away so quickly and so completely, he has the appearance of wishing to discard all at once all the fetters of the early implanted opinions belonging to his age and nation; but he does this only apparently and for a moment, in order at once to assume them again, and hold them all the more firmly; and it is just the same with all his successors down to Kant. Goethe's verses are therefore very applicable to a free and independent thinker of this kind:

> "Saving thy gracious presence, he to me
> A long-legged grasshopper appears to be,
> That springing flies, and flying springs,
> And in the grass the same old ditty sings." [3]

Kant had reasons for looking as if *he* too had only this in view. But the pretended leap that was allowed, because it was known that it leads back to the grass, this time became a flight; and now those who stand below are able only to follow him with their eyes, and no longer to catch him again.

Kant therefore ventured to demonstrate by his teaching the impossibility of our being able to prove all those dogmas that were alleged to have been proved. Speculative theology and the rational psychology connected with it received from him their death-blow.

["O my ailing mind, what prevents you from bringing forth;
  Do you offer your work to this unworthy age?
 Whenever shadows are borne over the lands,
  Raise your summit, O my mount, high into the ether." Tr.]

Whoever reads this principal work of his as well as the rest of his Italian works, formerly so rare but now accessible to everyone through a German edition, will find, as I did, that of all philosophers he alone somewhat approaches Plato as regards the strong blend of poetical force and tendency together with the philosophical, and this he also shows in a particularly dramatic way. Imagine the tender, spiritual, thoughtful being, as he appears to us in this work of his, in the hands of coarse and enraged priests as his judges and executioners, and thank Time that produced a brighter and gentler age, so that posterity, whose curse was to fall on those fiendish fanatics, is the present generation.

[3] *Faust,* Bayard Taylor's translation. [Tr.]

They have since vanished from German philosophy, and we must not let ourselves be misled by the fact that the word is retained here and there after the thing has been given up, or that some miserable professor of philosophy has the fear of his master in view and leaves truth to look after itself. Only he who has observed the pernicious influence of those conceptions on natural science, as well as on philosophy, in all the writers, even the best, of the seventeenth and eighteenth centuries can estimate the magnitude of this merit of Kant's. The change of tone and of the metaphysical background that has appeared in German works on natural science since Kant is remarkable; before him things were the same as they still are in England. This merit of Kant is connected with the fact that the unreflecting pursuit of the laws of the phenomenon, the enhancement of these to eternal truths, and the raising of the fleeting phenomenon to the real inner being of the world, in short, *realism,* not disturbed in its delusion by any reflection, had been wholly prevalent in all preceding philosophy of ancient, medieval, and modern times. Berkeley, who like Malebranche before him had recognized its one-sidedness and indeed its falseness, was unable to overthrow it, since his attack was confined to *one* point. It was therefore reserved for Kant to help the fundamental idealistic view to obtain the ascendancy in Europe, at any rate in philosophy, a view which prevails in the whole of non-Mohammedan Asia, and is in essence even that of religion. Thus before Kant we were *in* time; now time is in us, and so on.

Ethics was also treated by that realistic philosophy according to the laws of the phenomenon, which it regarded as absolute and holding good even of the thing-in-itself. Therefore ethics was based now on a doctrine of perfect happiness, now on the will of the Creator, and finally on the notion of perfection. In and by itself, such a concept is entirely empty and void of content, for it denotes a mere relation that acquires significance only from the things to which it is applied. "To be perfect" means nothing more than "to correspond to some concept presupposed and given," a concept which must therefore be first framed, and without which the perfection is an unknown abstract quantity and consequently means nothing at all when expressed alone. Now if we want to make the concept "mankind" into a tacit assumption, and accordingly to set it up as a moral principle for aspiring to human perfection, then in this case we merely say: "Men ought to be as they ought to be," and we are just as wise as we were before. In fact, "perfect" is very nearly a mere synonym of "numerically complete," since it signifies that, in a given case or individual, all the predicates that lie in the concept of its species appear in support of it, and hence are actually present.

Therefore, the concept of "perfection," if used absolutely and in the abstract, is a word devoid of idea, and so also is all talk about the "most perfect of all beings," and the like. All this is a mere idle display of words. Nevertheless, in the eighteenth century this concept of perfection and imperfection had become current coin; indeed, it was the hinge on which almost all questions of morality and even of theology turned. It was on everyone's lips, so that ultimately it became a real nuisance. We see even the best authors of the time, Lessing for example, entangled most deplorably in perfections and imperfections and wrestling with them. Here any thinking man was bound to feel, vaguely at any rate, that this concept is without any positive content, since, like an algebraical symbol, it indicates a mere relation *in abstracto*. Kant, as we have already said, entirely separated the undeniable, great ethical significance of actions from the phenomenon and its laws, and showed that the former directly concerned the thing-in-itself, the innermost nature of the world, whereas the latter, i.e., time and space, and all that fills them and is arranged in them according to the causal law, are to be regarded as an unstable and insubstantial dream.

The little I have said, which by no means exhausts the subject, may be sufficient evidence of my recognition of Kant's great merits, a recognition recorded here for my own satisfaction, and because justice demanded that those merits should be recalled to the mind of everyone who wishes to follow me in the unsparing exposure of his mistakes, to which I now turn.

* * *

That Kant's great achievements were bound to be accompanied by great errors is easy to understand on merely historical grounds. For although he effected the greatest revolution in philosophy, and did away with scholasticism, which in the above-mentioned wider sense had lasted for fourteen hundred years, in order really to begin an entirely new third world-epoch in philosophy, the immediate result of his appearance was, however, in practice only negative, not positive. For, since he did not set up a completely new system to which his followers could have adhered only for a period, all observed indeed that something very great had happened, but no one rightly knew what. They certainly saw that all previous philosophy had been a fruitless dreaming, from which the new age awakened; but they did not know what they ought to adhere to now. A great void, a great lack, had occurred; the universal attention even of the general public was attracted. Induced by this, but not urged by inner inclination and feeling of power (which express themselves even at the most unfavourable moment, as in the case of Spinoza), people without any conspicuous talent made many different, feeble, absurd, and sometimes insane attempts, to which the public, now interested, gave its attention, and with great patience, such as is found only in Germany, long lent its ear.

The same thing must once have happened in nature, when a great revolution altered the whole surface of the earth, sea and land changed places, and the scene was levelled for a new creation. It was then a long time before nature could produce a new series of lasting forms, each in harmony with itself and with the rest. Strange and monstrous organisms appeared which did not harmonize with themselves or with one another, and could not last. But it is just the remains of these, still in existence, which have brought down to us the memorial of that wavering and tentative procedure of nature forming herself anew. Now since a crisis quite similar to this and an age of monstrous abortions were produced by Kant, as we all know, it may be concluded that his merit was not complete, but was burdened with great defects, and must have been negative and one-sided. These defects we will now investigate.

* * *

First of all, we will clearly present to ourselves and examine the fundamental idea in which lie the plan and purpose of the whole *Critique of Pure Reason.* Kant took up the point of view of his predecessors, the dogmatic philosophers, and accordingly started with them from the following assumptions. (1) Metaphysics is the science of that which lies beyond the possibility of all experience. (2) Such a thing can never be found according to fundamental principles that are themselves first drawn from experience (*Prolegomena,* § 1); but only what we know *prior to,* and hence *independently of,* experience can reach farther than possible experience. (3) In our reason (*Vernunft*), some fundamental principles of the kind are actually to be found; they are comprehended under the name of knowledge from pure reason. So far Kant agrees with his predecessors, but now he parts company from them. They say: "These fundamental principles, or knowledge from pure reason, are expressions of the absolute possibility of things, *aeternae veritates,* sources of ontology; they stand above the world-order, just as with the ancients fate stood above the gods." Kant says that they are mere forms of our intellect, laws, not of the existence of things, but of our representations of them; therefore they are valid merely for our apprehension of things, and accordingly cannot extend beyond the possibility of experience, which is what was aimed at according to the first assumption. For it is precisely the *a priori* nature of these forms of knowledge, since it can rest only on their subjective origin, that cuts us off for ever from knowledge of the being-in-itself of things, and confines us to a world of mere phenomena, so that we cannot know things as they may be in themselves, even *a posteriori,* not to mention *a priori.* Accordingly, metaphysics is impossible, and in its place we have criticism of pure reason. In face of the old dogmatism, Kant is here wholly triumphant; hence all dogmatic attempts that have since appeared, have had to pursue courses quite different from the earlier ones. I shall now go on to the justification of my attempt in accordance with the expressed intention of the present criticism. Thus, with a more careful examination of the above argumentation, we shall have to confess that its first fundamental assumption is a *petitio principii;*[4] it lies in the proposition (clearly laid down especially in *Prolegomena,* § 1): "The source of metaphysics cannot be empirical at all; its fundamental principles and concepts can never be taken from experience, either inner or outer." Yet nothing at all is advanced to establish this cardinal assertion except the etymological argument from the word metaphysics. In truth, however, the matter stands thus: The world and our own existence present themselves to us necessarily as a riddle. It is now assumed, without more ado, that the solution of this riddle cannot result from a thorough understanding of the world itself, but must be looked for in something quite different from the world (for this is the meaning of "beyond the possibility of all experience"); and that everything of which we can in any way have *immediate* knowledge (for this is the meaning of possible experience, inner as well as outer) must be excluded from that solution. On the contrary, this solution must be sought only in what we can arrive at merely indirectly, namely by means of inferences from universal principles *a priori.* After the principal source of all knowledge had thus been excluded, and the direct path to truth closed, it is not surprising that the dogmatic attempts failed, and that Kant was able to demonstrate the necessity of this failure. For it had been assumed beforehand that metaphysics and knowledge *a priori* were identical; yet for this it would have been necessary first to demonstrate that the material for solving the riddle of the world cannot possibly be contained in the world itself, but is to be sought only outside it, in something we can reach only under the guidance of those forms of which we are *a priori* conscious. But so

---

[4] "Begging of the question." [Tr.]

long as this is not proved, we have no ground for shutting ourselves off from the richest of all sources of knowledge, inner and outer experience, in the case of the most important and most difficult of all problems, in order to operate with empty forms alone. Therefore, I say that the solution to the riddle of the world must come from an understanding of the world itself; and hence that the task of metaphysics is not to pass over experience in which the world exists, but to understand it thoroughly, since inner and outer experience are certainly the principal source of all knowledge. I say, therefore, that the solution to the riddle of the world is possible only through the proper connexion of outer with inner experience, carried out at the right point, and by the combination, thus effected, of these two very heterogeneous sources of knowledge. Yet this is so only within certain limits inseparable from our finite nature, consequently so that we arrive at a correct understanding of the world itself without reaching an explanation of its existence which is conclusive and does away with all further problems. Consequently, *est quadam prodire tenus,*[5] and my path lies midway between the doctrine of omniscience of the earlier dogmatism and the despair of the Kantian Critique. But the important truths discovered by Kant, by which the previous metaphysical systems were overthrown, have furnished my system with data and material. Compare what I have said about my method in chapter 17 of volume two. So much for Kant's fundamental idea; we will now consider the argument and its detail.

* * *

Kant's style bears throughout the stamp of a superior mind, a genuine, strong individuality, and a quite extraordinary power of thought. Its characteristic quality can perhaps be appropriately described as a *brilliant dryness,* on the strength of which he was able to grasp concepts firmly and pick them out with great certainty, and then toss them about with the greatest freedom, to the reader's astonishment. I find the same brilliant dryness again in the style of Aristotle, though that is much simpler. Nevertheless, Kant's exposition is often indistinct, indefinite, inadequate, and occasionally obscure. This obscurity is certainly to be excused in part by the difficulty of the subject and the depth of the ideas. Yet whoever is himself clear to the bottom, and knows quite distinctly what he thinks and wants, will never write indistinctly, never set up wavering and indefinite concepts, or pick up from foreign languages extremely diffi-

---

[5] "It is right to go up to the boundary (if there is no path beyond)." [Tr.]

cult and complicated expressions to denote such concepts, in order to continue using such expressions afterwards, as Kant took words and formulas from earlier, even scholastic, philosophy. These he combined with one another for his own purpose, as for example, "transcendental synthetic unity of apperception," and in general "unity of synthesis," which he always uses where "union" or "combination" would be quite sufficient by itself. Moreover, such a man will not always be explaining anew what has already been explained once, as Kant does, for example, with the understanding, the categories, experience, and other main concepts. Generally, such a man will not incessantly repeat himself, and yet, in every new presentation of an idea that has already occurred a hundred times, leave it again in precisely the same obscure passages. On the contrary, he will express his meaning once distinctly, thoroughly, and exhaustively, and leave it at that. *Quo enim melius rem aliquam concipimus, eo magis determinati sumus ad eam unico modo exprimendam,*[6] says Descartes in his fifth letter. But the greatest disadvantage of Kant's occasionally obscure exposition is that it acted as *exemplar vitiis imitabile;*[7] in fact it was misinterpreted as a pernicious authorization. The public had been forced to see that what is obscure is not always without meaning; what was senseless and without meaning at once took refuge in obscure exposition and language. Fichte was the first to grasp and make vigorous use of this privilege; Schelling at least equalled him in this, and a host of hungry scribblers without intellect or honesty soon surpassed them both. But the greatest effrontery in serving up sheer nonsense, in scrabbling together senseless and maddening webs of words, such as had previously been heard only in madhouses, finally appeared in Hegel. It became the instrument of the most ponderous and general mystification that has ever existed, with a result that will seem incredible to posterity, and be a lasting monument of German stupidity. Meanwhile, Jean Paul wrote in vain his fine paragraph, "Higher appreciation of philosophical madness in the professor's chair, and of poetical madness in the theatre" (*Aesthetische Nachschule*); for in vain had Goethe already said:

"They prate and teach, and no one interferes;
All from the fellowship of fools are shrinking.
Man usually believes, if only words he hears,
That also with them goes material for thinking." [8]

---

[6] "For the better we understand a thing, the more are we resolved to express it in a unique way." [Tr.]

[7] "An example inducing one to imitate its defects." [Tr.]

[8] *Faust,* Bayard Taylor's translation. [Tr.]

But let us return to Kant. We cannot help admitting that he entirely lacks grand, classical simplicity, *naïveté, ingénuité, candeur.* His philosophy has no analogy with Greek architecture which presents large, simple proportions, revealing themselves at once to the glance; on the contrary, it reminds us very strongly of the Gothic style of architecture. For an entirely individual characteristic of Kant's mind is a peculiar liking for *symmetry* that loves a variegated multiplicity, in order to arrange this, and to repeat this arrangement in subordinate forms, and so on indefinitely, precisely as in Gothic churches. In fact, he sometimes carries this to the point of trifling, and then, in deference to this tendency, goes so far as to do open violence to truth, and treats it as nature was treated by old-fashioned gardeners, whose works are symmetrical avenues, squares and triangles, trees shaped like pyramids and spheres, and hedges in regular and sinuous curves. I will illustrate this with facts.

After discussing space and time isolated from everything else, and then disposing of the whole of this world of perception, filling space and time, in which we live and are, with the meaningless words "the empirical content of perception is *given* to us," he immediately arrives in one jump at the *logical basis of his whole philosophy, namely the table of judgements.* From this table he deduces an exact dozen of categories, symmetrically displayed under four titles. These later become the fearful Procrustean bed on to which he violently forces all things in the world and everything that occurs in man, shrinking from no violence and disdaining no sophism in order merely to be able to repeat everywhere the symmetry of that table. The first thing that he symmetrically deduces from it is the pure physiological table of universal principles of natural science, namely the axioms of intuition, anticipations of perception, analogies of experience, and postulates of empirical thought in general. Of these fundamental principles the first two are simple; but each of the last two symmetrically sends out three shoots. The mere categories were what he calls *concepts,* but these fundamental principles of natural science are *judgements.* In consequence of his highest guiding line to all wisdom, namely symmetry, the series is now to prove itself fruitful in the *inferences* or *syllogisms;* and this indeed they do again symmetrically and rhythmically. For as, by applying the categories to sensibility, experience together with its *a priori* principles sprang up for the *understanding,* so by applying the *syllogisms* to the categories, a task performed by *reason (Vernunft)* according to its alleged principle of looking for the unconditioned, the *Ideas* of reason arise. This takes place as follows: The three categories of relation give to syllogisms the three only possible kinds of major premisses, and accordingly syllogisms also are divided into three kinds, each of which is to be regarded as an egg from which the faculty of reason hatches an Idea; from the categorical kind of syllogism, the Idea of the *soul;* from the hypothetical, the Idea of the *world;* and from the disjunctive, the Idea of *God.* In the middle one, namely the Idea of the world, the symmetry of the table of categories is once more repeated, since its four titles produce four theses, each of which has its antithesis as a symmetrical pendant.

We express our admiration for the really extremely acute combination that produced this elegant structure, but later on we shall thoroughly examine its foundations and its parts. First, however, we must make the following remarks.

* * *

It is astonishing how Kant, without further reflection, pursues his way, following his symmetry, arranging everything according to it, without ever considering by itself one of the subjects thus dealt with. I will explain myself in more detail. After taking intuitive knowledge into consideration merely in mathematics, he entirely neglects the rest of knowledge of perception in which the world lies before us, and sticks solely to abstract thinking. Such thinking, however, receives the whole of its meaning and value only from the world of perception, which is infinitely more significant, more universal, and more substantial than is the abstract part of our knowledge. In fact, and this is a main point, he has nowhere clearly distinguished knowledge of perception from abstract knowledge, and in this way, as we shall see later, he becomes implicated in inextricable contradictions with himself. After disposing of the whole world of the senses with the meaningless "it is given," he now, as we have said, makes the logical table of judgements the foundation-stone of his structure. But here again he does not reflect for a moment on what really lies before him. These forms of judgements are indeed *words* and *word-combinations.* Yet first of all it should have been asked what these directly denote; it would be found that they are *concepts.* Then the next question would be about the nature of *concepts.* From the answer to it we should have seen what relation these have to the representations of perception in which the world exists, for perception and reflection would have been separated. It would then have been necessary to examine not merely how pure and only formal intuition *a priori,* but also how its content, namely empirical perception, enters consciousness. But then it would have been seen what share the *understanding* has in this, and so also in general what the *understanding* is, and, on the other hand, what *reason* (*Vernunft*) really is, the critique of which was being written. It is very remarkable that he does not once properly and adequately define the latter, but only occasionally, and as required by the context in each case, gives incomplete and inaccurate explanations of it, in entire contradiction to the rule of Descartes already quoted.[9] For example, on p. 11 (V, 24) of the *Critique of Pure Reason*, it is the faculty of the principles *a priori;* again on p. 299 (V, 356) he says that reason is the faculty of the *principles,* and that it is opposed to the understanding, which is the faculty of *rules!* Now one would think that there must be a vast difference between principles and rules, for it entitles us to assume a particular faculty of knowledge for each of them. But this great distinction is said to lie merely in the fact that what is known *a priori* through pure intuition or perception, or through the forms of the understanding, is a *rule,* and only what results *a priori* from mere concepts is a principle. We shall return later to this arbitrary and inadmissible distinction when dealing with the Dialectic. On p. 330 (V, 386) reason is the faculty of inference; mere judging (p. 69; V, 94) he often declares to be the business of the understanding. Now by this he really says that judging is the business of the understanding, so long as the ground of the judgement is empirical, transcendental, or metalogical (*On the Principle of Sufficient Reason,* §§ 31, 32, 33); but if it is logical, and the syllogism consists in this, then a quite special, and much more important, faculty of knowledge, namely of reason, is here at work. Indeed, what is more, on p. 303 (V, 360) it is explained that the immediate inferences from a proposition are still a matter of the understanding, and that only those where a mediating concept is used would be carried out by our faculty of reason. The example quoted is that from the proposition "All men are mortal," the inference "Some mortals are men" is drawn by the mere understanding; on the other hand: "All scholars are mortal" is an inference demanding a quite different and far more important faculty, that of reason. How was it possible for a great thinker to produce anything like this? On p. 553 (V. 581) reason is all of a sudden the constant condition of all arbitrary actions. On p. 614 (V, 642)

---

[9] Here it must be noted that I everywhere quote the *Critique of Pure Reason* according to the pagination *of the first edition,* for in the Rosenkranz edition of the collected works this pagination is always given in addition. Moreover, I add the pagination of the fifth edition, preceded by a V. All the other editions from the second onwards are like the fifth, and so also is their pagination.

[*Translator's addition:* Professor F. Max Müller's English translation of the *Critique of Pure Reason* indicates in square brackets the original pagination of the first German edition.]

it consists in our being able to give an account of our assertions; on pp. 643, 644 (V, 671, 672) it consists in the fact that it unites the concepts of the understanding into Ideas, just as the understanding unites the manifold of objects into concepts. On p. 646 (V, 674) it is nothing but the faculty of deriving the particular from the general.

The *understanding* is also being constantly explained afresh. It is explained in seven passages of the *Critique of Pure Reason:* thus, on p. 51 (V, 75) it is the faculty of producing representations themselves; on p. 69 (V, 94) it is the faculty of judging, i.e., of thinking, i.e., of knowing through concepts; on p. 137 of the fifth edition,[10] it is the faculty of knowledge in general; on p. 132 (V, 171) it is the faculty of rules, but on p. 158 (V, 197) he says that "It is not only the faculty of rules, but the source of fundamental principles (*Grundsätze*) according to which everything is under rules"; and yet previously it was opposed to reason, because reason alone was the faculty of principles (*Principien*). On p. 160 (V, 199) the understanding is the faculty of concepts; but on p. 302 (V, 359) it is the faculty of the unity of phenomena by means of rules.

Against such really confused and groundless utterances on the question (although they come from Kant) I shall have no need to defend the explanations I have advanced of these two faculties of knowledge, for such explanations are fixed, precise, definite, simple, and always agree with the use of language in all nations and all ages. I have quoted them merely as proofs of my reproach that Kant pursues his symmetrical, logical system without reflecting sufficiently on the subject with which he thus deals.

Now, as I have said above, if Kant had seriously investigated to what extent two such different faculties of knowledge, one of which is the distinctive characteristic of mankind, come to be known, and what reason and understanding mean according to the use of language in all nations and by all philosophers, then he would never have divided reason into theoretical and practical without any further authority than the *intellectus theoreticus* and *practicus* of the scholastics, who use the terms in an entirely different sense, and he would never have made practical reason the source of virtuous conduct. In the same way, Kant should really have investigated what a *concept* is in general, before separating so carefully concepts of the understanding (by which he understands partly his categories, partly all common concepts) and concepts of reason (his so-called Ideas), and making them both the material of his philosophy, which

---

[10] Para. 17. [Tr.]

for the most part deals only with the validity, application, and origin of all these concepts. But this very necessary investigation, unfortunately, has also been omitted, and this has greatly contributed to the terrible confusion of intuitive and abstract knowledge which I shall shortly demonstrate. The same want of adequate reflection with which he passed over such questions as: What is perception? What is reflection? What is concept? What is reason? What is understanding? caused him also to pass over the following investigations just as absolutely necessary, namely: What do I call the *object* which I distinguish from the *representation?* What is existence? What is object? What is subject? What are truth, illusion, error? But he pursues, without reflecting or looking about him, his logical schema and his symmetry. The table of judgements shall and must be the key to all wisdom.

* * *

I have mentioned it above as Kant's principal merit that he distinguished the phenomenon from the thing-in-itself, declared this whole visible world to be phenomenon, and therefore denied to its laws all validity beyond the phenomenon. It is certainly remarkable that he did not trace that merely relative existence of the phenomenon from the simple, undeniable truth which lay so near to him, namely *"No object without a subject,"* in order thus, at the very root, to show that the object, because it always exists only in relation to a subject, is dependent thereon, is conditioned thereby, and is therefore mere phenomenon that does not exist in itself, does not exist unconditionally. Berkeley, to whose merit Kant does not do justice, had already made that important proposition the foundation-stone of his philosophy, and had thus created an immortal reputation for himself. Yet even he did not draw the proper conclusions from that proposition, and so was in part misunderstood, and in part insufficiently attended to. In my first edition, I explained Kant's avoidance of this Berkeleian principle as resulting from a visible fear of decided idealism, whereas, on the other hand, I found this distinctly expressed in many passages of the *Critique of Pure Reason,* and accordingly accused Kant of contradicting himself. And this reproach was well founded, in so far as the *Critique of Pure Reason* was at that time known to me only in its second edition, or in the five subsequent editions printed from it. Now when later I read Kant's principal work in the first edition, which had already become scarce, I saw, to my great joy, all those contradictions disappear. I found that, although Kant does not use the formula "No object without subject," he nevertheless, with just as much emphasis as do Berkeley and I, declares the external world lying before us in space and time to be mere representation of the subject that knows it. Thus, for example, he says there (p. 383) without reserve: "If I take away the thinking subject, the whole material world must cease to exist, as it is nothing but the phenomenon in the sensibility of our subject, and a species of its representations." However, the whole passage from p. 348 to p. 392, in which Kant expounds his decided idealism with great beauty and clarity, was suppressed by him in the second edition. On the other hand, he introduced a number of remarks that controverted it. In this way, the text of the *Critique of Pure Reason,* as it was in circulation from the year 1787 to 1838, became disfigured and spoilt; it was a self-contradictory book, whose sense therefore could not be thoroughly clear and comprehensible to anyone. In a letter[11] to Professor Rosenkranz, I discussed this in detail, as well as my conjectures regarding the grounds and the weaknesses that could have induced Kant to disfigure his immortal work in such a way. The main passage of this letter was included by Rosenkranz in his preface to the second volume of the edition of Kant's collected works edited by him, to which therefore I refer. In consequence of my representations, Professor Rosenkranz was induced in 1838 to restore the *Critique of Pure Reason* to its original form, for in the second volume, just mentioned, he had it printed according to the *first* edition of 1781. In this way he rendered an inestimable service to philosophy; indeed he has possibly rescued from destruction the most important work of German literature; and for this we must always be grateful to him. But let no one imagine he knows the *Critique of Pure Reason,* and has a clear conception of Kant's teaching, if he has read only the second or one of the subsequent editions. This is absolutely impossible; for he has read only a mutilated, spoilt, and, to a certain extent ungenuine text. It is my duty to state this here emphatically, as a warning to everyone.

However, the way in which Kant introduces the *thing-in-itself* stands in undeniable contradiction to the fundamental, emphatic, and idealistic view so clearly expressed in the first edition of the *Critique of Pure Reason.* Without doubt this is mainly why, in the second edition, he suppressed the principal idealistic passage previously referred to, and declared himself directly opposed to Berkeley's idealism. By doing this, however, he only introduced inconsistencies into his work, without being able to remedy its main de-

---

[11] Dated 24 August 1837. [Tr.]

fect. It is well known that this defect is the introduction of the *thing-in-itself* in the way he chose, whose inadmissibility was demonstrated in detail by G. E. Schulze in *Aenesidemus,* and which was soon recognized as the untenable point of his system. The matter can be made clear in a very few words. Kant bases the assumption of the thing-in-itself, although concealed under many different turns of expression, on a conclusion according to the law of causality, namely that empirical perception, or more correctly *sensation* in our organs of sense from which it proceeds, must have an external cause. Now, according to his own correct discovery, the law of causality is known to us *a priori,* and consequently is a function of our intellect, and so is of *subjective* origin. Moreover, sensation itself, to which we here apply the law of causality, is undeniably *subjective;* and finally, even space, in which, by means of this application, we place the cause of the sensation as object, is a form of our intellect given *a priori,* and is consequently *subjective.* Therefore the whole of empirical perception remains throughout on a *subjective* foundation, as a mere occurrence in us, and nothing entirely different from and independent of it can be brought in as a *thing-in-itself,* or shown to be a necessary assumption. Empirical perception actually is and remains our mere representation; it is the world as representation. We can arrive at its being-in-itself only on the entirely different path I have followed, by means of the addition of self-consciousness, which proclaims the will as the in-itself of our own phenomenon. But then the thing-in-itself becomes something *toto genere* different from the representation and its elements, as I have explained.

The great defect of the Kantian system in this point, which, as I have said, was soon demonstrated, is an illustration of the beautiful Indian proverb: "No lotus without a stem." Here the stem is the faulty deduction of the thing-in-itself, though only the method of deduction, not the recognition of a thing-in-itself belonging to the given phenomenon. But in this last way Fichte misunderstood it, and this was possible only because he was concerned not with truth, but with making a sensation for the furtherance of his personal ends. Accordingly, he was foolhardy and thoughtless enough altogether to deny the thing-in-itself, and to set up a system in which not the merely formal part of the representation, as with Kant, but also the material, namely its whole content, was ostensibly deduced *a priori* from the subject. He quite correctly reckoned here on the public's lack of judgement and stupidity, for they accepted wretched sophisms, mere hocus-pocus, and senseless twaddle as proofs, so that he succeeded in turning the public's attention from Kant to himself, and in giving to German philosophy the direction in which it was afterwards carried farther by Schelling, finally reaching its goal in the senseless sham wisdom of Hegel.

I now return to Kant's great mistake, already touched on above, namely that he did not properly separate knowledge of perception from abstract knowledge; from this there arose a terrible confusion which we have now to consider more closely. If he had sharply separated representations of perception from concepts thought merely *in abstracto,* he would have kept these two apart, and would have known with which of the two he had to deal in each case. Unfortunately this was not the case, although the reproach for this has not yet become known, and is therefore perhaps unexpected. His "object of experience," of which he is constantly speaking, the proper subject of the categories, is not the representation of perception, nor is it the abstract concept; it is different from both, and yet is both at the same time, and is an utter absurdity and impossibility. For, incredible as it seems, he lacked the good sense or the good will to come to an understanding with himself about this, and to explain clearly to others whether his "object of experience, i.e., of the knowledge brought about by the application of the categories," is the representation of perception in space and time (my first class of representations), or merely the abstract concept. Strange as it is, there is constantly running through his mind something between the two, and so there comes about the unfortunate confusion that I must now bring to light. For this purpose I shall have to go over the whole elementary theory in general.

* * *

The *Transcendental Aesthetic* is a work of such merit that it alone would be sufficient to immortalize the name of Kant. Its proofs have such a complete power of conviction that I number its propositions among the incontestable truths. They are also undoubtedly among those that are richest in results, and are therefore to be regarded as that rarest thing in the world, a real and great discovery in metaphysics. The fact, which he strictly demonstrates, that we are *a priori* conscious of a part of our knowledge, admits of no other explanation at all except that this constitutes the forms of our intellect; indeed this is not so much an explanation as merely the distinct expression of the fact itself. For *a priori* means nothing but "not gained on the path of experience, and hence not come into us from without." Now that which is present in the intellect yet has not come from without, is just that which originally belongs to the intellect itself, namely its own nature. If that which is thus present in the intellect itself consists in the mode and manner in which all its objects must present themselves to it, then this is equivalent to saying that what is thus present is the intellect's forms of knowing, in other words, the mode and manner, settled once for all, in which it fulfils this its function. Accordingly, "knowledge *a priori*" and "the intellect's own forms" are fundamentally only two expressions for the same thing, and so are, to a certain extent, synonyms.

Therefore, I knew of nothing to take away from the theories of the Transcendental Aesthetic, but only of something to add to them. Kant did not pursue his thought to the very end, especially in not rejecting the whole of the Euclidean method of demonstration, even after he had said on p. 87 (V, 120) that all geometrical knowledge has direct evidence from perception. It is most remarkable that even one of his opponents, in fact the cleverest of them, G. E. Schulze (*Kritik der theoretischen Philosophie,* ii, 241), draws the conclusion that an entirely different treatment of geometry from what is actually in use would result from Kant's teaching. He thus imagines that he is bringing an apagogical argument against Kant, but as a matter of fact, without knowing it, he is beginning a war against the Euclidean method. I refer to § 15 in the first book of the present work.

After the detailed discussion of the universal *forms* of all perception, given in the Transcendental Aesthetic, we necessarily expect to receive some explanation of its *content,* of the way in which *empirical* perception enters our consciousness, of how knowledge of this whole world, for us so real and so important, originates in us. But about this the whole of Kant's teaching really contains nothing but the oft-repeated meaningless expression: "The empirical part of perception is *given* from without." Therefore, here also from the *pure forms of intuition,* Kant arrives with one jump at *thinking,* at the *Transcendental Logic.* At the very beginning of the Transcendental Logic (*Critique of Pure Reason,* p. 50; V, 74), where Kant cannot help touching on the material content of empirical perception, he takes the first false step, he commits the πρῶτον ψεῦδος. "Our knowledge," he says, "has two sources, receptivity of impressions and spontaneity of concepts: the former is the capacity of receiving representations; the latter is the capacity for knowing an object through these representations. Through the first an *object* is given to us, through the second it is thought." This is false, for according to this the *impression,* for which alone we have mere receptivity, which therefore comes from without and alone is really *"given,"* would be already a *representation,* in fact even an *object.* But it is nothing more than a mere *sensation* in the sense-organ, and only by the application of the *understanding* (i.e., of the law of causality), and of the forms of perception, of space and time, does our *intellect* convert this mere *sensation* into a *representation.* This representation now exists as *object* in space and time, and cannot be distinguished from the latter (the object) except in so far as we ask about the thing-in-itself; in other respects it is identical with the object. I have discussed this point in detail in the essay *On the Principle of Sufficient Reason,* § 21. But with this the business of the understanding and of knowledge of perception is finished, and for this no concepts and no thinking are needed in addition; therefore the animal also has these representations. If concepts are added, if thinking is added, to which spontaneity can certainly be attributed, then knowledge of *perception* is entirely abandoned, and a completely different class of representations, namely non-perceptible, abstract concepts, enters consciousness. This is the activity of *reason* (*Vernunft*), which nevertheless has the whole content of its thinking only from the perception that precedes this thinking, and from the comparison of this with other perceptions and concepts. But in this way Kant brings thinking into perception, and lays the foundation for the terrible confusion of intuitive and abstract knowledge which I am here engaged in condemning. He allows perception, taken by itself, to be without understanding, purely sensuous, and thus entirely passive, and only through thinking (category of the understanding) does he allow an *object* to be apprehended; thus he brings *thinking into perception.* But then again, the object of *thinking* is an individual, real object; in this way, thinking loses its essential character of universality and abstraction, and, instead of universal concepts, receives as its object individual things; thus he again brings *perception into thinking.* From this springs the terrible confusion referred to, and the consequences of this first false step extend over the whole of his theory of knowledge. Through the whole of this, the utter confusion of the representation of perception with the abstract representation tends to a cross between the two, which he describes as the object of knowledge through the understanding and its categories, and this knowledge he calls *experience.* It is difficult to believe that, in the case of this object of the understanding, Kant pictured to himself something quite definite and really distinct. I shall now prove this by the tremendous contradiction, running through the whole of the Transcendental Logic, which is the real source of the obscurity that envelops it.

Thus in the *Critique of Pure Reason,* pp. 67-69 (V, 92-94); pp. 89, 90 (V, 122, 123); further, V, 135, 139, 153, he repeats and insists that the understanding is no faculty of perception, that its knowledge is not intuitive but discursive; that the understanding is the faculty of judging (p. 69: V, 94), and a judgement is indirect knowledge, representation of a representation (p. 68: V, 93); that the understanding is the faculty of thinking, and thinking is knowledge through concepts (p. 69: V, 94); that the categories of the understanding are by no means the conditions under which objects are given in perception (p. 89: V, 122), and perception in no way requires the functions of thinking (p. 91: V, 123); that our understanding can only think, not perceive (V, pp. 135, 139). Further, in the *Prolegomena,* § 20, he says that perception, intuition, *perceptio* belongs merely to the senses; that judgement belongs only to the understanding; and in § 22, that the business of the senses is to perceive, that of the understanding to think, i.e., to judge. Finally, in the *Critique of Practical Reason,* fourth edition, p. 247 (Rosenkranz's edition, p. 281) he says that the understanding is discursive, its representations are thoughts, not perceptions. All this is in Kant's own words.

From this it follows that this world of perception would exist for us even if we had no understanding at all, that it comes into our head in an entirely inexplicable way; this he frequently indicates by his curious expression that perception is *given,* without ever explaining this indefinite and metaphorical expression any further.

Now all that has been quoted is contradicted most flagrantly by all the rest of his doctrine of the understanding, of its categories, and of the possibility of experience, as he explains this in the Transcendental Logic. Thus in the *Critique of Pure Reason,* p. 79 (V, 105) the understanding through its categories brings unity into the manifold of *perception,* and the pure concepts of the understanding refer *a priori* to objects of *perception.* On p. 94 (V, 126) he says that "the categories are the condition of experience, whether of *perception* or of thinking that is met with in it." In V, 127,[12] the understanding is the originator of experience. In V, 128,[12] the categories determine the *perception* of the objects. In V, p. 130,[13] all that we represent to ourselves as combined in the object (which is of course something perceptible and not an abstraction), has been combined by an act of the understanding. In V, p. 135,[14] the understanding is explained anew as the faculty of combining *a priori,* and bringing the manifold of given representations under the unity of apperception. According to all ordinary use of language, however, apperception is not the thinking of a concept, but *perception.* In V, p. 136,[14] we find even a supreme principle of the possibility of all perception

---

[12] Para. 14. [Tr.]
[13] Para. 15. [Tr.]
[14] See generally paras. 15-27. [Tr.]

in relation to the understanding. In V, p. 143,[15] it is given even as a heading that all sensuous perception is conditioned by the categories. At the very same place, the *logical function of the judgements* also brings the manifold of given *perceptions* under an apperception in general, and the manifold of a given perception stands necessarily under the categories. In V, p. 144,[15] unity comes into *perception* by means of the categories through the understanding. In V, p. 145,[15] the thinking of the understanding is very strangely explained by saying that the understanding synthetizes, combines, and arranges the manifold of *perception*. In V, p. 161,[15] experience is possible only through the categories, and consists in the connexion of *perceptions* (*Wahrnehmungen*) which, however, are just intuitions (*Anschauungen*). In V, p. 159,[15] the categories are *a priori* knowledge of the objects of *perception* in general. Moreover, here and in V, pp. 163 and 165,[15] one of Kant's main doctrines is expressed, namely *that the understanding first of all makes nature possible,* since it prescribes for her laws *a priori,* and nature accommodates herself to the constitution of the understanding, and so on. Now nature is certainly perceptible and not an abstraction; accordingly, the understanding would have to be a faculty of perception. In V, p. 168[15] it is said that the concepts of the understanding are the principles of the possibility of experience, and this is the determining of phenomena in space and time generally, phenomena which, however, certainly exist in perception. Finally, pp. 189-211 (V, 232-265) there is the long proof (whose incorrectness is shown in detail in my essay *On the Principle of Sufficient Reason,* § 23), that the objective succession and also the coexistence of the objects of experience are not sensuously apprehended, but are brought into nature only through the understanding, and that nature herself first becomes possible in this way. But it is certain that nature, the sequence of events, and the coexistence of states, is something purely perceptible, and not something merely thought in the abstract.

I invite everyone who shares my respect for Kant to reconcile these contradictions, and to show that, in his doctrine of the object of experience and of the way in which this object is determined by the activity of the understanding and its twelve functions, Kant conceived something quite distinct and definite. I am convinced that the contradiction I have pointed out, which extends through the whole Transcendental Logic, is the real reason for the great obscurity of its language. In fact, Kant was vaguely aware of the contradiction, inwardly struggled with it, but yet would not or could

---

[15] See generally paras. 15-27. [Tr.]

not bring it to clear consciousness. He therefore wrapped it in mystery for himself and for others, and avoided it by all kinds of subterfuges. Possibly from this it can also be inferred why he made from the faculty of knowledge so strange and complicated a machine, with so many wheels, such as the twelve categories, the transcendental synthesis of imagination, of the inner sense, of the transcendental unity of apperception, also the schematism of the pure concepts of the understanding, and so on. And notwithstanding this great apparatus, not even an attempt is made to explain the perception of the external world, which is after all the main thing in our knowledge, but this pressing claim is very miserably rejected always by the same meaningless metaphorical expression: "Empirical perception is given to us." On p. 145[16] of the fifth edition, we learn further that perception is given through the object; consequently, the object must be something different from perception.

Now if we endeavour to examine Kant's innermost meaning, which he himself does not distinctly express, we find that actually such an object different from *perception,* which, however, is by no means a *concept,* is for him the proper object for the understanding; indeed that it really must be by the strange assumption of such an object, incapable of representation, that perception first becomes experience. I believe that an old, deep-rooted prejudice in Kant, dead to all investigation, is the ultimate reason for the assumption of such an *absolute object* that is an object in itself, i.e., one without a subject. It is certainly not the *perceived object,* but through the concept it is added to perception by thought as something corresponding to perception; and now perception is experience, and has value and truth that it consequently receives only through the relation to a concept (in diametrical opposition to our exposition, according to which the concept obtains value and truth only from perception). It is then the proper function of the categories to add by thought on to perception this object that is not capable of direct representation. "The object is given only through perception, and it is afterwards thought in accordance with the category" (*Critique of Pure Reason,* first edition, p. 399). This becomes particularly clear from a passage, p. 125[17] of the fifth edition: "It is now asked whether concepts *a priori* do not also come first as conditions under which alone something is, although *not perceived,* yet *conceived* as *object* in general," a question he answers in the affirmative. Here the source of the error and the confusion that surrounds it are clearly seen. For the *object* as such exists always only for and in *perception;*

---

[16] Para. 22. [Tr.]
[17] Para. 14. [Tr.]

now perception may be brought about through the senses, or, in the absence of the object, through the power of imagination. What is *thought,* on the other hand, is always a universal, non-perceptible *concept,* which can at all events be the concept of an object in general. Only indirectly, however, by means of concepts, is thinking related to *objects,* and these objects themselves always are and remain *perceptible.* For our thinking does not help to impart reality to perceptions; this they have in so far as they are capable of it (empirical reality) through themselves; but our thinking does serve to comprehend and embrace the common element and the results of perceptions, in order to be able to preserve them and manipulate them more easily. Kant, however, ascribes the objects themselves to *thinking,* in order thus to make experience and the objective world dependent on the *understanding,* yet without letting the understanding be a faculty of *perception.* In this connexion, he certainly distinguishes perceiving from thinking, but he makes particular things the object sometimes of perception and sometimes of thinking. But actually they are only the object of perception; our empirical perception is at once *objective,* just because it comes from the causal nexus. Things, and not representations different from them, are directly its object. Individual things as such are perceived in the understanding and through the senses; the *one-sided* impression on these is at once completed by the power of the imagination. On the other hand, as soon as we pass over to *thinking,* we leave individual things, and have to do with universal concepts without perceptibility, although afterwards we apply the results of our thinking to individual things. If we stick to this, the inadmissibility is apparent of the assumption that the perception of things obtains reality and becomes experience only through the thought of these very things applying the twelve categories. On the contrary, in perception itself empirical reality, and consequently experience, is already given; but perception can also come about only by the application of knowledge of the causal nexus, the sole function of the understanding, to the sensation of the senses. Accordingly, perception is really intellectual, and this is just what Kant denies.

Besides the passage quoted, Kant's assumption here criticized is also found expressed with admirable clearness in the *Critique of Judgement,* § 36, at the very beginning; likewise in the *Metaphysical Rudiments of Natural Science,* in the note to the first explanation of "Phenomenology." But with a naïvety which Kant ventured on least of all in connexion with this doubtful point, it is found most distinctly laid down in the book of a Kantian, namely, Kiesewetter's *Grundriss einer allgemeinen Logik,* third edition, Part I, p. 434 of the explanation, and Part II, §§ 52 and 53 of the explanation; like-wise in Tieftrunk's *Denklehre in rein Deutschem Gewande* (1825). There it is clearly seen how the disciples of every thinker, who do not think for themselves, become the magnifying mirror of his mis-takes. Having once decided on his doctrine of the categories, Kant always trod warily when expounding it; the disciples, on the con-trary, are quite bold, and thus expose its falseness.

In accordance with what has been said, the object of the cate-gories with Kant is not exactly the thing-in-itself, but yet is very closely akin to it. It is the *object-in-itself,* an object requiring no subject, an individual thing, and yet not in time and space, because not perceptible; it is object of thinking, and yet not abstract concept. Accordingly, Kant makes a triple distinction: (1) the representation; (2) the object of the representation; (3) the thing-in-itself. The first is the concern of sensibility, which for him includes, simul-taneously with sensation, also the pure forms of perception, namely space and time. The second is the concern of the understanding, that adds it in *thought* through its twelve categories. The third lies beyond all possibility of knowledge. (As proof of this, see pp. 108 and 109 of the first edition of the *Critique of Pure Reason.*) The distinction between the representation and the object of the repre-sentation is, however, unfounded. Berkeley had already demonstrated this, and it follows from the whole of my discussion in the first book, especially from Chapter I of the supplements; in fact it follows from Kant's own wholly idealistic point of view in the first edition. But if we did not wish to reckon the object of the representation as belonging to the representation, and to identify it therewith, we should have to attribute it to the thing-in-itself; in the end this de-pends on the sense we attach to the word object. However, this much is certain, that, when we reflect clearly, nothing can be found except representation and thing-in-itself. The unwarranted introduc-tion of that hybrid, the object of the representation, is the source of Kant's errors. Yet, when this is removed, the doctrine of the categories as concepts *a priori* also falls to the ground; for they con-tribute nothing to perception, and are not supposed to hold good of the thing-in-itself, but by means of them we conceive only those "objects of the representations," and thus convert representation into experience. For every empirical perception is already experience; but every perception that starts from sensation is empirical. By means of its sole function (namely *a priori* knowledge of the law of causality), the understanding refers this sensation to its cause. In this way the cause presents itself in space and time (forms of pure intuition or perception) as object of experience, material object, enduring in space through all time, but yet as such always remaining representation, just like space and time themselves. If we wish to go beyond this representation, we arrive at the question as to the thing-in-itself, the answer to which is the theme of my whole work, as of all metaphysics in general. Kant's error, here discussed, is connected with the mistake of his which we previously condemned, namely that he gives no theory of the origin of empirical perception, but, without more ado, treats it as *given,* identifying it with the mere sensation to which he adds only the forms of intuition or perception, namely space and time, comprehending both under the name of sensibility. But still there does not arise any objective representation from these materials. On the contrary, this positively demands a relation of the sensation to its cause, and hence the application of the law of causality, and thus understanding. For without this, the sensation still remains always subjective, and does not put an object into space, even when space is given with it. But according to Kant, the understanding could not be applied to perception; it was supposed merely to *think,* in order to remain within the Transcendental Logic. With this again is connected another of Kant's mistakes, namely that he left it to me to furnish the only valid proof of the rightly recognized *a priori* nature of the law of causality, in other words, the proof from the possibility of objective, empirical perception itself. Instead of this, he gives an obviously false proof, as I have shown in my essay *On the Principle of Sufficient Reason,* § 23. From the above, it is clear that Kant's "object of the representation" (2) is made up of what he has stolen partly from the representation (1) and partly from the thing-in-itself (3). If experience actually came about only by our understanding applying twelve different functions, in order to *think* through just as many concepts *a priori* the objects that were previously merely perceived, then every real thing as such would have to have a number of determinations, which, being given *a priori,* just like space and time, could not possibly be thought away, but would belong quite essentially to the existence of the thing, and yet could not be deduced from the properties of space and time. But only a single determination of this kind is to be found, that of causality. On this rests materiality, for the essence of matter consists in action, and it is through and through causality. (See Vol. 2, chap. 4.) But it is materiality alone that distinguishes the real thing from the picture of the imagination, that picture then being only representation. For matter, as permanent, gives the thing permanence through all time according to its matter, while the forms change in conformity with causality. Everything else in the thing is either determinations of space or of time, or its empirical properties, all of which relate to its activity, and are thus fuller determinations of causality. Causality, however, already enters as a condition into empirical perception, and this is accordingly a concern of the understanding, which makes perception possible, but, apart from the law of causality, contributes nothing to experience and its possibility. What fills the old ontologies, apart from what is stated here, is nothing more than relations of things to one another, or to our reflection, and is a scrambled-up hotch-potch.

The style and language of the doctrine of the categories afford an indication of its groundlessness. What a difference in this respect between the Transcendental *Aesthetic* and the Transcendental *Analytic!* In the *former,* what clearness, definiteness, certainty, firm conviction, openly expressed and infallibly communicated! All is full of light, no dark lurking-places are left; Kant knows what he wants, and knows he is right. In the *latter,* on the other hand, all is obscure, confused, indefinite, wavering, uncertain; the language is cautious and uneasy, full of excuses and appeals to what is coming, or even to what is withheld. The entire second and third sections of the Deduction of the Pure Concepts of the Understanding are completely changed in the second edition, because they did not satisfy Kant himself, and have become quite different from those in the first edition, although no clearer. We actually see Kant in conflict with the truth, in order to carry out the hypothesis that he has once settled. In the Transcendental *Aesthetic,* all his propositions are actually demonstrated and proved from undeniable facts of consciousness; in the Transcendental *Analytic,* on the other hand, when we consider it closely, we find mere assertions that so it is and so it must be. Therefore here, as everywhere, the style bears the stamp of the thinking from which it has arisen, for style is the physiognomy of the mind. Moreover it is to be noted that, whenever Kant wishes to give an example for the purpose of fuller discussion, he almost always takes for this purpose the category of causality, and then what is said turns out to be correct; precisely because the law of causality is the real, but also the only, form of the understanding, and the remaining eleven categories are merely blind windows. The deduction of the categories is simpler and plainer in the first edition than in the second. He endeavours to explain how, according to the perception given by sensibility, the understanding brings about experience by means of thinking the categories. In this connexion, the expressions recognition, reproduction, association, apprehension, transcendental unity of apperception, are repeated *ad nauseam,* and yet no clarity is reached. It is very remarkable, however, that in this explanation he does not once touch on what must occur to everyone first of all, the relation of the sensation to its external cause. If he did not wish to admit this relation, he should have expressly denied it, but he does not do even this. He therefore furtively manoeuvres round it, and all the Kantians have stealthily evaded it in precisely the same way. The secret motive for this is that he reserves the causal nexus under the name "ground of the phenomenon" for his false deduction of the thing-in-itself, and then that, through the relation to the cause, perception would become intellectual, a thing which he dare not admit. Moreover, he seems to have been afraid that, if the causal nexus were allowed to hold good between sensation and object, the latter would at once become the thing-in-itself, and would introduce Locke's empiricism. But the difficulty is removed by reflection constantly reminding us that the law of causality is of subjective origin, just as is the sensation itself; moreover our own body, in so far as it appears in space, already belongs to representations. But Kant was prevented from admitting this by his fear of Berkeleian idealism.

"The combination of the manifold of perception" is repeatedly stated to be the essential operation of the understanding by means of its twelve categories. Yet this is never properly explained, nor is it shown what this manifold of perception is before the combination by the understanding. Now time and space, the latter in all its three dimensions, are *continua,* i.e., all their parts are originally not separated but combined. But they are the universal forms of our perception; hence everything that exhibits itself (is given) in them also appears originally as *continuum,* in other words, its parts already appear as combined, and require no additional combination of the manifold. If, however, we wish to interpret that combination of the manifold of perception by saying that I refer the different sense-impressions of an object only to this one, thus, for example, when perceiving a bell, I recognize that what affects my eye as yellow, my hands as smooth and hard, my ear as emitting sounds, is yet only one and the same body, then this is rather a consequence of the knowledge *a priori* of the causal nexus (of this actual and sole function of the understanding). By virtue of this knowledge, all those different impressions on my different organs of sense nevertheless lead me only to a common cause of them, namely the constitution of the body that stands before me, so that my understanding, in spite of the variety and plurality of the effects, still apprehends the unity of the cause as a single object exhibiting itself in just this way in perception. In the fine recapitulation of his teaching which Kant gives in the *Critique of Pure Reason,* pp. 719-726 (V, 747-754), he explains the categories, possibly more clearly than anywhere else, as "the mere rule of the synthesis of what perception or observation may give *a posteriori.*" It seems that something is present in his mind to the effect that in the construction of the triangle the angles furnish the rule for the composition of the lines; at any rate, by this picture we can best explain to ourselves what he says about the function of the categories. The preface to the *Metaphysical Rudiments of Natural Science* contains a long note, also furnishing an explanation of the categories, and stating that they "differ in no respect from the formal acts of the understanding in judging," except that in the latter, subject and predicate can at all events change places. Then in the same passage the judgement in general is defined as "an act through which the given representations first become knowledge of an object." According to this, as the animals do not judge, they too must necessarily have no knowledge whatever of objects. Generally, according to Kant, there are only concepts of *objects,* no perceptions. On the other hand, I say that objects exist primarily only for perception, and that concepts are always abstractions from this perception. Therefore abstract thinking must be conducted exactly according to the world present in perception, for only the relation to this world gives content to the concepts, and we cannot assume for the concepts any other *a priori* determined form than the faculty for reflection in general. The essential nature of this faculty is the formation of concepts, i.e., of abstract nonperceptible representations, and this constitutes the sole function of our faculty of *reason,* as I have shown in the first book. Accordingly, I demand that we throw away eleven of the categories, and retain only that of causality, but that we see that its activity is indeed the condition of empirical perception, this being therefore not merely sensuous but intellectual, and that the object thus perceived, the object of experience, is one with the representation from which only the thing-in-itself can still be distinguished.

After repeated study of the *Critique of Pure Reason* at different periods of my life, a conviction has forced itself on me with regard to the origin of the Transcendental Logic, and I mention it here as being very useful for its understanding. The sole discovery, based on objective apprehension and the highest human thought, is the *aperçu* that time and space are known by us *a priori.* Gratified by this lucky find, Kant wanted to pursue this vein still farther, and his love for architectonic symmetry gave him the clue. Just as he had found a pure intuition or perception *a priori* attributed as a condition to empirical *perception,* so he imagined that certain *pure concepts,* as presupposition in our faculty of knowledge, would also lie at the root of the empirically acquired *concepts*. He imagined that empirical, actual thinking would be possible first of all through a pure thinking *a priori,* which would have no objects at all in itself, but would have to take them from perception. Thus he thought that, just as the *Transcendental Aesthetic* establishes an *a priori* basis for mathematics, so must there also be such a basis for logic, and so the former then received a symmetrical pendant in a *Transcendental Logic.* From now on, Kant was no longer unprejudiced; he was no longer in a condition of pure investigation and observation of what is present in consciousness, but was guided by an assumption and pursued a purpose, that of finding what he presupposed, in order to add to the Transcendental Aesthetic, so fortunately discovered, a Transcendental Logic analogous to it, and thus symmetrically corresponding to it, as a second storey. For this he hit upon the table of judgements, from which he formed as well as he could the *table of categories,* as the doctrine of twelve pure concepts *a priori* which were to be the condition of our *thinking* those very *things* whose *perception* is conditioned *a priori* by the two forms of sensibility. Thus a *pure understanding* corresponded symmetrically to a *pure sensibility.* After this, there occurred to him yet another consideration that offered him a means of increasing the plausibility of the thing, by assuming the *schematism* of the pure concepts of the understanding. But precisely in this way is his method of procedure, to him unconscious, most clearly betrayed. Thus, since he aimed at finding for every empirical function of the faculty of knowledge an analogous *a priori* function, he remarked that, between our empirical perceiving and our empirical thinking, carried out in abstract non-perceptible concepts, a connexion very frequently, though not always, takes place, since every now and then we attempt to go back from abstract thinking to perceiving. We attempt this, however, merely in order really to convince ourselves that our abstract thinking has not strayed far from the safe ground of perception, and has possibly become somewhat high-flown or even a mere idle display of words, much in the same way as, when walking in the dark, we stretch out our hand every now and then to the wall that guides us. We then go back to perception only tentatively and for the moment, by calling up in imagination a perception corresponding to the concept that occupies us at the moment, a perception which yet can never be quite adequate to the concept, but is a mere *representative* of it for the time being. I have already undertaken the necessary discussion of this in my essay *On the Principle of Sufficient Reason,* § 28. Kant calls a fleeting phantasm of this kind a *schema* in contrast to the perfected picture of the imagination. He says that it is, so to speak, a monogram of the imagination, and asserts that, just as such a schema stands midway between our abstract thinking of empirically acquired concepts and our clear perception occurring through the senses, so also do there exist *a priori* similar *schemata of the pure concepts of the understanding* between the faculty of perception *a priori* of pure sensibility and the faculty of thinking *a priori* of the pure understanding (hence the categories). He describes these schemata one by one as monograms of the pure imagination *a priori,* and assigns each of them to the category corresponding to it, in the strange "Chapter on the Schematism of the Pure Concepts of the Understanding," which is well known for its great obscurity, since no one has ever been able to make anything out of it. But its obscurity is cleared up if we consider it from the point of view here given; but here more than anywhere else do the intentional nature of Kant's method of procedure and the resolve, arrived at beforehand, to find what would correspond to the analogy, and what might assist the architectonic symmetry, clearly come to light. In fact, this is the case to such a degree that the thing borders on the comical. For, by assuming schemata of the pure (*void of content*) concepts *a priori* of the understanding (categories) analogous to the empirical schemata (or representatives of our actual concepts through the imagination), he overlooks the fact that the purpose of such schemata is here entirely wanting. For the purpose of the schemata in the case of empirical (actual) thinking is related solely to the *material content* of such concepts. For, since these concepts are drawn from empirical perception, we assist ourselves and see where we are, in the case of abstract thinking, by casting now and then a fleeting, retrospective glance at perception from which the concepts are taken, in order to assure ourselves that our thinking still has real content. This, however, necessarily presupposes that the concepts which occupy us have sprung from perception; and it is a mere glance back at their material content, in fact a mere remedy for our weakness. But with concepts *a priori,* which still have no content at all, obviously this is of necessity omitted; for these have not sprung from perception, but come to it from within, in order first to receive a content from it. Therefore they have as yet nothing on which they could look back. I discuss this point at length, because it is precisely this that throws light on the mysterious method of the Kantian philosophizing. This accordingly consists in the fact that, after the happy discovery of the two forms of intuition or perception *a priori,* Kant attempts, under the guidance of analogy, to demonstrate for every determination of our empirical knowledge an analogue *a priori,* and this finally extends in the schemata even to a merely psychological fact. Here the apparent depth of thought and the difficulty of the discussion merely serve to conceal from the reader the fact that its content remains an entirely undemonstrable and merely arbitrary assumption. But whoever finally penetrates the meaning of such an exposition is easily induced to regard this laboriously acquired comprehension as a conviction of the truth of the matter. On the other hand, if Kant had here maintained an unprejudiced and purely observant attitude, as with the discovery of the intuitions or perceptions *a priori,* he could not but have found that what is added to the pure intuition or perception of space and time, when an empirical perception comes from it, is the sensation on the one hand, and knowledge of causality on the other. This converts the mere sensation into objective empirical perception; yet it is not on this account borrowed and learnt from sensation, but exists *a priori,* and is just the form and function of the pure understanding. It is also, however, its sole form and function, yet one so rich in results that all our empirical knowledge rests on it. If, as has often been said, the refutation of an error is complete only by our demonstrating psychologically the way in which it originated, then I believe I have achieved this in what I have said above with regard to Kant's doctrine of the categories and of their schemata.

* * *

After Kant had introduced such great mistakes into the first simple outlines of a theory of the representation-faculty, he took into his head a variety of very complicated assumptions. In connexion with these, we have first of all the synthetic unity of apperception, a very strange thing very strangely described. "The *I think* must be able to accompany all my representations." Must be able: this is a problematical-apodictic enunciation, or, in plain English, a proposition taking away with one hand what it gives with the other. And what is the meaning of this proposition balanced on a point? That all representing is thinking? Not so: that indeed would be terrible, for then there would be nothing but abstract concepts, or at any rate a pure perception free from reflection and from will, like that of the beautiful, the deepest comprehension of the true essence of things, in other words, of their Platonic Ideas. Then again, the animals would be bound either to think, or not even to have representations. Or is the proposition supposed to mean: No object without subject? This would be very badly expressed by it, and would come too late. If we summarize Kant's utterances, we shall find that what he understands by the synthetic unity of apperception is, so to speak, the extensionless centre of the sphere of all our representations, whose radii converge on it. It is what I call the subject of knowing, the correlative of all representations, and is at the same time what I have described and discussed at length in chapter 22 of the second volume as the focus on which the rays of the brain's activity converge. To that chapter I therefore refer, so as not to repeat myself.

* * *

That I reject the whole doctrine of the categories, and number it among the groundless assumptions with which Kant burdened the theory of knowledge, follows from the criticism of it given above. In the same way it follows from the demonstration of the contradictions in the Transcendental Logic which had their ground in the confusion of knowledge from perception with abstract knowledge; further, from the demonstration of the want of a distinct and definite conception of the nature of the understanding and of the faculty of reason. Instead of this we found in Kant's works only incoherent, inconsistent, inadequate, and incorrect expressions about those two faculties of the mind. Finally, it results from the explanations that I myself have given in the first book and its supplements, and in even greater detail in the essay *On the Principle of Sufficient Reason,* §§ 21, 26, and 34, about the same faculties of the mind. These explanations are very definite and distinct, and clearly result from a consideration of the nature of our knowledge; moreover, they fully agree with the conceptions of those two faculties of knowledge that appear in the language and writings of all ages and all nations, but were not brought to distinct expression. Their defence against the very different Kantian description has for the most part been already given with the exposure of the errors of that description. Now, as the table of judgements, which Kant makes the basis of his theory of thinking and indeed of his whole philosophy, is yet correct in itself and as a whole, it is still incumbent on me to demonstrate how these universal forms of all judgements arise in our faculty of knowledge, and to make them agree with my description of it. In this discussion I shall always associate with the concepts understanding and reason (*Vernunft*) the sense given to them in my explanation, with which therefore I assume the reader to be familiar.

An essential difference between Kant's method and that which I follow is to be found in the fact that he starts from indirect, reflected knowledge, whereas I start from direct and intuitive knowledge. He is comparable to a person who measures the height of a tower from its shadow; but I am like one who applies the measuring-rod directly to the tower itself. Philosophy, therefore, is for him a science *of* concepts, but for me a science *in* concepts, drawn from knowledge of perception, the only source of all evidence, and set down and fixed in universal concepts. He skips over this whole world of perception which surrounds us, and which is so multifarious and rich in significance, and he sticks to the forms of abstract thinking. Although he never states the fact, this procedure is founded on the assumption that reflection is the ectype of all perception, and that everything essential to perception must therefore be expressed in reflection, and indeed in very contracted, and therefore easily comprehensible, forms and outlines. Accordingly, what is essential and conformable to law in abstract knowledge would place in our hands all the threads that set in motion before our eyes the many-coloured puppet-show of the world of perception. If only Kant had expressed this highest principle of his method plainly, and had then followed it consistently, he would at least have been obliged clearly to separate the intuitive from the abstract, and we would not have had to contend with inextricable contradictions and confusions. But from the way in which he has solved his problem we see that that fundamental principle of his method was only very indistinctly present in his mind, and thus we still have to guess at it, even after a thorough study of his philosophy.

Now as regards the method stated and the fundamental maxim itself, there is much to be said for it, and it is a brilliant idea. The real nature of all science consists indeed in our comprehending the endless manifold of the phenomena of perception under comparatively few abstract concepts, and arranging out of these a system from which we have all those phenomena wholly in the power of our knowledge, can explain the past and determine the future. The sciences, however, divide among themselves the extensive sphere of phenomena according to the special and manifold classes of these latter. It was a bold and happy idea to isolate what is absolutely essential to the concepts as such and apart from their content, in order to see from the forms of all thinking, found in this way, what is also essential to all intuitive knowledge, and consequently to the world as phenomenon in general. Now since this would be found *a priori* on account of the necessity of those forms of thought, it would be of subjective origin, and would lead exactly to the ends Kant had in view. Then before going farther, what the relation of reflection to knowledge of perception is should have been investigated (and this naturally presupposes the clear separation of the two, which Kant neglected); in what way reflection really reproduces and represents knowledge of perception. It should have been investigated whether such reflection remains quite pure, or is changed and partially disguised by assimilation into its own (reflection's) forms, whether the form of abstract reflective knowledge becomes more definite through the form of knowledge of perception, or through the nature or quality that unalterably belongs to itself, i.e., to reflective knowledge. In this way, even what is very heterogeneous in intuitive knowledge can no longer be distinguished, the moment it has entered reflective knowledge; and conversely, many distinctions observed by us in the reflective method of knowledge have also sprung from this knowledge itself, and in no way indicate corresponding differences in intuitive knowledge. As a result of this investigation, however, it would have been seen that knowledge of perception, on being taken up into reflection, undergoes nearly as much change as food does when assimilated into the animal organism, whose forms and combinations are determined by itself, so that from their composition the nature and quality of the food can no longer be recognized at all. Or (for this is saying a little too much) at any rate, it would have appeared that reflection is in no way related to knowledge of perception as a reflection in water is to the objects reflected, and hardly even as the shadow of these objects is to the objects themselves. Such a shadow reproduces only a few external outlines, but it also unites the most manifold into the same form, and presents the most varied through the same outline. Thus, starting from it, we could not possibly construct the shapes or forms of things with completeness and certainty.

The whole of reflective knowledge, or reason (*Vernunft*), has only one main form, and that is the abstract concept. It is peculiar to our faculty of reason itself, and has no direct necessary connexion with the world of perception. This world of perception, therefore, exists for the animals entirely without reflective knowledge, and even if it were to be a totally different world, that form of reflection would nevertheless suit it just as well. But the combination of concepts for judging has certain definite and regular forms which, found by induction, constitute the table of judgements. For the most part, these forms can be derived from the nature of reflective knowledge itself, and hence directly from the faculty of reason, especially in so far as they spring from the four laws of thought (which I call metalogical truths) and from the *dictum de omni et nullo*.[18] Others of these forms, however, have their ground in the nature of knowledge of perception, and hence in the understanding; yet they do not

---

[18] "Whatever is affirmed (denied) of an entire class or kind may be affirmed (denied) of any part." [Tr.]

by any means point to an equal number of special forms of the understanding, but can be deduced wholly and entirely from the sole function that the understanding has, namely direct knowledge of cause and effect. Finally, still others of these forms have sprung from the concurrence and combination of the reflective and intuitive methods of knowledge, or really from the taking up of the latter into the former. I shall now go through the moments of the judgement individually, and demonstrate the origin of each from the sources mentioned. From this it follows automatically that a deduction of categories from them falls to the ground, and that the assumption thereof is just as groundless as its exposition has been found to be confused and self-conflicting.

(1) The so-called *quantity* of judgements springs from the essential nature of concepts as such. It therefore has its ground solely in our faculty of reason, and has absolutely no direct connexion with the understanding and with knowledge of perception. As explained in the first book, it is in fact essential to concepts as such that they have a range, a sphere, and that the wider and less definite concept includes the narrower and more definite. The latter can therefore be separated out, and this can be done in two ways; either we express the narrower concept merely as an indefinite part of the wider concept in general, or we define it and completely separate it by means of the addition of a special name. The judgement that is the carrying out of this operation is called in the first case a particular, in the second case a universal judgement. For example, one and the same part of the sphere of the concept "tree" can be isolated through a particular and through a universal judgement, thus: "Some trees bear gall-nuts," or "All oaks bear gall-nuts." We see that the difference of the two operations is very slight, in fact that its possibility depends on the richness of the language. Nevertheless, Kant has declared that this difference reveals two fundamentally different actions, functions, categories of the pure understanding that just through these determines experience *a priori*.

Finally, we can also use a concept in order to arrive by its means at a definite, particular representation of perception, from which, and at the same time from many others, this concept itself is drawn off; this is done through the singular judgement. Such a judgement indicates only the boundary between abstract knowledge and knowledge of perception, and passes directly over to the latter: "This tree here bears gall-nuts." Kant has made a special category of this also.

After all that has been said, there is no need here of further polemic.

(2) In the same way, the *quality* of judgements lies entirely within

the province of our faculty of reason, and is not an adumbration of any law of the understanding that makes perception possible; in other words, it does not point or refer thereto. The nature of abstract concepts, which is just the inner nature of our faculty of reason itself objectively comprehended, entails the possibility of uniting and separating their spheres, as already explained in the first book, and on this possibility, as their presupposition, rest the universal laws of thought, the laws of identity and of contradiction. Since they spring purely from our faculty of reason, and cannot be further explained, I have attributed to them *metalogical* truth. They determine that what is united must remain united, and what is separated must remain separated, and hence that what is settled and established cannot at the same time be again eliminated. Thus they presuppose the possibility of the combination and separation of spheres, in other words, judgement. But according to the *form,* this lies simply and solely in our faculty of reason, and this form has not, like the *content* of the judgements, been taken over from the perceptible knowledge of the understanding, and therefore no correlative or analogue of it is there to be looked for. After perception has arisen through the understanding and for the understanding, it exists complete, subject to no doubt or error; accordingly it knows neither affirmation nor denial. For it expresses itself, and has not, like the abstract knowledge of our faculty of reason, its value and content in the mere relation to something outside it, according to the principle of the ground of knowing. It is therefore nothing but reality; all negation is foreign to its nature; that can be added in thought only through reflection, but on this very account it always remains in the province of abstract thinking.

To the affirmative and negative Kant adds the infinite judgements, making use of a fad of the old scholastics, a cunningly contrived stop-gap not even requiring an explanation, a blind window, like many others employed by him for the sake of his architectonic symmetry.

(3) Under the very wide concept of relation Kant has brought three entirely different properties of judgements, which we must therefore examine individually in order to recognize their origin.

(a) The *hypothetical judgement* in general is the abstract expression of that most universal form of all our knowledge, the principle of sufficient reason. In my essay on this principle, I showed in 1813 that it has four entirely different meanings, and that in each of these it originates primarily from a different faculty of knowledge, just as it also concerns a different class of representations. From this it is sufficiently clear that the origin of the hypothetical judgement in general, of this universal form of thought, cannot be, as Kant would have it, merely the understanding and its category of causality; but that the law of causality, the only form of knowledge of the pure understanding according to my description, is only one of the forms of the principle of sufficient reason embracing all pure or *a priori* knowledge. This principle, on the other hand, has in each of its meanings this hypothetical form of judgement as its expression. Here we see quite clearly how kinds of knowledge quite different in their origin and significance nevertheless appear, when thought by our faculty of reason *in abstracto,* in one and the same form of combination of concepts and judgements. In this form they can no longer be distinguished at all, but in order to distinguish them we must go back to knowledge of perception, leaving abstract knowledge altogether. Therefore the path followed by Kant for finding the elements and also the inner mechanism of intuitive knowledge from the standpoint of abstract knowledge was quite the wrong one. Moreover, the whole of my introductory essay *On the Principle of Sufficient Reason* is to be regarded to a certain extent merely as a thorough discussion of the significance of the hypothetical form of judgement; I shall therefore not dwell on it any more here.

(b) The form of the *categorical judgement* is nothing but the form of the judgement in general, in the strictest sense. For, strictly speaking, judging simply means thinking the combination, or the irreconcilability, of the spheres of concepts. Therefore, the hypothetical and disjunctive combinations are not really special forms of the judgement, for they are applied only to judgements already completed, in which the combination of the concepts remains unchanged, namely the categorical. But they again connect these judgements, since the hypothetical form expresses their dependence on one another, and the disjunctive their incompatibility. But mere concepts have only one kind of relation to one another, namely those relations expressed in the categorical judgement. The fuller determination, or the subspecies of this relation, are the intersection and the complete separateness of the concept-spheres, and thus affirmation and negation. Out of these Kant has made special categories under quite a different title, that of *quality*. Intersection and separateness again have subspecies, according as the spheres lie within one another completely or only partially, a determination constituting the *quantity* of the judgements. Out of these Kant has again made a quite special title of categories. Thus he separated what is quite closely related and even identical, namely the easily surveyed modifications of the only possible relations of mere concepts to one another; on the other hand, he united under this title of relation that which is very different.

Categorical judgements have as their metalogical principle the laws of thought of identity and contradiction. But the *ground* of the connexion of concept-spheres giving *truth* to the judgement, that is nothing but this connexion, can be of a very varied nature, and, as a result of this, the truth of the judgement is either logical, or empirical, or transcendental, or metalogical. This has already been discussed in the introductory essay, §§ 30-33, and need not here be repeated. But it follows from this how very different the immediate kinds of knowledge can be, all of which exhibit themselves in the abstract through the combination of the spheres of two concepts as subject and predicate, and that we cannot by any means set up a single function of the understanding as corresponding to and producing it. For example, the judgements: "Water boils"; "The sine measures the angle"; "The will decides"; "Employment distracts"; "Distinction is difficult," express through the same logical form the most varied kinds of relations. From this we obtain once more the sanction, however wrong the beginning, to place ourselves at the standpoint of abstract knowledge, in order to analyse direct, intuitive knowledge. For the rest, the categorical judgement springs from a knowledge of the understanding proper, in my sense, only where a causality is expressed through it; but this is the case also with all judgements expressing a physical quality. For if I say: "This body is heavy, hard, fluid, green, sour, alkaline, organic," and so on, this always expresses its action or effect, and thus a knowledge that is possible only through the pure understanding. Now after this knowledge, like much that is quite different from it (e.g., the subordination of highly abstract concepts), has been expressed in the abstract through subject and predicate, these mere relations of concepts have been transferred back to knowledge of perception, and it has been supposed that the subject and predicate of the judgement must have a special correlative of their own in perception, namely substance and accident. But later on I shall clearly show that the concept "substance" has no other true content than that of the concept "matter." Accidents, however, are quite synonymous with kinds of effects, so that the supposed knowledge of substance and accident is still always that of the pure understanding of cause and effect. But how the representation of matter really arises is discussed partly in our first book, § 4, and still more clearly in the essay *On the Principle of Sufficient Reason* at the end of § 21. To some extent we shall see it still more closely when we investigate the principle that substance is permanent.

(c) The *disjunctive judgements* spring from the law of thought of the excluded middle, which is a metalogical truth; they are therefore entirely the property of pure reason, and do not have their origin in the understanding. The deduction of the category of community or *reciprocal effect* from them, however, is a really glaring example of the acts of violence on truth which Kant ventures to commit, merely in order to satisfy his love for architectonic symmetry. The inadmissibility of that deduction has already often been rightly censured, and has been demonstrated on various grounds, especially by G. E. Schulze in his *Kritik der theoretischen Philosophie* and by Berg in his *Epikritik der Philosophie*. What actual analogy is there in fact between the problematical determination of a concept by predicates that exclude one another, and the idea of reciprocal effect? The two indeed are quite opposed, for in the disjunctive judgement the actual statement of one of the two terms of division is necessarily at the same time an elimination of the other. On the other hand, if we imagine two things in the relation of reciprocal effect, the statement of the one is necessarily the statement of the other also, and *vice versa*. Therefore the actual logical analogue of reciprocal effect is unquestionably the *circulus vitiosus,* for in it, just as ostensibly in the case of reciprocal effect, what is established is also the ground, and conversely. And just as logic rejects the *circulus vitiosus,* so also is the concept of reciprocal effect to be banished from metaphysics. For I now intend quite seriously to prove that there is no reciprocal effect at all in the proper sense, and that this concept, so extremely popular precisely on account of the indefiniteness of the idea, appears on closer consideration to be empty, false, and invalid. First of all, let us recall what causality in general is, and, to assist in this, let us look up my discussion about it in the introductory essay, § 20, also in my essay *On the Freedom of the Will,* chap. 3, pp. 27 *seq.* (2nd ed., pp. 26 *seq.*), and finally in the fourth chapter of the second volume of the present work. Causality is the law according to which the *states or conditions* of matter that appear determine their positions in time. With causality it is a question merely of states or conditions, in fact, really only of *changes,* and not of matter as such or of persistence without change. *Matter* as such is not under the law of causality, for it neither comes into being nor passes away; thus the whole *thing,* as we commonly say, does not come under this law, but only the *states or conditions* of matter. Further, the law of causality has nothing to do with *permanence,* for where nothing *changes* there is no producing of *effects* and no causality, but a continuing state of rest. If such a state or condition is changed, then the newly arisen state is again either permanent, or it is not, and it at once produces a third condition or state. The necessity with which this happens is just the law of causality, which is a form of the principle of sufficient reason, and thus cannot be further explained, since the principle of sufficient reason is the very principle of all explanation and all necessity. From this it is clear that the existence of cause and effect is closely connected with, and necessarily related to, the *sequence of time.* Only in so far as state A precedes state B in time, but their succession is necessary and not an accidental one, in other words, is no mere sequence but a consequence—only to this extent is state A the cause and state B the effect. But the concept of *reciprocal effect* contains this, that each is cause and each is effect of the other; but this is equivalent to saying that each of the two is the earlier and the later at the same time, which is absurd. For that both *states* are simultaneous, and indeed necessarily simultaneous, cannot be accepted, since, as they necessarily belong together and are simultaneous, they constitute only *one* state. The enduring presence of all its determinations is certainly required for the persistence of this state, but then there is no longer any question of change and causality, but of duration and rest. Nothing is said except that, if *one* determination of the whole state is changed, the resultant new state cannot continue, but becomes the cause of the change of all the other determinations of the first state also, whereby a new, third state appears. All this happens merely in accordance with the simple law of causality, and does not establish a new law, that of reciprocal effect.

I also positively assert that the concept of *reciprocal effect* cannot be illustrated by a single example. All that we should like to pass off as such is either a state of rest, to which the concept of causality, having significance only in regard to changes, finds no application whatever; or it is an alternating succession of states of the same name that condition one another, for the explanation of which simple causality is quite sufficient. An example of the first class is afforded by a pair of scales brought to rest by equal weights. There is no effect at all here, for there is no change; it is a state of rest; gravity acts, uniformly distributed, as it does in every body supported at its centre of gravity, but it cannot manifest its force through any effect. That the taking away of *one* weight produces a second state that at once becomes the cause of a third, namely the sinking of the other scale, happens according to the simple law of cause and effect. It requires no special category of the understanding, not even a special name. An example of the other class is the continuous burning of a fire. The combination of oxygen with the combustible body is the cause of the heat, and the heat again is the cause of the renewed occurrence of that chemical combination. But this is nothing but a chain of causes and effects, the alternate links of which, however, bear *the same name.* The burning A produces free heat B; this produces a new burning C (i.e., a new effect having the same name as the cause A, but not individually the same with it); this produces a new heat D (which is not really identical with the effect B, but is the same only according to the concept, in other words, it has the *same name* as B), and so on indefinitely. A good example of what in ordinary life is called reciprocal effect is afforded by a theory of deserts given by Humboldt (*Ansichten der Natur,* second edition, vol. II, p. 79). In sandy deserts it does not rain, but it rains on the wooded mountains that border them. The cause is not the attraction of the clouds by the mountains, but the column of heated air, rising from the sandy plain, which prevents the particles of vapour from disintegrating, and drives the clouds upwards. On the mountain range the vertically rising current of air is weaker, the clouds descend, and the rainfall ensues in the cooler air. Thus want of rain and the absence of plants in the desert stand in the relation of reciprocal effect. It does not rain, because the heated surface of sand radiates more heat; the desert does not become a steppe or prairie, because it does not rain. But obviously we have again here, as in the above example, only a succession of causes and effects of the same names, and absolutely nothing essentially different from simple causality. It is just the same with the swinging of a pendulum, and even, in fact, with the self-maintenance of the organic body, where every state likewise produces a new one. This state is of the same kind as the one by which it was itself brought about, but individually it is new. Only here the matter is more complicated, since the chain no longer consists of links of two kinds, but of links of many kinds, so that a link of the same name recurs only after several others have intervened. However, we always see before us only an application of the single and simple law of causality which affords the rule of the sequence of states or conditions, but not something that needs to be comprehended by a new and special function of the understanding.

Or will it be said as a proof of the concept of reciprocal effect that action and reaction are equal to each other? But this is to be found precisely in what I urge so strongly, and have discussed at length, in the essay *On the Principle of Sufficient Reason,* namely that the cause and the effect are not two bodies, but two successive states of bodies. Consequently, each of the two states also implicates all the bodies concerned, and hence the effect, i.e., the newly appearing state, e.g., in the case of impact, extends to both bodies in the same proportion; therefore the impelled body undergoes just as great a change as does the impelling body (each in proportion to its mass and velocity). If we choose to call this reciprocal effect, then absolutely every effect is a reciprocal effect, and no new concept arises on this account, still less a new function of the understanding for it, but we have only a superfluous synonym for causality. Kant, however, thoughtlessly expresses just this view in the *Metaphysical Rudiments of Natural Science,* where the proof of the fourth proposition of mechanics begins: "All external effect in the world is reciprocal effect." Then how are different functions to lie *a priori* in the understanding for simple causality and for reciprocal effect; in fact, how is the real succession of things to be possible and knowable only by means of causality, and their coexistence only by means of reciprocal effect? Accordingly, if all effect is reciprocal effect, succession and simultaneity would be the same thing, and consequently everything in the world would be simultaneous. If there were true reciprocal effect, then the *perpetuum mobile* would also be possible, and even *a priori* certain. On the other hand, the *a priori* conviction that there is no true reciprocal effect and no form of the understanding for such an effect, is the basis for asserting that perpetual motion is impossible.

Aristotle also denies reciprocal effect in the strict sense, for he remarks that two things can indeed be reciprocally causes of each other, but only in so far as we understand this in a different sense of each, for example, that one thing acts on the other as motive, but the latter acts on the former as the cause of its movement. Thus we find the same words in two passages: *Physics,* Bk. ii, c. 3, and *Metaphysics,* Bk. v, c. 2. Ἔστι δέ τινα καὶ ἀλλήλων αἴτια· οἷον τὸ πονεῖν αἴτιον τῆς εὐεξίας, καὶ αὕτη τοῦ πονεῖν· ἀλλ' οὐ τὸν αὐτὸν τρόπον, ἀλλὰ τὸ μὲν ὡς τέλος, τὸ δὲ ὡς ἀρχὴ κινήσεως. (*Sunt praeterea quae sibi sunt mutuo causae, ut exercitium bonae habitudinis, et haec exercitii: at non eodem modo, sed haec ut finis, illud ut principium motus.*)[19] Moreover, if he assumed a reciprocal effect proper, he would introduce it here, for in both passages he is concerned with enumerating all the possible kinds of causes. In the *Posterior Analytics,* Bk. ii, c. 11, he speaks of a rotation of causes and effects, but not of a reciprocal effect.

---

[19] "There are also things that are the cause of one another; thus, for example, gymnastics is the cause of good health, and *vice versa;* yet not in the same way, but the one as the end of the movement, the other as its beginning." [Tr.]

(4) The categories of *modality* have the advantage over all the others, since what is expressed through each of them actually corresponds to the form of judgement from which it is derived. With the other categories this is hardly ever the case, since they are usually deduced from the forms of judgement with the most arbitrary violence.

Therefore, that the concepts of the possible, of the actual, and of the necessary give rise to the problematical, the assertory, and the apodictic forms of judgement, is perfectly true; but that those concepts are special, original cognitive forms of the understanding incapable of further derivation, is not true. On the contrary, they spring from the single form of all knowledge, which is original and therefore known to us *a priori,* namely the principle of sufficient reason; and in fact knowledge of *necessity* springs directly from this. On the other hand, only by applying reflection to this do the concepts of contingency, possibility, impossibility, and actuality arise. Therefore all these do not in any way originate from *one* faculty of the mind, the understanding, but arise through the conflict of abstract knowledge with intuitive, as will be seen in a moment.

I maintain that to be necessary and to be consequent from a given ground or reason are absolutely reciprocal concepts, and completely identical. We can never know or even think anything as necessary, except in so far as we regard it as the consequent from a given ground or reason. The concept of necessity contains absolutely nothing more than this dependence, this being established through another thing, and this inevitably following from it. Thus it arises and exists simply and solely by applying the principle of sufficient reason. Therefore, according to the different forms of this principle, there are a physically necessary (the effect from the cause), a logically necessary (through the ground of knowing, in analytical judgements, syllogisms, and so on), a mathematically necessary (according to the ground of being in space and time), and finally a practically necessary. With this last we wish to express not some determination through a so-called categorical imperative, but the necessarily appearing action with the given empirical character according to the motives presented to it. But everything necessary is so only relatively, namely on the presupposition of the ground or reason from which it follows; therefore absolute necessity is a contradiction. For the rest, I refer to § 49 of the essay *On the Principle of Sufficient Reason.*

The contradictory opposite, in other words, the denial of necessity, is *contingency.* The content of this concept is therefore negative, and so nothing more than absence of the connexion expressed by the principle of sufficient reason. Consequently even the contingent is always only relative; thus it is contingent in relation to something that is not *its* ground or reason. Every object, of whatever kind it be, e.g., every event in the actual world, is always at the same time both necessary and contingent; *necessary* in reference to the one thing that is its cause; *contingent* in reference to everything else. For its contact in time and space with everything else is a mere coincidence without necessary connexion; hence also the words *chance, contingency,* σύμπτωμα, *contingens.* Therefore an absolute contingency is just as inconceivable as an absolute necessity, for the former would be just an object that did not stand to any other in the relation of consequent to ground. The inconceivability of such a thing, however, is precisely the content of the principle of sufficient reason negatively expressed. This principle, therefore, would first have to be overthrown if we were to conceive an absolute contingency. But then this itself also would have lost all meaning, for the concept of the contingent has meaning only in reference to that principle, and signifies that two objects do not stand to each other in the relation of ground to consequent.

In nature, in so far as this is representation of perception, everything that happens is necessary, for it proceeds from its cause. If, however, we consider this individual thing in relation to everything else that is not its cause, we recognize it as contingent; but this is already an abstract reflection. Now if further, in the case of an object of nature, we abstract entirely from its causal relation to everything else, and hence from its necessity and contingency, then the concept of the *actual* comprehends this kind of knowledge. In the case of this concept we consider only the *effect,* without looking about for the cause, in reference to which we should otherwise have to call it *necessary,* and in reference to everything else *contingent.* All this rests ultimately on the fact that the modality of the judgement indicates not so much the objective quality of things as the relation of our knowledge to that quality. But as in nature everything proceeds from a cause, everything *actual* is also *necessary;* yet only in so far as it is *at this time, in this place;* for only thus far does determination through the law of causality extend. But if we leave nature of perception, and pass over to abstract thinking, we can in reflection represent to ourselves all the laws of nature, known to us partly *a priori,* partly only *a posteriori.* This abstract representation contains all that is in nature at *any* time, in *any* place, but with abstraction from every definite place and time; and in just this way, through such reflection, we have entered the wide realm of *possibility.* But what finds no place even here is the *impossible.*

It is obvious that possibility and impossibility exist only for reflection, for the abstract knowledge of our faculty of reason, not for the knowledge of perception, although it is the pure forms of such knowledge which suggest to our reason determination of the possible and the impossible. According as the laws of nature, from which we start when thinking of the possible and the impossible, are known *a priori* or *a posteriori,* is the possibility or impossibility metaphysical or only physical.

From this exposition, which requires no proof because it rests directly on knowledge of the principle of sufficient reason and on the development of the concepts of the necessary, the actual, and the possible, it is clear enough how entirely groundless is Kant's assumption of three special functions of the understanding for those three concepts; here again we see that he did not let himself be disturbed by any scruple in achieving his architectonic symmetry.

In addition to this, however, there is also the very great mistake, namely his confusion with each other of the concepts of necessary and contingent, of course after the example of previous philosophy. This earlier philosophy misused abstraction in the following way. It was obvious that that of which the ground is set, follows inevitably, in other words, cannot fail to be, and so necessarily is. But men held to this last determination alone, and said that that is necessary which cannot be otherwise, or whose opposite is impossible. But they disregarded the ground and the root of such necessity, overlooked the relativity of all necessity that results therefrom, and thus made the utterly inconceivable fiction of an *absolutely necessary,* in other words, of something whose existence would be as inevitable as the consequent from the reason or ground, yet which would not be consequent from a ground, and would thus depend on nothing. This addition is just an absurd *petitio principii,* since it is contrary to the principle of sufficient reason. Now starting from this fiction they declared, in diametrical opposition to the truth, that everything established through a ground or reason was contingent, since they looked at the relative nature of its necessity, and compared this with the entirely fictitious *absolute* necessity that is self-contradictory in its concept.[20]

---

[20] See Christian Wolff's *Vernünftige Gedanken von Gott, Welt, und Seele,* §§ 577-579. It is strange that he declares to be contingent only what is necessary according to the principle of sufficient reason of becoming, i.e., what takes place from causes. On the other hand, he recognizes as necessary what is necessary according to the other forms of the principle of sufficient reason, e.g., what follows from the *essentia* (definition), hence analytical judgements, and further mathematical truths also. As the reason for this, he states that only the law of causality gives infinite series, but the other kinds of grounds give only finite series. This, however, is by no means the case with the forms

Now Kant also retains this fundamentally perverse definition of the contingent, and gives it as explanation: *Critique of Pure Reason,* V, pp. 289-291; 243 (V, 301); 419, 458, 460 (V, 447, 486, 488). Here indeed he falls into the most obvious contradiction with himself, since he says on p. 301: "Everything contingent has a cause," and adds: "That is contingent, of which the non-existence is possible." But whatever has a cause cannot possibly not be; therefore it is necessary. For the rest, the origin of the whole of this false explanation of the necessary and the contingent is to be found in Aristotle in *De Generatione et Corruptione,* Bk. ii, chaps. 9 and 11, where the necessary is declared to be that of which the non-existence is impossible; opposed to it is that of which the existence is impossible. And between these two lies that which can be and also not be—hence that which arises and passes away, and this would then be the contingent. According to what has been said above, it is clear that this explanation, like so many of Aristotle's, has resulted from sticking to abstract concepts without going back to the concrete and perceptible, in which, however, lies the source of all abstract concepts, and by which they must therefore always be controlled. "Something of which the non-existence is impossible" can certainly be thought in the abstract, but if we go with it to the concrete, the real, the perceptible, we find nothing to illustrate the thought, even only as something possible—as merely the aforesaid consequent of a given ground, whose necessity, however, is relative and conditioned.

I take this opportunity to add a few more remarks on these concepts of modality. As all necessity rests on the principle of sufficient reason, and on this very account is relative, all *apodictic* judgements are originally, and in their ultimate significance, *hypothetical.* They become *categorical* only by the introduction of an *assertory* minor, hence in the consequent of a syllogism. If this minor is still undecided, and this indecision is expressed, this gives the *problematical* judgement.

What in general (as rule) is apodictic (a law of nature), is always in reference to a particular case only problematical, since first the condition which puts the case under the rule must actually appear. Conversely, what in the particular as such is necessary (apodictic) (every particular change necessary through its cause), is again in general, and expressed universally, only problematical, since

---

of the principle of sufficient reason in pure space and time, but holds good only of the logical ground of knowledge. However, he regarded mathematical necessity as such a logical ground. Compare the essay *On the Principle of Sufficient Reason,* § 50.

the cause that appears concerns only the particular case, and the apodictic, always hypothetical, judgement invariably states only universal laws, not particular cases directly. All this has its ground in the fact that the possible exists only in the province of reflection and for our faculty of reason, the actual in the province of perception and for our understanding, the necessary for both. In fact, the distinction between necessary, actual, and possible really exists only in the abstract and according to the concept; in the real world all three coincide in one. For all that happens, happens *necessarily,* because it happens from causes, but these themselves in turn have causes, so that the whole course of events in the world, great as well as small, is a strict concatenation of what necessarily takes place. Accordingly, everything actual is at the same time something necessary, and in reality there is no difference between actuality and necessity. In just the same way there is no difference between actuality and possibility, for what has not happened, in other words has not become actual, was also not possible, since the causes without which it could never take place have themselves not happened, nor could they happen, in the great concatenation of causes; thus it was an impossibility. Accordingly, every event is either necessary or impossible. All this holds good merely of the empirically real world, in other words, of the complex of individual things, and thus of the wholly particular or individual as such. On the other hand, if by means of our faculty of reason we consider things in general, comprehending them in the abstract, then necessity, actuality, and possibility are again separated. We then know everything as generally possible according to *a priori* laws belonging to our intellect, and that which corresponds to the empirical laws of nature as possible in this world, even if it has never become actual; thus we clearly distinguish the possible from the actual. The actual is in itself always also necessary, but it is understood as being such only by the man who knows its cause; apart from this, it is and is called contingent. This consideration also gives us the key to that *contentio* περὶ δυνάτων[21] between the Megaric Diodorus and Chrysippus the Stoic, which Cicero mentions in his book *De Fato.* Diodorus says: "Only what becomes actual has been possible, and all that is actual is also necessary." On the other hand, Chrysippus says: "Much that is possible never becomes actual, for only the necessary becomes actual." We can explain this as follows: Actuality is the conclusion of a syllogism for which possibility provides the premises. Yet for it not only the major, but also the minor is required; only the two

---

[21] "Contention over possibility." [Tr.]

give complete possibility. Thus the major gives a merely theoretical, general possibility *in abstracto;* but this in itself still does not make anything possible at all, in other words, capable of becoming actual. For this the minor is still needed, which gives the possibility for the particular case, since it brings the case under the rule. Precisely in this way the case at once becomes actuality. For example:

Maj. All houses (consequently mine also) can be destroyed by fire.

Min. My house is catching fire.

Concl. My house is being destroyed by fire.

For every general proposition, and hence every major, establishes things with regard to actuality only under a presupposition, and consequently hypothetically; for example, the ability to be destroyed by fire has the catching fire as a presupposition. This presupposition is brought out in the minor. The major always loads the gun, but only when the minor applies the fuse does the shot, i.e., the conclusion, follow. This holds good everywhere of the relation of possibility to actuality. Now as the conclusion, which is the assertion of actuality, follows *necessarily,* it is clear from this that everything that is actual is also necessary; this can also be seen from the fact that necessity means simply being consequent of a given ground or reason. With the actual this ground is a cause; hence everything actual is necessary. Accordingly, we see the concepts of the possible, the actual, and the necessary coincide, and not merely the last presuppose the first, but also *vice versa.* What keeps them apart is the limitation of our intellect through the form of time; for time is the mediator between possibility and actuality. The necessity of the individual event can be seen perfectly from the knowledge of all its causes, but the coincidence of all these different causes, independent of one another, seems to us to be *contingent;* in fact their independence of one another is just the concept of contingency. However, as each of them was the necessary consequence of *its* cause, and the chain of causes is beginningless, it is clear that contingency is a merely subjective phenomenon, arising out of the limitation of the horizon of our understanding, and is just as subjective as is the optical horizon in which the heavens touch the earth.

As necessity is identical with consequent from a given ground or reason, it must also appear as a special necessity in the case of each form of the principle of sufficient reason, and also have its opposite in the possibility and impossibility which always arise only through the application of our reason's abstract reflection to the object. Opposed to the above-mentioned four kinds of necessity are the same number of kinds of impossibility, that is, physical, logical, mathematical, and practical. In addition it may be observed that, if we keep entirely within the province of abstract concepts, possibility always belongs to the more general concept, necessity to the more limited. For example "An animal *may* be a bird, a fish, an amphibious creature, and so on." "A nightingale *must* be a bird, a bird *must* be an animal, an animal *must* be an organism, an organism *must* be a body." This is really because logical necessity, whose expression is the syllogism, goes from the general to the particular, and never *vice versa*. In nature of perception (the representations of the first class), on the contrary, everything is really necessary through the law of causality. Only added reflection can at the same time comprehend it as contingent, comparing it with that which is not its cause, and also as simply and solely actual, by disregarding all causal connexion. Only with this class of representations does the concept of the *actual* really occur, as is also indicated by the derivation of the word from the concept of causality. If we keep entirely within the third class of representations, pure mathematical perception, there is nothing but necessity. Possibility also arises here merely through reference to the concepts of reflection; for example, "A triangle *may* be right-angled, obtuse-angled, or equiangular, but it *must* have three angles amounting to two right angles." Thus here we arrive at the *possible* only by passing from the perceptible to the abstract.

After this discussion, which assumes a recollection of what was said in the essay *On the Principle of Sufficient Reason* as well as in the first book of the present work, it is hoped that there will be no further doubt about the true and very heterogeneous origin of those forms of judgements laid before us by the table, and likewise no doubt about the inadmissibility and utter groundlessness of the assumption of twelve special functions of the understanding for their explanation. Many particular observations, easily made, also furnish information on this latter point. Thus, for example, it requires great love of symmetry and much confidence in a guiding line taken from it, to assume that an affirmative, a categorical, and an assertory judgement are three things so fundamentally different as to justify the assumption of a quite special function of the understanding for each of them.

Kant himself betrays an awareness of the untenability of his doctrine of categories by the fact that, in the third section of the Analysis of Principles (*phaenomena et noumena*), in the second edition he omitted several long passages from the first (namely pp. 241, 242, 244-246, 248-253) which showed too openly the weakness of that doctrine. Thus, for example, he there (p. 241) says that he has not

defined the individual categories, because he could not do so even
if he had wished, since they were incapable of any definition. He
had forgotten that on p. 82 of the same first edition he had said: "I
purposely dispense with the definition of the categories, although
I may be in possession of it." This was therefore—*sit venia verbo*[22]
wind. But he has allowed this last passage to stand; and so all those
passages afterwards prudently omitted betray the fact that nothing
distinct can be thought in connexion with the categories, and that
this whole doctrine stands on a weak foundation.

This table of categories is now supposed to be the guiding line
along which every metaphysical, and in fact every scientific, speculation is to be conducted (*Prolegomena*, § 39). In fact, it is not only
the foundation of the whole Kantian philosophy, and the type according to which its symmetry is carried through everywhere, as I
have already shown above, but it has also really become the
Procrustean bed on to which Kant forces every possible consideration
by means of a violence that I shall now consider somewhat more
closely. But with such an opportunity, what were the *imitatores,
servum pecus*[23] bound to do? We have seen. That violence is therefore committed in the following way. The meaning of the expressions
that denote the titles, forms of judgements, and categories, is entirely set aside and forgotten, and only the expressions themselves
retained. These have their origin partly in Aristotle's *Analytica
priora*, i, 23 (περὶ ποιότητος καὶ ποσότητος τῶν τοῦ συλλογισμοῦ ὅρων:
de qualitate et quantitate terminorum syllogismi),[24] but they are
arbitrarily chosen; for the extent of the concepts could certainly have
been expressed otherwise than by the word *quantity*, although this
word is better suited to its object than are the remaining titles of
the categories. Even the word *quality* has obviously been chosen
merely from the habit of opposing quality to quantity; for the name
quality is indeed taken arbitrarily enough for affirmation and denial.
But in every inquiry conducted by Kant, every quantity in time and
space, and every possible quality of things, physical, moral, and so
on, is brought under those category-titles, although between these
things and those titles of the forms of judging and thinking there is
not the least thing in common, except the accidental and arbitrary
nomenclature. We must be mindful of the high esteem due to Kant
in other respects, in order not to express our indignation at this
procedure in harsh terms. The pure physiological table of general
principles of natural science at once furnishes us with the nearest

[22] "If the term may be excused." [Tr.]
[23] "Imitators, slavish mob!" [Tr.]
[24] "On the quality and quantity of the terms of the syllogism." [Tr.]

example. What in the world has the quantity of judgements to do with the fact that every perception has an extensive magnitude? What has the quality of judgements to do with the fact that every sensation has a degree? On the contrary, the former rests on the fact that space is the form of our external perception, and the latter is nothing more than an empirical, and moreover quite subjective, observation or perception drawn merely from the consideration of the nature of our sense-organs. Further, in the table that lays the foundation for rational psychology (*Critique of Pure Reason,* p. 344; V, 402), the *simple, uncompounded nature* of the soul is cited under quality; but this is precisely a quantitative property, and has no reference at all to affirmation or denial in the judgement. But quantity had to be filled up by the *unity* of the soul, although that is already included in its simple nature. Modality is then ludicrously forced in; the soul thus stands in connexion with *possible* objects; but connexion belongs to relation; relation, however, is already taken possession of by substance. Then the four cosmological Ideas that are the material of the antinomies are traced back to the titles of the categories. We shall speak of these in greater detail later on, when we examine these antinomies. Several examples, if possible even more glaring, are furnished by the table of the *categories of freedom* in the *Critique of Practical Reason;* further by the *Critique of Judgement,* first book, which goes through the judgement of taste according to the four titles of the categories; finally by the *Metaphysical Rudiments of Natural Science* which are cut out entirely in accordance with the table of categories. Possibly the false, which is mixed up here and there with what is true and excellent in this important work, was mainly brought about precisely in this way. Let us see, at the end of the first chapter, how the unity, plurality, and totality of the directions of lines are supposed to correspond to the categories, so named according to the quantity of the judgements.

* * *

The principle of the *permanence of substance* is derived from the category of subsistence and inherence. We know this, however, only from the form of categorical judgements, in other words, from the connexion of two concepts as subject and predicate. Hence how violently is that great metaphysical principle made dependent on this simple, purely logical form! But this is done only *pro forma* and for the sake of symmetry. The proof given here for this principle entirely sets aside its alleged origin from the understanding and the category, and is produced from the pure intuition or perception of time. But this proof also is quite incorrect. It is false to say that in mere time there are *simultaneity* and *duration;* these representations first result from the union of *space* with time, as I have already shown in the essay *On the Principle of Sufficient Reason,* § 18, and have discussed more fully in § 4 of the present work. I must assume an acquaintance with these two discussions for an understanding of what follows. It is false to say that time itself *remains* in spite of all change; on the contrary, it is precisely time itself that is fleeting; a permanent time is a contradiction. Kant's proof is untenable, however much he has supported it with sophisms; in fact he falls here into the most palpable contradiction. Thus, after falsely setting up *coexistence* as a mode of time (p. 177; V, 219), he says (p. 183; V, 226) quite correctly: *"Coexistence* is not a mode of time, for in it absolutely no parts are simultaneous, but all are in succession." In truth, space is just as much implicated in coexistence as time is. For if two things are simultaneous and yet not one, they are different through space; if two states or conditions of *one* thing are simultaneous (e.g., the glow and the heat of iron), then they are two coexistent effects of *one* thing; hence they presuppose matter, and matter presupposes space. Strictly speaking, the simultaneous is a negative determination, merely indicating that two things or states are not different through time; thus their difference is to be sought elsewhere. But our knowledge of the persistence of substance, i.e., of matter, must of course rest on an insight *a priori,* for it is beyond all doubt, and cannot therefore be drawn from experience. I derive it from the fact that the principle of all becoming and passing away, namely the law of causality, of which we are conscious *a priori,* essentially concerns only *changes,* i.e., successive *states or conditions* of matter. It is therefore limited to the form, but leaves *matter* untouched, which thus exists in our consciousness as the foundation of all things. This foundation is not subject to any becoming or passing away; consequently, it has always been and always continues to be. A deeper proof of the permanence of substance, drawn from the analysis of our perceptible representation of the empirical world in general, is found in our first book, § 4, where it was shown that the essential nature of *matter* consists in the complete *union of space and time,* a union that is possible only by means of the representation of causality, and consequently only for the understanding, that is nothing but the subjective correlative of causality. Matter is therefore never known otherwise than as operative or causative, in other words, as causality through and through. To be and to act are with it identical, as is indeed indicated by the word *actuality* (*Wirklichkeit*). Intimate union of space and time—causality, matter, actuality—are therefore one, and the subjective correlative of this one is the understanding. Matter must carry in itself the conflicting properties of the two factors from which it arises, and it is the representation of causality which eliminates the contradictory element in both, and renders their coexistence conceivable to the understanding. Matter is through and for the understanding alone, and the whole faculty of the understanding consists in the knowledge of cause and effect. Thus for the understanding there is united in matter the inconstant and unstable flux of time, appearing as change of accidents, with the rigid immobility of space, exhibiting itself as the permanence of substance. For if substance passed away just as the accidents do, the phenomenon would be completely torn away from space, and would belong only to mere time; the world of experience would be dissolved by the destruction of matter, by annihilation. Therefore from the share that *space* has in matter, i.e., in all the phenomena of actuality—since it is the opposite and the reverse of time, and thus, in itself and apart from union with time, knows absolutely no change—that principle of the permanence of substance, which everyone recognizes as *a priori* certain, had to be deduced and explained; not, however, from mere time, to which for this purpose Kant quite falsely attributed a *permanence*.

In the essay *On the Principle of Sufficient Reason,* § 23, I have demonstrated in detail the incorrectness of the proof (which now follows) of the *a priori* nature and the necessity of the law of causality from the mere chronological sequence of events; I can therefore only refer to it here.[25] It is just the same with the proof of reciprocal effect, the concept of which I had to demonstrate previously as invalid. What is necessary about modality has also been said already, and the working out of its principles now follows.

I should have to refute a good many more particulars in the further course of the Transcendental Analytic, if I were not afraid of trying the patience of the reader; I therefore leave them to his own reflection. But again and again in the *Critique of Pure Reason* we come across that principal and fundamental error of Kant's which I have previously censured in detail, namely the complete absence of any distinction between abstract, discursive knowledge and intuitive knowledge. It is this that spreads a permanent obscurity over the whole of Kant's theory of the faculty of knowledge. It never lets the reader know what is at any time really being talked about, so that instead of understanding he is always merely guessing and con-

---

[25] The reader may like to compare my refutation of the Kantian proof with the earlier attacks on it by Feder, *Ueber Zeit, Raum und Kausalität,* § 28; and by G. E. Schulze, *Kritik der theoretischen Philosophie,* Vol. II, pp. 422-442.

jecturing, since he tries every time to understand what is said alternately about thinking and about perceiving, and always remains in suspense. In the chapter "On the Differentiation of all Objects into Phenomena and Noumena," that incredible want of reflection on the real nature of the representation of perception and of the abstract representation leads Kant, as I shall explain more fully in a moment, to the monstrous assertion that without thought, and hence without abstract concepts, there is absolutely no knowledge of an object, and that, because perception is not thought, it is also not knowledge at all, and in general is nothing but mere affection of sensibility, mere sensation! Nay more, that perception without concept is absolutely empty, but that concept without perception is still something (p. 253; V, 309). Now this is the very opposite of the truth, for concepts obtain all meaning, all content, only from their reference to representations of perception, from which they have been abstracted, drawn off, in other words, formed by the dropping of everything inessential. If, therefore, the foundation of perception is taken away from them, they are empty and void. Perceptions, on the other hand, have immediate and very great significance in themselves (in them, in fact, is objectified the will, the thing-in-itself); they represent themselves, express themselves, and have not merely borrowed content as concepts have. For the principle of sufficient reason rules over them only as the law of causality, and as such determines only their position in space and time. It does not, however, condition their content and their significance, as is the case with concepts, where it holds good of the ground or reason of knowing. For the rest, it looks as if just here Kant really wants to set about distinguishing the representation of perception from the abstract representation. He reproaches Leibniz and Locke, the former with having made everything into abstract representations, the latter with having made everything into representations of perception. But yet no distinction is reached, and although Locke and Leibniz actually did make these mistakes, Kant himself is burdened with a third mistake that includes both these, namely that of having mixed up the perceptible and the abstract to such an extent that a monstrous hybrid of the two resulted, an absurdity of which no clear mental picture is possible, and which therefore inevitably merely confused and stupefied students, and set them at variance.

Certainly in the chapter referred to "On the Differentiation of all Objects into Phenomena and Noumena," thought and perception are separated more than anywhere else; but here the nature of this distinction is a fundamentally false one. Thus it is said on p. 253 (V, 309): "If I take away all thought (through categories) from empirical knowledge, there is left absolutely no knowledge of an object; for through mere perception nothing at all is thought, and that this affection of sensibility is in me does not constitute any relation at all of such a representation to any object." To a certain extent, this sentence contains all Kant's errors in a nutshell, since it clearly brings out that he falsely conceived the relation between sensation, perception, and thinking. Accordingly, he identifies perception, the form of which is supposed to be space, and indeed space in all three dimensions, with the mere subjective sensation in the organs of sense, but he admits knowledge of an object only through thinking, which is different from perceiving. On the other hand, I say that objects are first of all objects of perception, not of thinking, and that all knowledge of *objects* is originally and in itself perception. Perception, however, is by no means mere sensation, but with it the understanding already proves itself active. *Thought,* that is added only in the case of man, not in that of the animals, is mere abstraction from perception, does not furnish fundamentally new knowledge, does not establish objects that did not exist previously. It merely changes the form of the knowledge already gained through perception, makes it into an abstract knowledge in concepts, whereby its perceptible nature is lost, but, on the other hand, its combination becomes possible, and this immeasurably extends its applicability. On the other hand, the *material* of our thinking is none other than our perceptions themselves, and not something which perception does not contain, and which would be added only through thought. Therefore the material of everything that occurs in our thinking must be capable of verification in our perception, as otherwise it would be an empty thinking. Although this material is elaborated and transformed by thought in many different ways, it must nevertheless be capable of being restored from this; and it must be possible for thought to be traced back to this material—just as a piece of gold is ultimately reduced from all its solutions, oxides, sublimates, and compounds, and is again presented reguline and undiminished. This could not be, if thought itself had added something, indeed the main thing, to the object.

The whole chapter on the amphiboly, which follows this, is merely a criticism of the Leibnizian philosophy, and as such is on the whole correct, although the whole form or arrangement is made merely for the sake of architectonic symmetry which here also affords the guiding line. Thus to bring out the analogy with the Aristotelian Organon, a transcendental topic is set up. This consists in our having to consider every concept from four points of view, in order to make out to which faculty of knowledge it should be brought. But those four points of view are assumed quite arbitrarily, and ten more could be added with just as much right; but their fourfold number corresponds to the titles of the categories. Therefore the chief doctrines of Leibniz are divided among them as best may be. Through this criticism, what were merely Leibniz's false abstractions are also to a certain extent stamped as natural errors of the faculty of reason. Instead of learning from his great philosophical contemporaries, Spinoza and Locke, Leibniz preferred to serve up his own strange inventions. In the chapter on the amphiboly of reflection, it is said finally that there can perhaps be a perception entirely different from ours, to which however our categories can nevertheless be applicable. Therefore, the objects of that supposed perception would be *noumena,* things that could be merely *thought* by us; but as the perception that would give meaning to that thinking is lacking in us, and is in fact wholly problematical, the object of that thinking would also be merely a quite indefinite possibility. I have shown above through quoted passages that Kant, in the greatest contradiction with himself, sets up the categories, now as the condition of the representation of perception, now as the function of merely abstract thinking. Here they now appear in the latter meaning, and it seems quite as if he wants to ascribe to them merely a discursive thinking. But if this is really his opinion, then necessarily at the beginning of the Transcendental Logic, before specifying at such great length the different functions of thought, he should have characterized thought in general, and consequently distinguished it from perception. He should have shown what knowledge is given by mere perception, and what new knowledge is added in thought. He would then have known what he was really talking about, or rather he would have spoken quite differently, first about perceiving, and then about thinking. Instead of this, he is now concerned with something between the two, which is an impossibility. Then also there would not be that great gap between the Transcendental Aesthetic and the Transcendental Logic, where, after describing the mere form of perception, he disposes of its content, all that is empirically apprehended, with the phrase "it is *given.*" He does not ask how it comes about, *whether with or without understanding,* but with a leap passes over to abstract thinking, and not even to thinking in general, but at once to certain forms of thought. He does not say a word about what thinking is, what the concept is, what the relation of abstract and discursive to concrete and intuitive is, what the difference between the knowledge of man and that of the animal is, and what the faculty of reason is.

But it was just this difference between abstract knowledge and knowledge of perception, entirely overlooked by Kant, which the ancient philosophers denoted by φαινόμενα and νοούμενα.[26] Their contrast and incommensurability occupied those philosophers so much in the philosophemes of the Eleatics, in Plato's doctrine of the Ideas, in the dialectic of the Megarics, and later the scholastics in the dispute between nominalism and realism, whose seed, so late in developing, was already contained in the opposite mental tendencies of Plato and Aristotle. But Kant who, in an unwarrantable manner, entirely neglected the thing for the expression of which those words φαινόμενα and νοούμενα had already been taken, now takes possession of the words, as if they were still unclaimed, in order to denote by them his things-in-themselves and his phenomena.

* * *

After having had to reject Kant's doctrine of the categories, just as he himself rejected that of Aristotle, I will indicate here by way of suggestion a third method of reaching what is intended. Thus, what both Kant and Aristotle looked for under the name of the categories were the most universal concepts under which all things, however different, must be subsumed, and through which, therefore, everything existing would ultimately be thought. This is just why Kant conceived them as the *forms* of all thinking.

Grammar is related to logic as are clothes to the body. Those highest of all concepts, this ground-bass of our faculty of reason, are the foundation of all more special thinking, and therefore without the application of this, no thinking whatever can take place. Should not such concepts, therefore, ultimately lie in those which, just on account of their exceeding generality (transcendentality), have their expression not in single words, but in whole classes of words, since one of them is already thought along with every word, whatever it may be, and accordingly their designation would have to be looked for not in the lexicon, but in the grammar? Therefore, ought they not ultimately to be those distinctions of concepts by virtue of which the word that expresses them is either a substantive or an adjective, a verb or an adverb, a pronoun, a preposition, or some other particle, in short the *partes orationis* (parts of speech)? For unquestionably these denote the forms which all thinking assumes in the first instance, and in which it immediately moves. Precisely on this account, they are the essential forms of speech, the

---

[26] See Sextus Empiricus, *Pyrrhoniae hypotyposes*, Bk. i, ch. 13, νοούμενα φαινομένοις ἀντετίθη ᾽Αναξαγόρας (*intelligibilia apparentibus opposuit Anaxagoras*). ("Anaxagoras opposed what is thought to what is perceived.") [Tr.]

fundamental constituent elements of every language, so that we cannot imagine any language that would not consist at least of substantives, adjectives, and verbs. To these fundamental forms there could then be subordinated those forms of thought which are expressed through their inflexions, through declension and conjugation; and here in the main thing it is inessential whether we make use of the article and the pronoun for denoting them. But we will examine the matter somewhat more closely, and raise anew the question: What are the forms of thinking?

(1) Thinking consists throughout of judging; judgements are the threads of its whole texture, for without the use of a verb our thinking makes no progress, and whenever we use a verb, we judge.

(2) Every judgement consists in recognizing the relation between a subject and a predicate, which are separated or united by it with various restrictions. It unites them by the recognition of the actual identity of the two, an identity that can occur only with convertible concepts; then in the recognition that the one is always thought along with the other, although not conversely—in the universal affirmative proposition; up to the recognition that the one is sometimes thought along with the other, in the particular affirmative proposition. Negative propositions take the reverse course. Accordingly, in every judgement it must be possible to find subject, predicate, and copula, the last affirmative or negative, although not every one of these is denoted by a word of its own, though that is generally the case. *One* word often denotes predicate and copula, as "Caius ages"; occasionally one word denotes all three, as *concurritur,* i.e., "The armies come to close quarters." From this it is clear that we have not to look for the forms of thinking precisely and directly in words, or even in the parts of speech; for the same judgement can be expressed in different languages, indeed by different words in the same language, and even by different parts of speech. However, the thought nevertheless remains the same, and consequently its form also; for the thought could not be the same with a different form of thought itself. But with the same idea and with the same form of the idea the form of words can very well be different, for it is merely the outward expression of the thought, and that, on the other hand, is inseparable from *its* form. Therefore grammar explains only the clothing of the forms of thought; hence the parts of speech can be derived from the original thought-forms themselves, which are independent of all languages; their function is to express these forms of thought with all their modifications. They are the instrument, the clothing, of the forms of thought, which must be

made to fit their structure accurately, so that that structure can be recognized in it.

(3) These actual, unalterable, original forms of thinking are certainly those of Kant's *logical table of judgements;* only that in this table are to be found blind windows for the sake of symmetry and of the table of categories, which must therefore be omitted; likewise a false arrangement. Thus:

(a) *Quality:* affirmation or denial, i.e., combination or separation of concepts: two forms. It belongs to the copula.

(b) *Quantity:* the subject-concept is taken wholly or in part: totality or plurality. To the former also belong individual subjects: Socrates means "all Socrateses." Hence only two forms. It belongs to the subject.

(c) *Modality:* has actually three forms. It determines the quality as necessary, actual, or contingent. Consequently, it also belongs to the copula.

These three forms of thought spring from the laws of thought of contradiction and of identity. But from the principle of sufficient reason and from that of the excluded middle there arises

(d) *Relation:* This appears only when we decide about ready and completed judgements, and can consist only in the fact that it either states the dependence of one judgement on another (also in the plurality of both), and hence combines them in the *hypothetical* proposition; or else states that judgements exclude one another, and hence separates them in the *disjunctive* proposition. It belongs to the copula, that here separates or combines the completed judgements.

The *parts of speech* and grammatical forms are modes of expression of the three constituent elements of the judgement, that is, the subject, the predicate, and the copula, and also of their possible relations, and thus of the thought-forms just enumerated, and of the closer determinations and modifications thereof. Therefore substantive, adjective, and verb are essential and fundamental constituents of language in general; and so they are bound to be found in all languages. Yet a language could be imagined in which adjective and verb were always amalgamated, as they sometimes are in all languages. For the time being, it can be said that substantive, article, and pronoun are intended to express the *subject;* adjective, adverb, preposition, to express the *predicate;* the verb to express the *copula.* But with the exception of *esse* (to be), the verb already contains the predicate. Philosophical grammar has to tell us about the precise mechanism of the expression of the thought-forms, just as logic has to inform us about the operations with the thought-forms themselves.

Note.—As a warning against a wrong path, and to illustrate the above, I mention S. Stern's *Vorläufige Grundlage zur Sprachphilosophie* (1835) as being a wholly abortive attempt to construct the categories out of the grammatical forms. He has entirely confused thinking with perceiving, and therefore, instead of the categories of thinking, he has claimed to deduce the supposed categories of perceiving from the grammatical forms; consequently, he has put the grammatical forms in direct relation to *perception.* He is involved in the great error that *language* is directly related to *perception,* instead of its being directly related merely to *thought* as such, and hence to the *abstract concepts,* and primarily by means of these to perception. But they have to perception a relation that brings about an entire change of the form. What exists in perception, and hence also the relations which spring from time and space, certainly becomes an object of thinking. Therefore there must also be forms of language to express it, yet always only in the abstract, as concepts. Concepts are always the first material of thought, and the forms of logic are related only to these as such, never *directly* to perception. Perception always determines only the material, never the formal, truth of propositions, as the formal truth is determined according to the logical rules alone.

*   *   *

I return to the Kantian philosophy, and come to the *Transcendental Dialectic.* Kant opens it with the explanation of *reason* (*Vernunft*), which faculty is supposed to play the principal role in it; for hitherto only sensibility and understanding were on the scene. In discussing his different explanations of reason, I have already spoken about the one given here, that "it is the faculty of principles." Here it is now taught that all *a priori* knowledge hitherto considered, which makes pure mathematics and pure natural science possible, gives us mere *rules,* but not *principles,* because it proceeds from perceptions and forms of knowledge, not from mere *concepts,* which are required if we are to speak of principles. Accordingly, such a principle should be a knowledge *from mere concepts* and yet *synthetical.* But this is absolutely impossible. From mere concepts nothing but *analytical* propositions can ever result. If concepts are to be combined synthetically and yet *a priori,* this combination must necessarily be brought about through a third thing, namely a pure intuition or perception of the formal possibility of experience, just as synthetic judgements *a posteriori* are brought about through empirical perception; consequently, a synthetic proposition *a priori* can never proceed from mere concepts. In general, however, we are *a priori* conscious of nothing more than the principle of sufficient reason in its different forms, and therefore no synthetic judgements *a priori* are possible other than those resulting from that which gives content to that principle.

Nevertheless, Kant finally comes forward with a pretended principle of reason[27] answering to his demand, but only with this *one,* from which other conclusions and corollaries subsequently follow. It is the principle set up and elucidated by Chr. Wolff in his *Cosmologia,* sect. 1, c. 2, § 93, and his *Ontologia,* § 178. Now just as previously under the title of the amphiboly, mere Leibnizian philosophemes were taken to be natural and necessary aberrations of the faculty of reason, and were criticized as such, so precisely the same thing is done here with the philosophemes of Wolff. Kant still presents this principle of reason (*Vernunft*) in a faint light through indistinctness, indefiniteness, and by cutting it up (p. 307; V, 364, and 322; V, 379). Clearly expressed, however, it is as follows: "If the conditioned is given, then the totality of its conditions must also be given, and consequently also the *unconditioned,* by which alone that totality becomes complete." We become most vividly aware of the apparent truth of this proposition if we picture to ourselves the conditions and the conditioned as the links of a pendent chain, whose upper end, however, is not visible; thus it might go on to infinity. As the chain does not fall but hangs, there must be *one* link above, which is the first, and is fixed in some way. Or more briefly, our faculty of reason would like to have a point of contact for the causal chain that reaches back to infinity; this would be convenient for it. We wish, however, to examine the proposition not figuratively, but in itself. Synthetic it certainly is, for analytically nothing more follows from the concept of the conditioned than that of the condition. However, it has not *a priori* truth, or even *a posteriori,* but surreptitiously obtains its semblance of truth in a very subtle way that I must now disclose. Immediately and *a priori,* we have the different kinds of knowledge expressed by the principle of sufficient reason in its four forms. From this immediate knowledge all abstract expressions of the principle of sufficient reason are already derived, and are thus indirect; but their conclusions and corollaries are even more so. I have discussed above how *abstract* knowledge often unites many different kinds of *intuitive* knowledge into *one* form or *one* concept, so that they are now no longer dis-

---

[27] *Princip der Vernunft* is the German term. [Tr.]

tinguishable. Thus abstract knowledge is related to intuitive as the shadow is to real objects, whose great variety and multiplicity it reproduces through *one* outline comprehending them all. Now the pretended principle of reason (*Vernunft*) makes use of this shadow. In order from the principle of sufficient ground or reason (*Grund*) to deduce the unconditioned that flatly contradicts this principle, it cleverly and cunningly abandons the immediate, perceptible knowledge of the content of the principle of sufficient reason in its particular forms, and makes use only of abstract concepts drawn from it and having value and meaning only through it, in order to smuggle its unconditioned in some way into the wide sphere of those concepts. Its procedure becomes most distinct through dialectical expression; thus: "If the conditioned exists, its condition must also be given, and that indeed entirely, hence completely, thus the totality of its conditions; consequently, if they constitute a series, the whole series, and so also its first beginning, thus the unconditioned." Here it is already false that the conditions to a conditioned as such can constitute a *series*. On the contrary, the totality of the conditions to every conditioned must be contained in its *nearest* reason or ground from which it directly proceeds, and which only thus is a *sufficient* reason or ground. Thus, for example, the different determinations of the state or condition that is the cause, all of which must have come together before the effect appears. But the series, for example the chain of causes, arises merely from the fact that what was just now the condition is again regarded by us as a conditioned; but then the whole operation begins again from the beginning, and the principle of sufficient reason appears anew with its demand. But to a conditioned there can never be a real successive *series* of conditions that would exist merely as such, and on account of what is finally and ultimately conditioned. On the contrary, it is always an alternating series of conditioneds and conditions; as each link is laid aside, the chain is broken, and the demand of the principle of sufficient reason is entirely removed. This demand arises anew by the condition becoming the conditioned. Thus the principle of *sufficient* ground or reason always demands only the completeness of the *nearest or next condition,* never the completeness of a *series.* But this very concept of the completeness of the condition leaves it indefinite whether such a completeness is to be simultaneous or successive; and since the latter is now chosen, there arises the demand for a complete *series* of conditions following one another. Merely through an arbitrary abstraction is a series of causes and effects regarded as a series of nothing but causes that would exist merely on account of the last effect, and would therefore be demanded as its *sufficient* reason or ground. On the other hand, from a closer and more intelligent consideration, and by descending from the indefinite generality of abstraction to the particular, definite reality, it is found that the demand for a *sufficient* reason or ground extends merely to the completeness of the determinations of the *nearest* cause, not to the completeness of a series. The demand of the principle of sufficient reason is extinguished completely in each given sufficient reason or ground. It at once arises anew, since this reason or ground is again regarded as a consequent; but it never demands immediately a series of reasons or grounds. On the other hand, if, instead of going to the thing itself, we keep within the abstract concepts, those differences disappear. Then a chain of alternating causes and effects, or of alternating logical reasons and consequents, is given out as a chain of nothing but causes or reasons of the last effect, and the *completeness of the conditions* through which a reason or ground first becomes *sufficient,* appears as a completeness of that assumed *series* of nothing but grounds or reasons, which exists only on account of the last consequent. There then appears very boldly the abstract principle of reason (*Vernunft*) with its demand for the unconditioned. But in order to recognize the invalidity of this demand, there is no need of a critique of reason by means of antinomies and their solution, but only of a critique of reason understood in my sense. Such a critique would be an examination of the relation of abstract knowledge to immediate intuitive knowledge by descending from the indefinite generality of the former to the fixed definiteness of the latter. It follows from this that the essential nature of reason (*Vernunft*) by no means consists in the demand for an unconditioned; for, as soon as it proceeds with full deliberation, it must itself find that an unconditioned is really an absurdity. As a faculty of knowledge, our reason can always be concerned only with objects; but every object for the subject is necessarily and irrevocably subordinated and given over to the principle of sufficient reason, *a parte ante* as well as *a parte post.*[28] The validity of the principle of sufficient reason is so much involved in the form of consciousness that we simply cannot imagine anything objectively of which no "why" could be further demanded; hence we cannot imagine an absolute absolute like a blank wall in front of us. That this or that person's convenience bids him stop somewhere, and arbitrarily assume such an absolute, is of no avail against that incontestable certainty *a priori,* even if he assumes an air of importance in doing so. In fact, the whole talk about the absolute, that almost

---

[28] In other words, with the object is posited the principle of sufficient reason, and *vice versa.* [Tr.]

sole theme of the philosophies attempted since Kant's time, is nothing but the cosmological proof *incognito*. In consequence of the case brought against this proof by Kant, it is deprived of all rights and is outlawed; it dare not any longer appear in its true form. It therefore appears in all kinds of disguises, now in distinguished form under the cloak of intellectual intuition or of pure thinking, now as a suspected vagabond, half begging, half demanding what it wants, in the more unassuming philosophemes. If the gentlemen absolutely want to have an absolute, I will place in their hands one that satisfies all the demands made on such a thing much better than their misty and extravagant phantoms do; I mean matter. It is beginningless and imperishable, hence it is independent and *quod per se est et per se concipitur*.[29] From its womb everything comes, and to it everything returns; what more can we demand of an absolute? But to those on whom no critique of reason has had any effect, we ought rather to exclaim:

> Are ye not like women who ever
> Return merely to their first word,
> Though one has talked reason for hours? [30]

That the return to an unconditioned cause, to a first beginning, is by no means established in the nature of our faculty of reason is, moreover, proved in practice by the fact that the original religions of our race, which even now have the greatest number of followers on earth, I mean Brahmanism and Buddhism, neither know nor admit such assumptions, but carry on to infinity the series of phenomena that condition one another. On this point I refer to the note given below with the criticism of the first antinomy, and we can also look up Upham's *Doctrine of Buddhaism* (p. 9), and generally every genuine account of the religions of Asia. We should not identify Judaism with reason (*Vernunft*).

Kant, who by no means wishes to maintain his pretended principle of reason (*Vernunft*) as objectively valid, but only as subjectively necessary, deduces it even as such only by a shallow sophism, p. 307 (V, 364). He says that, because we try to subsume every truth known to us under a more general truth, as long as this method goes on, this should be nothing but the pursuit of the unconditioned that we already presuppose. In truth, however, by such an attempt we do nothing more than apply and appropriately use our faculty of reason for the simplification of our knowledge by a

---

[29] "That which exists in itself and is conceived through itself." [Tr.]

[30] From Schiller's *Wallensteins Tod*, II, 3. [Tr.]

comprehensive survey. Our reason is that faculty of abstract universal knowledge which distinguishes the prudent, thoughtful human being, endowed with speech, from the animal, the slave of the present moment. For the use of the faculty of reason consists precisely in our knowing the particular through the universal, the case through the rule, the rule through the more general rule, and thus in our looking for the most universal points of view. Through such a survey our knowledge is so facilitated and perfected that from it arises the great difference between animal and human life, and again between the life of the educated man and that of the uneducated. Now the series of *grounds of knowledge,* existing only in the sphere of the abstract, and thus of our faculty of reason, certainly always finds an end in the indemonstrable, in other words, in a representation that is not further conditioned according to this form of the principle of sufficient reason, and thus in the *a priori* or *a posteriori* immediately perceptible ground of the highest proposition of the chain of reasoning. I have already shown in the essay *On the Principle of Sufficient Reason,* § 50, that here the series of the grounds of knowledge really passes over into the series of the grounds of becoming or of being. However, we can try to put forward this circumstance, in order to demonstrate an unconditioned according to the law of causality, even if it be merely as a demand, only when we have not yet distinguished the forms of the principle of sufficient reason, but, keeping to the abstract expression, have confused them all. Kant, however, tries to establish this confusion even by a mere play on the words *Universalitas* (universality) and *Universitas* (totality), p. 322 (V, 379). It is therefore fundamentally false to say that our search for higher grounds of knowledge, for more general truths, springs from the assumption of an object unconditioned as regards its existence, or that it has anything whatever in common therewith. Moreover, how could it be essential to our faculty of reason to presuppose something that it must recognize as an absurdity as soon as it reflects? On the contrary, the origin of that concept of the unconditioned can never be demonstrated in anything but in the indolence of the individual who by means of it wishes to get rid of all questions, his own and those of others, although without any justification.

Now Kant himself denies objective validity to this pretended principle of reason (*Vernunft*), yet he gives it as a necessary subjective assumption, and thus introduces into our knowledge an unsolvable split that he soon renders more conspicuous. For this purpose, he further unfolds that principle of reason (*Vernunft*), p. 322 (V, 379), according to his favourite method of architectonic symmetry. From the three categories of relation spring three kinds of syllogism, each of which gives the guiding line to the discovery of a special unconditioned, of which therefore there are again three, namely soul, world (as object-in-itself and totality complete in itself), God. Now we must at once observe here a great contradiction, of which, however, Kant takes no notice, since it would be very dangerous to the symmetry. Indeed, two of these unconditioneds are themselves in turn conditioned by the third, namely soul and world by God, who is their originating cause. Thus the two former by no means have the predicate of unconditionedness in common with the latter, and yet this is the point here, but only the predicate of being inferred according to principles of experience beyond the sphere of the possibility of experience.

Setting this aside, we find again in the three unconditioneds to which, according to Kant, everyone's faculty of reason, following its essential laws, must come, the three main subjects round which the whole of philosophy, under the influence of Christianity, from the scholastics down to Christian Wolff, has turned. Accessible and familiar as those concepts have become through all those philosophers, and now also through the philosophers of pure reason (*Vernunft*), it is by no means certain from this that, even without revelation, they were bound to result from the development of everyone's faculty of reason, as a creation peculiar to the nature of this reason itself. To decide this, it would be necessary to make use of historical research, and to find out whether the ancient and non-European nations, especially those of Hindustan, and many of the oldest Greek philosophers actually arrived at those concepts, or whether only we, by translating the Brahma of the Hindus and the Tien of the Chinese quite falsely as "God," charitably ascribe such concepts to them, just as the Greeks encountered their gods everywhere; whether it is not rather the case that theism proper is to be found only in the Jewish religion, and the two religions that have sprung from it. On this very account, the adherents of these religions comprehend the followers of all other religions on earth under the name of heathen. Incidentally, the word heathen is an extremely silly and crude expression that should be banished, at any rate from the writings of scholars, since it identifies and mixes up indiscriminately Brahmans, Buddhists, Egyptians, Greeks, Romans, Germans, Gauls, Iroquois, Patagonians, Caribbeans, Tahitians, Australians, and many others. Such an expression is suitable for parsons, but in the learned world it must be shown the door at once; it can travel to England, and take up its abode at Oxford. It is a thoroughly established fact that Buddhism in particular, the religion with the greatest number of representatives on earth, contains absolutely no theism, indeed rejects it out of hand. As regards Plato, I am of the opinion that he owes to the Jews the theism that periodically comes over him. This is why Numenius (according to Clement of Alexandria, *Stromata,* i, c. 22, Eusebius, *Praeparatio evangelica,* xiii, 12, and Suidas, under "Numenius") called him the *Moses graecizans:* Τί γάρ ἐστι Πλάτων, ἢ Μωσῆς ἀττικίζων;[31] and he reproaches him with having stolen (ἀποσύλησας) his doctrines of God and the creation from the Mosaic writings. Clement often repeats that Plato knew and made use of Moses, e.g., *Stromata,* i, 25; v, 14, § 90 etc.; *Paedagogus,* ii, 10, and iii, 11; also in the *Cohortatio ad gentes,* c. 6, where, after in the previous chapter monkishly scolding and ridiculing all the Greek philosophers for not having been Jews, he exclusively praises Plato and breaks out into pure exultation that, as he (Plato) learned his geometry from the Egyptians, his astronomy from the Babylonians, magic from the Thracians, and a great deal from the Assyrians, so he learned his theism from the Jews: Οἶδά σου τοὺς διδασκάλους κἄν ἀποκρύπτειν ἐθέλῃς, . . . δόξαν τὴν τοῦ θεοῦ παρ' αὐτῶν ὠφέλησαι τῶν Ἑβραίων (*tuos magistros novi, licet eos celare velis, . . . illa de Deo sententia suppeditata tibi est ab Hebraeis.*[32] A touching scene of recognition. But in what follows I see unusual confirmation of the matter. According to Plutarch (*Marius*), and better according to Lactantius (i, 3, 19), Plato thanked nature for his having been born a human being and not an animal, a man and not a woman, a Greek and not a barbarian. Now in Isaac Euchel's *Gebete der Juden,* from the Hebrew second edition, 1799, p. 7,[32A] there is a morning prayer in which the Jews thank and praise God that they have been born Jews and not heathens, free men and not slaves, men and not women. Such a historical investigation would have saved Kant from an unfortunate necessity in which he is now involved, for he represents those three concepts as springing necessarily from the nature of our faculty of reason, and yet he shows that they are untenable and cannot be established by this faculty, thus making our reason itself the sophist, for he says, p. 339 (V, 397): "There are sophistications not of people, but of pure reason itself, from which even the wisest man cannot free himself, and though possibly after much trouble he can avoid error, yet he can never get rid of the illusion that incessantly mocks and tor-

---

[31] "For what is Plato but a Moses speaking Attic?" [Tr.]

[32] "I know your masters, although you would like to conceal them; you are directly indebted to the Hebrews for belief in God." [Tr.]

[32A] Compare the *Authorised Daily Prayer Book of the United Hebrew Congregations of the British Empire,* pp. 5-6. [Tr.]

ments him." Accordingly, these Kantian "Ideas of Reason" might be compared to the focus in which the converging reflected rays from a concave mirror meet several inches in front of its surface; in consequence of which, through an inevitable process of the understanding, an object presents itself to us there which is a thing without reality.

But the name *Ideas* is very unfortunately chosen for these three ostensibly necessary productions of pure theoretical reason. It was forcibly taken from Plato, who denoted by it the imperishable forms that, multiplied by time and space, become imperfectly visible in the innumerable, individual, fleeting things. In consequence of this, Plato's *Ideas* are in every way perceptible, as is so definitely indicated through the word he chose, which could be adequately translated only through things perceptible or visible. Kant has appropriated it to denote what lies so far from all possibility of perception that even abstract thinking can only half attain to it. The word "Idea," first introduced by Plato, has retained ever since, through twenty-two centuries, the meaning in which he used it; for not only all the philosophers of antiquity, but also all the scholastics, and even the Church Fathers and the theologians of the Middle Ages, used it only with that Platonic meaning, in the sense of the Latin word *exemplar,* as Suarez expressly mentions in his twenty-fifth Disputation, Sect. 1. That Englishmen and Frenchmen were later induced through the poverty of their languages to misuse the word is bad enough, but not important. Kant's misuse of the word *Idea* by the substitution of a new significance, drawn in on the slender thread of not-being-object-of-experience, a significance that it has in common with Plato's Ideas, but also with all possible chimeras, is therefore altogether unjustifiable. Now, as the misuse of a few years is not to be considered against the authority of many centuries, I have used the word always in its old original, Platonic significance.

*   *   *

The refutation of *rational psychology* is very much more detailed and thorough in the first edition of the *Critique of Pure Reason* than in the second and subsequent editions; here, therefore, we must certainly make use of the first edition. On the whole, this refutation has very great merit, and much that is true. But I am definitely of the opinion that it is merely from Kant's love of symmetry that he derives as necessary the concept of the soul from that paralogism by applying the demand for the unconditioned to the concept of *substance,* which is the first category of relation. Accordingly he maintains that the concept of a soul arises in this way in every speculative reason (*Vernunft*). If this concept actually had its origin in the assumption of a final subject of all the predicates of a thing, then one would have assumed a soul not only in man, but also just as necessarily in every inanimate thing, for such a thing also requires a final subject of all its predicates. In general, however, Kant makes use of a wholly inadmissible expression when he speaks of something that can exist only as subject and not as predicate (e.g., *Critique of Pure Reason,* p. 323; V, 412; *Prolegomena,* §§ 4 and 47); although a precedent for this is to be found in Aristotle's *Metaphysics,* iv, chap. 8. Nothing whatever exists as subject and predicate, for these expressions belong exclusively to logic, and denote the relation of abstract concepts to one another. In the world of perception, their correlative or representative must be substance and accident. But we need not look further for that which exists always only as substance and never as accident, but we have it directly in matter. It is the substance to all the properties of things that are its accidents. If we wish to retain Kant's expression just condemned, matter is actually the final subject of all the predicates of every empirically given thing, what is left after removing all its properties of every kind. This holds good of man as well as of the animal, plant, or stone, and it is so evident that, in order not to see it, there is needed a determined will not to see. I shall soon show that it is actually the prototype of the concept substance. Subject and predicate, however, are related to substance and accident rather as the principle of sufficient reason or ground in logic is to the law of causality in nature, and the confusion or identification of the two former is just as inadmissible as is that of the two latter. But in the *Prolegomena,* § 46, Kant carries this confusion and identification to the fullest extent, in order to represent the concept of the soul as arising from the concept of the final subject of all predicates, and from the form of the categorical syllogism. To discover the sophistry of this paragraph, we need only reflect that subject and predicate are purely logical determinations that concern simply and solely abstract concepts, and this indeed according to their relation in the judgement. On the other hand, substance and accident belong to the world of perception and to its apprehension in the understanding; but they are found there only as identical with matter and form or quality. A few more remarks on this in a moment.

The antithesis that has given rise to the assumption of two fundamentally different substances, body and soul, is in truth the antithesis of the objective and subjective. If man apprehends himself objectively in external perception, he finds a being spatially extended,

and in general entirely corporeal. On the other hand, if he apprehends himself in mere self-consciousness, and thus purely subjectively, he finds a merely willing and perceiving being, free from
all forms of perception, and thus without any of the properties belonging to bodies. He now forms the concept of the soul, like all the
transcendent concepts Kant calls Ideas, by applying the principle
of sufficient reason, the form of every object, to what is not object,
and here indeed to the subject of knowing and willing. Thus he
regards knowing, thinking, and willing as effects, of which he is
looking for the cause; he cannot assume the body to be this cause,
and therefore assumes one that is entirely different from the' body.
In this way, the first and the last dogmatists prove the existence of
the soul, Plato in the *Phaedrus,* and also Wolff, namely from thinking and willing as the effects leading to that cause. Only after the
concept of an immaterial, simple, indestructible being or essence
had arisen in this way by the hypostasizing of a cause corresponding
to the effect, did the school develop and demonstrate this from the
concept of *substance.* But the school had previously formed this
concept itself expressly for this purpose by the following noteworthy
dodge.

With the first class of representations, in other words, the real
world of perception, the representation of matter is also given, since
the law of causality, ruling in that class, determines the change of
conditions or states, and these states themselves presuppose something permanent of which they are the change. When discussing the
principle of the permanence of substance, I showed by reference
to previous passages that this representation of matter arises because
in the understanding, for which alone it exists, time and space are
intimately united by the law of causality (the understanding's sole
form of knowledge), and the share of space in this product exhibits
itself as the permanence of *matter,* while the share of time shows
itself as the change of *states* of matter. Purely by itself, matter can
be thought only in the abstract, but cannot be perceived; for to
perception it always appears in form and quality. Now from this
concept of *matter, substance* is again an abstraction, consequently
a higher *genus.* It arose through the fact that of the concept of matter only the predicate of permanence was allowed to stand, while all
its other essential properties, such as extension, impenetrability,
divisibility, and so on, were thought away. Therefore, like every
higher *genus,* the concept *substance* contains *less in itself* than does
the concept *matter,* but it does not in return for this contain, as
the higher *genus* usually does, *more under itself,* since it does not

include several lower *genera* besides matter. On the contrary this remains the only true subspecies of the concept of substance, the only demonstrable thing by which its content is realized and obtains a proof. Thus the purpose for which our reason (*Vernunft*) usually produces a higher concept by abstraction, that is in order to think simultaneously in this concept several subspecies that are different through secondary determinations, has here no place at all. Consequently, that abstraction is either quite purposelessly and uselessly undertaken, or has a secret secondary purpose. This secret purpose now comes to light, since under the concept substance a second species is coordinated with matter its genuine subspecies, namely the immaterial, simple, indestructible substance, soul. But the surreptitious introduction of this concept occurred through following an unauthorized and illogical method in the formation of the higher concept *substance*. In its legitimate working, our reason (*Vernunft*) always forms a higher generic concept by placing several specific concepts side by side; and, comparing them, it proceeds discursively, and by omitting their differences and retaining the qualities in which they agree, obtains the generic concept that includes them all, but contains less. From this it follows that the specific concepts must always precede the generic concept; but in the present case it is quite the reverse. Only the concept matter existed before the generic concept *substance,* which without occasion, and consequently without justification, was formed superfluously from the former concept by the arbitrary omission of all its determinations except one. Only subsequently was the second ungenuine subspecies placed beside the concept matter, and thus foisted in. But for the formation of this, nothing more was now required but an express denial of what had already been tacitly omitted previously in the higher generic concept, namely extension, impenetrability, and divisibility. Thus the concept *substance* was formed merely in order to be the vehicle for surreptitiously introducing the concept of the immaterial substance. Consequently, it is very far from being able to pass for a category or necessary function of the understanding; on the contrary, it is an exceedingly superfluous concept, because its only true content already lies in the concept of matter, beside which it contains only a great void. This void can be filled up by nothing except the surreptitiously introduced secondary species *immaterial substance;* and that concept was formed solely to take up this secondary species. Strictly speaking, therefore, the concept of substance must be entirely rejected, and that of matter be everywhere put in its place.

* * *

The categories were a Procrustean bed for every possible thing, but the three kinds of syllogism are such only for the three so-called Ideas. The Idea of the soul had been forced to find its origin in the categorical form of the syllogism. It is now the turn of the dogmatic representations concerning the universe, in so far as this is thought of as an object-in-itself between two limits, that of the smallest (atom) and that of the largest (limits of the universe in time and space). These must now proceed from the form of the hypothetical syllogism. For this in itself no particular violence is necessary. For the hypothetical judgement has its form from the principle of sufficient reason; and from the senseless and unqualified application of this principle, and from then arbitrarily laying it aside, we do in fact get all those so-called Ideas, and not the cosmological alone. Thus, according to the principle of sufficient reason, only the dependence of one object on another is always sought, until finally the exhaustion of the imagination puts an end to the journey. Here the fact is lost sight of that every object, indeed the whole series of objects and the principle of sufficient reason itself, are in a much closer and greater dependence, that is, in dependence on the knowing subject, for whose objects, i.e., representations, that principle alone is valid, since their mere position in space and time is determined by it. Therefore, as the form of knowledge from which only the cosmological Ideas are here derived, namely the principle of sufficient reason, is the origin of all hair-splitting hypostases, there is in this case no need of any sophisms; but the need thereof is all the greater in order to classify those Ideas according to the four titles of the categories.

(1) The cosmological Ideas with regard to time and space, and thus of the limits of the world in both, are boldly regarded as determined through the category of *quantity,* with which they obviously have nothing in common except the accidental indication in logic of the extent of the subject-concept in the judgement by the word *quantity,* a figurative expression, instead of which another might just as well have been chosen. However, this is enough for Kant's love of symmetry, in order to make use of the fortunate accident of this nomenclature, and to tie up with it the transcendent dogmas of the world's extension.

(2) Even more boldly does Kant tie up the transcendent Ideas about matter with *quality,* in other words, the affirmation or negation in a judgement. For this there is no foundation even in an accidental similarity of words; for it is precisely to the quantity and not to the *quality* of matter that its mechanical (not chemical) divisibility is related. But, what is more, this whole Idea of divisi-

bility by no means belongs to the inferences according to the principle of sufficient reason, from which, however, as from the content of the hypothetical form, all the cosmological Ideas should flow. For the assertion on which Kant here relies, namely that the relation of the parts to the whole is that of condition to conditioned, and thus a relation according to the principle of sufficient reason, is certainly a subtle yet groundless sophism. On the contrary, that relation is based on the principle of contradiction; for the whole is not through the parts, nor are the parts through the whole, but the two are necessarily together because they are one, and their separation is only an arbitrary act. It rests on this, according to the principle of contradiction, that if the parts are thought away, the whole is thought away, and conversely. But it does not by any means rest on the fact that the parts as *ground* condition the whole as *consequent,* and that therefore, according to the principle of sufficient reason, we should necessarily be urged to look for the ultimate parts, in order to understand the whole from them as its ground. Such great difficulties are overcome here by the love of symmetry.

(3) Now the Idea of the first cause of the world would quite properly come under the title of *relation.* Kant, however, must keep this for the fourth title, that of *modality,* otherwise there would be nothing left for that title. He then forces that Idea under it by saying that the contingent or accidental (in other words, every consequent from its ground, according to his explanation which is diametrically opposed to the truth) becomes the necessary through the first cause. Therefore, for the sake of symmetry, the concept of *freedom* here appears as a third Idea. With this concept, however, as is distinctly stated in the note to the thesis of the third antinomy, only the Idea of the world-cause, which alone is suitable here, is really meant. The third and fourth antinomies are therefore at bottom tautological.

About all this, however, I find and maintain that the whole antinomy is a mere sham fight. Only the assertions of the *antitheses* actually rest on the forms of our faculty of knowledge, in other words, if we express it objectively, on the necessary, *a priori* certain, most universal laws of nature. Their proofs alone are therefore furnished from objective grounds. On the other hand, the assertions and proofs of the *theses* have no ground other than a subjective one, and rely simply and solely on the weakness of the subtly reasoning individual. His imagination grows weary with an endless regression, and he therefore puts an end to this by arbitrary assumptions which he tries to gloss over as best he can; moreover in this case his power of judgement is paralysed by early and deeply imprinted prejudices. Therefore the proof of the thesis in all four antinomies is everywhere

only a sophism, whereas that of the antithesis is an inevitable inference of our faculty of reason from the laws of the world as representation, known to us *a priori*. Moreover, only with great pains
and skill has Kant been able to sustain the thesis, and to enable it
to make apparent attacks on the opponent, which is endowed with
original force and strength. Now his first and usual artifice here is
that he does not stress and bring out the *nervus argumentationis*,[33]
as anyone does when he is conscious of the truth of his proposition,
and thus present it in as isolated, bare, and distinct a form as possible. On the contrary he introduces the same argument on both sides,
concealed under, and mixed up with, a whole host of superfluous
and prolix sentences.

Now the theses and antitheses, which here appear in conflict, remind one of the δίκαιος and ἄδικος λόγος[34] which Socrates, in Aristophanes' *Clouds,* represents as contending. But this resemblance
extends only to the form, and not to the content, as those would
gladly assert who ascribe to these most speculative of all questions
of theoretical philosophy an influence on morality, and therefore
seriously regard the thesis as the δίκαιος (just), and the antithesis
as the ἄδικος (unjust) λόγος. However, I shall not accommodate
myself and pay heed to such small, narrow, and perverse minds;
and paying honour not to them but to truth, I shall expose as
sophisms the proofs furnished by Kant for the individual theses,
whereas I shall show that the proofs of the antitheses are quite fair,
correct, and drawn from objective grounds. I assume that, in this
investigation, the reader always has before him the Kantian antinomy itself.

If the proof of the thesis in the first antinomy is to be admitted,
it proves too much, since it would be just as applicable to time itself
as to change in time, and would therefore prove that time itself must
have had a beginning, which is absurd. Besides, the sophism consists
in this, that, instead of the beginninglessness of the series of conditions or states, which was primarily the question, the endlessness
(infinity) of the series is suddenly substituted. It is now proved,
what no one doubts, that completeness logically contradicts this endlessness, and yet every present is the end of a past. But the end of
a beginningless series can always be *thought* without detracting from
its beginninglessness, just as conversely the beginning of an endless
series can also be *thought*. But against the really correct argument
of the antithesis, namely that the changes of the world absolutely

---

[33] "The salient point of the argument." [Tr.]
[34] "The just and the unjust cause." [Aristophanes, *Clouds,* 889, 1104. Tr.]

and necessarily presuppose an infinite series of changes *retrogressively,* nothing at all is advanced. We can imagine the possibility of the causal series one day ending in an absolute standstill, but we cannot by any means imagine the possibility of an absolute beginning.[35]

With regard to the spatial limits of the world, it is proved that, if it is to be called a *given whole,* it must necessarily have limits. The logical conclusion is correct, only it was just its first link which was to be proved, and this is left unproved. Totality presupposes limits, and limits presuppose totality; but here the two together are arbitrarily presupposed. For this second point, however, the antithesis affords no such satisfactory proof as for the first, because the law of causality provides us with necessary determinations merely in regard to time, not to space, and affords us *a priori* the certainty that no occupied time could ever be bounded by a previous empty time, and that no change could ever be the first, but not that an occupied space can have no empty space beside it. To this extent, no decision *a priori* on the latter point would be possible; yet the difficulty of imagining the world as limited in space is to be found in the fact that space itself is necessarily infinite, and that therefore a limited, finite world in space, however large it may be, becomes an infinitely small magnitude. In this incongruity the imagination finds an insuperable obstacle, since accordingly there is left to it only the choice of thinking the world as either infinitely large or infinitely small. The ancient philosophers already saw this: Μητρόδωρος, ὁ καθηγητὴς Ἐπικούρου, φησὶν ἄτοπον εἶναι ἐν μεγάλῳ

---

[35] That the assumption of a limit to the world in time is by no means a necessary idea of our faculty of reason can be demonstrated even historically, since the Hindus do not teach any such thing even in the religion of the people, not to mention in the *Vedas.* On the contrary, they try to express mythologically through a monstrous chronology the infinity of this world of appearance, of this unstable and unsubstantial web of Maya, since at the same time they bring out very ingeniously the relative nature of all periods of time in the following myth (Polier, *Mythologie des Indous,* Vol. II, p. 585). The four ages, in the last of which we live, together embrace 4,320,000 years. Each day of the creator Brahma has a thousand such periods of four ages, and his night again has a thousand such periods. His year has 365 days and as many nights. He lives a hundred of his years, always creating; and when he dies, a new Brahma is at once born, and so on from eternity to eternity. The same relativity of time is also expressed by the special myth that is quoted from the *Puranas* in Polier's work, Vol. II, p. 594. In it a Raja, after a visit of a few moments to Vishnu in his heaven, finds on his return to earth that several million years have elapsed, and that a new age has appeared, since every day of Vishnu is equal to a hundred recurrences of the four ages.

πεδίῳ ἕνα στάχυν γεννηθῆναι, καὶ ἕνα κόσμον ἐν τῷ ἀπείρῳ (*Metrodorus, caput scholae Epicuri, absurdum ait, in magno campo spicam unam produci, et unum in infinito mundum*). Stobaeus, *Ecl.,* I, c. 23.[36] Therefore many of them taught (as immediately follows), ἀπείρους κόσμους ἐν τῷ ἀπείρῳ (*infinitos mundos in infinito*).[37] This is also the sense of the Kantian argument for the antithesis, though he has disfigured it by a scholastic and stilted mode of expression. The same argument could also be used against setting limits to the world in time, if we did not already have a much better one under the guidance of causality. Further, with the assumption of a world limited in space, there arises the unanswerable question what advantage the filled part of space would have over the infinite space that remained empty. In the fifth dialogue of his book *Del Infinito, Universo e Mondi,* Giordano Bruno gives a detailed and very readable account of the arguments for and against the finiteness of the world. For the rest, Kant himself seriously, and on objective grounds, asserts the infinity of the world in space in his *Natural History and Theory of the Heavens,* Part II, chap. 7. Aristotle also acknowledges the same thing in *Physics,* iii, chap. 4. This chapter, together with those that follow, is well worth reading with regard to this antinomy.

In the second antinomy, the thesis at once commits a *petitio principii*[38] that is not in the least subtle, since it begins: *"Every compound* substance consists of simple parts." From the compoundness, here arbitrarily assumed, it of course very easily demonstrates afterwards the simple parts. But the proposition, "All matter is compound," which is just the point, remains unproved, because it is just a groundless assumption. Thus the opposite of the simple is not the compound, but the extended, that which has parts, the divisible. But here it is really tacitly assumed that the parts existed before the whole, and were gathered together, and that in this way the whole came into existence; for this is what the word "compound" means. Yet this can be asserted just as little as the opposite. Divisibility implies merely the possibility of splitting the whole into parts; it by no means implies that the whole was compounded out of parts, and thus came into existence. Divisibility merely asserts the parts *a parte post;* compoundness asserts them *a parte ante.* For there is essentially no time-relation between the parts and the whole; rather do they condition each other reciprocally, and to this extent

---

[36] "Metrodorus, the head of the Epicurean school, says it is absurd for there to spring into existence only one ear of corn in a large field, and only one world in infinite space." [Tr.]

[37] "That there exists in infinite space an infinite number of worlds." [Tr.]

[38] "Begging of the question." [Tr.]

they are always simultaneous; for only in so far as both exist does the spatially extended exist. Therefore what Kant says in the note to the thesis: "Space should really not be called a *compositum,* but a *totum,*" and so on, holds good entirely of matter as well, since matter is simply space that has become perceptible. On the other hand, the infinite divisibility of matter, asserted by the antithesis, follows *a priori* and incontestably from that of space which it fills. This proposition has nothing at all against it; therefore Kant also, p. 513 (V, 541), presents it as objective truth, when he is speaking seriously and in his own person, and no longer as the mouthpiece of the ἄδικος λόγος. Likewise in the *Metaphysical Rudiments of Natural Science* (page 108, first edition), the proposition: "Matter is divisible to infinity" stands as an established and certain truth at the head of the proof of the first proposition in mechanics, after it had appeared and been demonstrated in dynamics as the fourth proposition. Here, however, Kant spoils the proof of the antithesis by the greatest confusion of style and a useless torrent of words, with the cunning intention that the evidence of the antithesis shall not put the sophisms of the thesis too much in the shade. Atoms are not a necessary idea of our faculty of reason, but merely a hypothesis for explaining the differences in the specific gravity of bodies. But Kant himself has shown in the Dynamics of his *Metaphysical Rudiments of Natural Science* that we can also explain this otherwise, and even better and more simply, than by atomism; before him, however, was Priestley, *On Matter and Spirit,* Sect. I. In fact, even in Aristotle, *Physics,* iv, 9, the fundamental idea of this is to be found.

The argument for the third thesis is a very subtle sophism, and is really Kant's pretended principle of pure reason (*Vernunft*) itself entirely unadulterated and unchanged. It attempts to prove the finiteness of the series of causes by saying that, to be *sufficient,* a cause must contain the complete sum of the conditions from which the following state, the effect, results. For this completeness of the determinations *simultaneously* in the state or condition that is the cause, the argument now substitutes the completeness of the *series* of causes by which that state itself first arrived at actuality; and because completeness presupposes a state of being closed in, and this again presupposes finiteness, the argument infers from this a first cause closing the series and therefore unconditioned. But the juggling is obvious. In order to conceive state A as a sufficient cause of state B, I assume that it contains the completeness of the determinations necessary for this, from whose coexistence state B inevitably ensues. In this way my demand on it as a *sufficient* cause is entirely satisfied, and that demand has no direct connexion with the question how state A itself arrived at actuality. On the contrary, this belongs to an entirely different consideration in which I regard the self-same state A no longer as cause, but as itself effect, in which case another state must be related to it, just as it itself is related to B. The presupposition of the finiteness of the series of causes and effects, and accordingly of a first beginning, nowhere appears as necessary in this, any more than the presence of the present moment has as assumption a beginning of time itself; such assumption is added only by the indolence of the speculating individual. That this presupposition lies in the acceptance of a cause as *sufficient reason or ground,* is therefore surreptitiously obtained, and is false, as I have already shown in detail when considering the Kantian principle of reason (*Vernunft*) which coincides with this thesis. To illustrate the assertion of this false thesis, Kant has the effrontery, in his note thereon, to give as an example of an unconditioned beginning his rising from his chair, as though it were not just as impossible for him to rise without motive as for the ball to roll without cause. I certainly do not need to prove the groundlessness of his appeal to the philosophers of antiquity, which he makes from a feeling of weakness, from Ocellus Lucanus, the Eleatics, etc., not to speak of the Hindus. As in the case of the previous ones, nothing can be said against the argument of this antithesis.

The fourth antinomy is, as I have already remarked, really tautological with the third. The proof of the thesis is also essentially the same as that of the preceding. His assertion that every conditioned presupposes a complete *series* of conditions, and thus a series ending with the unconditioned, is a *petitio principii*[39] that must be absolutely denied. Every conditioned presupposes nothing but its condition; the fact that this is again conditioned raises a new consideration not directly contained in the first.

A certain plausibility is not to be denied to the antinomy; yet it is remarkable that no part of the Kantian philosophy has met with so little contradiction, indeed, has found so much acknowledgement and approbation, as this exceedingly paradoxical doctrine. Almost all philosophical groups and text-books have admitted and repeated it, and even elaborated it, whereas almost all the other doctrines of Kant have been disputed. In fact there has never been a lack of warped minds which rejected even the Transcendental Aesthetic. The unanimous assent which the antinomy, on the other hand, has met with, may in the end spring from the fact that some people re-

---

[39] "Begging of the question." [Tr.]

gard with inward gratification the point where the understanding is really supposed to be brought to a standstill, since it has hit upon something that at the same time is and is not, and accordingly they actually have here before them the sixth trick of Philadelphia in Lichtenberg's broadsheet.[39A]

Now if we examine the real meaning of Kant's *critical resolution* of the cosmological argument which follows, it is not what he gives it out to be, namely the solution of the dispute by disclosing that both sides, starting from false assumptions, are wrong in the first and second antinomies, but right in the third and fourth. On the contrary, it is in fact the confirmation of the antitheses by the explanation of their assertion.

Kant first of all asserts in this solution, obviously wrongly, that both sides started from the assumption, as the first principle, that with the conditioned, the completed (hence closed) *series* of its conditions is given. Merely the *thesis* laid down this proposition, namely Kant's principle of pure reason (*Vernunft*), as the foundation of its assertions; the antithesis, on the other hand, everywhere expressly denied it, and maintained the contrary. Kant further charges both sides with this assumption that the world exists in itself, in other words, independently of its being known and of the forms of that knowledge. But once more this assumption is made only by the thesis; it is so far from forming the basis of the assertions of the antithesis as to be even quite inconsistent with them. For that it is entirely given is absolutely contradictory to the concept of an infinite series. It is therefore essential to it that it exists always only with reference to the process of going through it, but not independently thereof. On the other hand, in the assumption of definite limits lies also the assumption of a whole that exists absolutely and independently of the process of measuring it. Hence only the thesis makes the false assumption of a universe existing in itself, in other words, of a universe given prior to all knowledge, to which knowledge came as a mere addition. The antithesis at the outset is absolutely at variance with this assumption; for the infinity of the series, which it asserts merely on the guidance of the principle of sufficient reason, can exist only in so far as the regressus is carried out, not independently thereof. Just as the object in general presupposes the subject, so does the object, determined as an *endless* chain of conditions, also necessarily presuppose in the subject the kind of knowledge corresponding thereto, namely the *constant pursuit* of the links. This, however, is just what Kant gives as the solu-

---

[39A] See Lichtenberg, *Vermischte Schriften*, vol. iii, p. 187, Göttingen, 1844. [Tr.]

tion of the dispute, and so often repeats: "The infinite magnitude of the world is only *through* the regressus, not *before* it." This solution that he gives to the antinomy is therefore really only the decision in favour of the antithesis. That truth already lies in the assertion of the antithesis, just as it is entirely inconsistent with the assertions of the thesis. If the antithesis had asserted that the world consisted of infinite series of grounds and consequents, and yet existed independently of the representation and its regressive series, and thus in itself, and therefore constituted a given whole, then it would have contradicted not only the thesis, but itself also. For an infinite can never be *entirely* given, nor can an *endless* series exist, except in so far as it is endlessly run through; nor can a boundless constitute a whole. Therefore that assumption, of which Kant asserted that it had misled both sides, belongs only to the thesis.

It is a doctrine of Aristotle that an infinite can never be *actu,* in other words, actual and given, but merely *potentiâ.* Οὐκ ἔστιν ἐνεργείᾳ εἶναι τὸ ἄπειρον· . . . ἀλλ' ἀδύνατον τὸ ἐντελεχείᾳ ὂν ἄπειρον (*infinitum non potest esse actu: . . . sed impossible, actu esse infinitum*).[40] *Metaphysics,* x.10. Further: κατ' ἐνέργειαν μὲν γὰρ οὐδέν ἐστιν ἄπειρον, δυνάμει δὲ ἐπὶ τὴν διαίρεσιν (*nihil enim actu infinitum est, sed potentia tantum, nempe divisione ipsa*).[41] *De Generatione et Corruptione,* i, 3. He deals with this at great length in the *Physics,* iii, 5 and 6, where to a certain extent he gives the perfectly correct solution of all the antinomic theses and antitheses. In his brief way, he describes the antinomies, and then says: "A mediator (διαιτητής) is required"; according to which he gives the solution that the infinite, both of the world in space and in time and in division, is never *before* the regressus or progressus, but *in* it. This truth, therefore, lies in the correctly apprehended concept of the infinite. We therefore misunderstand ourselves if we imagine we conceive the infinite, be it of whatever kind it may, as something objectively present and finished, and independent of the regressus.

Indeed, if, reversing the procedure, we take as the starting-point that which Kant gives as the solution of the antinomy, the assertion of the antithesis already follows therefrom. Thus, if the world is not an unconditioned whole, and does not exist in itself, but only in the representation; and if its series of grounds and consequents do not exist *before* the regressus of the representations of them, but only *through* this regressus, then the world cannot contain definite and

---

[40] "It is not possible for the infinite to exist in actuality; . . . but infinity existing in actuality is impossible." [Tr.]

[41] "For according to actuality there is no infinity (i.e., no infinitely small), but potentially there is in regard to division." [Tr.]

finite series, since their determination and limitation would necessarily be independent of the representation that then comes only as an addition; on the contrary, all its series must be endless, in other words, incapable of exhaustion by any representation.

On p. 506 (V, 534) Kant tries to prove from the falseness of both sides the transcendental ideality of the phenomenon, and begins: "If the world is a whole existing in itself, it is either finite or infinite." But this is false; a whole existing in itself cannot possibly be infinite. On the contrary, that ideality could be inferred in the following way from the infinity of the series in the world: If the series of grounds and consequents in the world are absolutely without end, then the world cannot be a given whole independent of the representation, for such a thing always presupposes definite limits, just as, on the contrary, infinite series presuppose infinite regressus. Therefore, the presupposed infinity of the series must be determined through the form of ground and consequent, and this in turn through the form of knowledge of the subject. Hence the world, as it is known, must exist only in the mental picture or representation of the subject.

I am unable to decide whether Kant himself was or was not aware that his critical decision of the argument was really a statement in favour of the antithesis. For it depends on whether what Schelling has somewhere very appropriately called Kant's system of accommodation extended so far, or whether Kant's mind was here involved in an unconscious accommodation to the influence of his time and environment.

* * *

The solution of the third antinomy, whose subject was the Idea of freedom, merits special consideration, in so far as for us it is very remarkable that Kant is obliged precisely here, in connexion with the *Idea of freedom,* to speak in greater detail about the *thing-in-itself,* hitherto seen only in the background. This is very easy for us to understand after we have recognized the thing-in-itself as the *will.* In general, this is the point where Kant's philosophy leads to mine, or mine springs from his as its parent stem. We shall be convinced of this if we read with attention pp. 536 and 537 (V, 564 and 565) of the *Critique of Pure Reason,* and further compare with this passage the introduction to the *Critique of Judgement,* pp. xviii and xix of the third edition, or p. 13 of the Rosenkranz edition, where it is even said: "The concept of freedom can in its object (for this indeed is the will) present a thing-in-itself to our minds.

but not in perception; the concept of nature, on the other hand, can present its object to our minds in perception, but not as thing-in-itself." But in particular, let us read § 53 of the *Prolegomena* concerning the solution of the antinomies, and then honestly answer the question whether all that is said does not sound like a riddle to which my teaching is the solution. Kant did not arrive at a conclusion to his thinking; I have merely carried his work into effect. Accordingly, what Kant says merely of the human phenomenon, I have extended to every phenomenon in general which differs from the human only in degree, namely that their essence-in-itself is something absolutely free, in other words, a will. How fruitful this insight is in connexion with Kant's doctrine of the ideality of space, time, and causality, follows from my work.

Kant has nowhere made the thing-in-itself the subject of a special discussion or clear deduction, but whenever he makes use of it, he at once brings it in through the conclusion that the phenomenon, and hence the visible world, must have a ground or reason, an intelligible cause, which is not phenomenon, and which therefore does not belong to any possible experience. This he does after having incessantly urged that the categories, and thus also the category of causality, had a use in every way restricted only to possible experience; that they were mere forms of the understanding serving to spell out the phenomena of the world of sense, beyond which, on the other hand, they had no significance at all, and so on. He therefore most strictly forbids their application to things beyond experience, and rightly explains, and at the same time overthrows, all previous dogmatism as resulting from a violation of this law. The incredible inconsistency Kant here committed was soon noticed, and used by his first opponents for attacks to which his philosophy could not offer any resistance. For we certainly apply the law of causality, wholly *a priori* and prior to all experience, to the changes felt in our organs of sense. But on this very account this law is just as much of subjective origin as these sensations themselves are; and therefore it does not lead to the thing-in-itself. The truth is that on the path of the representation we can never get beyond the representation; it is a closed whole, and has in its own resources no thread leading to the essence of the thing-in-itself, which is *toto genere* different from it. If we were merely representing beings, the way to the thing-in-itself would be entirely cut off from us. Only the other side of our own inner nature can vouchsafe us information regarding the other side of the being-in-itself of things. I have pursued this path. However, Kant's inference of the thing-in-itself, forbidden by himself, obtains some extenuation from the following. He does not, as truth demanded, lay down the object simply and positively as conditioned by the subject, and *vice versa,* but only the manner of the object's appearance as conditioned by the subject's forms of knowledge, which therefore also come *a priori* to consciousness. Now what, in contrast to this, is known merely *a posteriori,* is for him already immediate effect of the thing-in-itself, which becomes phenomenon only in its passage through those forms that are given *a priori.* From this point of view, it is to some extent clear how he could fail to notice that being-object in general belongs to the form of the phenomenon, and is just as much conditioned by being-subject in general as the object's mode of appearing is conditioned by the subject's forms of knowledge; hence that, if a thing-in-itself is to be assumed, it cannot be an object at all, which, however, he always assumes it to be; but such a thing-in-itself would have to lie in a sphere *toto genere* different from the representation (from knowing and being known), and therefore could least of all be inferred according to the laws of the connexion of objects among themselves.

Precisely the same thing happened to Kant with the demonstration of the thing-in-itself as with the demonstration of the *a priori* nature of the law of causality; both doctrines are correct, but their proof is false. They belong therefore to correct conclusions from false premisses. I have retained both, yet I have established them in an entirely different way and with certainty.

I have not introduced the thing-in-itself surreptitiously or inferred it according to laws that exclude it, since they already belong to its phenomenon; moreover, in general I have not arrived at it by roundabout ways. On the contrary, I have demonstrated it directly, where it immediately lies, namely in the will that reveals itself to everyone immediately as the in-itself of his own phenomenon.

It is also from this immediate knowledge of one's own will that in human consciousness the concept of *freedom* arises; for certainly the will as world-creating, as thing-in-itself, is free from the principle of sufficient reason, and thus from all necessity, and hence is completely independent, free, and indeed almighty. Yet actually this holds good only of the will in itself, not of its phenomena, not of the individuals, who, just through the will itself, are unalterably determined as its phenomena in time. But in the ordinary consciousness not clarified by philosophy, the will is at once confused with its phenomenon, and what belongs only to the will is attributed to the phenomenon. In this way arises the delusion of the individual's unconditioned freedom. Precisely on this account, Spinoza rightly says that even the projected stone would believe, if it had consciousness, that it was flying of its own free will. For the in-itself even of the stone is certainly the one and only free will; but, as in all its phenomena, so here also where it appears as stone, it is already fully determined. Enough has already been said about all this, however, in the main part of this work.

By failing to recognize and overlooking this immediate origin of the concept of freedom in every human consciousness, Kant now (p. 533; V, 561) places the origin of that concept in a very subtle speculation. Thus through this speculation, the unconditioned, to which our reason (*Vernunft*) must always tend, leads to the hypostasizing of the concept of freedom, and the practical concept of freedom is supposed to be based first of all on this transcendent Idea of freedom. In the *Critique of Practical Reason*, § 6, and p. 185 of the fourth (p. 235 of the Rosenkranz) edition, he again derives this last concept differently, namely from the fact that the categorical imperative presupposes it. Accordingly, he says that the speculative Idea is only the primary source of the concept of freedom for the sake of this presupposition, but that here it really obtains significance and application. Neither, however, is the case; for the delusion of a perfect freedom of the individual in his particular actions is most vivid in the conviction of the least cultured person who has never reflected. It is therefore not founded on any speculation, though it is often assumed by speculation from without. On the other hand, only philosophers, and indeed the profoundest of them, and also the most thoughtful and enlightened authors of the Church, are free from the delusion.

Therefore it follows from all that has been said that the real origin of the concept of freedom is in no way essentially an inference either from the speculative Idea of an unconditioned cause, or from the fact that the categorical imperative presupposes it, but springs directly from consciousness. In consciousness everyone recognizes himself at once as the *will*, in other words, as that which, as thing-in-itself, has not the principle of sufficient reason for its form, and itself depends on nothing, but rather everything else depends on it. Not everyone, however, recognizes himself at once with the critical and reflective insight of philosophy as a definite phenomenon of this will which has already entered time, one might say as an act of will distinguished from that will-to-live itself. Therefore, instead of recognizing his whole existence as an act of his freedom, he looks for freedom rather in his individual actions. On this point I refer to my essay *On the Freedom of the Will.*

Now if Kant, as he here pretends, and also apparently did on previous occasions, had merely inferred the thing-in-itself, and that moreover with the great inconsistency of an inference absolutely forbidden by himself, what a strange accident it would then be that here, where for the first time he comes nearer to the thing-in-itself and elucidates it, he should at once recognize in it the *will*, the free will proclaiming itself in the world only through temporal phenomena! Therefore I actually assume, though it cannot be proved, that whenever Kant spoke of the thing-in-itself, he always thought indistinctly of the will in the obscure depths of his mind. Evidence of this is given in the preface to the second edition of the *Critique of Pure Reason,* pp. xxvii and xxviii in the Rosenkranz edition, p. 677 of the supplements.[42]

For the rest, it is just this intended solution of the sham third antinomy that gives Kant the opportunity to express very beautifully the profoundest ideas of his whole philosophy; thus in the whole of the "Sixth Section of the Antinomy of Pure Reason"; but above all, the discussion of the contrast between the empirical and intelligible characters, pp. 534-550 (V, 562-578), which I number among the most admirable things ever said by man. (We can regard as a supplementary explanation of this passage a parallel passage in the *Critique of Practical Reason,* pp. 169-179 of the fourth, or pp. 224-231 of the Rosenkranz edition). But it is all the more regrettable that this is not in its right place here, in so far as, on the one hand, it is not found in the way stated by the exposition, and could thus be deduced otherwise than it is, and, on the other, in so far as it does not fulfil the purpose for which it is there, namely the solution of the pretended antinomy. From the phenomenon is inferred its intelligible ground or reason, the thing-in-itself, by the inconsistent use, already sufficiently condemned, of the category of causality beyond all experience. For this case the will of man (to which Kant gives the title of reason or *Vernunft* quite inadmissibly and by an unpardonable breach of all linguistic usage) is set up as this thing-in-itself with an appeal to an unconditioned ought, to the categorical imperative that is postulated without more ado.

Now instead of all this, the plain, open procedure would have been to start directly from the will, to demonstrate this as the in-itself of our own phenomenon, recognized without any mediation, and then to give that description of the empirical and intelligible characters, to explain how all actions, though necessitated by motives, are nevertheless ascribed both by their author and by the independent judge necessarily and positively to the former himself and alone, as depending solely on him, to whom guilt and merit are therefore attributed in respect of them. This alone was the straight path to the

---

[42] P. 688 *seq.* of Prof. Max Müller's English translation. [Tr.]

knowledge of that which is not phenomenon, of that which in consequence is not found in accordance with the laws of the phenomenon, but which reveals itself through the phenomenon, becomes knowable, objectifies itself, namely the will-to-live. Then this would have had to be described, merely by analogy, as the in-itself of every phenomenon. But then, of course, it could not have been said (p. 546; V, 574) that in the case of inanimate, and indeed animal, nature no faculty can be thought except as sensuously conditioned. In Kant's language, this is really to say that the explanation according to the law of causality also exhausts the innermost essence of those phenomena, whereby in their case the thing-in-itself, very inconsistently, is abolished. Through the wrong position and the roundabout deduction conforming with it which the thing-in-itself has received in Kant's work, the whole conception of it has been falsified. For the will or thing-in-itself, found by investigating an unconditioned cause, here appears related to the phenomenon as the cause to the effect. This relation, however, occurs only within the phenomenon, and therefore presupposes it. It cannot connect the phenomenon itself with that which lies outside the phenomenon, and is *toto genere* different from it.

Further, the purpose intended, namely the solution of the third antinomy by the decision that both sides, each in a different sense, are right, is not achieved at all. For neither the thesis nor the antithesis speaks in any way of the thing-in-itself, but entirely of the phenomenon, of the objective world, of the world as representation. It is this, and absolutely nothing else, of which the thesis tries to show, by means of the sophism we have exposed, that it contains unconditioned causes; and it is also this of which the antithesis rightly denies that it contains such causes. Therefore the whole exposition of the transcendental freedom of the will, here given in justification of the thesis, namely in so far as the will is thing-in-itself, is nevertheless really and truly a μετάβασις εἰς ἄλλο γένος,[43] excellent as it is in itself. For the transcendental freedom of the will which is expounded is by no means the unconditioned causality of a cause, which the thesis asserts, because a cause must be essentially phenomenon, not something *toto genere* different lying beyond every phenomenon.

If it is a question of cause and effect, then the relation of the will to its phenomenon (or of the intelligible character to the empirical) must never be drawn in, as is done here, for it is entirely differ-

---

[43] "A transition to another genus"; in other words, the logical mistake of jumping into another dimension, e.g., from the line to the surface, from the surface to the solid. [Tr.]

ent from the causal relation. However, here also, in this solution of the antinomy, it is said with truth that man's empirical character, like that of every other cause in nature, is unalterably determined, and hence that actions necessarily result from it in accordance with external influences. Therefore in spite of all transcendental freedom (i.e. independence of the will-in-itself of the laws of the connexion of its phenomenon), no person has the capacity of himself to begin a series of actions, a thing which, on the contrary, was asserted by the thesis. Therefore freedom also has no causality, for only the will is free, and it lies outside nature or the phenomenon. The phenomenon is only the objectification of the will, and does not stand to it in a relation of causality. Such a relation is met with only within the phenomenon, and thus presupposes this; it cannot include the phenomenon itself, and connect it with what is expressly not phenomenon. The world itself is to be explained only from the will (for it is the will itself in so far as this will appears), and not through causality. But *in the world,* causality is the sole principle of explanation, and everything happens solely in accordance with laws of nature. Therefore right is entirely on the side of the antithesis; for this sticks to the point in question, and uses the principle of explanation which is valid with regard thereto; hence it needs no apology. The thesis, on the other hand, is supposed to be drawn by an apology from the matter, that first passes over to something quite different from the point in question, and then takes over a principle of explanation which cannot be applied there.

The fourth antinomy, as I have said already, is according to its innermost meaning tautological with the third. In the solution to it, Kant develops still more the untenability of the thesis. On the other hand, he advances no grounds for its truth and its pretended compatibility with the antithesis, just as, conversely, he is unable to bring any against the antithesis. He introduces the assumption of the thesis only in the form of a request, and yet he himself calls it (p. 562; V, 590) an arbitrary presupposition, whose object in itself might well be impossible, and shows merely an utterly impotent attempt to provide for it somewhere a snug little place, secure from the prevailing might of the antithesis, simply in order not to disclose the emptiness of the whole of his favourite pretence of the necessary antinomy in man's faculty of reason.

* * *

There now follows the chapter on the Transcendental Ideal, which at once takes us back to the rigid scholasticism of the Middle Ages.

We think we are listening to Anselm himself. The *ens realissimum,* the comprehensive totality of all realities, the content of all affirmative propositions, appears, and in fact claims to be a necessary idea of our faculty of reason! I for my part must confess that to my faculty of reason such an idea is impossible, and that from the words which express it I am unable to think of anything definite.

Moreover, I do not doubt that Kant was compelled to write this strange chapter, so unworthy of him, merely by his fondness for architectonic symmetry. The three principal objects of scholastic philosophy (which if understood in the wider sense, as we have said, can be regarded as continuing down to Kant), namely the soul, the world, and God, were supposed to be derived from the three possible major premisses of syllogisms, although it is obvious that they have arisen and can arise simply and solely through the unconditioned application of the principle of sufficient reason. After the soul had been forced into the categorical judgement, and the hypothetical was used for the world, there was nothing left for the third Idea but the disjunctive major premiss. Fortunately, there was to be found in this sense a preparatory work, namely the *ens realissimum* of the scholastics, together with the ontological proof of the existence of God, put forward in a rudimentary fashion by Anselm, and then perfected by Descartes. This was gladly made use of by Kant, for he was also reminded somewhat of an earlier Latin work of his youth. However, the sacrifice Kant made in this chapter to his love for architectonic symmetry is exceedingly great. In defiance of all truth, what must be regarded as the grotesque notion of a comprehensive totality of all possible realities is made into an idea that is necessary and essential to reason (*Vernunft*). For deriving this, Kant resorts to the false allegation that our knowledge of individual things arises from a progressive limitation of universal concepts, and consequently even of a most universal concept of all, which would contain all reality *in itself.* Here he is just as much in contradiction with his own teaching as he is with the truth; for the very reverse is the case. Our knowledge, starting from the particular, is extended to the general, and all general concepts result through abstraction from real, individual things known through perception, and this can be continued right up to the most universal of all concepts, which then includes everything under it, but almost nothing *in it.* Thus Kant has here turned the procedure of our faculty of knowledge completely upside down. Therefore he might well be accused of having given rise to a philosophical charlatanism that has become famous in our day. Instead of recognizing concepts as ideas abstracted from things, this charlatanism, on the contrary, makes the concepts the first thing, and sees in things only concrete concepts, thus coming forward with a world turned upside down as a philosophical buffoonery naturally bound to meet with great acceptance.

Even if we assume that everyone's faculty of reason must, or at any rate can, attain to the concept of God, even without revelation, this obviously happens only under the guidance of causality; this is so evident that it requires no proof. Therefore, Chr. Wolff also says (*Cosmologia Generalis,* praef., p. 1): *Sane in theologia naturali existentiam Numinis e principiis cosmologicis demonstramus. Contingentia universi et ordinis naturae, una cum impossibilitate casus, sunt scala, per quam a mundo hoc adspectabili ad Deum ascenditur.*[44] And before him Leibniz had said with reference to the law of causality: *Sans ce grand principe nous ne pourrions jamais prouver l'existence de Dieu*[45] (*Théodicée,* § 44). Likewise in his controversy with Clarke, § 126: *J'ose dire que sans ce grand principe on ne saurait venir à la preuve de l'existence de Dieu.*[46] On the other hand, the idea worked out in this chapter is so far from being one necessary and essential to the faculty of reason, that it is rather to be regarded as a real specimen of the monstrous creations of an age that through strange circumstances fell into the most singular aberrations and absurdities. Such was the age of scholasticism, one which is without parallel in the history of the world, and can never recur. When this scholasticism had reached a state of perfection it certainly furnished the principal proof of the existence of God from the concept of the *ens realissimum,* and only in addition to this, as accessory, did it use the other proofs. This, however, is a mere method of instruction, and proves nothing about the origin of theology in the human mind. Here Kant has taken the procedure of scholasticism for that of our faculty of reason, and he has done this frequently. If it were true that, according to the essential laws of our faculty of reason, the Idea of God arose from the disjunctive syllogism under the form of an Idea of the most real of all beings, then this Idea would also have appeared in the philosophers of antiquity. But of the *ens realissimum* there is nowhere a trace in any of the ancient philosophers, although some of them certainly speak of a world-creator, yet only as the giver of form to matter that exists without him, a

---

[44] "We prove conclusively in natural theology the existence of the Supreme Being from cosmological principles. The contingent aspect of the universe and of the order of nature, simultaneously with the impossibility of a (pure) accident, are the steps on which we ascend from this visible world to God." [Tr.]

[45] "Without this great principle we should never be able to prove the existence of God." [Tr.]

[46] "I venture to say that, without this great principle, we could never obtain proof of the existence of God." [Tr.]

δημιουργός, whom, however, they infer, simply and solely in accordance with the law of causality. It is true that Sextus Empiricus (*Adversus Mathematicos,* ix, 88) quotes an argument of Cleanthes which some regard as the ontological proof. However, it is not that, but a mere inference from analogy, because experience teaches that on earth one being is always superior to another, and that man indeed, as the most preeminent, closes the series, but still has many faults; then there must be still more excellent beings, and finally the most excellent of all (κράτιστον, ἄριστον), and this would be God.

* * *

On the detailed refutation of speculative theology which now follows, I have only briefly to remark that it, as well as the whole criticism of the three so-called Ideas of reason (*Vernunft*) in general, and hence the whole Dialectic of pure reason, is to a certain extent the aim and object of the whole work. But this polemical part has not really, like the preceding doctrinal part, i.e., the Aesthetic and Analytic, an entirely universal, permanent, and purely philosophical, but rather a temporal and local interest, since it stands in special reference to the main points of the philosophy that prevailed in Europe up to Kant's time. Yet the complete overthrow of that philosophy through this polemic stands to Kant's immortal merit. He has eliminated theism from philosophy; for in philosophy, as a science and not a doctrine of faith, only that can find a place which either is empirically given or is established through tenable and solid proofs. Naturally, there is here meant only real, seriously understood philosophy, directed to truth and nothing else, and certainly not the facetious philosophy of the universities, in which, now as ever, speculative theology plays the principal part, and where also, now as ever, the soul appears without ceremony as a well-known person. For that is the philosophy endowed with emoluments and fees, and even with titles, honours, and awards. Proudly looking down from its height, it remains for forty years entirely unaware of little men like me; it would be heartily glad to be rid of old Kant and his Critiques, in order deeply and cordially to drink Leibniz's health. Further, it is to be remarked here that, as Kant was admittedly induced to bring forward his teaching of the *a priori* nature of the concept of causality by Hume's scepticism with regard to that concept, perhaps in just the same way Kant's criticism of all speculative theology has its origin in Hume's criticism of all popular theology. Hume had given this in his *Natural History of Religion,* a book very well worth reading, and the *Dialogues on Natural Re-*

ligion. It may be, in fact, that Kant wanted to a certain extent to supplement this. For the first-named work of Hume is really a criticism of popular theology, the pitiable state whereof it attempts to show, while on the other hand it points to rational or speculative theology as genuine and worthy of esteem. But Kant uncovers the groundlessness of the latter; on the other hand, he leaves popular theology untouched, and even sets it up in a more dignified form as a faith founded on moral feeling. This was later distorted by the philosophasters into apprehensions of reason (*Vernunft*), consciousness of God, or intellectual intuitions of the supersensible, the divine, and so on. On the other hand, when Kant demolished old and revered errors, and knew the danger of the business, he had only wanted to substitute here and there through moral theology a few weak props, so that the ruin would not fall on top of him, and he would have time to get away.

Now as regards the performance of the task, no *Critique of Reason* was at all necessary to refute the *ontological* proof of the existence of God, since, even without presupposing the Aesthetic and Analytic, it is very easy to make clear that this ontological proof is nothing but a cunning and subtle game with concepts, without any power of conviction. In Aristotle's *Organon* there is a chapter as completely adequate for refuting the ontotheological proof as if it had been intentionally written for the purpose; the seventh chapter of the second book of the *Posterior Analytics*. Among other things, it expressly says there: τὸ δὲ εἶναι οὐκ οὐσία οὐδενί, in other words, *existentia nunquam ad essentiam rei pertinet.*[47]

The refutation of the *cosmological* proof is an application to a given case of the doctrine of the Critique expounded up to that point, and there is nothing to be said against it. The *physico-theological* proof is a mere amplification of the cosmological, which it presupposes; and it finds its detailed refutation only in the *Critique of Judgement.* In this connexion I refer the reader to the heading "Comparative Anatomy" in my work *On the Will in Nature.*

As I have said, in the criticism of these proofs Kant is concerned only with speculative theology, and restricts himself to the School. On the other hand, if he had had life and popular theology in view, he would still have had to add to the three proofs a fourth, which with the mass of the people is really the effective one, and in Kant's terminology could be most appropriately called the *ceraunological.* This is the proof founded on man's feeling of need, distress, impotence, and dependence in face of natural forces infinitely superior,

---

[47] "Existence in the case of any thing never belongs to its essence." [Tr.]

unfathomable, and for the most part ominous and portentous. To this is added man's natural inclination to personify everything; finally there is the hope of effecting something by entreaty and flattery, and even by gifts. With every human undertaking there is something that is not within our power, and does not come into our calculations; the desire to gain this for ourselves is the origin of the gods. *Primus in orbe Deos fecit timor*[48] is an old and true saying of Petronius. Hume criticizes mainly this proof; in every respect he appears to be Kant's forerunner in the works above-mentioned. Those whom Kant has permanently embarrassed by his criticism of speculative theology are the professors of philosophy. Drawing their salaries from Christian governments, they dare not abandon the chief article of faith.[49] Now how do these gentlemen help themselves? They just assert that the existence of God is a matter of course. Indeed! After the ancient world, at the expense of its conscience, had performed miracles to prove it, and the modern world, at the expense of its understanding, had placed in the field ontological, cosmological, and physico-theological proofs—it is a matter of course with these gentlemen. And from this self-evident God they then explain the world; this is their philosophy.

Until the time of Kant, there was a real and well-established dilemma between materialism and theism, in other words, between the assumption that a blind chance, or an intelligence arranging from without according to purposes and concepts, had brought about the world, *neque dabatur tertium*.[50] Therefore, atheism and materialism were the same thing; hence the doubt whether there could in fact be an atheist, in other words, a person who really could attribute to blind chance an arrangement of nature, especially of organic nature, which is immense, inexhaustible, and appropriate. See, for ex-

---

[48] "Fear was the first origin of the belief in Gods." [Petronius, Fragm. 27 (Tr.)]

[49] Kant said: "It is very absurd to expect enlightenment from reason (*Vernunft*), and yet to prescribe to it beforehand on which side it must necessarily turn out." (*Critique of Pure Reason*, p. 747; V, 775). On the other hand, the following naïvety is the utterance of a professor of philosophy in our own times: "If a philosophy denies the reality of the fundamental ideas of Christianity, it is either false, or, *even if true, it is nevertheless useless* . . ." that is to say, for professors of philosophy. It was the late Professor Bachmann who in the *Jena'sche Litteraturzeitung* of July 1840, No. 126, so indiscreetly blurted out the maxim of all his colleagues. Moreover, it is worth noting as a characteristic of university philosophy how, if truth will not accommodate and adapt herself, she is shown the door without ceremony, with the remark: "Get out! We cannot *use* you. Do we owe you anything? Do you pay us? Then get out!"

[50] "And there was no third possibility." [Tr.]

ample, Bacon's *Essays* (*Sermones fideles*), Essay 16, "On Atheism." In the opinion of the great mass of people and of Englishmen, who in such things belong entirely to the great mass (the mob), this is still the case, even with their most famous men of learning. One has only to look at R. Owen's *Ostéologie comparée* of 1855, preface, pp. 11, 12, where he always stands before the old dilemma between Democritus and Epicurus on the one hand, and an intelligence on the other, in which *la connaissance d'un être tel que l'homme a existé avant que l'homme fit son apparition.*[51] All suitability and appropriateness must have started from an *intelligence;* he does not even dream of doubting this. Yet in the reading of this now somewhat modified preface given on 5 September 1853, in the *Académie des Sciences,* he said with childish naivety: *La téléologie, ou la théologie scientifique* (*Comptes rendus,* Sept. 1853),[52] these are for him directly one and the same thing! If something in nature is suitable and appropriate, it is a work of intention, of deliberation, of intelligence. Now, I ask, what is the *Critique of Judgement,* or even my book *On the Will in Nature,* to such an Englishman and to the *Académie des Sciences?* These gentlemen do not see so far beneath them. These *illustres confrères*[53] indeed look down on metaphysics and the *philosophie allemande;*[54] they stick to frock-philosophy. But the validity of that disjunctive major premiss, of that dilemma between materialism and theism, rests on the assumption that the world that lies before us is the world of things-in-themselves, and that, in consequence, there is no other order of things than the empirical. But after the world and its order had become through Kant the mere phenomenon, whose laws rest mainly on the forms of our intellect, the existence and inner nature of things and of the world no longer needed to be explained on the analogy of changes perceived or effected by us *in* the world; nor can that which we comprehend as means and end have arisen in consequence of such knowledge. Therefore, by depriving theism of its foundation through his important distinction between phenomenon and thing-in-itself, Kant, on the other hand, opened the way to entirely different and deeper explanations of existence.

In the chapter on the ultimate aims of the natural dialectic of reason (*Vernunft*), it is alleged that the three transcendent Ideas are of value as regulative principles for the advancement of the

---

[51] "The cognition of a being such as man existed before man made his appearance." [Tr.]

[52] "Teleology or scientific theology." [Tr.]

[53] "Illustrious colleagues." [Tr.]

[54] "German philosophy." [Tr.]

knowledge of nature. But Kant can hardly have been serious in making this assertion. At any rate, its opposite, namely that those assumptions are restrictive and fatal to all investigation of nature, will be beyond doubt to every natural philosopher. To test this by an example, let us consider whether the assumption of a soul as an immaterial, simple, thinking substance would have been necessarily useful, or in the highest degree a hindrance, to the truths so beautifully expounded by Cabanis, or to the discoveries of Flourens, Marshall Hall, and Ch. Bell. In fact, Kant himself says (*Prolegomena*, § 44), that "the Ideas of reason (*Vernunft*) are opposed and an impediment to the maxims of the rational knowledge of nature."

It is certainly not one of the least merits of Frederick the Great that under his government Kant was able to develop, and was allowed to publish, the *Critique of Pure Reason*. Under hardly any other government would a salaried professor have dared to do such a thing. To the successor of the great King Kant had to promise not to write any more.

* * *

I might consider that I could dispense here with the criticism of the ethical part of the Kantian philosophy, seeing that I furnished, twenty-two years later, a more detailed and thorough criticism than the present one in *Die Beiden Grundprobleme der Ethik*. However, what is retained here from the first edition, and for the sake of completeness could not be omitted, may serve as a suitable introduction to that later and much more thorough criticism, to which, in the main, I therefore refer the reader.

In consequence of the love for architectonic symmetry, theoretical reason (*Vernunft*) also had to have a *pendant*. The *intellectus practicus* of scholasticism, which again springs from the νοῦς πρακτικός of Aristotle (*De Anima*, iii, 10, and *Politics*, vii, c. 14; ὁ μὲν γὰρ πρακτικός ἐστι λόγος, ὁ δὲ θεωρητικός),[55] suggests the word to us. Yet here something quite different is denoted by it, not the faculty of reason that is directed to technical science as with Aristotle. Here with Kant practical reason (*Vernunft*) appears as the source and origin of the undeniable, ethical significance of human conduct, as well as of all virtue, all noble-mindedness, and every attainable degree of holiness. Accordingly, all this would come from mere *reason* (*Vernunft*), and would require nothing but this. To behave rationally and to act in a virtuous, noble, and holy manner would be one

---

[55] "Reason is practical on the one hand, theoretical on the other." [Tr.]

and the same thing; and to act selfishly, wickedly, and viciously would be merely to behave irrationally. However, all times and all nations and languages have always clearly distinguished the two, and regarded them as two entirely different things; and so also do all those even at the present day who know nothing of the language of the modern school, in other words, the whole world with the exception of a small handful of German savants. All except these understand by virtuous conduct and a rational course of life two entirely different things. To say that the sublime founder of the Christian religion, whose course of life is presented to us as the pattern of all virtue, had been the *most rational of all* men, would be called a very unworthy, and even blasphemous, way of speaking, and almost as much so if it were said that his precepts contained only the best advice for a completely *rational life*. Further, that the person who, according to these precepts, instead of thinking first of himself and of his own future needs, always relieves the present greater want of others without further regard, in fact presents the whole of his property to the poor, in order then, destitute of all resources, to go and preach to others the virtue he himself has practised; this everyone rightly respects, but who ventures to extol it as the height of *reasonableness?* And finally, who praises it as an extremely *rational* deed that Arnold von Winkelried with boundless magnanimity grasped and held the hostile spears against his own body, in order to obtain victory and deliverance for his countrymen? On the other hand, we see a man intent from his youth upwards with rare deliberation on how to procure for himself the means to a living free from care, for the support of wife and children, to a good name among mankind, to outward honour and eminence. In this he does not allow himself to be led astray, or induced ever to lose sight of his goal, by the charm of present pleasures, or the gratification of defying the arrogance of those in authority, or the desire to avenge unmerited humiliation and insults he has suffered, or the power of attraction of useless aesthetic or philosophical mental occupation and travel to countries worth seeing; but with the greatest consistency he works solely towards this goal. Who ventures to deny that such a Philistine is *rational* to quite a remarkable degree, even if he may have allowed himself to employ some means that are not praiseworthy, but yet are without danger? Let us consider further. A villain helps himself to riches, honours, and even thrones and crowns with deliberate cunning in accordance with a well-thought-out plan. Then, with the most subtle craftiness, he ensnares neighbouring countries, subdues them one by one, and becomes a world-conqueror. In this he does not allow himself to be led astray by any regard for right or by humaneness, but with harsh consistency crushes and pulverizes everything that opposes his plan; he plunges millions without pity into every kind of misery, and condemns millions to bleed and die. Nevertheless, he royally rewards his adherents and helpers, and always protects them, never forgetting anything, and thus attains his end. Who does not see that such a person was bound to go to work in a thoroughly rational way? Who does not see that, just as a powerful understanding was required to draw up the plans, so a perfect command of the faculty of *reason,* indeed of really *practical reason,* was needed to carry them out? Or are the precepts *irrational* which the clever and consistent, the deliberate and far-seeing Machiavelli gives to the prince? [56]

Just as wickedness is quite compatible with the faculty of reason, in fact is really terrible only in this combination, so, conversely, nobility of mind is sometimes found in combination with want of reason. We can attribute to this the action of Coriolanus. After he had applied all his strength for years in order to obtain revenge on the Romans, he then, when the time ultimately came, let himself be softened by the entreaties of the Senate and the tears of his mother and wife. He gave up the revenge he had so long and laboriously prepared for; and in fact, by thus incurring the righteous anger of the Volscians, he died for those Romans whose ingratitude he knew and wanted so strenuously to punish. Finally, for the sake of completeness, it may be mentioned that the faculty of reason can quite well be united with want of understanding. This is the case when a stupid maxim is chosen, but is consistently carried into effect. An example of this kind was afforded by Princess Isabella, daughter of Philip II, who vowed that, so long as Ostend had not been conquered, she would not put on a clean shift, and for three years kept her word. Generally all vows are of this class, the origin whereof is always a want of insight in accordance with the law of causality, in other words, want of understanding. Nevertheless, it is rational to fulfil them, if one is of so limited an understanding as to make them.

---

[56] Incidentally, Machiavelli's problem was the solution to the question how the prince could *unconditionally* keep himself on the throne, in spite of internal and external enemies. Thus his problem was by no means the ethical one whether a prince, as a man, should want to do so or not, but purely the political problem how to carry it out, *if* he wants to. He gives the solution to this, just as a person writes instructions for playing chess, in which it would be foolish to regret the failure to answer the question whether it is morally advisable to play chess at all. To reproach Machiavelli with the immorality of his work is just as much out of place as it would be to reproach a fencing master with not opening his instruction with a moral lecture against murder and manslaughter.

In keeping with what has been mentioned, we see the authors who appeared just before Kant place conscience, as the seat of the moral impulses, in opposition to reason (*Vernunft*). Thus Rousseau in the fourth book of *Émile*: *La raison nous trompe, mais la conscience ne trompe jamais;* and a little farther on: *Il est impossible d'expliquer par les conséquences de notre nature le principe immédiat de la conscience indépendant de la raison même.* Further: *Mes sentimens naturels parlaient pour l'intérêt commun, ma raison rapportait tout à moi. . . . On a beau vouloir établir la vertu par la raison seule, quelle solide base peut-on lui donner?* [57] In the *Rêveries du promeneur*, prom. 4ème, he says: *Dans toutes les questions de morale difficiles je me suis toujours bien trouvé de les résoudre par le dictame de la conscience, plutôt que par les lumières de la raison.*[58] In fact, Aristotle already expressly says (*Ethica Magna*, i, 5), that the virtues have their seat in the ἀλόγῳ μορίῳ τῆς ψυχῆς (*in parte irrationali animi*) and not in the λόγον ἔχοντι (*in parte rationali*). Accordingly, Stobaeus says (*Ecl.* ii, *c.* 7) speaking of the Peripatetics: Τὴν ἠθικὴν ἀρετὴν ὑπολαμβάνουσι περὶ τὸ ἄλογον μέρος γίγνεσθαι τῆς ψυχῆς, ἐπειδὴ διμερῆ πρὸς τὴν παροῦσαν θεωρίαν ὑπέθεντο τὴν ψυχήν, τὸ μὲν λόγικον ἔχουσαν, τὸ δ'ἄλογον. Καὶ περὶ μὲν τὸ λογικὸν τὴν καλοκἀγαθίαν γίγνεσθαι, καὶ τὴν φρόνησιν, καὶ τὴν ἀγχίνοιαν, καὶ σοφίαν, καὶ εὐμάθειαν, καὶ μνήμην, καὶ τὰς ὁμοίους· περὶ δὲ τὸ ἄλογον, σωφροσύνην, καὶ δικαιοσύνην, καὶ ἀνδρείαν, καὶ τὰς ἄλλας τὰς ἠθικὰς καλουμένας ἀρετάς. (*Ethicam virtutem circa partem animae ratione carentem versari putant, cum duplicem, ad hanc disquisitionem, animam ponant, ratione praeditam, et ea carentem. In parte vero ratione praedita collocant ingenuitatem, prudentiam, perspicacitatem, sapientiam, docilitatem, memoriam, et reliqua; in parte vero ratione destituta temperantiam, justitiam, fortitudinem, et reliquas virtutes, quas ethicas vocant.*)[59] And Cicero (*De Natura Deorum*, iii, c. 26-31)

---

[57] "Reason deceives us, but never conscience;—It is impossible to explain through the consequences of our nature the immediate principle of conscience that is independent of reason itself.—My natural feelings spoke in favour of the common interest, but my reason referred everything to myself. . . . We try in vain to base virtue on reason alone, but what solid foundation can we give it?" [Tr.]

[58] "In all the difficult questions of morality I have always found it better to solve them through the dictates of conscience than by the light of reason." [Tr.]

[59] "About ethical virtue, they think that it concerns the irrational part of the soul, for as far as the present consideration is concerned, they assume that the soul consists of two parts, a rational and an irrational; and to the rational part belong magnanimity, prudence, sagacity, wisdom, docility, memory, and the like; to the irrational part, on the contrary, belong temperance, justice, fortitude, and the rest of the so-called ethical virtues." [Tr.]

explains at length that the faculty of reason is the necessary means and the instrument for all crimes.

I have declared *reason* to be the *faculty of concepts*. It is this quite special class of general, non-perceptible representations, symbolized and fixed only by words, that distinguishes man from the animal, and gives him the mastery of the earth. If the animal is the slave of the present, knows no other motives than immediately sensuous ones, and therefore, when these are presented to it, is necessarily attracted or repelled by them as iron by the magnet, then, on the other hand, deliberation and reflection have arisen in man through the gift of reason (*Vernunft*). This enables him easily to survey his life and the course of the world in both directions as a whole; it makes him independent of the present, enables him to go to work deliberately, systematically, and with forethought, for evil as well as for good. But what he does is done with complete self-consciousness; he knows exactly how his will decides, what he chooses in each case, and what other choice was possible according to the case in point; and from this self-conscious willing he becomes acquainted with himself, and mirrors himself in his actions. In all these references to man's conduct the faculty of reason can be called *practical;* it is theoretical only in so far as the objects with which it is concerned have no reference to the conduct of the thinker, but purely theoretical interest, of which very few people are capable. What in this sense is called *practical reason* is very nearly what is expressed by the Latin word *prudentia;* according to Cicero (*De Natura Deorum,* ii, 22), this is a contraction of *providentia.* On the other hand, *ratio,* used of a mental faculty, signifies for the most part theoretical reason proper, although the ancients do not observe the distinction strictly. In nearly all men the faculty of reason has an almost exclusively practical tendency. If this too is abandoned, then thought loses control over action, wherefore it is then said: *Video meliora, proboque, deteriora sequor,*[60] or *"Le matin je fais des projets, et le soir je fais des sottises."* [61] Thus the man lets his conduct be guided not by his thinking, but by the impression of the present moment, almost after the fashion of the animal; and so he is called *irrational* (without in this way reproaching him with moral depravity), although he does not really lack the faculty of reason, but merely the ability to apply it to his own conduct; and to a cer-

---

[60] "I see and applaud what is better, but I follow what is worse." [Ovid, *Metamorphoses,* vii, 20. Tr.]

[61] "In the morning I make plans, and in the evening I commit absurdities." [Tr.]

tain extent it might be said that his faculty of reason is purely theoretical, and not practical. In this connexion, he may be really good, like many a man who cannot see anyone in misfortune without helping him, even at the cost of sacrifices, but who nevertheless leaves his debts unpaid. Such an irrational character is quite incapable of committing great crimes, since the systematic planning, the dissimulation and self-control, always necessary in this connexion are for him impossible. Yet he will hardly reach a very high degree of virtue, for, however much he may be inclined by nature to do good, those individual vicious and wicked outbursts to which every person is subject cannot fail to appear, and where the faculty of reason, not showing itself practically, holds up to them.unalterable maxims and fixed intentions, they are bound to become deeds.

Finally, the faculty of *reason* shows itself quite specially as *practical* in those really rational characters who on this account are in ordinary life called practical philosophers. They are distinguished by an unusual calmness in unpleasant as well as in pleasant circumstances, an equable disposition, and a fixed adherence to decisions once made. In fact, it is the prevalence of the faculty of reason in them, in other words, the abstract rather than intuitive knowledge, and therefore the survey of life by means of concepts, in general, as a whole and on a large scale, which has made them acquainted once and for all with the deception of the momentary impression, with the instability of all things, with the shortness of life, the emptiness of pleasures, the fickleness of fortune, and the great and little tricks and whims of chance. Therefore nothing comes to them unexpectedly, and what they know in the abstract does not surprise or disconcert them when it confronts them in real life and in the particular case. This happens, however, to those characters who are not so rational. On these the present, the perceptible, and the actual exerts such force that the cold and colourless concepts withdraw entirely into the background of consciousness, and such characters, forgetting resolutions and maxims, are abandoned to emotions and passions of every kind. I have already explained at the end of the first book that, in my opinion, the ethics of Stoicism was originally nothing but a guide to a really rational life in this sense. Such a life is also repeatedly extolled by Horace in very many passages. Connected with this are his *nil admirari*,[62] and also the Delphic Μηδὲν

---

[62] "Not to let oneself be disconcerted," correctly explained by Schopenhauer, only that the concept is even wider, and needs to be superior not only to desire but also to fear. It is ἀταραξία, "unshakable serenity or peace of mind," regarded by Stoics, Epicureans, and Sceptics as the highest goal, which they all in different ways attempted to reach. [Tr.]

ἄγαν.[63] To translate *nil admirari* as "to admire nothing" is quite wrong. This saying of Horace does not concern the theoretical so much as the practical, and really means: "Do not value any object unconditionally; do not become infatuated with anything; do not believe that the possession of anything can confer perfect happiness on you. Every inexpressible longing for an object is only a taunting chimera that one can just as well, and much more easily, get rid of by knowledge made clear as by possession attained with effort." In this sense Cicero also uses *admirari* (*De Divinatione,* ii, 2). What Horace means is therefore the ἀθαμβία (fearlessness) and ἀκατάπληξις (want of admiration), also ἀθαυμασία (imperturbability), which Democritus already prized as the highest good (see Clement of Alexandria, *Stromata,* ii, 21, and cf. Strabo, i, 98 and 105). There is really no question of virtue and vice in such reasonableness of conduct, but this practical use of the faculty of reason constitutes man's real prerogative over the animal; and only in this regard has it a meaning, and is it permissible, to speak of a dignity of man.

In all the cases described, and in all conceivable cases, the distinction between rational and irrational conduct goes back to the question whether the motives are abstract concepts or representations of perception. Therefore the explanation of reason (*Vernunft*) that I have given agrees exactly with the usage of language at all times and among all peoples, a circumstance that will not be regarded as something just accidental or arbitrary. It will be seen that it has arisen precisely from the distinction, of which every man is conscious, between the different mental faculties; he speaks in accordance with such consciousness, but of course does not raise it to the distinctness of abstract definition. Our ancestors did not make words without attaching a definite meaning to them, so that these would lie ready for philosophers who might possibly come centuries later, and determine what should be thought in connexion with them; but they denoted by them quite definite concepts. The words, therefore, are no longer unappropriated, and to read into them a meaning entirely different from that which they have had hitherto is to misuse them, to introduce a licence according to which anyone could use any word in any sense he chose, in which way endless confusion would inevitably result. Locke has already shown at length that most disagreements in philosophy arise from a false use of words. For the sake of illustration, let us glance for a moment at the scandalous misuse of the words substance, consciousness, truth, and so on,

---

[63] "Nothing to excess." [Tr.]

made at the present day by philosophasters destitute of ideas. Moreover, the statements and explanations of all philosophers of all ages,
with the exception of the most modern, concerning reason (*Vernunft*), agree just as much with my explanation of it as do the concepts prevailing among all nations of that prerogative of man. Let
us see what Plato, in the fourth book of the *Republic* [440 c], and
in innumerable scattered passages, calls the λόγικον or λογιστικὸν
τῆς ψυχῆς,[64] what Cicero says (*De Natura Deorum*, iii, 26-31),
what Leibniz and Locke say about this in the passages already
quoted in the first book. There would be no end to the quotations
here, if we wished to show how all philosophers before Kant generally spoke of reason (*Vernunft*) in my sense, although they did
not know how to explain its nature with complete definiteness and
distinctness by reducing it to a point. What was understood by
reason shortly before Kant appeared is shown on the whole by two
essays of Sulzer in the first volume of his miscellaneous philosophical writings, one entitled *Analysis of the Concept of Reason*, and
the other *On the Mutual Influence of Reason and Language*. On the
other hand, if we read how in the most recent times people speak
of reason (*Vernunft*), through the influence of the Kantian error
that afterwards increased like an avalanche, then we are obliged to
assume that all the sages of antiquity, as well as the philosophers
before Kant, had absolutely no faculty of reason at all; for the immediate perceptions, intuitions, apprehensions, and presentiments of
reason, now discovered, remained as foreign to them as the sixth
sense of bats is to us. Moreover, as regards myself, I must confess
that, in my narrow-mindedness, I too cannot grasp or imagine in
any other way than as the sixth sense of bats a faculty of reason
that directly perceives, or apprehends, or has an intellectual intuition of, the supersensible, the Absolute, together with long narratives
accompanying it. We must, however, say this in favour of the invention or discovery of such a faculty of reason that perceives at
once and directly anything we choose, that it is an incomparable
expédient for withdrawing ourselves and our favourite fixed ideas
from the affair in the easiest way in the world, in spite of all the
Kants and their Critiques of Reason. The invention and the recep-
tion it has met with do honour to the age.

Therefore, although what is essential to *reason* (τὸ λόγικον, ἡ
φρόνησις, *ratio, raison, Vernunft*) was, on the whole and in general,
rightly recognized by all the philosophers of all ages, though not
defined sharply enough or reduced to a point, yet, on the other hand,

---

[64] "The rational part of the soul." [Tr.]

it was not so clear to them what the *understanding* (νοῦς, διάνοια, *intellectus, esprit, intellect, Verstand*) is. Hence they often confuse it with reason, and on this very account do not reach a thoroughly complete, pure, and simple explanation of the nature of the faculty of reason. With the Christian philosophers, the concept of reason obtained an entirely extraneous, subsidiary meaning by contrast with revelation. Starting from this, many then assert, quite rightly, that knowledge of the obligation to virtue is possible even from mere reason, in other words, even without revelation. This consideration certainly had influence even on Kant's exposition and use of words. But that contrast is really of positive, historical significance, and is thus an element foreign to philosophy. From it philosophy must be kept free.

We might have expected that, in his critiques of theoretical and practical reason, Kant would have started with a description of the nature of reason (*Vernunft*) in general, and, after thus defining the *genus,* would have gone on to an explanation of the two *species,* showing how one and the same faculty of reason manifests itself in two such different ways, and yet, by retaining the principal characteristic, proves to be the same. But of all this we find nothing. I have already shown how inadequate, wavering, and inconsistent are the explanations given by him in the *Critique of Pure Reason,* here and there by the way, of the faculty he is criticizing. *Practical* reason (*Vernunft*) is already found unannounced in the *Critique of Pure Reason,* and subsequently stands in the *Critique* expressly devoted to it as a settled and established thing. This is left without any further account of it, and without the linguistic usage of all times and peoples, which is trampled under foot, or the conceptdefinitions of the greatest of earlier philosophers daring to raise their voices. On the whole, we can infer from particular passages that Kant's meaning is as follows: Knowledge of principles *a priori* is an essential characteristic of the faculty of reason; now, as knowledge of the ethical significance of conduct is not of empirical origin, it too is a *principium a priori,* and accordingly springs from our reason that is thus to this extent *practical.* I have already said enough about the incorrectness of that explanation of the faculty of reason. But apart from this, how superficial and shallow it is to use here the single quality of being independent of experience, in order to combine the most heterogeneous things, while overlooking their fundamental, essential, and immeasurable difference in other respects! For even assuming, though not admitting, that knowledge of the ethical significance of conduct springs from an imperative that lies within us, from an unconditioned *ought,* yet how fundamentally different would such an imperative be from those universal *forms of knowledge!* In the *Critique of Pure Reason* Kant shows that we are conscious of these a priori, and that by virtue of such consciousness we can express beforehand an unconditioned *must,* valid for all experience possible to us. But the difference between this *must,* this necessary form of every object already determined in the subject, and that *ought* of morality is so immense and obvious, that we can make use of their agreement in the criterion of the non-empirical form of knowledge as a witty comparison indeed, but not as a philosophical justification for identifying the origin of the two.

Moreover, the birthplace of this child of practical reason, the *absolute ought* or categorical imperative, is not in the *Critique of Practical Reason,* but in the *Critique of Pure Reason,* p. 802 (V, 830). The birth is violent, and is achieved only by means of the forceps of a *therefore* that stands up boldly and audaciously, we might say shamelessly, between two propositions utterly foreign to each other and having no connexion, in order to combine them as ground and consequent. Thus Kant starts from the proposition that we are determined not merely by perceptible, but also by abstract, motives, and expresses it in the following manner: "Not merely what excites, i.e., directly affects the senses, determines man's free choice, but we have a faculty for overcoming the impressions on our sensuous appetitive faculty through representations of what is itself in a more remote way useful or harmful. These deliberations about what is worth desiring in regard to our whole condition, i.e., what is good and useful, rest on reason." (Perfectly right; would that he always spoke so rationally about reason!) "Reason *therefore* (!) also gives laws which are imperatives, i.e., objective laws of freedom, and which say what *ought* to happen, although possibly it never does happen"! Thus, without further credentials, the categorical imperative leaps into the world, in order to command there with its *unconditioned ought*—a sceptre of wooden iron. For in the concept *ought* there exists absolutely and essentially consideration of threatened punishment or promised reward as the necessary condition, and this is not to be separated from it without abolishing the concept itself, and depriving it of all meaning. Therefore, an *unconditioned ought* is a *contradictio in adjecto.*[65] This mistake had to be censured, closely connected as it otherwise is with Kant's great service to ethics, which consists in the fact that he freed ethics from all principles of the world of experience, particularly from all direct or indirect eudaemonism, and showed quite properly that the kingdom

---

[65] Contradiction of a subsidiary determination contrary to the concept to which it is united, as hot snow or cold fire. [Tr.]

of virtue is not of this world. This service is all the greater since all the ancient philosophers, with the single exception of Plato, thus the Peripatetics, the Stoics, and the Epicureans, tried by very different devices either to make virtue and happiness dependent on each other according to the principle of sufficient reason, or to identify them according to the principle of contradiction. This reproach is just as much levelled at the philosophers of modern times down to Kant. His merit in this respect, therefore, is very great; yet justice requires that we also remember here, firstly that his exposition and argument are often not in keeping with the tendency and spirit of his ethics, as we shall see in a moment, and secondly that, even so, he is not the first to have purged virtue of all principles of happiness. For Plato, especially in the *Republic,* of which the main tendency is precisely this, expressly teaches that virtue is to be chosen for its own sake alone, even if unhappiness and ignominy should be inevitably associated with it. But still more does Christianity preach a wholly unselfish virtue, that is also practised not for the sake of the reward in a life after death, but quite gratuitously out of love for God, inasmuch as works do not justify, but only faith which virtue accompanies, as its mere symptom so to speak, and which therefore appears quite gratuitously and of its own accord. See Luther's *De Libertate Christiana.* I will not take at all into account the Indians, in whose sacred books the hope of a reward for our works is everywhere described as the path of darkness which can never lead to the blissful state. However, we do not find Kant's doctrine of virtue so pure; or rather the presentation falls far short of the spirit, and has in fact lapsed into inconsistency. In his *highest good,* which he subsequently discussed, we find virtue wedded to happiness. Yet the ought, originally so unconditioned, does postulate afterwards a condition for itself, really in order to be rid of the inner contradiction, burdened with which it cannot live. Now supreme happiness in the highest good should not really be the motive for virtue; yet it is there like a secret article, the presence of which makes all the rest a mere sham contract. It is not really the reward of virtue, but yet is a voluntary gift for which virtue, after work has been done, stealthily holds its hand open. We can convince ourselves of this from the *Critique of Practical Reason* (pp. 223-266 of the fourth, or pp. 264-295 of the Rosenkranz edition). The whole of Kant's moral theology also has the same tendency, and on this very account morality really destroys itself through moral theology. For I repeat that all virtue in any way practised for the sake of a reward is based on a prudent, methodical, far-seeing egoism.

Now the purport of the absolute ought, the fundamental law of practical reason, is the famous: "So act that the maxim of your will might always be valid at the same time as the principle of a universal legislation." This principle gives to the person who demands a regulation for his own will, the task of seeking a regulation for the will of all. The question then arises how such a regulation is to be found. Obviously, to discover the rule of my conduct, I ought not to have regard to myself alone, but to the sum-total of all individuals. Then instead of my own well-being, the well-being of all without distinction becomes my object and aim. This aim, however, still always remains well-being. I then find that all can be equally well off only if each makes the egoism of others the limit of his own. It naturally follows from this that I ought not to injure anyone, so that, since this principle is assumed to be universal, *I* also may not be injured. This, however, is the only ground on account of which I, not yet possessing a moral principle but only looking for one, can desire this to be a universal law. But obviously in this way the desire for well-being, in other words egoism, remains the source of this ethical principle. As the basis of political science it would be excellent; as the basis of ethics it is worthless. For the man who attempts to establish a regulation for the will of all, which is proposed in that moral principle, is himself in turn necessarily in need of a regulation, otherwise everything would be a matter of indifference to him. This regulation, however, can only be his own egoism, as the conduct of others influences this alone. Therefore only by means of this, and with respect to it, can that man have a will concerning the conduct of others, and is such conduct not a matter of indifference to him. Kant himself very naïvely intimates this (p. 123 of the *Critique of Practical Reason;* Rosenkranz edition, p. 192), where he thus carries out the search for the maxim for the will: "If everyone regarded the need of others with complete indifference, and *you also belonged* to such an order of things, would you consent thereto?" *Quam temere in nosmet legem sancimus iniquam!* [66] would be the regulation of the consent sought. Likewise in the *Foundation to the Metaphysics of Morals,* p. 56 of the third, p. 50 of the Rosenkranz edition: "A will that resolved to render no assistance to anyone in distress would contradict itself, since cases might occur *where it would need the love and sympathy of others,"* and so on. Closely examined, therefore, this principle of ethics, which is nothing but an indirect and disguised expression of the old simple principle, *Quod tibi fieri non vis, alteri ne feceris,*[67] is related pri-

---

[66] "How thoughtlessly we establish an unjust law which argues against ourselves!" [Horace, *Satires,* I, 3, 67. Tr.]

[67] "Do not to another what you do not wish should be done to you." [Tr.]

marily and directly to what is passive, to suffering, and only by means of this to action. Therefore, as we have said, it would be quite useful as a guide to the foundation of the *State,* which is directed towards preventing the *suffering of wrong,* and desires to procure for each and all the greatest sum of well-being. In ethics, however, where the object of investigation is *action* as *action* and in its immediate significance for the *doer of the action*—but not its consequence, namely suffering, or its reference to others—that consideration is altogether inadmissible, since at bottom it amounts to a principle of happiness, and hence to egoism.

Therefore we cannot share Kant's satisfaction that his principle of ethics is not material, in other words, a principle that sets up an object as motive, but merely formal, whereby it corresponds symmetrically to the formal laws with which the *Critique of Pure Reason* has made us acquainted. Of course, instead of a law, it is only the formula for discovering such a law. In the first place, however, we already had this formula more briefly and clearly in the *Quod tibi fieri non vis, alteri ne feceris;* in the second place, analysis of this formula shows that it is simply and solely regard for our own happiness which gives it content. Therefore it can serve only rational egoism, to which also every legal constitution owes its origin.

Another mistake which, because it offends the feelings of everyone, is often censured, and is satirized in an epigram by Schiller, is the pedantic rule that, to be really good and meritorious, a deed must be performed simply and solely out of regard for the known law and for the concept of duty, and according to a maxim known to reason (*Vernunft*) in the abstract. It must not be performed from any inclination, any benevolence felt towards others, any tenderhearted sympathy, compassion, or emotion of the heart. According to the *Critique of Practical Reason,* p. 213 (Rosenkranz edition, p. 257), these are even very irksome to right-thinking people, as they confuse their deliberate maxims. On the contrary, the deed must be performed unwillingly and with self-compulsion. Remember that hope of reward is nevertheless not to have any influence, and consider the great absurdity of the demand. But, what is more important, this is directly opposed to the genuine spirit of virtue; not the deed, but the willingness to do it, the love from which it results, and without which it is a dead work, this constitutes its meritorious element. Christianity, therefore, rightly teaches that all outward works are worthless if they do not proceed from that genuine disposition which consists in true readiness and pure affection. It also teaches that what makes blessed and redeems is not works done (*opera operata*), but faith, the genuine disposition, that is granted by the Holy Ghost alone, not produced by the free and deliberate will that has in view only the law. This demand by Kant that every virtuous action shall be done from pure, deliberate regard for and according to the abstract maxims of the law, coldly and without inclination, in fact contrary to all inclination, is precisely the same thing as if he were to assert that every genuine work of art must result from a well-thought-out application of aesthetic rules. The one is just as absurd as the other. The question, dealt with by Plato and Seneca, whether virtue can be taught, is to be answered in the negative. Finally, we shall have to decide to see what gave rise to the Christian doctrine of election by grace, namely that, as regards the main thing and its essence, virtue, like genius, is to a certain extent innate, and that just as all the professors of aesthetics with their combined efforts are unable to impart to anyone the capacity to produce works of genius, i.e., genuine works of art, so are all the professors of ethics and preachers of virtue just as little able to transform an ignoble character into one that is virtuous and noble. The impossibility of this is very much more obvious than is that of converting lead into gold. The search for an ethical system and a first principle thereof, which would have practical influence and would actually transform and improve the human race, is just like the search for the philosophers' stone. But I have spoken at length at the end of our fourth book on the possibility of an entire change of mind or conversion of man (regeneration, new birth), not by means of abstract (ethics), but of intuitive knowledge (effect of grace). The contents of that book relieve me in general of the necessity for dwelling on this point any longer.

Kant by no means penetrated into the real significance of the ethical content of actions, and this is shown finally by his doctrine of the highest good as the necessary combination of virtue and happiness, a combination indeed where virtue would merit happiness. Here the logical reproach is already levelled at him, that the concept of merit or desert, which is here the measure or standard, already presupposes an ethical system as its measure, and therefore could not be traced from it. The conclusion of our fourth book was that, after all genuine virtue has attained to its highest degree, it ultimately leads to a complete renunciation in which all willing comes to an end. Happiness, on the other hand, is a satisfied willing, and so the two are fundamentally irreconcilable. He who has been enlightened by my discussion needs no further explanation of the complete absurdity of this Kantian view regarding the highest good; and, independently of my positive exposition, I have no further negative exposition to give here.

Kant's love of architectonic symmetry is also met with in the *Critique of Practical Reason,* since he has given this the complete cut and shape of the *Critique of Pure Reason.* He has again introduced the same titles and forms in an obviously arbitrary manner, and this becomes particularly evident in the table of the categories of freedom.

*   *   *

The *Jurisprudence* is one of Kant's latest works, and is so feeble that, although I reject it entirely, I consider that a polemic against it is superfluous, for, just as if it were not the work of this great man, but the production of an ordinary mortal, it is bound to die a natural death through its own weakness. Therefore, as regards the *Jurisprudence,* I renounce the negative method of procedure, and refer to the positive, and hence to the brief outline of it laid down in our fourth book. A few general remarks on Kant's *Jurisprudence* only may be made here. The mistakes that I have censured when considering the *Critique of Pure Reason* as everywhere adhering to Kant are found to such an excess in the *Jurisprudence* that we often think that we are reading a satirical parody of the Kantian style, or at any rate are listening to a Kantian. The two principal errors, however, are the following. He tries (and many have tried since) to separate jurisprudence sharply from ethics, yet not to make the former dependent on positive legislation, i.e., on arbitrary obligation, but to allow the concept of right to exist by itself pure and *a priori.* But this is not possible, since conduct, apart from its ethical significance, and from the physical relation to others and thus to external obligation, does not admit of a third view, even as a mere possibility. Consequently when he says: "Legal obligation is that which *can* be enforced," this *can* is either to be understood physically, and then all law and justice are positive and arbitrary, and again all arbitrariness that can be enforced is also law; or this *can* is to be understood ethically, and we are again in the province of ethics. With Kant, therefore, the concept of law or right hovers between heaven and earth, and has no ground on which it can set foot; with me it belongs to ethics. In the second place, his definition of the concept of law or right is wholly negative, and thus inadequate:[68] "Right is that which is consistent with the coexistence and compatibility of the freedoms of individuals in juxtaposition to one an-

---

[68] Although the concept of law or right is really negative in contrast to that of wrong, which is the positive starting-point, the explanation of these concepts cannot be completely and entirely negative.

other, in accordance with a universal law." Freedom (here the empirical, i.e., physical, not the moral freedom of the will) means not being hindered or obstructed, and is therefore a mere negation; again, compatibility or coexistence has exactly the same meaning. Thus we are left with mere negations, and do not obtain any positive concept; in fact, we do not get to know at all what is really being talked about, unless we already know it in a different way. In the subsequent discussion the most absurd views are developed, such as that in the natural condition, in other words, outside the State, there is absolutely no right to property. This really means that all right or law is positive, and thus natural law is based on positive law, instead of which the reverse should be the case. Further, there are the establishment of legal acquisition through seizure and occupation; the ethical obligation to set up a civil constitution; the grounds for the right to punish, and so on, all of which, as I have said, I do not regard as at all worth a special refutation. However, these Kantian errors have exercised a very injurious influence; they have confused and obscured truths long since known and expressed, and given rise to strange theories and to much writing and controversy. This of course cannot last, and already we see how truth and sound reason (*Vernunft*) are again making headway. As evidence of the latter, there is in particular J. C. F. Meister's *Naturrecht,* in contrast to so many queer and crazy theories, although I do not on this account regard the book as a pattern of attained perfection.

* * *

After what has been said so far, I can also be very brief concerning the *Critique of Judgement.* We are bound to wonder how Kant, to whom certainly art remained very foreign, and who in all probability had little susceptibility to the beautiful, in fact probably never had the opportunity to see an important work of art, and who seems finally to have had no knowledge even of Goethe, the only man of his century and country fit to be placed by his side as his giant brother—it is, I say, wonderful how, in spite of all this, Kant was able to render a great and permanent service to the philosophical consideration of art and the beautiful. His merit lies in the fact that, much as men had reflected on the beautiful and on art, they had really always considered the matter from the empirical point of view alone; and, supported by facts, they investigated what quality distinguished the object of any kind called *beautiful* from other objects of the same kind. On this path they first arrived at quite special principles, and then at more general ones. They attempted to separate genuine artistic beauty from the spurious, and to discover characteristics of this genuineness which could then serve again as rules. What pleases us as beautiful, what does not, hence what is to be imitated, to be aimed at, what to be avoided, what rules, at any rate negative rules, are to be fixed, in short, what are the means for exciting aesthetic pleasure, in other words, what are for this the conditions residing in the *object*—this was almost exclusively the theme of all considerations on art. This path had been taken by Aristotle, and on the same path we find, even in the most recent times, Home, Burke, Winckelmann, Lessing, Herder, and many others. It is true that the universality of the aesthetic principles discovered ultimately led back to the subject, and it was observed that, if the effect were properly known in the subject, the cause of its residing in the object could also be determined *a priori,* and in this way alone could this method of consideration attain to the certainty of a science. Occasionally, this gave rise to psychological discussions; but in particular, Alexander Baumgarten produced with this intention a general aesthetic of all that is beautiful, in which he started from the concept of the perfection of knowledge of the senses, and hence of knowledge of perception. But in his case also, the subjective part is at once done with as soon as this concept is established, and he proceeds to the objective part, and to that which is practical and is related thereto. But even here, the merit was reserved for Kant of investigating seriously and profoundly *the stimulation itself,* in consequence of which we call the object giving rise to it *beautiful,* in order, if possible, to discover its constituent elements and conditions in our nature. His investigation, therefore, took the entirely subjective direction. This path was obviously the right one, since, in order to explain a phenomenon given in its effects, we must first know accurately this effect itself, so as thoroughly to determine the nature of the cause. In this respect, however, Kant's merit does not really extend much farther than his having shown the right path, and having given, by a provisional attempt, an example of how, roughly, we must follow it. For what he gave cannot be considered as objective truth and a real gain. He suggested the method for this investigation, paved the way, but otherwise missed the mark.

With the *Critique of Aesthetic Judgement* there is first of all forced on us the observation that Kant retained the method which is peculiar to his whole philosophy, and which I have previously considered in detail. I refer to the method of starting from abstract knowledge, in order to investigate knowledge of perception, so that the former serves him, so to speak, as a *camera obscura* in which to gather and survey the latter. Just as in the *Critique of Pure Reason* the forms of judgements were supposed to give him information about the knowledge of our whole world of perception, so in this *Critique of Aesthetic Judgement* he does not start from the beautiful itself, from the direct, beautiful object of perception, but from the *judgement* concerning the beautiful, the so-called, and very badly so-called, judgement of taste. This is the problem for him. His attention is specially aroused by the circumstance that such a judgement is obviously the expression of something occurring in the subject, but is nevertheless as universally valid as if it concerned a quality of the object. It is this that struck him, not the beautiful itself. He always starts only from the statements of others, from the judgement concerning the beautiful, not from the beautiful itself. Therefore it is as if he knew it entirely from hearsay alone, and not immediately. A very intelligent blind person could almost in the same way combine a theory of colours from accurate statements that he heard about them. And actually we can regard Kant's philosophemes on the beautiful as being in much the same position. We shall then find that his theory is very ingenious, in fact here and there pertinent, and true general remarks are made. His real solution to the problem, however, is so very inadequate, and remains so far beneath the dignity of the subject, that it can never occur to us to regard it as objective truth. I therefore consider myself exempt from a refutation of it, and here too I refer to the positive part of my work.

With regard to the form of his whole book, it is to be noted that it originated from the idea of finding in the concept of *suitableness* or *expediency* the key to the problem of the beautiful. This idea or notion is deduced, and this is nowhere difficult, as we have learnt from Kant's successors. Thus we now have the queer combination of the knowledge of the beautiful with that of the suitableness of natural bodies into *one* faculty of knowledge called *power of judgement,* and the treatment of the two heterogeneous subjects in one book. With these three powers of knowledge, namely faculty of reason, judgement, and understanding, many different symmetrical-architectonic diversions and amusements are subsequently undertaken, the liking for which in general shows itself in this book in many ways; for example, in the pattern of the *Critique of Pure Reason* being forcibly adapted to the whole, but especially in the antinomy of aesthetic judgement being dragged in by the hair. One might almost frame a charge of great inconsistency from the fact that, after it has been incessantly repeated in the *Critique of Pure Reason* that the understanding is the ability to judge, and after the forms of its judgements are made the foundation-stone of all philosophy, a quite peculiar power of judgement now appears which is entirely different from that ability. However, what I call power of judgement, namely the capacity to translate knowledge of perception into abstract knowledge, and in turn to apply the latter correctly to the former, is discussed in the positive part of my work.

By far the most excellent thing in the *Critique of Aesthetic Judgement* is the theory of the sublime. It is incomparably more successful than that of the beautiful, and gives not only, as that does, the general method of investigation, but also a part of the right way to it, so much so that, although it does not provide the real solution to the problem, it nevertheless touches on it very closely.

In the *Critique of the Teleological Judgement* we can, on account of the simplicity of the subject-matter, recognize perhaps more than anywhere else Kant's peculiar talent for turning an idea about and about, and expressing it in many different ways, until a book has come out of it. The whole book tries to say only this: that although organized bodies necessarily seem to us as though they were constructed according to a conception of purpose which preceded them, this still does not justify us in assuming it to be objectively the case. For our intellect, to which things are given from without and indirectly, which therefore never knows their inner nature whereby they arise and exist, but merely their exterior, cannot comprehend a certain quality peculiar to the organized productions of nature otherwise than by analogy, since it compares this quality with the works intentionally made by man, whose quality is determined by a purpose and by the conception thereof. This analogy is sufficient to enable us to comprehend the agreement of all their parts with the whole, and thus to serve even as a guide to their investigation. But it cannot by any means be made on this account the actual ground for explaining the origin and existence of such bodies. For the necessity of so conceiving them is of subjective origin. I should summarize in some such way as this Kant's teaching on this point. In the main, he had already expounded it in the *Critique of Pure Reason,* pp. 692-702 (V, 720-730). However, even in the knowledge of *this* truth, we find David Hume as Kant's meritorious forerunner; he had also keenly disputed that assumption in the second section of his *Dialogues concerning Natural Religion.* The difference between Hume's criticism of that assumption and Kant's is mainly that Hume criticizes it as an assumption based on experience, Kant, on the other hand, as an *a priori* assumption. Both are right, and their accounts supplement each other. In fact, we find what is essential to the Kantian teaching on this point already expressed in the commentary of

Simplicius to the *Physics* of Aristotle: ἡ δὲ πλάνη γέγονεν αὐτοῖς ἀπὸ τοῦ ἡγεῖσθαι, πάντα τὰ ἕνεκα τοῦ γινόμενα κατὰ προαίρεσιν γενέσθαι καὶ λογισμόν, τὰ δὲ φύσει μὴ οὕτως ὁρᾶν γινόμενα. (*Error iis ortus est ex eo, quod credebant, omnia, quae propter finem aliquem fierent, ex proposito et ratiocinio fieri, dum videbant, naturae opera non ita fieri.*) *Schol. in Arist. Phys.*, Berlin edition, p. 354.[69] Kant is perfectly right in the matter; it was also necessary that, after it was demonstrated how the concept of cause and effect was inapplicable to the whole of nature in general according to its existence, it was also shown how, according to its state or quality, nature could not be thought of as effect of a cause guided by motives (concepts of purpose). When we consider the great plausibility of the physico-theological proof which even Voltaire regarded as irrefutable, it was of the greatest importance to show that what is subjective in our comprehension, for which Kant claimed space, time, and causality, extends also to our judgement of natural bodies. Accordingly, the urge we feel to conceive them as having arisen through premeditation according to concepts of purpose, and hence on a path *where the representation of them would have preceded their existence,* is just as much of subjective origin as is the perception of space that manifests itself so objectively; consequently, it cannot be accepted as objective truth. Apart from its wearisome prolixity and repetition, Kant's explanation of the matter is admirable. He rightly asserts that we shall never reach an explanation of the constitution of organic bodies from merely mechanical causes, by which he understands the unconscious, unpremeditated, regular effect of all the universal forces of nature. However, I find yet another defect here. Thus he denies the possibility of such an explanation merely in regard to the appropriateness and apparent deliberateness or premeditation of *organic* bodies. But we find that, even where this does not occur, the grounds of explanation cannot be transferred from one province of nature to another, but forsake us as soon as we enter a new province; and instead of them new fundamental laws appear, whose explanation cannot at all be expected from those of the former province. Thus in the province of the really mechanical, the laws of gravity, cohesion, rigidity, fluidity, and elasticity prevail. In themselves (apart from my explanation of all natural forces as lower grades of the will's objectification), they exist as manifestations of forces incapable of further explanation; but they themselves constitute

---

[69] "[Democritus and Epicurus] fell into the error of imagining that everything that happens for the sake of an end or purpose can rest only on design and deliberation; and yet they observed that the productions of nature do not originate in this way." [Tr.]

the principle of all further explanation, which consists merely in a reduction to them. If we leave this province, and come to the phenomena of chemistry, electricity, magnetism, crystallization, those principles can no longer be used at all; in fact, those previous laws are no longer valid. These forces are overcome by others, and the phenomena take place in direct contradiction to them, according to new fundamental laws, which, just like those other laws, are original and inexplicable, in other words, cannot be reduced to more universal laws. Thus, for instance, we shall never succeed in explaining even the solution of a salt in water according to the laws of mechanics proper, not to mention the more complicated phenomena of chemistry. All this has already been discussed at greater length in the second book of the present work. A discussion of this kind, it seems to me, would have been of great use in the *Critique of the Teleological Judgement,* and would have thrown much light on what is said there. Such a discussion would have been particularly favourable to Kant's excellent suggestion that a deeper knowledge of the inner being-in-itself, the phenomenon of which are the things in nature, would find both in the mechanical (according to law) and in the apparently intentional working of nature one and the same ultimate principle that could serve as the common ground of explanation of them both. I hope I have given such a principle by establishing the will as the real thing-in-itself. Generally in accordance with this, the insight into the inner being of the apparent appropriateness, harmony, and agreement of the whole of nature has perhaps become clearer and deeper in our second book and its supplements, but particularly in my work *On the Will in Nature.* Therefore I have nothing more to say about it here.

The reader interested in this criticism of the Kantian philosophy should not fail to read the supplement to it given in the second essay of the first volume of my *Parerga and Paralipomena* under the title "A Few more Elucidations of the Kantian Philosophy." For it must be borne in mind that my writings, few as they are, have not been composed all at the same time, but successively in the course of a long life, and at wide intervals. Accordingly, it cannot be expected that all I have said on a subject will appear all together in one place.

A CATALOG OF SELECTED
DOVER BOOKS
IN ALL FIELDS OF INTEREST

A CATALOG OF SELECTED DOVER
BOOKS IN ALL FIELDS OF INTEREST

CONCERNING THE SPIRITUAL IN ART, Wassily Kandinsky. Pioneering work by father of abstract art. Thoughts on color theory, nature of art. Analysis of earlier masters. 12 illustrations. 80pp. of text. 5⅜ x 8½. 0-486-23411-8

CELTIC ART: The Methods of Construction, George Bain. Simple geometric techniques for making Celtic interlacements, spirals, Kells-type initials, animals, humans, etc. Over 500 illustrations. 160pp. 9 x 12. (Available in U.S. only.) 0-486-22923-8

AN ATLAS OF ANATOMY FOR ARTISTS, Fritz Schider. Most thorough reference work on art anatomy in the world. Hundreds of illustrations, including selections from works by Vesalius, Leonardo, Goya, Ingres, Michelangelo, others. 593 illustrations. 192pp. 7⅛ x 10¼. 0-486-20241-0

CELTIC HAND STROKE-BY-STROKE (Irish Half-Uncial from "The Book of Kells"): An Arthur Baker Calligraphy Manual, Arthur Baker. Complete guide to creating each letter of the alphabet in distinctive Celtic manner. Covers hand position, strokes, pens, inks, paper, more. Illustrated. 48pp. 8¼ x 11. 0-486-24336-2

EASY ORIGAMI, John Montroll. Charming collection of 32 projects (hat, cup, pelican, piano, swan, many more) specially designed for the novice origami hobbyist. Clearly illustrated easy-to-follow instructions insure that even beginning papercrafters will achieve successful results. 48pp. 8¼ x 11. 0-486-27298-2

BLOOMINGDALE'S ILLUSTRATED 1886 CATALOG: Fashions, Dry Goods and Housewares, Bloomingdale Brothers. Famed merchants' extremely rare catalog depicting about 1,700 products: clothing, housewares, firearms, dry goods, jewelry, more. Invaluable for dating, identifying vintage items. Also, copyright-free graphics for artists, designers. Co-published with Henry Ford Museum & Greenfield Village. 160pp. 8¼ x 11. 0-486-25780-0

THE ART OF WORLDLY WISDOM, Baltasar Gracian. "Think with the few and speak with the many," "Friends are a second existence," and "Be able to forget" are among this 1637 volume's 300 pithy maxims. A perfect source of mental and spiritual refreshment, it can be opened at random and appreciated either in brief or at length. 128pp. 5⅜ x 8½. 0-486-44034-6

JOHNSON'S DICTIONARY: A Modern Selection, Samuel Johnson (E. L. McAdam and George Milne, eds.). This modern version reduces the original 1755 edition's 2,300 pages of definitions and literary examples to a more manageable length, retaining the verbal pleasure and historical curiosity of the original. 480pp. 5⅜₆ x 8¼. 0-486-44089-3

ADVENTURES OF HUCKLEBERRY FINN, Mark Twain, Illustrated by E. W. Kemble. A work of eternal richness and complexity, a source of ongoing critical debate, and a literary landmark, Twain's 1885 masterpiece about a barefoot boy's journey of self-discovery has enthralled readers around the world. This handsome clothbound reproduction of the first edition features all 174 of the original black-and-white illustrations. 368pp. 5⅜ x 8½. 0-486-44322-1

FRENCH STORIES/CONTES FRANÇAIS: A Dual-Language Book, Wallace Fowlie. Ten stories by French masters, Voltaire to Camus: "Micromegas" by Voltaire; "The Atheist's Mass" by Balzac; "Minuet" by de Maupassant; "The Guest" by Camus, six more. Excellent English translations on facing pages. Also French-English vocabulary list, exercises, more. 352pp. 5⅜ x 8½. 0-486-26443-2

CHICAGO AT THE TURN OF THE CENTURY IN PHOTOGRAPHS: 122 Historic Views from the Collections of the Chicago Historical Society, Larry A. Viskochil. Rare large-format prints offer detailed views of City Hall, State Street, the Loop, Hull House, Union Station, many other landmarks, circa 1904-1913. Introduction. Captions. Maps. 144pp. 9⅜ x 12¼. 0-486-24656-6

OLD BROOKLYN IN EARLY PHOTOGRAPHS, 1865-1929, William Lee Younger. Luna Park, Gravesend race track, construction of Grand Army Plaza, moving of Hotel Brighton, etc. 157 previously unpublished photographs. 165pp. 8⅞ x 11¾. 0-486-23587-4

THE MYTHS OF THE NORTH AMERICAN INDIANS, Lewis Spence. Rich anthology of the myths and legends of the Algonquins, Iroquois, Pawnees and Sioux, prefaced by an extensive historical and ethnological commentary. 36 illustrations. 480pp. 5⅜ x 8½. 0-486-25967-6

AN ENCYCLOPEDIA OF BATTLES: Accounts of Over 1,560 Battles from 1479 B.C. to the Present, David Eggenberger. Essential details of every major battle in recorded history from the first battle of Megiddo in 1479 B.C. to Grenada in 1984. List of Battle Maps. New Appendix covering the years 1967-1984. Index. 99 illustrations. 544pp. 6½ x 9¼. 0-486-24913-1

SAILING ALONE AROUND THE WORLD, Captain Joshua Slocum. First man to sail around the world, alone, in small boat. One of great feats of seamanship told in delightful manner. 67 illustrations. 294pp. 5⅜ x 8½. 0-486-20326-3

ANARCHISM AND OTHER ESSAYS, Emma Goldman. Powerful, penetrating, prophetic essays on direct action, role of minorities, prison reform, puritan hypocrisy, violence, etc. 271pp. 5⅜ x 8½. 0-486-22484-8

MYTHS OF THE HINDUS AND BUDDHISTS, Ananda K. Coomaraswamy and Sister Nivedita. Great stories of the epics; deeds of Krishna, Shiva, taken from puranas, Vedas, folk tales; etc. 32 illustrations. 400pp. 5⅜ x 8½. 0-486-21759-0

MY BONDAGE AND MY FREEDOM, Frederick Douglass. Born a slave, Douglass became outspoken force in antislavery movement. The best of Douglass' autobiographies. Graphic description of slave life. 464pp. 5⅜ x 8½. 0-486-22457-0

FOLLOWING THE EQUATOR: A Journey Around the World, Mark Twain. Fascinating humorous account of 1897 voyage to Hawaii, Australia, India, New Zealand, etc. Ironic, bemused reports on peoples, customs, climate, flora and fauna, politics, much more. 197 illustrations. 720pp. 5⅜ x 8½. 0-486-26113-1

THE PEOPLE CALLED SHAKERS, Edward D. Andrews. Definitive study of Shakers: origins, beliefs, practices, dances, social organization, furniture and crafts, etc. 33 illustrations. 351pp. 5⅜ x 8½. 0-486-21081-2

THE MYTHS OF GREECE AND ROME, H. A. Guerber. A classic of mythology, generously illustrated, long prized for its simple, graphic, accurate retelling of the principal myths of Greece and Rome, and for its commentary on their origins and significance. With 64 illustrations by Michelangelo, Raphael, Titian, Rubens, Canova, Bernini and others. 480pp. 5⅜ x 8½. 0-486-27584-1

DRIED FLOWERS: How to Prepare Them, Sarah Whitlock and Martha Rankin. Complete instructions on how to use silica gel, meal and borax, perlite aggregate, sand and borax, glycerine and water to create attractive permanent flower arrangements. 12 illustrations. 32pp. 5⅜ x 8½. 0-486-21802-3

EASY-TO-MAKE BIRD FEEDERS FOR WOODWORKERS, Scott D. Campbell. Detailed, simple-to-use guide for designing, constructing, caring for and using feeders. Text, illustrations for 12 classic and contemporary designs. 96pp. 5⅜ x 8½. 0-486-25847-5

THE COMPLETE BOOK OF BIRDHOUSE CONSTRUCTION FOR WOODWORKERS, Scott D. Campbell. Detailed instructions, illustrations, tables. Also data on bird habitat and instinct patterns. Bibliography. 3 tables. 63 illustrations in 15 figures. 48pp. 5¼ x 8½. 0-486-24407-5

SCOTTISH WONDER TALES FROM MYTH AND LEGEND, Donald A. Mackenzie. 16 lively tales tell of giants rumbling down mountainsides, of a magic wand that turns stone pillars into warriors, of gods and goddesses, evil hags, powerful forces and more. 240pp. 5⅜ x 8½. 0-486-29677-6

THE HISTORY OF UNDERCLOTHES, C. Willett Cunnington and Phyllis Cunnington. Fascinating, well-documented survey covering six centuries of English undergarments, enhanced with over 100 illustrations: 12th-century laced-up bodice, footed long drawers (1795), 19th-century bustles, 19th-century corsets for men, Victorian "bust improvers," much more. 272pp. 5⅝ x 8¼. 0-486-27124-2

ARTS AND CRAFTS FURNITURE: The Complete Brooks Catalog of 1912, Brooks Manufacturing Co. Photos and detailed descriptions of more than 150 now very collectible furniture designs from the Arts and Crafts movement depict davenports, settees, buffets, desks, tables, chairs, bedsteads, dressers and more, all built of solid, quarter-sawed oak. Invaluable for students and enthusiasts of antiques, Americana and the decorative arts. 80pp. 6½ x 9¼. 0-486-27471-3

WILBUR AND ORVILLE: A Biography of the Wright Brothers, Fred Howard. Definitive, crisply written study tells the full story of the brothers' lives and work. A vividly written biography, unparalleled in scope and color, that also captures the spirit of an extraordinary era. 560pp. 6⅛ x 9¼. 0-486-40297-5

THE ARTS OF THE SAILOR: Knotting, Splicing and Ropework, Hervey Garrett Smith. Indispensable shipboard reference covers tools, basic knots and useful hitches; handsewing and canvas work, more. Over 100 illustrations. Delightful reading for sea lovers. 256pp. 5⅜ x 8½. 0-486-26440-8

FRANK LLOYD WRIGHT'S FALLINGWATER: The House and Its History, Second, Revised Edition, Donald Hoffmann. A total revision–both in text and illustrations–of the standard document on Fallingwater, the boldest, most personal architectural statement of Wright's mature years, updated with valuable new material from the recently opened Frank Lloyd Wright Archives. "Fascinating"–*The New York Times*. 116 illustrations. 128pp. 9¼ x 10¾. 0-486-27430-6

PHOTOGRAPHIC SKETCHBOOK OF THE CIVIL WAR, Alexander Gardner. 100 photos taken on field during the Civil War. Famous shots of Manassas Harper's Ferry, Lincoln, Richmond, slave pens, etc. 244pp. 10⅝ x 8¼. 0-486-22731-6

FIVE ACRES AND INDEPENDENCE, Maurice G. Kains. Great back-to-the-land classic explains basics of self-sufficient farming. The one book to get. 95 illustrations. 397pp. 5⅜ x 8½. 0-486-20974-1

CATALOG OF DOVER BOOKS

LIGHT AND SHADE: A Classic Approach to Three-Dimensional Drawing, Mrs. Mary P. Merrifield. Handy reference clearly demonstrates principles of light and shade by revealing effects of common daylight, sunshine, and candle or artificial light on geometrical solids. 13 plates. 64pp. 5⅜ x 8½. 0-486-44143-1

ASTROLOGY AND ASTRONOMY: A Pictorial Archive of Signs and Symbols, Ernst and Johanna Lehner. Treasure trove of stories, lore, and myth, accompanied by more than 300 rare illustrations of planets, the Milky Way, signs of the zodiac, comets, meteors, and other astronomical phenomena. 192pp. 8⅜ x 11. 0-486-43981-X

JEWELRY MAKING: Techniques for Metal, Tim McCreight. Easy-to-follow instructions and carefully executed illustrations describe tools and techniques, use of gems and enamels, wire inlay, casting, and other topics. 72 line illustrations and diagrams. 176pp. 8¼ x 10⅞. 0-486-44043-5

MAKING BIRDHOUSES: Easy and Advanced Projects, Gladstone Califf. Easy-to-follow instructions include diagrams for everything from a one-room house for bluebirds to a forty-two-room structure for purple martins. 56 plates; 4 figures. 80pp. 8¾ x 6⅜. 0-486-44183-0

LITTLE BOOK OF LOG CABINS: How to Build and Furnish Them, William S. Wicks. Handy how-to manual, with instructions and illustrations for building cabins in the Adirondack style, fireplaces, stairways, furniture, beamed ceilings, and more. 102 line drawings. 96pp. 8¾ x 6⅜. 0-486-44259-4

THE SEASONS OF AMERICA PAST, Eric Sloane. From "sugaring time" and strawberry picking to Indian summer and fall harvest, a whole year's activities described in charming prose and enhanced with 79 of the author's own illustrations. 160pp. 8¼ x 11. 0-486-44220-9

THE METROPOLIS OF TOMORROW, Hugh Ferriss. Generous, prophetic vision of the metropolis of the future, as perceived in 1929. Powerful illustrations of towering structures, wide avenues, and rooftop parks–all features in many of today's modern cities. 59 illustrations. 144pp. 8¼ x 11. 0-486-43727-2

THE PATH TO ROME, Hilaire Belloc. This 1902 memoir abounds in lively vignettes from a vanished time, recounting a pilgrimage on foot across the Alps and Apennines in order to "see all Europe which the Christian Faith has saved." 77 of the author's original line drawings complement his sparkling prose. 272pp. 5⅜ x 8½. 0-486-44001-X

THE HISTORY OF RASSELAS: Prince of Abissinia, Samuel Johnson. Distinguished English writer attacks eighteenth-century optimism and man's unrealistic estimates of what life has to offer. 112pp. 5⅜ x 8½. 0-486-44094-X

A VOYAGE TO ARCTURUS, David Lindsay. A brilliant flight of pure fancy, where wild creatures crowd the fantastic landscape and demented torturers dominate victims with their bizarre mental powers. 272pp. 5⅜ x 8½. 0-486-44198-9

Paperbound unless otherwise indicated. Available at your book dealer, online at **www.doverpublications.com**, or by writing to Dept. GI, Dover Publications, Inc., 31 East 2nd Street, Mineola, NY 11501. For current price information or for free catalogs (please indicate field of interest), write to Dover Publications or log on to **www.doverpublications.com** and see every Dover book in print. Dover publishes more than 500 books each year on science, elementary and advanced mathematics, biology, music, art, literary history, social sciences, and other areas.